Oracle Press™

OCA Oracle Database 12*c*: Installation and Administration Exam Guide

(Exam 1Z0-062)

ABOUT THE AUTHOR

John Watson (Oxford, UK) works for Skillbuilders Corporation, teaching and consulting throughout Europe and North America. He was with Oracle Corporation for several years in Johannesburg working for Internal Support and Oracle University, and has also worked for a number of companies, government departments, and NGOs in Europe and Africa. He is an Oracle Certified Master DBA, with many other accreditations for Oracle technologies. John has 30 years of experience in IT and first came across Oracle with database release 5, installing it on IBM ATs.

About the Technical Editor

Roopesh Ramklass (Canada) is an Oracle Certified Master with expertise in infrastructure, middleware, and database architecture. He has worked for Oracle Global Support, Advanced Customer Services, and Oracle University. He has run an IT consultancy and is experienced with infrastructure systems provisioning, software development, and systems integration. He has spoken at numerous Oracle Users Group conferences and is the author of several technology books.

OCA Oracle Database 12*c*: Installation and Administration Exam Guide

(Exam 1Z0-062)

John Watson

McGraw-Hill is an independent entity from Oracle Corporation and is not affiliated with Oracle Corporation in any manner. This publication and CD-ROM may be used in assisting students to prepare for the Oracle Database 12*c*: Installation and Administration exam 1Z0-062. Neither Oracle Corporation nor McGraw-Hill Education warrants that use of this publication and CD-ROM will ensure passing the relevant exam.

New York Chicago San Francisco
Athens London Madrid Mexico City
Milan New Delhi Singapore Sydney Toronto

Cataloging-in-Publication Data is on file with the Library of Congress

McGraw-Hill Education books are available at special quantity discounts to use as premiums and sales promotions, or for use in corporate training programs. To contact a representative, please visit the Contact Us pages at www.mhprofessional.com.

OCA Oracle Database 12c: Installation and Administration Exam Guide (Exam 1Z0-062)

4 5 6 7 8 9 QVS/QVS 22 21 20 19 18

ISBN: Book p/n 978-0-07-183125-3 and CD p/n 978-0-07-183126-0
of set 978-0-07-182923-6

MHID: Book p/n 0-07-183125-8 and CD p/n 0-07-183126-6
of set 0-07-182923-7

Sponsoring Editor
Tim Green

Editorial Supervisor
Jody McKenzie

Project Editor
Howie Severson,
Fortuitous Publishing

Acquisitions Coordinator
Mary Demery

Technical Editor
Roopesh Ramklass

Copy Editor
Bart Reed

Proofreader
Paul Tyler

Indexer
Jack Lewis

Production Supervisor
James Kussow

Composition
Cenveo® Publishing Services

Illustration
Cenveo Publishing Services

Art Director, Cover
Jeff Weeks

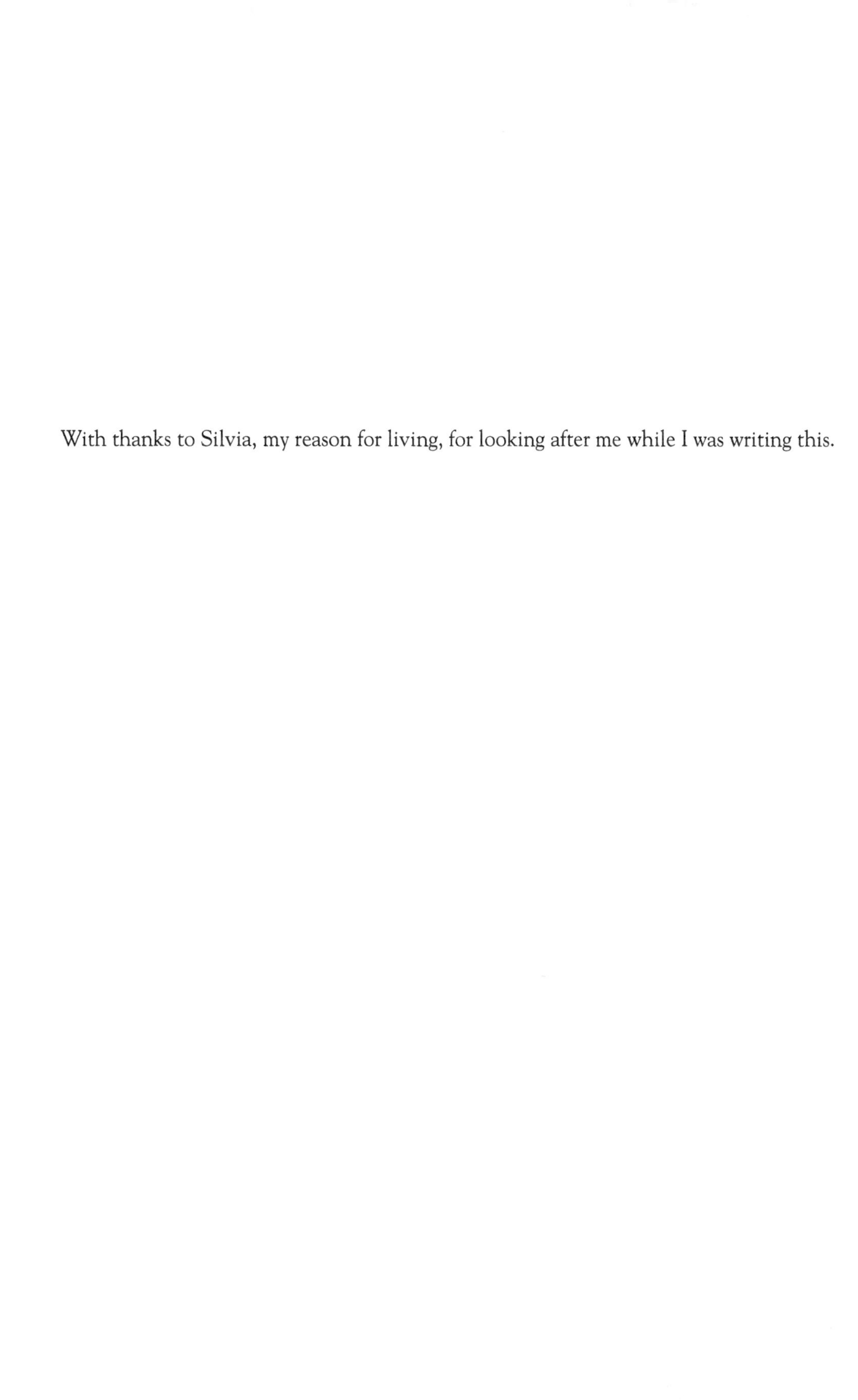

With thanks to Silvia, my reason for living, for looking after me while I was writing this.

CONTENTS AT A GLANCE

CONTENTS

PREFACE

The objective of this study guide is to prepare you for the 1Z0-062 exam by familiarizing you with the material tested in the exam. The primary focus of the book is to help you pass the test, but it is a lot more than that: it is intended to teach you to be a competent database administrator. And a competent DBA will pass the exam. To this end, there are numerous best practices scattered throughout the book, and there is plenty of discussion of concepts. We hope this book will serve you as a valuable professional resource: it is not merely an exam crammer.

Your study of Oracle database administration is about to begin—you can continue these studies for the rest of your working life. Enjoy!

In This Book

This book is organized in such a way as to serve as an in-depth review for the Oracle Database 12*c*: Installation and Administration exam for both experienced and beginner Oracle database professionals. Each chapter covers a major aspect of the exam, with an emphasis on the "why" as well as the "how to" of working with and supporting Oracle release 12*c* databases.

On the CD-ROM

For more information on the CD-ROM, please see the About the CD-ROM appendix at the back of the book.

Exam Objective Map

The exam consists of 30 top-level objectives, with a total of 86 subtopics. This book is structured for the most part with one chapter for each top-level objective. This rule has not been followed where the objectives are very small (perhaps only one subtopic) and should sensibly be combined. The chapter ordering is not exactly that of the topics as listed on the Oracle University website. For example, installing the database software and creating a database are our first two chapters—but they are almost at the end of the official objectives list. There is, however, a very close alignment of content with exam objectives.

At the end of the Introduction you will find an Exam Objective Map. This table has been constructed to allow you to cross-reference the official exam objectives with the objectives as they are presented and covered in this book. References have been provided for the objective exactly as the vendor presents it, the chapter title of the study guide that covers that objective, and a chapter number and page reference.

In Every Chapter

We've created a set of chapter components that call your attention to important items, reinforce important points, and provide helpful exam-taking hints. Take a look at what you'll find in every chapter:

- Every chapter begins with **Certification Objectives**—what you need to know in order to pass the section on the exam dealing with the chapter topic. The Certification Objective headings identify the objectives within the chapter, so you'll always know an objective when you see it.
- **Exam Watch** notes call attention to information about, and potential pitfalls in, the exam. These helpful hints are written by authors who have taken the exam and received their certification—who better to tell you what to worry about? They know what you're about to go through.
- **Step-by-Step Exercises** are interspersed throughout the chapters. These are typically designed as hands-on exercises that allow you to get a feel for the real-world experience you need in order to pass the exam. They help you master skills that are likely to be an area of focus on the exam. Don't just read through the exercises; they are hands-on practice that you should be comfortable completing. Learning by doing is an effective way to increase your competency with a product.

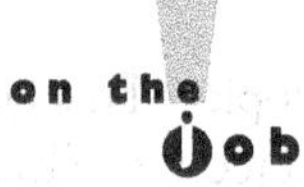

- **On the Job** notes describe the issues that come up most often in real-world settings. They provide a valuable perspective on certification- and product-related topics. They point out common mistakes and address questions that have arisen from on-the-job discussions and experience.

- The **Certification Summary** is a succinct review of the chapter and a restatement of salient points regarding the exam.
- ✓ The **Two-Minute Drill** at the end of every chapter is a checklist of the main points of the chapter. It can be used for last-minute review.
- Q&A The **Self Test** offers questions that cover the material found on the exam. They are not, of course, actual exam questions (that would be illegal). The answers to these questions, as well as explanations of the answers, can be found at the end of each chapter. By taking the Self Test after completing each chapter, you'll reinforce what you've learned from that chapter while becoming familiar with the structure of the exam questions.
- The **Lab Question** at the end of the Self Test section offers a unique and challenging question format that requires you to understand multiple chapter concepts in order to answer correctly. These questions are more complex and more comprehensive than the other questions, as they test your ability to take all the knowledge you've gained from reading the chapter and apply it to complicated, real-world situations. These questions are aimed to be more difficult than what you will find on the exam. If you can answer these questions, you have proven that you know the subject.

Some Pointers

Once you've finished reading this book, set aside some time to do a thorough review. You might want to return to the book several times and make use of all the methods it offers for reviewing the material:

1. *Reread all the Two-Minute Drills*, or have someone quiz you. You also can use the drills as a way to do a quick cram before the exam.
2. *Reread all the Exam Watch notes*. Remember that these notes are written by authors who have taken the exam and passed. They know what you should expect—and what you should be on the lookout for.
3. *Retake the Self Tests*. Taking the tests right after you've read the chapter is a good idea, because the questions help reinforce what you've just learned. However, it's an even better idea to go back later and answer all the questions in the book in a single sitting. Pretend that you're taking the live exam.

When you go through the questions the first time, you should mark your answers on a separate piece of paper. That way, you can run through the questions as many times as you need to until you feel comfortable with the material.

4. *Complete the Exercises*. Did you do the exercises when you read through each chapter? If not, do them. Construct your own variations as well. These exercises are designed to cover exam topics, and there's no better way to get to know this material than by practicing. Be sure you understand why you are performing each step in each exercise. If there is something you are not clear on, reread that section in the chapter.

INTRODUCTION

The Oracle Certification Program

There is an ever-increasing demand for staff with IT industry certification. The benefits to employers are significant—they can be certain that staff have a certain level of competence—and the benefits to the individuals, in terms of demand for their services, are equally great. Many employers are now requiring technical staff to have certifications, and many IT purchasers will not buy from firms that do not have certified staff. The Oracle certifications are among the most sought after. But apart from rewards in a business sense, knowing that you are among a relatively small pool of elite Oracle professionals and have proved your competence is a personal reward well worth attaining. Furthermore, studying is always enjoyable, and studying for an exam provides a nice target at which to aim.

There are several Oracle certification *tracks*—this book is concerned with the Oracle Database Administration certification track, specifically for release 12*c* of the database. There are three levels of DBA certification: Certified Associate (OCA), Certified Professional (OCP), and Certified Master (OCM). The OCA qualification is based on two examinations, the second of which is covered in this book. The OCP qualification requires passing a third examination. These examinations can be taken at any Pearson Vue testing center, and consist of a number of multiple-choice questions that must be completed within a time limit. The OCM qualification requires completing a further two-day evaluation at an Oracle testing center, involving simulations of complex environments and use of advanced techniques. Full details are on the Oracle University website, http://education.oracle.com.

To prepare for the second OCA examination you can attend an Oracle University instructor-led training course, you can study online learning material, or you can read this book. In all cases, you should also refer to the Oracle Documentation Library for detail of syntax. This book will be a valuable addition to other study methods, but is sufficient by itself. It has been designed with the examination objectives in mind, although it also includes a great deal of information that will be useful to you in the course of your work.

However, it is not enough to buy the book, place it under your pillow, and assume that knowledge will permeate into your brain by the process of osmosis: you must read it thoroughly, work through the exercises and sample questions, and experiment further with various commands. As you become more familiar with the Oracle environment, you will realize that there is one golden rule:

When it doubt, try it out.

In a multitude of cases, you will find that a simple test that takes a couple of minutes can save hours of speculation and poring through manuals. If anything is ever unclear, construct an example and see what happens. Test everything. This book was developed using Windows and Linux, but to carry out the exercises and your further investigations you can use any platform that is supported for Oracle.

The Examination

Now here are some suggestions for approaching the exam.

An OCA/OCP exam will consist of multiple-choice questions, but they are not always "choose the best answer." Sometimes the questions will ask you to "choose all correct answers" or "put the answers in the correct order." Some questions are easy, some are hard. Some are confusing. You might be asked (for example) to "choose the best answer," and you will think, "All the answers are wrong!" or perhaps "But two of the answers are correct!" In that case, read the question very carefully, and you may eventually see what they are wanting; the questions are often very precisely worded.

The questions are fair, and do not require feats of memory. You will not (for example) be asked if a view name is V$DATAFILE or V$DATA_FILE. But you might be asked whether V$DATAFILE or DBA_DATA_FILES is visible when the database is in mount mode. Fair enough: you should know whether a view is populated from the instance, from the controlfile, or from the data dictionary; you should know which of these structures is available in mount mode. This is not a matter of spelling; it is something you can work out.

The exam technique you should follow is to go through all the questions as quickly as possible: answer the ones you know, mark the ones you don't (there is an option to do that). That first run through will take you half the time. Then spend the rest of the time going over the questions you marked again, and again. At the end, there may still be a few questions where you have no idea: just guess—there are no deductions for errors. The mistake you must not make is to try to do the questions in order, because you will run out of time. And there might have been some very easy questions at the end that you never looked at.

All the detail of how to book an exam is available on the Oracle University website, http://education.oracle.com/certification.

Prerequisite Knowledge and Environment

This book was developed using Windows and Linux, from which come all the examples. These platforms were chosen because they are likely to be those most readily available to readers. The version of Windows was 64-bit Windows 8, and Linux was Oracle Enterprise Linux 5.8 for x86-64. As of the time of writing, release 12*c* is not available for any 32-bit operating system. To carry out the exercises and your further investigations you can use any platform on which the Oracle database can be installed. Do not get too hung up on whether your platform is supported. For example, Oracle does not support the database on any "home" edition of Windows—but it will work for learning purposes, no problem.

Clearly, you must be familiar with whatever command-line interface and graphical admin tools your environment offers. Oracle University uses Linux in the classroom, and some exam questions do have a Linux-y feel to them, so if at all possible try to do at least some preparation on a Linux machine.

A basic knowledge of SQL (Structured Query Language, pronounced *sequel)* is essential. No particularly complex statements are used, but if there are any commands or structures with which you are not familiar, you must look them up. Any DBA will have to know the SQL language—extremely well. But advanced SQL is not tested in the DBA exams. The same applies to PL/SQL, the principles of data normalization, and application and system design: a DBA must be proficient with these, but they are not tested.

The releases of the database used for developing this book were 12.1.0.0 (a beta release, as you may notice in some screenshots) and 12.1.0.1, the first production release. Great effort has been taken to ensure that the book is fully compatible with the production software. You should download and install whatever the latest release currently available to you happens to be. Oracle University validates the exams against the first production release. When a new release (perhaps 12.2.0.1) is issued, Oracle University will revalidate all questions against the new release, and adjust or remove any questions where changes in behavior could affect the answer. So for exam purposes, it should not matter what release you use—but for practical purposes, you want to be on the latest one.

A Word on Unauthorized Sample Questions (aka "Brain Dumps")

The chapter review and practice exam questions that come with this book are not actual Oracle exam questions. However, they do cover the knowledge you should have. There is no point in memorizing the questions and answers: treat them merely as a check of whether you have grasped the material. Some students like to go through many simulation exams, which you can buy (or perhaps download for free—though the legality of these should be confirmed), repeatedly until they have a perfect score. I strongly believe that this is poor preparation technique: it proves nothing more than that you can pass a particular simulated exam. The only value of such material is if you question the answers: that is, you work out why the supposedly correct answer is correct and why the wrong answers are wrong. That is the way to address all the questions in this book. If you really feel the need to do a trial exam, why not simply book the real thing? That will be real questions! And you never know, you might pass the first time.

Exam 1Z0-062 Exam Objective Map

Official Objective	Study Guide Coverage	Ch. No.	Pg. No.
1.2 Exploring the Oracle Database Architecture			
1.2.1 List the architectural components of Oracle Database	Exploring the Oracle Database Architecture	3	59
1.2.2 Explain the memory structure	Exploring the Oracle Database Architecture	3	59
1.2.3 Describe the background processes	Exploring the Oracle Database Architecture	3	59
1.2.4 Explain the relationship between logical and physical storage structures	Exploring the Oracle Database Architecture	3	59
1.3 Oracle Database Management Tools			
1.3.1 Use database management tools	Managing the Database Instance	4	107
1.4 The Oracle Database Instance	Managing the Database Instance	4	107
1.4.1 Understand initialization parameter files	Managing the Database Instance	4	107
1.4.2 Start up and shut down an Oracle database instance	Managing the Database Instance	4	107
1.4.3 View the alert log and access dynamic performance views	Managing the Database Instance	4	107

Official Objective	Study Guide Coverage	Ch. No.	Pg. No.
1.5 Configuring the Oracle Network Environment			
1.5.1 Configure Oracle Net Services	Configuring the Oracle Network Environment	5	147
1.5.2 Use tools for configuring and managing the Oracle network	Configuring the Oracle Network Environment	5	147
1.5.3 Configure client-side network	Configuring the Oracle Network Environment	5	147
1.5.4 Understand database resident connection pooling	Configuring the Oracle Network Environment	5	147
1.5.5 Configure communication between databases	Configuring the Oracle Network Environment	5	147
1.6 Administering User Security			
1.6.1 Create and manage database user accounts	Administering User Security	8	243
1.6.2 Grant and revoke privileges	Administering User Security	8	243
1.6.3 Create and manage roles	Administering User Security	8	243
1.6.4 Create and manage profiles	Administering User Security	8	243
1.7 Managing Database Storage Structures			
1.7.1 Describe the storage of table row data in blocks	Managing Database Storage Structures	6	185
1.7.2 Create and manage tablespaces	Managing Database Storage Structures	6	185
1.8 Managing Space			
1.8.1 Explain how Oracle database server automatically manages space	Managing Space	7	217
1.8.2 Save space by using compression	Managing Space	7	217
1.8.3 Proactively monitor and manage tablespace space usage	Managing Space	7	217
1.8.4 Use the Segment Advisor	Managing Space	7	217
1.8.5 Reclaim wasted space from tables and indexes by using the segment shrink functionality	Managing Space	7	217
1.8.6 Manage resumable space allocation	Managing Space	7	217

Official Objective	Study Guide Coverage	Ch. No.	Pg. No.
1.9 Managing Undo Data			
1.9.1 Explain DML and undo data generation	Managing Undo Data	9	281
1.9.2 Monitor and administer undo data	Managing Undo Data	9	281
1.9.3 Describe the difference between undo data and redo data	Managing Undo Data	9	281
1.9.4 Configure undo retention	Managing Undo Data	9	281
1.10 Managing Data Concurrency			
1.10.1 Describe the locking mechanism and how Oracle manages data concurrency	Managing Data Concurrency	10	317
1.10.2 Monitor and resolve locking conflicts	Managing Data Concurrency	10	317
1.11 Implementing Oracle Database Auditing			
1.11.1 Explain DBA responsibilities for security and auditing	Implementing Oracle Database Auditing	11	335
1.11.2 Enable standard database auditing and unified auditing	Implementing Oracle Database Auditing	11	335
1.12 Backup and Recovery Concepts			
1.12.1 Identify the importance of checkpoints, redo log files, and archive log files	Backup and Recovery: Concepts and Configuration	18	503
1.13 Backup and Recovery: Configuration			
1.13.1 Configure the fast recovery area	Backup and Recovery: Concepts and Configuration	18	503
1.13.2 Configure ARCHIVELOG mode	Backup and Recovery: Concepts and Configuration	18	503
1.14 Performing Database Backups			
1.14.1 Create consistent database backups	Backup and Recovery Operations	19	525
1.14.2 Back up your database without shutting it down	Backup and Recovery Operations	19	525
1.14.3 Create incremental backups	Backup and Recovery Operations	19	525

Official Objective	Study Guide Coverage	Ch. No.	Pg. No.
1.14.4 Automate database backups	Backup and Recovery Operations	19	525
1.14.5 Manage backups	Backup and Recovery Operations	19	525
1.15 Performing Database Recovery			
1.15.1 Determine the need for performing recovery	Backup and Recovery Operations	19	525
1.15.2 Use Recovery Manager (RMAN) and the Data Recovery Advisor to perform recovery of Control file, Redo log file, and Data file	Backup and Recovery Operations	19	525
1.16 Moving Data			
1.16.1 Describe ways to move data	Moving Data	17	475
1.16.3 Use SQL*Loader to load data from a non-Oracle database	Moving Data	17	475
1.16.4 Use external tables to move data via platform-independent files	Moving Data	17	475
1.16.6 Use Data Pump Export and Import to move data between Oracle databases	Moving Data	17	475
1.17 Performing Database Maintenance			
1.17.1 Manage the Automatic Workload Repository (AWR)	Performing Database Maintenance	12	351
1.17.2 Use the Automatic Database Diagnostic Monitor (ADDM)	Performing Database Maintenance	12	351
1.17.3 Describe and use the advisory framework	Performing Database Maintenance	12	351
1.17.4 Set alert thresholds	Performing Database Maintenance	12	351
1.17.6 Use automated tasks	Performing Database Maintenance	12	351
1.18 Managing Performance			
1.18.2 Use Automatic Memory Management	Managing Performance	13	377
1.18.3 Use the Memory Advisor to size memory buffers	Managing Performance	13	377

Official Objective	Study Guide Coverage	Ch. No.	Pg. No.
1.19 Managing Performance: SQL Tuning			
1.19.1 Manage optimizer statistics	Managing Performance: SQL Tuning	14	401
1.19.2 Use the SQL Tuning advisor	Managing Performance: SQL Tuning	14	401
1.19.3 Use the SQL Access Advisor to tune a workload	Managing Performance: SQL Tuning	14	401
1.20 Managing Resources Using Database Resource Manager			
1.20.1 Configure the Database Resource Manager	Managing Resources Using Database Resource Manager	15	423
1.20.2 Access and create resource plans	Managing Resources Using Database Resource Manager	15	423
1.20.3 Monitor the Resource Manager	Managing Resources Using Database Resource Manager	15	423
1.21 Automating Tasks by Using Oracle Scheduler			
1.21.1 Use Oracle Scheduler to simplify management tasks	Automating Tasks by Using Oracle Scheduler	16	453
1.21.2 Use job chains to perform a series of related tasks	Automating Tasks by Using Oracle Scheduler	16	453
1.21.3 Use Scheduler jobs on remote systems	Automating Tasks by Using Oracle Scheduler	16	453
1.21.4 Use advanced Scheduler features to prioritize jobs	Automating Tasks by Using Oracle Scheduler	16	453
2.2 Oracle Software Installation Basics			
2.2.1 Plan for an Oracle Database software installation	Installing Oracle Database Software	1	1
2.3 Installing Oracle Grid Infrastructure for a Standalone Server			
2.3.1 Configure storage for Oracle Automatic Storage Management (ASM)	Installing Oracle Grid Infrastructure for a Standalone Server	20	555
2.3.2 Install Oracle Grid Infrastructure for a standalone server	Installing Oracle Grid Infrastructure for a Standalone Server	20	555

Official Objective	Study Guide Coverage	Ch. No.	Pg. No.
2.4 Installing Oracle Database Software			
2.4.1 Install the Oracle Database software	Installing Oracle Database Software	1	1
2.5 Creating an Oracle Database Using DBCA			
2.5.1 Create a database by using the Database Configuration Assistant (DBCA)	Creating an Oracle Database Using DBCA	2	19
2.5.2 Generate database creation scripts by using DBCA	Creating an Oracle Database Using DBCA	2	19
2.5.3 Manage database design templates by using DBCA	Creating an Oracle Database Using DBCA	2	19
2.5.4 Configure database options by using DBCA	Creating an Oracle Database Using DBCA	2	19
2.6 Using Oracle Restart			
2.6.1 Use Oracle Restart to manage components	Using Oracle Restart	21	579
2.7 Upgrading Oracle Database Software			
2.7.1 Describe upgrade methods	Upgrading Oracle Database Software and Migrating Data	22	593
2.7.2 Describe data migration methods	Upgrading Oracle Database Software and Migrating Data	22	593
2.7.3 Describe the upgrade process	Upgrading Oracle Database Software and Migrating Data	22	593
2.8 Preparing to Upgrade to Oracle Database 12c			
2.8.1 Describe upgrade requirements when certain features or options are used in Oracle Database	Database Upgrade: Preparation, Upgrading, and Post-Upgrade Tasks	23	609
2.8.2 Use the pre-upgrade information tool before performing an upgrade	Database Upgrade: Preparation, Upgrading, and Post-Upgrade Tasks	23	609
2.8.3 Prepare the new Oracle Home prior to performing an upgrade	Database Upgrade: Preparation, Upgrading, and Post-Upgrade Tasks	23	609

Official Objective	Study Guide Coverage	Ch. No.	Pg. No.
2.9 Upgrading to Oracle Database 12*c*			
2.9.1 Upgrade the database to Oracle Database 12*c* by using the Database Upgrade Assistant (DBUA)	Database Upgrade: Preparation, Upgrading, and Post-Upgrade Tasks	23	609
2.9.2 Perform a manual upgrade to Oracle Database 12*c* by using scripts and tools	Database Upgrade: Preparation, Upgrading, and Post-Upgrade Tasks	23	609
2.10 Performing Post-Upgrade Tasks			
2.10.1 Migrate to unified auditing	Database Upgrade: Preparation, Upgrading, and Post-Upgrade Tasks	23	609
2.10.2 Perform post-upgrade tasks	Database Upgrade: Preparation, Upgrading, and Post-Upgrade Tasks	23	609
2.11 Migrating Data by Using Oracle Data Pump			
2.11.1 Migrate data by using Oracle Data Pump	Upgrading Oracle Database Software and Migrating Data	22	593

1

Installing Oracle Database Software

CERTIFICATION OBJECTIVES

1.01	Plan for an Oracle Database Software Installation	✓	Two-Minute Drill
1.02	Install the Oracle Database Software	Q&A	Self-Test

The Oracle Database software is installed with the Oracle Universal Installer (OUI). This is an Oracle product in its own right that is used to manage the installation and maintenance of many other products. The installation of Oracle software has, as far as possible, been standardized for all products on all platforms—but there are platform and product variations. Before installing anything, it is essential that you read the product's release notes for the platform concerned. This chapter goes through the process of planning the installation and then installing the Oracle Database 12*c* software, with examples from Linux and Windows.

CERTIFICATION OBJECTIVE 1.01

Plan for an Oracle Database Software Installation

The install process requires a number of prerequisites; principal among them are the availability of the software and a suitable machine. Once these are in place, the actual installation is straightforward, and (depending on hardware) should take around 15 minutes. Ideally, students will have their own installation on their own PC so that they may practice as much as desired. That is the environment described here.

Supported Platforms

Historically, the Oracle Database was supported on an extraordinarily wide range of platforms, which was one reason for the product's preeminence in the RDBMS market. In recent years, the number of platforms considered commercially viable has reduced, and Oracle Corporation has reduced support accordingly. Linux is always the first platform for release. The platforms most commonly available to students are Linux and Microsoft Windows, so these are the platforms most commonly referenced in the exams and in this guide.

Obtain the Oracle Database Software

Oracle Corporation has made the software available for public download without the need to buy a license. However, this public license is very restricted. One may download and install the product on one's own machine only for the purposes of application development and self-tuition. This is made clear in the license agreement. There are also legal restrictions on downloading in (or subsequently transferring to) certain countries. Furthermore, only the base release is publicly available. To obtain patches of any kind, it is necessary to have a support agreement. The base release is adequate for training purposes, though not necessarily for production use.

The two commonly used sources for software download are the Oracle Technology Network (OTN) and the Oracle Software Delivery Cloud. To reach the OTN download site, go to www.oracle.com, navigate through the Downloads tab to Oracle Database, and select the latest available release. To use the Oracle Software Delivery Cloud, go to http://edelivery.oracle.com and select the Oracle Database product pack. In either site, it is necessary to log on to an Oracle account (or create a new Oracle account) and then accept the license agreement. The software is in the form of ZIP files, and four are needed: two files for the Oracle Database software, and two for the Grid Infrastructure software. Unzip them (one directory for the Oracle Database software, a second directory for the Grid Infrastructure) and you are ready to go.

User Accounts

On any version of Unix or Linux, it is not possible to install the software as the root user. It is necessary to create accounts that will own the software. Best practice is to create one account that will own the database software and a second account that will own the Grid Infrastructure software: This permits separation of the duties between the database administration domain and the system administration domain. For the purposes of education, one account can be used for both functions. Traditionally, this account is named oracle and given the primary group of oinstall. A secondary group will be dba. These groups should be created before installing and should be assigned to the oracle account.

On Windows, it is not uncommon to install Oracle software under an account with Administrator privileges. Although this is certainly bad from a security perspective and should never be done on a production system, it will not cause a problem on a training system. The installer will create a group named ORA_DBA and assign it to the account from which the installer is run.

Disk Space and Directories

The installation requires around 5GB for the database Oracle Home. An Oracle Home is the location of an Oracle product installation—a set of files in a directory structure. Note that variations in size due to the platform, the type of file system, and the options selected may be substantial. The directory may be on a local file system or a clustered file system, but it must be a "cooked" file system—that is, not an ASM disk group or a raw device.

The recommended directory structure is known as Optimal Flexible Architecture, or OFA. OFA is intended to ease the process of organizing multiple software installations. The general idea is that each product should be installed into its own Oracle Home, beneath an Oracle Base. The Oracle Base is a directory that will contain one or more Oracle Homes as well as various other directories for administration purposes and also the actual database(s). The directory containing the OUI inventory exists outside the Oracle Base, which makes sense because it should be independent of any other product.

The recommended naming convention of Oracle Base is based on three variables:

/pm/s/u

And for each Oracle Home, add a literal and more variables:

/pm/s/u/product/v/type_[n]

The files that make up each database are in the Oracle Base, plus two variables:

/pm/s/u/q/d

Here are the variables and suggested values:

Variable	Description	Typical Values
pm	Mount point	Linux: /u01 Windows: D:\
s	Standard directory name	app
u	OS installer account	oracle
v	Software version	12.1.0
type	Type of product	dbhome
n	Install counter	1
q	Indication of the contents	oradata
d	Database name	orcl

Here are some examples:

- An Oracle Base of D:\app\oracle is an indication that all Oracle-related files exist on drive D: in a directory called \app, and that the installs were done by Windows user oracle.

- An Oracle Home of /u01/app/oracle/product/12.1.0/dbhome_1 suggests that the Oracle Base is /u01/app/oracle and that this directory contains the first installation of the 12*c* release 1 database software on this machine.
- The path D:\app\oracle\oradata\orcl would be the directory beneath Oracle Base containing the files of a database named orcl.
- The path /u01/app/oraInventory is the location of the OUI inventory files, next to the Oracle Base.

It is not essential to conform to the OFA directory structure, but OFA does make a DBA's life easier. Many DBAs, and some products, assume that OFA is in place, which means deviating from OFA will cause confusion.

The Prerequisite Checks

The installation release notes for each platform list the prerequisites. These will usually be hardware requirements (disk space and RAM), operating system versions, availability of certain utilities, security settings, kernel resource limits, and patch levels. Generally speaking, at this level Windows installations are simpler than Linux. This is because Windows is a tightly controlled environment, and the OUI can make many assumptions. Similarly, if the Linux distribution is Oracle Enterprise Linux, it is likely that a standard installation will fulfill all the prerequisites. A Red Hat, SUSE, or CentOS distribution may not conform by default and may therefore need some work before Oracle can be installed.

There are prerequisites for running OUI, and more prerequisites for particular products. The OUI prerequisites are coded in the file oraparam.ini and are very basic. Search for this file in the unzipped software. The following is from release 12.1.0.1.0 for 64-bit Linux:

```
[Generic Prereqs]
TEMP_SPACE=500
SWAP_SPACE=150
MIN_DISPLAY_COLORS=256
[end code]
```

The OUI will refuse to run if these conditions are not met. Then there are prerequisites for that product actually being installed. These are coded into the cvu_prereq.xml file and are checked by the OUI as part of the installation. It is possible to ignore failures to meet the prerequisites and proceed with installation, but if you do so there is no guarantee the installation will actually function correctly.

on the job

Often the problem with prereq failures is not that the products won't work, it is deciding whether they matter. For example, on Linux, some of the kernel settings and packages are not really needed for an entry-level installation. However, a problem may occur with support. If you ever raise an SR (an SR is a Service Request, which is passed to Oracle Support Services through My Oracle Support) and your system does not conform to the prereqs, the support analysts might refuse to help you. Therefore, if you have to break one of the rules to get an installation through, be sure to fix it as soon as possible afterward.

CERTIFICATION OBJECTIVE 1.02

Install the Oracle Database Software

The OUI gives several options for installation. The suggested installation, discussed next, will be suitable for any studies up to the Oracle Certified Professional level. The Oracle Certified Master curriculum includes RAC, the installation of which is not covered here. One option is whether to chain the installation of the software with the creation of a database. This option is not going to be discussed here, however, because creating a database is dealt with as a separate topic.

The OUI Inventory

OUI creates an inventory, which is a set of XML files that record exactly what Oracle products have been installed on the machine, with details of where the Oracle Homes are and what patches (if any) have been applied to each Home. In order to prevent this inventory from being corrupted, a locking mechanism prevents running the OUI (or the Opatch patching routine) concurrently in two or more sessions. Whenever OUI or Opatch is run, the first thing it does is locate the inventory and check whether it is already locked. The location of the inventory and the operating system group that owns it are stored in a pointer file. The pointer file has a platform-specific name and location. On Linux, it is /etc/oracle/oraInst.loc, as in this example, which shows that the inventory is located in the /u01/app/oraInventory directory:

```
db121a $
db121a $ cat /etc/oraInst.loc
inventory_loc=/u01/app/oraInventory
inst_group=oinstall
db121a $
```

On Solaris or AIX, the pointer file resides in the /var/opt/oracle directory. On Windows, the inventory location is defined in a registry key:

HKEY_LOCAL_MACHINE/SOFTWARE/ORACLE/inst_loc

The OUI is written in Java, using JDK1.5, which is included in the product. This means that OUI is the same on all platforms, with the exception of certain trivial variations in the Java user interface, such as whether windows have square or rounded corners. The OUI can be installed as a self-contained product in its own Oracle Home, but this is not usually necessary because it is shipped with every other Oracle product and can be launched from the product installation CD (or DVD); it will install itself into the Oracle Home along with the product. There are different versions of the OUI, and if a product comes with a version earlier than the one already installed on the machine, it's usually a good idea (and may indeed be necessary) to install the product using the already-installed version, from the existing Oracle Home. When the OUI prompts for the location of the products.xml file, specify the DVD or directory with the product you want to install.

on the job ***Always use the latest version of the OUI you have available. There can be issues with updating the OUI inventory if you try to revert to earlier versions after using a later version. Also note that some products (such as the WebLogic server) still do not use OUI and are installed independently. You can download the latest OUI from the Oracle Technology Network.***

The OUI Dialog: Interactive Install

To launch the OUI, run the runInstaller.sh shell script (Linux) or the setup.exe program (Windows) from the root of the directory in which the software was unzipped. For an interactive install, a graphical terminal must be available. For Windows, this is no problem. For Linux, it means an X terminal of some kind. If you are logged on to the console through one of the standard Linux X Window managers (such as Gnome), OUI will run straight away. If you are connecting remotely, you will have to use a connection method that allows display of graphics, such as a VNC desktop or an X Window server. There is nothing special about this: Any Linux tutorial or any experienced Linux user can explain it. However, this topic is beyond the scope of an Oracle tutorial.

The use of the OUI dialog is detailed in the exercise at the end of this chapter. In summary, here is the information requested by the 12 steps of the installer on Linux (Windows is slightly different):

Step	Description
1: Configure Security Updates	Login credentials for My Oracle Support (optional).
2: Download Software Updates	Enable automatic downloads of CPUs or PSUs (optional).
3: Select Installation Option	Choose whether to chain the install to creating or upgrading a database.
4: Grid Installation Options	Create an installation for single instance, RAC, or RAC One Node.
5: Select Product Languages	By default, only English is selected.
6: Select Database Edition	Choose Enterprise Edition, Standard Edition, or Standard Edition 1.
7: Specify Installation Location	Specify the Oracle Base and Oracle Home directories.
8: Privileged Operating System Groups	Nominate the groups that will manage the Oracle Home.
9: Perform Prerequisite Checks	Validate the environment.
10: Summary	Summary of the dialog.
11: Install Product	Progress monitor.
12: Finish	Successful completion.

Step 9 may fail on some tests. This is unlikely on Windows, but on Linux (if you're not using an Oracle-validated version of Linux, such as OEL5.8) you may face a number of issues. Typically, these involve kernel parameter settings and the availability of certain RPMs. Every issue will be flagged as "warning" or "critical." Clicking the Fix and Check Again button will generate a script and prompt you to run it as root, which will fix many "fixable" issues (such as kernel limits). However, it cannot fix all of them. Therefore, any unfixable issues (such as missing critical RPMs) should be addressed before proceeding. If it is not possible to fix the issues, clicking the Ignore All check box will allow you to proceed, but with no guarantee that the installation will succeed.

Step 11, on Linux, includes a prompt to run the script root.sh as the root user. This script accomplishes certain tasks that require root privileges, such as creating files in /etc and changing ownership and access modes on certain files in the Oracle Home.

Silent Install and Response Files

Running the OUI interactively is fine for a one-off install. However, if you are installing on multiple machines or perhaps designing a repeatable and automated procedure, it is necessary to use another technique: driving OUI with a response file. A response file is read by OUI and contains answers to all the questions posed by the interactive dialog. When using a response file, you'll usually want to disable all graphical output. This allows you to carry out installations on systems where no graphical terminal device is available, such as blade servers with no console attached.

Creating a response file from scratch is beyond the capability of most DBAs. However, a template response file is provided: the file db_install.rsp in the /response/ directory beneath the root of the installation software. It is well documented, with descriptions of every value required. But even veteran DBAs will try to avoid writing a response file by hand. And there is no need to because you can generate one with an interactive run of OUI. Launch OUI and go through the dialog. On the final screen you'll see a check box next to the question "Generate response file?" At this point you nominate a location for an automatically generated response file based on the preceding dialog and then cancel the install.

To run a silent install later (perhaps on a different machine), edit the generated file to match the environment and then launch OUI with the following syntax (for Windows):

```
setup.exe -silent -responseFile db_install.rsp
```

You can pass many other command-line switches to the installer. Here's how to display them all in Linux:

```
./runInstaller -help
```

A particularly useful switch is -ignoreSysPrereqs, which allow a silent or interactive install to proceed even if the prerequisite checks fail.

Windows and Linux Variations

Discussing the details of platform variations is beyond the scope of the OCP syllabus. However, as it is possible that students may find the differences confusing, so here is a summary of the principal differences.

- **User ID on Linux** An operating system user who will own the software must be pre-created and must be a member of operating system groups to be used to own the Oracle Home and for database administration. It is customary to name the user oracle and the groups oinstall and dba. Run OUI as this user; you cannot run the OUI as root.

- **User ID on Windows** The OUI must be run as a user with administration privileges, and it prompts for the user who owns the Oracle home. If the user does not exist, it will be created.
- **Operating system groups on Linux** At least one group must be pre-created, the OSDBA group. You can call it anything you want, but dba is the customary group name, and the user running the installer must be a member of this group. A second group, customarily called oinstall, should be the primary group of the user running OUI.
- **Operating system groups on Windows** The names are hard coded and will be created by OUI. The nominated user will be made a member of these groups automatically.
- **Root scripts on Linux** At the end of the installation, a shell script must be run as the root user. This script makes certain changes that require root privileges. Execute it when prompted. Windows does not require this step because the OUI must itself have been run as a user with administration rights.

EXERCISE 1-1

Install the Oracle Database Software

In this exercise, you will install an Oracle Home but you won't create a database at this point.

Prepare your training system by creating appropriate directories and a user; then launch the OUI and follow the wizard. The steps and prompts are slightly different between the Windows and Linux dialogs, but overall the process is very similar and self-explanatory, with context-sensitive assistance available via the Help button. Following is an example of the OUI dialog for Windows, followed by a dialog for Linux. Of course, you must adjust the process to your own circumstances. You can use these two examples to assist you in your installation.

The Windows Installation Dialog

This dialog was captured by running the OUI setup.exe on a 64-bit Windows 8.0 machine. You may need to adjust the suggested responses to your environment.

1. **Configure Security Updates** Deselect the "I wish to receive security updates" check box. Leave the other fields blank, click Next, and then click Yes when warned about not providing an e-mail address.

2. **Download Software Updates** Select the Skip Software Updates radio button and then click Next.
3. **Select Installation Option** Select the Install Database Software Only radio button and then click Next.
4. **System Class** Select the Server Class radio button. This has no technical significance, but does ensure that you will subsequently see all possible options. Click Next.
5. **Grid Installation Options** Select the Single Instance Database Installation radio button and then click Next.
6. **Select Install Type** Select the Advanced Install radio button and then click Next.
7. **Select Product Languages** Add any languages you need and then click Next.
8. **Select Database Edition** Select the Enterprise Edition radio button and then click Next.
9. **Specify Oracle Home User** Enter the name and password of either an existing user who will own the installation or a new user to be created by the OUI. A commonly used username is "oracle" (in all lowercase). Click Next.
10. **Specify Installation Location** Enter an Oracle Base directory, such as C:\app\oracle, and a software location, such as C:\app\oracle\product\12.1.0\dbhome_1. Click Next.
11. **Perform Prerequisite Checks** OUI will perform its checks. Fix any issues.
12. **Summary** A summary of the installation will be displayed. It is possible to make changes here, or to navigate back through the dialog with the Back button. Click Install to proceed.

The Linux Installation Dialog

This dialogue was captured by running the OUI runInstaller.sh on a 64-bit Linux 5.8 machine. You may need to adjust the suggested responses to your environment..

1. **Configure Security Updates** Deselect the "I wish to receive security updates" check box. Leave the other fields blank, click Next, and then click Yes when warned about not providing an e-mail address.
2. **Download Software Updates** Select the Skip Software Updates radio button and then click Next.

3. **Select Installation Option** Select the Install Database Software Only radio button and then click Next.
4. **Grid Installation Options** Select the Single Instance Database Installation radio button and then click Next.
5. **Select Product Languages** Add any languages you need and then click Next.
6. **Select Database Edition** Select the Enterprise Edition radio button and then click Next.
7. **Specify Installation Location** Enter an Oracle Base directory on which your Linux user has full permissions, such as /u01/apporacle, and a software location within it, such as /u01/app/oracle/product/12.1.0/dbhome_1. Click Next.
8. **Privileged Operating System Groups** Select an operating system group from each drop-down box. The list will be dependent on the group membership of the user under which you are running the OUI. Selecting "dba", if available, is usually a good choice. Click Next.
9. **Perform Prerequisite Checks** OUI will perform its checks. Fix any issues.
10. **Summary** A summary of the installation will be displayed. It is possible to make changes here, or to navigate back through the dialog with the Back button. Click Install to proceed.
11. **Install Product** The OUI copies the software into the Oracle home, links it, and runs various configuration scripts.
12. **Execute Configuration Scripts** A popup window (make sure it is not hiding behind another window!) will prompt you to run a shell script as root. Run this, accepting defaults for all the prompted values. Then click OK in the popup window. The installation is now complete; click Close to exit from the installer.

CERTIFICATION SUMMARY

The OUI is the tool used to install an Oracle Home. A successful installation requires a certain amount of preparatory work by the system administrator, such as creating an operating system user account and groups as well as a directory into which the software will be installed. The OUI runs various prerequisite checks and will even generate a script to fix some shortcomings. Although it is possible to ignore any failures, this may lead to problems later.

TWO-MINUTE DRILL

Plan for an Oracle Database Software Installation

- ❑ Create operating system groups and users.
- ❑ Create a directory beneath which the Oracle Base will exist.
- ❑ Download the appropriate version of the installation DVDs.

Install the Oracle Database Software

- ❑ Launch the OUI: setup.exe (Windows) or runInstaller.sh (Linux).
- ❑ Follow the OUI dialog.

SELF TEST

Plan for an Oracle Database Software Installation

1. Which statement best describes the relationship between the Oracle Base and the Oracle Home? (Choose the best answer.)
   A. The Oracle Base exists inside the Oracle Home.
   B. The Oracle Base can contain Oracle Homes for different products.
   C. One Oracle Base is required for each product, but versions of the product can exist in their own Oracle Homes within their Oracle Base.
   D. The Oracle Base is created when you run the orainstRoot.sh script, and contains a pointer to the Oracle Home.
2. What does Optimal Flexible Architecture (OFA) describe? (Choose the best answer.)
   A. A directory structure
   B. Distributed database systems
   C. A multitier processing architecture
   D. All the above
3. What environment variable must be set on Linux before running the Oracle Universal Installer for an interactive installation? (Choose the best answer.)
   A. ORACLE_HOME
   B. ORACLE_BASE
   C. ORACLE_SID
   D. DISPLAY

Install the Oracle Database Software

4. If the OUI detects that a prerequisite has not been met, what can you do? (Choose the best answer.)
   A. You must cancel the installation, fix the problem, and launch OUI again.
   B. A silent install will fail; an interactive install will continue.
   C. Instruct the OUI to continue (at your own risk).
   D. The options will depend on how far into the installation the OUI is when the problem is detected.

5. What type of devices can the OUI install an Oracle Home onto? (Choose all correct answers.)
   A. Regular file systems
   B. Clustered file systems
   C. Raw devices
   D. ASM disk groups
6. Which command-line switch can be used to prevent the OUI from stopping when prerequisite tests fail? (Choose the best answer.)
   A. –silent
   B. –record
   C. –responsefile
   D. –ignoresysprereqs
7. When does an OUI inventory get created? (Choose the best answer.)
   A. Every time a new Oracle Home is created
   B. Every time a new Oracle Base is created
   C. Before the first run of the OUI
   D. During the first run of the OUI

LAB QUESTION

Use the OUI to instantiate another Oracle Home. Then launch OUI again and take the option to deinstall an Oracle Home. This will prompt you to run a shell script (Linux) or batch file (Windows) to accomplish the deinstallation. Repeat! It is important to become completely comfortable with all the options of OUI.

SELF TEST ANSWERS

Plan for an Oracle Database Software Installation

1. ☑ **B.** The Oracle Base directory contains all the Oracle Homes, which can be any versions of any products.
   ☒ **A, C,** and **D** are incorrect. **A** is incorrect because it inverts the relationship. **C** is incorrect because there is no requirement for a separate base for each product. **D** is incorrect because it misunderstands the purpose of the orainstRoot.sh script, which is to create the oraInst.loc file, not to create the Oracle Base directory.
2. ☑ **A.** The rather grandly named Optimal Flexible Architecture is nothing more than a naming convention for directory structures.
   ☒ **B, C,** and **D** are incorrect. These are incorrect because they go way beyond OFA.
3. ☑ **D.** Without a DISPLAY set, the OUI will not be able to open any windows.
   ☒ **A, B,** and **C** are incorrect. These are incorrect because although they can be set before the OUI is launched, the OUI will prompt for values for them.

Install the Oracle Database Software

4. ☑ **C.** Perhaps not advisable, but you can certainly do this.
   ☒ **A, B,** and **D** are incorrect. **A** is incorrect because while it might be a good idea, it is not something you have to do. **B** is incorrect because the interactive installation will halt. **D** is incorrect because all prerequisites are checked at the same time.
5. ☑ **A** and **B.** The Oracle Home must exist on a file system, but it can be local or clustered.
   ☒ **C** and **D** are incorrect. Raw devices and ASM devices can be used for databases, but not for an Oracle Home.
6. ☑ **D.** The –ignoresysprereqs switch stops OUI from running the tests.
   ☒ **A, B,** and **C** are incorrect. **A** is incorrect because this switch will suppress generation of windows, not running tests. **B** is incorrect because this is the switch to generate a response file. **C** is incorrect because this is the switch to read a response file.
7. ☑ **D.** If the OUI cannot find an inventory, it will create one.
   ☒ **A, B,** and **C** are incorrect. **A** and **B** are incorrect because one inventory can manage any number of Homes in any Base. **C** is incorrect because the inventory is created at the end of the process, not the beginning.

LAB ANSWER

The OUI "Welcome" window features a button labeled Deinstall Products. Clicking this button will present a list of Oracle Homes. Selecting one will enable a Remove button. Click this button, and on Windows a pop-up will tell you to run a command such as the following:

```
c:\app\oracle\product\12.1.0\dbhome_2/deinstall/deinstall
```

On Linux, the result is similar (although the use of forward and backward slashes is more consistent).

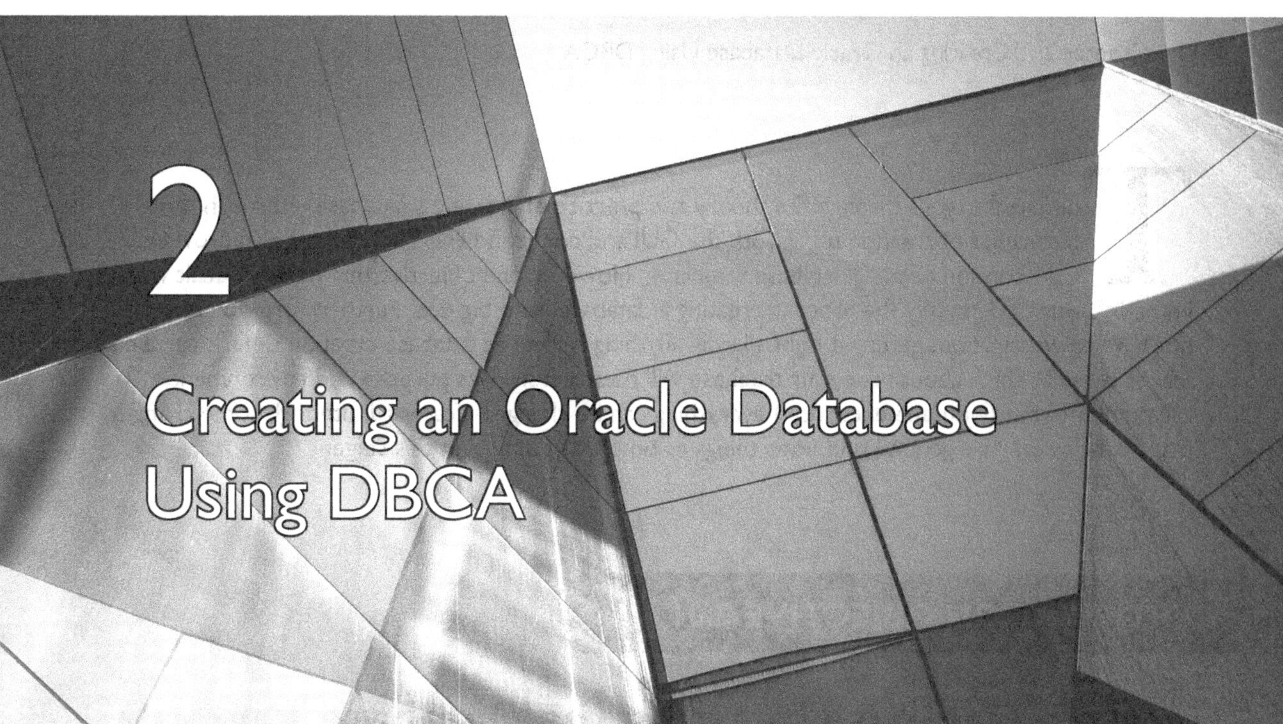

2 Creating an Oracle Database Using DBCA

CERTIFICATION OBJECTIVES

2.01	Create a Database by Using the Database Configuration Assistant (DBCA)	2.04	Configure Database Options by Using DBCA
2.02	Generate Database Creation Scripts by Using DBCA	2.05	Certification Summary
		✓	Two-Minute Drill
2.03	Manage Database Design Templates by Using DBCA	Q&A	Self-Test

This chapter goes through the theory and practice of creating a database—through the mechanics of creation using both the GUI and command line. This chapter also provides a description of using database templates. However, one objective that must be dealt with immediately is to demystify the process: creating a database is no big deal. Furthermore, you really do not have to worry about getting it right. Hardly anything is fixed at database-creation time. It certainly makes sense to think about how your database will be structured, its purpose and environment, at creation time, but (with one exception) everything can be changed afterward, although some changes may be awkward. As a general rule, keep things as simple as possible at this stage.

CERTIFICATION OBJECTIVE 2.01

Create a Database by Using the Database Configuration Assistant (DBCA)

Although creating a database is not difficult (the process can be quick and simple—a single two-word command will do it—and it may take less than 10 minutes), there are some concepts you should understand before proceeding with the creation process—namely, the instance, the database, and the data dictionary.

The Instance, the Database, and the Data Dictionary

An Oracle server is an instance and a database; the two are separate but connected. The instance is composed of memory structures and processes, in your RAM and on your CPU(s). Its existence is transient; it can be started and stopped. The database is composed of files on disk; once created, it persists until it is deleted. Creating an instance is nothing more than building the memory structures and starting the processes. Creating a database is done by the instance as a once-off operation, and the instance can then subsequently open and close the database many times. The database is inaccessible without the instance.

Within the database is a set of tables and other objects called the data dictionary. The data dictionary describes all the logical and physical structures in the database, including all the segments that store user data. The database creation process involves creating the bare minimum of physical structures needed to support the data dictionary and then creating the data dictionary within them.

An instance is defined by an instance parameter file. The parameter file contains directives that define (among other things) how the instance should be built in memory, including the size of the memory structures and the behavior of the background processes. After the instance has been built, it is said to be in "no mount" mode. In no mount mode, the instance exists but has not connected to a database. Indeed, the database may not have been created at this point.

All parameters, either specified by the parameter file or set implicitly, have defaults, except for the DB_NAME parameter. This parameter names the database to which the instance will connect. This name is also embedded in the controlfile. One parameter, CONTROL_FILES, tells the instance the location of the controlfile. This parameter defines the connection between the instance and the database. When the instance reads the controlfile (which it will find by reading the CONTROL_FILES parameter or by relying on the default value), if there is a mismatch in database names, the database will not mount. In mount mode, the instance has successfully connected to the controlfile. If the controlfile is damaged or nonexistent, it will be impossible to mount the database. The controlfile is small, but vital.

Within the controlfile are pointers to the other files (the online redo log files and the datafiles) that make up the rest of the database. Having mounted the database, the instance can open the database by locating and opening these other files. An open database is a database where the instance has opened all the available online redo log files and datafiles. Also within the controlfile is a mapping of datafiles to tablespaces. This lets the instance identify the datafile(s) that make(s) up the SYSTEM tablespace. In the SYSTEM tablespace, it will find the data dictionary. The data dictionary lets the instance resolve references to objects referred to in SQL code to the segments in which they reside, and work out where, physically, the objects are.

The creation of a database server must therefore involve these steps:

1. Create the instance.
2. Create the database.
3. Create the data dictionary.

In practice, though, there is a fourth step:

4. Make the database usable.

The data dictionary, as initially created with the database, is fully functional but unusable. It has the capability for defining and managing user data but cannot be used by normal human beings because its structure is too abstruse. Before users (or DBAs) can actually use the database, a set of views must be created on top of the data dictionary that will present it in a human-understandable form. Also, many PL/SQL packages are required to add functionality.

The data dictionary itself is created by running a set of SQL scripts that exist in the ORACLE_HOME/rdbms/admin directory. These are called by the **CREATE DATABASE** command. The first is sql.bsq, which then calls several other scripts. These scripts issue a series of commands that create all the tables and other objects that make up the data dictionary.

The views and other objects that make the database usable are generated with more scripts in the ORACLE_HOME/rdbms/admin directory and have a "cat" prefix. Examples of these are catalog.sql and catproc.sql, which should always be run immediately after database creation. There are many other optional "cat" scripts that will enable certain features—some of these can be run at creation time; others might be run subsequently to install the features at a later date.

Using the DBCA to Create a Database

Here are the steps to follow to create a database:

1. Create a parameter file and (optionally) a password file.
2. Use the parameter file to build an instance in memory.
3. Issue the **CREATE DATABASE** command. This will generate, at a minimum, a controlfile, two online redo log files, one datafile each for the SYSTEM and SYSAUX tablespaces, and a data dictionary. The syntax does allow a lot more to be done at this point.
4. Run SQL scripts to generate the data dictionary views and the supplied PL/SQL packages.
5. Run SQL scripts to generate the Enterprise Manager Database Express as well as any options (such as Java) the database will require.
6. On Windows systems, there is an additional step because Oracle runs as a Windows service. Oracle provides a utility, oradim.exe, to assist you in creating this service.

These steps can be executed interactively from the SQL*Plus prompt or through a GUI tool, the Database Configuration Assistant (DBCA). Alternatively, you can automate the process by using scripts or the DBCA with a response file.

Regardless of the platform you are running on, the easiest way to create a database is through the DBCA. It creates a parameter file and a password file and then generates scripts that will start the instance, create the database, and generate the data dictionary and the data dictionary views. Alternatively, you can create the parameter file and password file by hand and then do the rest from a SQL*Plus session. Many DBAs combine the two techniques: they use the DBCA to generate the files and scripts, and then look at them and perhaps edit them before running them from SQL*Plus.

To launch the DBCA on Windows, take the shortcut on the Start menu. Here's the navigation path:

1. Start
2. Programs
3. Oracle – OraDB12Home1
4. Configuration and Migration Tools
5. Database Configuration Assistant

Note that the precise path will vary depending on the name given to the Oracle Home at install time. Alternatively, run the dbca.bat script from a CMD prompt. Following a standard installation, it will be included in your Windows search path.

To launch the DBCA on Linux, first set the environment variables that should always be set for any Linux DBA session: DISPLAY, ORACLE_BASE, ORACLE_HOME, and PATH. Here is an example of a script that will do this:

```
export DISPLAY=myhost:0.0
export ORACLE_BASE=/u01/app/oracle
export ORACLE_HOME=$ORACLE_BASE/product/12.1.0/dbhome_1
export PATH=$ORACLE_HOME/bin:$PATH
```

Note that the Base and Home will vary according to choices made at install time. The variables also exist in a Windows environment, but are usually defined as registry variables set by the Oracle Universal Installer (OUI) rather than shell variables. The DISPLAY variable must, of course, be set to the address of your X server. To launch the DBCA, run the dbca shell script, which is located in the $ORACLE_HOME/bin directory.

on the job

Be sure to have the $ORACLE_HOME/bin directory at the start of your search path, in case there are any Linux executables with the same name as Oracle executables. A well-known case in point is rman, which is the name of both an Oracle tool and a SUSE Linux utility.

Remember that (with one exception) every choice made at database creation time can be changed later but that some changes are awkward and will involve downtime. Therefore, it is not vital to get everything right—but the more you can get right, the better.

The DBCA Dialog

The DBCA dialog consists of 13 steps, as illustrated in Figures 2-1 through 2-13.

Step 1: Database Operation

The radio buttons available in this first step allow you to select the type of operation you want to perform:

- **Create Database** You can launch a dialog that will prompt you to create an instance and a database.

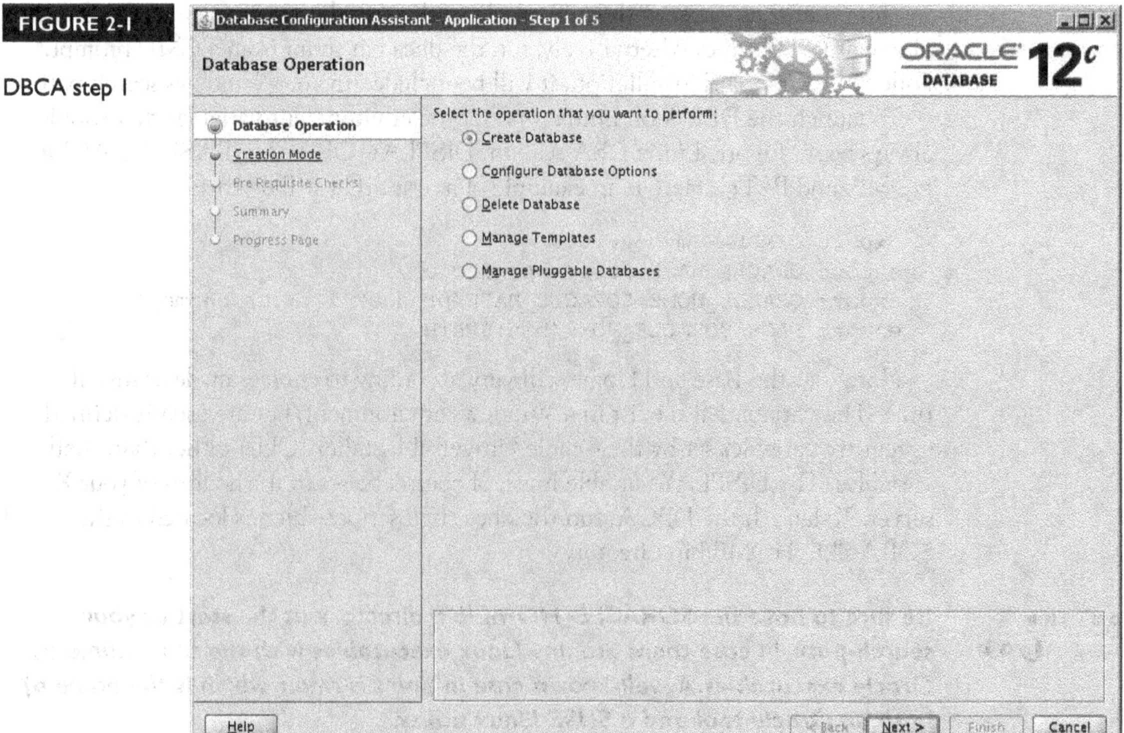

FIGURE 2-1 DBCA step 1

- **Configure Database Options** You can adjust an existing database, perhaps by installing additional capabilities.
- **Delete Database** You can remove any existing instances and databases.
- **Manage Templates** A template is a stored, preconfigured database. Some templates are supplied, or you can create your own from an existing database.
- **Manage Pluggable Databases** Pluggable databases are a new feature in 12*c* and are beyond the scope of the OCA curriculum.

Step 2: Creation Mode

The "Create a database with default configuration" option gives you access to a small subset of the DBCA's capabilities. The Advanced Mode option, on the other hand, gives you access to all the possibilities.

FIGURE 2-2 DBCA step 2

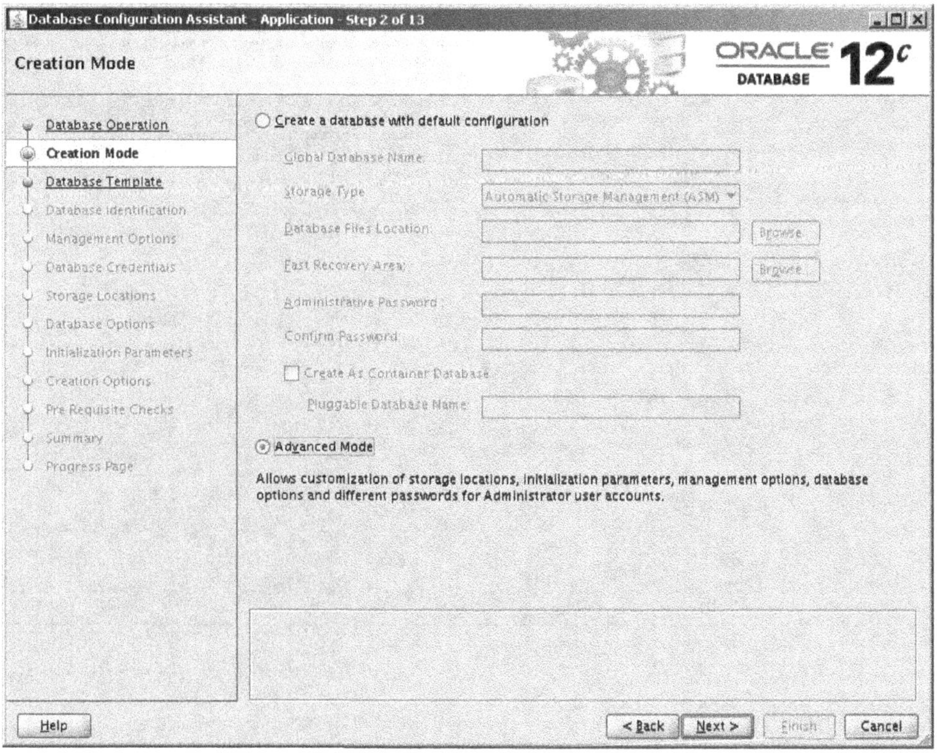

Step 3: Database Template

A template is a stored version of a preconfigured database from which you can generate a new database. Creating a database from a template is much faster than creating it from nothing, but not all options are configurable. Oracle supplies two demonstration templates: a general-purpose template, which is configured for nothing in particular, and a data warehouse template, which is supposedly optimized for query processing rather than transaction processing. The Custom Database option generates a dialog that will give you complete freedom in how the database is configured, with no predefined limits.

FIGURE 2-3

DBCA step 3

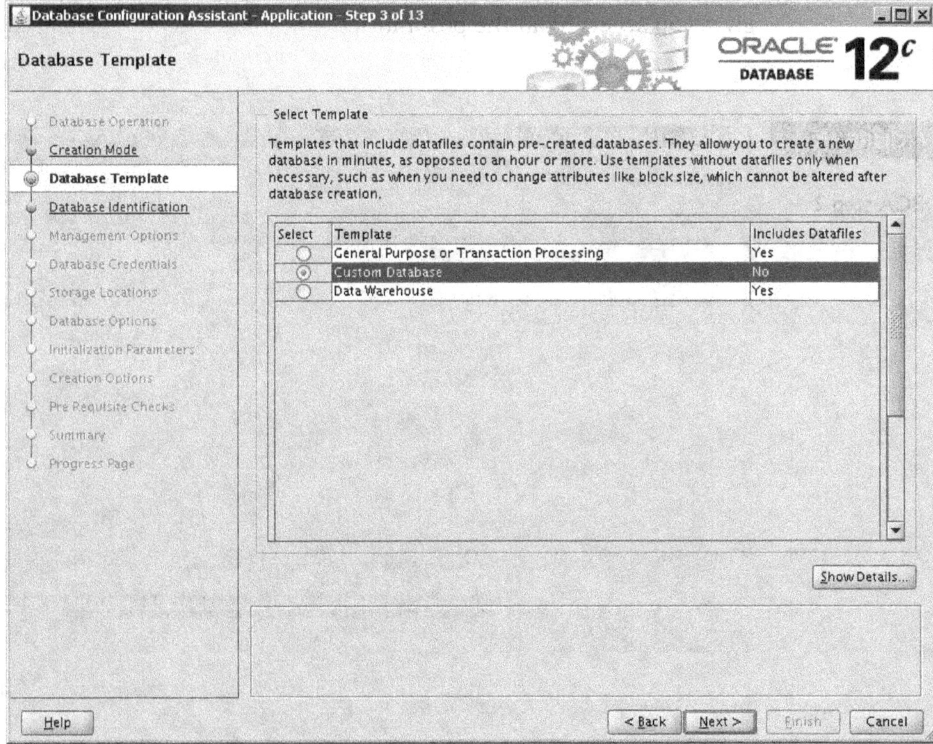

Step 4: Database Identification

The database must have a global database name. The global name consists of a database name and, optionally, a database domain. The database name is embedded in the controlfile, will be specified as the DB_NAME instance parameter, and must be unique on the server machine. The name may be up to eight characters long, including alphanumeric characters, underscore (_), number sign (#), and dollar sign ($), and the first character must be alphabetic. Case sensitivity may vary from one platform to another. The database name is an example of a value you want to get right: it can be changed later, but to do so requires downtime.

The database domain may be up to 128 characters long, including alphanumeric characters and the number sign (#). Dots may be used as separators for the different elements of the domain. The domain is used for the DB_DOMAIN instance parameter. Note that although it is possible to construct a global name that resembles the fully qualified domain names (FQDNs) used on TCP networks, there is no relationship between them.

FIGURE 2-4 DBCA step 4

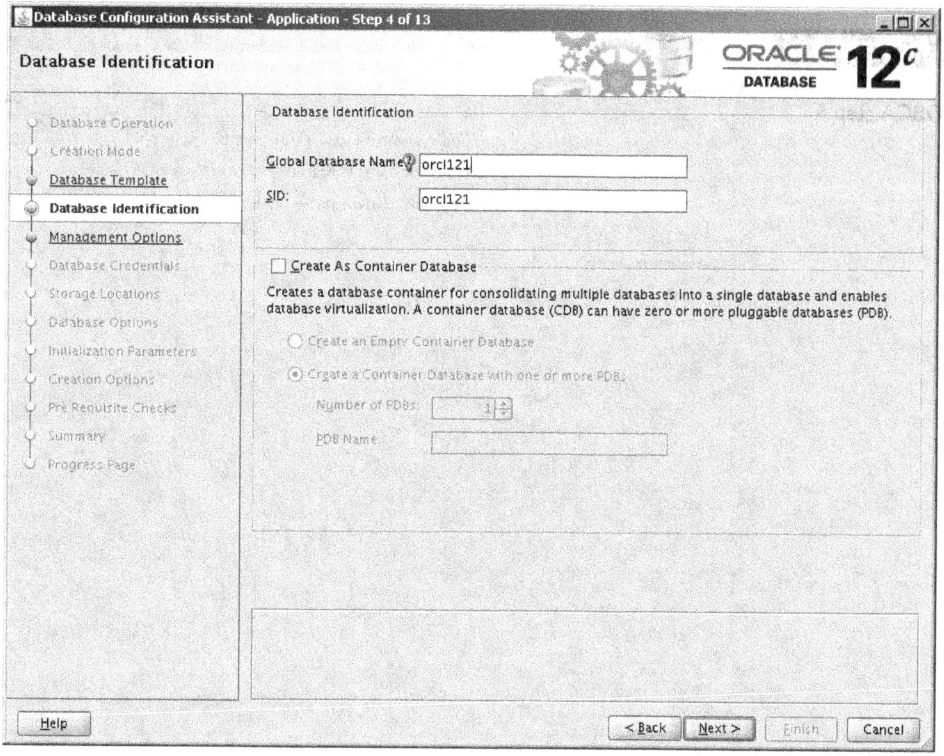

The second required value is the system identifier, or SID. This is the name of the Oracle instance to be created, and is used for the ORACLE_SID parameter. There is no reason for this to be the same as the DB_NAME, but for the sake of your sanity you will usually keep it the same. It must be unique on the database server machine.

on the job

Using global names with a domain may help distinguish databases on different machines that happen to have the same DB_NAME. Many DBAs will append the machine's FQDN as the DB_DOMAIN for this purpose. But there is no need to use a DB_DOMAIN at all: Some DBAs consider domains to be a liability, possibly because they can cause confusion due to their impact on database links and database global name.

Step 5: Management Options

Use of Oracle Enterprise Manager (OEM) is entirely optional. If you want to use it, you have two possibilities: Enterprise Manager Database Express and Enterprise Manager Cloud Control. Enterprise Manager Database Express is a version of OEM

FIGURE 2-5

DBCA step 5

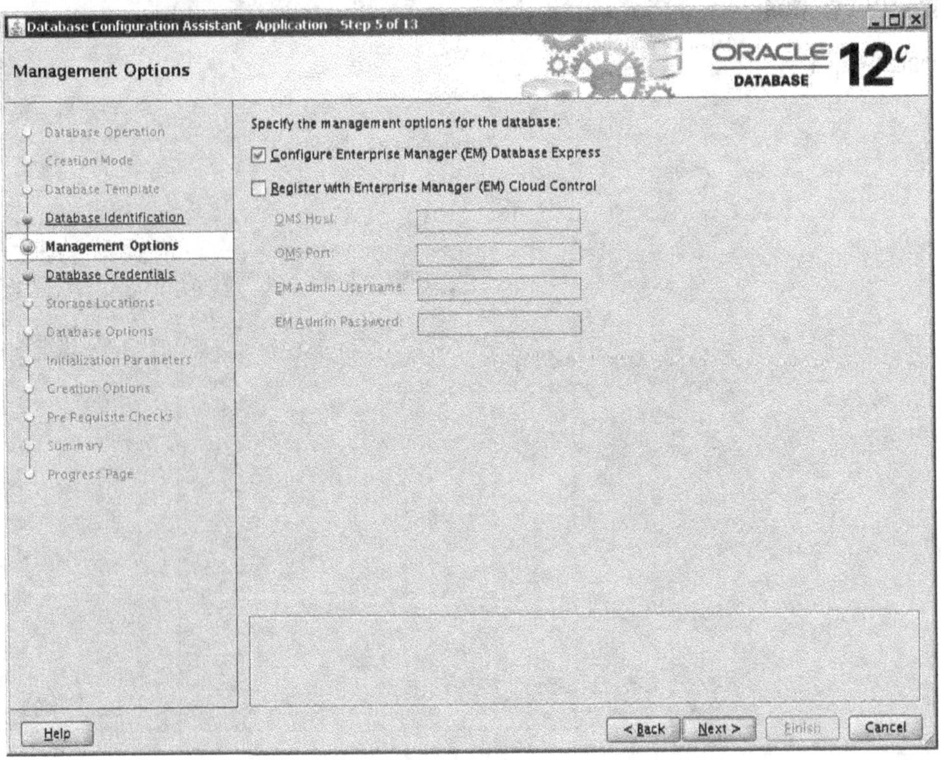

that is configured within the one managed database. If you install a second database, you will require a separate instance of Database Express, configured within that database. Enterprise Manager Cloud Control is Oracle's universal management system, which usually runs on a dedicated machine (or machines) with agents running on each managed server. If you have a Cloud Control installation available, DBCA needs to know how to log on to it.

Step 6: Database Credentials

In this step you provide passwords for the SYS and SYSTEM schemas. SYS is the schema that owns the data dictionary itself, and the password is written out to the external password file. The SYS user is very special, and the password may be required for some critical functions (such as startup and shutdown). The SYSTEM schema is really just a user like any other, but it is given many powerful privileges.

Oracle best practice is that these passwords should be at least eight characters, including a mix of upper- and lowercase letters and at least one digit. The characters

FIGURE 2-6

DBCA step 6

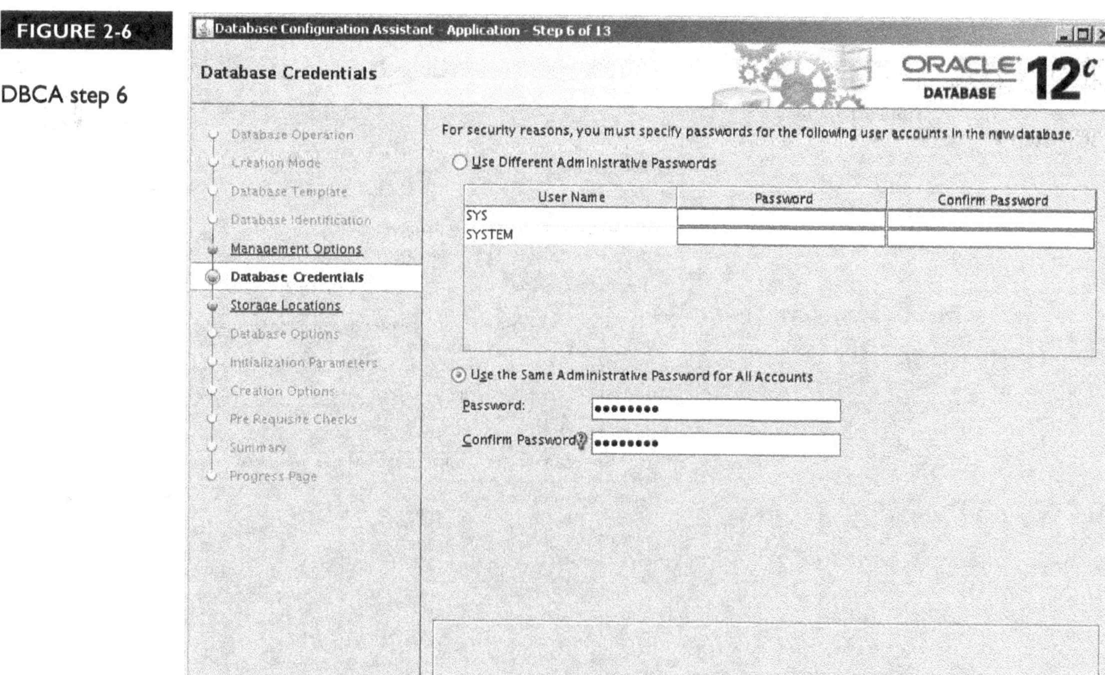

are any included in your database character set (detailed later on). If you specify a password considered too simple, DBCA will complain but will let you proceed nonetheless.

A Windows variation at this point is that you will be prompted for the password of the operating system account that owns the Oracle Home.

on the job

It is often considered best practice to stick to a small range of characters for the passwords (upper- and lowercase letters, digits, and the more common punctuation marks) and to begin with a leading alphabetic character. Some command shell interpreters may have problems with the more unusual characters.

Step 7: Storage Locations

The database may be created on either an Automatic Storage Management disk group or in a file system directory. Either way, you can nominate the destination or let DBCA decide where to store the database files, based on its derived value for

FIGURE 2-7

DBCA step 7

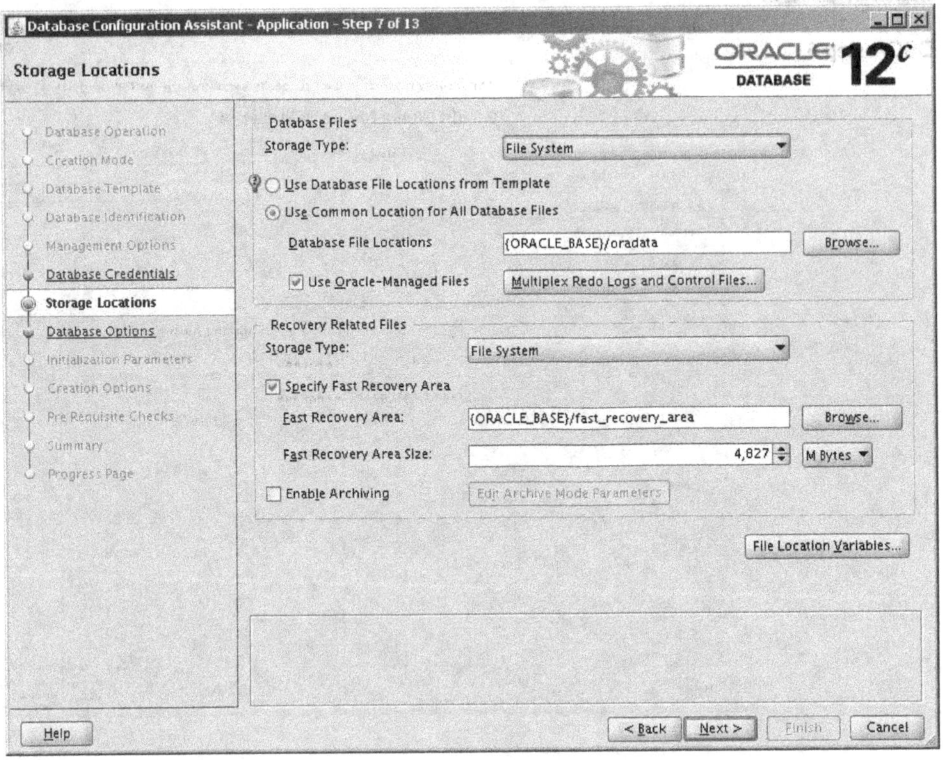

the ORACLE_BASE environment variable. Both storage types can also optionally use Oracle Managed Files, or OMF. OMF lets Oracle take control of naming all your database files and constructing a suitable directory structure within which to store them.

The Recovery Related Files section of this step lets you nominate a Fast Recovery Area to be used as a default location for backups and other files related to recovery, and also to enable the archive log mode of operation. Most (if not all) production databases will run in archive log mode, but it can be enabled at any time subsequent to database creation.

Step 8: Database Options

Figure 2-8 shows those options selected by default if the Oracle Home is an Enterprise Edition installation. Some of these are in fact separately licensed and must be deselected if your license does not include them. The Sample Schemas tab will cause DBCA to install the demonstration schemas into their own tablespace.

FIGURE 2-8

DBCA step 8

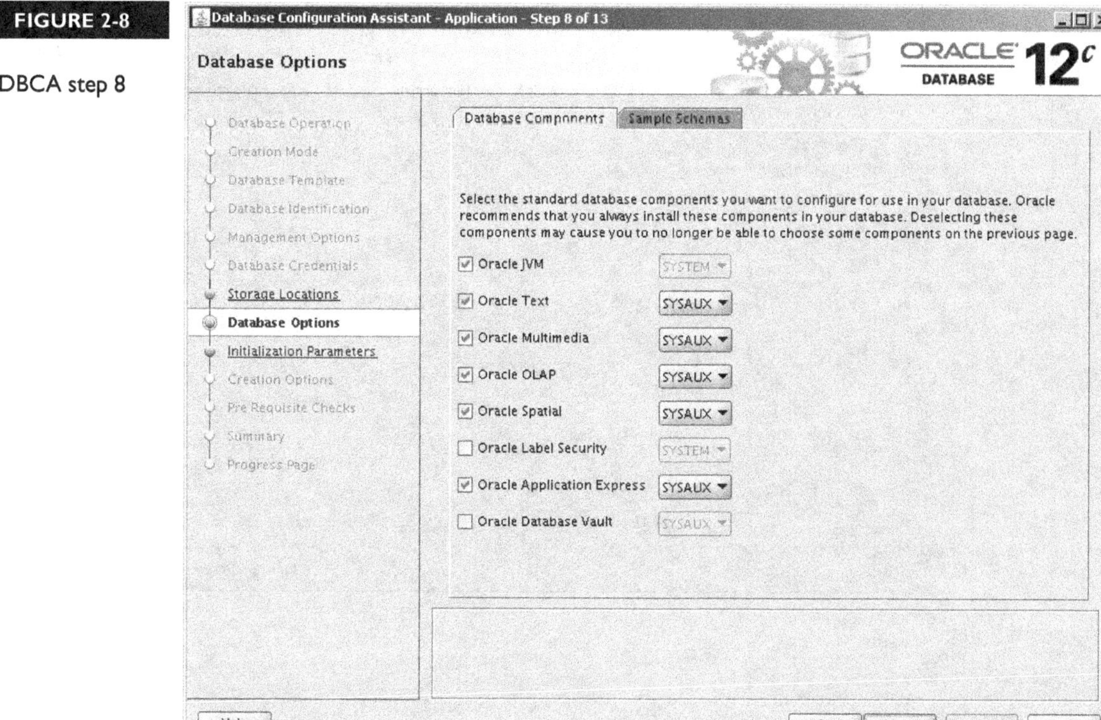

The navigation at this point can produce some surprises. For example, deselecting Java will automatically deselect several other components. Deselecting some other components will disable the option to install the sample schemas.

Step 9: Initialization Parameters

There are over three hundred publicly visible initialization parameters, and thousands more so-called "hidden" parameters. DBCA provides prompts for the bare minimum, with a link to an editor where you can see its defaults for the others and set any you want. Figure 2-9 shows the Memory tab of the step 9 window: You can

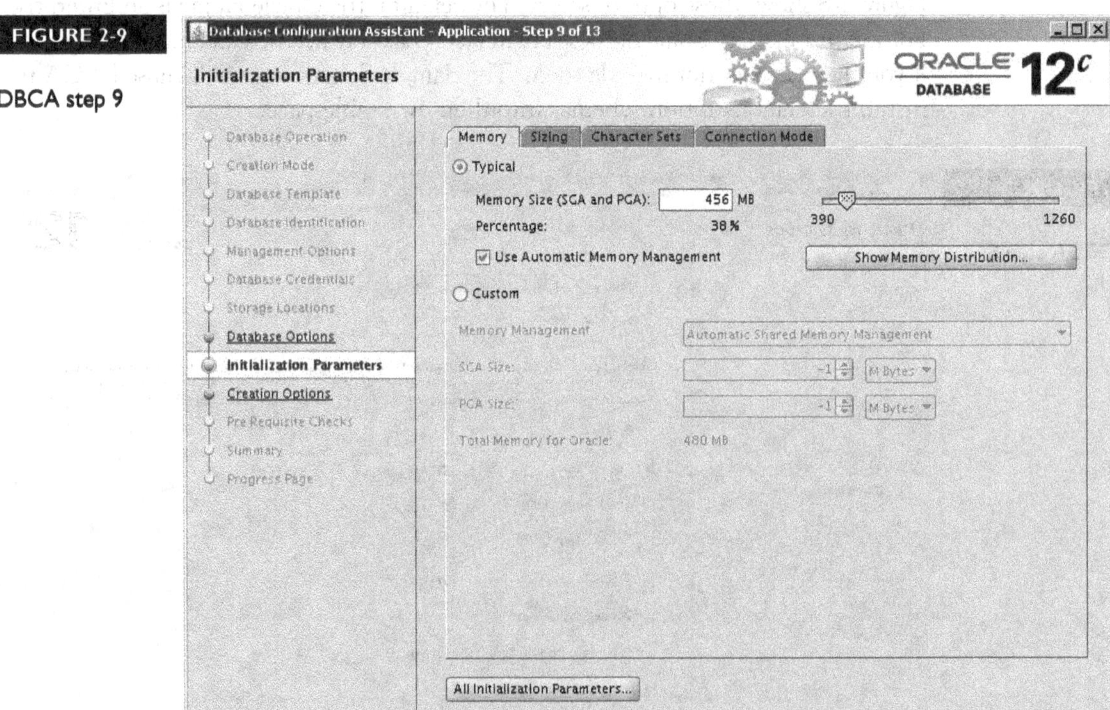

FIGURE 2-9 DBCA step 9

either specify an overall total for memory to be used by the instance (as illustrated) or choose Custom and specify values for the System Global Area (SGA) and the Program Global Area (PGA). SGA is used by the instance and is accessible from all sessions; it is divided into many substructures, some of which can be individually tuned. PGA is divided into private memory areas for each connected session and process. This stage of the DBCA dialog sets some of the memory parameters.

The Sizing tab shows two parameters: DB_BLOCK_SIZE (although the prompt is just "Block Size") and PROCESSES. DB_BLOCK_SIZE is critical: it is the one parameter that can never be changed after database creation. This is because it specifies the size of the blocks into which the SYSTEM tablespace datafile is formatted. The SYSTEM tablespace stores the data dictionary, and to change this would require re-creating the data dictionary, which would be equivalent to creating a new database. The default DB_BLOCK_SIZE is 8K. The legal values are 2K, 4K, 8K, 16K, and (on some platforms) 32K.

The Character Sets tab lets you choose the database character set and the alternative National Character Set. The database character set is used for the data dictionary and all character data types except NVARCHAR2, NCHAR, and NCLOB, which use the National Character Set. It is theoretically possible to change the character set at any time after database creation, but this is a potentially dangerous process and not one on which to embark lightly. Many DBAs (including this author) believe that best practice is not to use the default (which is derived from your operating system) but to use Unicode—specifically, AL32UTF8.

The Connection Mode tab lets you configure the shared server. This topic is discussed in Chapter 5.

on the job

No DBA has ever been fired for choosing 8K, the default value, as his DB_BLOCK_SIZE. There is rarely any reason to use anything else. But the default character set may well be inappropriate, particularly if you are ever likely to have clients using languages other than American English.

Step 10: Creation Options

In this step, the Create Database check box will launch the actual creation. The Save as a Database Template check box will generate a stored template based on the preceding dialog, which can subsequently be used many times (this is selected at step 3).

FIGURE 2-10

DBCA step 10

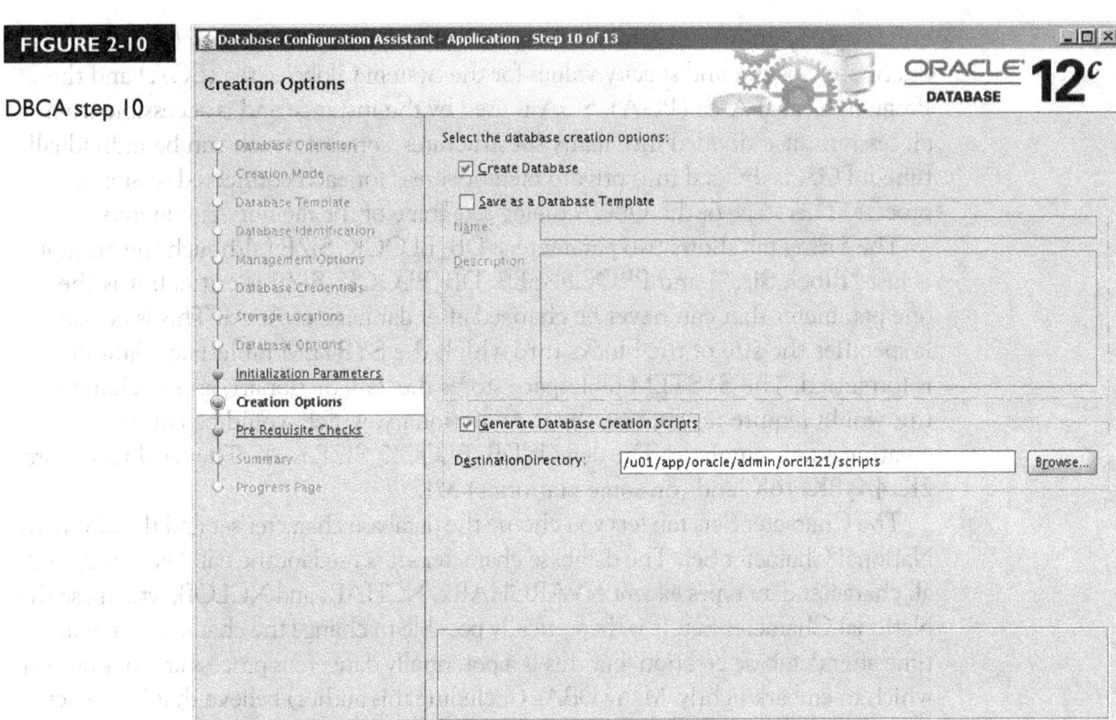

Finally, the Generate Database Creation Scripts check box will generate and save a set of scripts that can be run manually to create the database.

Step 11: Pre Requisite Checks

DBCA runs a few brief "sanity checks" to confirm that the creation will work. If there are any failures, they really should be addressed before proceeding. However, you can choose to ignore them and proceed regardless.

FIGURE 2-11

DBCA step 11

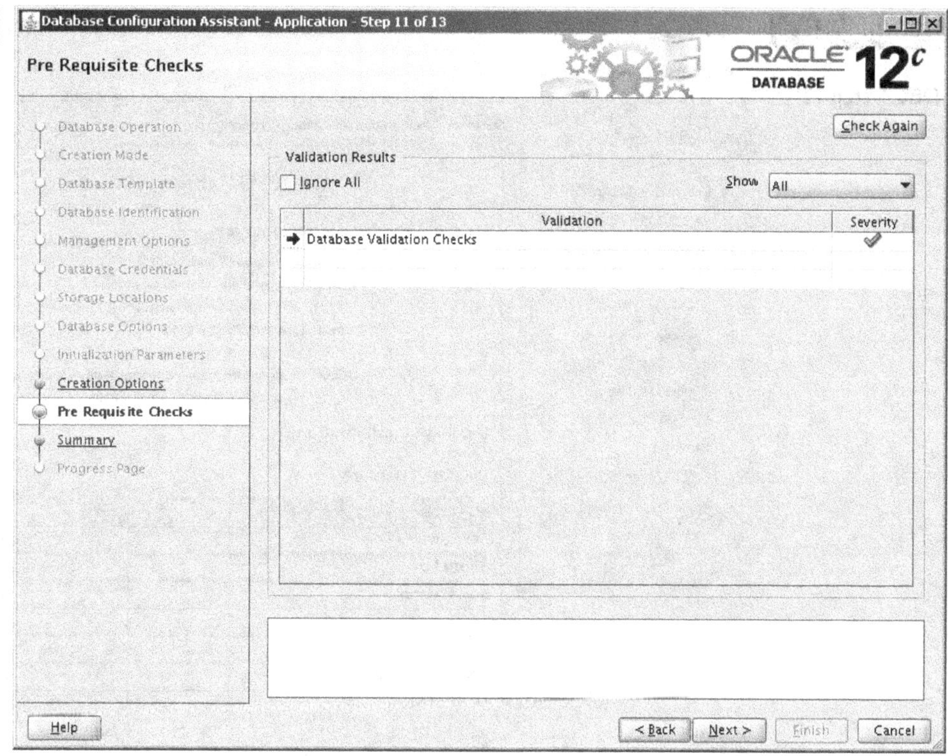

on the job

The DBCA validation checks are not comprehensive. Errors may show up only during step 13. Typical of these are memory issues. For instance, if at step 9 you specify Automatic Memory Management with a total that is more that the shared memory configured on your system, you will not get an error at this point.

Step 12: Summary

The Summary window shows what DBCA intends to do. Scan through the report, and if you see anything you do not like, this would be a good time to use the Back button and make changes.

FIGURE 2-12

DBCA step 12

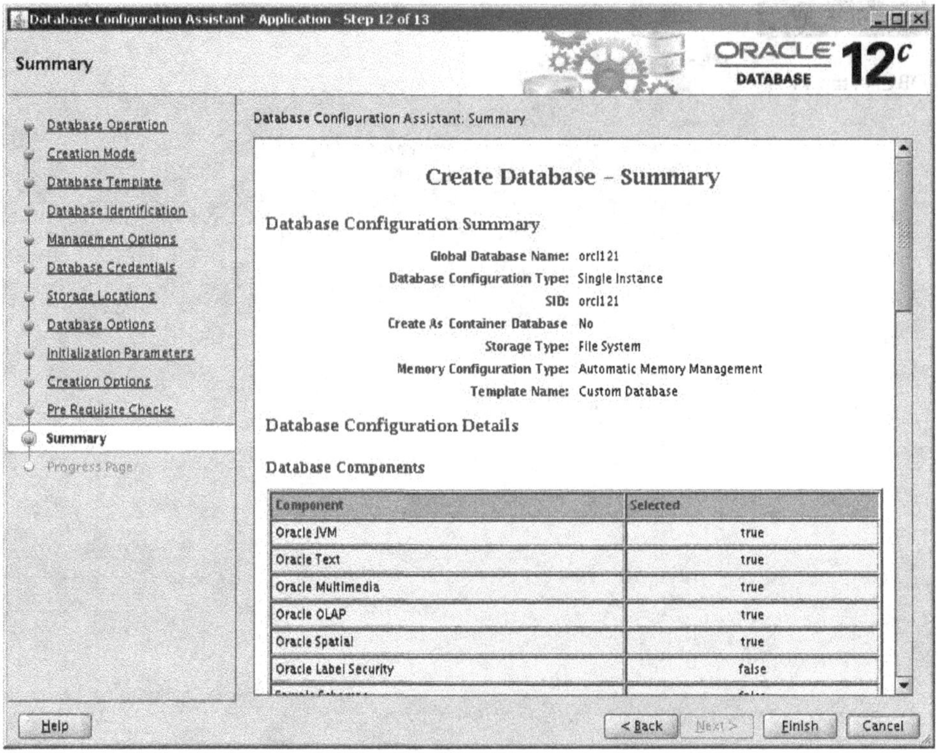

Step 13: Progress Page

The Progress Page window shows the creation of the scripts (if they were requested) and then the various stages of database creation. This may take 10 minutes, or it may take an hour or more. The difference is largely dependent on whether a template was used, what options were selected, and the hardware specifications.

FIGURE 2-13

DBCA step 13

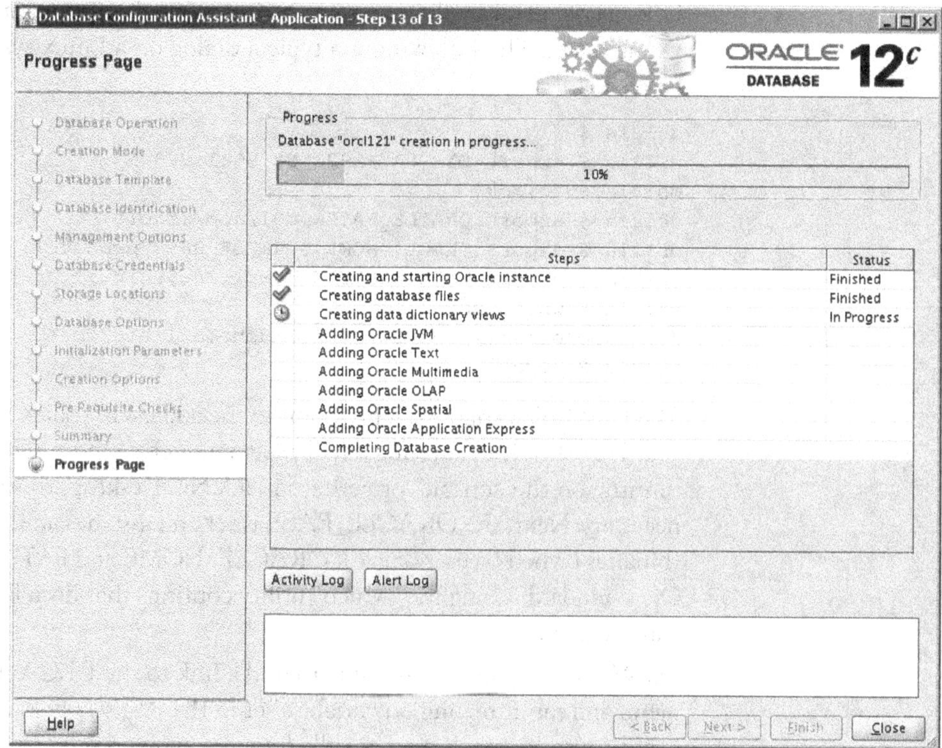

EXERCISE 2-1

Create a Database with DBCA

Using the graphical DBCA tool, create a database. Repeat the exercise as many times as you can, deleting any previously created database(s) first if you are short on RAM or disk space. It is important to become comfortable with the process and to experiment with the various options presented by the dialog.

Some of the responses will vary depending on whether the platform is Windows, Linux, or something else. The variations will be obvious and most commonly have to do with directory naming conventions. Here are the steps to follow:

1. Log on to the server machine.

   Connect to the server as the operating system user who did the installation. The standard account name is oracle.

2. Launch the DBCA.

From a command shell, make sure that you have the appropriate environment variables set. The following is a typical dialog on a Linux system using the bash shell:

```
db121a $
db121a $ export DISPLAY=192.168.56.1:0.0
db121a $ xclock
db121a $ export ORACLE_BASE=/u01/app/oracle
db121a $ export ORACLE_HOME=$ORACLE_BASE/product/12.1.0/dbhome_1
db121a $ export PATH=$ORACLE_HOME/bin:$PATH
db121a $ which dbca
/u01/app/oracle/product/12.1.0/dbhome_1/bin/dbca
db121a $ dbca
```

The DISPLAY variable is set to point to the address of your X server (typically your PC). Test it by running any X program, such as the X-Clock. If you are running on the console, or perhaps in a VNC Desktop, this will not be necessary. Next, the ORACLE_BASE is set and assumes an OFA installation (binaries owned by user oracle). ORACLE_HOME and PATH continue the OFA standard. Using the "which" utility confirms that dbca is on the search path, so launch it.

On Windows, it may be possible to find a link to the DBCA in the Start menu and run it relying on variables set in the Registry. Alternatively, you could control everything manually from a command prompt, again assuming an OFA install:

```
c:\> set ORACLE_BASE=c:\app\oracle
c:\> set ORACLE_HOME=%ORACLE_BASE%\product\12.1.0\dbhome_1
c:\> set PATH=%ORACLE_HOME%\bin;%PATH%
c:\> where dbca
c:\app\oracle\product\12.1.0\dbhome_1\BIN\dbca.bat
c:\> dbca
```

3. Respond to the prompts as follows:
   a. Select the Create Database radio button. Click Next.
   b. Select the Advanced Mode radio button. Click Next.
   c. Select the Custom Database radio button. Click Next.

      Note that at this point, depending on whether the Grid Infrastructure product has already been installed on the server, you may get a prompt regarding Oracle Restart. Ignore this and continue.

d. Specify both the Global Database Name and the SID as orcl121. Click Next.

e. Select the Configure Enterprise Manager (EM) Database Express check box. Click Next.

f. Select the radio button for Use the Same Administrative Password for All Accounts and enter **Oracle121**. Click Next.

g. Select File System in the Storage Type drop-down box, and select the radio button for Use Database File Locations from Template. Leave everything else at the default. This will cause DBCA to create both the database and the Fast Recovery Area beneath the ORACLE_BASE. Click Next.

h. On the Database Components tab, leave everything at the default. Click the Sample Schemas tab and select the Sample Schemas check box. Click Next.

i. Acceptable memory settings will depend on your environment, and the default may or may not be suitable. We'll use values that usually work, even on very low-spec systems.

   Therefore, on the Memory tab, select the Typical radio button, set the value of Memory Size (SGA and PGA) to 640MB, and deselect the Use Automatic Memory Management check box.

   On the Character Sets tab, select the Use Unicode (AL32UTF8) radio button. Click Next.

j. Select the check boxes for both Create Database and Generate Database Creation Scripts. Note the directory where the scripts will be created. Click Next.

k. This should not require any input.

l. Study the summary. Click Finish.

m. The scripts will be generated, followed by a small modal window telling you where they are (if you don't see this window, make sure that it isn't hiding beneath something else). Click OK.

   As the wizards run, you will notice that the first two, which create the instance and the database, complete in just a few minutes. The others, which create the data dictionary views and the various components, will take much longer.

On completion, you will be presented with a success window that shows the URL for accessing Enterprise Manager Database Express. It will resemble this:

http://db121a.example.com:5500/em

Note this URL for future use.

4. Post-installation, confirm that you can log on to the newly created database using SQL*Plus.

From an operating system prompt, set your ORACLE_SID environment variable to the name of the database instance, and then log on and off, as in this example for Windows:

```
c:\>
c:\>set ORACLE_SID=orcl121
c:\>sqlplus / as sysdba
c:\> SQL*Plus: Release 12.1.0.0.2 Beta on Sat Apr 6 12:10:42 2013
Copyright (c) 1982, 2012, Oracle.  All rights reserved.
Connected to:
Oracle Database 12c Enterprise Edition Release 12.1.0.0.2 - 64bit Beta
With the Partitioning, OLAP, Data Mining and Real Application Testing
options
orcl121> exit
Disconnected from Oracle Database 12c Enterprise Edition
Release 12.1.0.0.2 - 64bit Beta
With the Partitioning, OLAP, Data Mining and Real Application Testing
options
c:\>
```

Alternatively, use this example for Linux:

```
db121a orcl121$ db121a orcl121$ export ORACLE_SID=orcl121
db121a orcl121$ sqlplus / as sysdba
SQL*Plus: Release 12.1.0.0.2 Beta on Sat Apr 6 14:08:35 2013
Copyright (c) 1982, 2012, Oracle.  All rights reserved.
Connected to:
Oracle Database 12c Enterprise Edition Release 12.1.0.0.2 - 64bit Beta
With the Partitioning, OLAP, Data Mining and Real Application Testing
options
orcl121> exit
Disconnected from Oracle Database 12c Enterprise Edition
Release 12.1.0.0.2 - 64bit Beta
With the Partitioning, OLAP, Data Mining and Real Application Testing
options
db121a orcl121$
```

5. Repeat ad infinitum.

   Go through this exercise as often as you can, making your own variations, until you are happy with all the options. At "Step 1: Database Operation," you may wish to select the Delete Database radio button to remove the previous creation.

CERTIFICATION OBJECTIVE 2.02

Generate Database Creation Scripts by Using DBCA

There is no reason not to create a database interactively with DBCA, but in many situations it is better to create a database from the command line. Why? Perhaps for one of the following reasons:

- The server machine may not have graphics capability.
- Change control procedures may require tested scripts.
- You may have to create a dozen identical databases.
- You do not wish to sit in front of a screen responding to prompts.

Whatever the reason, it is straightforward to create a database manually, if you have the scripts. And the easiest way to write the scripts is to let DBCA do it for you.

Generating the Scripts

To generate the scripts, launch the DBCA and go through the dialog, taking whatever options are appropriate. At step 10, shown in Figure 2-10, select the appropriate check box and choose a directory. The default location is beneath the ORACLE_BASE. The typical locations for a database named orcl121 on Windows would be

```
c:\app\oracle\admin\orcl121\scripts
```

and on Linux, they would be

```
/u01/app/oracle/admin/orcl121/scripts
```

Whatever the platform, the scripts have the same structure. A shell script named after the database (for example, orcl121.sh for Linux, orcl121.bat for Windows) does some OS work and then launches SQL*Plus to run a SQL script (called oracle121.sql). The SQL script drives the rest of the database creation. Studying these scripts and the scripts they call is very instructive.

The Creation Scripts

The starting point is the shell script. Let's take a look at a Linux example:

```
#!/bin/sh
OLD_UMASK=`umask`
umask 0027
mkdir -p /u01/app/oracle/admin/orcl121/adump
mkdir -p /u01/app/oracle/admin/orcl121/dpdump
mkdir -p /u01/app/oracle/admin/orcl121/pfile
mkdir -p /u01/app/oracle/audit
mkdir -p /u01/app/oracle/cfgtoollogs/dbca/orcl121
mkdir -p /u01/app/oracle/fast_recovery_area
mkdir -p /u01/app/oracle/fast_recovery_area/orcl121
mkdir -p /u01/app/oracle/oradata/orcl121
mkdir -p /u01/app/oracle/product/12.1.0/dbhome_1/dbs
umask ${OLD_UMASK}
ORACLE_SID=orcl121; export ORACLE_SID
PATH=$ORACLE_HOME/bin:$PATH; export PATH
echo You should Add this entry in the /etc/oratab:
orcl121:/u01/app/oracle/product/12.1.0/dbhome_1:Y
/u01/app/oracle/product/12.1.0/dbhome_1/bin/sqlplus /nolog
@/u01/app/oracle/admin/orcl121/scripts/orcl121.sql
```

This creates a few directories, using values calculated from the ORACLE_BASE and ORACLE_HOME environment variables, provided in the DBCA dialog, or from defaults with appropriate access permissions. It then concludes with the call to SQL*Plus, to launch the SQL script orcl121.sql. A variation on Windows will be calls to the ORADIM utility (described later) that create the Windows service under which the instance will run.

The driving SQL script will vary greatly, depending on the options taken in the DBCA dialog. Here is one example:

```
set verify off
ACCEPT sysPassword CHAR PROMPT 'Enter new password for SYS: ' HIDE
ACCEPT systemPassword CHAR PROMPT 'Enter new password for SYSTEM: ' HIDE
host /u01/app/oracle/product/12.1.0/dbhome_1/bin/orapwd file=/u01/app/
```

```
oracle/product/12.1.0/dbhome_1/dbs/orapworcl121 force=y extended=y
@/u01/app/oracle/admin/orcl121/scripts/CreateDB.sql
@/u01/app/oracle/admin/orcl121/scripts/CreateDBFiles.sql
@/u01/app/oracle/admin/orcl121/scripts/CreateDBCatalog.sql
@/u01/app/oracle/admin/orcl121/scripts/sampleSchema.sql
@/u01/app/oracle/admin/orcl121/scripts/apex.sql
@/u01/app/oracle/admin/orcl121/scripts/postDBCreation.sql
@/u01/app/oracle/admin/orcl121/scripts/lockAccount.sql
```

The ACCEPT commands prompt for passwords for the SYS and SYSTEM schemas. Then the script invokes a host shell to run the orapwd utility. This utility creates the external password file, with a name that is platform specific. On Linux it will be $ORACLE_HOME/dbs/orapw<DBNAME> (where <DBNAME> is the name of the database), and on Windows it will be %ORACLE_HOME%\database\PWD<DBNAME>.ora.

Following this is a set of calls to other SQL scripts, beginning with CreateDB.sql:

```
SET VERIFY OFF
connect "SYS"/"&&sysPassword" as SYSDBA
set echo on
spool /u01/app/oracle/admin/orcl121/scripts/CreateDB.log append
startup nomount pfile="/u01/app/oracle/admin/orcl121/scripts/init.ora";
CREATE DATABASE "orcl121"
MAXINSTANCES 8
MAXLOGHISTORY 1
MAXLOGFILES 16
MAXLOGMEMBERS 3
MAXDATAFILES 100
DATAFILE '/u01/app/oracle/oradata/orcl121/system01.dbf' SIZE 700M
REUSE AUTOEXTEND ON NEXT  10240K MAXSIZE UNLIMITED
EXTENT MANAGEMENT LOCAL
SYSAUX DATAFILE '/u01/app/oracle/oradata/orcl121/sysaux01.dbf' SIZE 550M
REUSE AUTOEXTEND ON NEXT  10240K MAXSIZE UNLIMITED
SMALLFILE DEFAULT TEMPORARY TABLESPACE TEMP TEMPFILE '/u01/app/oracle/
oradata/orcl121/temp01.dbf' SIZE 20M
REUSE AUTOEXTEND ON NEXT  640K MAXSIZE UNLIMITED
SMALLFILE UNDO TABLESPACE "UNDOTBS1" DATAFILE  '/u01/app/oracle/oradata/
orcl121/undotbs01.dbf' SIZE 200M
REUSE AUTOEXTEND ON NEXT  5120K MAXSIZE UNLIMITED
CHARACTER SET AL32UTF8
NATIONAL CHARACTER SET AL16UTF16
LOGFILE GROUP 1 ('/u01/app/oracle/oradata/orcl121/redo01.log') SIZE
51200K,
GROUP 2 ('/u01/app/oracle/oradata/orcl121/redo02.log') SIZE 51200K,
```

```
GROUP 3 ('/u01/app/oracle/oradata/orcl121/redo03.log') SIZE 51200K
USER SYS IDENTIFIED BY "&&sysPassword" USER SYSTEM IDENTIFIED BY
"&&systemPassword";
spool off
```

The second line connects as user SYS using the supplied password. The fifth line starts the database in no mount mode using a parameter file named init.ora. This file will be populated with parameters set by default or specified in the DBCA dialog. The next command (which continues to the end of the file) creates the database.

Note: Remember the modes: nomount means "build the memory structures and start the processes."

Following the CREATE DATABASE "orcl121" line are some settings for limits (such as MAXDATAFILES=100, meaning that this database will be restricted to 100 datafiles) and then clauses for four tablespaces:

- The SYSTEM tablespace (where the data dictionary lives) will be in a datafile named system01.dbf with a size of 700MB.
- The SYSAUX tablespace (objects that are not associated with the data dictionary but are very closely related) will be in a datafile named sysaux01.dbf with a size of 550MB.
- A default temporary tablespace (for temporary data—space needed by sessions for, one hopes, only a brief period) named TEMP will be in tempfile temp01.dbf, with a size of 20MB. An undo tablespace (used for undo segments, which are necessary to ensure transactional consistency) named UNDOTBS1 will use the datafile undotbs01.dbf, with a size of 200MB.

Then the character sets for the database and national language are specified. In the example, they are Unicode. The LOGFILE section specifies that the database should have three online log file groups, each consisting of one file (the log file member) that's 50MB in size. Finally, the passwords for SYS and SYSTEM are set.

This database creation command takes only a couple minutes to run. All it does is create the minimal structures necessary for a database, most importantly the data dictionary. Control then returns to the calling SQL script, which (in the example) launches more scripts:

- CreateDBFiles.sql will create a tablespace called USERS, to be used as the default tablespace for storing permanent objects (such as tables).
- CreateDBCatalog.sql calls a set of scripts to generate the required views onto the data dictionary and the various supplied PL/SQL packages.

- A set of scripts (JServer.sql through apex.sql) then generate various options that were selected in the DBCA dialog.
- postDBCreation.sql runs anything necessary immediately after creation, such as applying bundled patches and converting the pfile to an spfile.
- lockAccount.sql locks all pre-seeded accounts (with a few exceptions) and finally restarts the database.

The scripts generated and their contents vary greatly, depending on the DBCA dialog. For example, if at step 3 you choose to create a database from a template, the whole process is much simpler because the database does not need to be created, and most of the work is done via calls to the RMAN Recovery Manager procedures, which in effect restore a database from a backup in the template.

The Initialization Parameter File

In order to start the database instance, DBCA must create an initialization parameter file. This is generated whether you take the option to create a database or to generate scripts. The file is generated in the same directory as the other script and is nominated on the STARTUP command in the CreateDB.sql script:

```
startup nomount pfile="/u01/app/oracle/admin/orcl121/scripts/init.ora";
```

Here is the file generated by the dialog from Exercise 2-1 (comment lines removed for brevity):

```
db_block_size=8192
open_cursors=300
db_domain=""
db_name="orcl121"
control_files=("/u01/app/oracle/oradata/orcl121/control01.ctl",
"/u01/app/oracle/fast_recovery_area/orcl121/control02.ctl")
db_recovery_file_dest="/u01/app/oracle/fast_recovery_area"
db_recovery_file_dest_size=5061476352
compatible=12.0.0.0.0
diagnostic_dest=/u01/app/oracle
processes=300
sga_target=503316480
audit_file_dest="/u01/app/oracle/admin/orcl121/adump"
audit_trail=db
```

```
remote_login_passwordfile=EXCLUSIVE
dispatchers="(PROTOCOL=TCP) (SERVICE=orcl121XDB)"
pga_aggregate_target=167772160
undo_tablespace=UNDOTBS1
```

All these parameters will be covered in later chapters. The file has just 16 parameters specified out of hundreds, and is the bare minimum needed to get a typical database running. Many more parameters will usually be added subsequently according to the requirements for the environment, scale, and performance.

EXERCISE 2-2

Generate Database Creation Scripts by Using DBCA

Use DBCA to generate several sets of database creation scripts. Perform as many iterations of this as you wish, supplying a different database name and SID each time, and selecting different options. Here are the steps to follow:

1. Launch the DBCA. Respond to the prompts as follows:
    a. Select the Create Database radio button. Click Next.
    b. Select the radio button for Advanced Mode. If you choose the button for "Create a database with default configuration," you do not get a prompt to generate scripts. Click Next.
    c. Select the radio button for General Purpose or Transaction Processing. Click Next.
    d. Specify the value **gpdb** for both Global Database Name and SID. Click Next.
    e. Deselect everything. Click Next.
    f. Enter the passwords as Oracle121. Click Next.
    g. Choose Storage Type: File System. Leave everything else at the default. Click Next.
    h. Leave everything at the default. Click Next.
    i. Leave everything at the default. Click Next.
    j. Deselect the check boxes for Create Database and Save as a Database Template. Select the check box for Generate Database Creation Scripts. Note the destination directory. Click Next.

k. No input needed.
l. Study the summary. Note that the install from a template will include all the options that were prompted for in the previous exercise, and will also have values for various parameters. Click Finish.
m. The scripts will be generated. Click OK and then Close.

2. Study the scripts.

   Attempt to reverse-engineer the creation process. Note that the process is much simpler when using a template. Compare the scripts generated by this exercise with those generated by the previous exercise.

3. Repeat.

   And repeat again, with variations. It is vital to become familiar with the DBCA dialog, and with the scripts that it generates.

CERTIFICATION OBJECTIVE 2.03

Manage Database Design Templates by Using DBCA

A template is a stored definition of a database. This definition can be subsequently used to create any number of databases, and it's portable across platforms. Templates come in one of two forms:

- **Structure only** A "structure only" template contains the structural information (database options selected, storage details, initialization parameters) but does not include the actual datafiles. When this template is used, the database will be created from nothing. It is not possible for any user-defined data to be included.
- **Structure and data** A "structure and data" template also includes the datafiles. Databases created from this template will be identical to the database from which the template was generated, as of the time of generation.

Templates are managed through DBCA. If at step 1 of the DBCA dialog (refer to Figure 2-1) you choose the radio button for Manage Templates, you will prompted whether to delete a template or create one from one of three sources:

- An already existing template
- An existing database, structure only
- An existing database, structure and data

The template or database must already exist on the machine from which DBCA is running. Note that the template creation from a running database will require a restart of the source database if the template includes datafiles, but not if it is structure only.

The DBCA dialog is perfectly straightforward: You are prompted for the source and type of the template and, if it includes datafiles, for the location of the file that will store the compressed database. Once the template has been created, it will be visible as a source for a new database on step 3 of the DBCA dialog.

The underlying storage for a template is from files in the ORACLE_HOME/assistants/dbca/templates directory. Copying these files to another Oracle Home will make the template available there.

EXERCISE 2-3

Manage Database Design Templates by Using DBCA

Use DBCA to create a template from the database created in this chapter's first exercise. Here are the steps to follow:

1. Launch the DBCA. Respond to the prompts as follows:
   a. Select the Manage Templates radio button. Click Next.
   b. Select the radio buttons for "Create a database template" and "From an existing database" (structure as well as data). Click Next.
   c. Select orcl121 from the Database Instance drop-down box. Click Next.
   d. Give the template a name and description. Note that the name is used for the name of the template datafile in ORACLE_HOME/assistants/dbca/templates. Click Next.

   e. Select the radio button for converting the file locations to use OFA structure. This is usually the best option because it makes it simpler to use the template on another machine with a different file system. Click Next.
   f. Note the summary information. Click Finish.
   g. The template will be created, restarting the source database if it is running. This is necessary for the copy of the datafiles to be consistent: The copy is made with the database in mount mode. Click OK and then Close.
2. Use the template.

   Use the template (if you want) to create a database. Launch the DBCA, and respond to the prompts as follows:
   a. Select the radio button for Create Database. Click Next.
   b. Select the radio button for Advanced Mode. Click Next.
   c. The list of templates presented will include the newly created template. Note that it does include data files. Select its radio button, and click the Show Details button. This will generate the equivalent of the summary information previously displayed when the source database was created. Study this and then dismiss the window.
3. Exit from DBCA. Click the Cancel button and then confirm to exit.

CERTIFICATION OBJECTIVE 2.04

Configure Database Options by Using DBCA

The final topic on database creation is modifying databases subsequent to creation. The concept to hang on to is that a database option, generally speaking, is a combination of executable code in the Oracle Home and necessary objects (such as tables and PL/SQL procedures) in the database. The software installation will have installed the executable code. But for any one database running off that Home, the options will be enabled only if the objects have been created. The DBCA database creation dialog (shown previously in Figure 2-8) prompts for which options to install, which determines the scripts called by the driving database creation script. It will by now be apparent why when using a template with datafiles it is not possible to control the options: They either will or will not have existed in the database from which the template was generated.

Using DBCA to configure options causes DBCA to generate calls to scripts that will install options in the database. It is not possible to uninstall options through DBCA. To see the installed options, log on to the database and query the DBA_REGISTRY view. Here's an example:

```
orcl121> select comp_name,version,status from dba_registry order by 1;
COMP_NAME                           VERSION          STATUS
----------------------------------- --------------- ------
OLAP Catalog                        12.1.0.0.2       VALID
Oracle Application Express          4.1.1.00.23      VALID
Oracle Database Catalog Views       12.1.0.0.2       VALID
Oracle Database Packages and Types  12.1.0.0.2       VALID
Oracle Expression Filter            12.1.0.0.2       VALID
5 rows selected.
orcl121>
```

EXERCISE 2-4

Configure Database Options by Using DBCA

In this exercise, you'll use DBCA to add an option that was not selected for the original database creation. Here are the steps to follow:

1. Confirm the list of options installed.

   From an operating system prompt, log on to the database and run this query:

   ```
   select comp_name from dba_registry;
   ```

2. Launch the DBCA. Respond to the prompts as follows:
   a. Select the Configure Database Options radio button. Click Next.
   b. Select the radio button for the orcl21 database. Click Next.
   c. DBCA will present the list of components given at creation time (refer Figure 2-8), with those previously selected grayed out and any remaining available for selection. Note that it is not possible to add the sample schemas with this method.

      Select the check box for Oracle Label Security. Click Next.

   d. Deselect the check box for Oracle Database Vault. Click Next.
   e. Leave everything at the default. Click Next.
   f. The summary will show what is to be installed. Click Finish.
   g. The option will install. Click OK and Close.
3. Confirm the installation.

   Rerun the query against DBA_REGISTRY and note that Label Security is now an installed component.

CERTIFICATION SUMMARY

This chapter covers in great detail what you can do with DBCA. But more important is to understand what DBCA is doing for you: It is generating scripts. Few practicing DBAs will create production databases with DBCA from the supplied templates. But equally few will create their production databases by typing freehand commands into SQL*Plus. DBCA's greatest value is in generating scripts that can be studied, edited, and saved for reuse.

The template capability can be invaluable for automating creation of identical databases. Create one database, get it right, and save it as a template. The only issue is space: If the database on which the template is based is a couple of terabytes, you will need a lot of space for the template. Best to use templates for replicating near-empty databases (and the RMAN duplicate-from-backup technique to replicate fully populated databases).

TWO-MINUTE DRILL

Create a Database by Using the Database Configuration Assistant (DBCA)

- DBCA is written in Java and requires a graphical display.
- The dialog prompts for all necessary information to create an instance and a database.
- At the conclusion of the creation, the database is ready for use.

Generate Database Creation Scripts by Using DBCA

- The generation includes a shell script that calls a set of SQL scripts.
- Also generated are a parameter file and a password file.
- The scripts can optionally be edited and then run manually.

Manage Database Design Templates by Using DBCA

- A template is a saved database definition from which more databases can be created.
- Templates include structural information and, optionally, datafiles.
- A "structure only" template cannot include references to user objects.
- A "structure plus data" template permits only minimal changes at creation time.

Configure Database Options by Using DBCA

- Options are installed by running scripts against an existing database.
- It is not possible to uninstall options through DBCA.

SELF TEST

Create a Database by Using the Database Configuration Assistant (DBCA)

1. Which of these operations can be accomplished with the DBCA? (Choose all correct answers.)

A. Create a database

B. Remove a database

C. Upgrade a database

D. Add database options

E. Remove database options

2. To create a database, in what mode must the instance be? (Choose the best answer.)

A. Not started

B. Started in NOMOUNT mode

C. Started in MOUNT mode

D. Started in OPEN mode

3. Several actions are necessary to create a database. Place these in the correct order:

1. Create the data dictionary views.
2. Create the parameter file.
3. Create the password file.
4. Issue the **CREATE DATABASE** command.
5. Issue the **STARTUP** command.

(Choose the best answer.)

A. 2, 3, 5, 4, 1

B. 3, 5, 2, 4, 1

C. 5, 3, 4, 2, 1

D. 2, 3, 1, 4, 5

4. What instance parameter cannot be changed after database creation? (Choose the best answer.)

A. All instance parameters can be changed after database creation.

B. All instance parameters can be changed after database creation, if it is done while the instance is in MOUNT mode.

C. CONTROL_FILES.

D. DB_BLOCK_SIZE.

5. What files are created by the **CREATE DATABASE** command? (Choose all correct answers.)
   A. The controlfile
   B. The server parameter file
   C. The online redo log files
   D. The password file
   E. The static initialization parameter file
   F. The SYSAUX tablespace datafile
   G. The SYSTEM tablespace datafile
6. What will happen if you do not run the CATALOG.SQL and CATPROC.SQL scripts after creating a database? (Choose the best answer.)
   A. It will not be possible to open the database.
   B. It will not be possible to create any user tables.
   C. It will not be possible to use PL/SQL.
   D. It will not be possible to query the data dictionary views.
   E. It will not be possible to connect as any user other than SYS.

Manage Database Design Templates by Using DBCA

7. What tools can be used to manage templates? (Choose all correct answers.)
   A. The Database Configuration Assistant
   B. The Database Upgrade Assistant
   C. SQL*Plus
   D. Database Express
   E. The Oracle Universal Installer
8. At what point can you not choose or change the database character set? (Choose the best answer.)
   A. At database creation time, if you are using a DBCA template
   B. At database creation time, if you are using a DBCA template that includes datafiles
   C. At database creation time, if you are not using a DBCA template
   D. After database creation, using DBCA to install options

Configure Database Options by Using DBCA

9. If there are several databases created off the same Oracle Home, how will Database Express be configured? (Choose the best answer.)

A. Database Express will give access to all the databases created from the one Oracle Home through one URL.
B. Database Express will give access to each database through different ports.
C. Database Express need only be configured in one database and can then be used to connect to all of them.
D. Database Express can manage only one database per Oracle Home.

10. The SYSAUX tablespace is mandatory. What will happen if you attempt to issue a **CREATE DATABASE** command that does not specify a datafile for the SYSAUX tablespace? (Choose the best answer.)
    A. The command will fail.
    B. The command will succeed, but the database will be inoperable until the SYSAUX tablespace is created.
    C. A default SYSAUX tablespace and datafile will be created.
    D. The SYSAUX objects will be created in the SYSTEM tablespace.

Generate Database Creation Scripts by Using DBCA

11. What files are generated when you choose the option to Generate Database Creation Scripts in the Database Configuration Assistant? (Choose all correct answers.)
    A. A shell script
    B. SQL scripts
    C. A parameter file
    D. A password file
    E. A response file

LAB QUESTION

Create a database manually by following these steps:

1. Create an initialization file with the bare minimum of parameters.
2. Issue a **CREATE DATABASE** command.
3. Run a few queries to see what has been created.
4. Delete the database.

SELF TEST ANSWERS

Create a Database by Using the Database Configuration Assistant (DBCA)

1. ☑ **A, B, D.** The DBCA can create and remove databases, and also install options into existing databases.
   ☒ **C** and **E** are incorrect. A database upgrade would require the DBUA (the Database Upgrade Assistant), not the DBCA. Removing options cannot be done through any wizard: It is a manual process.

2. ☑ **B.** The instance must be running before you create a database.
   ☒ **A, C,** and **D** are incorrect. The instance must be started, but it cannot be mounted (because there is no controlfile) or opened (because there are no datafiles).

3. ☑ **A.** This is the correct sequence (although 2 and 3 could be done the other way round).
   ☒ **B, C,** and **D** are incorrect. None of these sequences are possible.

4. ☑ **D.** This is the one parameter that can never be changed after creation.
   ☒ **A, B,** and **C** are incorrect. **A** and **B** are incorrect because DB_BLOCK_SIZE cannot be changed no matter when you try to do it. **C** is incorrect because the CONTROL_FILES parameter can certainly be changed, although this will require a shutdown and restart.

5. ☑ **A, C, F,** and **G.** All of these will always be created, by default, if they are not specified.
   ☒ **B, D,** and **E** are incorrect. **B** and **D** are incorrect because these should exist before the instance is started. **E** is incorrect because the conversion of the static parameter file to a dynamic parameter file only occurs, optionally, after the database is created.

6. ☑ **D.** The database will function, but without the data dictionary views and PL/SQL packages created by these scripts, it will be unusable.
   ☒ **A, B, C,** and **E** are incorrect. **A** is incorrect because the database will open; in fact, it must be open to run the scripts. **B** is incorrect because tables and other objects can certainly be created. **C** is incorrect because PL/SQL will be available; it is the supplied packages that will be missing. **E** is incorrect because although the scripts need to be run by SYS, you can connect as other users.

Manage Database Design Templates by Using DBCA

7. ☑ **A.** The DBCA is the only tool that can manage templates.
   ☒ **B, C, D,** and **E** are incorrect. These are all incorrect because only the DBCA offers template management.

8. ☑ **D.** It is not possible to change character sets after database creation with DBCA: Character sets are not installed as options.
   ☒ **A, B,** and **C** are incorrect. **A** and **B** are incorrect because templates are not relevant. If the template includes datafiles, the DBCA will change the character set behind the scenes. **C** is incorrect because creation without a template gives you complete control, including your choice of character set.

Configure Database Options by Using DBCA

9. ☑ **B.** Database Express can be used for each database and will be configured with a different port for each one.
   ☒ **A, C,** and **D** are incorrect. **A** is incorrect because this would require Cloud Control. **C** is incorrect because Database Express must be installed in every database that will use it. **D** is incorrect because although a Database Express instance is only for one database, every database can have its own.

10. ☑ **C.** There are defaults for everything, including the SYSAUX tablespace and datafile definitions.
    ☒ **A, B,** and **D** are incorrect. **A** is incorrect because the command will succeed. **B** and **D** are incorrect because these are not the way the defaults work.

Generate Database Creation Scripts by Using DBCA

11. ☑ **A, B, C, D. One shell script is generated which calls a set of SQL scripts. There is also a password file to allow SYSDBA connections, and a parameter file to start the instance.**
    ☒ **E.** This is incorrect because response files are generated by the Oracle Universal Installer, not by the Configuration Assistant.

LAB ANSWER

Here is a Windows example of the parameter file:

```
db_name=manualdb
db_create_file_dest=c:\app\oracle\oradata\manualdb
audit_file_dest= c:\app\oracle\manualdb\audit
```

Name the file initmanualdb.ora and place it in the directory %ORACLE_HOME%\database. Create the two directories specified in the file. If you're working on Linux, adjust the directory names appropriately and place the file in $ORACLE_HOME/dbs.

Next, set your ORACLE_SID environment variable. Here it is on Windows:

```
set ORACLE_SID=manualdb
```

And here it is on Linux:

```
export ORACLE_SID=manualdb
```

Also, set your ORACLE_HOME and PATH variables as usual. On Windows, create the service

```
oradim -new -sid manualdb
```

and then launch SQL*Plus and issue a **CREATE DATABASE** command, relying on defaults for everything:

```
sqlplus / as sysdba
startup nomount;
create database;
```

Next, here are some queries:

```
select instance_name, status from v$instance;
select name,open_mode from v$database;
select name from v$datafile;
select * from v$controlfile;
select member from v$logfile;
```

To remove the database, run the **DROP DATABASE** command from within SQL*Plus:

```
shutdown immediate;
startup mount restrict;
drop database;
```

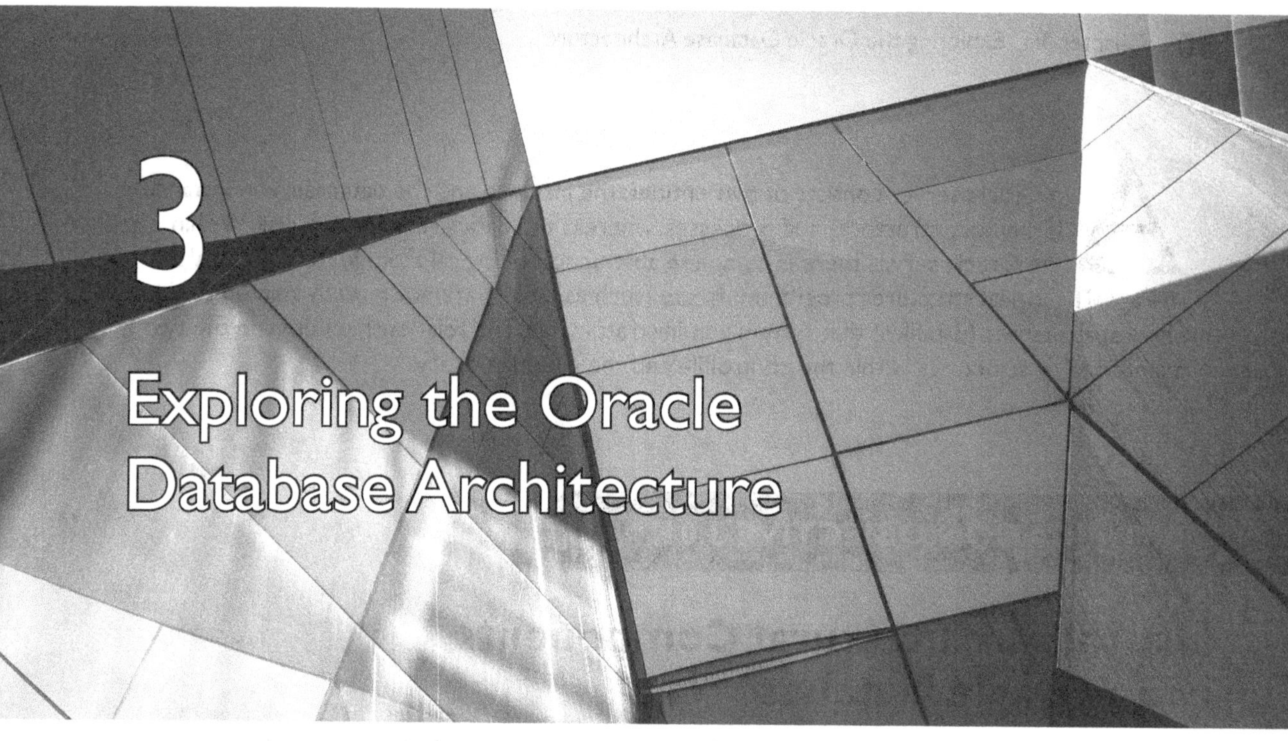

CERTIFICATION OBJECTIVES

3.01	List the Architectural Components of an Oracle Database	3.04	Explain the Relationship Between Logical and Physical Storage Structures
3.02	Explain the Memory Structures	✓	Two-Minute Drill
3.03	Describe the Background Processes	Q&A	Self-Test

An Oracle server consists of two entities: the instance and the database. The instance is memory structures and processes, whereas the database is files on disk. Within the Oracle server there is complete abstraction of logical storage from physical storage. The logical structures programmers see (such as tables) are not directly related to the physical structures (datafiles) that system administrators see. The relationship between the two is maintained by structures within the controlfile and the data dictionary.

CERTIFICATION OBJECTIVE 3.01

List the Architectural Components of an Oracle Database

For the most part in this book, you will be dealing with the simplest database environment: one instance on one computer, opening a database stored on local disks. The more complex distributed architectures, involving multiple instances and multiple databases, are beyond the scope of the OCP examination (although not the OCM qualification), although you may realistically expect to see high-level summary questions on distributed architecture.

Single-Instance Database Architecture

The instance consists of memory structures and processes. Its existence is transient, in your RAM and on your CPU(s). When you shut down the running instance, all trace of its existence goes away at the same time. The database consists of physical files on disk. Whether the instance is running or stopped, these files remain. Thus, the lifetime of the instance is only as long as it exists in memory: It can be started and stopped. By contrast, the database, once created, persists indefinitely—that is, until you deliberately delete the files that are associated with the database.

The processes that make up the instance are known as *background processes* because they are present and running at all times while the instance is active. These processes are for the most part completely self-administering, although in some cases it is possible for the DBA to influence the number of them and their operation. The memory structures, which are implemented in shared memory segments provided by the operating system, are known as the *System Global Area*, or SGA. The SGA is allocated at instance startup and released on shutdown. Within certain limits, the SGA in the 12*c* instance and the components within it can be resized while the instance is running, either automatically or in response to the DBA's instructions.

User sessions consist of a user process running locally to the user machine connecting to a server process running locally to the instance on the server machine. The technique for launching the server processes, which are started on demand for each session, is covered in Chapter 4. The connection between user process and server process is usually across a local area network (LAN) and uses Oracle's proprietary Oracle Net protocol layered on top of an industry-standard protocol (usually TCP). The user-process/server-process split implements the client-server architecture: User processes generate SQL, server processes execute SQL. The server processes are sometimes referred to *foreground processes*, in contrast with the background processes that make up the instance. Associated with each server process is an area of nonshareable memory, called the *Program Global Area*, or PGA. This is private to the session, unlike the SGA, which is available to all the foreground and background processes. Note that background processes also have a PGA. The size of any one session's PGA will vary according to the memory needs of the session at any one time; the DBA can define an upper limit for the total of all the PGAs, and Oracle manages the allocation of this to sessions dynamically.

on the job

You will sometimes hear the term* shadow process. *Be cautious of using this term. Some people use it to refer to foreground processes; others use it to refer to background processes. Never mind which is correct—just make sure you know what they are talking about.

Memory management in 12*c* can be totally automatic: The DBA need do nothing more than specify an overall memory allocation for both the SGA and the PGA and then let Oracle manage this memory as it thinks best. Alternatively, the DBA can control memory allocations himself. As an in-between technique, the DBA can define certain limits on what the automatic management can do.

exam watch

SGA memory is shared across all background and foreground processes; PGA memory can be accessed only by the foreground process of the session to which it has been allocated. Both SGA and PGA memory can be automatically managed.

The physical structures that make up an Oracle database are the datafiles, the online redo log files, and the controlfile. Within the physical structures of the database, which the system administrators see, are the logical structures that the end users (developers, business analysts, data warehouse architects, and so on) see. The Oracle architecture guarantees abstraction of the logical from the physical: There is no way a programmer can determine where, physically, a bit of data is located. Programmers address only logical structures, such as tables. Similarly, it is impossible for system administrators to know what bits of data are in any physical structure: All they can see is the operating system files, not what is within them. It is only you, the database administrator, who is permitted (and required) to see both sides of the story.

The abstraction of logical storage from physical storage is part of the RDBMS standard. If it were possible for a programmer to determine the physical location of a row, then successful execution of the code would be totally dependent on the one environment for which it was written. Changing the platform, moving the datafiles, and even renaming a file would break the application. It is, in fact, possible to determine where a table (and even one row within a table) actually is, but not through standard SQL. The language does not permit it. Tools are supplied for the database administrator's use for doing this, should it ever be necessary.

Data is stored in datafiles. There is no practical limit to the number or size of datafiles, and the abstraction of logical storage from physical storage means that datafiles can be moved or resized and more datafiles can be added without the application developers being aware of this. The relationship between physical and logical structures is maintained and documented in the data dictionary, which contains metadata describing the whole database. By querying certain views in the data dictionary, the DBA can determine precisely where every part of every table is.

The data dictionary is a set of tables stored within the database. There is a recursive problem here: The instance needs to be aware of the physical and logical structure of the database, but the information describing this is itself within the database. The solution to this problem lies in the staged startup process, which is detailed in Chapter 4.

A requirement of the RDBMS standard is that the database must not lose data. This means that it must be backed up; furthermore, any changes made to data between backups must be captured in a manner such that they can be applied to a restored backup. This is the forward recovery process. Oracle implements the capture of changes through the *redo log*, which is a sequential record of all *change vectors* applied to data. A change vector is the alteration made by a DML (Data Manipulation Language) statement (such as INSERT, UPDATE, DELETE, or MERGE). Whenever a user session makes any changes, the data itself in the data block is changed, and the change vector is written out sideways to the redo log, in a form that makes it repeatable. Then, in the event of damage to a datafile, a backup of the file can be restored and Oracle will extract the relevant change vectors from the redo log and apply them to the data blocks within the file. This ensures that work will never be lost—unless the damage to the database is so extensive as to lose not only one or more datafiles, but also either their backups or the redo log.

The controlfile stores the details of the physical structures of the database and is the starting point for the link to the logical structures. When an instance opens a database, it does so by first reading the controlfile. Within the controlfile is information the instance can then use to connect to the rest of the database, and the data dictionary within it.

The architecture of a single-instance database, represented graphically in Figure 3-1, can be summarized as consisting of four interacting components:

- A user interacts with a user process.
- A user process interacts with a server process.
- A server process interacts with an instance.
- An instance interacts with a database.

The *user process* is the user interface software. It could be a simple tool such as SQL*Plus, or something more complicated, such as Microsoft Access plus the ODBC driver, something written in C, or a Java process running on an application server. Whatever it is, it is the tool with which the user interacts, on the client side. It is absolutely impossible for any client-side process to have any contact with the

FIGURE 3-1

The indirect connection between a user and a database

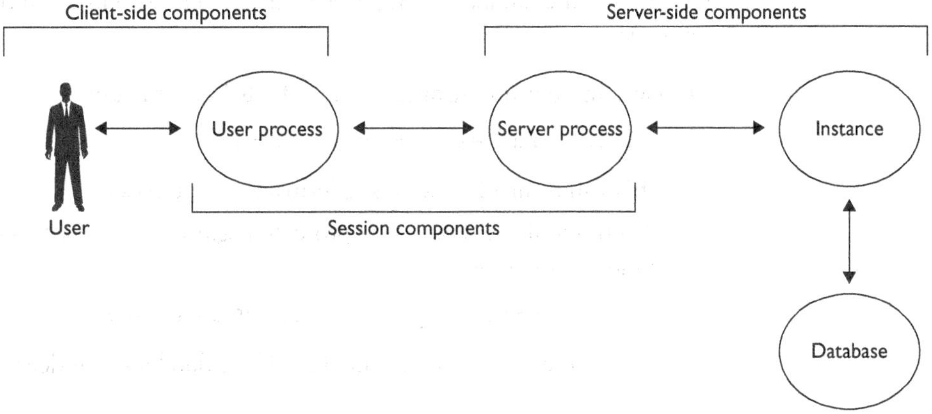

database. The client-server split is between the user process (which generates SQL) and the server process (which executes it).

Distributed Systems Architectures

In the single-instance environment, one instance opens one database. In a distributed environment, there are various possibilities for grouping instances and databases:

- **Real Application Clusters (RAC)** Multiple instances open one database.
- **Streams** Multiple Oracle servers propagate transactions between each other.
- **Data guard** A primary database updates one or more standby databases to keep them all synchronized.

Combinations of these options can deliver a distributed system that can achieve the goal of 100-percent uptime and zero percent data loss, with limitless scalability and performance.

EXERCISE 3-1

Identify the Components of the Database Server

In this exercise you will run queries to determine whether the database is a self-contained system or is part of a larger distributed environment, and you will also identify the major components.

Connect to the database using SQL*Plus as user SYSTEM and then follow these steps:

1. Determine if the instance is part of a RAC database:

```
select parallel from v$instance;
```

This will return NO for a single-instance database.

2. Determine if the database is protected against data loss by a Data Guard standby database:

```
select protection_level from v$database;
```

This will return UNPROTECTED if the database is indeed unprotected.

3. Determine whether Streams has been configured in the database:

```
select * from dba_streams_administrator;
```

This will return no rows if Streams has never been configured.

4. Identify the physical structures of the database:

```
select name,bytes from v$datafile;select name,bytes from
v$tempfile;
select member from v$logfile;
select * from v$controlfile;
```

Can you deduce any directory and file naming standards?

5. Identify the memory and process structures.
For a Linux environment, from an operating system prompt use the **ipcs** command to display shared memory segments and the **ps** command to show the oracle processes:

```
ipcs -m
ps -ef|grep ora_
```

Figure 3-2 shows some sample output. **ipcs** shows two blocks of shared memory owned by user oracle that make up the SGA, and ps shows the background processes of an instance called orcl. Your output will vary depending on how your database instance was named.

For a Windows environment, launch the Windows Task Manager. Search for an image named oracle.exe and adjust the column display to show the number of threads within the process and the committed memory. The threads are the background processes, the committed memory is the total of SGA and PGA for the instance.

FIGURE 3-2 SGA and processes, as seen in Linux

```
oracle@db121a:~
db121a orcl$
db121a orcl$ ipcs -m

------ Shared Memory Segments --------
key        shmid      owner      perms      bytes      nattch     status
0x00000000 1769473    root       644        80         2
0x00000000 1802242    root       644        16384      2
0x00000000 1835011    root       644        280        2
0x51c21dfc 1998853    oracle     660        14680064   96
0x00000000 2031622    oracle     660        448790528  48

db121a orcl$ ps -ef|grep ora_
oracle     9081      1  0 16:24 ?        00:00:02 ora_pmon_orcl
oracle     9085      1  1 16:24 ?        00:00:07 ora_psp0_orcl
oracle     9089      1  1 16:24 ?        00:00:07 ora_vktm_orcl
oracle     9093      1  0 16:24 ?        00:00:01 ora_gen0_orcl
oracle     9097      1  0 16:24 ?        00:00:01 ora_mman_orcl
oracle     9105      1  0 16:24 ?        00:00:03 ora_diag_orcl
oracle     9109      1  0 16:24 ?        00:00:01 ora_ofsd_orcl
```

CERTIFICATION OBJECTIVE 3.02

Explain the Memory Structures

An Oracle instance consists of a block of shared memory known as the System Global Area, or SGA, and a number of background processes. At a minimum, the SGA will contain three data structures:

- The database buffer cache default pool
- The log buffer
- The shared pool

It may, optionally, also contain the following:

- A large pool
- A Java pool
- A Streams pool
- Additional buffer cache pools

User sessions also need memory on the server side. This is nonshareable and is known as the Program Global Area, or PGA. Each session will have its own private PGA.

Which SGA structures are required, and which are optional? The database buffer cache, log buffer, and shared pool are required; the large pool, Java pool, and Streams pool are optional.

The Database Buffer Cache

The database buffer cache is Oracle's work area for executing SQL. When updating data, users' sessions don't directly do so on disk. The data blocks containing the data of interest are first copied into the database buffer cache. Changes (such as inserting new rows and deleting or modifying existing rows) are applied to these copies of the data blocks in the database buffer cache. The blocks will remain in the cache for some time afterward, until the buffer they are occupying is needed for caching another block.

When querying data, it also goes via the cache. The session works out which blocks contain the rows of interest and copies them into the database buffer cache; the projected columns of relevant rows are then transferred into the session's PGA for further processing. And again, the blocks remain in the database buffer cache for some time afterward.

Take note of the term *block*. Datafiles are formatted into fixed-sized blocks. Table rows, and other data objects such as index keys, are stored in these blocks. The database buffer cache is formatted into memory buffers, each sized to hold one block. Unlike blocks, rows are of variable length; the length of a row will depend on the number of columns defined for the table, whether the columns actually have anything in them, and, if so, what. Depending on the size of the blocks (which is chosen by the DBA) and the size of the rows (which is dependent on the table design and usage), there may be several rows per block or possibly a row may stretch over several blocks. The structure of a data block will be described in the section "The Datafiles," later in this chapter.

Ideally, all the blocks containing data that is frequently accessed will be in the database buffer cache, thus minimizing the need for disk I/O. As a typical use of the database buffer cache, consider an end user retrieving an employee record and updating it with these statements:

```
select last_name, salary, job_id from employees where employee_id=100;
update employees set salary=salary * 1.1 where employee_id=100;
commit;
```

The user process will have prompted the user for the employee number and constructed the SELECT statement. The SELECT retrieves some details to be sent to the user process, where they will be formatted for display. To execute this statement, the session's server process will read the data block containing the relevant row from a datafile into a buffer. The user process will then initiate a screen dialog to prompt for some change to be made and verified; then the UPDATE statement and the COMMIT statement will be constructed and sent to the server process for execution. Provided that an excessive period of time has not elapsed, the block with the row will still be available in the cache when the UPDATE statement is executed. In this example, the buffer cache hit ratio will be 50 percent: two accesses of a block in the cache, but only one read of the block from disk. A well-tuned database buffer cache can result in a cache hit ratio well over 90 percent.

A buffer storing a block whose image in the cache is not the same as the image on disk is often referred to as a "dirty" buffer. A buffer will be "clean" when a block is first copied into it: At that point, the block image in the buffer is the same as the block image on disk. The buffer will become dirty when the block in it is updated. Eventually, dirty buffers must be written back to the datafiles, at which point the buffer will be clean again. Even after being written to disk, the block remains in memory; it is possible that the buffer will not be overwritten with another block for some time.

exam watch ***Changed blocks may be written to datafiles before or after COMMIT. In the course of normal running, it is not unusual for uncommitted data to be written to the datafiles, or for committed changes not to have been written.***

Note that there is no correlation between the frequency of updates to a buffer (or the number of COMMITs) and when it gets written back to the datafiles.

The size of the database buffer cache is critical for performance. The cache should be sized adequately for caching all the frequently accessed blocks (whether clean or dirty), but not so large that it caches blocks that are rarely needed. An undersized cache will result in excessive disk activity, as frequently accessed blocks are continually read from disk, used, overwritten by other blocks, and then read from disk again. An oversized cache is not so bad (so long as it is not so large that the operating system is having to swap pages of virtual memory in and out of real memory) but can cause problems; for example, startup of an instance is slower if it involves formatting a massive database buffer cache.

on the job ***Determining the optimal size of the database buffer cache is application specific and a matter of performance tuning. It is impossible to give anything but the vaguest guidelines without making observations, but it is probably true to say that the majority of databases will operate well with a cache sized in hundreds of megabytes up to a couple of dozen gigabytes. Very few applications will perform well with a cache smaller than this, and not many will need a cache of hundreds of gigabytes.***

exam watch ***The size of the database buffer cache can be adjusted dynamically, and it can be automatically managed.***

The database buffer cache is allocated at instance startup time and can be resized up or down at any time. This resizing can be either manual or automatic, according to the workload if the automatic mechanism has been enabled.

The Log Buffer

The log buffer is a small, short-term staging area for change vectors before they are written to the redo log on disk. A *change vector* is a modification applied to something; executing DML statements generates change vectors applied to data. The redo log is the database's guarantee that data will never be lost: Whenever a data block is changed, the change vectors applied to the block are written out to the redo log, from where they can be extracted and applied to datafile backups if it is ever necessary to restore a datafile. Thus, the datafile can be brought up to date.

Redo is not written directly to the redo log files by session server processes. If it were, the sessions would have to wait for disk I/O operations to complete whenever they executed a DML statement. Instead, sessions write redo to the log buffer, in memory. This is much faster than writing to disk. The log buffer (which will contain change vectors from many sessions, interleaved with each other) is then written out to the redo log files. One write of the log buffer to disk may therefore be a batch of many change vectors from many transactions. Even so, the change vectors in the log buffer are written to disk in very nearly real time—and when a session issues a COMMIT statement, the log buffer write really does happen in real time. The writes are done by the log writer background process, the LGWR.

What does LGWR do when you COMMIT? It flushes the entire log buffer to disk. What does the DBWn do on COMMIT? Nothing.

The log buffer is small (in comparison with other memory structures) because it is a very short-term storage area. Change vectors are inserted into it and are streamed to disk in near real time. There is no need for it to be more than a few megabytes at the most, and indeed making it much bigger than the default value can be seriously bad for performance. The default is determined by the Oracle server and is based on the number of CPUs on the server node. The default is usually correct.

Understanding COMMIT processing is vital. When a COMMIT statement is issued, part of the COMMIT processing involves writing the contents of the log buffer to the redo log files on disk. This write occurs in real time, and while it is in progress the session that issued the COMMIT will hang. The guarantee that a committed transaction will never be lost is based on this: The commit-complete message is not returned to the session until the data blocks in the cache have been changed (which means that the transaction has been completed) and the change vectors have been written to the redo log on disk (and therefore the transaction could be recovered, if necessary).

on the job

Raising the log buffer size above the default may be necessary for some applications, but as a rule you should start tuning with the log buffer on default.

watch

The size of the log buffer is static, fixed at instance startup. It cannot be automatically managed.

The log buffer is allocated at instance startup, and it can never be resized subsequently without restarting the instance. It is a circular buffer. As server processes write change vectors to it, the current write address moves around. The log writer process writes the vectors out in batches, and as it does so, the space they occupied becomes available and can be overwritten by more change vectors. It is possible that at times of peak activity, change vectors will be generated faster than the log writer process can write them out. If this happens, all DML activity will cease (for a few milliseconds) while the log writer clears the buffer.

The process of flushing the log buffer to disk is one of the ultimate bottlenecks in the Oracle architecture. You cannot do DML faster than the LGWR can flush the change vectors to the online redo log files.

on the job

If redo generation is the limiting factor in a database's performance, the only option is to go to RAC. In a RAC database, each instance has its own log buffer and its own LGWR.

The Shared Pool

The shared pool is the most complex of the SGA structures. It is divided into hundreds of substructures, all of which are managed internally by the Oracle server. This discussion of architecture will only mention four of the shared pool components (and only briefly):

- The library cache
- The data dictionary cache
- The PL/SQL area
- The SQL query and PL/SQL function result cache

Some other structures will be described in later chapters. All the structures within the shared pool are automatically managed. Their size will vary according to the

The shared pool size is dynamic and can be automatically managed.

pattern of activity against the instance, within the overall size of the shared pool. The shared pool itself can be resized dynamically, either in response to the DBA's instructions or through being managed automatically.

The Library Cache

The library cache is a memory area for storing recently executed code, in its parsed form. Parsing is the conversion of code written by programmers into something executable, and it is a process that Oracle does on demand. Because parsed code is cached in the shared pool so that it can be reused without reparsing, performance can be greatly improved. Parsing SQL code takes time. Consider a simple SQL statement:

```
select * from employees where last_name='KING';
```

Before this statement can be executed, the Oracle server has to work out what it means and how to execute it. To begin with, what is "employees"? Is it a table, a synonym, or a view? Does it even exist? Then there is the asterisk (*). What are the columns that make up the employees table (if it is a table)? Does the user have permission to see the table? Answers to these questions and many others have to be found by querying the data dictionary.

on the job

The algorithm used to find SQL in the library cache is based on the ASCII values of the characters that make up the statement. The slightest difference (even something as trivial as SELECT instead of select) means that the statement will not match and will therefore be parsed again. Code that is not reusable is very bad for performance.

Having worked out what the statement actually means, the server has to decide how best to execute it. Is there an index on the last_name column? If so, would it be quicker to use the index to locate the row or to scan the whole table? More queries against the data dictionary are needed. It is quite possible for a simple one-line query against a user table to generate dozens of queries against the data dictionary, and for the parsing of a statement to take many times longer than eventually executing it. The purpose of the library cache of the shared pool is to store statements in their parsed form, ready for execution. The first time a statement is issued, it has to be parsed before execution—the second time, it can be executed immediately. In a well-designed application, it is possible that statements may be parsed once and executed millions of times. This saves a huge amount of time.

The Data Dictionary Cache

The data dictionary cache is sometimes referred to as the *row cache*. Whichever term you prefer, it stores recently used object definitions: descriptions of tables, indexes, users, and other metadata definitions. Keeping such definitions in memory in the SGA, where they are immediately accessible to all sessions, rather than each session having to read them repeatedly from the data dictionary on disk, enhances parsing performance. The cached object definitions can be used to parse many different statements.

The data dictionary cache stores object definitions so that when statements do have to be parsed, they can be parsed fast—without having to query the data dictionary. Consider what happens if these statements are issued consecutively:

```
select sum(salary) from employees;
select * from employees where last_name='KING';
```

Both statements must be parsed because they are different statements—but parsing the first SELECT statement will have loaded the definition of the employees table and its columns into the data dictionary cache, so parsing the second statement will be faster than it would otherwise have been, because no data dictionary access will be needed.

on the job

Shared pool tuning is usually oriented toward making sure that the library cache is the right size. This is because the algorithms Oracle uses to allocate memory in the SGA are designed to favor the dictionary cache, so if the library cache is correct, the dictionary cache will already be correct.

The PL/SQL Area

Stored PL/SQL objects are procedures, functions, packaged procedures and functions, object type definitions, and triggers. These are all stored in the data dictionary, as source code and also in their compiled form. When a stored PL/SQL object is invoked by a session, it must be read from the data dictionary. To prevent repeated reading, the objects are then cached in the PL/SQL area of the shared pool.

The first time a PL/SQL object is used, it must be read from the data dictionary tables on disk, but subsequent invocations will be much faster, because the object will already be available in the PL/SQL area of the shared pool.

PL/SQL can be issued from user processes, rather than being stored in the data dictionary. This is called* anonymous *PL/SQL. Anonymous PL/SQL cannot be cached and reused, and it must be compiled dynamically. It will therefore always perform worse than stored PL/SQL. Developers should be encouraged to convert all anonymous PL/SQL into stored PL/SQL.

The SQL Query and PL/SQL Function Result Cache

In many applications, the same query is executed many times, by either the same session or many different sessions. Creating a result cache lets the Oracle server store the results of such queries in memory. The next time the query is issued, rather than running the query, the server can retrieve the cached result. The result cache mechanism is intelligent enough to track whether the tables against which the query was run have been updated. If this has happened, the query results will be invalidated, and the next time the query is issued it will be rerun. There is therefore no danger of ever receiving an out-of-date cached result.

The PL/SQL result cache uses a similar mechanism. When a PL/SQL function is executed, its return value can be cached ready for the next time the function is executed. If the parameters passed to the function, or the tables that the function queries, are different, the function will be reevaluated, but otherwise the cached value will be returned.

By default, use of the SQL query and PL/SQL function result cache is disabled, but if enabled programmatically, it can often dramatically improve performance. The cache is within the shared pool: Unlike the other memory areas described previously, it does afford DBAs some control in that they can specify a maximum size.

Sizing the Shared Pool

Sizing the shared pool is critical for performance. It should be large enough to cache all the frequently executed code and frequently needed object definitions (in the library cache and the data dictionary cache) but not so large that it caches statements that have only been executed once. An undersized shared pool cripples performance because server sessions have repeatedly had to grab space in it for parsing statements, which are then overwritten by other statements and therefore have to be parsed again when they are re-executed. An oversized shared pool can impact badly on performance because it takes too long to search it. If the shared pool is less than the optimal size, performance will degrade. However, there is a minimum size below which statements will fail.

Memory in the shared pool is allocated according to an LRU (least recently used) algorithm. When the Oracle server needs space in the shared pool, it will overwrite the object that has not been used for the longest time. If the object is later needed again, it will have to be reloaded—possibly overwriting another object.

on the job ***Determining the optimal size is a matter for performance tuning, but it is probably safe to say that most databases will need a shared pool of several hundred megabytes to a few gigabytes. Few applications will perform adequately with less than a hundred megabytes, and few will need double-digit gigabytes.***

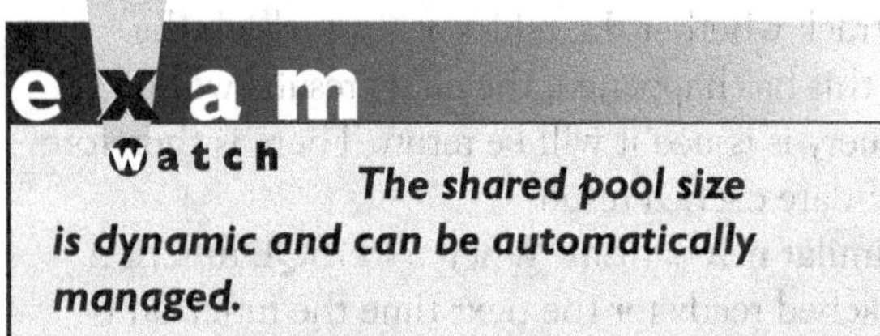

The shared pool size is dynamic and can be automatically managed.

The shared pool is allocated at instance startup time. Prior to release 9*i* of the database, it was not possible to resize the shared pool subsequently without restarting the database instance, but from 9*i* onward it can be resized up or down at any time. This resizing can be either manual or (from release 10g onward) automatic, according to workload, if the automatic mechanism has been enabled.

The Large Pool

The large pool is an optional area that, if created, will be used automatically by various processes that would otherwise take memory from the shared pool. One major use of the large pool is by shared server processes, described in Chapter 5 in the discussion of the shared (or multithreaded) server architecture. Parallel execution servers will also use the large pool, if there is one. In the absence of a large pool, these processes will use memory from the shared pool. This can cause bad contention for the shared pool: If shared servers or parallel servers are being used, a large pool should always be created. Some I/O processes may also make use of the large pool, such as the processes used by the Recovery Manager when it is backing up to a tape device.

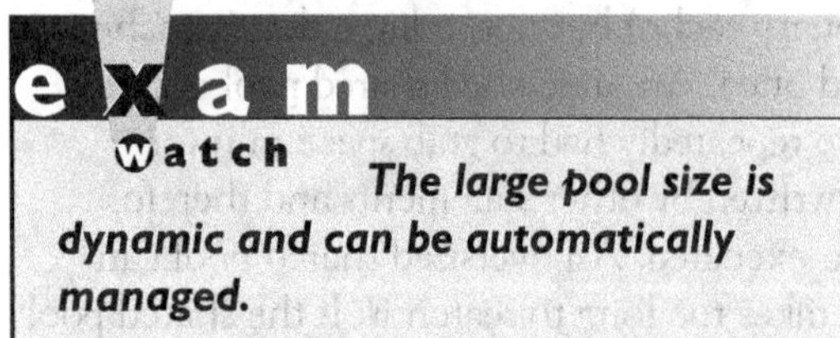

The large pool size is dynamic and can be automatically managed.

The Java Pool

The Java pool is only required if your application is going to run Java-stored procedures within the database: It is used for the heap space needed to instantiate the Java objects. However, a number of Oracle options are written in Java, so the Java pool is considered standard nowadays. Note that Java code is not cached in the Java pool: It is cached in the shared pool, in the same way that PL/SQL code is cached.

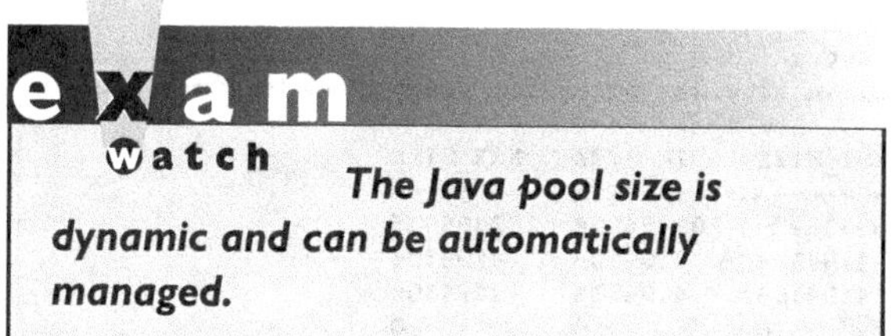

The Java pool size is dynamic and can be automatically managed.

The Streams Pool

The Streams pool is used by Oracle Streams. This is an advanced tool that is beyond the scope of the OCP examinations or this book, but for completeness a short description follows.

The mechanism used by Streams involves extracting change vectors from the redo log and from these reconstructing the statements that were executed—or statements that would have the same effect. These statements are executed at the remote database. The processes that extract changes from redo and the processes that apply the changes need memory: This memory is the Streams pool. From database release 10*g* onward, it is possible to create and resize the Streams pool after instance startup; this creation and sizing can be completely automatic. With earlier releases it had to be defined at startup and was a fixed size.

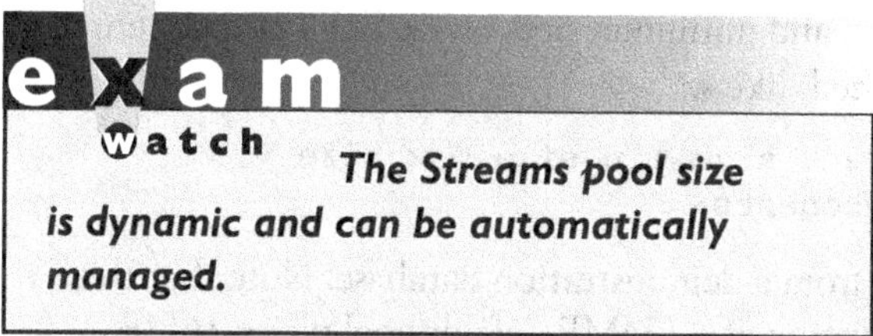

The Streams pool size is dynamic and can be automatically managed.

EXERCISE 3-2

Investigate the Memory Structures of the Instance

In this exercise, you will run queries to determine the current sizing of various memory structures that make up the instance. Here are the steps:

1. Connect to the database as user SYSTEM.
2. Use the **SHOW SGA** command to display summarized information.

FIGURE 3-3 Example of SGA configuration

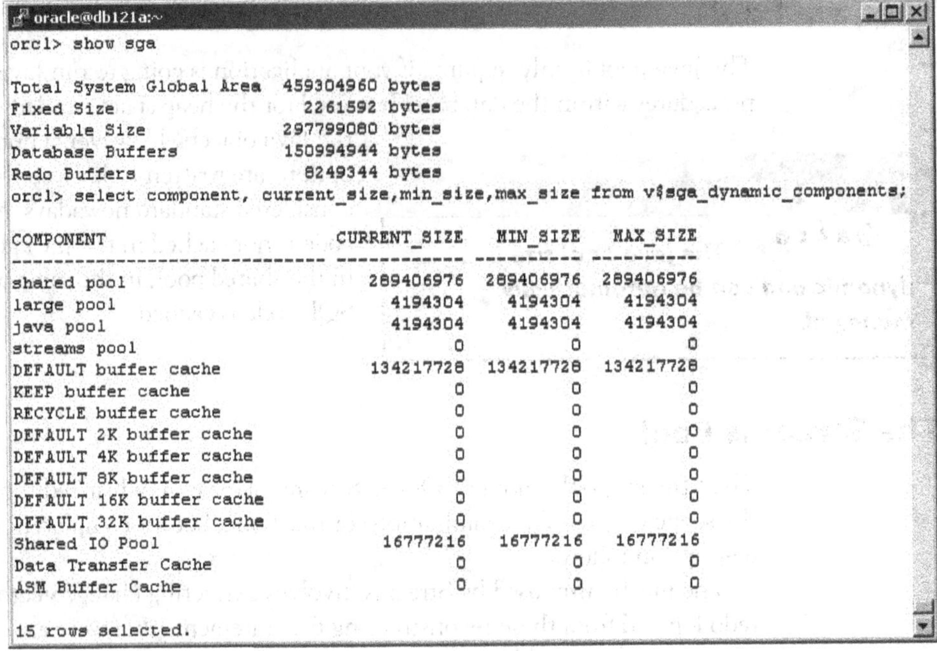

```
orcl> show sga

Total System Global Area  459304960 bytes
Fixed Size                  2261592 bytes
Variable Size             297799080 bytes
Database Buffers          150994944 bytes
Redo Buffers                8249344 bytes
orcl> select component, current_size,min_size,max_size from v$sga_dynamic_components;

COMPONENT                        CURRENT_SIZE   MIN_SIZE   MAX_SIZE
-------------------------------- ------------ ---------- ----------
shared pool                         289406976  289406976  289406976
large pool                            4194304    4194304    4194304
java pool                             4194304    4194304    4194304
streams pool                                0          0          0
DEFAULT buffer cache                134217728  134217728  134217728
KEEP buffer cache                           0          0          0
RECYCLE buffer cache                        0          0          0
DEFAULT 2K buffer cache                     0          0          0
DEFAULT 4K buffer cache                     0          0          0
DEFAULT 8K buffer cache                     0          0          0
DEFAULT 16K buffer cache                    0          0          0
DEFAULT 32K buffer cache                    0          0          0
Shared IO Pool                       16777216   16777216   16777216
Data Transfer Cache                         0          0          0
ASM Buffer Cache                            0          0          0

15 rows selected.
```

3. Show the current, maximum, and minimum sizes of the SGA components that can be dynamically resized, like so:

```
select component, current_size,min_size,max_size
from v$sga_dynamic_components;
```

   Figure 3-3 shows the results from a demonstration database. Note that the buffer cache is 150MB, consisting of a 134MB default pool plus a 16MB shared I/O pool (this last component is a section of the cache used for LOBs), and that no components have been resized since startup.

4. Determine how much memory has been, and is currently, allocated to Program Global Areas:

```
select name,value from v$pgastat where name in
('maximum PGA allocated','total PGA allocated');
```

CERTIFICATION OBJECTIVE 3.03

Describe the Background Processes

The instance background processes are the processes that are launched when the instance is started and run until it is terminated. Five background processes have a long history with Oracle and are the first five described in the sections that follow: System Monitor (SMON), Process Monitor (PMON), Database Writer (DBWn), Log Writer (LGWR), and Checkpoint Process (CKPT). A number of others have been introduced with the more recent releases; notable among these are Manageability Monitor (MMON) and Memory Manager (MMAN). There are also some that are not essential but will exist in most instances. These include the Archiver (ARCn) and Recoverer (RECO) processes. Others will exist only if certain options have been enabled. This last group includes the processes required for RAC and Streams. Additionally, some processes exist that are not properly documented (or are not documented at all). The processes described here are those that every OCP candidate will be expected to know.

First, though, a platform variation must be cleared up before discussing processes. On Linux and Unix, all the Oracle processes are separate operating system processes, each with a unique process number. On Windows, there is one operating system process (called ORACLE.EXE) for the whole instance, and the Oracle processes run as separate threads within this one process.

on the job

In release 12c, it is in fact possible to run Oracle in a multithreaded model (rather than the default multiprocess model) as it runs on Windows. This is enabled with the THREADED_EXECUTION instance parameter, which is beyond the scope of the OCP exam.

SMON, the System Monitor

SMON initially has the task of mounting and opening a database. The steps involved in this are described in detail in Chapter 4. In brief, SMON *mounts* a database by locating and validating the database controlfile. It then *opens* a database by locating and validating all the datafiles and online log files. Once the database is opened and in use, SMON is responsible for various housekeeping tasks, such as collating free space in datafiles.

PMON, the Process Monitor

A user session is a user process that is connected to a server process. The server process is launched when the session is created and destroyed when the session ends. An orderly exit from a session involves the user logging off. When this occurs, any work they were doing will be completed in an orderly fashion, and their server process will be terminated. If the session is terminated in a disorderly manner (perhaps because the user's PC is rebooted), the session will be left in a state that must be cleared up. PMON monitors all the server processes and detects any problems with the sessions. If a session has terminated abnormally, PMON will destroy the server process, return its PGA memory to the operating system's free memory pool, and roll back any incomplete transaction that may have been in progress.

on the job ***If a session terminates abnormally, what will happen to an active transaction? It will be rolled back by the PMON background process.***

DBWn, the Database Writer

Always remember that sessions do not as a general rule write to disk. They write data (or changes to existing data) to buffers in the database buffer cache. It is the database writer that subsequently writes the buffers to disk. It is possible for an instance to have several database writers (up to a maximum of 100) that will be called DBW0 to DBW9 then DBWa to DBWz: hence the use of the term DBWn to refer to "the" database writer. Writers beyond 36 are named BW36 to BW99. The default number is one database writer per eight CPUs, rounded up.

on the job ***How many database writers do you need? The default number may well be correct. Adding more may help performance, but usually you should look at tuning memory first. As a rule, before you optimize disk I/O, ask why there is any need for disk I/O.***

DBWn writes dirty buffers from the database buffer cache to the datafiles—but it does not write the buffers as they become dirty. On the contrary: It writes as few buffers as it can get away with. The general idea is that disk I/O is bad for performance, so don't do it unless it really is needed. If a block in a buffer has been written to by a session, there is a reasonable possibility that it will be written to again—by that session, or a different one. Why write the buffer to disk if it may well be dirtied again in the near future? The algorithm DBWn uses to select dirty buffers

What will cause DBWn to write? No free buffers, too many dirty buffers, a three-second timeout, or a checkpoint.

for writing to disk (which will clean them) will select only buffers that have not been recently used. So if a buffer is very busy, because sessions are repeatedly reading or writing to it, DBWn will not write it to disk for some time. There could be hundreds or thousands of writes to a buffer before DBWn cleans it. It could be that in a buffer cache of a million buffers, a hundred thousand of them are dirty—but DBWn might only write a few hundred of them to disk at a time. These will be the few hundred that no session has been interested in for some time.

DBWn writes according to a very lazy algorithm: as little as possible, as rarely as possible. Four circumstances will cause DBWn to write: no free buffers, too many dirty buffers, a three-second timeout, and when there is a checkpoint.

The first circumstance is when there are no free buffers. If a server process needs to copy a block into the database buffer cache, it must find a *free buffer*, which is a buffer that is neither dirty (updated, and not yet written back to disk) nor pinned (a pinned buffer is one that is being used by another session at that very moment). A dirty buffer must not be overwritten because if it were, the changed data would be lost, and a pinned buffer cannot be overwritten because the operating system's memory protection mechanisms will not permit this. If a server process takes "too long" (as determined by Oracle internally) to find a free buffer, it signals the DBWn to write some dirty buffers to disk. Once this is done, they will be clean—and thus free and available for use.

The second circumstance is when there are too many dirty buffers ("too many" being another internal threshold). No one server process may have had a problem finding a free buffer, but overall, there could be a large number of dirty buffers: This will cause DBWn to write some of them to disk.

The third circumstance is the three-second timeout. Every three seconds, DBWn will clean a few buffers. In practice, this event may not be significant in a production system because the two previously described circumstances will be forcing the writes, but the timeout does mean that even if the system is idle, the database buffer cache will eventually be cleaned.

Fourth, there may be a checkpoint requested. The three reasons already given will cause DBWn to write a limited number of dirty buffers to the datafiles. When a checkpoint occurs, all dirty buffers are written.

Writing buffers for the first three reasons mentioned is referred to as an *incremental checkpoint*, or as *advancing the incremental checkpoint position*. This is all

exam watch

What does DBWn do when a transaction is committed? It does absolutely nothing.

that should happen in the course of normal running, and is optimized such that buffers will be made available as needed without impacting performance by stressing the I/O system.

The only moment when a full checkpoint is absolutely necessary is when the database is closed and the instance is shut down—a full description of this sequence is given in Chapter 4. A checkpoint writes all dirty buffers to disk: This synchronizes the buffer cache with the datafiles, and the instance with the database. During normal running, the datafiles are always out of date: They may be missing changes (committed and uncommitted). This does not matter, because the copies of blocks in the buffer cache are up to date, and it is these that the sessions work on. But on shutdown, it is necessary to write everything to disk. Automatic checkpoints only occur on shutdown, but a checkpoint can be forced at any time with this statement:

```
alter system checkpoint;
```

watch

Is there a full checkpoint on log switch? No, not since release 8i. Many DBAs, including some who should know better, have never learned this change in behavior that happened many years ago.

The checkpoint described so far is a full checkpoint. Partial checkpoints that force DBWn to write all the dirty buffers containing blocks from just one or more datafiles, rather than the whole database, occur more frequently: for example, when a datafile or tablespace is taken offline, when a tablespace is put into backup mode, or when a tablespace is made read-only. These are less drastic than full checkpoints, and occur automatically whenever the relevant event happens.

To conclude, the DBWn writes on a very lazy algorithm—as little as possible, as rarely as possible—except when a full checkpoint occurs. Then, all dirty buffers are written to disk, as fast as possible.

LGWR, the Log Writer

LGWR writes the contents of the log buffer to the online log files on disk. A write of the log buffer to the online redo log files is often referred to as *flushing* the log buffer.

When a session makes any change (by executing INSERT, UPDATE, or DELETE commands) to blocks in the database buffer cache, before it applies the change to the block it writes out the change vector that it is about to apply to the log buffer. In order that no work is lost, these change vectors must be written to disk with only minimal delay. To this end, the LGWR streams the contents of the log buffer to the online redo log files on disk in near real time. And when a session issues a COMMIT, the LGWR writes in real time: the session hangs while LGWR writes the buffer to disk. Only then is the transaction recorded as committed and therefore nonreversible.

Three circumstances will cause LGWR to flush the log buffer: if a session issues a COMMIT, if the log buffer is one-third full, and if DBWn is about to write dirty buffers.

The first circumstance is the write-on-commit. To process a COMMIT, the server process inserts a commit record into the log buffer. It will then hang while LGWR flushes the log buffer to disk. Only when this write has completed is a commit-complete message returned to the session, and the server process can then continue working. This is the guarantee that transactions will never be lost: every change vector for a committed transaction will be available in the redo log on disk and can therefore be applied to datafile backups. Therefore, if the database is ever damaged, it can be restored from backup and all work done since the backup was made can be redone.

Second, when the log buffer is one-third full, LGWR will flush it to disk. This is about performance. If the log buffer is small (as it usually should be), this one-third-full trigger will force LGWR to write the buffer to disk in near real time, even if no one is committing transactions. The log buffer for many applications will be optimally sized at only a few megabytes. The application will generate enough redo to fill one third of this in a fraction of a second, so LGWR will be forced to stream the change vectors to disk continuously, in near real time. Then, when a session does COMMIT, there will be hardly anything to write, so the COMMIT will complete almost instantaneously.

Third, when DBWn needs to write dirty buffers from the database buffer cache to the datafiles, it will signal LGWR to flush the log buffer to the online redo log files. This is to ensure that it will always be possible to reverse an uncommitted transaction. The mechanism of transaction rollback is fully explained in Chapter 9. For now, you just need to know that it is perfectly possible for DBWn to write an uncommitted transaction to the datafiles. This is fine, so long as the undo data needed to reverse the transaction is guaranteed to be available. Generating undo data also generates change vectors, and because these will be in the redo log files before the datafiles are updated, the undo data needed to roll back a transaction (should this be necessary) can be reconstructed if needed.

Watch ***When will LGWR flush the log buffer to disk? On COMMIT, when the buffer is one-third full, and just before DBWn writes.***

Note that it can be said that there is a three-second timeout that causes LGWR to write. In fact, the timeout is on DBWn. However, because LGWR will always write just before DBWn, in effect there is a three-second timeout on LGWR as well.

CKPT, the Checkpoint Process

The CKPT keeps track of where in the redo stream the incremental checkpoint position is, and if necessary instructs DBWn to write out some dirty buffers in order to push the checkpoint position forward. The current checkpoint position is the point in the redo stream at which recovery must begin in the event of an instance crash. CKPT continually updates the controlfile with the current checkpoint position.

MMON, the Manageability Monitor

MMON is the enabling process for many of the self-monitoring and self-tuning capabilities of the database. The database instance gathers a vast number of statistics about activity and performance. These statistics are accumulated in the SGA, and their current values can be interrogated by issuing SQL queries against various V$ views. For performance tuning and also for trend analysis and historical reporting, it is necessary to save these statistics to long-term storage. MMON regularly (by default, every hour) captures statistics from the SGA and writes them to the data dictionary, where they can be stored indefinitely (though, by default, they are kept for only eight days).

Every time MMON gathers a set of statistics (known as a *snapshot*), it also launches the Automatic Database Diagnostic Monitor, the ADDM. The ADDM is a tool that analyses database activity using an expert system developed over many years by many DBAs. It studies two snapshots (by default, the current and previous snapshots) and makes observations and recommendations regarding performance during the period covered. Chapter 12 describes the use of ADDM (and other tools) for performance tuning. As well as gathering snapshots, MMON continuously monitors the database and the instance to check whether any alerts should be raised.

exam Watch ***By default, MMON gathers a snapshot and launches the ADDM every hour.***

MMNL, the Manageability Monitor Light

MMNL is a process that assists the MMON. There are times when MMON's scheduled activity is not enough. For example, MMON flushes statistical information accumulated in the SGA to the database according to a schedule (by default, every hour). If the memory buffers used to accumulate this information fill before MMON is due to flush them, MMNL will take responsibility for flushing the data.

MMAN, the Memory Manager

MMAN can completely automate memory management: All the DBA needs to do is set an overall target for memory usage, and MMAN will observe the demand for PGA memory and SGA memory and then allocate memory to sessions and to SGA structures, as needed, while keeping the total allocated memory within a limit set by the DBA.

on the job

The automation of memory management is one of the major technical advances of the later releases, automating a large part of the DBA's job and giving huge benefits in performance and resource utilization. MMAN does it better than you can.

LREG, the Listener Registration Process

A database instance will attempt to register itself with a database listener. This is to allow users to connect via the listener. In an advanced environment such as a clustered database with several instances offering many services, LREG will also update the listener with information regarding workload and performance. This allows the listener to direct sessions intelligently to appropriate instances. In earlier releases, this function was performed by the PMON process, but in release 12*c* a dedicated process (namely, LREG) has been added to do this.

ARCn, the Archiver

This is an optional process as far as the database is concerned, but usually a required process for the business. Without one or more ARCn processes (there can be from one to 30, named ARC0, ARC1, and so on), it is possible to lose data. The process and purpose of launching ARCn to create archive log files is described in detail in Chapter 18. For now, only a summary is needed.

All change vectors applied to data blocks are written out to the log buffer (by the sessions making the changes) and then to the *online* redo log files (by the LGWR).

The online redo log files are of fixed size and number: Once they have been filled, LGWR will overwrite them with more redo data. The time that must elapse before this happens is dependent on the size and number of the online log files, and the amount of DML activity (and therefore the amount of redo generated) against the database. This means that the online redo log only stores change vectors for recent activity. In order to preserve a complete history of all changes applied to the data, the online log files must be copied as they are filled and before they are reused. The ARCn is responsible for doing this. Provided that these copies, known as *archive* redo log files, are available, it will always be possible to recover from any damage to the database by restoring datafile backups and applying change vectors to them extracted from all the archive log files generated since the backups were made.

exam watch

LGWR writes the online log files; ARCn reads them. During normal running, no other processes touch them at all.

on the job

The progress of the ARCn processes and the state of the destination(s) to which they are writing must be monitored. If archiving fails, the database will eventually hang. This monitoring can be done through the alert system.

RECO, the Recoverer Process

A *distributed transaction* is a transaction that involves updates to two or more databases. Distributed transactions are designed by programmers and operate through database links. Consider this example:

```
update employees set salary=salary * 1.1
where employee_id=1000;
update employees@dev set salary=salary * 1.1
where employee_id=1000;
commit;
```

The first update applies to a row in the local database; the second applies to a row in a remote database identified by the database link DEV. The **COMMIT** command instructs both databases to commit the transaction, which consists of both statements. Distributed transactions require a *two-phase commit*. The commit in each database must be coordinated: If one were to fail and the other were to succeed, the data overall would be in an inconsistent state. A two-phase commit prepares each database by instructing their LGWRs to flush the log buffer to disk (the first phase), and once this is confirmed, the transaction is flagged as committed everywhere (the second phase). If anything goes wrong anywhere between the two phases, RECO takes action to cancel the commit and roll back the work in all databases.

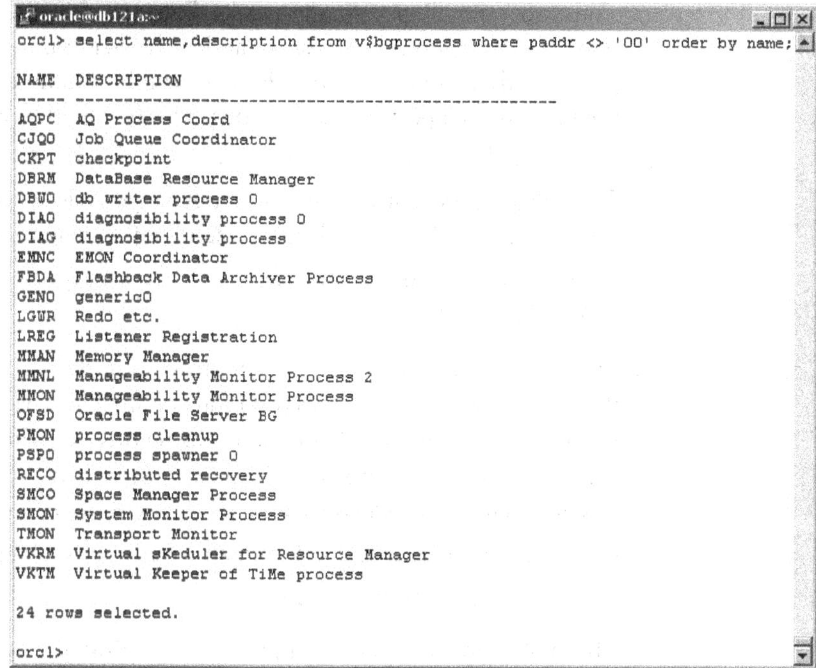

FIGURE 3-4 The background processes typically present in a single instance

Some Other Background Processes

It is unlikely that processes other than those already described will be examined, but for completeness descriptions of the remaining processes usually present in an instance follow. Figure 3-4 shows a query that lists all the processes running in an instance on a Linux system. Many more processes may exist, depending on certain options being enabled, but those shown in the figure will be present in most instances.

EXERCISE 3-3

Investigate the Processes Running in Your Instance

In this exercise, you will run queries to see what background processes are running on your instance. You may use either SQL Developer or SQL*Plus. Here are the steps to follow:

1. Connect to the database as user SYSTEM.
2. Determine what processes are running and how many of each:

```
select program,paddr from v$session order by program;
select program,addr from v$process order by program;
```

These queries will give similar results: Each process must have a session (even the background processes), and each session must have a process. The processes that can occur multiple times will have a numeric suffix, except for the processes supporting user sessions, which will all have the same name.

3. Investigate how many processes could be running.

   The v$bgprocess view has one row for every possible process. Processes that are actually running have an address, which is a join column to v$process view:

```
select name,description,paddr from v$bgprocess
order by paddr;
```

4. Observe that the launching of server processes as sessions is made by counting the number of server processes (on Linux or any Unix platform) or the number of Oracle threads (on Windows). The technique is different on the two platforms: On Linux/Unix, the Oracle processes are separate operating system processes, but on Windows they are threads within one operating system process.

   On Linux, run this command from an operating system prompt:

```
ps -ef | grep LOCAL | wc -l
```

   This will count the number of processes running that have the string LOCAL in their name, and will include all the session server processes.

   Launch a SQL*Plus session and then rerun the preceding command: Use the **host** command to launch an operating shell from within the SQL*Plus session. You will see that the number of processes has increased. Exit the session, and you will see that the number has dropped down again. Figure 3-5 demonstrates this.

   Observe in the figure how the number of processes changes from 3 to 4 and back again: The difference is the launching and terminating of the server process supporting the SQL*Plus session.

   On Windows, launch the Task Manager. Configure it to show the number of threads within each process: On the View button, take the Select Columns option and tick the Thread Count check box. Look for the ORACLE.EXE process, and note the number of threads. In Figure 3-6, this is currently at 33. Launch a new session against the instance, and you will see the thread count increment. Exit the session, and it will decrement.

FIGURE 3-5

Counting session server processes

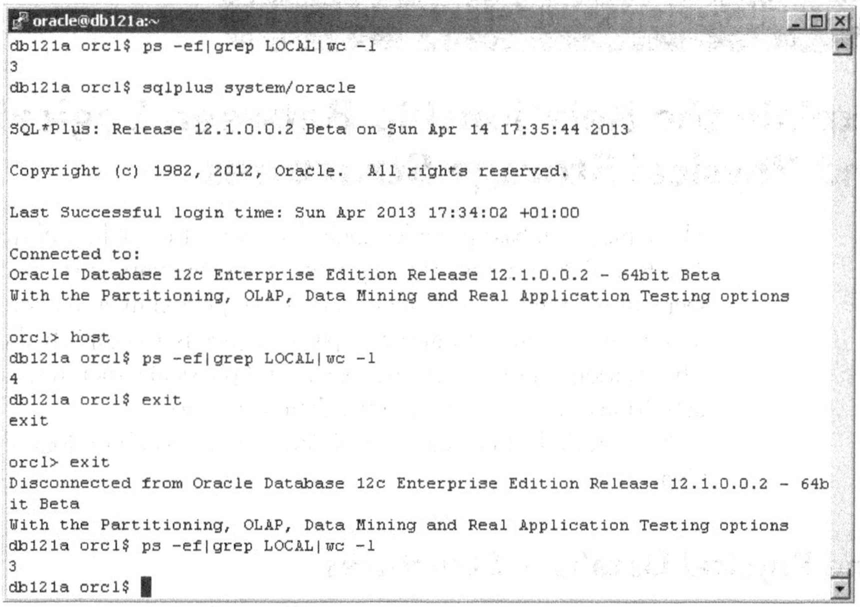

```
oracle@db121a:~
db121a orcl$ ps -ef|grep LOCAL|wc -l
3
db121a orcl$ sqlplus system/oracle

SQL*Plus: Release 12.1.0.0.2 Beta on Sun Apr 14 17:35:44 2013

Copyright (c) 1982, 2012, Oracle.  All rights reserved.

Last Successful login time: Sun Apr 2013 17:34:02 +01:00

Connected to:
Oracle Database 12c Enterprise Edition Release 12.1.0.0.2 - 64bit Beta
With the Partitioning, OLAP, Data Mining and Real Application Testing options

orcl> host
db121a orcl$ ps -ef|grep LOCAL|wc -l
4
db121a orcl$ exit
exit

orcl> exit
Disconnected from Oracle Database 12c Enterprise Edition Release 12.1.0.0.2 - 64b
it Beta
With the Partitioning, OLAP, Data Mining and Real Application Testing options
db121a orcl$ ps -ef|grep LOCAL|wc -l
3
db121a orcl$
```

FIGURE 3-6

Display the thread count within the Oracle executable image

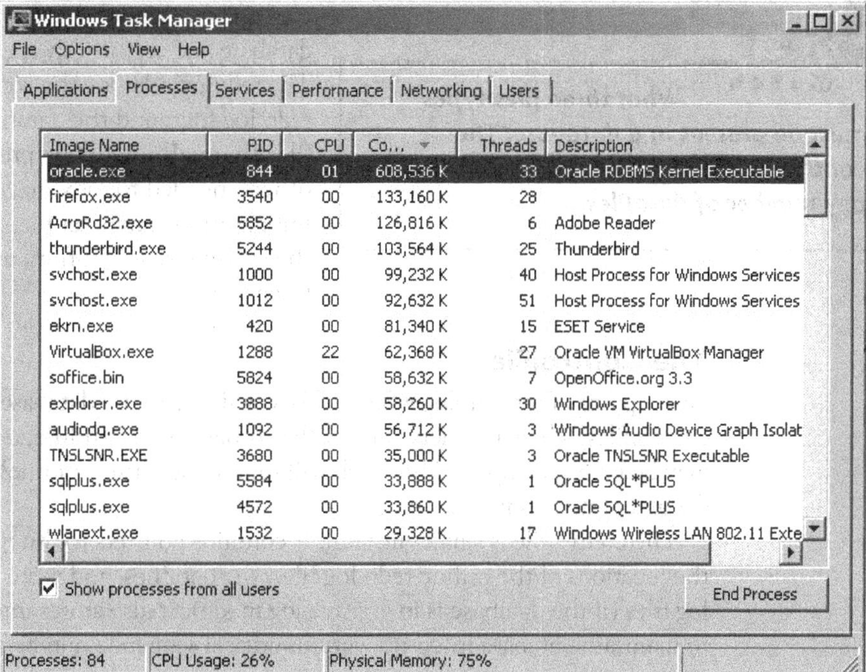

CERTIFICATION OBJECTIVE 3.04

Explain the Relationship Between Logical and Physical Storage Structures

The Oracle database provides complete abstraction of logical storage from physical. The logical data storage is in *segments*. There are various segment types; a typical segment is a table. The segments are stored physically in datafiles. The abstraction of the logical storage from the physical storage is accomplished through tablespaces. The relationships between the logical and physical structures, as well as their definitions, are maintained in the data dictionary.

You can find a full treatment of database storage, both logical and physical, in Chapter 6.

The Physical Database Structures

What three files types must be present in a database? The controlfile, the online redo log files, and any number of datafiles.

Three file types make up an Oracle database, plus a few others that exist externally to the database and are, strictly speaking, optional. The required files are the controlfile, the online redo log files, and the datafiles. The external files that will usually be present (there are others, needed for advanced options) are the initialization parameter file, the password file, the archive redo log files, and the log and trace files.

The Controlfile

First a point of terminology: Some DBAs will say that a database can have multiple controlfiles, whereas others will say that it has one controlfile, of which there may be multiple copies. This book will follow the latter terminology. The Oracle documentation is inconsistent.

The controlfile is small but vital. It contains pointers to the rest of the database: the locations of the online redo log files, the datafiles, and more recently the archive log files (if the database is in archive log mode). It also stores information required to maintain database integrity: various critical sequence numbers and timestamps, for example. If the Recovery Manager tool is being used for backups, the details of these backups will also be stored in the controlfile. The controlfile will usually be no more than a few megabytes in size, but you can't survive without it.

Every database has one controlfile, but a good DBA will always create multiple copies of the controlfile so that if one copy is damaged, the database itself will survive. If all copies of the controlfile are lost, it is possible (though perhaps awkward) to recover, but you should never find yourself in that situation. You don't have to worry about keeping multiplexed copies of the controlfile synchronized—Oracle will take care of that. Its maintenance is automatic; your only control is how many copies to have, and where to put them.

If you get the number of copies, or their location, wrong at database creation time, you can add or remove copies later, or move them around. However, you should bear in mind that any such operations will require downtime, so it is a good idea to get it right at the beginning. There is no right or wrong answer when determining how many copies to have. The minimum is one; the maximum possible is eight. All organizations should have a DBA standards handbook that states something like "all production databases will have three copies of the controlfile, on three separate devices" (three being a number picked for illustration purposes only, but a number with which many organizations are happy). If no such guidelines are in place, someone should write them (and perhaps the "someone" should be you). There is no rule that says two copies are too few, or seven copies are too many; there are only corporate standards, and the DBA's job is to ensure that the databases conform to these standards.

Damage to any controlfile copy will cause the database instance to terminate immediately. There is no way to avoid this: Oracle Corporation does not permit operating a database with less than the number of controlfiles requested.

The Online Redo Log Files

The redo log stores a continuous chain in chronological order of every change vector applied to the database. This will be the bare minimum of information required to reconstruct, or redo, all the work that has been done. If a datafile (or the whole database) is damaged or destroyed, these change vectors can be applied to datafile backups to redo the work, bringing them forward in time until the moment that the damage occurred. The redo log consists of two file types: the online redo log files (which are required) and the archive log files (which are optional).

Every database has at least two online redo log files, but as with the controlfile, a good DBA creates multiple copies of each online redo log file. The online redo log

exam watch *Every database must have at least two online redo log file groups to function. Each group should have at least two members for safety.*

consists of groups of online redo log files, each file being known as a member. An Oracle database requires at least two groups of at least one member each to function. You may create more than two groups for performance reasons, and more than one member per group for security (as the old joke goes, "this isn't just data security, it is job security"). The requirement for a minimum of two groups is so that one group can be accepting the current changes while the other group is being backed up (or *archived*, to use the correct term).

One of the groups is the *current* group: Changes are written to the current online redo log file group by LGWR. As user sessions update data in the database buffer cache, they also write out the minimal change vectors to the redo log buffer. LGWR continually flushes this buffer to the files that make up the current online redo log file group. Log files are fixed size; therefore, eventually the files making up the current group will fill. LGWR will then perform what is called a *log switch*, which makes the second group current and starts writing to that. If your database is configured appropriately, the ARCn process(es) will then archive (in effect, back up) the log file members making up the first group. When the second group fills, LGWR will switch back to the first group, making it current and overwriting it; ARCn will then archive the second group. Thus, the online redo log file groups (and therefore the members making them up) are used in a circular fashion, and each log switch will generate an archive redo log file.

As with the controlfile, if you have multiple members per group (and you should!), you don't have to worry about keeping them synchronized. LGWR will ensure that it writes to all of them, in parallel, thus keeping them identical. If you lose one member of a group, as long as you have a surviving member, the database will continue to function.

The size and number of your log file groups are a matter of tuning. In general, you will choose a size appropriate to the amount of activity you anticipate. The minimum size is 50MB, but some very active databases will need to raise this to several gigabytes if they are not to fill every few minutes. A very busy database can generate megabytes of redo a second, whereas a largely static database may generate only a few megabytes an hour. The number of members per group will be dependent on what level of fault tolerance is deemed appropriate, and is a matter to be documented in corporate standards. However, you don't have to worry about this at database creation time. You can move your online redo log files around, add or drop them, and create ones of different sizes as you please at any time later on. Such operations are performed "online" and don't require downtime; they are therefore transparent to the end users.

The Datafiles

The third required file type making up a database is the datafile. At a minimum, you must have three datafiles (all to be created at database creation time): one each for the SYSTEM tablespace (which stores the data dictionary), the SYSAUX tablespace (which stores data that is auxiliary to the data dictionary), and the UNDO tablespace (which stores the undo segments required to protect transactions). You will have many more than that when your database goes live, and will often create a few more to begin with.

Datafiles are the repository for data. Their size and numbers are effectively unlimited. A small database might have just half a dozen datafiles of only a few hundred megabytes each. A larger database could have thousands of datafiles, whose size is limited only by the capabilities of the host operating system and hardware.

The datafiles are the physical structures visible to the system administrators. Logically, they are the repository for the *segments* containing user data that the programmers see, and also for the segments that make up the data dictionary. A segment is a storage structure for data; typical segments are tables and indexes. Datafiles can be renamed, resized, moved, added, or dropped at any time in the lifetime of the database, but remember that some operations on some datafiles may require downtime.

At the operating system level, a datafile consists of a number of operating system blocks. Internally, datafiles are formatted into *Oracle blocks*. These blocks are consecutively numbered within each datafile. The block size is fixed when the datafile is created, and in most circumstances it will be the same throughout the entire database. The block size is a matter for tuning and can range (with limits, depending on the platform) from 2KB up to 32KB. There is no necessary relationship between the Oracle block size and the operating system block size.

Figure 3-7 shows the Oracle storage model in the form of an entity-relationship diagram. The left column shows the logical structures next to the physical structures. For completeness, the diagram also shows the ASM entities in the two right-most columns, which are covered in Chapter 19. These are an alternative to the file system storage discussed here.

on the job

Many DBAs like to match the operating system block size to the Oracle block size. For performance reasons, the operating system blocks should never be larger than the Oracle blocks, but there is no reason not to have them smaller. For instance, having a 1KB operating block size and an 8KB Oracle block size is perfectly acceptable.

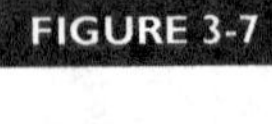
FIGURE 3-7

The Oracle storage model

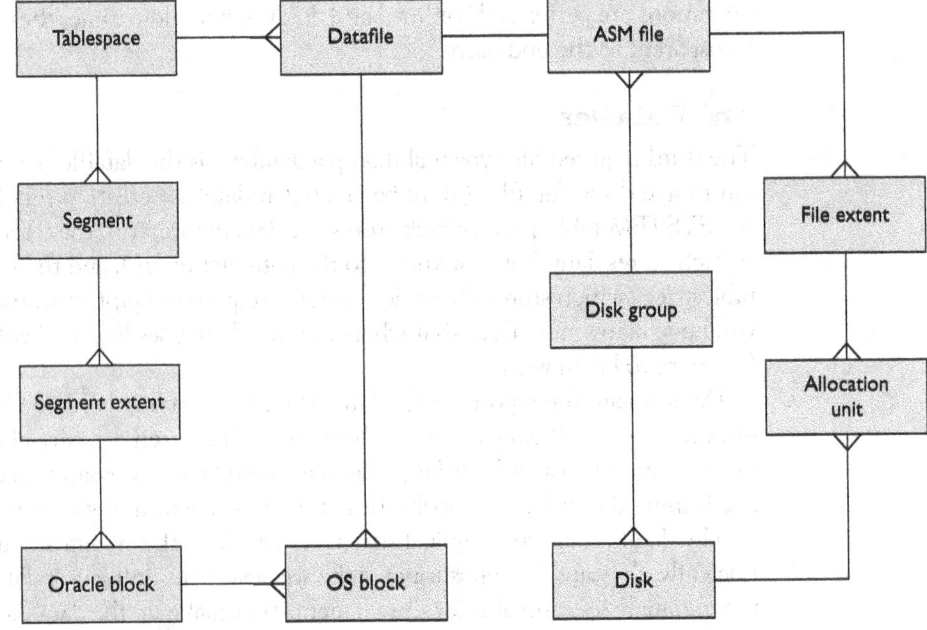

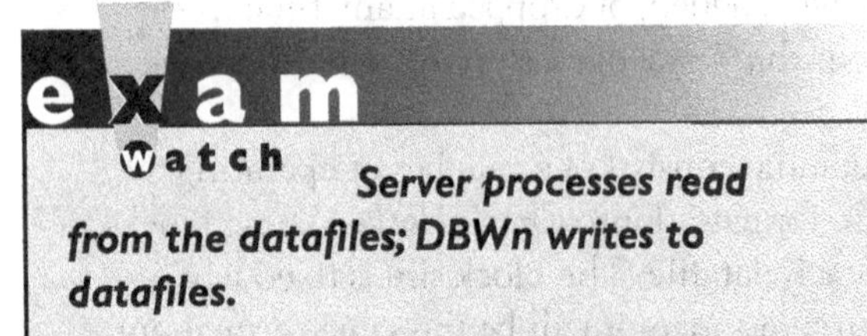

Server processes read from the datafiles; DBWn writes to datafiles.

Within a block is a header section, a data area, and possibly some free space. The header section contains information such as the row directory, which lists the location within the data area of the rows in the block (if the block is being used for a table segment) and also row locking information if there is a transaction (or several concurrent transactions) working on the rows in the block. The data area contains the data itself, such as rows if it is part of a table segment, or index keys if the block is part of an index segment.

Other Database Files

These files exist outside the database. They are necessary for practical purposes, but are not, strictly speaking, part of the database:

- **Instance parameter file** When an Oracle instance is started, the SGA structures build in memory and the background processes start according to settings in the parameter file. This is the only file that needs to exist in order to start an instance. There are several hundred parameters, but only one is required: the DB_NAME parameter. All others have defaults. Therefore, the parameter file can be quite small, but it must exist.

- **Password file** Users establish sessions by presenting a username and password. The Oracle server authenticates these against user definitions stored in the data dictionary. The data dictionary is a set of tables in the database; it is therefore inaccessible if the database is not open. There are occasions when a user needs to be authenticated before the data dictionary is available: when they need to start the database, or indeed to create it. An external password file is one means of doing this. It contains a small number of (typically less than half a dozen) usernames and passwords that exist outside the data dictionary that can be used to connect to an instance before the data dictionary is available.

- **Archive redo log files** When an online redo log file fills, the ARCn process copies it out of the database to an archive redo log file. Once this is done, the archive log is no longer part of the database. It is, however, essential if it's ever necessary to restore a datafile backup, and Oracle does provide facilities for managing the archive redo log files.
- **Alert log and trace files** The alert log is a continuous stream of messages regarding certain critical operations affecting the instance and the database. Not everything is logged: only events that are considered to be really important (such as startup and shutdown), changes to the physical structures of the database, and changes to the parameters that control the instance. Trace files are generated by background processes when they detect error conditions, and sometimes to report certain actions.

The Logical Database Structures

The physical structures that make up a database are visible as operating system files to your system administrators. Your users see logical structures such as tables. Oracle uses the term *segment* to describe any structure that contains data. A typical segment is a table, containing rows of data, but there are more than a dozen possible segment types in an Oracle database. Of particular interest (for examination purposes) are table segments, index segments, and undo segments, all of which are investigated in detail later on. For now, you don't need to know any more than that tables contain rows of information, that indexes are a mechanism for giving fast access to any particular row, and that undo segments are data structures used for storing the information that might be needed to reverse, or roll back, any transactions you do not wish to make permanent.

The SYSAUX tablespace must be created at database creation time. If you do not specify it, one will be created by default.

So system administrators see physical datafiles; programmers see logical segments. Oracle abstracts the logical storage from the physical storage by means of the *tablespace*, which is logically a collection of one or more segments and physically a collection of one or more datafiles. Put in terms of relational analysis, there is a many-to-many relationship between segments and datafiles: One table may be cut across many datafiles, one datafile may contain bits of many tables. By inserting the tablespace entity between the segments and the files, Oracle resolves this many-to-many relationship.

A segment will consist of a number of blocks. Datafiles are formatted into blocks, and these blocks are assigned to segments as the segments grow. Because managing space one block at a time would be a time-consuming process, blocks are grouped into *extents*. An extent is a series of blocks that are consecutively numbered within a datafile, and segments grow by having new extents added to them. These extents need not be adjacent to each other, or even in the same datafile; they can come from any datafile that is part of the tablespace within which the segment resides.

Figure 3-7 (seen earlier) shows the Oracle data storage hierarchy, with the separation of logical from physical storage. The figure shows the relationships between the storage structures. Logically, a tablespace can contain many segments, each consisting of many extents. An *extent* is a set of Oracle blocks. Physically, a datafile consists of many operating system blocks assigned by whatever file system the operating system is using. The two parts of the model are connected by the relationships showing that one tablespace can consist of multiple datafiles, and at the lowest level that one Oracle block will consist of multiple operating system blocks.

The Data Dictionary

The data dictionary is metadata: data about data. It describes the database, both physically and logically, and its contents. User definitions, security information, integrity constraints, and performance monitoring information are all part of the data dictionary. It is stored as a set of segments in the SYSTEM and SYSAUX tablespaces.

In many ways, the segments that make up the data dictionary are segments like any other: just tables and indexes. The critical difference is that the data dictionary tables are generated at database creation time, and you are not allowed to access them directly. There is nothing to stop an inquisitive DBA from investigating the data dictionary directly, but if you do any updates to it, you may cause irreparable damage to your database—and certainly Oracle Corporation will not support you. Creating a data dictionary is part of the database creation process. It is maintained subsequently by Data Definition Language (DDL) commands. When you issue the **CREATE TABLE** command, you are in fact inserting rows into data dictionary tables, as you are with commands such as **CREATE USER** and **GRANT**.

exam watch ***Which view will show you*** *all* ***the tables in the database? DBA_TABLES, not ALL_TABLES.***

For querying the dictionary, Oracle provides a set of views. The views come in three forms, prefixed DBA_, ALL_, or USER_. Most of the views come in all three forms. Any view prefixed USER_ will be populated with rows describing objects owned by the user querying the view. Therefore, no two people will see the same contents. If user SCOTT queries USER_TABLES, he will see information about his tables; if you query USER_TABLES, you will see information about your tables. Any view prefixed ALL_ will be populated with rows describing objects to which you have access. Therefore, ALL_TABLES will contain rows describing your own tables, plus rows describing tables belonging to anyone else you have been given permission to see. Any view prefixed DBA_ will have rows for every object in the database, so DBA_TABLES will have one row for every table in the database, no matter who created it. These views are created as part of the database creation process, along with a large number of PL/SQL packages that are provided by Oracle to assist database administrators in managing the database and programmers in developing applications. PL/SQL code is also stored in the data dictionary.

The relationship between tablespaces and datafiles is maintained in the database controlfile. This lists all the datafiles, stating which tablespace they are a part of. Without the controlfile, there is no way an instance can locate the datafiles and then identify those that make up the SYSTEM tablespace. Only when the SYSTEM tablespace has been opened is it possible for the instance to access the data dictionary, at which point it becomes possible to open the database.

EXERCISE 3-4

Investigate the Storage Structures in Your Database

In this exercise, you will create a table segment and then work out where it is physically. Follow these steps:

1. Connect to the database as user SYSTEM.
2. Create a table without nominating a tablespace—it will be created in your default tablespace, with one extent:

```
create table tab34 (c1 varchar2(10))
segment creation immediate;
```

3. Identify the tablespace in which the table resides, the size of the extent, the file number the extent is in, and at which block of the file the extent starts:

```
select tablespace_name, extent_id, bytes, file_id, block_id
from dba_extents where owner='SYSTEM' and segment_name='TAB34';
```

4. Identify the file by name (substitute the file_id from the previous query when prompted):

```
select name from v$datafile where file#=&file_id;
```

5. Work out precisely where in the file the extent is, in terms of how many bytes into the file it begins. This requires finding out the tablespace's block size. Enter the block_id and tablespace_name returned by the query in step 3 when prompted.

```
select block_size * &block_id from dba_tablespaces
where tablespace_name='&tablespace_name';
```

Figure 3-8 shows these steps, executed from SQL*Plus.

The figure shows that the table exists in one extent (extent number zero) that is 64KB in size. This extent is in the file /u01/app/oracle/oradata/orcl/system01.dbf and begins about 826MB into the file.

FIGURE 3-8 Determining the physical location of a logical object

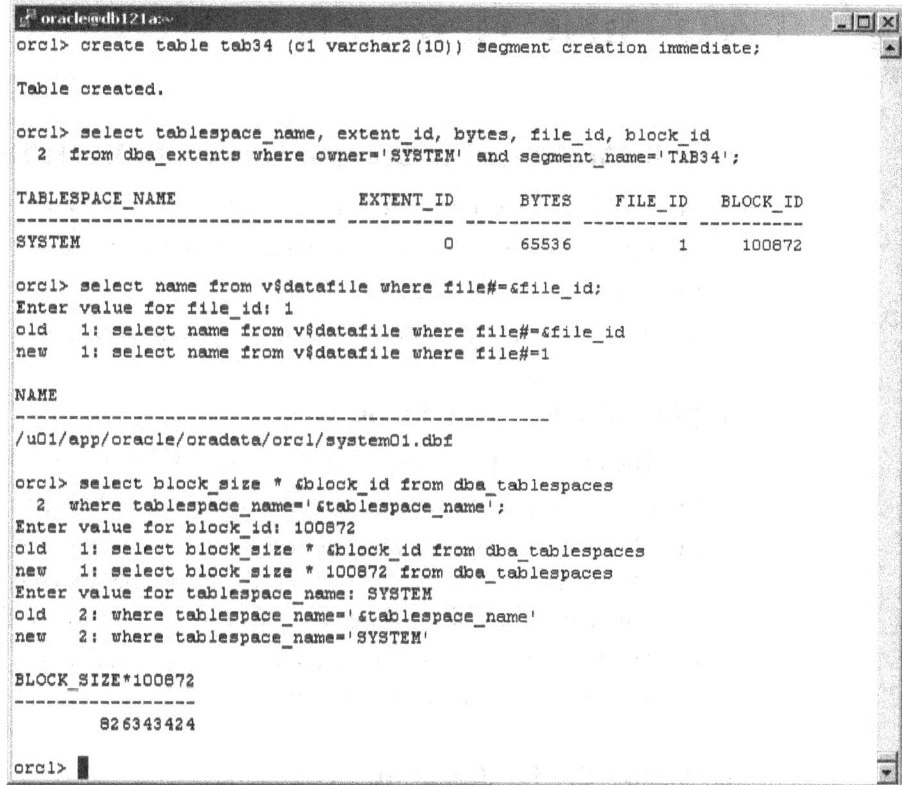

```
orcl> create table tab34 (c1 varchar2(10)) segment creation immediate;

Table created.

orcl> select tablespace_name, extent_id, bytes, file_id, block_id
  2  from dba_extents where owner='SYSTEM' and segment_name='TAB34';

TABLESPACE_NAME                 EXTENT_ID      BYTES    FILE_ID   BLOCK_ID
------------------------------ ---------- ---------- ---------- ----------
SYSTEM                                  0      65536          1     100872

orcl> select name from v$datafile where file#=&file_id;
Enter value for file_id: 1
old   1: select name from v$datafile where file#=&file_id
new   1: select name from v$datafile where file#=1

NAME
--------------------------------------------------
/u01/app/oracle/oradata/orcl/system01.dbf

orcl> select block_size * &block_id from dba_tablespaces
  2  where tablespace_name='&tablespace_name';
Enter value for block_id: 100872
old   1: select block_size * &block_id from dba_tablespaces
new   1: select block_size * 100872 from dba_tablespaces
Enter value for tablespace_name: SYSTEM
old   2: where tablespace_name='&tablespace_name'
new   2: where tablespace_name='SYSTEM'

BLOCK_SIZE*100872
-----------------
        826343424

orcl>
```

CERTIFICATION SUMMARY

This chapter covers the Oracle instance and database architecture. Many topics will be given a fuller treatment in later chapters, but at this point the overall architecture of the instance (consisting of shared memory structures and processes), the database (consisting of files on disk), and a user session (a user process and a server process) should be clear.

TWO-MINUTE DRILL

List the Architectural Components of an Oracle Database

- An Oracle server is an instance connected to a database.
- An instance is a block of shared memory and a set of background processes.
- A database is a set of files on disk.
- A user session is a user process connected to a server process.

Explain the Memory Structures

- The instance shared memory is the System Global Area (the SGA).
- A session's private memory is its Program Global Area (the PGA).
- The SGA consists of a number of substructures, some of which are required (the database buffer cache, the log buffer, and the shared pool) and some of which are optional (the large pool, the Java pool, and the Streams pool).
- The SGA structures can be dynamically resized and automatically managed, with the exception of the log buffer.

Describe the Background Processes

- Session server processes are launched on demand when users connect.
- Some background processes are launched at instance startup and persist until shutdown; others start/stop as needed.
- Server processes read from the database; background processes write to the database.
- Some background processes will always be present (in particular SMON, PMON, DBWn, LGWR, CKPT, and MMON); others will run depending on what options have been enabled.

Explain the Relationship Between Logical and Physical Storage Structures

- ❑ There are three required file types in a database: the controlfile, the online redo log files, and the datafiles.
- ❑ The controlfile stores integrity information and pointers to the rest of the database.
- ❑ The online redo logs store recent change vectors applied to the database.
- ❑ The datafiles store the data.
- ❑ External files include the parameter file, the password file, archive redo logs, and the log and trace files.
- ❑ Logical data storage (segments) is abstracted from physical data storage (datafiles) by tablespaces.
- ❑ A tablespace can consist of multiple datafiles.
- ❑ Segments consist of multiple extents, which consist of multiple Oracle blocks, which consist of multiple operating system blocks.
- ❑ A segment can have extents in several datafiles.

SELF TEST

List the Architectural Components of an Oracle Database

1. What statements regarding instance memory and session memory are correct? (Choose all correct answers.)
   A. SGA memory is private memory segments; PGA memory is shared memory segments.
   B. Sessions can write to the PGA, not the SGA.
   C. The SGA is written to by all sessions; a PGA is written by one session.
   D. The PGA is allocated at instance startup.
   E. The SGA is allocated at instance startup.
2. How do sessions communicate with the database? (Choose the best answer.)
   A. Server processes use Oracle Net to connect to the instance.
   B. Background processes use Oracle Net to connect to the database.
   C. User processes read from the database and write to the instance.
   D. Server processes execute SQL received from user processes.

Explain the Memory Structures

3. What memory structures are a required part of the SGA? (Choose all correct answers.)
   A. The database buffer cache
   B. The Java pool
   C. The large pool
   D. The log buffer
   E. The Program Global Area
   F. The shared pool
   G. The Streams pool
4. Which SGA memory structure(s) cannot be resized dynamically after instance startup? (Choose all correct answers.)
   A. The database buffer cache.
   B. The Java pool.
   C. The large pool.
   D. The log buffer.
   E. The shared pool.
   F. The Streams pool.
   G. All SGA structures can be resized dynamically after instance startup.

5. Which SGA memory structure(s) cannot be resized automatically after instance startup? (Choose all correct answers.)
   A. The database buffer cache.
   B. The Java pool.
   C. The large pool.
   D. The log buffer.
   E. The shared pool.
   F. The Streams pool.
   G. All SGA structures can be resized automatically after instance startup.

Describe the Background Processes

6. When a session changes data, where does the change get written? (Choose the best answer.)
   A. To the data block in the cache, and the redo log buffer.
   B. To the data block on disk, and the current online redo log file.
   C. The session writes to the database buffer cache, and the log writer writes to the current online redo log file.
   D. Nothing is written until the change is committed.
7. Which of these background processes is optional? (Choose the best answer.)
   A. ARCn, the archive process
   B. CKPT, the checkpoint process
   C. DBWn, the database writer
   D. LGWR, the log writer
   E. MMON, the manageability monitor
8. What happens when a user issues a COMMIT? (Choose the best answer.)
   A. The CKPT process signals a checkpoint.
   B. The DBWn process writes the transaction's changed buffers to the datafiles.
   C. The LGWR flushes the log buffer to the online redo log.
   D. The ARCn process writes the change vectors to the archive redo log.
9. An Oracle instance can have only one of some processes, but several of others. Which of these processes can occur several times? (Choose all correct answers.)
   A. The archive process
   B. The checkpoint process
   C. The database writer process
   D. The log writer process
   E. The session server process

Explain the Relationship Between Logical and Physical Storage Structures

10. One segment can be spread across many datafiles. How? (Choose the best answer.)

A. By allocating extents with blocks in multiple datafiles

B. By spreading the segment across multiple tablespaces

C. By assigning multiple datafiles to a tablespace

D. By using an Oracle block size that is larger than the operating system block size

11. Which statement is correct regarding the online redo log? (Choose the best answer.)

A. There must be at least one log file group, with at least one member.

B. There must be at least one log file group, with at least two members.

C. There must be at least two log file groups, with at least one member each.

D. There must be at least two log file groups, with at least two members each.

12. Where is the current redo byte address, also known as the incremental checkpoint position, recorded? (Choose the best answer.)

A. In the controlfile

B. In the current online log file group

C. In the header of each datafile

D. In the System Global Area

LAB QUESTION

Simulate a situation a DBA will find themselves in many times: You have been asked to take on management of a database that you have not seen before, and for which the documentation is woefully inadequate. Write a series of queries that will begin to document the system. Following are some of the views that will help. Describe each view and then query the relevant columns. To see the views, it will be necessary to connect as a user with high privileges, such as user SYSTEM.

V$DATABASE

V$CONTROLFILE

VLOG, VLOGFILE

V$TABLESPACE, V$DATAFILE, V$TEMPFILE

On what operating system is the database is running?

Where is the controlfile? Is it multiplexed?

How many online log file groups are there?

How many members are in each group, and what are they called?

How big are they?

What tablespaces exist in the database?

What datafiles are assigned to each tablespace?

What are they called, and how big are they?

SELF TEST ANSWERS

List the Architectural Components of an Oracle Database

1. ☑ **C, E.** The SGA is shared memory, updated by all sessions; PGAs are private to each session. The SGA is allocated at startup time (but it can be modified later).
☒ **A, B,** and **D** are incorrect. **A** is incorrect because it reverses the situation: It is the SGA that exists in shared memory, not the PGA. **B** is incorrect because sessions write to both their own PGA and to the SGA. **D** is incorrect because (unlike the SGA) the PGA is only allocated on demand.

2. ☑ **D.** This is the client-server split: User processes generate SQL, and server processes execute SQL.
☒ **A, B,** and **C** are incorrect. **A** and **B** are incorrect because they get the use of Oracle Net wrong. Oracle Net is the protocol between a user process and a server process. **C** is incorrect because it describes what server processes do, not what user processes do.

Explain the Memory Structures

3. ☑ **A, D, F.** Every instance must have a database buffer cache, a log buffer, and a shared pool.
☒ **B, C, E,** and **G** are incorrect. **B, C,** and **G** are incorrect because the Java pool, the large pool, and the Streams pool are only needed for certain options. **E** is incorrect because the PGA is not part of the SGA at all.

4. ☑ **D.** The log buffer is fixed in size at startup time.
☒ **A, B, C, E, F,** and **G** are incorrect. **A, B, C, E,** and **F** are incorrect because these are the SGA's resizable components. **G** is incorrect because the log buffer is static.

5. ☑ **D.** The log buffer cannot be resized manually, never mind automatically.
☒ **A, B, C, E, F,** and **G** are incorrect. **A, B, C, E,** and **F** are incorrect because these SGA components can all be automatically managed. **G** is incorrect because the log buffer is static.

Describe the Background Processes

6. ☑ **A.** The session updates the copy of the block in memory and writes out the change vector to the log buffer.
☒ **B, C,** and **D** are incorrect. **B** is incorrect because although this will happen, it does not happen when the change is made. **C** is incorrect because it confuses the session making changes in memory with LGWR propagating changes to disk. **D** is incorrect because all changes to data occur in memory as they are made—the COMMIT is not relevant.

7. ☑ **A.** Archiving is not compulsory (although it is usually a good idea).
   ☒ **B, C, D,** and **E** are incorrect. CKPT, DBWn, LGWR, and MMON are all necessary processes.

8. ☑ **C.** On COMMIT, the log writer flushes the log buffer to disk. No other background processes need do anything.
   ☒ **A, B,** and **D** are incorrect. **A** is incorrect because full checkpoints only occur on request, or on orderly shutdown; partial checkpoints are automatic as needed. **B** is incorrect because the algorithm DBWn uses to select buffers to write to the datafiles is not related to COMMIT processing, but to how busy the buffer is. **D** is incorrect because ARCn only copies filled online redo logs; it doesn't copy change vectors in real time.

9. ☑ **A, C, E.** Both **A** and **C** are correct because the DBA can choose to configure multiple archive and database writer processes. **E** is correct because one server process will be launched for every concurrent session.
   ☒ **B** and **D** are incorrect. An instance can have only one log writer process and only one checkpoint process.

Explain the Relationship Between Logical and Physical Storage Structures

10. ☑ **C.** If a tablespace has several datafiles, segments can have extents in all of them.
    ☒ **A, B,** and **D** are incorrect. **A** is incorrect because one extent consists of consecutive blocks in any one datafile. **B** is incorrect because one segment can only exist in one tablespace (although one tablespace can contain many segments). **D** is incorrect because although this can certainly be done, one block can only exist in one datafile.

11. ☑ **C.** Two groups of one member is the minimum required for the database to function.
    ☒ **A, B,** and **D** are incorrect. **A** and **B** are incorrect because at least two groups are always required. **D** is incorrect because although it is certainly advisable to multiplex the members, it is not a technical requirement.

12. ☑ **A.** The checkpoint process writes the redo byte address (RBA) to the controlfile.
    ☒ **B, C,** and **D** are incorrect. The online logs, the datafiles, and the SGA have no knowledge of where the current RBA is.

LAB ANSWER

Possible queries follow:

```
select platform_name from v$database;
```

This will return the operating system that database is running on.

```
select name from v$controlfile;
```

This will return one row for each copy of the controlfile. If there is only one row, it is not multiplexed.

```
select group#,bytes,members from v$log;
select group#,member from v$logfile;
```

The first query will show how many groups exist, their size, and how many members each group has. The second lists the name of each member and the group to which it belongs.

```
select t.name tname,d.name fname,bytes
from v$tablespace t join v$datafile d
on t.ts#=d.ts#
order by t.ts#;
```

This query will list the tablespaces, with their datafile(s). This query is, in fact, incomplete: It will only list *permanent* tablespaces. To complete your picture of the physical layout of the database, the following query must be run too:

```
select t.name tname,d.name fname,bytes
from v$tablespace t join v$tempfile d
on t.ts#=d.ts# order by t.ts#;
```

This query will show the *temporary* tablespaces.

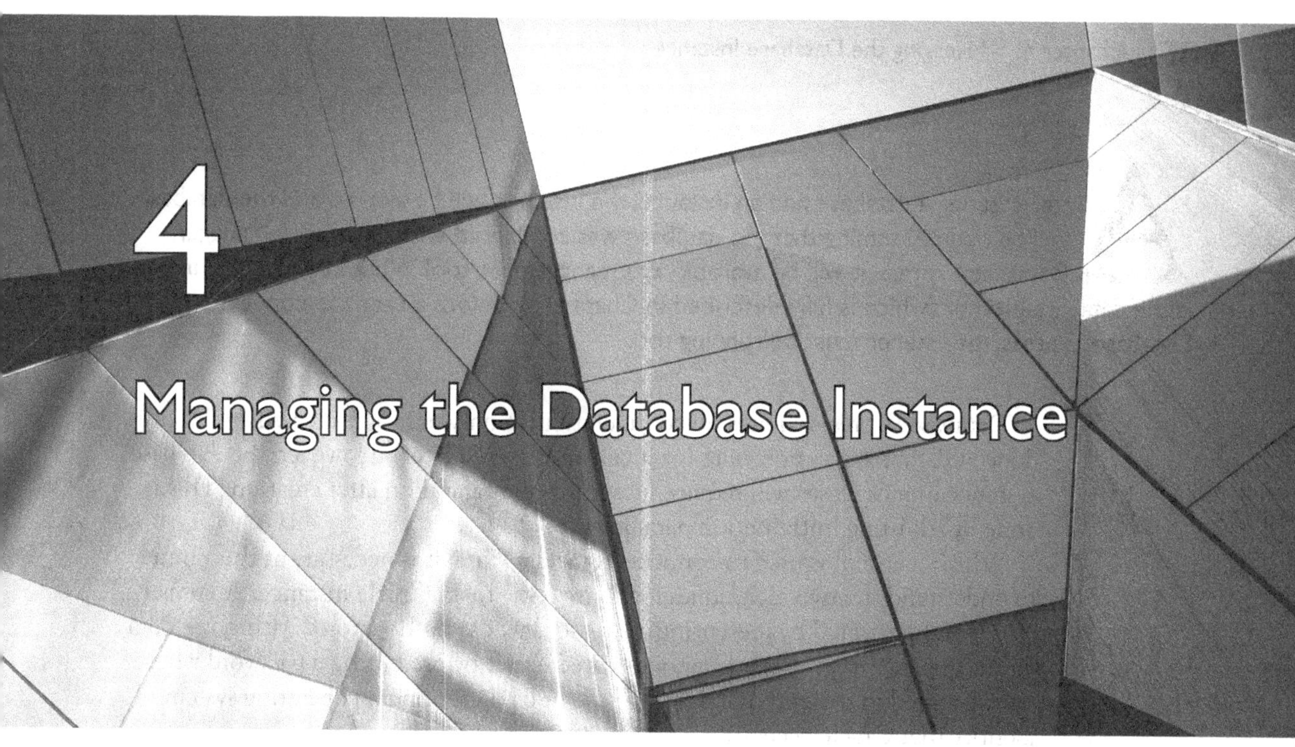

4 Managing the Database Instance

CERTIFICATION OBJECTIVES

4.01	Use Database Management Tools
4.02	Understand Initialization Parameter Files
4.03	Start Up and Shut Down an Oracle Database Instance
4.04	View the Alert Log and Access Dynamic Performance Views
✓	Two-Minute Drill
Q&A	Self-Test

After creating a database and an instance, the instance will be started and the database will be open. Assuming that the database was configured with Enterprise Manager Database Express, it will be available as a management tool. What may not be running is the database listener (which is fully described in Chapter 5). Before a user can connect to Database Express, the listener must be running too.

Database Express requires no configuration. It only has to be created, and that is done at database creation time (or it can be installed later). However, the database instance in most cases will require substantial configuration after creation. This is done by adjusting initialization parameters.

Whichever tool is used to connect to the database, it is necessary at this point to understand the two techniques for connecting to an Oracle instance. A *normal* user is authenticated by presenting a password whose hash is stored within the data dictionary. A *privileged* user is authenticated either by presenting a password whose hash is stored in the external password file or by presenting an operating system identity that Oracle accepts.

CERTIFICATION OBJECTIVE 4.01

Use Database Management Tools

The tools discussed in this section are the SQL*Plus command-line utility, the Database Express graphical utility, and the SQL Developer graphical utility. Some sites will have access to Cloud Control as well, which in some ways is a superior management tool, but is beyond the scope of the OCP exams.

Working with SQL*Plus

Working with SQL*Plus couldn't be simpler. It is just an elementary process for issuing ad-hoc SQL commands to a database. SQL*Plus is a client-server tool. On Windows systems, either launch it from a command prompt or use the shortcut to the sqlplus.exe executable file in your Start menu that the standard installation of Oracle will have created. On Unix, it is called sqlplus. On either operating system you will find the executable program in your ORACLE_HOME/bin directory.

A variation you need to be aware of is the NOLOG switch. By default, the SQL*Plus program immediately prompts you for an Oracle username, password, and database connect string. To launch SQL*Plus without a login prompt, use the /NOLOG switch:

```
sqlplus /nolog
```

This will give you a SQL prompt from which you can connect with a variety of syntaxes, to be detailed in the next section.

If SQL*Plus does not launch, or throws errors when it does launch, the most likely reason is that your operating system session environment is not set up correctly: The ORACLE_HOME variable or the PATH variable will be wrong or missing. Figure 4-1 shows examples of this problem, and how to correct it, for Linux. The same technique is applicable on Windows.

on the Job ***Many DBAs always work from SQL*Plus when trying to resolve problems. It is a simple tool that does not conceal error messages and is always available.***

Log On as a Normal or Privileged User

Chapter 7 goes through security in detail, but an understanding of how to connect with SYSDBA privileges is necessary at this point.

FIGURE 4-1 Launching SQL*Plus from an operating system command prompt

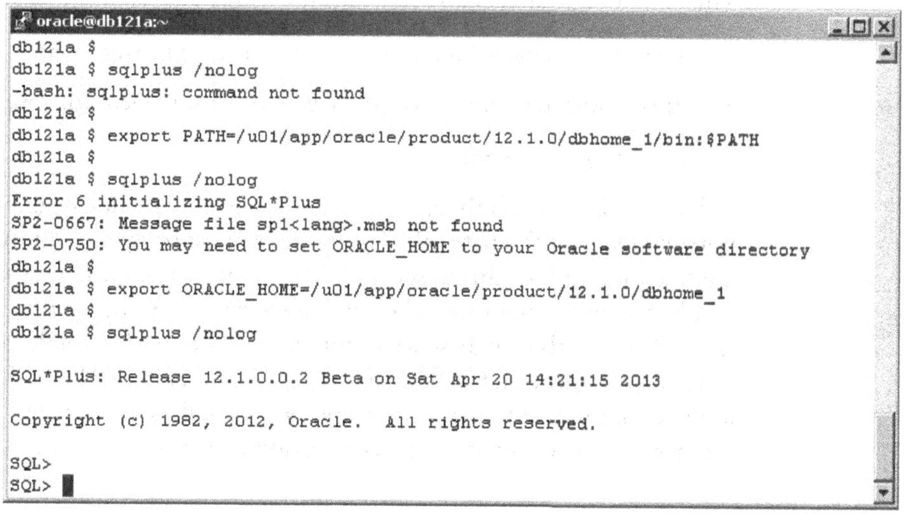

```
oracle@db121a:~
db121a $
db121a $ sqlplus /nolog
-bash: sqlplus: command not found
db121a $
db121a $ export PATH=/u01/app/oracle/product/12.1.0/dbhome_1/bin:$PATH
db121a $
db121a $ sqlplus /nolog
Error 6 initializing SQL*Plus
SP2-0667: Message file sp1<lang>.msb not found
SP2-0750: You may need to set ORACLE_HOME to your Oracle software directory
db121a $
db121a $ export ORACLE_HOME=/u01/app/oracle/product/12.1.0/dbhome_1
db121a $
db121a $ sqlplus /nolog

SQL*Plus: Release 12.1.0.0.2 Beta on Sat Apr 20 14:21:15 2013

Copyright (c) 1982, 2012, Oracle.  All rights reserved.

SQL>
SQL>
```

A normal user logon requires presenting a username and a password. The username is stored in the data dictionary, along with a hashed version of the password. This technique for logon requires the database to be open. If the database were not open, it would not be possible to query the data dictionary. This raises the question of how one can log on to a database that is not open—or, indeed, to an instance that has not been started. The answer is that Oracle offers two techniques for authenticating oneself that do not require the database to be open: password file authentication and operating system authentication. Both of these give you the option to connect with the SYSDBA or SYSOPER privilege. Only SYSDBA is discussed here (see Chapter 7 for SYSOPER).

Password file authentication compares a username and the hash of a presented password with values stored in the external password file. This is the file that was created with the orapwd utility before the database was created (see Chapter 2 for details). If the values match, the user is logged on as user SYS.

Operating system authentication delegates the authentication to the operating system. At install time, an OS group was nominated as the SYSDBA group (see Chapter 3). If your Unix or Windows user is a member of that group, Oracle will permit you to connect as user SYS with the SYSDBA privilege without presenting a password at all.

The choice of authentication method is made by the syntax used when connecting. Here's how to connect as a normal user from a SQL prompt:

```
connect username/password [ @connect_String ]
```

This is how to connect as a privileged user using password file authentication:

```
connect username/password [ @connect_string ] as sysdba
```

And this is how to connect as a privileged user using operating system authentication:

```
connect / as sysdba
```

Figure 4-2 shows all three connection syntaxes. The first example connects as a normal user, over the network. The database must be open (and the database listener must be running) for this to succeed. The second example connects as the privileged user SYS over the network. The database listener must be running, but this would succeed even if the database were shut down. The third example uses operating system authentication to obtain a privileged connection: The SQL*Plus session must be running on the same machine as the database. Neither the database nor the listener need be running for the connection to succeed.

FIGURE 4-2

Syntax for login with SQL*Plus

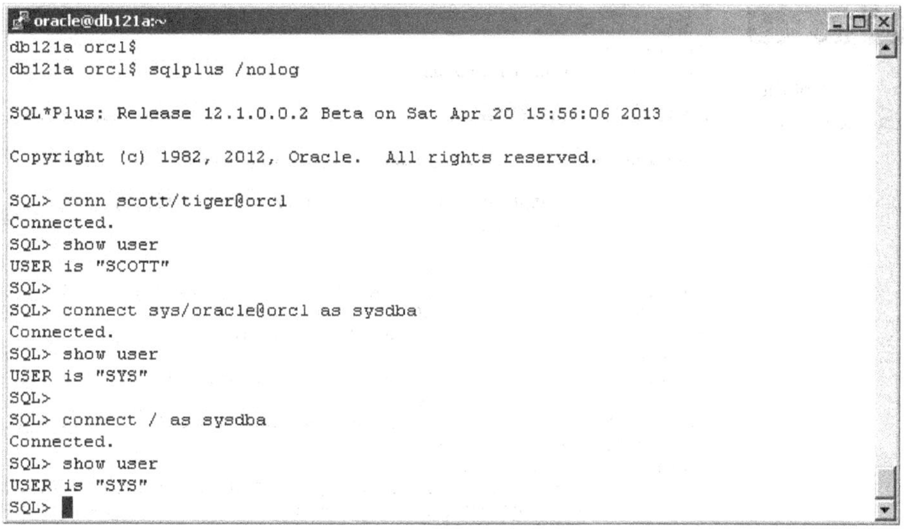

```
db121a orcl$
db121a orcl$ sqlplus /nolog

SQL*Plus: Release 12.1.0.0.2 Beta on Sat Apr 20 15:56:06 2013

Copyright (c) 1982, 2012, Oracle.  All rights reserved.

SQL> conn scott/tiger@orcl
Connected.
SQL> show user
USER is "SCOTT"
SQL>
SQL> connect sys/oracle@orcl as sysdba
Connected.
SQL> show user
USER is "SYS"
SQL>
SQL> connect / as sysdba
Connected.
SQL> show user
USER is "SYS"
SQL>
```

Working with Database Express

Database Express is a Java servlet application. Users communicate with it from a browser, over an HTTP connection established by the database listener. The application generates pages of HTML that are sent to browsers; users can use these pages to retrieve information or to send updates back. Because it consists of code stored within the database, Database Express cannot be used to start up or shut down a database.

The URL to access Database Express will have been displayed by the DBCA at the conclusion of the database creation. By default, it will be the following:

```
http://<database-host-name>:5500/em
```

To determine the HTTP listening port if it is not the default of 5500, log on to the database with SQL*Plus and run this query:

```
SQL>
SQL>  select dbms_xdb.gethttpport from dual;
GETHTTPPORT
-----------
       5500
SQL>
```

In this example, the listening port is 5500 and the protocol is HTTP. Use the lsnrctl utility to show the status of the listener, as in Figure 4-3.

FIGURE 4-3

The status of the database listener

```
oracle@db121a:/u01/app/oracle/product/12.1.0/dbhome_1/bin
db121a orcl$
db121a orcl$ lsnrctl status

LSNRCTL for Linux: Version 12.1.0.0.2 - Beta on 20-APR-2013 17:35:48

Copyright (c) 1991, 2012, Oracle.  All rights reserved.

Connecting to (ADDRESS=(PROTOCOL=tcp)(HOST=)(PORT=1521))
STATUS of the LISTENER
------------------------
Alias                     LISTENER
Version                   TNSLSNR for Linux: Version 12.1.0.0.2 - Beta
Start Date                20-APR-2013 16:03:47
Uptime                    0 days 1 hr. 32 min. 1 sec
Trace Level               off
Security                  ON: Local OS Authentication
SNMP                      OFF
Listener Log File         /u01/app/oracle/product/12.1.0/dbhome_1/log/diag/tnslsn
r/db121a/listener/alert/log.xml
Listening Endpoints Summary...
  (DESCRIPTION=(ADDRESS=(PROTOCOL=tcp)(HOST=db121a.example.com)(PORT=1521)))
  (DESCRIPTION=(ADDRESS=(PROTOCOL=tcp)(HOST=db121a.example.com)(PORT=5500))(Prese
ntation=HTTP)(Session=RAW))
Services Summary...
Service "orcl" has 1 instance(s).
  Instance "orcl", status READY, has 5 handler(s) for this service...
The command completed successfully
db121a orcl$
```

In the figure, the lsnrctl utility is run with the status switch. In the STATUS section of the output, you can see that the listener has been running for an hour and a half and that it is listening on two endpoints: port 1521 and port 5500, both on the address db121a.example.com. Port 1521 is the default port for database connections over Oracle Net. Note that port 5500 is listening for HTTP; therefore, this is the port for Database Express, and it is now possible to deduce what the URL for Database Express is:

```
http://db121a.example.com:5500/em
```

If the **lsnrctl status** command returns any sort of error, it is probable that the listener has not been started. In this case, start it with this:

```
lsnrctl start
```

The Database Express login window prompts for a username and password, with the option to specify that the connection should be made AS SYSDBA. If you want to connect as a privileged user, give the username SYS and the password and then check the box for AS SYSDBA. Otherwise, give any username and password that are valid for the database.

on the job

Database Express does require the Adobe Flash plugin. Without this, it is not possible to log on.

Database Express can be installed in a database at database creation time. The DBCA tool prompts for this. It can also be installed subsequently, either by running scripts or (much easier) by using DBCA and taking the option to Configure Database Options. The prerequisites for using Database Express are as follows: First, an HTTP(S) listening port must have been created. To confirm whether this has been done (and to correct the situation if it has not), use the DBMS_XDB package:

```
orclz>
orclz> select dbms_xdb.gethttpport from dual;

GETHTTPPORT
-----------
          0

orclz> exec dbms_xdb.sethttpport(5500)

PL/SQL procedure successfully completed.

orclz> select dbms_xdb.gethttpport from dual;

GETHTTPPORT
-----------
       5500

orclz>
```

Also, if you prefer to use HTTPS for Database Express, use the procedure DBMS_XDB.SETHTTPSPORT rather than DBM_XDB.SETHTTPPORT.

Finally, all access to Database Express is through the shared server mechanism, described in Chapter 5. This requires the existence of a DISPATCHER process; one will be running by default.

exam watch

What are the prerequisites for using Database Express? The listener must be running, a dispatcher must be running, and the XDB must have been used to enable a listening port.

Working with SQL Developer

SQL Developer is more suited to application development than to database administration, but it may still be useful to a DBA on occasion. A version is shipped with the database. Launch it by running sqldeveloper.exe (Windows) or sqldeveloper.sh (Linux) from the directory ORACLE_HOME/sqldeveloper.

EXERCISE 4-1

Use Database Management Tools

In this exercise, you become familiar with the techniques for connecting as a privileged user, with both SQL*Plus and Database Express. Explore the Database Express user interface by following these steps:

1. From an operating system prompt, confirm that your account is in the DBA group. On Linux, use the **id** command:

```
db121a $ id
uid=54321(oracle) gid=54321(oinstall) groups=54321(oinstall)
,54322(dba)
db121a $
```

   This output shows that the user is logged on as user oracle and is a member of the groups oinstall and dba. These are the default names for the groups that own the Oracle software and have SYSDBA privilege within the database.

   On Windows, use the **whoami** command:

```
c:\>
c:\>whoami /user /groups /fo list
USER INFORMATION
----------------
User Name: jwdell\john
SID:       S-1-5-21-3642582072-1318583595-1076227079-1000
GROUP INFORMATION
-----------------
Group Name: Everyone
Type:       Well-known group
SID:        S-1-1-0
Attributes: Mandatory group, Enabled by default, Enabled
Group Name: jwdell\ora_dba
Type:       Alias
SID:        S-1-5-21-3642582072-1318583595-1076227079-
Attributes: Mandatory group, Enabled by default, Enabled
```

This output shows that the user is a member of the group ora_dba, which is the name of the DBA group on Windows.

2. Set the necessary environment variables. This is a Linux example:

```
export ORACLE_BASE=/u01/app/oracle
export ORACLE_HOME=$ORACLE_BASE/product/12.1.0/dbhome_1
export PATH=$ORACLE_HOME/bin:$PATH
export ORACLE_SID=orcl
```

And this is a Windows example:

```
set ORACLE_BASE=c:\app\oracle
set ORACLE_HOME=%ORACLE_BASE%\product\12.1.0\dbhome_1
set PATH=%ORACLE_HOME%\bin;%PATH%
set ORACLE_SID=orcl
```

Substitute whatever values are appropriate for your installation.

3. Launch SQL*Plus and then connect as a privileged user using operating system authentication:

```
sqlplus /nolog
connect / as sysdba
show user
exit
```

This must show that you are connected as user SYS.

4. Launch a browser and then issue this URL:

```
http://<server_address>:5500/em
```

This will present you with a logon screen. Enter the username **sys** and password **oracle** (or whatever password you specified when creating the database) and select the "as sysdba" check box.

5. Explore the Database Express user interface. Select any tabs or links that look interesting. You will need to become familiar with all of them.

CERTIFICATION OBJECTIVE 4.02

Understand Initialization Parameter Files

An instance is defined by the parameters used to build it in memory. It can be changed after startup by adjusting these parameters—if the parameters are ones that can be changed. Some are fixed at startup time and can only be changed by shutting down the instance and starting it again.

Static and Dynamic Parameter Files

Parameter files come in two flavors: the static parameter file (also known a pfile or an init file) and the dynamic server parameter file (also known as the spfile). Either way, the initialization parameter file stores values for parameters used to build the instance in memory and to start the background processes. There are three default filenames. On Unix they are

```
$ORACLE_HOME/dbs/spfile<SID>.ora
$ORACLE_HOME/dbs/spfile.ora
$ORACLE_HOME/dbs/init<SID>.ora
```

and on Windows they are

```
%ORACLE_HOME%\database\SPFILE<SID>.ORA
%ORACLE_HOME%\database\SPFILE.ORA
%ORACLE_HOME%\database\INIT<SID>.ORA
```

In all cases, <SID> refers to the name of the instance that the parameter file will start. The preceding order is important! Unless a pfile is specified in the **startup** command, Oracle will work its way down the list, using the first file it finds and ignoring the rest. If none of them exist (and a nondefault pfile is not specified), the instance will not start.

The spfile is a server-side file, and it cannot be renamed or relocated. It is read by the SMON background process when the instance is started. The spfile is a binary file, and it cannot be edited by hand. Any attempt to edit will usually corrupt it and make it unusable. The pfile is a client-side file. It exists by default in the ORACLE_HOME directory, but it is in fact read by the user process that issues the command to start the instance. You can rename or move the pfile as you wish, but if you do this it will not be found by default and you must specify its name and location on your **startup** command. The pfile is an ASCII text file: Edit it with any text editor you like (perhaps the Windows notepad.exe or the Unix vi editor). The spfile is a binary file and cannot be edited manually. To change any values in it, use the ALTER SYSTEM SET.... commands from SQL*Plus or the parameter-editing facilities of Database Express.

To create a pfile, just type in the parameter=value pairs, one per line, and save the file with a name that conforms to the standard. To create an spfile, use a SQL*Plus command:

```
CREATE SPFILE [ = filename ] FROM PFILE [ = filename]
```

This command will read the nominated text pfile file and then use its contents to generate the binary spfile. By default, the files read and written will be those with the standard names in the standard directories. To convert an spfile into a text file that can be edited, use the reverse command:

```
CREATE PFILE [ = filename ] FROM SPFILE [ = filename]
```

The **CREATE PFILE** and **CREATE SPFILE** commands can be run from SQL*Plus at any time, even before the instance has been started.

on the Job

The file spfile<SID>.ora is undoubtedly the most convenient file to use as your parameter file. Normally, you will only use spfile.ora in a RAC environment, where one file may be used to start several instances. You will only use an init<SID>.ora file if for some reason you need to make manual edits; spfiles are binary files and cannot be edited by hand.

Static and Dynamic Parameters and the Initialization Parameter File

To view the parameters and their current values, a query such as this will do:

```
select name,value from v$parameter order by name;
```

This query may give slightly different results:

```
select name,value from v$spparameter order by name;
```

The difference is the view from which the parameter names and values are taken. V$PARAMETER shows the parameter values currently in effect in the running instance. V$SPPARAMETER shows the values in spfile on disk. Usually, these will be the same, but not always. Some parameters can be changed while the instance is running; others, known as static parameters, are fixed at instance startup time. A change made to the changeable parameters will have an immediate effect and can optionally be written out to the spfile. If this is done, the change will be permanent: The next time the instance is stopped and started, the new value will be read from the spfile. If the change is not saved to the spfile, the change will only persist until the instance is stopped. To change a static parameter, the change must be written to the spfile, and then it will come into effect at the next startup. If the output of the two preceding queries differs, this will typically be because the DBA has done some tuning work that he has not yet made permanent, or he has found it necessary to adjust a static parameter and hasn't yet restarted the instance.

If the instance is started with a pfile rather than an spfile, the V$SPPARAMETER view will show a NULL as the value for every parameter. Any attempt to change a parameter in the spfile will return an error. For example:

```
orclz>
orclz> alter system set sga_max_size=8g scope=spfile;
alter system set sga_max_size=8g scope=spfile
*
ERROR at line 1:
ORA-32001: write to SPFILE requested but no SPFILE in use
orclz>
```

The views can also be seen through Database Express. From the home page, select the Configuration tab and the Initialization Parameters link. On the subsequent window, shown in Figure 4-4, are two subtabs: Current shows the values currently in effect in the running instance, and SPFile shows those recorded in the spfile.

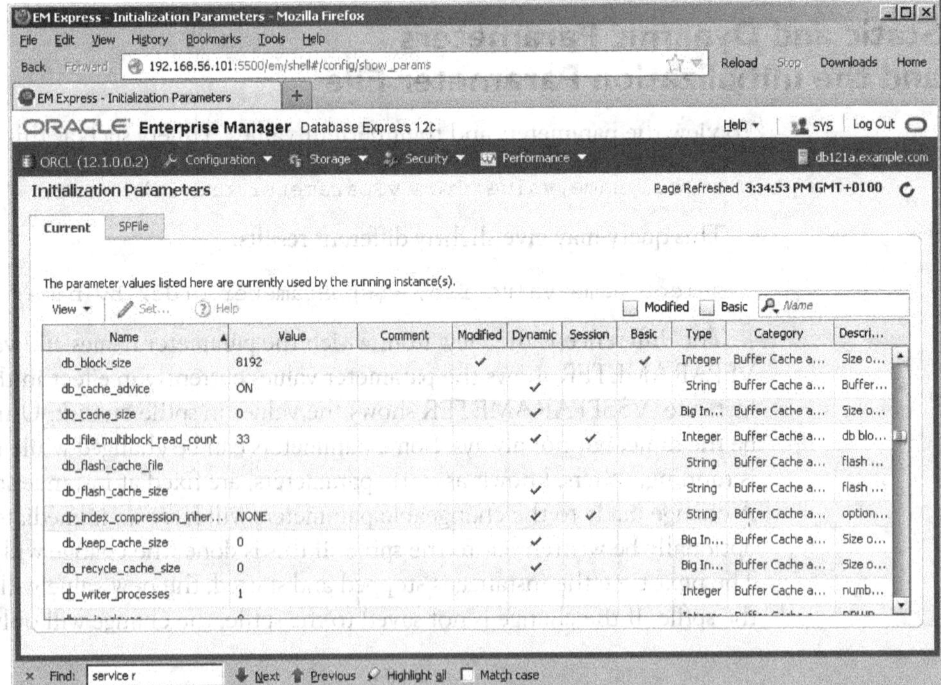

FIGURE 4-4 Initialization parameters, as seen through Database Express

The changeable parameters can be adjusted through the same window. The values for the first parameter shown (DB_BLOCK_SIZE) cannot be changed; it is not a dynamic parameter. But the next three parameters can be changed. To change the static parameters, it is necessary to select the SPFile subtab and make the changes there.

The Basic Parameters

The instance parameters considered to be "basic" are those that should be considered for every database. To view the basic parameters and their current values, a query such as this will do:

```
select name,value from v$parameter
where isbasic='TRUE' order by name;
```

A query that may give slightly different results is:

```
select s.name,s.value
from v$spparameter s join v$parameter p on s.name=p.name
where p.isbasic='TRUE' order by name;
```

The difference will be because some parameter changes may have been applied to the instance but not the spfile (or vice versa). The join is necessary because there is no column on V$SPPARAMETER to show whether a parameter is basic or advanced. Table 4-1 summarizes the basic parameters.

TABLE 4-1 Thirty Basic Parameters

Parameter	Purpose
cluster_database	Is the database a RAC or a single instance? That this is basic indicates that RAC is considered a standard option.
compatible	The release that the instance will emulate. Normally this would be the actual release, unless you are nervous about new features.
control_files	The name and location of the controlfile copies.
db_block_size	The default block size for formatting datafiles.
db_create_file_dest	The default location for datafiles.
db_create_online_log_dest_1	The default location for online redo log files.
db_create_online_log_dest_2	The default location for multiplexed copies of online redo log files.
db_domain	The domain name that can be suffixed to the db_name to generate a globally unique name.
db_name	The name of the database (the only parameter with no default).

TABLE 4-1 Thirty Basic Parameters (*continued*)

Parameter	Purpose
db_recovery_file_dest	The location of the flash recovery area.
db_recovery_file_dest_size	The amount of data that may be written to the flash recovery area.
db_unique_name	A unique identifier necessary in a Data Guard environment.
instance_number	Used to distinguish multiple RAC instances opening the same database.
ldap_directory_sysauth	Enables LDAP authentication for SYSDBA connections.
log_archive_dest_1	The destination for archiving redo log files.
log_archive_dest_2	The destination for multiplexed copies of archived redo log files.
log_archive_dest_state_1	An indicator for whether the destination is enabled or not.
log_archive_dest_state_2	An indicator for whether the destination is enabled or not.
nls_language	The language of the instance (provides many default formats).
nls_territory	The geographical location of the instance (which provides even more default formats).
open_cursors	The number of SQL work areas that a session can open at once.
pga_aggregate_target	The total amount of memory the instance can allocate to PGAs.
processes	The maximum number of processes (including session server processes) allowed to connect to the instance.
remote_listener	The addresses of listeners on other machines with which the instance should register (relevant only for RAC).
remote_login_passwordfile	Whether or not to use an external password file, to permit password file authentication.
sessions	The maximum number of sessions allowed to connect.
sga_target	The size of the SGA, within which Oracle will manage the various SGA memory structures.
shared_servers	The number of shared server processes to launch, for sessions that are not established with dedicated server processes.
star_transformation_enabled	Whether to permit the optimizer to rewrite queries that join the dimensions of a fact table.
undo_tablespace	The tablespace where the undo data will reside.

All these basic parameters are discussed in the appropriate chapters, as well as some of the advanced parameters.

Changing Parameters

To change parameters with SQL*Plus, use the **ALTER SYSTEM** command. Figure 4-5 shows examples.

The first query in Figure 4-5 shows that the value for the parameter DB_FILE_MULTIBLOCK_READ_COUNT is on default: It does not exist in the spfile on disk. The next two commands adjust the parameter in both memory and the spfile to different values, using the SCOPE keyword to determine where the change is made. The results are seen in the second query. The final command uses RESET to remove the stored value from the spfile; it will remain in effect within the instance at its current value until the instance is restarted, at which time it will return to the default. Here is the syntax:

```
ALTER SYSTEM SET <name> = <value> SCOPE = MEMORY | SPFILE | BOTH
```

FIGURE 4-5 Changing and querying parameters with SQL*Plus

```
oracle@db121a:/u01/app/oracle/diag/tnslsnr/db121a/listener/trace
SQL> select p.value in_effect, s.value in_file from v$parameter p join v$spparameter s
  2  on p.name=s.name where p.name='db_file_multiblock_read_count';

IN_EFFECT            IN_FILE
-------------------- --------------------
33

SQL> alter system set db_file_multiblock_read_count=16 scope=memory;

System altered.

SQL> alter system set db_file_multiblock_read_count=64 scope=spfile;

System altered.

SQL> select p.value in_effect, s.value in_file from v$parameter p join v$spparameter s
  2  on p.name=s.name where p.name='db_file_multiblock_read_count';

IN_EFFECT            IN_FILE
-------------------- --------------------
16                   64

SQL> alter system reset db_file_multiblock_read_count;

System altered.

SQL>
```

Note that the default for the scope clause is BOTH, meaning that if you do not specify a SCOPE, the update will be applied to the running instance and written to the spfile. Therefore, it will become a permanent change.

exam watch

An attempt to change a static parameter will fail unless the SCOPE is specified as SPFILE. The default SCOPE is BOTH (the running instance and the spfile). If the instance is started with a pfile, then SCOPE=SPFILE will fail.

An example of a static parameter is LOG_BUFFER. If you want to resize the log buffer to 10MB and issue the command

```
alter system set log_buffer=10m;
```

it will fail with the message "ORA-02095: specified initialization parameter cannot be modified." It must be changed with the SCOPE=SPFILE clause, and the instance must be restarted to take effect.

on the job

The default log buffer size is probably correct. If you raise it, you may find that COMMIT processing takes longer. If you make it smaller than the default, it may in fact be internally adjusted up to whatever Oracle thinks is necessary.

An example of a parameter that applies to the whole instance but can be adjusted for individual sessions is OPTIMIZER_MODE. This influences the way in which Oracle will execute statements. A common choice is between the values ALL_ROWS and FIRST_ROWS. The value ALL_ROWS instructs the optimizer to generate execution plans that will run statements to completion as quickly as possible, whereas FIRST_ROWS instructs it to generate plans that will get something back to the user as soon as possible, even if the whole statement takes longer to complete. Therefore, if your database is generally used for long DSS-type queries but some users use it for interactive work, you might issue the command

```
alter system set optimizer_mode=all_rows;
```

and let the individual users issue

```
alter session set optimizer_mode=first_rows;
```

if they want to.

on the job

Logon triggers can be used to adjust session parameters to values suitable for different users, depending on the username with which they log on.

EXERCISE 4-2

Query and Set Initialization Parameters

In this exercise, use either SQL*Plus or Database Express to manage initialization parameters. The examples use SQL*Plus, but only because it is clearer to give exact commands than to provide navigation paths through a GUI. Here are the steps to follow:

1. Connect to the database (which must be open!) as user SYS, with the SYSDBA privilege. Use either operating system authentication or password file authentication.
2. Display all the basic parameters, checking whether they have all been set or are still at their default, and note the values for PROCESSES and SESSIONS:

   ```
   select name,value,isdefault from v$parameter
   where isbasic='TRUE' order by name;
   ```

   Any basic parameters that are at their default should be investigated to see if the default is appropriate. In fact, all the basic parameters should be considered. Read up on all of them in the Oracle documentation now. The volume you need is titled "Oracle Database Reference." Part 1, Chapter 1 has a paragraph describing every initialization parameter.
3. Change the PROCESSES parameter to 200. This is a static parameter. It is therefore necessary to specify a SCOPE and then to bounce the database. Figure 4-6 shows the sequence of commands. The **STARTUP FORCE** command is explained in the next section.
4. Rerun the query from step 2. Note the new value for PROCESSES, and also for SESSIONS. PROCESSES limits the number of operating system processes allowed to connect to the instance, and SESSIONS limits the number of sessions. These figures are related, because each session will require a process. The default value for SESSIONS is derived from PROCESSES, so if SESSIONS was on default, it will now have a new value.
5. Change the value for the NLS_LANGUAGE parameter for your session. Choose whatever mainstream language you want (Oracle supports 67 languages

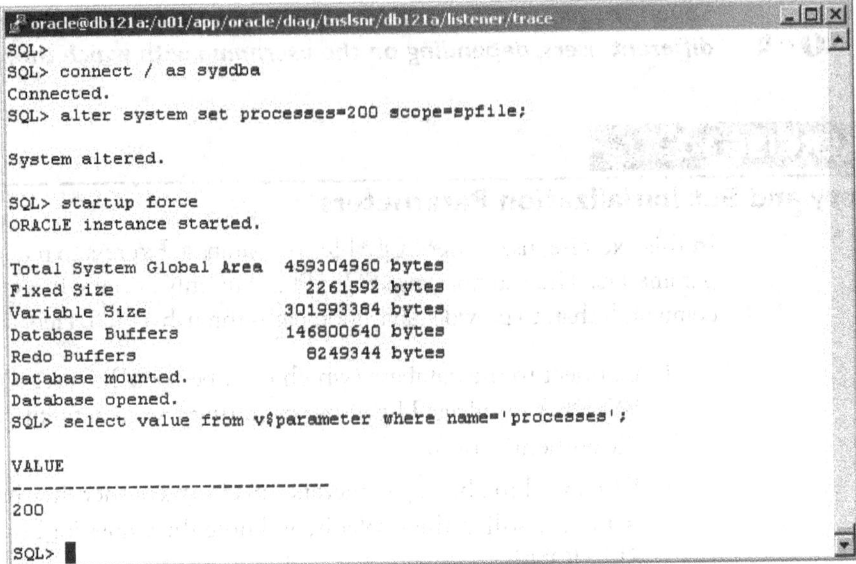

oracle@db121a:/u01/app/oracle/diag/tnslsnr/db121a/listener/trace
SQL>
SQL> connect / as sysdba
Connected.
SQL> alter system set processes=200 scope=spfile;
System altered.
SQL> startup force
ORACLE instance started.
Total System Global Area 459304960 bytes
Fixed Size 2261592 bytes
Variable Size 301993384 bytes
Database Buffers 146800640 bytes
Redo Buffers 8249344 bytes
Database mounted.
Database opened.
SQL> select value from v$parameter where name='processes';
VALUE

200
SQL>

FIGURE 4-6 How to change a static parameter

at the time of writing), but the language must be specified in English (for example, you would use "German," not "Deutsch"):

```
alter session set nls_language=French;
```

6. Confirm that the change has worked by querying the system date:

```
select to_char(sysdate,'day month') from dual;
```

You may want to change your session language back to what it was before (such as English) with another **ALTER SESSION** command. If you don't, be prepared for error messages to be in the language your session is now using.

7. Change the OPTIMIZER_MODE parameter, but restrict the scope to the running instance only; do not update the parameter file. This exercise enables the deprecated rule-based optimizer, which might be needed while testing some old code, but you would not want the change to be permanent:

```
alter system set optimizer_mode=rule scope=memory;
```

8. Confirm that the change has been effected but not written to the parameter file:

```
select value from v$parameter where name='optimizer_mode'
union
select value from v$spparameter where name='optimizer_mode';
```

9. Return the OPTIMIZER_MODE to its standard value, in both the running instance and the parameter file:

```
alter system set optimizer_mode=all_rows scope=both;
```

Note that the scope clause is not actually needed, because BOTH is the default.

CERTIFICATION OBJECTIVE 4.03

Start Up and Shut Down an Oracle Database Instance

Oracle Corporation's recommended sequence for starting a database is to start the database listener and then the database. Starting the database is itself a staged process.

Starting the Database Listener

The database listener is a process that monitors a port for database connection requests. These requests (and all subsequent traffic once a session is established) use Oracle Net, Oracle's proprietary communications protocol. Oracle Net is a layered protocol running over whatever underlying network protocol is in use (probably TCP/IP). Managing the listener is fully described in Chapter 5, but it is necessary to know how to start it now.

There are two ways to start the database listener:

- With the lsnrctl utility
- As a Windows service (Windows only, of course)

The lsnrctl utility is in the ORACLE_HOME/bin directory. The key commands are

```
lsnrctl start [ <listener> ]
lsnrctl status [ <listener> ]
```

where <listener> is the name of the listener. This will have defaulted to LISTENER, which is correct in most cases. You will know if you have created a listener with another name. Figure 4-3, from earlier in the chapter, shows the output of the **lsnrctl status** command when the listener (which is indeed named LISTENER) is running.

Note that the first DESCRIPTION line of the output in the figure shows the host address and port on which the listener is listening, and the third line from the bottom states that the listener will accept connections for the service "orcl," which is offered by an instance called "orcl." These are the critical bits of information needed to connect to the database. Following a successful database creation with DBCA, it can be assumed that they are correct. If the listener is not running, the output of **lsnrctl status** will make this very clear.

Under Windows, the listener runs as a Windows service. It is therefore possible to control it through the services interface. To identify the name of the listener service, use the Services management console. Control it either through the Services console or from a command prompt:

```
c:\>
c:\>net stop OracleOraDb12c_home1TNSListener
The OracleOraDb12c_home1TNSListener service is stopping.
The OracleOraDb12c_home1TNSListener service was stopped successfully.

c:\>net start OracleOraDb12c_home1TNSListener
The OracleOraDb12c_home1TNSListener service is starting.
The OracleOraDb12c_home1TNSListener service was started successfully.

c:\>
```

Database Startup and Shutdown

If one is being precise (always a good idea, if you want to pass the OCP examinations), one does not start or stop a database. An instance may be started and stopped; a database is mounted and opened, and then dismounted and closed. This can be done with SQL*Plus, using the **STARTUP** and **SHUTDOWN** commands. On a Windows system, it may also be done by controlling the Windows service under which the instance runs.

Connecting with an Appropriate Privilege

Ordinary users cannot start up or shut down a database. You must therefore connect with some form of external authentication: You must be authenticated either by the operating system, as being a member of the group that owns the Oracle software, or by giving a username/password combination that exists in an external password file.

You tell Oracle that you wish to use external authentication by using the appropriate syntax in the **CONNECT** command you give in your user process.

If you are using SQL*Plus, the syntax of the CONNECT command tells Oracle what type of authentication you wish to use: the default of data dictionary authentication, password file authentication, or operating system authentication. Here are the possibilities:

- connect user/pass[@connect_alias]
- connect user/pass[@connect_alias] as sysdba
- connect user/pass[@connect_alias] as sysoper
- connect / as sysdba
- connect / as sysoper

SYSDBA and SYSOPER are not users; they are privileges that can be granted to users. By default, only user SYS has these privileges until they are deliberately granted to other users.

In these examples, "user" is the username and "pass" is the password. The connect_alias will be resolved to a connect string, as described in Chapter 5. Either SYSDBA or SYSOPER is needed to perform a STARTUP or SHUTDOWN. Figure 4-7 shows examples of connecting with these privileges.

FIGURE 4-7 Use of operating system and password file authentication

```
oracle@db121a:/u01/app/oracle/diag/tnslsnr/db121a/listener/trace
db121a orcl$ export ORACLE_SID=orcl
db121a orcl$ sqlplus /nolog

SQL*Plus: Release 12.1.0.0.2 Beta on Sun Apr 21 16:57:18 2013

Copyright (c) 1982, 2012, Oracle.  All rights reserved.

SQL> connect / as sysdba
Connected.
SQL> show user
USER is "SYS"
SQL> conn / as sysoper
Connected.
SQL> sho user
USER is "PUBLIC"
SQL> connect sys/oracle@db121a.example.com:1521/orcl as sysdba
Connected.
SQL> show user
USER is "SYS"
SQL> conn sys/oracle@orcl as sysoper
Connected.
SQL> sho user
USER is "PUBLIC"
SQL>
```

Use of the SYSDBA privilege logs you on to the instance as user SYS, the most powerful user in the database and the owner of the data dictionary. Use of the SYSOPER privilege connects you as user PUBLIC. PUBLIC is not a user in any normal sense; they are a notional user with administration privileges, but with no privileges that let them see or manipulate data.

Startup: NOMOUNT, MOUNT, and OPEN

Remember that the instance and the database are separate entities; they can exist independently of each other. The startup process is therefore staged:

1. You build the instance in memory.
2. You enable a connection to the database by mounting the controlfile.
3. You open the database for use.

At any moment, a database will be in one of four states:

- SHUTDOWN
- NOMOUNT
- MOUNT
- OPEN

When the database is SHUTDOWN, all files are closed and the instance does not exist. In NOMOUNT mode, the instance has been built in memory (the SGA has been created and the background processes started, according to whatever is specified in its parameter file), but no connection has been made to a database. It is indeed possible that the database does not yet exist. In MOUNT mode, the instance locates and reads the database controlfile. In OPEN mode, all database files are located and opened and the database is made available for use by end users. The startup process is staged: Whenever you issue a startup command, it will go through these stages. It is possible to stop the startup partway. For example, if your controlfile is damaged, or a multiplexed copy is missing, you will not be able to mount the database, but by stopping in NOMOUNT mode you may be able to repair the damage.

At any stage, how does the instance find the files it needs, and exactly what happens? Start with NOMOUNT. When you issue a startup command, Oracle will attempt to locate a parameter file, following the naming convention given earlier.

If no parameter file exists, the instance will not start. The only file used in NOMOUNT mode is the parameter file. The parameters in the parameter file are used to build the SGA in memory and to start the background processes.

Where is the alert log? In the location calculated from the DIAGNOSTIC_DEST parameter. This will have defaulted to the ORACLE_BASE (remember OFA from Chapter 2?) directory. Within the DIAGNOSTIC_DEST is a standard directory structure. The alert log will be located and named thus:

```
<DIAGNOSTIC_DEST>/diag/rdbms/<DBNAME>/<INSTANCE_NAME>/trace/
alert_<instance_name>.log
```

For a database and instance named orcl, the values (Windows and Linux) would typically be the following:

```
c:\app\oracle\diag\rdbms\orcl\orcl\trace\alert_orcl.log
/u01/app/oracle/diag/rdbms/orcl/orcl/trace/alert_orcl.log
```

If the log already exists, it will be appended to. Otherwise, it will be created. If any problems occur during this stage, trace files may also be generated in the same location.

Once the instance is successfully started in NOMOUNT mode, it may be transitioned to MOUNT mode by reading the controlfile. It locates the controlfile by using the CONTROL_FILES parameter, which it knows from having read the parameter file used when starting in NOMOUNT mode. If the controlfile (or any multiplexed copy of it) is damaged or missing, the database will not mount and you will have to take appropriate action before proceeding further. All copies of the controlfile must be available and identical if the mount is to be successful.

As part of the mount, the names and locations of all the datafiles and online redo logs are read from the controlfile, but Oracle does not yet attempt to find them. This will happen during the transition to OPEN mode. If any files are missing or damaged, the database will remain in MOUNT mode and cannot be opened until you take appropriate action. Furthermore, even if all the files are present, they must be synchronized before the database opens. If the last shutdown was orderly, with all database buffers in the database buffer cache being flushed to disk by DBWn, then everything will be synchronized: Oracle will know that all committed transactions are safely stored in the datafiles and that no uncommitted transactions are hanging about waiting to be rolled back. However, if the last shutdown was disorderly (such as from a loss of power or from the server being rebooted), Oracle must repair the damage, and the database is considered to be in an inconsistent state. The mechanism for this process (known as *instance recovery*) is described in Chapter 18. The process that mounts and opens the database (and carries out repairs, if the previous shutdown was disorderly) is the SMON process. Only once the database has been successfully opened will Oracle permit user sessions to be established with normal data dictionary authentication.

Shutdown should be the reverse of startup. During an orderly shutdown, the database is first closed and then dismounted, and finally the instance is stopped. During the close phase, all sessions are terminated: Active transactions are rolled back, completed transactions are flushed to disk by DBWn, and the datafiles and redo log files are closed. During the dismount, the controlfile is closed. Then the instance is stopped by deallocating the SGA and terminating the background processes.

on the job

The startup command STARTUP FORCE can save you time. It is two commands in one: a SHUTDOWN ABORT followed by a STARTUP NORMAL.

Shutdown: NORMAL, TRANSACTIONAL, IMMEDIATE, and ABORT

Here are the options that may be used on the **shutdown** command, all of which require either a SYSDBA or a SYSOPER connection:

```
shutdown [ normal | transactional | immediate | abort ]
```

- **Normal** This is the default. No new user connections will be permitted, but all current connections are allowed to continue. Only once all users have (voluntarily!) logged off will the database actually shut down.
- **Transactional** No new user connections are permitted. Existing sessions that are not in a transaction will be terminated; sessions currently in a transaction are allowed to complete the transaction and will then be terminated. Once all sessions are terminated, the database will shut down.
- **Immediate** No new sessions are permitted, and all currently connected sessions are terminated. Any active transactions are rolled back, and the database will then shut down.
- **Abort** As far as Oracle is concerned, this is the equivalent of a power cut. The instance terminates immediately. Nothing is written to disk, and there is no attempt to terminate transactions in progress in any orderly fashion.

on the job

Typically, a normal shutdown is useless because there is always someone logged on, even if it is only a Cloud Control agent, so the command just hangs forever.

The normal, immediate, and transactional shutdown modes are usually referred to as "clean" or "consistent" shutdowns. After all sessions are terminated, PMON will roll back any incomplete transactions. A checkpoint is then issued that forces the DBWn process to write all updated data from the database buffer cache down to the datafiles. LGWR also flushes any change vectors still in memory to the log files. Then the file headers are updated and the file handles closed. This means that the database is in a "consistent" state: All committed transactions are in the datafiles, there are no uncommitted transactions hanging about that need to be rolled back, and all datafiles and log files are synchronized.

on the job

If someone were in the middle of a long-running update statement or, for example, were loading tables for a data warehouse when you had to shut down the database, the rollback phase, and therefore the time it takes the database to close and shut down cleanly, could be a long, long time (sometimes several hours).

The abort mode leaves the database in an "inconsistent" state: it is quite possible that committed transactions have been lost because they existed only in memory and DBWn had not yet written them to the datafiles. Equally, there may be uncommitted transactions in the datafiles that have not yet been rolled back. This is a definition of a corrupted database: It may be missing committed transactions or storing uncommitted transactions. These corruptions must be repaired by instance recovery (described in Chapter 17). It is exactly as though the database server had been switched off, or perhaps rebooted, while the database was running.

on the job

A shutdown abort will not damage the database, but some operations (such as backups) are not possible after an abort.

An orderly shutdown is a staged process, and it is theoretically possible to control the stages. The SQL*Plus commands are

```
alter database close;
alter database dismount;
```

These commands will exactly reverse the startup sequence. In practice, however, there is no value to them; a SHUTDOWN is all any DBA will ever use.

EXERCISE 4-3

Start Up and Shut Down an Oracle Database Instance

Use SQL*Plus to start an instance and open a database. If the database is already open, do this in the opposite order. Note that if you are working in Windows, the Windows service for the database must be running. It will have a name of the form OracleService*SID*, where *SID* is the name of the instance.

1. Log on to the computer as a member of the operating system group that owns the ORACLE_HOME and then set the environment variables appropriately for ORACLE_HOME and PATH and ORACLE_SID, as described previously.
2. Connect as SYS with operating system authentication:
   ```
   sqlplus / as sysdba
   ```
3. Start the instance only:
   ```
   startup nomount
   ```
4. Mount the database:
   ```
   alter database mount;
   ```
5. Open the database:
   ```
   alter database open;
   ```
6. Confirm that the database is open:
   ```
   select open_mode from v$database;
   ```
   This will return READ WRITE if the database is open.
7. Shut down the database:
   ```
   shutdown immediate
   ```
   Figure 4-8 shows that entire sequence of steps 2 through 7.
8. Restart the database:
   ```
   startup
   ```
   Observe that the default startup mode is OPEN.

FIGURE 4-8

Database startup and shutdown

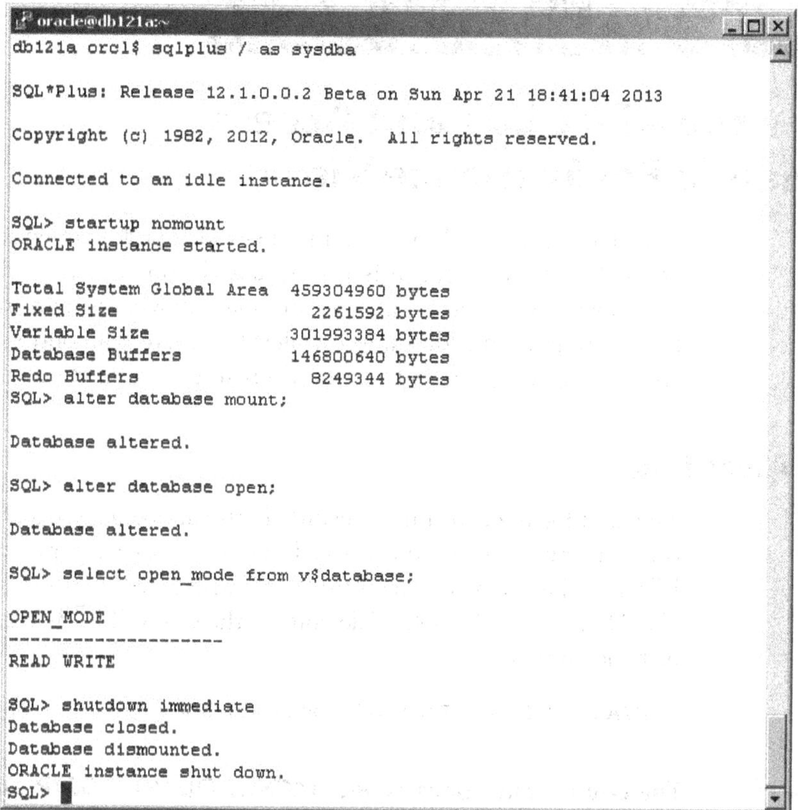

oracle@db121a:~
db121a orcl$ sqlplus / as sysdba
SQL*Plus: Release 12.1.0.0.2 Beta on Sun Apr 21 18:41:04 2013
Copyright (c) 1982, 2012, Oracle. All rights reserved.
Connected to an idle instance.
SQL> startup nomount
ORACLE instance started.
Total System Global Area 459304960 bytes
Fixed Size 2261592 bytes
Variable Size 301993384 bytes
Database Buffers 146800640 bytes
Redo Buffers 8249344 bytes
SQL> alter database mount;
Database altered.
SQL> alter database open;
Database altered.
SQL> select open_mode from v$database;
OPEN_MODE

READ WRITE
SQL> shutdown immediate
Database closed.
Database dismounted.
ORACLE instance shut down.
SQL>

CERTIFICATION OBJECTIVE 4.04

View the Alert Log and Access Dynamic Performance Views

The alert log is a vital source of information regarding important events in the life of the database instance. It is a continuous historical record of events. The dynamic performance views give real-time information: what is happening right now, or in the recent past. In addition to the alert log, there is an optionally enabled DDL log and a debug log generated automatically in the event of certain errors.

The Alert Log

The alert log is a continuous record of critical operations applied to the instance and the database. Its location is derived from the instance parameter DIAGNOSTIC_DEST, and its name is alert_<SID>.log, where <SID> is the name of the instance. The DIAGNOSTIC_DEST defaults to the ORACLE_BASE, and the alert log will be beneath that:

```
DIAGNOSTIC_DEST/diag/rdbms/<dbname>/<instancename>/trace
```

The two instance parameters BACKGROUND_DUMP_DEST and USER_DUMP_DEST give the full path to the location of the alert log. These parameters are officially deprecated, but showing them is the quickest way to locate the trace directory.

A copy of the alert log in XML format is also maintained in a different directory:

```
DIAGNOSTIC_DEST/diag/rdbms/<dbname>/<instancename>/alert
```

The critical operations recorded in the alert include the following:

- All startup and shutdown commands, including intermediate commands such as ALTER DATABASE MOUNT
- All errors internal to the instance (the ORA-600 errors, about which the DBA can do nothing other than investigate them using My Oracle Support and report them to Oracle Support if they are new issues)
- Any detected datafile block corruptions

- Any row-locking deadlocks that may have occurred
- All operations that affect the physical structure of the database, such as creating or renaming datafiles and online redo logs
- All ALTER SYSTEM commands that adjust the values of initialization parameters
- All log switches and log archives

The alert log entry for a startup shows all the initialization parameters specified in the parameter file. This information, together with the subsequent record of changes to the instance with ALTER SYSTEM and to the database physical structures with ALTER DATABASE, means that it is always possible to reconstruct the history of changes to the database and the instance. This can be invaluable when you are trying to backtrack in order to find the source of a problem.

on the job

For many DBAs, the first thing they do when they are asked to look at a database for the first time is locate the alert log and scan through it, just to get an idea of what has been going on.

Trace files are generated by the various background processes, usually when they hit an error. These files will be located in the trace directory, along with the alert log. If a background process has failed because of an error, the trace file generated will be invaluable in diagnosing the problem.

The DDL Log

Should the DBA choose to enable this, it is possible to record DDL commands in a log file. The statement used (without any supporting information, such as who issued it) is recorded in a text file named ddl_<instancename> in the directory

```
DIAGNOSTIC_DEST/diag/rdbms/<dbname>/<instancename>/log
```

with the same information in an XML file named log.xml.

To enable DDL logging, the instance parameter ENABLE_DDL_LOGGING must be set to TRUE (the default is FALSE).

on the job

DDL logging is of minimal value to the DBA because it captures nothing about who did it. It is of value only to Oracle Support, as part of the Incident Packaging Service. If you need to track DDL, do it by enabling audit of DDL statements.

The Dynamic Performance Views

There are more than 600 dynamic performance views. You will often hear them referred to as the "Vee dollar" views, because their names are prefixed with V$. In fact, the "Vee dollar" views are not views at all—they are synonyms to views that are prefixed with V_$, as shown in Figure 4-9.

The figure shows V$INSTANCE, which has one row with some summary information about the instance. The majority of the views are populated with information from the instance; the remainder are populated from the controlfile. All of them give real-time information. Dynamic performance views that are populated from the instance, such as V$INSTANCE or V$SYSSTAT, are available at all times, even when the instance is in NOMOUNT mode. Dynamic performance views that are populated from the controlfile, such as V$DATABASE and V$DATAFILE, cannot be queried unless the database has been mounted, which is when the controlfile is read. By contrast, the data dictionary views (prefixed DBA_, ALL_, or USER_) can be queried only after the database—including the data dictionary—has been opened.

FIGURE 4-9 A V$ view (or rather, a view and its V$ synonym)

```
oracle@db121a:~
SQL>
SQL> select owner,object_name,object_type from dba_objects
  2  where object_name like 'V%INSTANCE';

OWNER      OBJECT_NAME          OBJECT_TYPE
---------- -------------------- -----------------------
SYS        V_$INSTANCE          VIEW
PUBLIC     V$INSTANCE           SYNONYM

SQL> describe v$instance
 Name                                      Null?    Type
 ----------------------------------------- -------- ----------------------------
 INSTANCE_NUMBER                                    NUMBER
 INSTANCE_NAME                                      VARCHAR2(16)
 HOST_NAME                                          VARCHAR2(64)
 VERSION                                            VARCHAR2(17)
 STARTUP_TIME                                       DATE
 STATUS                                             VARCHAR2(12)
 PARALLEL                                           VARCHAR2(3)
 THREAD#                                            NUMBER
 ARCHIVER                                           VARCHAR2(7)
 LOG_SWITCH_WAIT                                    VARCHAR2(15)
 LOGINS                                             VARCHAR2(10)
```

exam Watch

Dynamic performance views (the V$ views) are populated from the instance or the controlfile, whereas the DBA_, ALL_, and USER_ views are populated from the data dictionary. This difference determines what views can be queried at the various startup stages.

The dynamic performance views are created at startup, updated during the lifetime of the instance, and dropped at shutdown. This means that they will contain values that have been accumulated since startup time; if your database has been open for six months nonstop, they will have data built up over that period. After a shutdown/startup, they will start from the beginning again.

on the Job

There is some overlap between V$ views and data dictionary views. For instance, V$TABLESPACE has a row for every tablespace, as does DBA_TABLESPACES. Note that as a general rule, V$ views are singular and data dictionary views are plural. But there are exceptions.

EXERCISE 4-4

Use the Alert Log and Dynamic Performance Views

In this exercise, you will locate the alert log and find the entries for the parameter changes made in Exercise 4-2 and the startups and shutdowns in Exercise 4-3.

1. Connect to your database with SQL*Plus and then display the value of the some parameters:

```
select value from v$parameter where name='diagnostic_dest';
select value from v$parameter where name='db_name';
select value from v$parameter where name='instance_name';
select value from v$parameter where name='background_dump_dest';
```

   Note the manner in which the name of the trace directory is derived.

2. Using whatever operating system tool you choose (such as Windows Explorer, or whatever file system browser your Linux session is using), navigate to the directory identified in step 1.
   Open the alert log. It will be a file called alert_<SID>.log, where <SID> is the name of the instance. Use any editor you please (but note that on

Windows, the Notepad may not be a good choice because of the way carriage returns are handled).
Go to the bottom of the file. You will see the ALTER SYSTEM commands of Exercise 4-2 and the results of the startup and shutdowns.

3. Use dynamic performance views to determine what datafile and tablespaces make up the database:

```
select t.name,d.name,d.bytes from v$tablespace t join
v$datafile d on t.ts#=d.ts# order by t.name;
```

Obtain the same information from data dictionary views:

```
select t.tablespace_name,d.file_name,d.bytes from
dba_tablespaces t
join dba_data_files d on t.tablespace_name=d.tablespace_name
order by tablespace_name;
```

4. Determine the location of all the controlfile copies, in two ways:

```
select * from v$controlfile;
select value from v$parameter where name='control_files';
```

5. Determine the location of the online redo log file members as well as their size. Because the size is an attribute of the group, not the members, you will have to join two views:

```
select m.group#,m.member,g.bytes from v$log g join v$logfile m
on m.group#=g.group# order by m.group#,m.member;
```

CERTIFICATION SUMMARY

Starting up a database is a staged process. Each stage requires various files to be available. Only when all stages are complete can regular users log on. Before that, only users with SYSDBA or SYSOPER privileges can connect, and they must use a form of authentication other than the data dictionary. The instance is built according to instance parameters stored in a parameter file. Many of these parameters can be adjusted while the instance is running, but others can only be written to the file and will then take effect the next time the instance is restarted. In the NOMOUNT and MOUNT modes, various dynamic performance views will be visible. Once in OPEN mode, the data dictionary can also be queried through views.

TWO-MINUTE DRILL

Use Database Management Tools

- ❑ SQL*Plus is always available. Database Express can make administration easy, but it depends on underlying database objects. It is therefore not available until the database is open.

Understand Initialization Parameter Files

- ❑ A database instance may be started from either a static parameter file (the init file) or a dynamic server parameter file (the spfile). If both exist, the spfile takes precedence.
- ❑ Static parameters cannot be changed without a shutdown/startup.
- ❑ Other parameters can be changed dynamically, for the instance or a session.
- ❑ Parameters can be seen in the dynamic performance views V$PARAMETER and V$SPPARAMETER.

Start Up and Shut Down an Oracle Database Instance

- ❑ The stages are NOMOUNT, MOUNT, and OPEN.
- ❑ NOMOUNT mode requires a parameter file.
- ❑ MOUNT mode requires the controlfile.
- ❑ OPEN mode requires the datafiles and online redo log files.

View the Alert Log and Access Dynamic Performance Views

- ❑ The alert log is a continuous stream of messages regarding critical operations.
- ❑ Trace files are generated by background processes, usually when they hit errors.
- ❑ The dynamic performance views are populated from the instance or the controlfile.
- ❑ The data dictionary views are populated from the data dictionary.
- ❑ Dynamic performance views accumulate values through the lifetime of the instance, and they are reinitialized at startup.
- ❑ Data dictionary views show information that persists across shutdown and startup.
- ❑ Both the data dictionary views and the dynamic performance views are published through synonyms.

SELF TEST

Use Database Management Tools

1. You issue the URL https://127.0.0.1:5500/em and receive an error. What could be the problem? (Choose all correct answers.)
   - A. You have not started the database listener.
   - B. Database Express is running on a different port.
   - C. You are not logged on to the database server node.
   - D. You have not started the Cloud Control agent.
   - E. You have not started the database.
2. What protocol(s) can be used to contact Database Express? (Choose all correct answers.)
   - A. HTTP
   - B. HTTPS
   - C. Oracle Net
   - D. IPC

Understand Initialization Parameter Files

3. What will be the setting of the OPTIMIZER_MODE parameter for your session after the next startup if you issue these commands:

```
alter system set optimizer_mode=all_rows scope=spfile;
alter system set optimizer_mode=rule;
alter session set optimizer_mode=first_rows;
```

   (Choose the best answer.)
   - A. all_rows
   - B. rule
   - C. first_rows
4. The LOG_BUFFER parameter is a static parameter. How can you change it? (Choose the best answer.)
   - A. You cannot change it because it is static.
   - B. You can change it only for individual sessions; it will return to the previous value for all subsequent sessions.
   - C. You can change it within the instance, but it will return to the static value at the next startup.
   - D. You can change it in the parameter file, but the new value will only come into effect at the next startup.

Start Up and Shut Down an Oracle Database Instance

5. Which files must be synchronized for a database to open? (Choose the best answer.)

A. Datafiles, online redo log files, and the controlfile.

B. Parameter file and password file.

C. All the multiplexed controlfile copies.

D. None. SMON will synchronize all files by instance recovery after opening the database.

6. During the transition from NOMOUNT to MOUNT mode, which files are required? (Choose the best answer.)

A. Parameter file

B. Controlfiles

C. Online redo logs

D. Datafiles

E. All of the above

7. You shut down your instance with SHUTDOWN IMMEDIATE. What will happen on the next startup? (Choose the best answer.)

A. SMON will perform automatic instance recovery.

B. You must perform manual instance recovery.

C. PMON will roll back uncommitted transactions.

D. The database will open without recovery.

8. You issue the command **SHUTDOWN**, and it seems to hang. What could be the reason? (Choose the best answer.)

A. You are not connected as SYSDBA or SYSOPER.

B. There are other sessions logged on.

C. You have not connected with operating system or password file authentication.

D. There are active transactions in the database; when they complete, the SHUTDOWN will proceed.

9. What action should you take after terminating the instance with SHUTDOWN ABORT? (Choose the best answer.)

A. Back up the database immediately.

B. Open the database and perform database recovery.

C. Open the database and perform instance recovery.

D. None, but some transactions may be lost.

E. None. Recovery will be automatic.

View the Alert Log and Access Dynamic Performance Views

10. Which of these actions will not be recorded in the alert log? (Choose all correct answers.)

A. ALTER DATABASE commands
B. ALTER SESSION commands
C. ALTER SYSTEM commands
D. Archiving an online redo log file
E. Creating a tablespace
F. Creating a user

11. Which parameter controls the location of background process trace files? (Choose the best answer.)

A. BACKGROUND_DUMP_DEST.
B. BACKGROUND_TRACE_DEST.
C. DB_CREATE_FILE_DEST.
D. DIAGNOSTIC_DEST.
E. No parameter. The location is platform specific and cannot be changed.

12. Which of these views can be queried successfully in NOMOUNT mode? (Choose all correct answers.)

A. DBA_DATA_FILES
B. DBA_TABLESPACES
C. V$DATABASE
D. V$DATAFILE
E. V$INSTANCE
F. V$SESSION

13. Which view will list all tables in the database? (Choose the best answer.)

A. ALL_TABLES
B. DBA_TABLES
C. USER_TABLES, when connected as SYS
D. V$FIXED_TABLE

LAB QUESTION

Prepare scripts for starting the Oracle environment on both Linux and Windows. The scripts should start the database instance and open the database and the database listener. For the Windows script, consider using services. Remember that some environment variables may be needed.

SELF TEST ANSWERS

Use Database Management Tools

1. ☑ **A, B, C, E.** Both the database listener and the database itself must be running to use Database Express. It is also possible the HTTP listening service may not be on the default port of 5500, and the loopback address will function only if you are running the browser on the database server machine.
   ☒ **D** is incorrect. The Cloud Control agent is not needed to use Database Express.

2. ☑ **A, B.** Both HTTP and HTTPS can be used, provided that an appropriate listening port has been configured with XDB.
   ☒ **C** and **D** are incorrect. Oracle Net and IPC are the protocols that can be used by user processes to contact the server, not by browsers to contact Database Express.

Understand Initialization Parameter Files

3. ☑ **B.** The default scope of ALTER SYSTEM is BOTH, meaning memory and spfile.
   ☒ **A** and **C** are incorrect. **A** is incorrect because this setting will have been replaced by the setting in the second command. **C** is incorrect because the session-level setting will have been lost during the restart of the instance.

4. ☑ **D.** This is the technique for changing a static parameter.
   ☒ **A, B,** and **C** are incorrect. **A** is incorrect because static parameters can be changed—but only with a shutdown. **B** and **C** are incorrect because static parameters cannot be changed for a running session or instance.

Start Up and Shut Down an Oracle Database Instance

5. ☑ **A.** These are the files that make up a database, and all must be synchronized if the database is to open.
   ☒ **B, C,** and **D** are incorrect. **B** is incorrect because these files are not, strictly speaking, part of the database. **C** is incorrect because a problem with a controlfile copy would mean that the database could not be mounted, never mind opened. **D** is incorrect because SMON's instance recovery mechanism can fix problems only in datafiles, not anything else.

6. ☑ **B.** Mounting the database is the process of opening the controlfile (all copies thereof).
   ☒ **A, C, D,** and **E** are incorrect. **A** is incorrect because the parameter file is needed only for NOMOUNT. **C, D,** and **E** are incorrect because these file types are only needed for OPEN mode.

7. ☑ **D.** An immediate shutdown is clean, so no recovery will be required.
☒ **A, B,** and **C** are incorrect. No recovery or rollback will be required; all the work will have been done as part of the shutdown.

8. ☑ **B.** The default shutdown mode is SHUTDOWN NORMAL, which will hang until all sessions have voluntarily disconnected.
☒ **A, C,** and **D** are incorrect. **A** and **C** are incorrect because these would cause an error, not a hang. **D** is incorrect because it describes SHUTDOWN TRANSACTIONAL, not SHUTDOWN NORMAL.

9. ☑ **E.** No required is action; recovery will be automatic.
☒ **A, B, C,** and **D** are incorrect. **A** is incorrect because this is one thing you should *not* do after an ABORT. **B** is incorrect because database recovery is not necessary, only instance recovery. **C** is incorrect because instance recovery will occur automatically in MOUNT mode at the next startup. **D** is incorrect because no transactions will ever be lost as a result of an ABORT.

View the Alert Log and Access Dynamic Performance Views

10. ☑ **B, F.** Neither of these affects the structure of the database or the instance; they are not important enough to generate an alert log entry.
☒ **A, C, D,** and **E** are incorrect. All of these are changes to physical or memory structures, and all such changes are recorded in the alert log.

11. ☑ **D.** This is the parameter used to determine the location of background trace files, and indeed the whole of the Automatic Diagnostic Repository.
☒ **A, B, C,** and **E** are incorrect. **A** is incorrect because although this parameter does still exist, it is deprecated. **B** is incorrect because there is no such parameter. **C** is incorrect because this is the default location for datafiles, not trace files. **E** is incorrect because although there is a platform-specific default, it can be overridden with a parameter.

12. ☑ **E, F.** These views are populated from the instance and will therefore be available at all times.
☒ **A, B, C,** and **D** are incorrect. **A** and **B** are data dictionary views, which can only be seen in open mode. **C** and **D** are dynamic performance views populated from the controlfile and are therefore only available in MOUNT mode or OPEN mode.

13. ☑ **B.** The DBA views list every appropriate object in the database.
☒ **A, C,** and **D** are incorrect. **A** is incorrect because this will list only the tables the current user has permissions on—which might be all the tables, but probably isn't. **C** is incorrect because it will list only the tables owned by SYS. **D** is incorrect because this is the view that lists all the dynamic performance views, not all the tables.

LAB ANSWER

Here is a possible Linux shell script:

```
export ORACLE_SID=orcl
export ORACLE_BASE=/u01/app/oracle
export ORACLE_HOME=$ORACLE_BASE/product/12.1.0/dbhome_1
export PATH=$ORACLE_HOME/bin:$PATH
export LD_LIBRARY_PATH=$ORACLE_HOME/lib:$LD_LIBRARY_PATH
lsnrctl start listener
sqlplus <<!
connect / as sysdba
startup
!
```

This script sets the relevant variables to start an instance called orcl. The first Oracle process launched is the database listener called LISTENER, which it will be called by default. Then SQL*Plus starts the instance using the technique for piping in commands.

Using Windows services, the batch file can be much shorter:

```
net start OracleOraDb12c_home1TNSListener
net start OracleServiceORCL
```

This script doesn't need any environment variables because they will be read from the registry by the services, but it does assume that the registry variable ORA_<SID>_AUTOSTART is set to TRUE. Unless this is done, the script will start the service but not go on to start the instance.

Here's an alternative script:

```
set ORACLE_BASE=d:\app\oracle
set ORACLE_HOME=%ORACLE_BASE%\12.1.0\dbhome_1
set PATH=%ORACLE_HOME%\bin;%PATH%
lsnrctl start listener
net start OracleServiceORCL
sqlplus <<!
connect / as sysdba
startup
!
```

This script explicitly sets environment variables. The instance service must be started with a **NET START** command, but it is assumed the service does not automatically start the instance itself and so it is started with SQL*Plus.

5

Configuring the Oracle Network Environment

CERTIFICATION OBJECTIVES

5.01 Configure Oracle Net Services

5.02 Use Tools for Configuring and Managing the Oracle Network

5.03 Configure Client-Side Network

5.04 Understand Database Resident Connection Pooling

5.05 Configure Communication Between Databases

✓ Two-Minute Drill

Q&A Self Test

Oracle Net is the enabling technology for Oracle's client-server architecture. It is the mechanism for establishing sessions against a database instance. Several tools can be used for setting up and administering Oracle Net, although it can be done with nothing more than an editor such as Windows Notepad. Whatever tool is used, the end result is a set of files that control a process (the database listener) that launches server processes in response to connection requests and defines the means by which a user process will locate the listener.

CERTIFICATION OBJECTIVE 5.01

Configure Oracle Net Services

Oracle's client-server architecture uses the Oracle Net protocol to establish and maintain the session between the client and the server. It is possible to use this with no configuration at all, but all sites will, in practice, configure it.

Oracle Net and the Client-Server Paradigm

There are many layers between the user and the database. In the Oracle environment, no user ever has direct access to the database—nor does the process that they are running. Client-server architecture guarantees that all access to data is controlled by the server.

A user interacts with a user process: this is the software that they run on their local terminal. For example, it could be Microsoft Access plus an ODBC driver on a Windows PC; it could be something written in C and linked with the Oracle Call Interface (or OCI) libraries; it could even be your old friend SQL*Plus. Whatever it is, the purpose of the user process is to prompt the user to enter information that the process can use to generate SQL statements. In the case of SQL*Plus, the process merely waits for you to type something in—a more sophisticated user process will paint a proper data-entry screen and validate your input, and then when you click the Submit button it will construct the statement and send it off to the server process.

The server process is a process running on the database server machine that executes the SQL it receives from the user process. This is the client-server split: a user process generating SQL, a server process executing SQL.

Oracle Net provides the mechanism for launching a server process to execute code on behalf of a user process. This is establishing a session. Then Oracle Net is responsible for maintaining the session: transmitting SQL from the user process to the server process, and fetching results from the server process back to the user process.

Figure 5-1 shows the various components of a session. A user interacts with a user process; a user process interacts with a server process, via Oracle Net; a server process interacts with the instance; and the instance, via its background processes, interacts with the database.

The client-server split between the user process and the server process will usually be physical as well as logical: there will be a network between the machines hosting the user processes and the machine hosting the server side, implemented by Oracle Net running on top of whatever communications protocol is supported by your operating system. The supported protocols are TCP/IP (versions 4 and 6, with or without SSL), Windows named pipes, and the Sockets Direct Protocol (SDP) designed for Infiniband networks. All operating systems also have an Inter-Process Communication (or IPC) protocol proprietary to the operating system. This, too, is available to Oracle Net for local connections where the user process is on the same machine as the server.

FIGURE 5-1 The database is protected from the user by several layers

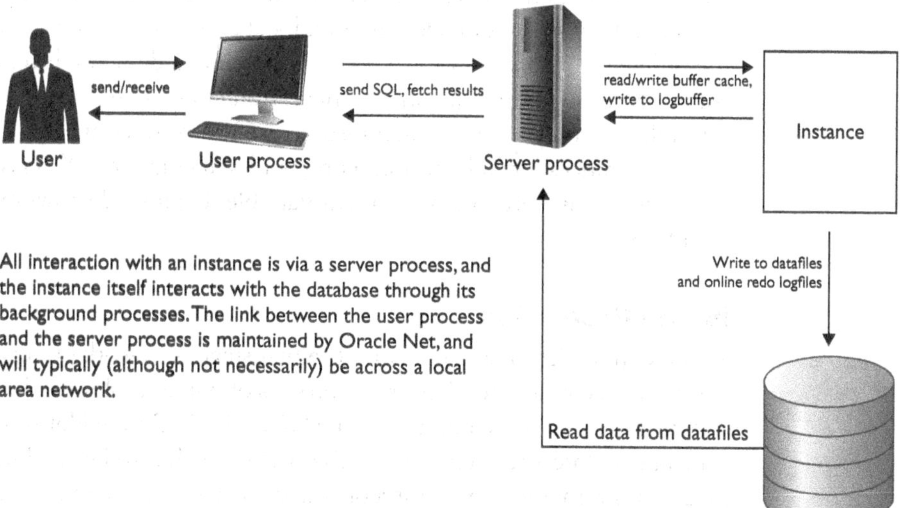
send/receive
send SQL, fetch results
read/write buffer cache,
write to logbuffer
Instance
User
User process
Server process
All interaction with an instance is via a server process, and the instance itself interacts with the database through its background processes. The link between the user process and the server process is maintained by Oracle Net, and will typically (although not necessarily) be across a local area network.
Write to datafiles
and online redo logfiles
Read data from datafiles
Database

Establishing a Session

When a user, through their user process, wishes to establish a session against an instance, they will issue a command such as this:

```
CONNECT SCOTT/TIGER@ORCL12C
```

What actually happens when that command is processed? First, break down the command into its components. There is a database username (SCOTT), followed by a database password (TIGER), and the two are separated by a delimiter (/). Then there is an @ symbol, followed by a connect string (ORCL12C). The @ symbol is an indication to the user process that a network connection is required. If the @ symbol and the connect string are omitted, the user process will assume that the instance the user wishes to connect to is running on the local machine and that the always-available IPC protocol can be used. If the @ symbol and a connect string are included, the user process will assume that the user is requesting a network connection to an instance on a remote machine—although, in fact, the user could be bouncing off the network card and back to the machine on to which they are logged.

Connecting to a Local Instance

Even when you connect to an instance running on your local machine, you still use Oracle Net. All Oracle sessions use a network protocol to implement the separation of user code from server code, but for a local connection the protocol is IPC. This is the only type of connection that does not require a database listener; indeed, local connections do not require any configuration at all. The only information needed is to tell your user process which instance you want to connect to. Remember that several instances could be running on your local computer. You give the process this information through an environment variable. Figure 5-2 shows examples of this on Windows.

Name Resolution

When connecting over a network, the first stage is to work out exactly what it is you want to connect to. This is the process of name resolution. If your connect statement includes the connect string "@orcl12c", Oracle Net has to work out what is meant by "orcl12c". This means that the string has to be resolved into certain pieces of information: the protocol you want to use (assume that this is TCP), the IP address on which the database listener is running, the port that the listener is

FIGURE 5-2

Local database connections on Windows

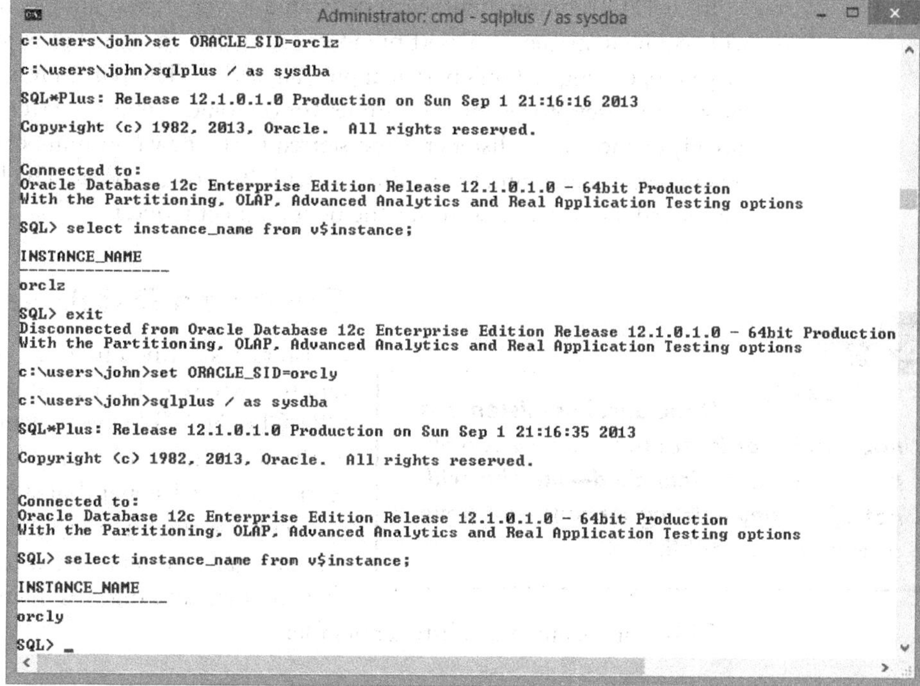

monitoring for incoming connection requests, and the name of the instance (which need not be the same as the connect string) to which you wish to connect. There are variations: rather than an IP address, the connect string can include a hostname, which then gets further resolved to an IP address by a DNS server. You can configure a number of ways of resolving connect strings to address and instance names, but one way or another the name resolution process gives your user process enough information to go across the network to a database listener and request a connection to a particular instance.

Administrator: cmd - sqlplus / as sysdba
c:\users\john>set ORACLE_SID=orclz
c:\users\john>sqlplus / as sysdba
SQL*Plus: Release 12.1.0.1.0 Production on Sun Sep 1 21:16:16 2013
Copyright (c) 1982, 2013, Oracle. All rights reserved.
Connected to:
Oracle Database 12c Enterprise Edition Release 12.1.0.1.0 - 64bit Production
With the Partitioning, OLAP, Advanced Analytics and Real Application Testing options
SQL> select instance_name from v$instance;
INSTANCE_NAME
----
orclz
SQL> exit
Disconnected from Oracle Database 12c Enterprise Edition Release 12.1.0.1.0 - 64bit Production
With the Partitioning, OLAP, Advanced Analytics and Real Application Testing options
c:\users\john>set ORACLE_SID=orcly
c:\users\john>sqlplus / as sysdba
SQL*Plus: Release 12.1.0.1.0 Production on Sun Sep 1 21:16:35 2013
Copyright (c) 1982, 2013, Oracle. All rights reserved.
Connected to:
Oracle Database 12c Enterprise Edition Release 12.1.0.1.0 - 64bit Production
With the Partitioning, OLAP, Advanced Analytics and Real Application Testing options
SQL> select instance_name from v$instance;
INSTANCE_NAME
----
orcly
SQL> _

Launching a Server Process

The database listener, running on the server machine, monitors one or more ports on one or more network interface cards for incoming connection requests. When it receives a connect request, the listener must first validate whether the instance requested is actually available. Assuming that it is, the listener will launch a new server process to service the user process. Thus, if you have a thousand users logging on concurrently to your instance, you will be launching a thousand server processes.

In the TCP environment, each dedicated server process launched by a listener will acquire a unique TCP port number. This will be assigned at process startup time by your operating system's port-mapping algorithm. The port number gets passed back to the user process by the listener (or on some operating systems, the socket already opened to the listener is transferred to the new port number), and the user process can then communicate directly with its server process. The listener has now completed its work and waits for the next connect request.

If the database listener is not running or is stopped, no new server processes can be launched—but this will not affect any existing sessions that have already been established.

Creating a Database Listener

A listener is defined in a file, the listener .ora file, whose default location is in the ORACLE_HOME/network/admin directory. As a minimum, the listener.ora file must include a section for one listener that states its name, the protocol, and the listening address it will use. You can configure several listeners in the one file, but they must all have different names and addresses.

This is an example of a listener.ora file:

```
LISTENER =
   (DESCRIPTION =
     (ADDRESS =
          (PROTOCOL = TCP)(HOST = jwlnx1)(PORT = 1521))
   )
LIST2 =
   (DESCRIPTION =
      (ADDRESS_LIST =
      (ADDRESS =
          (PROTOCOL = TCP)(HOST = 127.0.0.1)(PORT = 1522))
      (ADDRESS =
          (PROTOCOL = TCP)(HOST = jwlnx1.sb)(PORT = 1522))
      )
   )
```

The first section of this file defines a listener called LISTENER, monitoring the local hostname on the default port, 1521. The second section defines another listener called LIST2. This listener is monitoring port 1522 on both the hostname address and a loopback address.

To create a listener, you need do nothing more than create an entry in the listener .ora file and then start it. Under Windows, the listener will run as a Windows service, but there is no need to create the service explicitly; it will be created implicitly the first time the listener is started. From then on, if you wish, it can be started and stopped like any other Windows service.

on the job

You can run a listener completely on defaults, without a listener.ora file at all. It will listen on whatever address resolves to the machine's hostname, on port 1521. Don't do this, because it would be very confusing. Always configure the listener.ora file, to make your Oracle Net environment self-documenting.

Dynamic Service Registration

In order to launch sessions against an instance, the listener needs to know what instances are currently running on the server. This is the final part of the puzzle. It is possible to hardcode a list of instances in the listener.ora file, but this is not considered best practice. The approved technique is to rely on dynamic service registration.

Every database offers one or more services. A *service* is a logical name to which sessions can attach, through the instance. Different services within the database can have different characteristics (for instance, for fault tolerance). There will always be a default service named after the database, which is often the same name as the instance, which is often the same name as the Net service alias defined in a tnsnames.ora file and used in connect strings. When an instance starts, by default it will look for a listener on the address to which the machine's hostname resolves using port 1521. If there is indeed a listener running on that address:port, the database will register its service names(s) with the listener, and the listener will then be able to connect users. When the database is shut down, it will deregister itself from the listener. This is the process of dynamic registration.

It is the LREG background process that registers services with the listener.

During the lifetime of the instance, the LREG process repeatedly reregisters with the listener. Thus, if the listener is stopped and started, it will become aware of the database the next time LREG attempts to register.

Shared Server

The network architecture described so far is the *dedicated server* architecture: each user process is connected to a server process, launched by the listener for servicing that one session. An alternative is the *shared server* architecture, where a relatively small pool of server processes services a much larger number of user sessions.

The Limitations of Dedicated Server Architecture

As more users log on to your instance, more server processes get launched. This is not a problem as far as Oracle is concerned. The database listener can launch as many processes as required, although there may be operating system limits on the speed with which it can launch them. Then, once the sessions are established, there is no limit to the number that PMON can manage (although your operating system may have limits on the number of processes that it can support, limits to do with context switches and with memory).

A computer can only do one thing at a time unless it is an SMP machine, in which case each CPU can only do one thing at a time. The operating system simulates concurrent processing by using an algorithm to share CPU cycles across all the currently executing processes. This algorithm, often referred to as a *time-slicing* or *time-sharing algorithm*, takes care of allocating a few CPU cycles to each process in turn. The switch of taking one process off the CPU in order to put another process on the CPU is called a *context switch*. Context switches are very expensive: the operating system has to do a lot of work to restore the state of each process as it is brought on to the CPU and then save its state when it is switched off the CPU. As more users connect to the instance, the operating system has to context-switch between more and more server processes. Depending on your operating system, this can cause a severe degradation in performance. A decent mainframe operating system can context-switch between tens of thousands of processes without problems, but newer (and simpler) operating systems such as Unix and Windows may not be good at running thousands, or even just hundreds, of concurrent processes. Performance can degrade dramatically, because a large proportion of the computer's processing capacity is taken up with managing the context switches, leaving a relatively small amount of processing capacity available for actually doing work.

Also, memory problems may occur as more sessions are established. The actual server processes themselves are not an issue, because all modern operating systems use shared memory when the same process is loaded more than once. So launching a thousand server processes should take no more memory than launching one. The problem comes with the Program Global Area, or PGA. The PGA is a block of memory associated with each server process, to maintain the state of the session, and is a work area for operations such as sorting rows. Clearly, the PGAs cannot be in shared memory: they contain data unique to each session.

Therefore, in the dedicated server environment, performance may degrade if your operating system has problems managing a large number of concurrent processes, and the problem will be exacerbated if your server machine has insufficient memory. Note that it doesn't really matter whether or not the sessions are actually doing

> **exam watch**
>
> ***Oracle server processes are real processes, at the OS level, on Unix. They are threads within one operating system process on Windows.***

anything. Even if the sessions are idle, the operating system must still bring them on and off the CPU, and possibly page the appropriate PGA into main memory from swap files, according to its time-slicing algorithm. There comes a point when, no matter what you do in the way of hardware upgrades, performance begins to degrade because of the operating system inefficiencies in managing context switches and paging. These are not Oracle's problems, but to overcome them Oracle offers the option of the shared server architecture. This allows a large number of user processes to be serviced by a relatively small number of shared server processes, thus reducing dramatically the number of processes that the server's operating system has to manage. As a fringe benefit, memory usage may also reduce.

The Shared Server Architecture

One point to emphasize immediately is that the shared server is implemented purely on the server side. The user process and the application software have no way of telling that anything has changed. The user process issues a connect string that must resolve to the address of a listener and the name of a service (or of an instance). In return, it will receive the address of a server-side process that it will think is a dedicated server. It will then proceed to send SQL statements and receive back result sets; as far as the user process is concerned, absolutely nothing has changed. But the server side is very different.

> **exam watch**
>
> ***Shared server is configured at the server side, but the client can demand either a shared or dedicated server by specifying either SERVER=DEDICATED or SERVER=SHARED in the TNS connect string.***

Shared server is implemented by additional processes that are a part of the instance. They are background processes, launched at instance startup time. There are two process types: dispatchers and shared servers. There are also some extra queue memory structures within the SGA, and the database listener modifies its behavior for shared server. When an instance that is configured for shared server starts up, in addition to the usual background processes, one or more dispatcher processes also start. The dispatchers, like any other TCP process, run on a unique TCP port allocated by your operating system's port mapper. They contact the listener and register with it. One or more shared server processes also start. These are conceptually similar to a normal dedicated server process, but they are not tied to one session. They will receive SQL statements, parse and execute them, and generate a result set. However, they will not receive the SQL statements directly from a user process; instead, they will read them from a queue that will be populated with statements from any number of user processes. Similarly, the shared servers don't fetch result sets back to a user process directly; instead, they put the result sets onto a response queue.

The next questions are, how do the user-generated statements get onto the queue that is read by the server processes, and how do results get fetched to the users? This is where the dispatchers come in. When a user process contacts a listener, rather than launching a server process and connecting it to the user process, the listener passes back the address of a dispatcher. If there is only one dispatcher, the listener will connect it to all the user processes. If there are multiple dispatchers, the listener will load-balance incoming connection requests across them, but the end result is that many user processes will be connected to each dispatcher. Each user process will be under the impression that it is talking to a dedicated server process, but it isn't: it is sharing a dispatcher with many other user processes. At the network level, many user processes will have connections multiplexed through the one port used by the dispatcher.

> **exam watch** ***A session's connection to a dispatcher persists for the duration of the session, unlike the connection to the listener, which is transient.***

When a user process issues a SQL statement, it is sent to the dispatcher. The dispatcher puts all the statements it receives onto a queue. This queue is called the *common queue*, because all dispatchers share it. No matter which dispatcher a user process is connected to, all statements end up on the common queue.

All the shared server processes monitor the common queue. When a statement arrives on the common queue, the first available shared server picks it up. From then on, execution proceeds through the usual parse-bind-execute cycle, but when it comes to the fetch phase, it is impossible for the shared server to fetch the result set back to the user process: there is no connection between the user process and the shared server. So, instead, the shared server puts the result set onto a response queue that is specific to the dispatcher that received the job in the first place. Each dispatcher monitors its own response queue, and whenever any results are put on it, the dispatcher will pick them up and fetch them back to the user process that originally issued the statement.

> **exam watch** ***There is a common input queue shared by all dispatchers, but each dispatcher has its own response queue.***

A result of the mechanism of dispatchers and queues is that any statement from any user process could be executed by any available shared server. This raises the question of how the state of the session can be maintained. It would be quite possible for a user process to issue, for example, a SELECT FOR UPDATE, a DELETE, and a COMMIT. In a normal dedicated server connection, this isn't a problem because the PGA (which is tied to the one server process that is managing the session) stores information about what the session was doing, and therefore the dedicated server will know what to COMMIT and what locks to release. The PGA for a dedicated server session will store the session's session data, its cursor state, its sort space, and its stack space. But in the shared server environment, each statement might be picked off the common queue by a different shared server process, which will have no idea what the state of the transaction is. To get around this problem, a shared server session stores most of the session data in the SGA, rather than in a PGA. Then, whenever a shared server picks a job off the common queue, it will go to the SGA and connect to the appropriate block of memory to find out the state of the session. The memory used in the SGA for each shared server session is known as the User Global Area (the UGA) and includes all of what would have been in a PGA, with the exception of the session's stack space. This is where the memory saving will come from. Oracle can manage memory in the shared pool much more effectively than it can in many separate PGAs.

The following session memory structures are stored in the SGA when shared server is implemented:

- Sort area
- Hash area
- Bitmap creation area
- Bitmap merge area
- Cursor state
- User session data

The following session memory structures remain outside the SGA:

- Stack space
- Local variables

In shared server, what PGA memory structures do not go into the SGA? Stack space and local variables.

The part of the SGA used for storing UGAs is the large pool. This can be configured manually with the large_pool_size parameter, or it can be automatically managed.

It is impossible to use a shared server session to start up or shut down the instance. This is because the processes needed to support shared server (dispatchers and shared server processes) are themselves part of the instance.

Configuring the Shared Server

Being a server-side capability, there is no need for client configuration at all beyond perfectly normal client-side Oracle Net (the tnsnames.ora and sqlnet.ora files), as detailed previously. On the server side, shared server has nothing to do with the database—only the instance. The listener will be automatically configured for shared server through dynamic instance registration. It follows that shared server is configured though instance initialization parameters. There are a number of relevant parameters, but two are all that are usually necessary: dispatchers and shared_servers.

The first parameter to consider is shared_servers. This controls the number of shared servers that will be launched at instance startup time. Shared server uses a queuing mechanism, but the ideal is that there should be no queuing: there should always be a server process ready and waiting for every job that is put on the common queue by the dispatchers. Therefore, shared_servers should be set to the maximum number of concurrent requests you expect. But if there is a sudden burst of activity, you don't have to worry too much, because Oracle will launch additional shared servers, up to the value specified for max_shared_servers. By default, shared_servers is one if dispatchers is set. If the parameter max_shared_servers is not set, it defaults to one-eighth of the processes parameter.

The dispatchers parameter controls how many dispatcher processes to launch at instance startup time, and how they will behave. This is the only required parameter. There are many options for this parameter, but usually two will suffice: how many to start and what protocol they should listen on. Among the more advanced options are ones that allow you to control the port and network card on which the dispatcher will listen, and the address of the listener(s) with which it will register. However, you can usually let your operating system's port mapper assign a port, and use the local_listener parameter to control which listener the dispatchers will register The max_dispatchers parameter sets an upper limit to the number of dispatchers you can start, but unlike with shared servers, Oracle will not start extra dispatchers on demand. You can, however, launch additional dispatchers at any time, up to this limit.

For example, to enable the shared server architecture, adjust the to critical parameters as follows:

```
SQL> alter system set dispatchers='(dispatchers=2)(protocol=tcp)';
SQL> alter system set shared_servers=20;
```

Tuning the shared server is vital. There should always be enough shared servers to dequeue requests from the common queue as they arrive, and enough dispatchers that they can service incoming requests as they arrive and return results as they are enqueued to the response queues. Memory usage by shared server sessions in the SGA must be monitored. After converting from dedicated server to shared server, the SGA will need to be substantially larger.

When to Use the Shared Server

You will not find a great deal of hard advice in the Oracle documentation on when to use shared server, or how many dispatchers and shared servers you'll need. The main point to hang on to is that shared server is a facility you use because you are forced to, not something you use automatically. It increases scalability, but perhaps at the cost of reducing performance. It is quite possible that any one statement will take longer to execute in a shared server environment than if it were executing on a dedicated server, because it has to go via queues. It may also take more CPU resources because of this enqueuing and dequeuing activity. But overall, the scalability of your system will increase dramatically. Even if each request is marginally slower, you will be able to carry out many more requests per second through the instance.

on the job

It is often said that you should think about using shared server when your number of concurrent connections is in the low hundreds. If you have less than a hundred concurrent connections, you almost certainly don't need it. But if you have more than a thousand, you probably do. The critical factor is whether your operating system performance is beginning to degrade.

Consider an OLTP environment, such as hundreds of telephone operators in a call center. Each operator may spend one or two minutes per call, collecting the caller details and entering them into the user process. Then, when the operator clicks the Submit button, the user process constructs an insert statement and sends it off to the server process. The server process might go through the whole parse/bind/execute/fetch cycle for the statement in just a few hundredths of a second. Clearly, no matter how fast the clerks work, their server processes are idle 99.9 percent of the time. But the operating system still has to switch all those processes on and off the CPU, according to its time-sharing algorithm. By contrast, consider a data warehouse environment. Here, users submit queries that may run for a long time. The batch uploads of data will be equally long running. Whenever one of these large jobs is submitted, the server process for that session could be working flat out for hours on just one statement.

It should be apparent that shared server is ideal for managing many sessions doing short transactions, where the bulk of the work is on the client side of the client-server divide. In these circumstances, one shared server will be able to service dozens of sessions. But for batch processing work, dedicated servers are much better. If you submit a large batch job through a shared server session, it will work—but it will tie up one of your small pool of shared server processes for the duration of the job, leaving all your other users to compete for the remaining shared servers. The amount of network traffic involved in batch uploads from a user process and in fetching large result sets back to a user process will also cause contention for dispatchers.

A second class of operations that are better done through a dedicated server is database administration work. Index creation, table maintenance operations, and backup and recovery work through the Recovery Manager will perform much better through a dedicated server. And it is logically impossible to issue startup or shutdown commands through a shared server: the shared servers are part of the instance and therefore not available at the time you issue a startup command. So the administrator should always have a dedicated server connection.

The Default Shared Server Configuration

A 12*c* database instance will run shared server by default, but only for connections through the XDB. These queries show the default configuration, which is adequate for running Database Express (remember from Chapter 4 that Database Express requires XDB to be configured):

```
orcl> select name,value from v$parameter
where name like '%dispatchers';
NAME                 VALUE
-------------------- -----------------------------------
dispatchers          (PROTOCOL=TCP) (SERVICE=orclXDB)
max_dispatchers
orcl>
orcl> select name,value from v$parameter
```

```
where name like '%shared_servers';
NAME                 VALUE
-------------------- ------------------------------------
shared_servers       1
max_shared_servers
orcl>
```

CERTIFICATION OBJECTIVE 5.02

Use Tools for Configuring and Managing the Oracle Network

Configuring Oracle Net is nothing more than creating the configuration files. There are three of them:

- The configuration file listener.ora exists on the server side and defines the operation of the database listener.
- The configuration file tnsnames.ora is a client-side file used for name resolution. There will usually be a copy on the server as well, to facilitate running clients on the server machine.
- The configuration file sqlnet.ora is an optional file that may exist on both the client and server sides. It sets various defaults that will affect all clients and listeners.

Two graphical tools are provided for creating and editing these files: the Net Manager and the Net Configuration Assistant.

The Net Manager

To launch the Net Manager, run netmgr from a Unix prompt; on Windows you will find it on the Start menu.

The Net Manager navigation tree has three branches. The Profile branch creates or edits the sqlnet.ora file and is used to set options that may apply to both the client and server sides of Oracle. This is where, for example, you can configure detailed tracing of Oracle Net sessions or (as in Figure 5-3) enable certain name-resolution methods. The Service Naming branch is used to configure

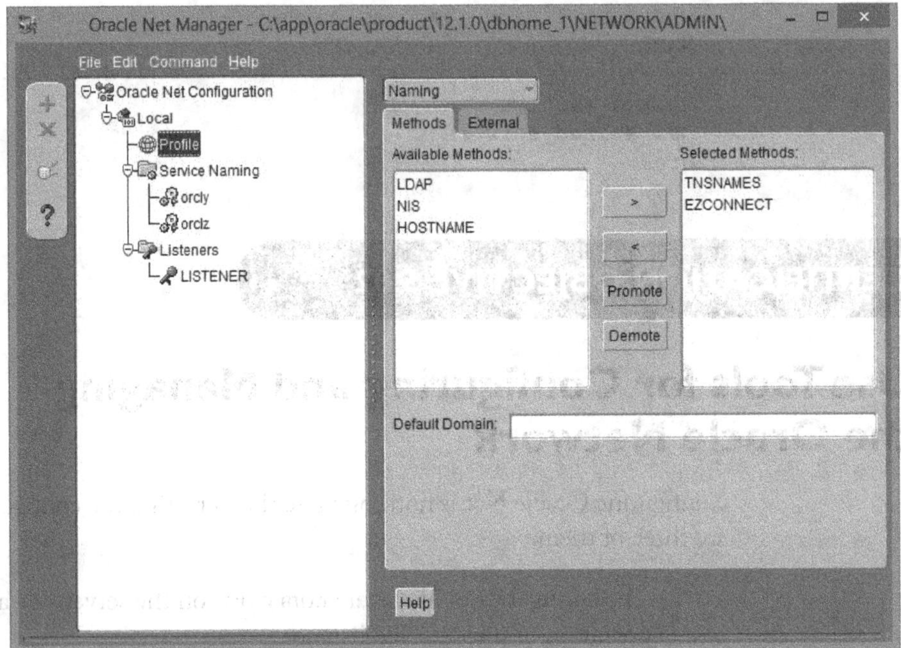

FIGURE 5-3 Net Manager's Profile editor

client-side name resolution, in the tnsnames.ora file. The Listeners branch is used to configure database listeners in the listener.ora file.

The Net Configuration Assistant

Launch netca by running the executable $ORACLE_HOME/bin/netca on Linux, or by navigating through the Start menu on Windows. Net Configuration Assistant is very simple to use. It does not have all the functionality of the Net Manager and can configure only database listeners and tnsnames connect strings.

The Listener Control Utility

The Listener Control utility is the executable $ORACLE_HOME/bin/lsnrctl on Linux, or %ORACLE_HOME%\bin\lsnrctl.exe on Windows. **lsnrctl** commands can be run directly from an operating system prompt, or through a simple user interface. For all the commands, you must specify the name of the listener, if it is not the default name of LISTENER. Figure 5-4 shows how to check the status

FIGURE 5-4

Starting the default listener

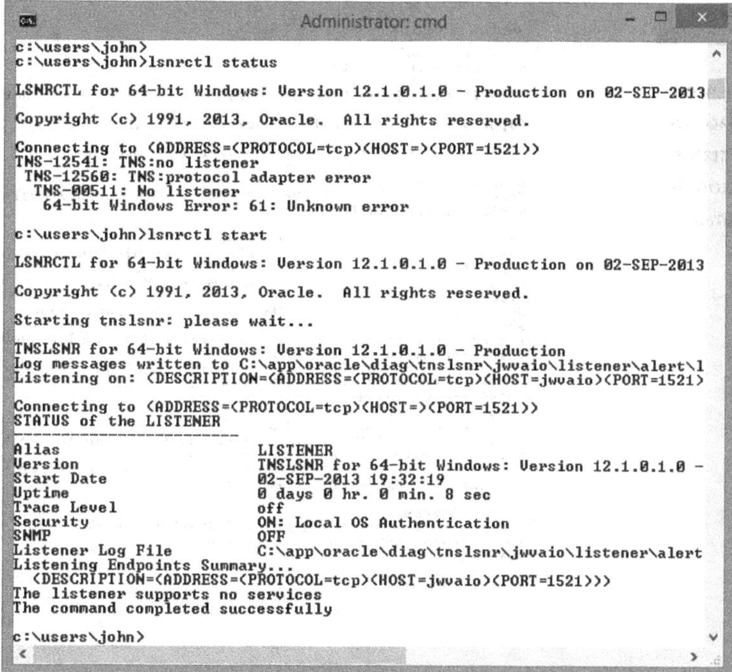

of the default listener named LISTENER and start it. Note that the listener starts listening on the address jwvaio on port 1521, but it is not offering a connection to any services. This is because it has only just started, and no database instances have registered with it. The registration will happen automatically within a minute, as instances find that it is started.

The lsnrctl utility does have a simple user interface. Figure 5-5 shows starting the interface, checking the status of the default listener, shutting it down, and exiting from the tool. Note the output of the **STATUS** command. The listener is listening on port 1521 for incoming TCP connections. These will be logon requests. It is also listening on port 5500 for HTTP over TCPS. This is for connections from browsers to Database Express.

The TNS_ADMIN Environment Variable

Configuring Oracle Net, manually or through the graphical tools, is nothing more than creating and editing the three text files: tnsnames.ora, sqlnet.ora, and listener .ora. Where do these files reside? The default location where Oracle processes will

FIGURE 5-5

Using the lsnrctl user interface to check the status and then stop the listener named LISTENER

```
Administrator: cmd
c:\users\john>
c:\users\john>lsnrctl

LSNRCTL for 64-bit Windows: Version 12.1.0.1.0 - Production on 02-SEP-2013

Copyright (c) 1991, 2013, Oracle.  All rights reserved.

Welcome to LSNRCTL, type "help" for information.

LSNRCTL> status
Connecting to (DESCRIPTION=(ADDRESS=(PROTOCOL=TCP)(HOST=jwvaio)(PORT=1521)
STATUS of the LISTENER
------------------------
Alias                     LISTENER
Version                   TNSLSNR for 64-bit Windows: Version 12.1.0.1.0 -
Start Date                02-SEP-2013 19:32:19
Uptime                    0 days 0 hr. 10 min. 15 sec
Trace Level               off
Security                  ON: Local OS Authentication
SNMP                      OFF
Listener Log File         C:\app\oracle\diag\tnslsnr\jwvaio\listener\alert
Listening Endpoints Summary...
  (DESCRIPTION=(ADDRESS=(PROTOCOL=tcp)(HOST=jwvaio)(PORT=1521)))
  (DESCRIPTION=(ADDRESS=(PROTOCOL=tcps)(HOST=jwvaio)(PORT=5500))(Security=
t))(Presentation=HTTP)(Session=RAW))
Services Summary...
Service "orclz" has 1 instance(s).
  Instance "orclz", status READY, has 1 handler(s) for this service...
Service "orclzXDB" has 1 instance(s).
  Instance "orclz", status READY, has 1 handler(s) for this service...
The command completed successfully
LSNRCTL>
LSNRCTL> stop
Connecting to (DESCRIPTION=(ADDRESS=(PROTOCOL=TCP)(HOST=jwvaio)(PORT=1521)
The command completed successfully
LSNRCTL> exit

c:\users\john>_
```

look for them is the directory $ORACLE_HOME/network/admin (Linux) or %ORACLE_HOME%\network\admin (Windows). In some circumstances, you will not want to use this directory. For example, if you have several Oracle products installed on one machine (multiple releases of the database, the Oracle client, and an application server, perhaps), each will be in its own Oracle home and therefore each will have its own copy of the files.

Keeping multiple copies of the files (particularly tnsnames.ora) identical can be awkward. The worst case is when hundreds of client PCs each have their own copy. One answer is to store the files in a central location (which could be a network mounted file system) and instruct all processes to read the files from this nondefault location. Do this by setting the TNS_ADMIN environment variable. Here is an example on Linux:

```
export TNS_ADMIN=/common/oracle/oraclenet
```

And here is an example on Windows:

```
set TNS_ADMIN=o:\common\oracle\oraclenet
```

CERTIFICATION OBJECTIVE 5.03

Configure Client-Side Network

The client side of Oracle Net is configured in a sqlnet.ora file and (typically) a tnsnames.ora file. The sqlnet.ora file is optional, and many sites will never use it. Most sites will, however, use a tnsnames file.

To establish a session against an instance, your user process must issue a connect string. That string resolves to the address of a listener and the name of an instance or service. Oracle provides four methods of name resolution: easy connect, local naming, directory naming, and external naming. It is probably true to say that the majority of Oracle sites use local naming, but there is no question that directory naming is the best method for a large and complex installation.

Easy Connect Name Resolution

The Easy Connect name resolution method is very easy to use—it requires no configuration at all. But it is limited to one protocol: TCP. The other name resolution methods can use any of the other supported protocols, such as TCP with secure sockets, or Named Pipes. Another limitation is that Easy Connect cannot be used with any of Oracle Net's more advanced capabilities, such as load balancing or connect-time failover across different network routes. It is fair to say that Easy Connect is a method you as a DBA will find very handy to use, but it is not a method of much use for your end users. Easy Connect is enabled by default. You invoke it with syntax such as the following connect string:

```
SQL> connect scott/tiger@jwvaio:1521/orclz
```

In this example, SQL*Plus will use TCP to go to port 1521 on the IP address to which the hostname jwvaio resolves. Then, if there is a listener running on that port and address, it will ask the listener to spawn a server process against an instance that is offering a service called orclz.

Local Naming Name Resolution

With local naming, the user supplies an alias, known as an Oracle Net service alias, for the connect string, and the alias is resolved by a local file into the full network address (protocol, address, port, and service or instance name). This local file is the infamous tnsnames.ora file, which has caused DBAs much grief over the years. Consider this example of a tnsnames.ora file:

```
orclz =
  (DESCRIPTION =
    (ADDRESS_LIST =
      (ADDRESS =
        (PROTOCOL = TCP)(HOST = jwvaio)(PORT = 1522))
    )
    (CONNECT_DATA =
      (service_name = orclz)
    )
  )
test =
  (DESCRIPTION =
    (ADDRESS_LIST =
     (ADDRESS =
     (PROTOCOL = TCP)
     (HOST = serv2.example.com)
     (PORT = 1521))
    )
    (CONNECT_DATA =
      (sid = testdb)
    )
  )
```

This tnsnames.ora file has two Oracle Net service aliases defined within it: orclz and test. These aliases are what your users will provide in their connect statements. The first entry, orclz, simply says that when the connect string @orclz is issued, your user process should use the TCP protocol to go the machine jwvaio, contact it on port 1521, and ask the listener monitoring that port to establish a session against the instance with the service name orclz. The second entry, test, directs users to a listener on a different machine, serv2.example.com, and asks for a session against the instance called testdb.

on the job ***There need be no relationship between the alias, the service name, and the instance name, but for the sake of your sanity you will usually keep them the same.***

Local naming supports all protocols and all the advanced features of Oracle Net, but maintaining tnsnames.ora files on all your client machines can be an extremely time-consuming task. The tnsnames.ora file is also notoriously sensitive to apparently trivial variations in layout. Using the GUI tools will help avoid such problems.

Directory Naming and External Naming

Directory naming points the user toward an LDAP directory server to resolve aliases. LDAP (the Lightweight Directory Access Protocol) is a widely used standard that Oracle Corporation (and other mainstream software vendors) is encouraging organizations to adopt. To use directory naming, you must first install and configure a directory server somewhere on your network. Oracle provides an LDAP server (the Oracle Internet Directory) as part of the Oracle Application Server, but you do not have to use that—if you already have a Microsoft Active Directory, that will be perfectly adequate. IBM and Novell also sell directory servers conforming to the LDAP standard.

Like local naming, directory naming supports all Oracle Net features—but unlike local naming, it uses a central repository, the directory server, for all your name resolution details. This is much easier to maintain than many tnsnames.ora files distributed across your whole user community.

External naming is conceptually similar to directory naming, but it uses third-party naming services such as Sun's Network Information Services (NIS+) or the Cell Directory Services (CDS) that are part of the Distributed Computing Environment (DCE).

The use of directories and external naming services is beyond the scope of the OCP syllabus.

Testing Oracle Net Connectivity

An invaluable tool is the tnsping utility. This accepts a connect string and then tests whether it works. It will show the name resolution method used, the Oracle Net configuration files being read, the details of what the string resolves to, and whether there is indeed a listener listening on those details. It does not test whether the database is actually running, but it does attempt to hit the listener and will return a suitable error message if it cannot.

Figure 5-6 shows the use of tnsping to test a connect string, first successfully, then unsuccessfully.

The first example tests the tnsconnect string orclz. The utility resolves the string using files located in the directory C:\app\oracle\product\12.1.0\dbhome_1\network\admin, which say that the address is a machine called jwvaio and port 1521. The requested service will be orclz. The test succeeds: there is indeed a listener on that address and port(tnsping does not test the existence of the service). The second test attempts to resolve the name orcla and fails, presumably because there is no such entry in the tnsnames.ora file.

FIGURE 5-6

Using the tnsping utility to test name resolution

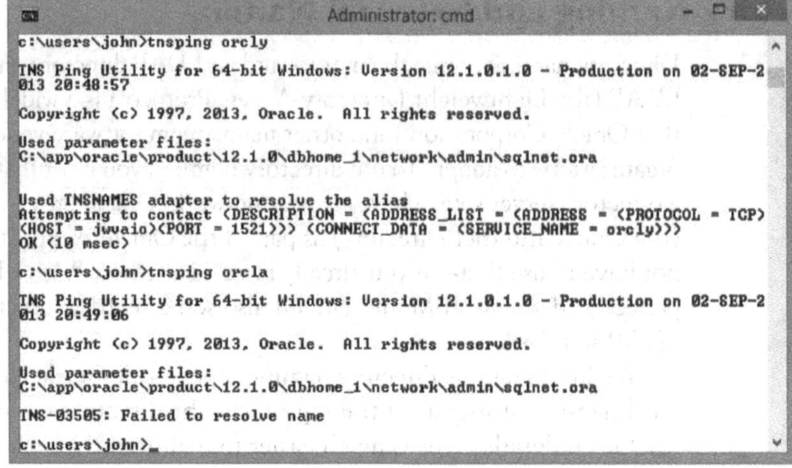

Administrator: cmd
c:\users\john>tnsping orcly
TNS Ping Utility for 64-bit Windows: Version 12.1.0.1.0 - Production on 02-SEP-2
013 20:48:57
Copyright (c) 1997, 2013, Oracle. All rights reserved.
Used parameter files:
C:\app\oracle\product\12.1.0\dbhome_1\network\admin\sqlnet.ora
Used TNSNAMES adapter to resolve the alias
Attempting to contact (DESCRIPTION = (ADDRESS_LIST = (ADDRESS = (PROTOCOL = TCP)
(HOST = jwvaio)(PORT = 1521))) (CONNECT_DATA = (SERVICE_NAME = orcly)))
OK (10 msec)
c:\users\john>tnsping orcla
TNS Ping Utility for 64-bit Windows: Version 12.1.0.1.0 - Production on 02-SEP-2
013 20:49:06
Copyright (c) 1997, 2013, Oracle. All rights reserved.
Used parameter files:
C:\app\oracle\product\12.1.0\dbhome_1\network\admin\sqlnet.ora
TNS-03505: Failed to resolve name
c:\users\john>_

EXERCISE 5-1

Configure Oracle Net

In this exercise, you will set up a complete Oracle Net environment using graphical and command-line tools. Any differences between Windows and Linux will be pointed out. These are the steps to follow:

1. Create a directory to be used for the Oracle Net configuration files and then set the TNS_ADMIN variable to point to this. It doesn't matter where the directory is, as long as the Oracle user has permission to create, read, and write it.

   On Linux:

   ```
   mkdir /u01/oracle/net
   export TNS_ADMIN=/u01/oracle/net
   ```

   Ensure that all work from now is done from a session where the variable has been set.

   On Windows:

   ```
   mkdir d:\oracle\net
   ```

Create and set the key TNS_ADMIN as a string variable in the registry in the Oracle Home branch. This will typically be

HKEY_LOCAL_MACHINE\SOFTWARE\ORACLE\KEY_OraDB12Home1

Check that the variable is being read by using the **TNSPING** command from an operating system prompt:

```
tnsping orcl
```

This will return the error "TNS-03505: Failed to resolve name" because there are no files in the TNS_ADMIN directory. On Windows, you may need to launch a new command prompt to pick up the new TNS_ADMIN value from the registry.

2. Start the Net Manager. On Linux, run netmgr from an operating system prompt; on Windows, launch it from the Start menu. The top line of the Net Manager window will show the location of the Oracle Net files. If this is not the new directory, the TNS_ADMIN variable has not been set correctly.
   a. Create a new listener by expanding the Local branch of the navigation tree, highlighting Listeners, and clicking +.
   b. Enter a listener name, **NEWLIST**, and click OK.
   c. Click Add Address.
   d. For Address 1, choose TCP/IP as the protocol and enter **127.0.0.1** as the host and **2521** as the port. Figure 5-7 shows this.
3. Create a new service name by highlighting Service Naming in the navigation tree and click +.
   a. Enter **NEW** as the net service name and click Next.
   b. Select TCP/IP as the protocol and click Next.
   c. Enter **127.0.0.1** as the hostname and **2521** as the port and then click Next.
   d. Enter **SERV1** as the service name and click Next.
   e. Click Finish. If you try the test, it will fail at this time. Figure 5-8 shows this.
4. Save the configuration by clicking File and Save Network Configuration. This will create the listener.ora and tnsnames.ora files in the TNS_ADMIN directory. Use an editor to check the two files.

LISTENER.ORA will look like this:

```
NEWLIST =
  (DESCRIPTION =
    (ADDRESS = (PROTOCOL = TCP)(HOST = 127.0.0.1)(PORT = 2521))
  )
```

And TNSNAMES.ora will look like this:

```
NEW =
  (DESCRIPTION =
    (ADDRESS_LIST =
      (ADDRESS = (PROTOCOL = TCP)(HOST = 127.0.0.1)(PORT = 2521))
    )
    (CONNECT_DATA =
      (SERVICE_NAME = SERV1)
    )
  )
```

5. From an operating system prompt, start the listener with lsnrctl start newlist.
6. From an operating system prompt, test the connect string with tnsping new.
7. Connect to your database using operating system authentication, bypassing any listener, with sqlplus / as sysdba.
8. Set the service_names and local_listener parameters for the running instance (memory only, not the parameter file) and register the new service name with the new, nondefault listener:

```
alter system set service_names=serv1 scope=memory;
alter system set local_listener=new scope=memory;
alter system register;
```

9. From an operating system prompt, confirm that the new service has registered with the new listener with lsnrctl services newlist.
10. Confirm that the new network environment is functional by logging on:

```
sqlplus system/oracle@new
```

11. Back out the changes to revert to default operation.
    a. Restart the database to return the parameters changed in step 8 to their default values.
    b. Stop the listener with lsnrctl stop newlist.
    c. Unset the TNS_ADMIN variable: on Linux, export TNS_ADMIN=''. On Windows, remove the TNS_ADMIN registry key.

FIGURE 5-7 Creating a listener with the Net Manager

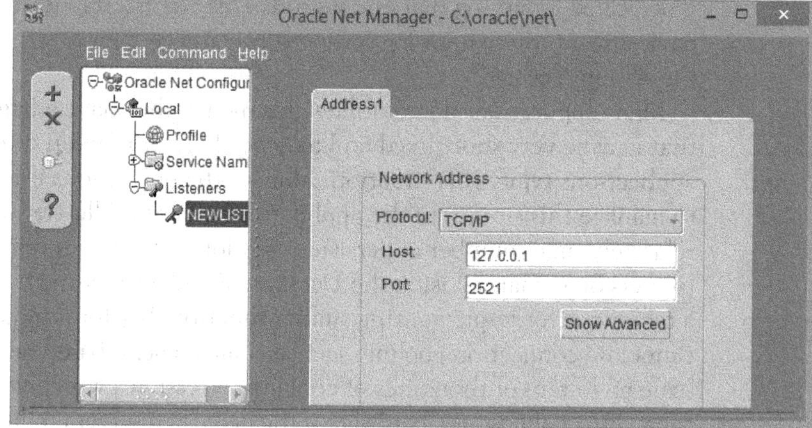

FIGURE 5-8 Creating a tnsnames service name alias with the Net Manager

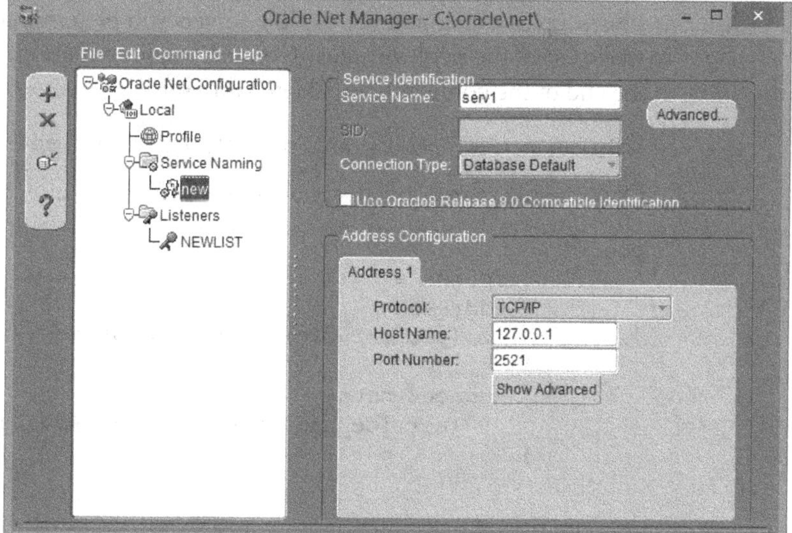

CERTIFICATION OBJECTIVE 5.04

Understand Database Resident Connection Pooling

The Oracle Net architecture described previously is the *dedicated server* architecture, where each connect request from a user process goes to a listener, and the listener spawns a server process. The server process persists until the session terminates, and is dedicated to serving that one session. This architecture is fine for a client-server environment where users log on and stay connected for a long time, making use of the session repeatedly.

Many applications do not follow this model: they have a large number of sessions that may be very short lived and may not log on/off in an orderly fashion. Web applications typify this situation. Many web applications use connection pooling to manage this situation: the application server middle-tier software establishes a relatively small number of persistent sessions, and passes temporary use of them to users on demand. Using the Database Resident Connection Pool (DRCP) is a technique for implementing similar functionality for middle-tier software that cannot do connection pooling, such as some Apache-based products. A DRCP can scale up to tens of thousands of concurrent sessions, which would be beyond the capability of almost any hardware if the dedicated server architecture is being used.

A DRCP is enabled by default, configured to launch a minimum of four server processes, up to a maximum of 40. Idle servers will be terminated after 300 seconds. To make use of the pool with Easy Connect name resolution, simply add **:POOLED** to the end of the connect string. Here's an example:

```
sqlplus scott/tiger@jwvaio:1521/orclz:pooled
```

Or you can go through a tnsnames.ora alias such as this:

```
pooled =
    (description =
        (address =
            (protocl=tcp)(host=jwvaio)(port=1521)
        )
        (connect_data=
            (service_name=orclz)(server=pooled)
        )
    )
```

When would one use a Database Resident Connection Pool? When many application server sessions connect to the same database schema, but use it for only short requests.

CERTIFICATION OBJECTIVE 5.05

Configure Communication Between Databases

So far, Oracle Net has been discussed in the context of users connecting to database instances. Oracle Net can also be used for communications between databases: a user session against one database can execute SQL statements against another database. This is done through a database link. There are several options for creating database links (all to do with security), but a simple example is shown here:

```
create database link prodscott
connect to fred identified by perry using 'prod';
```

This defines a database link from the current database to a remote database identified by the tnsnames.ora connect string PROD, and has embedded within it the logon credentials to be used when invoking code through the link. The link exists in the current user's schema, SCOTT, and only SCOTT can use it. When a statement such as

```
select * from score@prodscott;
```

is issued, the session will transparently launch a session against the remote database, log on to it as the user FRED, and run the query there. The results will be sent back to the local database session and then returned to the user process. Note that the name resolution occurs on the server, not the client. The client does not need any information regarding the connection details of the remote server; these details will need to be available in a tnsnames.ora file on the server side.

EXERCISE 5-2

Create and Use a Database Link

This exercise assumes that only one database is available, so the link will be a loopback link (out of the one database and back into it). Follow these steps:

1. Connected as user SYSTEM, create a database link:

   ```
   create database link l1
   connect to system identified by oracle using 'orcl';
   ```

   (Substitute a working tnsnames alias for 'orcl'. Note that this must be enclosed in single quotes.)

2. Test the link:

```
select * from all_users@l1;
```

3. Troubleshoot.

   The most common problems with database links are that the username/password embedded in the link are wrong, or that the tnsnames alias does not function. Other possible issues are that the listener is down and that the database dynamic registration with the listener has not yet happened.

CERTIFICATION SUMMARY

Oracle Net is the protocol used to connect to an Oracle database. A client user process issues a connect string, which identifies a database listener and requests connection to a database service. The listener (if the service exists) will launch a server process dedicated to supporting the session from the user process. This is the client-server split: a user process generates SQL, and its dedicated server process executes the SQL.

Oracle Net is configured with a set of parameter files. The TNSNAMES.ORA file is a client-side file that resolves connection requests. The LISTENER.ORA file is a server-side file that controls the operation of the listener. The SQLNET.ORA file may exist on both the client and the server and stores settings that control the overall operation of Oracle Net. These files can be configured manually or with graphical tools.

The usual method of communication between clients and servers is using a dedicated server architecture: one server process launched for every user process. Alternative architectures are shared servers (where many user processes go through a queueing mechanism to pass requests to a small number of shared server processes) and database resident connection pooling, where many users making short connections share a pool of persistent servers.

Distributed database environments, where transactions and queries can span databases, are implemented with database links. A database link is a data dictionary object that defines a connection to a remote database. The details are the net service name of the remote database (usually resolved by a TNSNAMES.ORA file on the database server) and the schema logon for the remote database.

TWO-MINUTE DRILL

Configure Oracle Net Services

- Oracle Net is configured with a set of three files: tnsnames.ora on the client side, listener.ora on the server side, and (optionally) sqlnet.ora on both sides. The database listener process spawns server sessions in response to connection requests from clients.
- The usual architecture is a dedicated server: one server process per user process, and the session consists of a persistent connection between the two. All session data is stored in PGA. An alternative is the shared server architecture, where user processes have persistent connections to dispatchers, which pass requests to a pool of shared server processes. In this architecture, most of the session information is stored in SGA, rather than PGA.

Use Tools for Configuring and Managing the Oracle Network

- Two configuration tools are provided: the Net Manager and the simpler Net Configuration Assistant. The listener is controlled with the Listener Control utility, lsnrctl.

Configure Client-Side Network

- Clients need the ability to resolve names into connection details. The details consist of the listening address of the database listener in the form of a hostname or IP address and a port as well as a database service name or instance name. The usual technique is to use a network alias, resolved by an entry in a tnsnames.ora file.

Understand Database Resident Connection Pooling

- A DRCP can be used for managing the problem of a large number of typically short-lived connections, such as those that come in through a website. Rather than spawning processes for each session, the DRCP passes out temporary use of one of a fixed number of persistent server processes on demand.

Configure Communication Between Databases

- Database links allow a session against one database to run SQL against another database. In effect, the first database becomes a client to the second. When a query is run through a link, a session is launched over Oracle Net from the first session to the linked database. The name resolution necessary to establish the remote session occurs on the server, not the client.

SELF TEST

Configure Oracle Net Services

1. Which protocols can Oracle Net 12*c* use? (Choose all correct answers.)
   - A. TCP
   - B. UDP
   - C. SPX/IPX
   - D. SDP
   - E. TCP with secure sockets
   - F. Named Pipes
   - G. LU6.2
   - H. NetBIOS/NetBEUI
2. Where is the division between the client and the server in the Oracle environment? (Choose the best answer.)
   - A. Between the instance and the database.
   - B. Between the user and the user process.
   - C. Between the server process and the instancc.
   - D. Between the user process and the server process.
   - E. The client-server split varies, depending on the stage of the execution cycle.
3. Which of the following statements about listeners is correct? (Choose the best answer.)
   - A. A listener can connect you to one instance only.
   - B. A listener can connect you to one service only.
   - C. Multiple listeners can share one network interface card.
   - D. An instance will only accept connections from the listener specified on the local_listener parameter.
4. You have decided to use local naming. Which file(s) must you create on the client machine? (Choose the best answer.)
   - A. tnsnames.ora and sqlnet.ora.
   - B. listener.ora only.
   - C. tnsnames.ora only.
   - D. listener.ora and sqlnet.ora.
   - E. None. You can rely on defaults if you are using TCP and your listener is running on port 1521.

5. If you stop your listener, what will happen to sessions that connected through it? (Choose the best answer.)
   A. They will continue if you have configured failover.
   B. They will not be affected in any way.
   C. They will hang until you restart the listener.
   D. You cannot stop a listener if it is in use.
   E. The sessions will error out.
6. Study this tnsnames.ora file:

```
test =
  (description =
    (address_list =
      (address = (protocol = tcp)(host = serv2)(port = 1521))
    )
    (connect_data =
      (service_name = prod)
    )
  )
prod =
  (description =
    (address_list =
      (address = (protocol = tcp)(host = serv1)(port = 1521))
    )
    (connect_data =
      (service_name = prod)
    )
  )
dev =
  (description =
    (address_list =
      (address = (protocol = tcp)(host = serv2)(port = 1521))
    )
    (connect_data =
      (service_name = dev)
    )
  )
```

   Which of the following statements are correct about the connect strings test, prod, and dev? (Choose all correct answers.)
   A. All three are valid.
   B. All three can succeed only if the instances are set up for dynamic instance registration.
   C. The test connection will fail, because the connect string doesn't match the service name.
   D. There will be a port conflict on serv2, because prod and dev try to use the same port.

7. Consider this line from a listener.ora file:

```
L1=(description=(address=(protocol=tcp)(host=serv1)(port=1521)))
```

What will happen if you issue this connect string:

```
connect scott/tiger@L1
```

(Choose the best answer.)

A. You will be connected to the instance L1.

B. You will only be connected to an instance if dynamic instance registration is working.

C. You can't tell—it depends on how the client side is configured.

D. If you are logged on to the server machine, IPC will connect you to the local instance.

E. The connection will fail if the listener is not started.

Use Tools for Configuring and Managing the Oracle Network

8. Which of these tools can configure a listener.ora file? (Choose two answers.)

A. The Database Configuration Assistant

B. Database Express

C. The lsnrctl utility

D. The Net Configuration Assistant

E. The Net Manager

Configure Client-Side Network

9. Consider this tnsnames.ora net service name:

```
orcl=(description=
(address=(protocol=tcp)(host=dbserv1)(port=(1521))
(connect_data=(service_name=orcl)(server=dedicated))
)
```

What will happen if shared server is configured and this net service name is used? (Choose the best answer)

A. The connect attempt will fail.

B. The connect will succeed with a shared server connection.

C. The connect will succeed with a dedicated server connection.

D. The connect will succeed only for SYSDBA or SYSOPER logons.

Understand Database Resident Connection Pooling

10. Under what circumstances would a connection through a Database Resident Connection Pool (SERVER=POOLED) connection be suitable?
    - A. When an application server needs a pool of persistent connections
    - B. When many short-lived connections share a schema
    - C. When many short-lived connections connect to different schemas
    - D. When many persistent connections make infrequent requests

Configure Communication Between Databases

11. When updating rows locally and through a database link in one transaction, what must you do to ensure a two-phase COMMIT?
    - A. Nothing special because two-phase COMMIT is automatic.
    - B. Issue a COMMIT locally first and then through the database link.
    - C. Issue a COMMIT through the link and then locally.
    - D. It is not possible to interleave local and remote updates.

LAB QUESTION

Use whatever tool you like (even a text editor) to create two listeners: one listening on address 127.0.0.2, port 1521, and the other listening on address 127.0.0.3, port 1521. This will simulate a server with two additional network cards. Start both listeners.

Use the Net Manager to create tnsnames entries for these addresses. Save the configuration and then test the entries with tnsping. Make an end-to-end test by connecting with SQL*Plus through the new tnsnames connect strings.

SELF TEST ANSWERS

Configure Oracle Net Services

1. ☑ **A, D, E, F.** TCP, SDP, TCPS, and NMP are the supported protocols with the current release.
☒ **B, C, G,** and **H** are incorrect. **B** and **H** are incorrect because UDP and NetBIOS/NetBEUI have never been supported. **C** and **G** are incorrect because SPX and LU6.2 are no longer supported.

2. ☑ **D.** The client-server split is between the user process and the server process.
☒ **A, B, C,** and **E** are incorrect. These all misrepresent the client-server architecture.

3. ☑ **C.** Many listeners can share one address, if they use different ports.
☒ **A, B,** and **D** are incorrect. **A** is incorrect because one listener can launch sessions against many instances. **B** is incorrect because a listener can connect you to a registered service. **D** is incorrect because the local_listener parameter controls which listener the instance will register with dynamically; it will also accept connections from any listener that has it statically registered.

4. ☑ **C.** This is the only required client-side file for local naming.
☒ **A, B,** and **D** are incorrect. **A** is incorrect because SQLNET.ORA is not essential. **B** and **D** are incorrect because they refer to server-side files. **E** is incorrect because some configuration is always necessary for local naming (though not for Easy Connect).

5. ☑ **B.** The listener establishes connections but is not needed for their maintenance.
☒ **A, C, D,** and **E** are incorrect. These are all incorrect because they assume that the listener is necessary for the continuance of an established session.

6. ☑ **A, B.** All three are valid but will only work if the services are registered with the listeners.
☒ **C** and **D** are incorrect. **C** is incorrect because there doesn't need to be a connection between the alias used in a connect string and the service name. **D** is incorrect because many services can be accessible through a single listening port.

7. ☑ **C.** Some client-side configuration is necessary, and without knowing what it is you have no idea what will happen.
☒ **A, B, D,** and **E** are incorrect. **A** is incorrect because the connect string could connect to any instance. **B** is incorrect because, although the listener L1 must use dynamic registration, this is not enough. **D** is incorrect because the use of IPC to bypass the listener is not relevant. **E** is incorrect because (although certainly true) you don't know if it is relevant.

Use Tools for Configuring and Managing the Oracle Network

8. ☑ **D, E.** Both netca and netman offer a graphical interface for editing the listener.ora file.
☒ **A, B,** and **C** are incorrect. **A** is incorrect because the DBCA cannot edit a listener, though it will edit the tnsnames.ora file. **B** is incorrect because Database Express has no capability for editing any file. **C** is incorrect because the lsnrctl utility can control a listener, but not configure the listener.ora file.

Configure Client-Side Network

9. ☑ **C.** The SERVER=DEDICATED directive requests a dedicated server, even if shared server is configured.
☒ **A, B,** and **D** are incorrect. **A** and **B** are incorrect because the client configuration takes precedence over the server configuration. **D** is incorrect because anyone can use this connect string. It will be necessary to use it rather than a shared server connection for SYSDBA connections; otherwise, startup/shutdown commands will fail.

Understand Database Resident Connection Pooling

10. ☑ **B.** This is exactly the environment for which DRCP is designed: many short-lived connections to a shared schema.
☒ **A, C,** and **D** are incorrect. **A** is incorrect because an application server would manage the pool itself. **C** is incorrect because a DRCP will pool connections to the same schema. **D** is incorrect because persistent connections would tie up the pooled servers.

Configure Communication Between Databases

11. ☑ **A.** Two-phase commit for distributed transactions is fully automatic.
☒ **B, C,** and **D** are incorrect. **B** and **C** are incorrect because a distributed transaction is, syntactically, committed exactly as a local transaction. **D** is incorrect because distributed transactions are no problem in the Oracle environment.

LAB ANSWER

The listeners (called, in this example, list2 and list3) will be defined by entries similar to these in the listener.ora file:

```
LIST3 =
  (DESCRIPTION =
    (ADDRESS = (PROTOCOL = TCP)(HOST = 127.0.0.2)(PORT = 1521))
  )
```

```
LIST2 =
  (DESCRIPTION =
    (ADDRESS = (PROTOCOL = TCP)(HOST = 127.0.0.3)(PORT = 1521))
  )
```

Start the listeners with these commands from an operating system prompt:

```
lsnrctl start list2
lsnrctl start list3
```

The tnsnames.ora entry (in this example, called NEW) will look like this:

```
NEW1 =
  (DESCRIPTION =
        (ADDRESS = (PROTOCOL = TCP)(HOST = 127.0.0.2)(PORT = 1521))
    (CONNECT_DATA =
      (SERVICE_NAME = orclz)
    )
  )

NEW2 =
  (DESCRIPTION =
        (ADDRESS = (PROTOCOL = TCP)(HOST = 127.0.0.3)(PORT = 1521))
    (CONNECT_DATA =
      (SERVICE_NAME = orclz)
    )
  )
```

To test the tnsnames entry and the listeners, type the following from an operating system prompt:

```
tnsping new1
tnsping new2
sqlplus system/oracle@new1
sqlplus system/oracle@new2
```

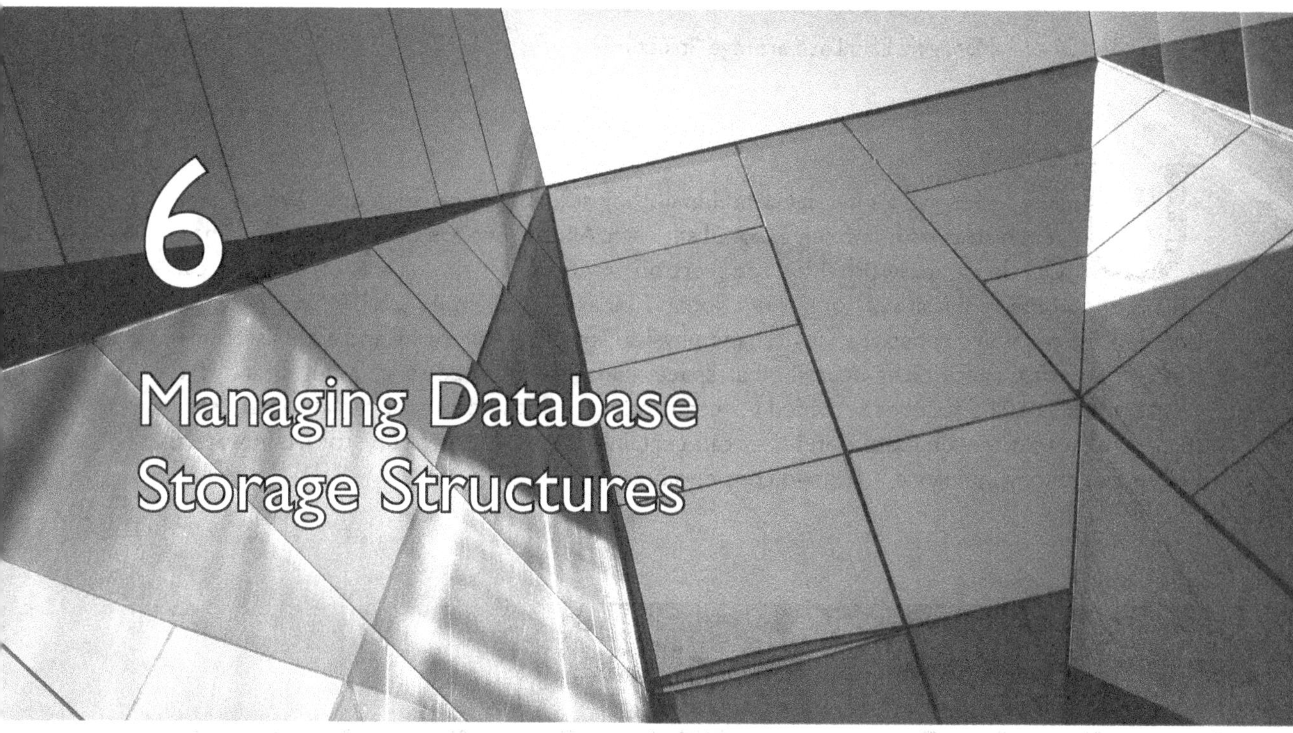

6 Managing Database Storage Structures

CERTIFICATION OBJECTIVES

6.01	Describe the Storage of Table Row Data in Blocks	✓	Two-Minute Drill
6.02	Create and Manage Tablespaces	Q&A	Self-Test

Users never see a physical datafile. All they see are logical segments. System administrators never see a logical segment. All they see are physical datafiles. The Oracle database provides complete abstraction of logical storage from physical. This is one of the requirements of the relational database paradigm. As a DBA, you must be aware of the relationship between logical and physical storage. Monitoring and administering these structures, a task often described as space management, used to be a huge part of a DBA's workload. The facilities provided in recent releases of the database can automate space management to a certain extent, and they can certainly let the DBA set up storage in ways that will reduce the maintenance workload considerably.

CERTIFICATION OBJECTIVE 6.01

Describe the Storage of Table Row Data in Blocks

At the lowest level, rows are stored in blocks. But there are several layers of storage above that, all of which must be understood before drilling down to the level of the row in the block. Start at the top, and work down.

The Oracle Data Storage Model

The separation of logical from physical storage is a necessary part of the relational database paradigm. It means that programmers have no possibility of finding out where, physically, an item of data is. If they could find out, their software would be tied to the one machine on which it was written. And even then, something as trivial as renaming or moving a file would break the application. The relational paradigm states that programmers should address only logical structures and let the database manage the mapping to physical structures. This means that physical storage can be reorganized, or the whole database moved to completely different hardware and operating system, and the application will not be aware of any change.

Figure 6-1 shows the Oracle storage model sketched as an entity-relationship diagram, with the logical structures to the left and the physical structures to the right.

There is one relationship, shown as a dotted line: a many-to-many relationship between segments and datafiles. This relationship is dotted because it shouldn't be there. As good relational engineers, DBAs do not permit many-to-many relationships.

FIGURE 6-1

The Oracle storage model

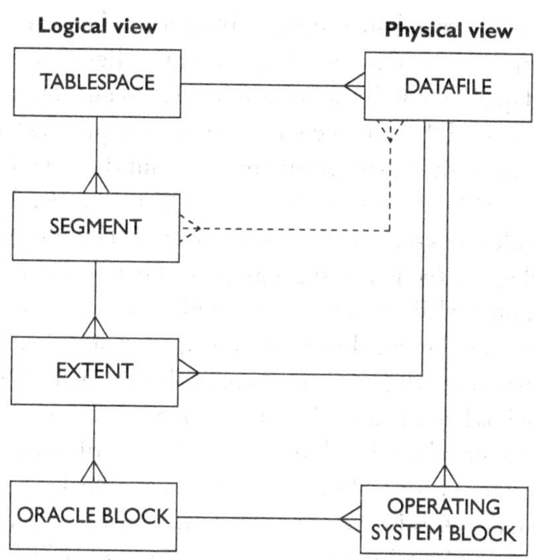

Resolving this relationship into a normalized structure is what the storage model is all about.

The tablespace entity resolves the many-to-many relationship between segments and datafiles. One tablespace can contain many segments and be made up of many datafiles. This means that any one segment may be spread across multiple datafiles, and any one datafile may contain all of or parts of many segments. This solves many storage challenges. Some older database management systems used a one-to-one relationship between segments and files: every table or index would be stored as a separate file. This raised two dreadful problems for large systems. First, an application might well have thousands of tables and even more indexes; managing many thousands of files was an appalling task for the system administrators. Second, the maximum size of a table is limited by the maximum size of a file. Even if modern operating systems do not have any practical limits, there may well be limitations imposed by the underlying hardware environment. Use of tablespaces bypasses both these problems. Tablespaces are identified by name, unique in the database.

The segment entity represents any database object that stores data and therefore requires space in a tablespace. Your typical segment is a table, but there are other segment types, notably index segments and undo segments. Any one segment can exist in only one tablespace, but the tablespace can spread it across all the files making up the tablespace. This means that the tables' sizes are not subject to any limitations imposed by the environment on maximum file size. Because many segments can share a single tablespace, it becomes possible to have far more segments than there are datafiles. Segments are schema objects, identified by the segment name and qualified with the owning schema name. Note that programmatic schema objects (such as PL/SQL procedures, views, or sequences) are not segments: they do not store data, and they exist as structures within the data dictionary.

The Oracle block is the unit of I/O for the database. Datafiles are formatted into Oracle blocks, consecutively numbered. The size of the Oracle blocks is fixed for a tablespace (generally speaking, it is the same for all tablespaces in the database); the default is 8KB. A row might be only a couple hundred bytes, so there could be many rows stored in one block. However, when a session wants a row, the whole block will be read from disk into the database buffer cache. Similarly, if just one column of one row has been changed in the database buffer cache, the DBWn will (eventually) write the whole block back into the datafile from which it came, overwriting the previous version. The size of an Oracle block can range from 2KB to 16KB on Linux or Windows and to 32KB on some other operating systems. The block size is controlled by the parameter DB_BLOCK_SIZE. This can never be changed after database creation because it is used to format the datafile(s) that make up the SYSTEM tablespace. If it becomes apparent later on that the block size is inappropriate, the only course of action is to create a new database and transfer everything into it. A block is uniquely identified by its number within a datafile: the block number alone is not enough.

The DB_BLOCK_SIZE is set at database creation and can never be changed.

Managing space one block at a time would be a crippling task, so blocks are grouped into extents. An *extent* is a set of consecutively numbered Oracle blocks within one datafile. Every segment will consist of one or more extents, also consecutively numbered. These extents may be in any and all of the datafiles that make up the tablespace. An extent can be identified from either the dimension of the segment (extents are consecutively numbered per segment, starting from zero) or the dimension of the datafile (every extent is in one file, starting at a certain Oracle block number).

on the job

Does block size matter? Probably not. You can cut your pizza into eight slices or 12. Does that make any difference to how big the box should be? Or how long it takes to eat?

A datafile is, physically, made up of a number of operating system blocks. How datafiles and the operating system blocks are structured is entirely dependent on the operating system's file system. Some file systems have well-known limitations and are therefore not widely used for modern systems (for example, the old MS-DOS FAT file system could handle files up to only 4GB, and only 512 of them per directory). Most databases will be installed on file systems with no practical limits, such as NTFS on Windows and ext3 on Linux. The alternatives to file systems for datafile storage are raw devices or ASM. Raw devices are no longer supported by Oracle for datafile storage. ASM is described in Chapter 20.

An operating system block is the unit of I/O for your file system. A process might want to read only one byte from disk, but the I/O system will have to read an operating system block. The operating system block size is configurable for some file systems (for example, when formatting an NTFS file system, you can choose from 512 bytes to 64KB), but typically system administrators leave it at the default (512 bytes for NTFS, 1KB for ext3). This is why the relationship between Oracle blocks and operating system blocks is usually one-to-many, as shown in Figure 6-1. There is no reason not to match the operating system block size to the Oracle block size if your file system lets you do this. A configuration that should always be avoided is one where the operating system blocks are bigger than the Oracle blocks.

Segments, Extents, Blocks, and Rows

Data is stored in segments. The data dictionary view DBA_SEGMENTS describes every segment in the database. This query shows the segment types in a simple database—the counts are low because there is no real application installed:

```
SQL> select segment_type,count(1) from dba_segments
    group by segment_type
    order by segment_type;
SEGMENT_TYPE         COUNT(1)
------------------ ----------
CLUSTER                    10
INDEX                    3185
INDEX PARTITION           324
LOB PARTITION               7
LOBINDEX                  760
LOBSEGMENT                760
NESTED TABLE               29
ROLLBACK                    1
TABLE                    2193
TABLE PARTITION           164
TYPE2 UNDO                 10
11 rows selected.
SQL>
```

In brief, and in the order they are most likely to concern a DBA, these segments types are as follows:

- **TABLE** These are the heap-structured tables: variable-length rows, in random order. Even though a typical segment is a table segment, never forget that the table is not the segment, and that there are more complex table organizations that use other segment types.
- **INDEX** Indexes are sorted lists of key values, each with a pointer, the ROWID, to the physical location of the row. The ROWID specifies which Oracle block of which datafile the row is in, and the row number within the block.
- **TYPE2 UNDO** The undo segments (no one refers to them as "type2 undo" segments) store the prechange versions of data necessary for providing transactional integrity: rollback, read consistency, and isolation.
- **TABLE PARTITION** A table can be divided into many partitions. If this is done, then the partitions will be individual segments, and the table itself will not be a segment at all: it exists only as the total of its partitions. Each table partition of a heap table is itself structured as a heap table, in its own segment. These segments can be in different tablespaces, meaning that it becomes possible to spread one table across multiple tablespaces.
- **INDEX PARTITION** An index will be in one segment, by default, but indexes can be partitioned. If you are partitioning your tables, you will usually partition the indexes on those tables as well.
- **LOBSEGMENT, LOBINDEX, LOB PARTITION** If a column is defined as a large object data type, then only a pointer is stored in the table itself: a pointer to an entry in a separate segment where the column data actually resides. LOBs can have indexes built on them for rapid access to data within the objects, and LOBs can also be partitioned.
- **CLUSTER** A cluster is a segment that can contain several tables. In contrast with partitioning, which lets you spread one table across many segments, clustering lets you denormalize many tables into one segment.
- **NESTED TABLE** If a column of a table is defined as a user-defined object type that itself has columns, then the column can be stored in its own segment, as a nested table.

- **ROLLBACK** Rollback segments should not be used in normal running from release 9*i* onward. Release 9*i* introduced automatic undo management, which is based on undo segments. There will always be one rollback segment that protects the transactions used to create a database (this is necessary because at that point, no undo segments exist), but it shouldn't be used subsequently.

Every segment has one or more extents. When a segment is created, Oracle will allocate an extent to it in whatever tablespace is specified. Eventually, as data is entered, the extent will fill. Oracle will then allocate a second extent, in the same tablespace but not necessarily in the same datafile. If you know that a segment is going to need more space, you can manually allocate an extent. Figure 6-2 shows how to identify precisely where each extent of a segment is.

In the figure, the first command creates the table SCOTT.NEWTAB, relying completely on defaults for the storage. Then a query against DBA_EXTENTS shows that the segment consists of just one extent, extent number 0. This extent is in file number 6 and is eight blocks long. The first of the eight blocks is block number 224. The size of the extent is 64KB, which shows that the block size is 8KB. The next command forces Oracle to allocate another extent to the segment, even though the first extent will not be full. The next query shows that this new extent, number 1, is also in file number 6 and starts immediately after extent 0. Note that it is not

FIGURE 6-2

Determining the physical location of a segment's extents

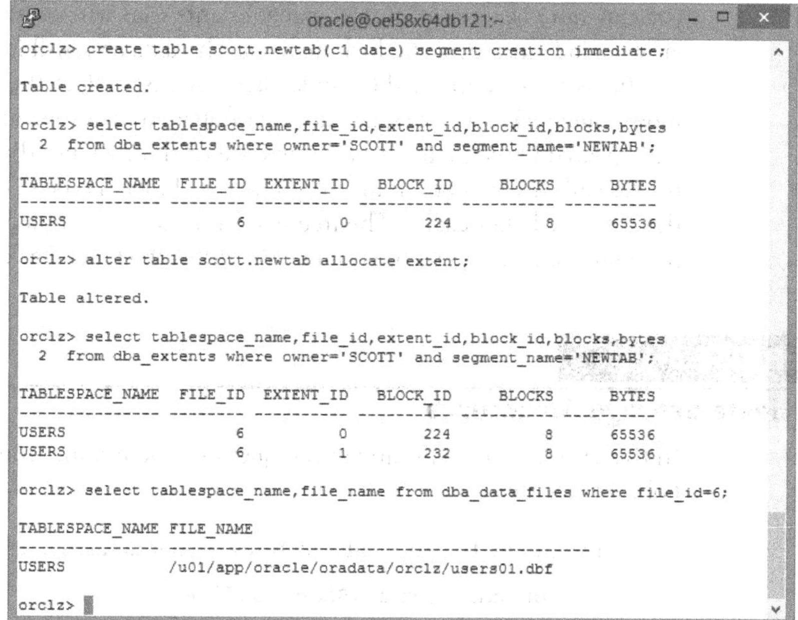

clear from this example whether or not the tablespace consists of multiple datafiles, because the algorithm Oracle uses to work out where to assign the next extent does not simply use datafiles in turn. If the tablespace does consist of multiple datafiles, you can override Oracle's choice with this syntax:

```
ALTER TABLE tablename ALLOCATE EXTENT STORAGE (DATAFILE 'filename');
```

The last query in Figure 6-2 goes to the view DBA_DATA_FILES to determine the name of the file in which the extents were allocated, and the name of the tablespace to which the datafile belongs. To identify the table's tablespace, you could also query DBA_SEGMENTS.

You can query DBA_TABLES to find out in which tablespace a table resides, but this will only work for nonpartitioned tables—not for partitioned tables, where each partition is its own segment and can be in a different tablespace. Partitioning lets one table (stored as multiple segments) span tablespaces.

An extent consists of a set of consecutively numbered blocks. Each block will have a header area and a data area. The header is of variable size and grows downward, if necessary, from the top of the block. Among other things, it contains a row directory (that lists where in the block each row begins) and row locking information. The data area fills from the bottom up. Between the two there may (or may not) be an area of free space. Events that will cause a block's header to grow include inserting and locking rows. The data area will initially be empty and will fill as rows are inserted (or index keys are inserted, in the case of a block of an index segment). The free space does get fragmented as rows are inserted, deleted, and updated (which may cause a row's size to change), but that is of no significance because all this happens in memory, after the block has been copied into a buffer in the database buffer cache. The free space is coalesced into a contiguous area, when necessary, and always before the DBWn writes the block back to its datafile.

EXERCISE 6-1

Investigate Storage Structures

In this exercise, you will run various queries to determine storage characteristics. Follow these steps:

1. Determine the physical structures of your database:

```
select name from v$controlfile;
select member,bytes from v$logfile
join v$log using (group#);
```

```
select t.name,d.name,d.bytes from v$tablespace t
join v$datafile d using (ts#)
union all
select t.name,d.name,d.bytes from v$tablespace t
join v$tempfile d using (ts#);
select tablespace_name,t.contents,d.file_name,d.bytes
from dba_tablespaces t
join dba_data_files d using (tablespace_name)
union all
select tablespace_name,t.contents,d.file_name,d.bytes
from dba_tablespaces t
join dba_temp_files d using (tablespace_name);
```

2. Create a table and determine where it is stored:

```
create table system.mytable as select * from
 all_objects;select tablespace_name from dba_tables
where owner='SYSTEM' and table_name='MYTABLE';
select tablespace_name,segment_type from dba_segments
where owner='SYSTEM' and segment_name='MYTABLE';
select file_name,extent_id,block_id from dba_data_files
join dba_extents using (file_id)
where owner='SYSTEM' and segment_name='MYTABLE';
```

What size are the extents? By default, this is thc size that will be used for the first 16 extents of a segment, after which extents of 128 blocks will be allocated.

3. Move the table:

```
alter table system.mytable move tablespace sysaux;
```

Where are the extents now?

4. Tidy up:

```
drop table system.mytable;
```

CERTIFICATION OBJECTIVE 6.02

Create and Manage Tablespaces

Tablespaces are repositories for schema data, including the data dictionary (which is the SYS schema). All databases must have a SYSTEM tablespace and a SYSAUX tablespace as well as (for practical purposes) a temporary tablespace and an undo tablespace. These four will usually have been created when the database was created. Subsequently, the DBA may create many more tablespaces for user data and possibly additional tablespaces for undo and temporary data.

Tablespace Creation

To create a tablespace with Database Express, from the database home page click the Storage tab and then the Tablespaces link. Figure 6-3 shows the result for the default database.

There are six tablespaces shown in the figure. For each tablespace, identified by name, the window shows:

- **Size** This is the current size of the datafile(s) assigned to the tablespace. It is based on the current size, not the maximum size to which it may be allowed to expand.
- **Free space** The space currently available within the tablespace.
- **Used (%)** This is the space occupied by segments in the tablespace that cannot be reclaimed.
- **Auto Extend** Indicates whether any files of the tablespace have the automatic extension facility enabled (they all do).

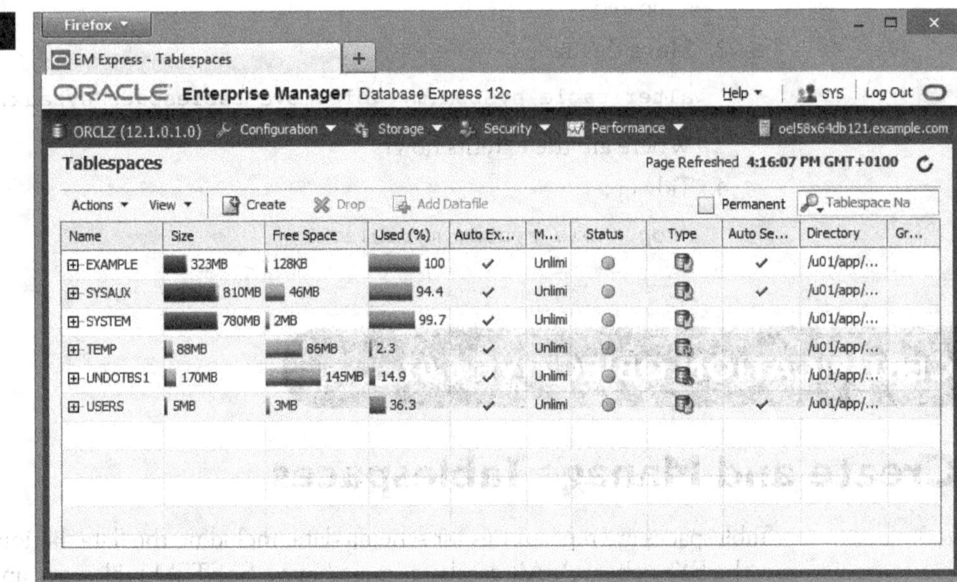

FIGURE 6-3 The tablespaces in the default ORCL database

- **Maximum size** If autoextensible, to what limit? In the figure, all are Unlimited, meaning the maximum possible.
- **Status** Green indicates that the tablespace is online and therefore that the objects within it should be accessible. An offline tablespace would be indicated in red.
- **Type** An icon indicating whether the tablespace stores permanent objects, temporary objects, or undo segments.
- **Auto segment management** A tick indicates that automatic segment space management is used by the tablespace.

This information could also be gleaned by querying the data dictionary views DBA_TABLESPACES, DBA_DATA_FILES, and DBA_FREE_SPACE as in this (partial) example, run against the same database as the figure:

```
orclz> with
  ts_size as (select tablespace_name,sum(bytes) bytes
  from dba_data_files group by tablespace_name),
  ts_free as (select tablespace_name,sum(bytes) free
  from dba_free_space group by tablespace_name)
  select tablespace_name, bytes,free,status
  from dba_tablespaces
  natural join ts_size natural join ts_free
  order by 1;
TABLESPACE_NAME              BYTES       FREE STATUS
-------------------- ---------- ---------- --------
EXAMPLE               338821120     131072 ONLINE
SYSAUX                849346560   47644672 ONLINE
SYSTEM                817889280    2424832 ONLINE
UNDOTBS1              178257920  151650304 ONLINE
USERS                   5242880    3342336 ONLINE
orclz>
```

Note that this query does not show the TEMP tablespace visible in Database Express. To include TEMP, the query would need a UNION to another query addressing DBA_TABLESPACES, DBA_TEMP_FILES, and DBA_TEMP_FREE_SPACE.

In Database Express, click the Actions button for a drop-down menu including Create to create a tablespace. The Create Tablespace window prompts for a tablespace name as well as the type of data (permanent, temporary, or undo) to be stored within it. The dialog continues with prompts for the datafile(s) definition and various attributes.

Database Express has a SHOW SQL button in most windows. This means that you can use it to construct syntactically correct statements that you can save (and edit) for future, scripted use. This is a typical statement generated by Database Express (line numbers added):

```
1  CREATE SMALLFILE TABLESPACE "JWTS"
2  DATAFILE '/u01/app/oracle/oradata/orclzjwts01.dbf'
3  SIZE 100M AUTOEXTEND ON NEXT 10M MAXSIZE 200M
4  LOGGING
5  DEFAULT NOCOMPRESS
6  ONLINE
7  EXTENT MANAGEMENT LOCAL AUTOALLOCATE
8  SEGMENT SPACE MANAGEMENT AUTO;
```

Look at this command line by line:

Line 1	The tablespace is a SMALLFILE tablespace. This means that it can consist of many datafiles. The alternative is BIGFILE, in which case it would be impossible to add a second datafile later (though the first file could be resized). SMALLFILE is the default.
Line 2	The datafile name and location.
Line 3	The datafile will be created as 100MB but when full can automatically extend in 10MB increments to a maximum of 200MB. By default, automatic extension is not enabled.
Line 4	All operations on segments in the tablespace will generate redo, unless it is explicitly disabled; this is the default. It is possible to disable redo generation for a very few operations (such as index generation).
Line 5	Objects in the tablespace will not, by default, be compressed. This is the default.
Line 6	The tablespace will be online (available for use) immediately. This is the default.
Line 7	The tablespace will use bitmaps for allocating extents, whose size will be set automatically; this is the default.
Line 8	Segments in the tablespace will use bitmaps for tracking block usage; this is the default.

A typical tablespace creation statement, as executed from the SQL*Plus command line, is shown in Figure 6-4, with a query confirming the result.

The tablespace GLTABS consists of two datafiles, neither of which will autoextend. The only deviation from defaults has been to specify a uniform extent size of 4MB. The first query in the figure shows that the tablespace is not a bigfile tablespace; if it were, it would not have been possible to define two datafiles.

The second query in the figure investigates the TEMP tablespace, used by the database for storing temporary objects. It is important to note that temporary tablespaces use *tempfiles*, not datafiles. Tempfiles are listed in the

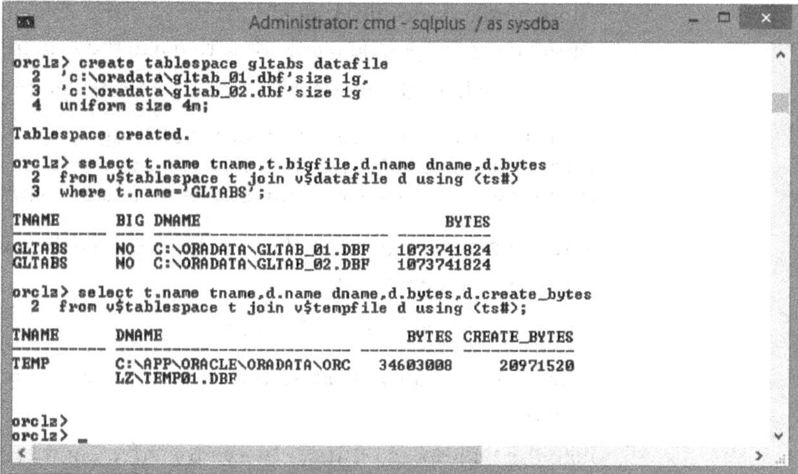
```
orclz> create tablespace gltabs datafile
  2  'c:\oradata\gltab_01.dbf'size 1g,
  3  'c:\oradata\gltab_02.dbf'size 1g
  4  uniform size 4m;

Tablespace created.

orclz> select t.name tname,t.bigfile,d.name dname,d.bytes
  2  from v$tablespace t join v$datafile d using (ts#)
  3  where t.name='GLTABS';

TNAME      BIG DNAME                          BYTES
---------- --- ------------------------- ----------
GLTABS     NO  C:\ORADATA\GLTAB_01.DBF   1073741824
GLTABS     NO  C:\ORADATA\GLTAB_02.DBF   1073741824

orclz> select t.name tname,d.name dname,d.bytes,d.create_bytes
  2  from v$tablespace t join v$tempfile d using (ts#);

TNAME      DNAME                          BYTES CREATE_BYTES
---------- ------------------------- ---------- ------------
TEMP       C:\APP\ORACLE\ORADATA\ORC   34603008     20971520
           LZ\TEMP01.DBF

orclz>
orclz> _
```

FIGURE 6-4 Tablespace creation and verification with SQL*Plus

views V$TEMPFILE and DBA_TEMP_FILES, whereas datafiles are listed in V$DATAFILE and DBA_DATA_FILES. Also note that the V$ views and the DBA views give different information. As the query shows, you can query V$TABLESPACE to find if a tablespace is a bigfile tablespace and V$TEMPFILE (or V$DATAFILE) to find how big a file was at creation time. This information is not shown in the DBA views. However, the DBA views give the detail of extent management and segment space management. The different information available in the views is because some information is stored only in the controlfile (and therefore visible only in V$ views) and some is stored only in the data dictionary (and therefore visible only in DBA views). Other information is duplicated.

EXERCISE 6-2

Create, Alter, and Drop Tablespaces

In this exercise, you will create tablespaces and change their characteristics. Follow these steps:

1. Connect to the database as user SYSTEM.
2. Create a tablespace in a suitable directory—any directory on which the Oracle owner has write permission will do. This is an example:

```
create tablespace newtbs
datafile '/home/db12c/oradata/newtbs_01.dbf' size 10m
extent management local autoallocate
segment space management auto;
```

This command specifies the options that are the default. Nonetheless, it may be considered good practice to do this, to make the statement self-documenting.

3. Create a table in the new tablespace and determine the size of the first extent:

```
create table newtab(c1 date) tablespace newtbs;
select extent_id,bytes from dba_extents
where owner='SYSTEM' and segment_name='NEWTAB';
```

4. Add extents manually and observe the size of each new extent by repeatedly executing the command

```
alter table newtab allocate extent;
```

followed by the query from step 3. Note the point at which the extent size increases.

5. Take the tablespace offline, observe the effect, and bring it back online:

```
alter tablespace newtbs offline;
delete newtab;
drop newtab;
alter tablespace newtbs online;
```

6. Make the tablespace read-only, observe the effect, and make it read-write again:

```
alter tablespace newtbs read only;
delete newtab;
drop newtab;
alter tablespace newtbs read write;
```

7. Tidy up by issuing the following command:

```
drop tablespace newtbs including contents and datafiles;
```

Altering Tablespaces

These are the changes commonly made to tablespaces after creation:

- Renaming
- Taking online and offline
- Flagging as read-write or read-only
- Resizing

Rename a Tablespace and Its Datafiles

The syntax is

```
ALTER TABLESPACE oldname RENAME TO newname;
```

This is very simple but can cause problems later. Many sites rely on naming conventions to relate tablespaces to their datafiles. All the examples in this chapter do just that: they embed the name of the tablespace in the name of the datafiles. Oracle doesn't care: internally, it maintains the relationships by using the tablespace number and the datafile (or tempfile) number. These are visible as the columns V$TABLESPACE.TS# and V$DATAFILE.FILE#. If your site does rely on naming conventions, it will be necessary to rename the files as well.

A tablespace can be renamed while it is in use, but to rename a datafile, it must be offline. This is because the file must be renamed at the operating system level, as well as within the Oracle environment, and this can't be done if the file is open: all the file handles would become invalid. It is, however, possible to move a datafile online.

Figure 6-5 shows an example of the whole process, using the GLTBS tablespace created in Figure 6-4.

In the figure, the first command renames the tablespace. Then the tablespace is taken offline (as described in the next section), and an operating system command renames one of the datafiles in the file system. An **ALTER DATABASE** command

FIGURE 6-5 Renaming a tablespace and its datafiles

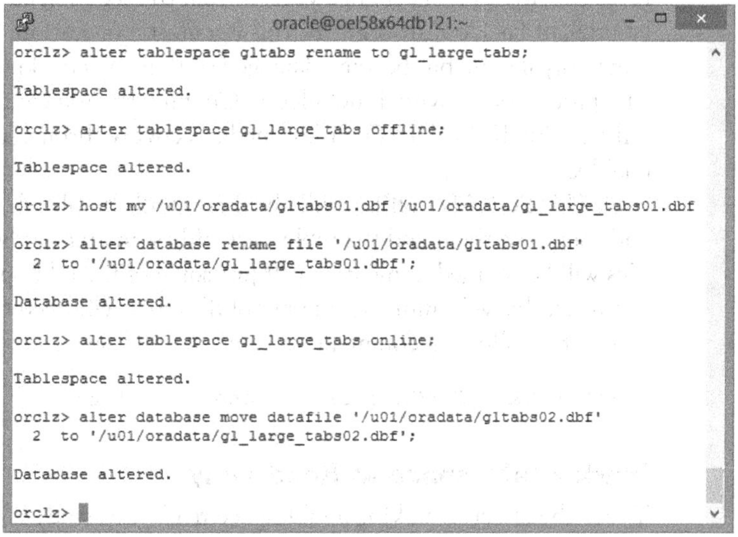

```
oracle@oel58x64db121:~
orclz> alter tablespace gltabs rename to gl_large_tabs;

Tablespace altered.

orclz> alter tablespace gl_large_tabs offline;

Tablespace altered.

orclz> host mv /u01/oradata/gltabs01.dbf /u01/oradata/gl_large_tabs01.dbf

orclz> alter database rename file '/u01/oradata/gltabs01.dbf'
  2  to '/u01/oradata/gl_large_tabs01.dbf';

Database altered.

orclz> alter tablespace gl_large_tabs online;

Tablespace altered.

orclz> alter database move datafile '/u01/oradata/gltabs02.dbf'
  2  to '/u01/oradata/gl_large_tabs02.dbf';

Database altered.

orclz>
```

changes the filename as recorded within the controlfile, so that Oracle will be able to find it. Finally, the tablespace is brought back online. The last command shows the alternative approach: it physically moves the other file and renames it (at both the file system level and within the controlfile) in one operation with zero downtime.

Taking a Tablespace Online or Offline

An *online* tablespace or datafile is available for use; an *offline* tablespace or datafile exists as a definition in the data dictionary and the controlfile but cannot be used. It is possible for a tablespace to be online but one or more of its datafiles to be offline. This is a situation that can produce interesting results and should generally be avoided. Here is the syntax for taking a tablespace offline:

```
ALTER TABLESPACE tablespacename
OFFLINE [ NORMAL | IMMEDIATE | TEMPORARY];
```

A NORMAL offline (which is the default) will force a checkpoint for all the tablespace's datafiles. Every dirty buffer in the database buffer cache that contains a block from the tablespace will be written to its datafile, and then the tablespace and the datafiles are taken offline.

At the other extreme is IMMEDIATE, which offlines the tablespace and the datafiles immediately, without flushing any dirty buffers. Following this, the datafiles will be corrupted (they may be missing committed changes) and will have to be recovered by applying change vectors from the redo log before the tablespace can be brought back online. Clearly, this is a drastic operation. It would normally be done only if a file has become damaged so that the checkpoint cannot be completed. The process of recovery is detailed in Chapter 18. You cannot take a tablespace offline using IMMEDIATE unless media recovery through archive logging has been enabled.

A TEMPORARY offline will checkpoint all the files that can be checkpointed and then take them and the tablespace offline in an orderly fashion. Any damaged files will be offlined immediately. If just some of the tablespace's datafiles have been damaged, this will limit the number of files that will need to be recovered.

Use the following command to bring the tablespace back online:

```
ALTER TABLESPACE tablespacename ONLINE;
```

Mark a Tablespace as Read-Only

To see the effect of making a tablespace read-only, study Figure 6-6.

FIGURE 6-6

Operations on a read-only tablespace

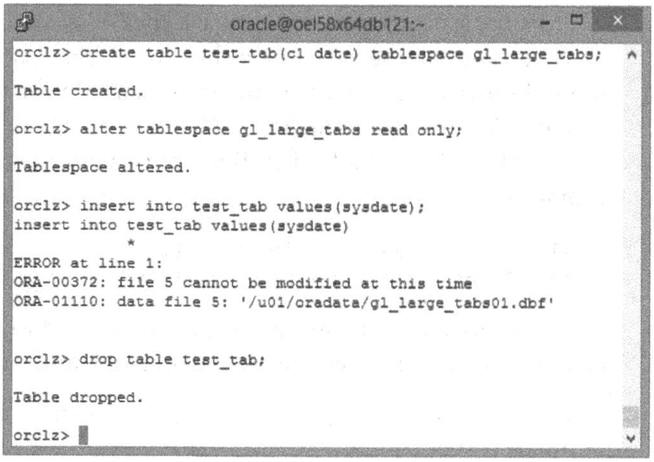

```
oracle@oel58x64db121:~
orclz> create table test_tab(c1 date) tablespace gl_large_tabs;

Table created.

orclz> alter tablespace gl_large_tabs read only;

Tablespace altered.

orclz> insert into test_tab values(sysdate);
insert into test_tab values(sysdate)
            *
ERROR at line 1:
ORA-00372: file 5 cannot be modified at this time
ORA-01110: data file 5: '/u01/oradata/gl_large_tabs01.dbf'


orclz> drop table test_tab;

Table dropped.

orclz>
```

The syntax is completely self-explanatory:

```
ALTER TABLESPACE tablespacename [READ ONLY | READ WRITE] ;
```

After a tablespace is made read-only, none of the objects within it can be changed with DML statements, as demonstrated in the figure. But they can be dropped. This is a little disconcerting but makes perfect sense when you think it through. Dropping a table doesn't actually affect the table. It is a transaction against the data dictionary that deletes the rows that describe the table and its columns; the data dictionary is in the SYSTEM tablespace, and that is not read-only.

on the job

Making a tablespace read-only can have advantages for backup and restore operations. Oracle will be aware that the tablespace contents cannot change and that it may not therefore be necessary to back it up repeatedly.

Resizing a Tablespace

A tablespace can be resized either by adding datafiles to it or by adjusting the size of the existing datafiles. The datafiles can be resized upward automatically as necessary if the AUTOEXTEND syntax were used at file creation time. Otherwise, you have to do it manually with an **ALTER DATABASE** command:

```
ALTER DATABASE DATAFILE 'filename' RESIZE n[M|G|T];
```

The M, G, and T refer to the units of size for the file (megabytes, gigabytes, and terabytes, respectively). This is an example:

```
alter database datafile '/oradata/users02.dbf' resize 10m;
```

From the syntax, you do not know if the file is being made larger or smaller. An upward resize can succeed only if there is enough space in the file system, and a resize downward can succeed only if the space in the file is not already in use by extents allocated to a segment.

To add another datafile of 2GB in size to a tablespace, using the following command:

```
alter tablespace gl_large_tabs
add datafile 'D:\ORADATA\GL_LARGE_TABS_03.DBF' size 2g;
```

Clauses for automatic extension can be included when creating the file. To enable automatic extension later, use a command such as this:

```
alter database datafile 'D:\ORADATA\GL_LARGE_TABS_03.DBF'
autoextend on next 100m maxsize 4g;
```

This will allow the file to double in size, increasing 100MB at a time.

A bigfile tablespace can be resized at the tablespace level, rather than the datafile level. This is because Oracle knows that the tablespace can have only one datafile, and therefore there is no ambiguity about which datafile should be resized. Figure 6-7 shows how to create and resize a bigfile tablespace.

One might think that limiting a tablespace to one file only would limit the storage capacity of the tablespace, but this is not the case. Whereas a smallfile tablespace can consist of up to 1,022 datafiles, each of which can be up to 4 million blocks, a bigfile tablespace can be one datafile of up to 4 billion blocks, so there is really no difference.

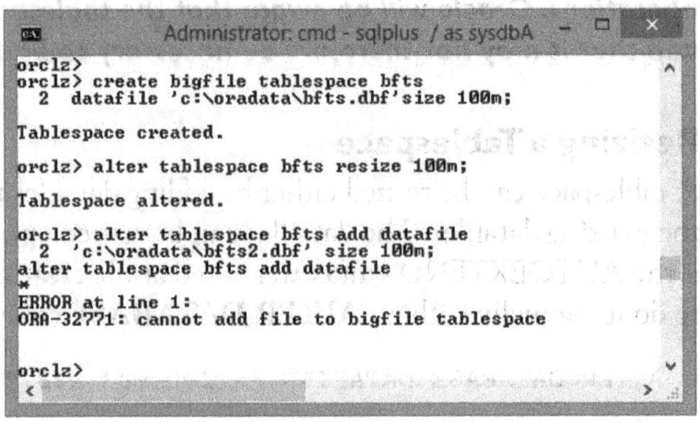

FIGURE 6-7 Working with bigfile tablespaces

```
Administrator: cmd - sqlplus / as sysdbA
orclz>
orclz> create bigfile tablespace bfts
  2  datafile 'c:\oradata\bfts.dbf'size 100m;

Tablespace created.

orclz> alter tablespace bfts resize 100m;

Tablespace altered.

orclz> alter tablespace bfts add datafile
  2  'c:\oradata\bfts2.dbf' size 100m;
alter tablespace bfts add datafile
*
ERROR at line 1:
ORA-32771: cannot add file to bigfile tablespace

orclz>
```

Dropping Tablespaces

To drop a tablespace, use the **DROP TABLESPACE** command. The syntax is

```
DROP TABLESPACE tablespacename
[INCLUDING CONTENTS [AND DATAFILES] ] ;
```

If the INCLUDING CONTENTS keywords are not specified, the drop will fail if there are any objects in the tablespace. Using these keywords instructs Oracle to drop the objects first, and then to drop the tablespace. Even this will fail in some circumstances, such as the tablespace containing a table that is the parent in a foreign key relationship with a table in another tablespace.

If the AND DATAFILES keywords are not specified, the tablespace and its contents will be dropped but the datafiles will continue to exist on disk. Oracle will know nothing about them anymore, and they will have to be deleted with operating system commands.

on the job

On Windows systems, you may find the datafiles are still there after using the INCLUDING CONTENTS AND DATAFILES clause. This is because of the way Windows flags files as "locked." It may be necessary to stop the Windows Oracle service (called something like OracleServiceORCL) before you can delete the files manually.

Extent Management

The extent management method is set per tablespace and applies to all segments in the tablespace. There are two techniques for managing extent usage: dictionary management or local management. The difference is clear: local management should always be used; dictionary management should never be used. Dictionary-managed extent management is still supported, but only just. It is a holdover from previous releases.

Dictionary extent management uses two tables in the data dictionary. SYS.UET$ has rows describing used extents, and SYS.FET$ has rows describing free extents. Every time the database needs to allocate an extent to a segment, it must search FET$ to find an appropriate bit of free space, and then carry out DML operations against FET$ and UET$ to allocate it to the segment. This mechanism causes bad problems with performance, because all space management operations in the database (many of which could be initiated concurrently) must serialize on the code that constructs the transactions.

Local extent management was introduced with release 8*i* and became the default with release 9*i*. It uses bitmaps stored in each datafile. Each bit in the bitmap covers a range of blocks, and when space is allocated, the appropriate bits are changed from zero to one. This mechanism is far more efficient than the transaction-based mechanism of dictionary management. The cost of assigning extents is amortized across bitmaps in every datafile that can be updated concurrently, rather than being concentrated (and serialized) on the two tables.

When creating a locally managed tablespace, an important option is *uniform size*. If uniform is specified, then every extent ever allocated in the tablespace will be that size. This can make the space management highly efficient, because the block ranges covered by each bit can be larger: only one bit per extent. Consider this statement:

```
create tablespace large_tabs
datafile 'large_tabs_01.dbf' size 10g
extent management local uniform size 160m;
```

Every extent allocated in this tablespace will be 160MB, so there will be about 64 of them. The bitmap needs only 64 bits, and 160MB of space can be allocated by updating just one bit. This is going to be very efficient—provided that the segments in the tablespace are large. If a segment were created that only needed space for a few rows, it would still get an extent of 160MB. Small objects need their own tablespace:

```
create tablespace small_tabs
datafile 'small_tabs_01.dbf' size 1g
extent management local uniform size 160k;
```

The alternative (and default) syntax would be this:

```
create tablespace any_tabs
datafile 'any_tabs_01.dbf' size 10g
extent management local autoallocate;
```

When segments are created in this tablespace, Oracle will allocate an eight-block (64KB) extent. As a segment grows and requires more extents, Oracle will allocate extents of this size up to 16 extents, after which it will allocate 128-block (1MB) extents. Thus, fast-growing segments will tend to be given space in larger chunks.

Oracle Corporation recommends AUTOALLOCATE, but if you know how big segments are likely to be and can place them accordingly, UNIFORM SIZE may well be the best option. Many applications are designed in this manner.

It is possible that if a database has been upgraded from previous versions, it will include dictionary-managed tablespaces. Check this with the following query:

```
select tablespace_name, extent_management
from dba_tablespaces;
```

Any dictionary-managed tablespaces should be converted to local management with this PL/SQL procedure call:

```
execute dbms_space_admin.tablespace_migrate_to_local(-
'tablespacename');
```

on the job

Converting tablespaces to local management is quick and easy, except for the SYSTEM tablespace, where some extra steps are required. These are well documented in the System Administrator's guide of the product documentation.

Segment Space Management

The segment space management method is set per tablespace and applies to all segments in the tablespace. There are two techniques for managing segment space usage: manual and automatic. The difference is clear: automatic management should always be used; manual management should never be used. Manual segment space management is still supported but never recommended. It is a holdover from previous releases.

Automatic segment space management was introduced with release 9*i* and became the default in release 11g. Every segment created in an automatic management tablespace has a set of bitmaps that describe how full each block is. There are five bitmaps for each segment, and each block will appear on exactly one bitmap. The bitmaps track the space used in bands: there is a bitmap for full blocks, and there are bitmaps for blocks that are 75-percent to 100-percent used, 50-percent to 75-percent used, 25-percent to 50-percent used, and 0-percent to 25-percent used. When searching for a block into which to insert a row, the session server process will look at the size of the row to determine which bitmap to search. For instance, if the block size is 4KB and the row to be inserted is 1,500 bytes, an appropriate block will be found by searching the "25 percent to 50 percent" bitmap. Every block on this bitmap is guaranteed to have at least 2KB of free space. As rows are inserted, are deleted, or change size through updates, the bitmaps get updated accordingly.

The old manual space management method used a simple list, known as the *freelist*, that stated which blocks were available for insert but without any information on how full they were. This method could cause excessive activity because blocks had to be tested for space at insert time, and often resulted in a large proportion of wasted space.

To see if any tablespaces are using manual management, run this query:

```
select tablespace_name,segment_space_management
from dba_tablespaces;
```

The only tablespaces that should be returned by this query are SYSTEM, undo tablespaces, and temporary tablespaces. The segments in these tablespaces are managed by Oracle, which does not require assistance from any automatic mechanism. It is not possible to convert tablespaces from manual to automatic segment space management. The only way is to create a new tablespace using automatic segment space management, move the segments into it (at which point the bitmap will be generated), and drop the old tablespaces.

Oracle Managed Files (OMF)

Use of OMF is intended to remove the necessity for the DBA to have any knowledge of the file systems. The creation of database files can be fully automated. To enable OMF, set some or all of these instance parameters:

```
DB_CREATE_FILE_DEST
DB_CREATE_ONLINE_LOG_DEST_1
DB_CREATE_ONLINE_LOG_DEST_2
DB_CREATE_ONLINE_LOG_DEST_3
DB_CREATE_ONLINE_LOG_DEST_4
DB_CREATE_ONLINE_LOG_DEST_5
DB_RECOVERY_FILE_DEST
```

The DB_CREATE_FILE_DEST parameter specifies a default location for all datafiles and online redo log files. The DB_CREATE_ONLINE_LOG_DEST_*n* parameters specify a default location for online redo log files, taking precedence over DB_CREATE_FILE_DEST. DB_RECOVERY_FILE_DEST sets up a default location for archive redo log files and Recovery Manager (RMAN) backup files; this will be discussed in later chapters on backup and recovery. As well as setting default file locations, OMF will generate filenames and (by default) set the file sizes. Setting these parameters can greatly simplify file-related operations. Once OMF has been enabled, it can always be overridden by specifying a datafile name on the **CREATE TABLESPACE** command.

Figure 6-8 shows an example of enabling and using OMF.

FIGURE 6-8

Using Oracle Managed Files

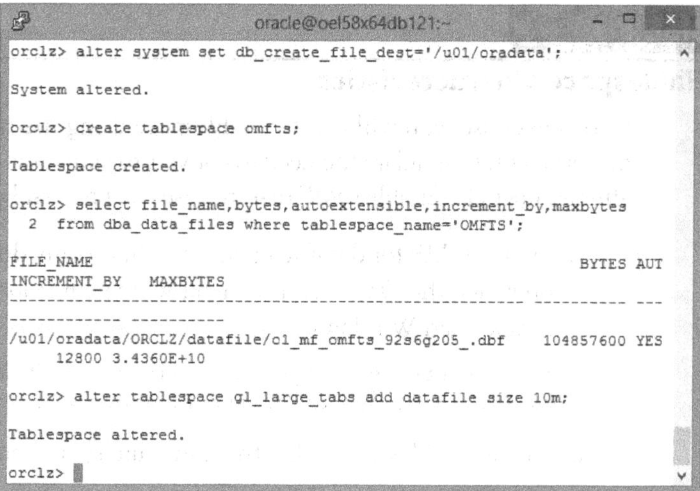
oracle@oel58x64db121:~
orclz> alter system set db_create_file_dest='/u01/oradata';
System altered.
orclz> create tablespace omfts;
Tablespace created.
orclz> select file_name,bytes,autoextensible,increment_by,maxbytes
2 from dba_data_files where tablespace_name='OMFTS';
FILE_NAME BYTES AUT
INCREMENT_BY MAXBYTES
/u01/oradata/ORCLZ/datafile/o1_mf_omfts_92s6g205_.dbf 104857600 YES
12800 3.4360E+10
orclz> alter tablespace gl_large_tabs add datafile size 10m;
Tablespace altered.
orclz>

In the figure, first the parameter is set. Note that the parameter is dynamic: you can change it at any time, and all OMF files created subsequently will be in the new location. Existing OMF files are not affected by any such change. Then the tablespace OMFTS is created, relying completely on the OMF defaults. The query shows what these are:

- **File name** Generated with a leading string (o1_mf), followed by the name of the tablespace, followed by eight random characters (to generate a unique name), and then a suffix (.dbf)
- **File size** 100MB
- **Autoextend** Enabled, in units of 12,800 blocks (100MB), up to 32GB

The final example in the figure shows adding an OMF file to an existing tablespace, overriding the OMF default for the file size.

The combination of OMF, bigfile tablespaces, and autoextend can make space management in an Oracle database extremely easy and completely automatic.

EXERCISE 6-3

Change Tablespace Characteristics

In this exercise, you will create a tablespace using the nondefault manual space management, to simulate the need to convert to automatic segment space management after an upgrade. Enable OMF first, to ease the process. Follow these steps:

1. Enable OMF for datafile creation. Choose any directory that exists and on which the Oracle user has read-write permissions. This is an example on Linux, then Windows:

```
alter system set db_create_file_dest='/home/oradata';
alter system set db_create_file_dest='c:\users\oracle\oradata';
```

2. Create a tablespace, using the minimum syntax now possible:

```
create tablespace omftbs;
```

3. Determine the characteristics of the OMF file:

```
select file_name,bytes,autoextensible,maxbytes,increment_by
from dba_data_files where tablespace_name='OMFTBS';
```

   Note the file is initially 100MB, autoextensible, with no upper limit.

4. Adjust the OMF file to have more sensible characteristics. Use whatever system-generated filename was returned by step 3:

```
alter database datafile
'/home/oradata/ORCL/datafile/o1_mf_omftbs_3olpn462_.dbf'
resize 500m;
alter database datafile
'/home/oradata/ORCL/datafile/o1_mf_omftbs_3olpn462_.dbf'
autoextend on next 100m maxsize 2g;
```

5. Drop the tablespace and use an operating system command to confirm that the file has indeed gone:

```
drop tablespace omftbs including contents and datafiles;
```

6. Create a tablespace using manual segment space management. Because OMF is enabled, there is no need for any datafile clause:

```
create tablespace manualsegs segment space management manual;
```

7. Confirm that the new tablespace is indeed using the manual technique:

```
select segment_space_management from dba_tablespaces
where tablespace_name='MANUALSEGS';
```

8. Create a table and an index in the tablespace:

```
create table mantab (c1 number) tablespace manualsegs;
create index mantabi on mantab(c1) tablespace manualsegs;
```

9. These segments will be created with freelists, not bitmaps. Create a new tablespace that will (by default) use automatic segment space management:

```
create tablespace autosegs;
```

10. Move the objects into the new tablespace:

```
alter table mantab move tablespace autosegs;
alter index mantabi rebuild online tablespace autosegs;
```

11. Confirm that the objects are in the correct tablespace:

```
select tablespace_name from dba_segments
where segment_name like 'MANTAB%';
```

12. Drop the original tablespace:

```
drop tablespace manualsegs including contents and datafiles;
```

13. Rename the new tablespace to the original name. This is often necessary, because some application software checks the tablespace names:

```
alter tablespace autosegs rename to manualsegs;
```

14. Tidy up by dropping the tablespace, first with this command:

```
drop tablespace manualsegs;
```

Note the error caused by the tablespace not being empty, and fix it:

```
drop tablespace manualsegs including contents and datafiles;
```

CERTIFICATION SUMMARY

The relational database paradigm requires a separation of logical storage, as seen by the programmers, from the physical storage seen by the system administrators. Oracle implements this with tablespaces. Within a tablespace, the segments are made of extents composed of Oracle blocks.

The current techniques of managing space with bitmaps, both for allocating extents to segments and for identifying blocks within a segment that are suitable for row insertion, are far superior to earlier techniques and should always be used. Combined with OMF and ASM, they can make space management completely automatic.

TWO-MINUTE DRILL

Describe the Storage of Table Row Data in Blocks

- ❑ One tablespace can span many datafiles.
- ❑ One tablespace can have many segments.
- ❑ One segment is one or more extents.
- ❑ One extent is many consecutive blocks, in one datafile.
- ❑ One Oracle block should be one or more operating system blocks.
- ❑ The Oracle block is the granularity of database I/O.
- ❑ A SMALLFILE tablespace can have many datafiles, but a BIGFILE tablespace can have only one.
- ❑ Tablespaces default to local extent management, automatic segment space management, but not to a uniform extent size.
- ❑ OMF datafiles are automatically named, are initially 100MB, and can autoextend without limit.
- ❑ A tablespace that contains segments cannot be dropped, unless an INCLUDING DATAFILES clause is specified.
- ❑ Tablespaces can be online or offline, read-write or read-only.
- ❑ Any one tablespace can store only one type of object: permanent objects, temporary objects, or undo segments.

Create and Manage Tablespaces

- ❑ Tablespaces can be resized by adding datafiles or by extending existing datafiles.
- ❑ Local extent management tracks extent allocation with bitmaps in each datafile.
- ❑ The UNIFORM SIZE clause when creating a tablespace forces all extents to be the same size.
- ❑ The AUTOALLOCATE clause lets Oracle determine the next extent size, which is based on how many extents are being allocated to a segment.
- ❑ Automatic segment space management tracks the free space in each block of an extent using bitmaps.
- ❑ It is possible to convert a tablespace from dictionary extent management to local extent management, but not from freelist segment management to automatic management.

SELF TEST

Describe the Storage of Table Row Data in Blocks

1. Examine the exhibit:

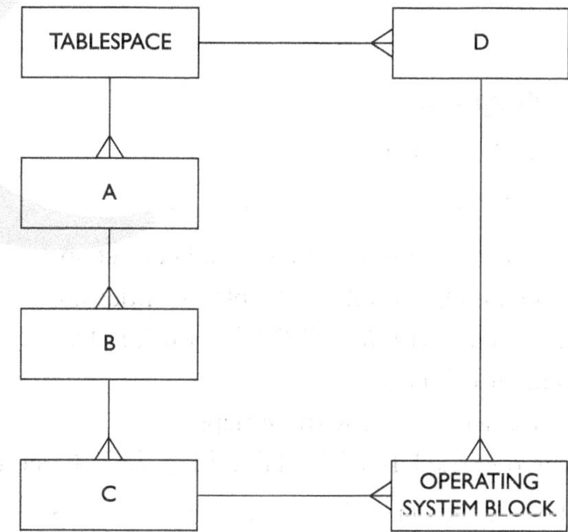

The exhibit shows the Oracle storage model, with four entities having letters for names. Match four of the following entities to the letters A, B, C, D:

DATAFILE
EXTENT
ORACLE BLOCK
ROW
SEGMENT
TABLE

2. What statements are correct about extents? (Choose all correct answers.)

A. An extent is a grouping of several Oracle blocks.
B. An extent is a grouping of several operating system blocks.
C. An extent can be distributed across one or more datafiles.
D. An extent can contain blocks from one or more segments.
E. An extent can be assigned to only one segment.

3. Which of these are types of segments? (Choose all correct answers.)
   A. Sequence
   B. Stored procedure
   C. Table
   D. Table partition
   E. View

Create and Manage Tablespaces

4. If a tablespace is created with the syntax

   ```
   create tablespace tbs1 datafile 'tbs1.dbf' size 10m;
   ```

   which of these characteristics will it have? (Choose all correct answers.)
   A. The datafile will autoextend, but only to double its initial size.
   B. The datafile will autoextend with MAXSIZE UNLIMITED.
   C. The extent management will be local.
   D. Segment space management will be with bitmaps.
   E. The file will be created in the DB_CREATE_FILE_DEST directory.
5. How can a tablespace be made larger? (Choose all correct answers.)
   A. Convert it from a SMALLFILE tablespace to a BIGFILE tablespace.
   B. If it is a SMALLFILE tablespace, add files.
   C. If it is a BIGFILE tablespace, add more files.
   D. Resize the existing file(s).
6. Which of these commands can be executed against a table in a read-only tablespace? (Choose the best answer.)
   A. DELETE
   B. DROP
   C. INSERT
   D. TRUNCATE
   E. UPDATE
7. What operation cannot be applied to a tablespace after creation? (Choose the best answer.)
   A. Convert from dictionary extent management to local extent management.
   B. Convert from manual segment space management to automatic segment space management.
   C. Change the name of the tablespace.
   D. Reduce the size of the datafile(s) assigned to the tablespace.
   E. All the above operations can be applied.

8. When the database is in mount mode, what views may be queried to find what datafiles and tablespaces make up the database? (Choose all correct answers.)
   A. DBA_DATA_FILES
   B. DBA_TABLESPACES
   C. DBA_TEMP_FILES
   D. V$DATABASE
   E. V$DATAFILE
   F. V$TABLESPACE
9. Which views could you query to find out about the temporary tablespaces and the files that make them up? (Choose all correct answers.)
   A. DBA_DATA_FILES
   B. DBA_TABLESPACES
   C. DBA_TEMP_TABLESPACES
   D. DBA_TEMP_FILES
   E. V$DATAFILE
   F. V$TABLESPACE
   G. V$TEMPTABLESPACE
   H. V$TEMPFILE

LAB QUESTION

Create a tablespace with one datafile. Use a uniform extent size of 64KB. Create two tables in this tablespace, and manually allocate a few extents to each in turn. Run a query to find the exact physical locations of each table: you will see that they are interleaved. Add a second datafile to the tablespace, and allocate a few more extents. Rerunning the query should demonstrate that Oracle is bringing the new file into use.

SELF TEST ANSWERS

Describe the Storage of Table Row Data in Blocks

1. ☑ A is SEGMENT, B is EXTENT, C is ORACLE BLOCK, and D is DATAFILE.
   ☒ Neither ROW nor TABLE is included in the model.
2. ☑ **A** and **E.** One extent is several consecutive Oracle blocks, and one segment consists of one or more extents.
   ☒ **B, C,** and **D** are incorrect. They misinterpret the Oracle storage model.
3. ☑ **C** and **D.** A table can be a type of segment, as is a table partition (in which case the table itself will not be a segment).
   ☒ **A, B,** and **E** are incorrect. They exist only as objects defined within the data dictionary. The data dictionary itself is a set of segments.

Create and Manage Tablespaces

4. ☑ **C** and **D.** Local extent management and automatic segment space management are enabled by default.
   ☒ **A, B,** and **E** are incorrect. **A** and **B** are incorrect because, by default, autoextension is disabled. **E** is incorrect because providing a filename will override the OMF mechanism.
5. ☑ **B** and **D.** A SMALLFILE tablespace can have many files, and all datafiles can be resized upward.
   ☒ **A** and **C** are incorrect. **A** is incorrect because you cannot convert between SMALLFILE and BIGFILE. **C** is incorrect because a BIGFILE tablespace can have only one file.
6. ☑ **B.** Objects can be dropped from read-only tablespaces.
   ☒ **A, C, D,** and **E** are incorrect. All of these commands will fail because they require writing to the table, unlike a DROP, which writes only to the data dictionary.
7. ☑ **B.** It is not possible to change the segment space management method after creation.
   ☒ **A, C, D,** and **E** are incorrect. **A** and **C** are incorrect because a tablespace can be converted to local extent management or renamed at any time. **D** is incorrect because a datafile can be resized downward, although only if the space to be freed up has not already been used. **E** is incorrect because you cannot change the segment space management without re-creating the tablespace.
8. ☑ **E** and **F.** Joining these views will give the necessary information.
   ☒ **A, B, C,** and **D** are incorrect. **A, B,** and **C** are incorrect because these views will not be available in mount mode. **D** is incorrect because there is no relevant information in V$DATABASE.

9. ☑ **B, D, F,** and **H.** V$TABLESPACE and DBA_TABLESPACE will list the temporary tablespaces, and V$TEMPFILE and DBA_TEMP_FILES will list their files.
   ☒ **A, C, E,** and **G** are incorrect. **A** and **E** are incorrect because V$DATAFILE and DBA_DATA_FILES do not include tempfiles. **C** and **G** are incorrect because there are no views with these names.

LAB ANSWER

Here's a possible solution using SQL*Plus:

```
create tablespace labtbs datafile 'labtbs_01.dbf'
size 10m uniform size 64k;
create table tab1(c1 date) tablespace labtbs;
create table tab2 tablespace labtbs as select * from tab1;
alter table tab1 allocate extent;
alter table tab2 allocate extent;
alter table tab1 allocate extent;
alter table tab2 allocate extent;
select segment_name,file_id,extent_id,block_id,blocks
from dba_extents where tablespace_name='LABTBS';
alter tablespace labtbs add datafile 'labtbs_02.dbf'
size 10m;
alter table tab1 allocate extent;
alter table tab2 allocate extent;
select segment_name,file_id,extent_id,block_id,blocks
from dba_extents where tablespace_name='LABTBS';
```

7 Managing Space

CERTIFICATION OBJECTIVES

7.01	Explain How Oracle Database Server Automatically Manages Space
7.02	Save Space by Using Compression
7.03	Proactively Monitor and Manage Tablespace Space Usage
7.04	Use the Segment Advisor
7.05	Reclaim Wasted Space from Tables and Indexes by Using the Segment Shrink Functionality
7.06	Manage Resumable Space Allocation
✓	Two-Minute Drill
Q&A	Self Test

Space management in an Oracle database can be (and usually should be) largely automatic. The DBA creates tablespaces consisting of one or more datafiles, gives the developers a quota on the tablespaces, and Oracle takes care of everything from then on. It is, however, important to understand how space is assigned to segments and within segments, as well as how to monitor space usage. Also, some facilities will permit more efficient use of space, such as compression and segment reorganization through the segment shrink capability.

When a user hits a space limit, an error will be returned and the statement that hit the limit will fail. This situation should of course be avoided, but if it does occur the user can be protected by enabling the resumable space allocation facility.

CERTIFICATION OBJECTIVE 7.01

Explain How Oracle Database Server Automatically Manages Space

Space is managed at three levels: the tablespace, the segment, and the block. Assigning space to tablespaces by creating and modifying datafiles was discussed in Chapter 6. Once these physical structures are in place, management moves to the logical level: how space is assigned to segments, and how space is used within segments. Figure 6-1 in Chapter 6 describes the Oracle storage model. If this is not completely clear, review the associated material before proceeding.

Extent Management

Space is allocated to a segment in the form of an extent, which is a set of consecutive Oracle blocks. Every datafile has a bitmap that describes the state of the block in the file: whether it is free or are a part of an extent that has been assigned to a segment. When a segment fills up and needs to extend, Oracle will search the bitmaps of the files of the tablespace for free space, select one file, and create a new extent of an appropriate size by modifying the bitmap. The extent can then be assigned to the segment.

A segment is a container for an object, but the two are not the same thing: it is possible for the object to exist without a segment. When a segment is first created, it will have at least one extent—but it is possible for some objects to exist without a segment. Study the code in Figure 7-1. The first two queries show the tables (four) and indexes (two) in the currently logged-on schema, with the flag that shows whether a segment has been created for them. The third query shows the segments. The table BONUS exists logically, but has no segment within which it can be contained.

on the Job

Deferred segment creation can have some odd effects. For example, problems with a quota will not show up when creating a table—only when inserting into it.

The key to understanding this situation is the instance parameter DEFERRED_SEGMENT_CREATION, which defaults to TRUE. If set to TRUE, this parameter instructs Oracle not to create a segment until the object actually contains some data. At table creation time, only the data dictionary structure describing the table is created. Only subsequently, when an attempt is made to insert a row into the table, is the segment created. It is possible to control this behavior, and to override the parameter setting, with the SEGMENT CREATION clause of the CREATE TABLE statement. Figure 7-2 demonstrates this, showing that a segment is created consisting of one extent when a row is inserted into a table.

FIGURE 7-1 Objects and segments

```
cmd - sqlplus scott/tiger
orclz> select table_name,segment_created from user_tables;

TABLE_NAME                     SEG
------------------------------ ---
SALGRADE                       YES
BONUS                          NO
EMP                            YES
DEPT                           YES

orclz> select index_name,segment_created from user_indexes;

INDEX_NAME                     SEG
------------------------------ ---
PK_DEPT                        YES
PK_EMP                         YES

orclz> select segment_name,segment_type from user_segments;

SEGMENT_NAME                   SEGMENT_TYPE
------------------------------ ------------------
DEPT                           TABLE
EMP                            TABLE
PK_DEPT                        INDEX
PK_EMP                         INDEX
SALGRADE                       TABLE

orclz> show parameter deferred_segment_creation

NAME                                 TYPE        VALUE
------------------------------------ ----------- ------------------------------
deferred_segment_creation            boolean     TRUE
orclz> _
```

FIGURE 7-2 Deferred segment creation

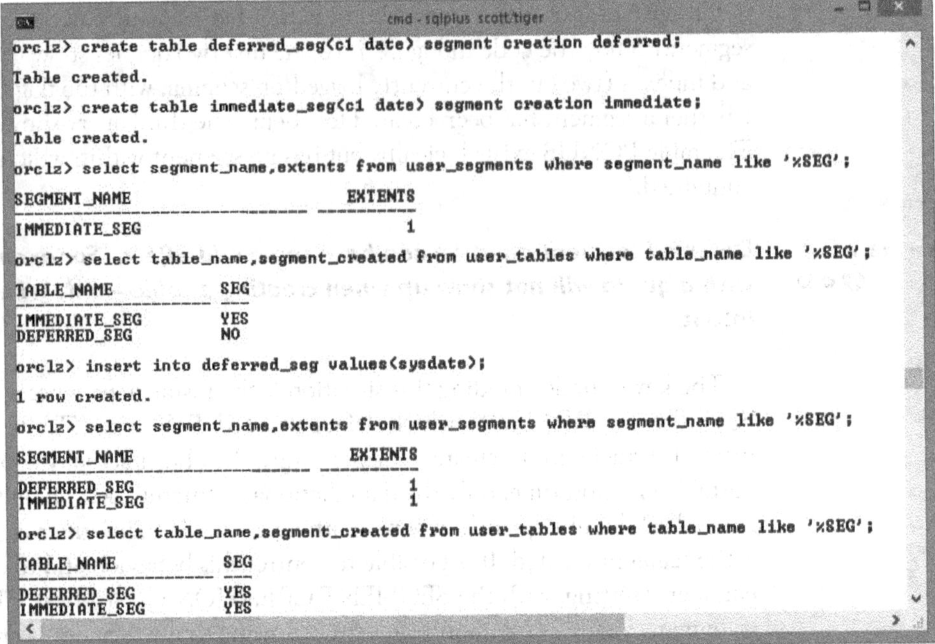


```
orclz> create table deferred_seg(c1 date) segment creation deferred;

Table created.

orclz> create table immediate_seg(c1 date) segment creation immediate;

Table created.

orclz> select segment_name,extents from user_segments where segment_name like '%SEG';

SEGMENT_NAME                      EXTENTS
------------------------------ ----------
IMMEDIATE_SEG                           1

orclz> select table_name,segment_created from user_tables where table_name like '%SEG';

TABLE_NAME                     SEG
------------------------------ ---
IMMEDIATE_SEG                  YES
DEFERRED_SEG                   NO

orclz> insert into deferred_seg values(sysdate);

1 row created.

orclz> select segment_name,extents from user_segments where segment_name like '%SEG';

SEGMENT_NAME                      EXTENTS
------------------------------ ----------
DEFERRED_SEG                            1
IMMEDIATE_SEG                           1

orclz> select table_name,segment_created from user_tables where table_name like '%SEG';

TABLE_NAME                     SEG
------------------------------ ---
DEFERRED_SEG                   YES
IMMEDIATE_SEG                  YES
```

exam watch

Segment creation is always immediate for objects created by internal users such as SYS or SYSTEM, no matter what the setting of the parameter. Attempting to use the SEGMENT CREATION DEFERRED clause as SYS returns an error.

EXERCISE 7-1

Segment Space Management

In this exercise, you observe the allocation of extents to segments.

1. Connect to the database as user SYSTEM.
2. Create a schema to work in for this exercise and then connect to it:

```
create user ex7 identified by ex7;
grant dba to ex7;
connect ex7/ex7;
```

3. Check that the DEFERRED_SEGMENT_CREATION parameter is set to TRUE, which is the default, and set it if it is not:

```
show parameter deferred_segment_creation
alter session set deferred_segment_creation=true;
```

4. Create tables and indexes as follows:

```
create table ex7a (c1 varchar2(10));
create table ex7b (c1 varchar2(10)) segment creation
deferred;
create table ex7c (c1 varchar2(10)) segment creation
immediate;
create index ex7ai on ex7a(c1);
create index ex7bi on ex7b(c1);
create index ex7ci on ex7c(c1);
```

5. Determine what segments have been created:

```
select segment_name from user_segments;
select table_name,segment_created from user_tables;
select index_name,segment_created from user_indexes;
```

6. Insert a row into EX7A and EX7B.
7. Run the queries from step 5 again.

Automatic Segment Space Management (ASSM)

A table segment consists of multiple blocks, in one or more extents. When an attempt is made to insert a row into the table, Oracle must make a decision: into which block should the row be placed? This is determined by a bitmap that reflects how full each block in the segment is. By inspecting the bitmap, Oracle can determine whether a block has sufficient space to accept the new row. The mapping is not precise, but rather works in 25-percent ranges: between 0 and 25 percent free space; 25 to 50 percent free space; 50 to 75 percent free space; and 75 to 100 percent free space. In addition, the bitmap shows whether the block is not actually formatted at all (that is, it is assigned to the segment but has not yet been used) or is classed as full and is therefore not available for inserts no matter how small the new row is.

As rows are inserted into blocks and deleted from blocks, the status of the block (in terms of to which of the 25-percent bands it belongs) is adjusted in the bitmap.

A problem related to the selection of a block for an insert is how to manage the situation where a row changes size. Some Oracle data types are of variable length: principally, the VARCHAR2 data type. If a VARCHAR2 column is updated such that it becomes longer, the row will become longer. Furthermore, if any columns are NULL when a row is inserted, they will take no space at all. It follows from this that when UPDATE statements are executed that expand a VARCHAR2 or populate a previously NULL column, the row will become bigger. It will therefore require more space in the block.

By default, Oracle reserves 10 percent of a block for row expansion. This is the PCTFREE (percent free) setting for the segment, set at segment creation time (though it can be modified later). A block whose usage has exceeded the PCTFREE setting for the segment is classed by the ASSM bitmap as FULL, and therefore the block is not available for insert even though it may in fact still have some free space. So if, on average, the rows in a block increase by no more than 10 percent during their lifetime, there is no problem: enough space will be available for the new versions of the rows. If a row expands such that there is not sufficient space in the block, it must be moved to a block with sufficient space. This is known as *row migration*.

exam watch

Row migration is caused by UPDATE statements. INSERT and DELETE can never result in row migration.

When a row is migrated, it is removed from the block in which it resides, and inserted into a different block with sufficient space. The new block will be located by searching the ASSM bitmap. So in effect, when a user executes an UPDATE, this becomes an INSERT and DELETE: a more expensive operation. Furthermore, the ROWID of the row (the physical locator of the row) is not changed. The ROWID still points to the original block, which now stores no more than a "forwarding address" for the row: the address of the block to which the row has been moved. The fact that the ROWID remains unchanged is good and bad. It is good because there is no need to adjust any indexes: they will still point to the original location. It is bad because when the row is retrieved through an index search, an extra I/O operation will be needed to read the row from its new location. This is, of course, transparent to SQL but may in extreme circumstances result in performance degradation.

Closely related to row migration is the issue of row chaining. A *chained row* is a row that is larger than the block. Clearly, if the blocksize is 8K and the row is 20K, then the row must be distributed across three blocks. At insert time, all three blocks will be located by searching the ASSM bitmap for blocks available for insertion, and when retrieving the row later all three blocks may be read (depending on which columns are projected by the query). The ROWID of a chained row points to the first block of the row, as is also the case with a migrated row.

CERTIFICATION OBJECTIVE 7.02

Save Space by Using Compression

Compression comes in various forms, some of which require a separate license: the Advanced Compression option. The primary purpose of compression is to reduce disk space requirements, but there is sometimes a fringe benefit: improved performance for subsequent queries. Compression may, however, cause performance degradation in some circumstances, and should therefore be approached with caution. An advisor capability will estimate the space savings that compression can achieve for a table.

Compression comes in three forms:

- Basic table compression compresses data within a block when rows are inserted through a direct load operation. Subsequent DML operations will cause the rows to be uncompressed (and possibly migrated as a result of this).
- Advanced row compression will compress rows no matter how they are inserted, and maintain the compression though DML. The compression is still on a block-by-block basis.
- Hybrid Columnar Compression (HCC) restructures data into compression units of several megabytes, and is available only on certain storage platforms.

Basic compression (which is the default type) is in fact de-duplication. If a repeating pattern of characters occurs within a block, the pattern is stored once only in a symbol table, with a reference to the symbol table stored in each row where the pattern occurs. Advanced row compression uses the same de-duplication technology. Either way, the compression is per block: the symbol tables are not usable outside of the block in which they exist. HCC is true compression, in that it uses compression algorithms to reduce the space needed to store data. HCC is not applied per block, but across groups of blocks, which further enhances the achievable compression ratios.

The type of compression is determined at table creation time. Compression can be added or removed after creation, but any such change will not affect existing rows.

To bring the change into effect, the table must be reorganized. Typically, this would be accomplished with an ALTER TABLE...MOVE statement.

The syntax to create a table with basic or advanced compression is a normal creation statement, with a suffix specifying the compression type:

```
CREATE TABLE.....COMPRESS [ BASIC ] ;
CREATE TABLE....ROW STORE COMPRESS ADVANCED
```

EXERCISE 7-2

Investigate Compression

In this exercise, you determine the effects of compression on storage requirements.

1. Connect to the EX7 schema created in the previous exercise.
2. Adjust a table to use basic compression:
```
alter table ex7b compress basic;
```
3. Insert 100,000 rows into the compressed and uncompressed tables, using a direct load:
```
insert /*+ append */ all
into ex7a values ('1111111111')
into ex7b values ('1111111111')
select * from dual connect by level  <= 100000;
```
4. Analyze the tables, and note the number of blocks used:
```
execute dbms_stats.gather_schema_stats(user);
select table_name,blocks from user_tables;
```
Note the effect of compression.
5. Update the rows:
```
update ex7a set c1='2222222222';
update ex7b set c1='2222222222';
```
6. Rerun the code from step 4. What does this tell you about basic compression and DML? Note that to preserve the compression ratio, rather than have it degrade to even worse than no compression at all, it would be necessary to implement advanced compression, not basic compression.

CERTIFICATION OBJECTIVE 7.03

Proactively Monitor and Manage Tablespace Space Usage

The database will automatically monitor tablespace usage, through the server alert system. Figure 7-3 shows a query against the DBA_THRESHOLDS view.

The first two lines of the output for Figure 7-3 show the system-generated thresholds for a temporary tablespace and the undo tablespace: tablespaces of these types are not monitored. This is because a simple check of free space is useless for tablespaces of these types, as they are usually fully occupied by temporary or undo segments. What matters is whether the temporary or undo segments within them are full: this is a more complex metric that is not configured by default.

The third line of the query's output shows the database-wide default alerts for all tablespaces that do not have an alert explicitly configured. The warning alert is set at greater than or equal to 85 percent, and the critical alert at greater than or equal to 97 percent.

In addition to the alert system, which will inform you of issues according to preconfigured thresholds, Oracle maintains a history of tablespace usage. This is stored in the AWR, the information being gathered as part of the AWR snapshots

FIGURE 7-3 Tablespace thresholds and usage

```
cmd - sqlplus / as sysdba
orclz> select object_name,warning_operator,warning_value,critical_operator,critical_value
  2  from dba_thresholds where metrics_name='Tablespace Space Usage';

OBJECT_NAME              WARNING_OPER WARNING_VALUE           CRITICAL_OPE CRITICAL_VALUE
------------------------ ------------ ----------------------- ------------ ------------------
TEMP                     DO NOT CHECK <SYSTEM-GENERATED DO_NOT_CHECK 0
UNDOTBS1                 DO NOT CHECK <SYSTEM-GENERATED DO_NOT_CHECK 0
                         GE           85                      GE           97
SMALL                    GT           50                      GT           75

orclz>
orclz> select rtime,name,tablespace_usedsize
  2  from v$tablespace v join dba_hist_tbspc_space_usage d on(v.ts#=d.tablespace_id)
  3  order by name,rtime desc;

RTIME                          NAME                           TABLESPACE_USEDSIZE
------------------------------ ------------------------------ -------------------
11/27/2013 20:00:52            EXAMPLE                                      41352
11/27/2013 19:45:49            EXAMPLE                                      41352
11/27/2013 19:30:48            EXAMPLE                                      41352
11/27/2013 19:15:47            EXAMPLE                                      41352
11/27/2013 19:00:47            EXAMPLE                                      41352
11/27/2013 18:45:46            EXAMPLE                                      41352
11/27/2013 18:30:45            EXAMPLE                                      41352
11/27/2013 18:15:44            EXAMPLE                                      41352
11/27/2013 18:00:43            EXAMPLE                                      41352
```

created by the MMON process. This information can be seen in the DBA_HIST_TBSPC_SPACE_USAGE view. The second query in Figure 7-3 joins this view to the V$TABLESPACE view (the join is necessary to retrieve the tablespace name) and shows the history of space usage for each tablespace. Note that there is one row per tablespace per snapshot. It can be seen that the snapshot frequency has been set to every 15 minutes and that (in the few lines displayed) there was no change in the usage within the EXAMPLE tablespace.

on the job

You may wish to write your own reporting code that queries DBA_HIST_TBSPC_SPACE_USAGE to gain a picture of how space is being used in the database, so that you can add space to tablespaces before alerts are raised.

CERTIFICATION OBJECTIVE 7.04

Use the Segment Advisor

The Segment Advisor is a tool that attempts to generate recommendations regarding reorganizing segments to reclaim space. The issue is that over time, in some circumstances, table and index segments may become larger than is necessary for the amount of data contained within them.

An obvious example is many rows having been deleted. Deletion frees up space within the segment, but the segment itself remains the same size. This will affect the table segment and all associated index segments. In most cases, if space has ever been assigned to a segment, then even if it is not needed now, it will be needed again. For example, the process of loading data into data warehouse tables often involves inserting many rows into a staging table, processing and deleting them. But even though the table may be empty at the end of the day's run, all the space will be needed again the next day.

It is therefore not enough to examine the current state of a table to determine if it is excessively large: one must also consider the history of space usage. The Segment Advisor can do this. It considers data in the AWR as well as the current state of the objects. The recommendations are based on a sampled analysis of the object, and also historical information used to predict future growth trends.

The Segment Advisor runs, by default, every night as an autotask scheduled job. The autotask does not attempt to analyze every segment. It selects segments on these criteria:

- Segments in tablespaces that have crossed a space usage threshold
- Segments that have had the most activity
- Segments that have the highest growth rate

To see the results of the autotask, use the DBMS_SPACE.ASA_RECOMMENDATIONS function. This function returns a table with the results of the last run. Figure 7-4 shows an example of querying the result of the Segment Advisor autotask, followed by the commands that implement its recommendations.

on the job

The Segment Advisor autotask runs by default. Many DBAs never look at its advice. You should either look at the results or disable the task.

FIGURE 7-4

Retrieving and implementing the Segment Advisor's autotask advice

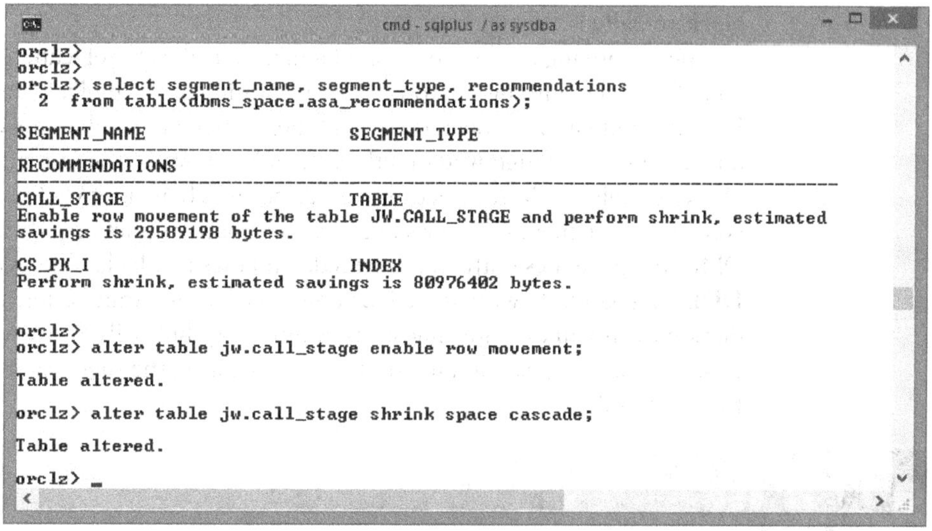

```
cmd - sqlplus / as sysdba
orclz>
orclz>
orclz> select segment_name, segment_type, recommendations
  2  from table(dbms_space.asa_recommendations);

SEGMENT_NAME                      SEGMENT_TYPE
--------------------------------- ------------------
RECOMMENDATIONS
------------------------------------------------------------------------------
CALL_STAGE                        TABLE
Enable row movement of the table JW.CALL_STAGE and perform shrink, estimated
savings is 29589198 bytes.

CS_PK_I                           INDEX
Perform shrink, estimated savings is 80976402 bytes.


orclz>
orclz> alter table jw.call_stage enable row movement;

Table altered.

orclz> alter table jw.call_stage shrink space cascade;

Table altered.

orclz> _
```

CERTIFICATION OBJECTIVE 7.05

Reclaim Wasted Space from Tables and Indexes by Using the Segment Shrink Functionality

When a row is deleted, the space it was occupying in its block becomes available for reuse when another row is inserted. However, the nature of the activity against a table can result in a significant amount of wasted space within the table. This could be reclaimed with a MOVE operation: following a move, all the blocks will be consecutively full of freshly reinserted rows. But during the move, the table is locked, and following it all the indexes must be rebuilt. For many environments, this makes use of MOVE to reorganize tables impossible. The **SHRINK** command avoids these problems. It can be run without any impact on end users. A limitation is that the table's tablespace must have been created to use automatic segment space management. Tables in tablespaces that use the older freelist technique for managing segment space usage cannot be shrunk, because (unlike the new bitmap method) the freelist does not include sufficient information for Oracle to work out how full each block actually is.

The underlying implementation of a table shrink is to relocate rows from the end of the table into blocks toward the beginning of the table, by means of matched INSERT and DELETE operations, and then, when all possible moves have been done, to bring the high water mark of the table down to the last currently used block and release all the space above this point. There are two distinct phases: the compact phase moves the rows in a series of small transactions, through normal DML that generates both undo and redo and uses row locks. The second phase is a **DDL** command. As with any DDL command, this is a transaction against the data dictionary: it will execute almost instantaneously, but will require a very short table lock. This last step is often referred to as "relocating the high water mark (HWM) of the segment."

exam watch

A table shrink operation generates undo and redo. Indexes are maintained, because the shrink is implemented as a set of DML transactions. There is no table lock during the compaction, but individual rows will be locked while they are being moved.

The syntax of the **SHRINK SPACE** command is as follows:

```
ALTER TABLE <table name> SHRINK SPACE [COMPACT] [CASCADE] ;
```

Using the keyword COMPACT carries out the first phase, but not the second: the rows are relocated, but the space is not actually released from the segment. The reason for using this is that while the compaction can occur during normal running hours (though it may take many hours to complete on a large table), it is possible that the DDL at the end will hang due to concurrency with other transactions, and it will also invalidate parsed SQL in the library cache. So it may be necessary to shrink the table with the COMPACT keyword first, and then again without COMPACT during a maintenance period: it will be fast, because the compaction will have already been done. The CASCADE keyword instructs Oracle also to shrink dependent objects, such as indexes.

exam watch ***The SHRINK SPACE COMPACT command reorganizes the contents of the segment, but does not return space to the tablespace.***

Before a table can be shrunk, you must enable row movement for the table:

```
ALTER TABLE <table name> ENABLE ROW MOVEMENT ;
```

Enabling row movement is necessary because the nature of the operation means that row IDs will be changing. The same row (no change to the primary key) will be in a different physical location and will therefore have a different row ID. This is something that Oracle will not permit unless row movement has been enabled.

exam watch ***A table must be in a tablespace with automatic segment space management and row movement must have been enabled, or it cannot be shrunk. If these conditions have not been met, a MOVE may be the only way to reorganize the table.***

Figure 7-4 shows enabling row movement for a table, followed by a SHRINK SPACE that reclaims space from both the table and its index.

on the job ***Compression is incompatible with SHRINK SPACE: you will need to uncompress before shrinking. To do this, use ALTER TABLE...NOCOMPRESS and ALTER TABLE...MOVE.***

CERTIFICATION OBJECTIVE 7.06

Manage Resumable Space Allocation

Many operations can fail for reasons of inadequate space. This typically shows up as an inability to add another extent to a segment, which itself can have several causes: a datafile could be full; an auto-extensible datafile or tempfile could be on a disk that is full; an undo segment could be in an undo tablespace that is full; an operation requiring temporary space could be using a temporary tablespace that is full; or a user could have reached their quota limit on a tablespace. Whatever the reason, space-related errors tend to be dreadfully time consuming.

Consider an exercise to load data into a data warehouse. The first time you attempt this, it fails because the destination tablespace runs out of space. The data that did go in must be rolled back (which may take as long as the insert), the tablespace extended, and the load done again. Then it fails because of inadequate undo space; therefore, you roll back, increase the undo tablespace, and try again. Then it fails during index rebuilding, because of a lack of temporary space. And so on. Exercises such as this are the bane of many DBAs' lives. The resumable space allocation feature can be the solution.

If you enable resumable space allocation, when an operation hits a space problem (any space problem at all), rather than failing with an error (and in many cases rolling back what it did manage to do) the operation will be suspended. To the user, this will show as the session hanging. When the error condition is resolved, it will continue. All suspended sessions (currently suspended and previously suspended but now running again) are listed in the view DBA_RESUMABLE.

To enable resumable space allocation at the session level, the command is

```
ALTER SESSION ENABLE RESUMABLE [ TIMEOUT <seconds> ] ;
```

The TIMEOUT option lets you specify for how long the statement should hang. If this time is reached without the problem being resolved, the error is returned and the statement fails. If there is no specified TIMEOUT, the session will hang indefinitely.

on the job

It is possible for a process to be suspended and resumed many times, without your knowledge. The DBA_RESUMABLE view will show you details of the current or the last suspension only.

It is also possible to enable resumable space for all sessions, by setting an instance parameter. This is a dynamic parameter. For example, here is how to set a timeout of one minute:

```
alter system set resumable_timeout=60;
```

This will cause all sessions that hit a space problem to be suspended for up to one minute.

on the job

The expdb and impdp Data Pump utilities have the command-line switch RESUMABLE=Y (the default is N), which will allow Data Pump jobs to suspend if they hit space problems. This is extremely useful.

There is little point in enabling resumable space allocation for a session or the instance if you don't do anything about the problem that caused a session to be suspended. Suspended sessions will, by default, be reported through the server alert system, be displayed by Database Control, and be listed in the DBA_RESUMABLE data dictionary view. Having spotted a problem, you can fix it interactively from another session. Or you can create an AFTER SUSPEND ON DATABASE trigger, which that will run whenever a session is suspended. This trigger could report the problem (perhaps by generating an e-mail), or it could include code to investigate the problem and fix it automatically.

on the job

The UTL_MAIL package is not available by default. You must create it by running the utlmail.sql and prvtmail.plb scripts.

For example, here is how to send an e-mail:

```
create trigger detect_suspend
after suspend on database
begin
utl_mail.send(sender=>'dba@mycompany.com',
recipients=>'dba@mycompany.com',
subject=>'DB session suspended',
message=>'resumable space allocation event occurred');

end;
```

on the job

If you create an AFTER SUSPEND ON DATABASE trigger that attempts to fix problems, remember that it might hit a space problem itself.

EXERCISE 7-3

Use Resumable Space Allocation

In this exercise, you will set up a space allocation problem and enable resumable space allocation to gain the opportunity to fix it without an error.

1. Connect to your database as user SYSTEM and create a tablespace to use for this exercise. Here is how with SQL*Plus:

```
create tablespace small datafile 'small1.dbf' size 2m;
```

2. Create a table in the tablespace, with fixed-length rows. It will be impossible to insert 2,000 rows without filling the tablespace:

```
create table toobig(c1 char(1000)) tablespace small;
```

3. Run this query to force an error:

```
insert into toobig
select 'a' from dual connect by level < 2000;
```

The illustration shows steps 1, 2, and 3.

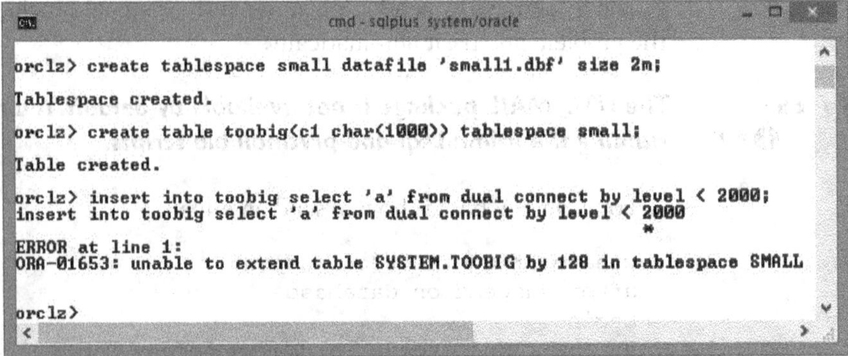

4. Note the error ORA-01653.
5. Alter the session to enable resumable space allocation:

```
alter session enable resumable name 'exercise 16-3';
```

6. Rerun the code from step 3. The session will hang.
7. Start another SQL*Plus session, connected as SYSTEM, and run this query:

```
select session_id,suspend_time,name ,sql_text,error_number
from dba_resumable;
```

Note that the ERROR_NUMBER column is reporting the error that would have been returned to the session, had it not been suspended.

8. From your second SQL*Plus session, fix the problem:

```
alter tablespace small add datafile 'small2.dbf' size 4m;
```

9. Observe that the query from step 6 will now complete successfully, with no intervention required.

10. Tidy up by dropping the tablespace:

```
drop tablespace small including contents and datafiles;
```

CERTIFICATION SUMMARY

This chapter describes the facilities within the database for managing space. Space management can be largely automatic. Space is allocated to segments on demand, in the form of extents. The extent size can be determined by the server, or fixed at a uniform size for all extents in the tablespace. Space within segments is used in the most efficient manner possible, using bitmaps that track the space usage of each block.

Compression can reduce the size of objects considerably. Basic compression works only for direct loads: rows inserted or updated by subsequent INSERT or UPDATE operations will not be compressed. Advanced row compression can maintain compression for all rows in all circumstances.

The Segment Advisor runs every night, as an autotask. It never implements its recommendations, but will detect segments where reorganization would result in a space saving. One method of reorganizing is to use the **SHRINK SPACE** command, which will compact all rows of a table into as few blocks as possible. By default, SHRINK SPACE will continue by releasing the free space from the segment and returning it to the tablespace for reuse elsewhere. The COMPACT keyword prevents this final step: the rows are compacted, but the space is not released. The CASCADE keyword propagates the shrink operation to all dependent objects, such as indexes.

If a statement hits a space error, it will fail, and any work it did will be rolled back. Enabling the resumable space allocation mechanism causes the statement to hang rather than fail, and to continue execution once the problem is fixed.

TWO-MINUTE DRILL

Explain How Oracle Database Server Automatically Manages Space

- ❑ Space is allocated to segments, on demand, in the form of extents. Extent usage is tracked by bitmaps.
- ❑ Space usage within a segment is tracked, in 25-percent bands, by bitmaps.

Save Space by Using Compression

- ❑ Basic compression de-duplicates data when inserted through a direct load.
- ❑ Advanced row compression can maintain the de-duplication compression through conventional DML.

Proactively Monitor and Manage Tablespace Space Usage

- ❑ The Server Alert system is preconfigured to raise alerts when a tablespace is 85-percent full (warning) and 97-percent full (critical).
- ❑ Alerts are not raised for temporary or undo tablespaces.
- ❑ Alert thresholds can be configured at any value for any tablespace individually.

Use the Segment Advisor

- ❑ The Segment Advisor runs every night as an autotask.
- ❑ The advice will be to shrink a table, if so doing would release a significant amount of space.
- ❑ The Segment Advisor considers historical usage as well as the current usage.

Reclaim Wasted Space from Tables and Indexes by Using the Segment Shrink Functionality

- ❑ A table shrink operation relocates rows toward the front of the segment, and (by default) releases free space at the end.
- ❑ A shrink is an online and in-place operation: it requires no additional space while running, and the table is not locked against other DML.

Manage Resumable Space Allocation

- ❑ Resumable space allocation can be enabled for a session or for the instance.
- ❑ If a session hits a space error, it will hang until the problem is fixed—or until a timeout expires.
- ❑ A database trigger can be configured to fire whenever a session is suspended.

SELF TEST

Explain How Oracle Database Server Automatically Manages Space

1. Which statements are correct about extents? (Choose all correct answers.)
   A. An extent is a consecutive grouping of Oracle blocks.
   B. An extent is a random grouping of Oracle blocks.
   C. An extent can be distributed across one or more datafiles.
   D. An extent can contain blocks from one or more segments.
   E. An extent can be assigned to only one segment.
2. Which of these are types of segment? (Choose all correct answers.)
   A. Sequence
   B. Stored procedure
   C. Table
   D. Table partition
   E. View

Save Space by Using Compression

3. Which form of compression uses compression algorithms rather than de-duplication algorithms? (Choose the best answer.)
   A. Compression implemented with COMPRESS BASIC.
   B. Compression implemented with ROW STORE COMPRESS ADVANCED.
   C. Hybrid Columnar Compression.
   D. All Oracle compression methods use compression algorithms.
   E. All Oracle compression methods use de-duplication algorithms.

Proactively Monitor and Manage Tablespace Space Usage

4. You receive an alert warning you that a tablespace is nearly full. What action could you take to prevent this becoming a problem, without any impact for your users? (Choose two correct answers.)
   A. Purge all recycle bin objects in the tablespace.
   B. Shrink the tables in the tablespace.
   C. Shrink the indexes in the tablespace.
   D. Move one or more tables to a different tablespace.
   E. Move one or more indexes to a different tablespace.

5. Which process is responsible for sending the alert when a tablespace usage critical threshold is reached? (Choose the best answer.)
   A. Database Control
   B. The DBMS_SERVER_ALERT package
   C. MMON, the Manageability Monitor process
   D. The server process of the session that detected the problem
   E. DBWn, the Database Writer, when it detects the problem

Use the Segment Advisor

6. When will the Segment Advisor run? (Choose two correct answers.)
   A. Every night, as an autotask
   B. On demand
   C. Automatically when a tablespace crosses a threshold for space usage
   D. Automatically when a session is suspended by the resumable space allocation mechanism

Reclaim Wasted Space from Tables and Indexes by Using the Segment Shrink Functionality

7. Which of the following commands will shrink space in a table or index segment and relocate the HWM?
   A. alter table employees shrink space compact hwm;
   B. alter table employees shrink space hwm;
   C. alter table employees shrink space compact;
   D. alter table employees shrink space;
   E. alter index employees shrink space cascade;
8. What is required before shrinking a table? (Choose all that apply.)
   A. Triggers must be disabled
   B. Indexes must be dropped.
   C. Row movement must be enabled.
   D. Automatic segment space management must be enabled.
   E. LOB columns must be dropped.

Manage Resumable Space Allocation

9. How can you enable the suspension and resumption of statements that hit space errors? (Choose all the correct answers.)
   A. Issue an **ALTER SESSION ENABLE RESUMABLE** command.
   B. Issue an **ALTER SYSTEM ENABLE RESUMABLE** command.
   C. Set the instance parameter RESUMABLE_STATEMENTS.
   D. Set the instance parameter RESUMABLE_TIMEOUT.
   E. Use the DBMS_RESUMABLE.ENABLE procedure.
10. If a statement is suspended because of a space error, what will happen when the problem is fixed? (Choose the best answer.)
   A. After the resumable timeout has expired, the statement will continue executing from the point it had reached.
   B. After the resumable timeout has expired, the statement will start executing from the beginning again.
   C. The statement will start executing from the beginning immediately after the problem is fixed.
   D. The statement will continue executing from the point it had reached immediately after the problem is fixed.

LAB QUESTION

Create a table containing 100,000 rows, all of which are different, and another table with the same number of identical rows. Analyze the tables to determine how many blocks they occupy:

```
create table diff (c1 varchar2(10));
create table ident(c1 varchar2(10));
insert into diff (select dbms_random.string('p',10)
from dual connect by level < 100000);
insert into ident (select '1111111111'
from dual connect by level < 100000);
execute dbms_stats.gather_table_stats(user,'diff')
execute dbms_stats.gather_table_stats(user,'ident')
```

How many blocks do the tables occupy? Enable compression for the tables. What compression ratio do you achieve?

Delete all the rows from one table, and truncate the other table. How many blocks do they occupy now? How would you reduce this?

SELF TEST ANSWERS

Explain How Oracle Database Server Automatically Manages Space

1. ☑ **A** and **E.** One extent is several consecutive Oracle blocks, and one segment consists of one or more extents.
   ☒ **B, C,** and **D** are incorrect. They misinterpret the Oracle storage model.
2. ☑ **C** and **D.** A table can be a type of segment, and so can a table partition.
   ☒ **A, B,** and **E** are incorrect. These exist only as objects defined within the data dictionary. The data dictionary itself is a set of segments.

Save Space by Using Compression

3. ☑ **C.** Hybrid Columnar Compression is true compression.
   ☒ **A, B, D,** and **E** are incorrect. **A** and **B** are incorrect because both BASIC and ADVANCED compression are in fact based on de-duplication. **D** and **E** are incorrect because Oracle can use either technique.

Proactively Monitor and Manage Tablespace Space Usage

4. ☑ **A** and **B.** Both purging dropped objects and shrinking tables will release space immediately, with no downtime.
   ☒ **C, D,** and **E** are incorrect. An index can be shrunk, but this will release space within the index, not return it to the tablespace. Relocating either indexes or tables has implications for the availability of the data.
5. ☑ **C.** The MMON background process raises alerts.
   ☒ **A, B, D,** and **E** are incorrect. **A** is incorrect because although Database Control reports alerts, it does not raise them. **B** is incorrect because the DBMS_SERVER_ALERT API is used to configure the alert system—it does not implement it. **D** and **E** are incorrect because foreground and background processes will encounter problems, not warn of their imminence.

Use the Segment Advisor

6. ☑ **A** and **B.** Unless the autotask has been disabled, it will run in every maintenance window. It can also be invoked on demand.
   ☒ **C** and **D** are incorrect. **C** is incorrect because although a tablespace usage alert will cause the autotask to analyze all objects in the tablespace in the next maintenance window, this does not happen when the alert is raised. **D** is incorrect because the only action triggered by suspension of a session is running the AFTER SUSPEND ON DATABASE trigger.

Reclaim Wasted Space from Tables and Indexes by Using the Segment Shrink Functionality

7. ☑ **D.** SHRINK SPACE both compacts the data and moves the HWM. While the HWM is being moved, DML operations on the table are blocked.
☒ **A, B, C,** and **E** are incorrect. **A, B,** and **E** are syntactically incorrect. **C** is incorrect because COMPACT only performs the shrink operation but does not move the HWM after shrinking the segment.

8. ☑ **C** and **D.** Row movement is necessary, because a shrink will change row IDs. ASSM is needed in order to give the necessary information on how full a block is.
☒ **A, B,** and **E** are incorrect. **A** is incorrect because triggers will not fire for the operation: they will continue to fire for any other DML. **B** is incorrect because indexes are maintained during a shrink. **E** is incorrect because LOB segments will not block a table shrink. They will be shrunk themselves if CASCADE is specified.

Manage Resumable Space Allocation

9. ☑ **A** and **D.** These are the only two methods to enable resumable space allocation.
☒ **B, C,** and **E** are incorrect. **B** and **C** are incorrect because resumable space allocation is enabled at the system level with the instance parameter RESUMABLE_TIMEOUT. **E** is incorrect because although there is a package called DBMS_RESUMABLE, it does not (rather annoyingly) include a procedure to enable resumable space allocation.

10. ☑ **D.** As "suspended" implies, the statement will continue from the point at which it stopped.
☒ **A, B,** and **C** are incorrect. The timeout controls how long the suspension can last before returning an error: it is the period during which the problem can be fixed.

LAB ANSWER

Here is a possible solution:

```
select table_name,blocks from user_tables;
alter table diff compress;
alter table ident compress;
alter table diff move;
alter table ident move;
select table_name,blocks from user_tables;
execute dbms_stats.gather_table_stats(user,'diff')
execute dbms_stats.gather_table_stats(user,'ident')
select table_name,blocks from user_tables;
```

```
delete from diff;
truncate table ident;
execute dbms_stats.gather_table_stats(user,'diff')
execute dbms_stats.gather_table_stats(user,'ident')
select table_name,blocks from user_tables;
alter table diff enable row movement;
alter table diff nocompress;
alter table diff move;
alter table diff shrink space;
execute dbms_stats.gather_table_stats(user,'diff')
select table_name,blocks from user_tables;
```

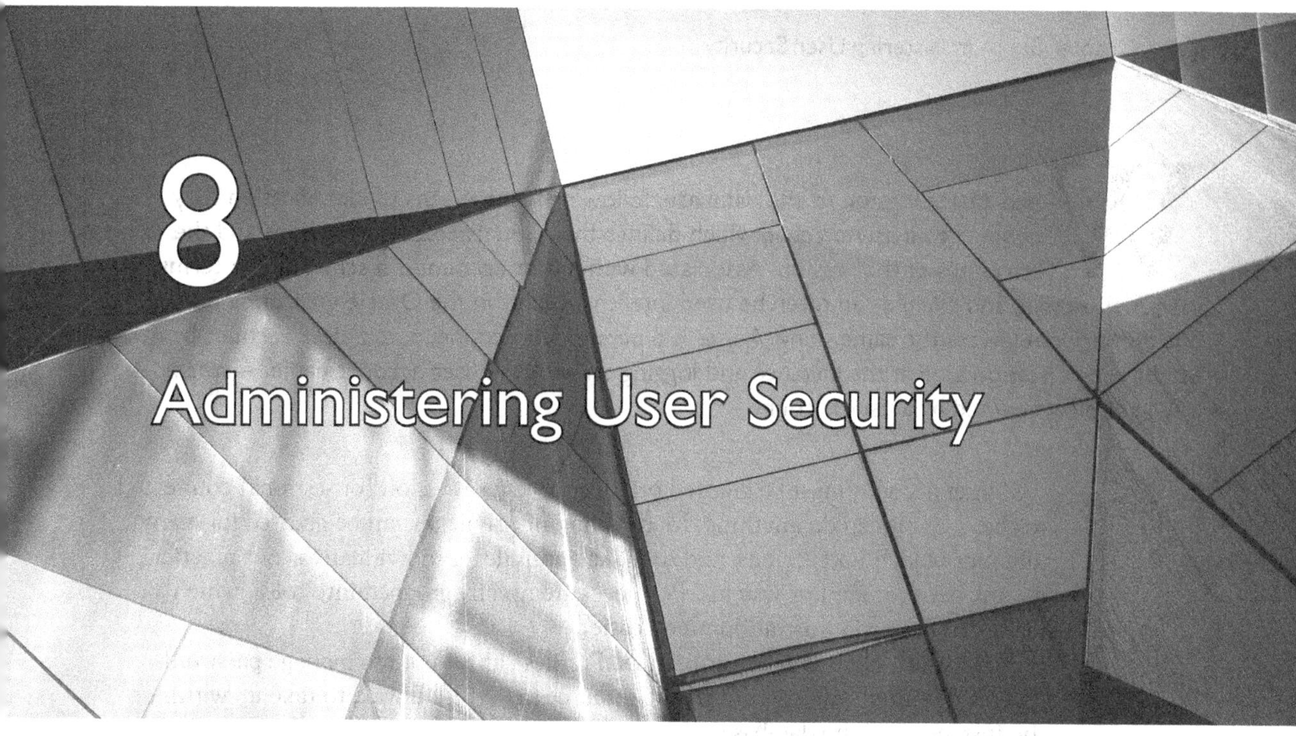

8 Administering User Security

CERTIFICATION OBJECTIVES

8.01	Create and Manage Database User Accounts
8.02	Grant and Revoke Privileges
8.03	Create and Manage Roles
8.04	Create and Manage Profiles
✓	Two-Minute Drill
Q&A	Self Test

When a user logs on to the database, following some means of identification they connect to a *user account*, which defines their initial access permissions and the attributes of the session. Associated with a user account is a schema. The terms *user*, *user account*, and *schema* can often be used interchangeably in the Oracle environment, but they are not always the same thing. A *user* is a person who connects to a user account by establishing a session against the instance and logging on with the user account name. A *schema* is a set of objects owned by a user account.

A user account must be granted privileges before a session (or sessions) connected to the account can do anything. Many different privileges can be granted for many different objects and actions, and to manage privileges individually is not practical for any but the simplest systems. Privileges are usually grouped into roles, which make privilege administration much easier.

Finally, this chapter looks at profiles. Profiles can be used to manage passwords and (to a limited extent) control the resources a user is allowed to take up within the instance and the database.

CERTIFICATION OBJECTIVE 8.01

Create and Manage Database User Accounts

To establish a session against an instance and a database, a user must connect to a user account. The account must be specified by name and authenticated by some means. The way the account was created will set up a range of attributes for the session, some of which can be changed later while the session is in progress.

User Account Attributes

A user account has a number of attributes defined at account creation time. These will be applied to sessions that connect to the account, although some can be modified by the session or the DBA while the session is running. These attributes are as follows:

- Username
- Authentication method

- Default tablespace
- Tablespace quotas
- Temporary tablespace
- User profile
- Account status

All of these should be specified when creating the user, although only username and authentication methods are mandatory; the others have defaults.

Username

The username must be unique in the database and must conform to certain rules. A username must begin with a letter, must be no more than 30 characters, and can consist of only letters, digits, and the dollar sign ($) and underscore (_) characters. A username may not be a reserved word. The letters are case sensitive but will be automatically converted to uppercase. All these rules (with the exception of the length) can be broken if the username is specified within double quotes, as shown on Figure 8-1.

In the first example in the figure, the username JOHN is created. This was entered in lowercase, but will have been converted to uppercase, as can be seen in the first query. The second example uses double quotes to create the user with

FIGURE 8-1

How to create users with nonstandard names

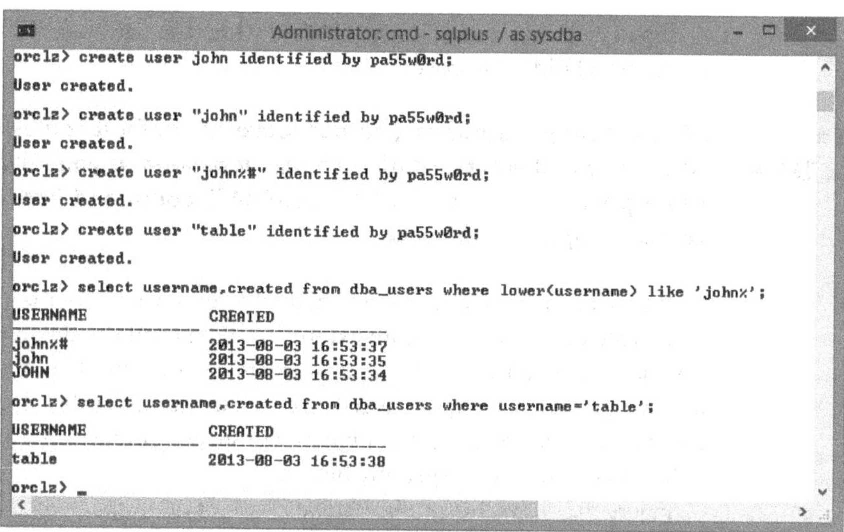

a name in lowercase. The third and fourth examples use double quotes to bypass the rules on characters and reserved words; both of these would fail without the double quotes. If a username includes lowercase letters or illegal characters or is a reserved word, then double quotes must always be used to connect to the account subsequently.

on the job

It is possible to use nonstandard usernames, but this may cause dreadful confusion. Some applications rely on the case conversion; others always use double quotes. It may be considered good practice always to use uppercase and only the standard characters; this means that double quotes can be used or not.

Default Tablespace and Quotas

Every user account has a *default tablespace*, which is the tablespace where any schema objects (such as tables or indexes) created by the user will reside. It is possible for a user to own objects in any tablespace on which he has been given a quota, but unless another tablespace is specified when creating the object, it will go into the user's default tablespace.

A database-wide default tablespace will be applied to all user accounts if a default tablespace is not specified when creating the user. The default can be set when creating the database and then changed later with

```
ALTER DATABASE DEFAULT TABLESPACE tablespace_name;
```

If a default tablespace is not specified when the database is created, it will be set to the SYSTEM tablespace.

on the job

After creating a database, do not leave the default tablespace as SYSTEM; this is very bad practice. Either change it as soon as you have created another tablespace, or after the* CREATE DATABASE *command has in fact let you create a default tablespace.

A *quota* is the amount of space in a tablespace that a user is allowed to occupy. He can create objects and allocate extents to them until the quota is reached. If he has no quota on a tablespace, he cannot create any objects at all. Quotas can be changed at any time. If a user's quota is reduced below the size of the objects he already owns (or even reduced to zero), the objects will survive and will still be usable, but they will not be permitted to get any bigger.

Figure 8-2 shows how to investigate and set quotas.

FIGURE 8-2

Managing user quotas

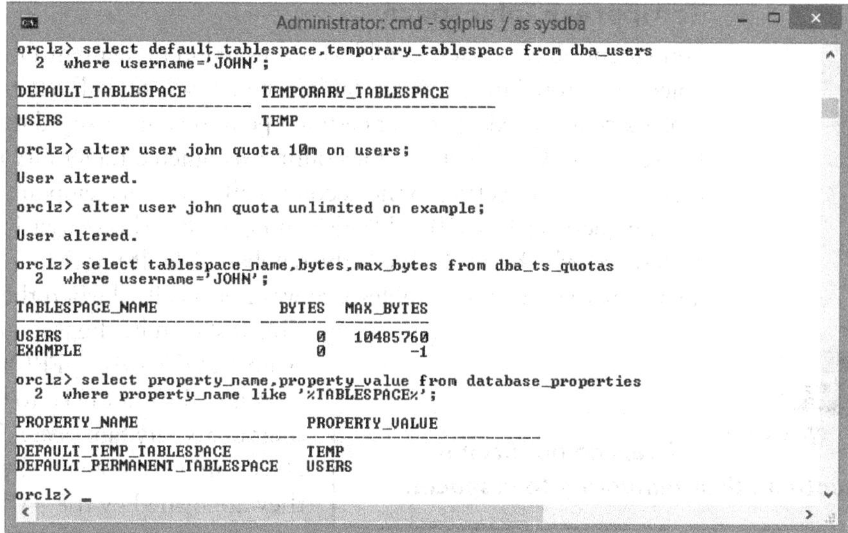
```
orclz> select default_tablespace,temporary_tablespace from dba_users
  2  where username='JOHN';

DEFAULT_TABLESPACE             TEMPORARY_TABLESPACE
------------------------------ ------------------------------
USERS                          TEMP

orclz> alter user john quota 10m on users;

User altered.

orclz> alter user john quota unlimited on example;

User altered.

orclz> select tablespace_name,bytes,max_bytes from dba_ts_quotas
  2  where username='JOHN';

TABLESPACE_NAME                     BYTES  MAX_BYTES
------------------------------ ---------- ----------
USERS                                   0   10485760
EXAMPLE                                 0         -1

orclz> select property_name,property_value from database_properties
  2  where property_name like '%TABLESPACE%';

PROPERTY_NAME                  PROPERTY_VALUE
------------------------------ ------------------------------
DEFAULT_TEMP_TABLESPACE        TEMP
DEFAULT_PERMANENT_TABLESPACE   USERS

orclz> _
```

The first query in the figure is against DBA_USERS and determines the default and temporary tablespaces for the user JOHN, created in Figure 8-1. DBA_USERS has one row for every user account in the database. User JOHN has picked up the database defaults for the default and temporary tablespaces, which are shown in the last query against DATABASE_PROPERTIES.

on the job

Most users will not need any quotas because they will never create objects. They will only have permissions against objects owned by other schemas. The few object-owning schemas will probably have QUOTA UNLIMITED on the tablespaces where their objects reside.

The two **ALTER USER** commands in Figure 8-2 give JOHN the capability to take up to 10MB of space in the USERS tablespace, and an unlimited amount of space in the EXAMPLE tablespace. The query against DBA_TS_QUOTAS confirms this; the number "–1" is how "unlimited" is represented. At the time the query was run, JOHN had not created any objects, so the figures for BYTES are zeros, indicating that he is not currently using any space in either tablespace.

exam watch

Before you can create a table, you must have both permission to execute CREATE TABLE and a quota on a tablespace in which to create it.

Temporary Tablespace

Permanent objects (such as tables) are stored in permanent tablespaces; temporary objects are stored in temporary tablespaces. A session will need space in a temporary tablespace if it needs space for certain operations that exceed the space available in the session's PGA. Every user account is assigned a temporary tablespace, and all user sessions connecting to the account will share this temporary tablespace.

The query against DBA_USERS in Figure 8-2 shows user JOHN's temporary tablespace, which in this case is the database default temporary tablespace because an alternative temporary tablespace was not specified when the user was created. This is shown by the last query in Figure 8-2, against DATABASE_PROPERTIES.

exam watch

Users do not need a quota on their temporary tablespaces.

A user does not need to be granted a quota on their temporary tablespace. This is because the objects in it are not actually owned by the user; they are owned by the SYS user, who has an unlimited quota on all tablespaces.

To change a user's temporary tablespace (which will affect all future sessions that connect to the account), use an **ALTER USER** command:

```
ALTER USER username TEMPORARY TABLESPACE tablespace_name;
```

If many users are logging on to the same user account, they will share use of one temporary tablespace. This can be a performance bottleneck, which may be avoided by using temporary tablespace groups.

Account Status

Every user account has a certain status, as listed in the ACCOUNT_STATUS column of DBA_USERS. There are five possibilities:

- **OPEN** The account is available for use.
- **LOCKED** This indicates that the DBA deliberately locked the account. No user can connect to a locked account.
- **EXPIRED** This indicates that the lifetime has expired. Passwords can have a limited lifetime. No user can connect to an EXPIRED account until the password is reset.

- **EXPIRED (GRACE)** This indicates that the *grace period* is in effect. A password need not expire immediately when its lifetime ends; it may be configured with a grace period during which users connecting to the account have the opportunity to change the password.
- **LOCKED (TIMED)** This indicates that the account is locked because of failed login attempts. An account can be configured to lock automatically for a period after an incorrect password is presented a certain number of times.

To lock and unlock an account, use these commands:

```
ALTER USER username ACCOUNT LOCK ;
ALTER USER username ACCOUNT UNLOCK ;
```

To force a user to change their password, use this command:

```
ALTER USER username PASSWORD EXPIRE;
```

This will immediately start the grace period, forcing the user to change their password at their next login attempt. There is no such command as "alter…unexpire." The only way to make the account fully functional again is to reset the password.

Authentication Methods

A user account must have an authentication method: some means whereby the database can determine if the user attempting to create a session connecting to the account is allowed to do so. The simplest technique is by presenting a password that will be matched against a password stored within the database, but there are alternatives. These are the possibilities:

- Operating system authentication
- Password file authentication
- Password authentication
- External authentication
- Global authentication

The first two techniques are used only for administrators; the last requires an LDAP directory server. The LDAP directory server is the Oracle Internet Directory, shipped as a part of the Oracle Fusion Middleware Suite.

Operating System and Password File Authentication

To enable operating system and password file authentication (the two go together) for an account, you must grant the user an administration role. There are six of these:

Admin Role	Group Name	Capabilities
SYSDBA	OSDBA	Startup and shutdown; all system privileges with admin. Total power.
SYSOPER	OSOPER	Startup and shutdown, nothing else. No privileges on users or data.
SYSASM	OSASM	Not relevant to an RDBMS instance. ASM only.
SYSBACKUP	OSBACKUPDBA	Startup and shutdown; create anything; no privileges on data.
SYSDG	OSDGDB	Startup and shutdown; privileges necessary to manage Data Guard.
SYSKM	OSKMDBA	Privileges necessary to manage data security and encryption.

Grant the roles as follows:

```
GRANT [SYSDBA | SYSOPER | SYSASM | SYSBACKUP | SYSDG | SYSKM] TO username ;
```

Granting any (or all) of these privileges will copy the user's password from the data dictionary into the external password file, where it can be read by the instance even if the database is not open. Following database creation, the only user with these privileges is SYS. It also allows the instance to authenticate users by checking whether the operating system user attempting the connection is a member of the operating system group mapped to the Oracle group name. On Linux, the operating system groups must be specified when installing the Oracle Home. On Windows, there is no choice. The groups are created implicitly with these names:

Oracle Group	Windows Group
OSDBA	ORA_DBA
OSOPER	ORA_OPER
OSASM	ORA_ASM
OSBACKUPDBA	ORA_%HOMENAME%_SYSBACKUP
OSDGDB	ORA_%HOMENAME%_SYSDG
OSKMDBA	ORA_%HOMENAME%_SYSDG

To use password file authentication, the user can connect with this syntax with SQL*Plus:

```
CONNECT username / password [@db_alias] AS [ SYSOPER | SYSDBA ] ;
```

Note that password file authentication can be used for a connection to a remote database over Oracle Net. This is a logical impossibility with operating system authentication because when using a remote database, one never logs on to the remote operating system.

To use operating system authentication, the user can connect with this syntax with SQL*Plus:

```
CONNECT / AS [ SYSOPER | SYSDBA ] ;
```

The operating system password is not stored by Oracle and therefore there are no issues with changing passwords.

The equivalent of these syntaxes is also available when connecting with Database Express, by selecting the AS SYSDBA check box in the Database Express login window. To determine to whom the SYSDBA and SYSOPER privileges have been granted, query the view V$PWFILE_USERS. Connection with operating system or password file authentication is always possible, no matter what state the instance and database are in, and is necessary to issue **STARTUP** and **SHUTDOWN** commands.

All user sessions must be authenticated. There is no such thing as an "anonymous" login, and some authentication method must be used. There is, however, a user ANONYMOUS: this account is used by APEX applications.

Password Authentication

The syntax for a connection with password authentication using SQL*Plus is

```
CONNECT username / password [@db_alias];
```

When the user connects with password authentication, the instance will validate the password given against the password hash stored with the user account in the data dictionary. For this to work, the database must be open; it is logically impossible to issue **STARTUP** and **SHUTDOWN** commands when connected with password authentication. The user SYS is not permitted to connect with password authentication; only password file, operating system, and LDAP authentication are possible for SYS.

Usernames are case sensitive but are automatically converted to uppercase unless specified within double quotes. Passwords are case sensitive and there is no automatic case conversion. It is not necessary to use double quotes; the password will always be read exactly as entered.

Any user can change their user account password at any time, or a highly privileged user (such as SYSTEM) can change any user account password. The syntax (whether you are changing your own password or another one) is

```
ALTER USER username IDENTIFIED BY password ;
```

External Authentication

If a user account is created with external authentication, Oracle will delegate the authentication to an external service; it will not prompt for a password. If the Advanced Security Option has been licensed, then the external service can be a number of third-party services, such as a Kerberos server or a RADIUS server. When a user attempts to connect to the user account, rather than authenticating the user itself, the database instance will accept (or reject) the authentication according to whether the external authentication service has authenticated the user. For example, if Kerberos is being used, the database will check that the user does have a valid Kerberos token.

Without the Advanced Security Option, the only form of external authentication that can be used is operating system authentication. This is a requirement for SYSDBA and SYSOPER accounts (as already discussed) but can also be used for normal users. The technique is to create an Oracle user account with the same name as the operating system user account but prefixed with a string specified by the instance parameter OS_AUTHENT_PREFIX. This parameter defaults to the string OPS$. To check its value, use a query such as this:

```
select value from v$parameter where name='os_authent_prefix';
```

On Linux or Unix, external operating system authentication is very simple. Assuming that the OS_AUTHENT_PREFIX is set to the default and that there is an operating system user called jwatson, if you create an oracle user and grant him the CREATE SESSION privilege, he will be able to log in with no password and will be connected to the database user account ops$jwatson:

```
create user ops$jwatson identified externally;
grant create session to ops$jwatson;
sqlplus /
```

Under Windows, when Oracle queries the operating system to find the identity of the user, Windows will usually (depending on the details of Windows security configuration) return the username prefixed with the Windows domain. Assuming that the Windows logon ID is John Watson (including a space), that the Windows domain is JWACER (which happens to be the machine name), and that the OS_AUTHENT_PREFIX is set to the default, the command will be as follows:

```
create user "OPS$JWACER\JOHN WATSON" identified externally;
```

Note that the username must be in uppercase, and because of the illegal characters (a backslash and a space) it must be enclosed in double quotes.

on the Job

Using external authentication can be very useful, but only if the users actually log on to the machine hosting the database. Users will rarely do this, so the technique is more likely to be of value for accounts used for running maintenance or batch jobs.

Creating Accounts

The **CREATE USER** command has only two required arguments: a username and a method of authentication. Optionally, it can accept a clause to specify a default tablespace and a temporary tablespace, one or more quota clauses, a named profile, and commands to lock the account and expire the password. This is a typical example (with line numbers added):

```
1     create user scott identified by tiger
2     default tablespace users temporary tablespace temp
3     quota 100m on users, quota unlimited on example
4     profile developer_profile
5     password expire
6     account unlock;
```

Only the first line is required; there are defaults for everything else. Break down the command, line by line:

1. Provide the username and a password for password authentication.
2. Provide the default and temporary tablespaces.
3. Set up quotas on the default and another tablespace.
4. Nominate a profile for password and resource management.

5. Force the user to change his password immediately.
6. Make the account available for use (which would have been the default).

Every attribute of an account can be adjusted later with **ALTER USER** commands, with the exception of the name. This is how to change the attributes:

```
alter user scott identified by lion;
alter user scott default tablespace hr_data temporary tablespace hr_temp;
alter user scott quota unlimited on hr_data, quota 0 on users;
alter user scott profile prod_profile;
alter user scott password expire;
alter user scott account lock;
```

Having created a user account, it may be necessary to drop it:

```
drop user scott;
```

This command will succeed only if the user does not own any objects—if the schema is empty. If you do not want to identify all the objects owned and drop them first, they can be dropped with the user by specifying CASCADE:

```
drop user scott cascade;
```

EXERCISE 8-1

Create Users

In this exercise, you will create some users to be used for the remaining exercises in this chapter. It is assumed that there is a permanent tablespace called EXAMPLE and a temporary tablespace called TEMP. If these don't exist, either create them or use any other suitable tablespaces. Here are the steps to follow:

1. Connect to your database with SQL*Plus as a highly privileged user, such as SYSTEM or SYS.
2. Create three users:

```
create user alois identified by alois
default tablespace example password expire;
create user afra identified by oracle
default tablespace example quota unlimited on example;
create user anja identified by oracle;
```

3. Confirm that the users have been created with Database Express. From the database home page, the navigation path is the Security tab | Users link. The users should look something like those shown in Figure 8-3.
4. From SQL*Plus, attempt to connect as user ALOIS:

```
connect alois/alois
```

5. When prompted, select a new password (such as "oracle"). This won't get you anywhere because ALOIS does not have the CREATE SESSION privilege.
6. Refresh the Database Express window and note that the status of the ALOIS account is no longer EXPIRED (indicated with the clock symbol) but rather OPEN (indicated with a tick) because his password has been changed.

FIGURE 8-3

Users displayed in Database Express

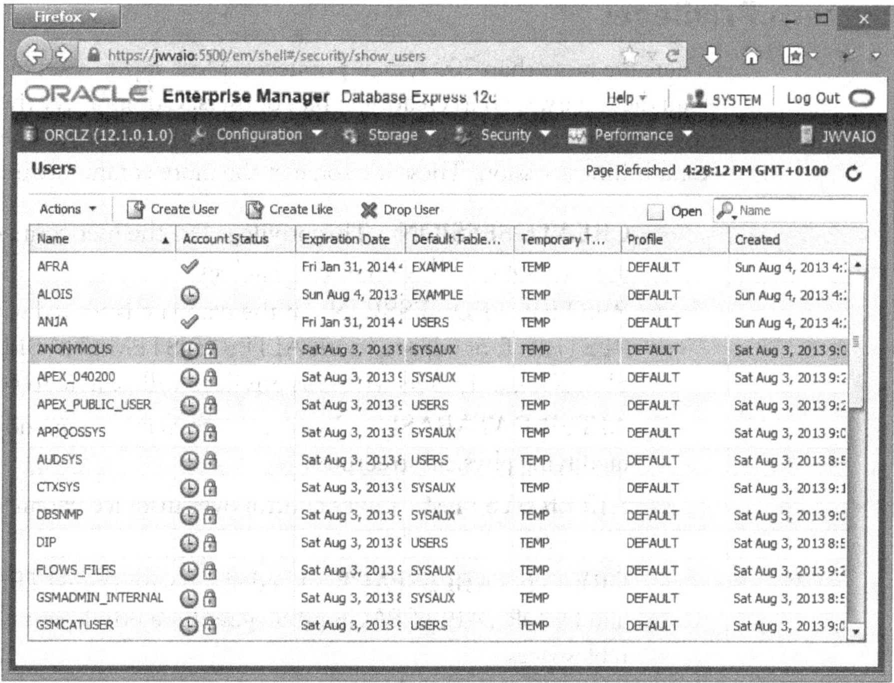

CERTIFICATION OBJECTIVE 8.02

Grant and Revoke Privileges

By default, no one can do anything in an Oracle database. A user cannot even connect without being granted a privilege. And once this has been done, they still can't do anything useful (or dangerous) without being given more privileges. Privileges are assigned to user accounts with a **GRANT** command and withdrawn with a **REVOKE**. Additional syntax can give a user the ability to grant any privileges they have to other users. By default, only the DBAs (SYS and SYSTEM) have the right to grant any but the most limited privileges.

Privileges come in two groups: system privileges, which (generally speaking) let users perform actions that affect the data dictionary, and object privileges, which let users perform actions that affect data.

System Privileges

There are more than 200 system privileges. Most apply to actions that affect the data dictionary, such as creating tables or users. Others affect the database or the instance, such as creating tablespaces, adjusting instance parameter values, and establishing a session. These are some of the more commonly used privileges:

- **CREATE SESSION** This privilege lets the user connect. Without it, the user cannot even log on to the database.
- **RESTRICTED SESSION** If the database is started with STARTUP RESTRICT, or adjusted with ALTER SYSTEM ENABLE RESTRICTED SESSION, only users with this privilege will be able to connect.
- **ALTER DATABASE** Gives access to many commands necessary for modifying physical structures.
- **ALTER SYSTEM** Gives control over instance parameters and memory structures.
- **CREATE TABLESPACE** Used along with the ALTER TABLESPACE and DROP TABLESPACE privileges; these privileges will let a user manage tablespaces.
- **CREATE TABLE** Lets the grantee create tables in his own schema; includes the ability to alter and drop them, to run **SELECT** and **DML** commands on them, and to create, alter, or drop indexes on them.

- **GRANT ANY OBJECT PRIVILEGE** Lets the grantee grant object permissions on all objects, including those he does not own, to others (but not to himself).
- **CREATE ANY TABLE** The grantee can create tables that belong to other users.
- **DROP ANY TABLE** The grantee can drop tables belonging to any other users.
- **INSERT ANY TABLE, UPDATE ANY TABLE, DELETE ANY TABLE** The grantee can execute these DML commands against tables owned by all other users.
- **SELECT ANY TABLE** The grantee can SELECT from any table in the database, with one provision: tables owned by SYS, including the data dictionary tables, are not visible.

The syntax for granting system privileges is

```
GRANT privilege [, privilege...] TO username;
```

After creating a user account, a command such as this will grant the system privileges commonly assigned to users who will be involved in developing applications:

```
grant create session, alter session,
create table, create view, create synonym, create cluster,
create database link, create sequence,
create trigger, create type, create procedure, create operator
to username;
```

These privileges let the user connect and configure his session and then create objects to store data and PL/SQL objects. These objects can only exist in their own schema; they will have no privileges against any other schema. The object creation will also be limited by the quota(s) they may (or may not) have been assigned on various tablespaces.

A variation in the syntax lets the grantee pass their privilege on to a third party. This is an example:

```
connect system/oracle;
grant create table to scott with admin option;
connect scott/tiger;
grant create table to jon;
```

watch ***Revocation of a system privilege will not cascade (unlike revocation of an object privilege).***

This gives SCOTT the ability to create tables in his own schema, and also to issue the **GRANT CREATE TABLE TO** command himself.

If a privilege is revoked from a user, any actions they performed using that privilege (such as creating tables) remain intact. Also, if the user has been granted and has used the ADMIN OPTION, any users to whom they passed on the privilege will retain it. There is no record kept of the grantor of a system privilege, so it is not possible for a REVOKE to cascade. Figure 8-4 illustrates this.

The ANY privileges give permissions against all relevant objects in the database. Thus,

```
grant select any table to scott;
```

will let SCOTT query every table in every schema in the database. It is often considered bad practice to grant the ANY privileges to any user other than the system administration staff.

on the job ***In fact, ANY is not as dangerous now as it was in earlier releases. It no longer includes tables in the SYS schema, so the data dictionary is still protected. However, ANY should still be used with extreme caution because it removes all protection from user tables.***

FIGURE 8-4

GRANT and REVOKE from SQL*Plus

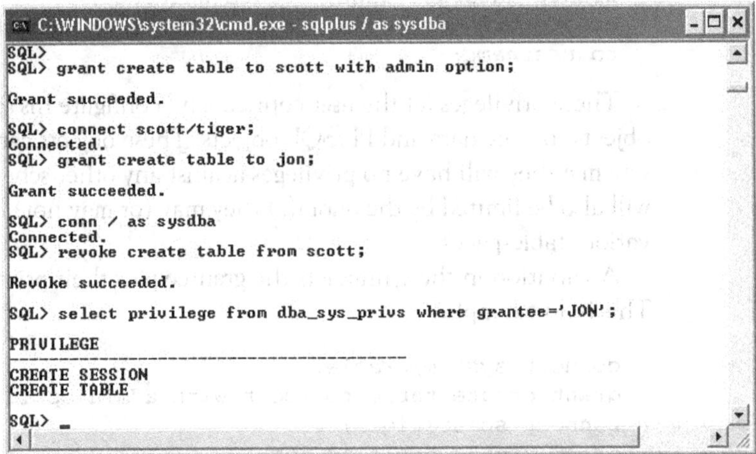

Object Privileges

Object privileges give the ability to perform **SELECT**, **INSERT**, **UPDATE**, and **DELETE** commands against tables and related objects as well as to execute PL/SQL objects. These privileges do not exist for objects in the users' own schemas; if a user has the system privilege CREATE TABLE, they can perform SELECT and DML operations against the tables they create with no further need for permissions.

The ANY privileges, which grant permissions against objects in every user account in the database, are not object privileges—they are system privileges.

The object privileges apply to different types of object:

Privilege	Granted On
SELECT	Tables, views, sequences, synonyms
INSERT	Tables, views, synonyms
UPDATE	Tables, views, synonyms
DELETE	Tables, views, synonyms
ALTER	Tables, sequences
EXECUTE	Procedures, functions, packages, synonyms

The syntax is

```
GRANT privilege ON schema.object TO username [WITH GRANT OPTION];
```

Here is an example:

```
grant select on hr.regions to scott;
```

Variations include the use of ALL, which will apply all the permissions relevant to the type of object, and nominating particular columns of views or tables:

```
grant select on hr.employees to scott;
grant update (salary) on hr.employees to scott;
grant all on hr.regions to scott;
```

This code will let SCOTT query all columns of HR's EMPLOYEES table but only write to one nominated column, SALARY. Then SCOTT is given all the object privileges (SELECT and DML) on HR's REGIONS table.

on the job

Granting privileges at the column level is often said to be bad practice because of the massive workload involved. If it is necessary to restrict people's access to certain columns, creating a view that shows only those columns will often be a better alternative.

watch

Revocation of an object privilege will cascade (unlike revocation of a system privilege).

Using WITH GRANT OPTION (or with Database Express, navigate to Security | Users | Privileges and Roles | Edit) lets a user pass their object privilege on to a third party. Oracle retains a record of who granted object privileges to whom; this allows a REVOKE of an object to cascade to all those in the chain. Consider this sequence of commands:

```
connect hr/hr;
grant select on employees to scott with grant option;
connect scott/tiger;
grant select on hr.employees to jon with grant option;
conn jon/jon;
grant select on hr.employees to sue;
connect hr/hr;
revoke select on employees from scott;
```

At the conclusion of these commands, neither SCOTT nor JON nor SUE has the SELECT privilege against HR.EMPLOYEES.

EXERCISE 8-2

Grant Direct Privileges

In this exercise, you will grant some privileges to the users created in Exercise 8-1 and prove that they work. Follow these steps:

1. Connect to your database as user SYSTEM with SQL*Plus and then grant CREATE SESSION to user ALOIS:

```
grant create session to alois;
```

2. Open another SQL*Plus session and connect as ALOIS. This time, the login will succeed:

```
connect alois/oracle
```

3. As ALOIS, attempt to create a table:

```
create table t1 (c1 date);
```

This will fail with the message "ORA-01031: insufficient privileges."

4. In the SYSTEM session, grant ALOIS the CREATE TABLE privilege:

```
grant create table to alois;
```

5. In the ALOIS session, try again:

```
create table t1 (c1 date) segment creation immediate;
```

This will fail with the message "ORA-01950: no privileges on tablespace 'EXAMPLE'."

6. In the SYSTEM session, give ALOIS a quota on the EXAMPLE tablespace:

```
alter user alois quota 1m on example;
```

7. In the ALOIS session, try again. This time, the creation will succeed.
8. As ALOIS, grant object privileges on the new table:

```
grant all on t1 to afra;
grant select on t1 to anja;
```

9. To retrieve information regarding these grants, as SYSTEM, run these queries:

```
select grantee,privilege,grantor,grantable from dba_tab_privs
where owner='ALOIS' and table_name='T1';
select * from dba_sys_privs where grantee='ALOIS';
```

10. Revoke the privileges granted to AFRA and ANJA:

```
revoke all on alois.t1 from afra;
revoke all on alois.t1 from anja;
```

11. Confirm the revocations by rerunning the first query from step 9.

CERTIFICATION OBJECTIVE 8.03

Create and Manage Roles

Managing security with directly granted privileges works but has two problems. First, it can be a huge workload: an application with thousands of tables and users could need millions of grants. Second, if a privilege has been granted to a user, that user has it in all circumstances: it is not possible to make a privilege active only in certain circumstances. Both these problems are solved by using roles. A *role* is a bundle of system and/or object privileges that can be granted and revoked as a unit, and having been granted can be temporarily activated or deactivated within a session.

Creating and Granting Roles

Roles are not schema objects: they aren't owned by anyone and therefore cannot be prefixed with a username. However, they do share the same namespace as users: it is not possible to create a role with the same name as an already-existing user, or a user with the same name as an already-existing role.

Create a role with the **CREATE ROLE** command:

```
CREATE ROLE rolename;
```

Then grant privileges to the role with the usual syntax, including WITH ADMIN or WITH GRANT OPTION, as desired.

For example, assume that the HR schema is being used as a repository for data to be used by three groups of staff: managerial staff have full access, senior clerical staff have limited access, and junior clerical staff have very restricted access. First, create a role that might be suitable for the junior clerks; all they can do is answer questions by running queries:

```
create role hr_junior;
grant create session to hr_junior;
grant select on hr.regions to hr_junior;
grant select on hr.locations to hr_junior;
grant select on hr.countries to hr_junior;
grant select on hr.departments to hr_junior;
grant select on hr.job_history to hr_junior;
grant select on hr.jobs to hr_junior;
grant select on hr.employees to hr_junior;
```

Anyone granted this role will be able to log on to the database and run SELECT statements against the HR tables. Next, create a role for the senior clerks, who can also write data to the EMPLOYEES and JOB_HISTORY tables:

```
create role hr_senior;
grant hr_junior to hr_senior with admin option;
grant insert, update, delete on hr.employees to hr_senior;
grant insert, update, delete on hr.job_history to hr_senior;
```

This role is first granted the HR_JUNIOR role (there is no problem granting one role to another) with the syntax that will let the senior users assign the junior role to others. Then it is granted DML privileges on just two tables. Now, create the managers' role, which can update all the other tables:

```
create role hr_manager;
grant hr_senior to hr_manager with admin option;
grant all on hr.regions to hr_manager;
grant all on hr.locations to hr_manager;
grant all on hr.countries to hr_manager;
grant all on hr.departments to hr_manager;
grant all on hr.job_history to hr_manager;
grant all on hr.jobs to hr_manager;
grant all on hr.employees to hr_manager;
```

This third role is given the HR_SENIOR role with the ability to pass it on, and then gets full control over the contents of all the tables. But note that the only system privilege this role has is CREATE_SESSION, acquired through HR_SENIOR, which acquired it through HR_JUNIOR. Not even this role can create or drop tables; that must be done by the HR user, or an administrator with CREATE ANY TABLE and DROP ANY TABLE system privileges.

Note the syntax WITH ADMIN OPTION, which is the same as that for granting system privileges. As with system privileges, revocation of a role will not cascade; there is no record kept of who has granted a role to whom.

Finally, grant the roles to the relevant staff. If SCOTT is a manager, SUE is a senior clerk, and JON and ROOP are junior clerks, the flow would be as shown in Figure 8-5.

Predefined Roles

There are dozens of predefined roles in an Oracle database. Here are some that every DBA should be aware of:

- **CONNECT** This role exists only for backward compatibility. In previous releases, it had the system privileges necessary to create data-storing objects, such as tables; with the current release, it only has CREATE SESSION.

FIGURE 8-5

Granting roles with SQL*Plus

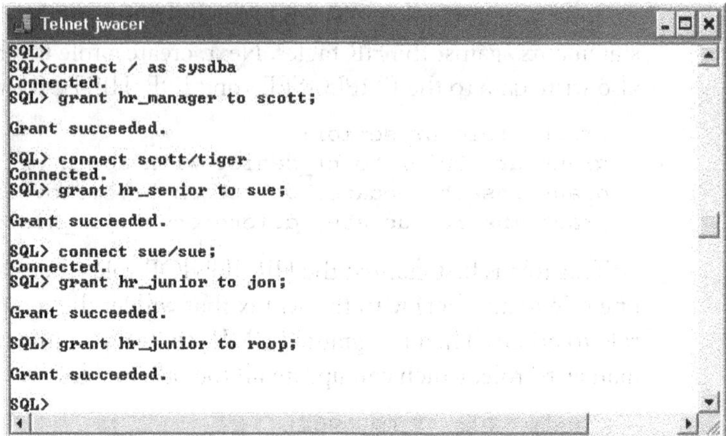
Telnet jwacer
SQL>
SQL>connect / as sysdba
Connected.
SQL> grant hr_manager to scott;
Grant succeeded.
SQL> connect scott/tiger
Connected.
SQL> grant hr_senior to sue;
Grant succeeded.
SQL> connect sue/sue;
Connected.
SQL> grant hr_junior to jon;
Grant succeeded.
SQL> grant hr_junior to roop;
Grant succeeded.
SQL>

- **RESOURCE** Also for backward compatibility, this role can create both data objects (such as tables) and procedural objects (such as PL/SQL procedures).
- **DBA** Has most of the system privileges as well as several object privileges and roles. Any user granted DBA can manage virtually all aspects of the database, except for startup and shutdown.
- **SELECT_CATALOG_ROLE** Has thousands of object privileges against data dictionary objects, but no system privileges or privileges against user data. Useful for junior administration staff who must monitor and report on the database but not be able to see user data.
- **SCHEDULER_ADMIN** Has the system privileges necessary for managing the Scheduler job-scheduling service.

Also, the predefined role PUBLIC is always granted to every database user account. It follows that if a privilege is granted to PUBLIC, it will be available to all users. Therefore, following the command

```
grant select on hr.regions to public;
```

all users will be able to query the HR.REGIONS table.

on the Job

The PUBLIC role is treated differently from any other role. It does not, for example, appear in the view DBA_ROLES. This is because the source code for DBA_ROLES, which can be seen in the cdsec.sql script called by the catalog .sql script, specifically excludes it.

Enabling Roles

By default, if a user has been granted a role, the role will be enabled. This means that the moment a session is established connecting to the user account, all the privileges (and other roles) granted to the role will be active. This behavior can be modified by making the role nondefault. Following the example given in the preceding section, this query shows what roles have been granted to JON:

```
SQL> select * from dba_role_privs where grantee='JON';
GRANTEE                       GRANTED_ROLE    ADM DEF
----------------------------- --------------- --- ---
JON                           HR_JUNIOR       NO  YES
```

JON has been granted HR_JUNIOR. He does not have administration on the role (so he cannot pass it on to anyone else), but it is a default role—he will have this role whenever he connects. This situation may well not be what you want. For example, JON has to be able to see the HR tables (it's his job) but that doesn't mean you want him to be able to dial in from home, at midnight, and hack into the tables with SQL*Plus. You want to arrange things such that he can see the tables only when he is at a terminal in the personnel office, running the HR application during working hours.

Here is how to change the default behavior:

```
alter user jon default role none;
```

Now when JON logs on, he will not have any roles enabled. Unfortunately, this means he can't log on at all—because it is only HR_JUNIOR that gives him the CREATE SESSION system privilege. This is easily fixed:

```
SQL> grant connect to jon;
Grant succeeded.
SQL> alter user jon default role connect;
User altered.
SQL> select * from dba_role_privs where grantee='JON';
GRANTEE                       GRANTED_ROLE    ADM DEF
----------------------------- --------------- --- ---
JON                           HR_JUNIOR       NO  NO
JON                           CONNECT         NO  YES
```

Now when JON connects, only his CONNECT role is enabled—and the current version of CONNECT is not dangerous at all. Within the application, software commands can be embedded to enable the HR_JUNIOR role. The basic command to enable a role within a session is

```
SET ROLE rolename;
```

which can be issued by the user at any time. So no security yet. But if the role is created with the syntax

```
CREATE ROLE rolename IDENTIFIED USING procedure_name;
```

then the role can only be enabled by running the PL/SQL procedure nominated by *procedure_name*. This procedure can make any number of checks: that the user is working on a particular TCP/IP subnet, that they are running a particular user process (probably not SQL*Plus), that the time is in a certain range, and so on. Embedding calls to the enabling procedures at appropriate points in an application can switch roles on and off, as required, while leaving them disabled at all times when a connection is made with an ad hoc SQL tool such as SQL*Plus.

Privilege Analysis

It is sometimes difficult to identify what privileges a user has and what privileges he actually uses, particularly when roles are involved. For this reason, Oracle provides the Privilege Analysis mechanism. The flow is as follows:

- Define the scope of what should be analyzed: privilege usage throughout the entire database; privileges used that were accessed through certain roles; privileges used by particular applications.
- Start monitoring activity; allow users to work for a period; stop monitoring activity.
- Generate reports on what privileges were used, and what granted privileges were not used, during the analysis period.

The critical procedures are

- dbms_privilege_capture.create_capture
- dbms_privilege_capture.enable_capture
- dbms_privilege_capture.disable_capture
- dbms_privilege_capture.generate_result

and the critical views are

- dba_used_privs
- dba_unused_privs

EXERCISE 8-3

Create and Grant Roles

In this exercise, you will create some roles, grant them to the users, and demonstrate their effectiveness. Follow these steps:

1. Connect to your database with SQL*Plus as user SYSTEM.
2. Create two roles, as follows:

```
create role usr_role;
create role mgr_role;
```

3. Grant some privileges to the roles and then grant USR_ROLE to MGR_ROLE:

```
grant create session to usr_role;
grant select on alois.t1 to usr_role;
grant usr_role to mgr_role with admin option;
grant all on alois.t1 to mgr_role;
```

4. As user SYSTEM, grant the roles to AFRA and ANJA:

```
grant mgr_role to AFRA;
```

5. Connect to the database as user AFRA:

```
connect afra/oracle;
```

6. Grant the USR_ROLE to ANJA and then insert a row into ALOIS.T1:

```
grant usr_role to anja;
insert into alois.t1 values(sysdate);
commit;
```

7. Confirm that ANJA can connect and query ALOIS.T1 but do nothing else:

```
connect anja/oracle
select * from alois.t1;
insert into alois.t1 values(sysdate);
```

8. As user SYSTEM, adjust ANJA so that by default she can log on but do nothing else:

```
connect system/oracle
grant connect to anja;
alter user anja default role connect;
```

9. Demonstrate the enabling and disabling of roles:

```
connect anja/oracle
select * from alois.t1;
set role usr_role;
select * from alois.t1;
```

10. Query the data dictionary to identify their role usage:

```
connect system/oracle
select * from dba_role_privs
where granted_role in ('USR_ROLE','MGR_ROLE');
select grantee,owner,table_name,privilege,grantable
from dba_tab_privs where grantee in ('USR_ROLE','MGR_ROLE')
union all
select grantee,to_char(null),to_char(null),privilege,admin_option
from dba_sys_privs  where grantee in ('USR_ROLE','MGR_ROLE')
order by grantee;
```

CERTIFICATION OBJECTIVE 8.04

Create and Manage Profiles

A *profile* can be used to enforce a password. Profiles are always used, but the default profile (applied by default to all users, including SYS and SYSTEM) does very little.

Password Profile Limits

These are the limits that can be applied to passwords:

- **FAILED_LOGIN_ATTEMPTS** Specifies the number of consecutive errors on a password before the account is locked. If the correct password is given before this limit is reached, the counter is reset to zero.
- **PASSWORD_LOCK_TIME** The number of days to lock an account after FAILED_LOGIN_ATTEMPTS is reached.
- **PASSWORD_LIFE_TIME** The number of days before a password expires. It may still be usable for a while after this time, depending on PASSWORD_GRACE_TIME.

- **PASSWORD_GRACE_TIME** The number of days following the first successful login after the password has expired during which the password can be changed. The old password is still usable during this time.
- **PASSWORD_REUSE_TIME** The number of days before a password can be reused.
- **PASSWORD_REUSE_MAX** The number of password changes before a password can be reused.
- **PASSWORD_VERIFY_FUNCTION** The name of a function to run whenever a password is changed. The purpose of the function is assumed to be checking the new password for a required degree of complexity, but it can do pretty much anything you want.

on the job

Profiles can be also be used to limit resource usage, but a much more sophisticated tool to accomplish this is the Resource Manager.

To see which profile is currently assigned to each user, run this query:

```
select username,profile from dba_users;
```

By default, all users will be assigned the profile called DEFAULT. Then the view that will display the profiles themselves is DBA_PROFILES:

```
select * from dba_profiles where profile='DEFAULT';
```

The DEFAULT profile has these password limits:

Resource Name	Limit
FAILED_LOGIN_ATTEMPTS	10
PASSWORD_LIFE_TIME	180 days
PASSWORD_REUSE_TIME	unlimited
PASSWORD_REUSE_MAX	unlimited
PASSWORD_VERIFY_FUNCTION	null
PASSWORD_LOCK_TIME	1 day
PASSWORD_GRACE_TIME	7 days

These restrictions are not too strict: a password can be entered incorrectly 10 consecutive times before the account is locked for one day, and a password will expire after about six months with a one-week grace period for changing it after that. There is no check on password complexity.

Creating and Assigning Profiles

The simplest way to enable more sophisticated password management is to run code provided in a supplied script. On Unix or Linux, it is

```
$ORACLE_HOME/rdbms/admin/utlpwdmg.sql
```

On Windows, it is

```
%ORACLE_HOME%\rdbms\admin\utlpwdmg.sql
```

On either platform, the script creates a set of functions offering various degrees of password complexity checking.

To create a profile with SQL*Plus, use the **CREATE PROFILE** command, setting whatever limits are required. Any limits not specified will be picked up from the current version of the DEFAULT profile. For example, it could be the rules of the organization state that accounts should be locked after five consecutive failed login attempts for one hour, except for administrators, who should be locked after two attempts for a whole day, and that all passwords should be subject to the provided standard password complexity verification algorithm.

EXERCISE 8-4

Create and Use Profiles

In this exercise, you'll create, assign, and test a profile that forces some password control. Here are the steps to follow:

1. Connect to your database with SQL*Plus as user sys.
2. Execute the script that will create the supplied verification functions and then apply one to the default profile. Confirm that the function has been created and applied:

```
@?/rdbms/admin/utlpwdmg.sql
describe sys.ora12c_verify_function
select * from dba_profiles where resource_name=
'PASSWORD_VERIFY_FUNCTION';
```

3. Create a profile that will lock accounts after two wrong passwords for 10 minutes:

```
create profile two_wrong limit failed_login_attempts 2
password_lock_time 10/1440;
```

4. Assign this new profile to ALOIS:

```
alter user alois profile two_wrong;
```

5. Deliberately enter the wrong password for ALOIS a few times:

```
connect alois/wrongpassword
```

6. As user SYSTEM, check the status of the ALOIS account and unlock it:

```
select account_status from dba_users where username='ALOIS';
alter user alois account unlock;
select account_status from dba_users where username='ALOIS';
```

7. Check that ALOIS can now connect:

```
connect alois/oracle
```

8. Test the verification function by attempting to change the password a few times:

```
alter user alois identified by oracle;
```

9. Tidy up by dropping the profile, the roles, and the users. Note the use of CASCADE when dropping the profile to remove it from ALOIS as well as on the **DROP USER** command to drop his table as well. Roles can be dropped even if they are assigned to users. The privileges granted on the table will be revoked as the table is dropped.

```
connect system/oracle
drop profile two_wrong cascade;
alter profile default limit password_verify_function null;
drop role usr_role;
drop role mgr_role;
drop user alois cascade;
drop user anja;
drop user afra;
```

CERTIFICATION SUMMARY

User accounts define users who can connect to the database and are associated with a schema that stores the objects owned by the account. Privileges must be granted to an account (either directly or via roles) before the account is usable in any way.

Privileges come in two forms: system privileges, which control certain actions within the database (typically, actions that involve changes to the data dictionary), and object privileges, which control access to data. A role is a bundle of privileges. Unlike a privilege (which is always enabled once granted), a role can be enabled or disabled within a session.

Profiles give control over account passwords and resource usage. All user accounts have a profile (by default, the profile called DEFAULT). The DEFAULT profile can be adjusted, and the change will immediately apply to all users with the DEFAULT profile. Alternatively, additional profiles can be created and assigned explicitly to certain users.

TWO-MINUTE DRILL

Create and Manage Database User Accounts

- ❑ Users connect to a user account, which is connected to a schema.
- ❑ Some form of authentication is always required.
- ❑ A user must have a quota on a tablespace before they can create any objects.
- ❑ A user who owns objects cannot be dropped, unless the CASCADE keyword is used.

Grant and Revoke Privileges

- ❑ Privileges are of two types: object privileges and system privileges.
- ❑ By default, a user can do nothing. They can't even log on.
- ❑ A revocation of a system privilege does not cascade; a revocation of an object privilege does.

Create and Manage Roles

- ❑ Roles are not schema objects.
- ❑ Roles can contain both system and object privileges as well as other roles.
- ❑ A role can be enabled or disabled for a session.

Create and Manage Profiles

- ❑ Profiles can enforce password policies.
- ❑ Every user always has a profile (by default, the DEFAULT profile).

SELF TEST

Create and Manage Database User Accounts

1. How can you permit users to connect without requiring them to authenticate themselves? (Choose the best answer.)

A. Grant CREATE SESSION to PUBLIC.

B. Create a user such as this, without a password:

```
CREATE USER ANON IDENTIFIED BY '';
```

C. Create a profile that disables password authentication and assign it to the users.

D. You cannot do this because all users must be authenticated.

2. You create a user with this statement:

```
create user jon identified by oracle default tablespace example;
```

What more must be done before he can create a table in the EXAMPLE tablespace? (Choose all correct answers.)

A. Nothing more is necessary.

B. Give him a quota on EXAMPLE.

C. Grant him the CREATE TABLE privilege.

D. Grant him the CREATE SESSION privilege.

E. Grant him the MANAGE TABLESPACE privilege.

3. If a user owns tables in a tablespace, what will be the effect of attempting to reduce their quota on the tablespace to zero? (Choose the best answer.)

A. The tables will survive, but INSERTS will fail.

B. The tables will survive but cannot get bigger.

C. The attempt will fail unless the tables are dropped first.

D. The tables will be dropped automatically if the CASCADE keyword is used.

4. If you create a user without specifying a temporary tablespace, what temporary tablespace will be assigned? (Choose the best answer.)

A. You must specify a temporary tablespace.

B. SYSTEM.

C. TEMP.

D. The database default temporary tablespace.

E. The user will not have a temporary tablespace.

Grant and Revoke Privileges

5. You issue these commands:

```
a.grant select on hr.regions to jon;
b.grant all on hr.regions to jon;
c.grant dba to jon;
d.grant select on hr.regions to public;
```

Which grants should be revoked to prevent JON from seeing the contents of HR.REGIONS? (Choose the best answer.)

A. a, b, c, and d

B. a, c, and d

C. a and b

D. c and d

E. a, b, and c

6. Which of these statements about system privileges are correct? (Choose all correct answers.)

A. Only the SYS and SYSTEM users can grant system privileges.

B. If a system privilege is revoked from a user, it will also be revoked from all users to whom he granted it.

C. If a system privilege is revoked from a user, it will not be revoked from all users to whom he granted it.

D. CREATE TABLE is a system privilege.

E. CREATE ANY TABLE is a system privilege.

Create and Manage Roles

7. Study this script (line numbers have been added):

```
1     create role hr_role identified by pass;
2     grant create table to hr_role;
3     grant select table to hr_role;
4     grant connect to hr_role;
```

Which line will cause an error? (Choose the best answer.)

A. Line 1, because only users, not roles, have passwords.

B. Line 2, because only users, not roles, can create and own tables.

C. Line 3, because SELECT TABLE is not a privilege.

D. Line 4, because a role cannot have a system privilege in addition to table privileges.

8. Which of these statements is incorrect regarding roles? (Choose the best answer.)
   A. You can grant object privileges and system privileges as well as roles to a role.
   B. A role cannot have the same name as a table.
   C. A role cannot have the same name as a user.
   D. Roles can be enabled or disabled within a session.

Create and Manage Profiles

9. If a password profile is dropped, what will be the effect on users to whom it is assigned? (Choose the best answer.)
   A. You cannot drop the profile until it is unassigned from the users.
   B. The profile will be removed if you use the CASCADE keyword.
   C. The users will revert to the default profile.
   D. Users to whom it is assigned will continue to use it, but it can no longer be assigned to anyone else.
10. Which of these can be controlled by a password profile? (Choose all correct answers.)
   A. Two or more users choosing the same password
   B. Preventing the reuse of a password by the same user
   C. Forcing a user to change password
   D. Enabling or disabling password file authentication

LAB QUESTION

For this question, use Database Express where possible, if you wish, but it is usually necessary to use SQL*Plus to query views directly when trying to understand what is happening with access rights. There are often several ways of getting to a table, and it can be difficult to work out why a user can see it.

Create the user BERND, and give him the necessary permissions to log on to the database with password authentication and create tables in his own schema. Test this by connecting as BERND and creating a table called DATETAB, with a single column of type DATE. Insert a row into DATETAB and then commit the insert.

Now create the user CHRISTA. Give her these privileges:

```
CREATE SESSION
SELECT ON BERND.DATETAB
ALL ON BERND.DATETAB
```

Connect as CHRISTA, and check that she can read BERND.DATETAB. Revoke her SELECT privilege, and confirm that she can no longer select from BERND.DATETAB, although she can (perhaps oddly) insert rows into it. Why is this, when she was also granted ALL on BERND.DATETAB? Run queries against DBA_TAB_PRIVS at all stages to understand what is happening.

Create the user DORIS and grant her privileges as follows:

```
SELECT ON BERND.DATETAB to DORIS
SELECT ON BERND.DATETAB to PUBLIC
SELECT ANY TABLE to DORIS
DBA to DORIS
```

Confirm that DORIS can now read BERND.DATETAB. What privileges must be revoked before DORIS will no longer be able to see BERND.DATETAB? Check the permissions at all stages by querying DBA_TAB_PRIVS, DBA_SYS_PRIVS, and DBA_ROLE_PRIVS.

Tidy up by dropping the users. Remember to use CASCADE where appropriate.

SELF TEST ANSWERS

Create and Manage Database User Accounts

1. ☑ **D.** All users must be authenticated.
☒ **A, B,** and **C** are incorrect. **A** is incorrect because although this will give all users permission to connect, they will still have to authenticate. **B** is incorrect because a NULL is not acceptable as a password. **C** is incorrect because a profile can only manage passwords, not disable them.

2. ☑ **C, D.** All these actions are necessary.
☒ **A, B,** and **E** are incorrect. **A** is incorrect because without privileges and a quota, jon cannot connect and create a table. **E** is incorrect because this privilege lets you manage a tablespace, not create objects in it. **B** is not necessary because an unlimited quota is implicitly granted on the EXAMPLE tablespace to user jon.

3. ☑ **B.** It will not be possible to allocate further extents to the tables.
☒ **A, C,** and **D** are incorrect. **A** is incorrect because inserts will succeed as long as there is space in the extents already allocated. **C** is incorrect because there is no need to drop the tables. **D** is incorrect because CASCADE cannot be applied to a quota command.

4. ☑ **D.** There is always a database-wide default, which (by default) is SYSTEM. In many cases, it will have been set to TEMP.
☒ **A, B, C,** and **E** are incorrect. **A** is incorrect because there is a default. **B** is incorrect because the default temporary tablespace may have been changed. **C** is incorrect because although TEMP is frequently used by default, it may not be. **E** is incorrect because all user accounts must have a temporary tablespace.

Grant and Revoke Privileges

5. ☑ **B.** The grant of the DBA role and the grant to PUBLIC must be removed, as well as the directly granted SELECT privilege.
☒ **C, D,** and **E** are incorrect. They all leave one grant in place that must be revoked. **A** is incorrect because it is not necessary to revoke ALL as well as SELECT: either would be sufficient.

6. ☑ **C, D,** and **E.** Answer **C** is correct because the revocation of a system privilege does not cascade. **D** and **E** are correct because any action that updates the data dictionary is a system privilege.
☒ **A** and **B** are incorrect. **A** is incorrect because system privileges can be granted by any user who has been granted the privilege WITH ADMIN OPTION. **B** is incorrect because the revocation of a system privilege does not cascade.

Create and Manage Roles

7. ☑ **C.** There is no such privilege as SELECT TABLE; it is granted implicitly with CREATE TABLE.
   ☒ **A, B,** and **D** are incorrect. **A** is incorrect because roles can be password protected. **B** is incorrect because even though tables must be owned by users, permission to create them can be granted to a role. **D** is incorrect because a role can have any combination of object and system privileges.

8. ☑ **B.** Roles are not schema objects and therefore can have the same names as tables.
   ☒ **A, C,** and **D** are incorrect. **A** is incorrect because roles can have any combination of system, object, and role privileges. **C** is incorrect because roles cannot have the same names as users. **D** is incorrect because roles can be enabled and disabled at any time.

Create and Manage Profiles

9. ☑ **C.** Dropping a profile implicitly reassigns all relevant users to the default profile.
   ☒ **A, B,** and **D** are incorrect. **A** is incorrect because of the implicit reassignment of users. **B** is incorrect because there is no CASCADE keyword in the **DROP PROFILE** command: it isn't necessary. **D** is incorrect because the effect of dropping a profile is immediate.

10. ☑ **B** and **C.** These are both password limits.
    ☒ **A** and **D** are incorrect. **A** is incorrect because it is not possible to control this: Oracle has no knowledge of the actual password, only knowledge of the hash of the password. **D** is incorrect because this is controlled through the REMOTE_LOGIN_PASSWORDFILE instance parameter, not through profiles.

LAB ANSWER

Here is one possible solution. To begin, create BERND and the table:

```
conn system/oracle
create user bernd identified by bernd;
alter user bernd default tablespace example
quota unlimited on example;
grant create table,create session to bernd;
connect bernd/bernd
create table datetab (c1 date);
insert into datetab values(sysdate);
commit;
```

The experiment with CHRISTA follows:

```
connect system/oracle
create user christa identified by christa;
grant create session to christa;
grant select on bernd.datetab to christa;
select * from dba_tab_privs where grantee='CHRISTA';
grant all on bernd.datetab to christa;
select * from dba_tab_privs where grantee='CHRISTA';
connect christa/christa;
select * from bernd.datetab;
connect system/oracle
revoke select on bernd.datetab from christa;
select * from dba_tab_privs where grantee='CHRISTA';
connect christa/christa;
insert into bernd.datetab values(sysdate);
select * from bernd.datetab;
```

For the experiment with DORIS, the queries to be run to investigate the permissions could include the following:

```
select * from dba_tab_privs where owner='BERND'
and table_name='DATETAB';
select * from dba_tab_privs where GRANTEE in ('DORIS','PUBLIC')
and owner='BERND';
select * from dba_sys_privs where GRANTEE in ('DORIS','PUBLIC');
select * from dba_role_privs where grantee='DORIS';
select * from dba_sys_privs where privilege='SELECT ANY TABLE';
```

9 Managing Undo Data

CERTIFICATION OBJECTIVES

It is time to investigate what actually happens in memory and on disk when one executes a DML statement: how a change to a table generates both redo and undo. The DML commands change data in tables. They will also change data in indexes, but this is automatic and will happen without the programmer's knowledge.

The relational database paradigm defines the manner in which one or more DML statements must be grouped into *transactions*. This is not the place to go into detail on the relational database transactional paradigm—there are numerous academic texts on this—but a quick review of transaction theory is necessary before looking at how Oracle has implemented transaction management and DML, through the mechanisms of redo and undo.

CERTIFICATION OBJECTIVE 9.01

Explain DML and Undo Data Generation

Undo data is the information needed to reverse the effects of DML statements. It is often referred to as *rollback data*, but try to avoid that term. In earlier releases of Oracle, the terms *rollback data* and *undo data* were used interchangeably, but from 9*i* onward they are different: their function is the same, but their management is not. The old mechanism of rollback segments is long outdated, and all databases should use *automatic undo management*, which uses undo segments to store undo data.

Database Transactions

Oracle's mechanism for ensuring transactional integrity is the combination of undo segments and redo log files: this mechanism is undoubtedly the best of any database yet developed and conforms perfectly with the international standards for data processing. Other database vendors comply with the same standards with their own mechanisms, but with varying levels of effectiveness. In brief, any relational database must be able to pass the ACID test: it must guarantee atomicity, consistency, isolation, and durability.

A Is for Atomicity

The principle of atomicity states that either all parts of transaction must complete or none of them complete. For example, if your business analysts have said that every time you change an employee's salary, you must also change his grade, then the atomic transaction will consist of two updates. The database must guarantee that both go through, or neither do. If only one of the updates were to succeed, you would have an employee on a salary that was incompatible with his grade: a data corruption, in business terms. If anything (anything at all!) goes wrong before the transaction is complete, the database itself must guarantee that any parts that did go through are reversed; this must happen automatically. But although an atomic transaction sounds small (like an atom), it could be enormous. To take another example, it is logically impossible in accountancy terms for the nominal ledger of an accounting suite to be half in August and half in September: the end-of-month rollover is therefore (in business terms) one atomic transaction, which may affect millions of rows in thousands of tables as well as take hours to complete (or to roll back, if anything goes wrong). The rollback of an incomplete transaction is the reversal process and may be manual (as when you issue the **ROLLBACK** command), but it must be automatic and unstoppable in the case of an error.

C Is for Consistency

The principle of consistency states that the results of a query must be consistent with the state of the database at the time the query started. Imagine a simple query that averages the value of a column of a table. If the table is large, it will take many minutes to pass through the table. If other users are updating the column while the query is in progress, should the query include the new or the old values? Should it include rows that were inserted or deleted after the query started? The principle of consistency requires that the database ensure that changed values are not seen by the query: it will give you an average of the column as it was when the query started, no matter how long the query takes or what other activity is occurring on the tables concerned.

Through the use of undo segments, Oracle guarantees that if a query succeeds, the result will be consistent. However, if your undo segments are incorrectly configured, the query may not succeed: the famous Oracle error "ORA-1555: snapshot too old" is raised. This used to be an extremely difficult problem to fix with earlier releases of the database, but from release 9*i* onward you should always be able to avoid it.

I Is for Isolation

The principle of isolation states that an incomplete (that is, uncommitted) transaction must be invisible to the rest of the world. While the transaction is in progress, only the one session that is executing the transaction is allowed to see the changes: all other sessions must see the unchanged data, not the new values. The logic behind this is, first, that the full transaction might not go through (remember the principle of atomicity?) and therefore no other users should be allowed to see changes that might be reversed. And, second, during the progress of a transaction, the data is (in business terms) inconsistent: there is a short time when the employee has had their salary changed, but not their grade. Transaction isolation requires that the database must conceal transactions in progress from other users: they will see the pre-update version of the data, until the transaction completes, when they will see all the changes as a consistent set.

Oracle guarantees transaction isolation, consistency, and atomicity through the use of undo segments.

D Is for Durable

The principle of durability states that once a transaction completes, it must be impossible for the database to lose it. During the time that the transaction is in progress, the principle of isolation requires that no one (other than the session concerned) can see the changes it has made so far. But the instant the transaction completes, it must be broadcast to the world, and the database must guarantee that the change is never lost: a relational database is not allowed to lose data. Oracle fulfills this requirement through the use of log files. Log files come in two forms—online redo log files and archive redo log files—that store a record of every change applied to the database. Of course, data can be lost through user error, such as using inappropriate DML and dropping objects. But as far as Oracle and the DBA are concerned, such events are transactions like any other: according to the principle of durability, they are absolutely nonreversible.

If a database ever loses data, management's first reaction is often to fire the DBA. Everyone knows that Oracle won't lose data—that is why people buy it. Therefore, it must be the administrator's fault. Careers have been broken for this reason.

Undo Generation

Whenever a transaction changes data, the pre-update version of the data is written out to a rollback segment or to an undo segment. The difference is crucial. Rollback segments can still exist in a 12*c* database, but with release 9*i* of the database, Oracle introduced the undo segment as an alternative. Oracle strongly advises that all databases should use undo segments—rollback segments are retained for backward compatibility, but they are not referenced in the OCP exam and are therefore not covered in this book. But even though "rollback" as a noun should no longer be used in the Oracle environment, "roll back" as a verb is as relevant as ever.

To roll back a transaction means to use data from the undo segments to construct an image of the data as it was before the transaction occurred. This is usually done automatically following some sort of failure, but the flashback query capability (introduced with 9*i* and greatly enhanced since) leverages the power of the undo mechanism by giving you the option of querying the database as it was at some time in the past. And, of course, any user can use the **ROLLBACK** command interactively to back out any DML statements that they have issued and not committed.

The ACID test requires, first, that the database should keep pre-update versions of data in order that incomplete transactions can be reversed—either automatically in the case of an error or on demand through the use of the **ROLLBACK** command. This type of rollback is permanent and published to all users. Second, for consistency, the database must be able to present a query with a version of the database as it was at the time the query started. The server process running the query will go to the undo segments and construct what is called a "read-consistent image" of the blocks being queried, if they were changed after the query started. This type of rollback is temporary and visible only to the session running the query. Third, undo segments are also used for transaction isolation. This is perhaps the most complex use of undo data. The principle of isolation requires that no transaction can be in any way dependent upon another, incomplete transaction. In effect, even though a multiuser database will have many transactions in progress at once, the end result must be as though the transactions were executing one after another. The use of undo data combined with row and table locks guarantees transaction isolation: the impossibility of incompatible transactions. Even though several transactions may be running concurrently, isolation requires that the end result must be as if the transactions were serialized.

From release 9*i* onward, undo data can also be used for flashback queries. This is a completely optional but very powerful tool that allows users to query a past image of the database. For flashback queries, undo data is used to construct a version of one or more tables as they were at some previous time by applying undo data. As with rollback for the purposes of consistency, rollback for flashback purposes is only temporary and is visible only to the session concerned.

Use of undo segments is incompatible with the use of rollback segments: It is one or the other, depending on the setting of the UNDO_MANAGEMENT parameter.

As a final word on rollback as opposed to undo, observe the results of two queries against DBA_SEGMENTS, shown in Figure 9-1. This shows that within the database there is one segment of type ROLLBACK, and 10 segments of type TYPE2 UNDO.

FIGURE 9-1 Segment types within a 12c database

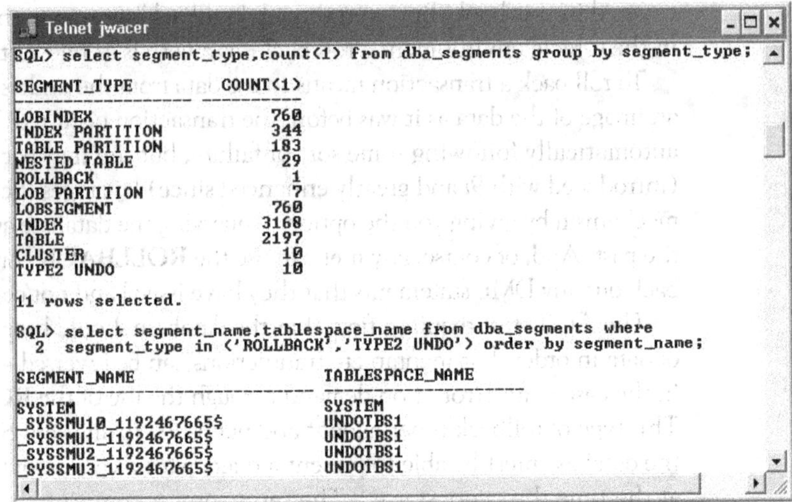

So rollback segments can (and one does) still exist in a 12c database. Undo segments can exist only in an undo tablespace; this is one of their features. But at database creation time, there may not be an undo tablespace. Therefore, at database creation time, Oracle creates a single old-fashioned rollback segment in the SYSTEM tablespace, along with the data dictionary. This is used during database creation but is never used in normal running. All user transactions will use undo segments, listed in DBA_SEGMENTS as segment type TYPE2 UNDO.

Executing SQL Statements

The whole of the SQL language is only a dozen or so commands. The ones we are concerned with here are

- SELECT
- INSERT
- UPDATE
- DELETE
- COMMIT
- ROLLBACK

Executing a SELECT Statement

The SELECT command retrieves data. The execution of a SELECT statement is a staged process: the server process executing the statement will first check whether the blocks containing the data required are already in memory, in the database buffer cache. If they are, then execution can proceed immediately. If they are not, the server must locate them on disk and then copy them into the database buffer cache.

> **exam watch** *Always remember that servers read blocks from datafiles into the database buffer cache; DBWn writes blocks from the database buffer cache to the datafiles.*

Once the data blocks required for the query are in the database buffer cache, any further processing (such as sorting or aggregation) is carried out in the PGA of the session. When the execution is complete, the result set is returned to the user process. How does this relate to the ACID test just described? For consistency, if the query encounters a block that has been changed since the time the query started, the server process will go to the undo segment that protected the change, locate the old version of the data, and (for the purposes of the current query only) roll back the change. Thus, any changes initiated after the query commenced will not be seen. A similar mechanism guarantees transaction isolation, although this is based on whether the change has been committed, not only on whether the data has been changed. Clearly, if the data needed to do this rollback is no longer in the undo segments, this mechanism will not work. That is when you get the "snapshot too old" error. Figure 9-2 shows a representation of the way a SELECT statement is processed.

FIGURE 9-2 The stages of execution of a SELECT

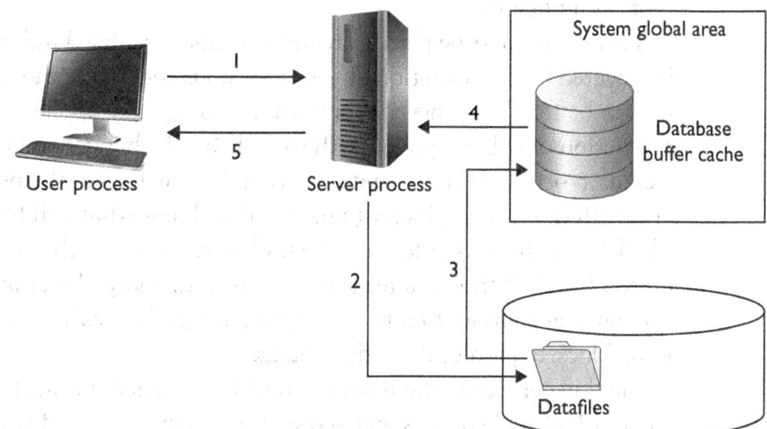

In the figure, step 1 is the transmission of the SELECT statement from the user process to the server process. The server will search the database buffer cache to find if the necessary blocks are already in memory. If they are, proceed to step 4. If they are not, step 2 is to locate the blocks in the datafiles, and step 3 is to copy them into the database buffer cache. Step 4 transfers the data to the server process, where there may be some further processing before step 5 returns the result of the query to the user process.

Executing an UPDATE Statement

For any DML operation, it is necessary to work on both data blocks and undo blocks, and also to generate redo: the A, C, and I of the ACID test require generation of the undo, and the D requires the generation of redo.

exam watch

Undo is not the opposite of redo! Redo protects all block changes, whether it is a change to a block of a table segment, an index segment, or an undo segment. As far as redo is concerned, an undo segment is just another segment, and any changes to it must be made durable.

The first step in executing DML is the same as executing SELECT: the required blocks must be found in the database buffer cache, or copied into the database buffer cache from the datafiles. The only change is that an empty (or expired—more of that later) block of an undo segment is needed too. From then on, things are a bit more complicated.

First, locks must be placed on any rows and associated index keys that are going to be affected by the operation. Then the redo is generated: the server process writes to the log buffer the change vectors that are going to be applied to the data blocks. This generation of redo is applied both to table block changes and to undo block changes: if a column of a row is to be updated, then the row ID and the new value of the column are written to the log buffer (which is the change that will be applied to the table block) as well as the old value (which is the change that will be applied to the undo block). If the column is part of an index key, the changes to be applied to the index are also written to the log buffer, together with a change to be applied to an undo block to protect the index change.

Having generated the redo, the update is carried out in the database buffer cache: the block of table data is updated with the new version of the changed column, and the old version of the changed column is written to the block of undo segment. From this point until the update is committed, all queries from other sessions addressing the changed row will be redirected to the undo data. Only the session that is doing the update will see the actual current version of the row in the table block. The same principle applies to any associated index changes.

As a simple example, consider this statement:

```
update emp set sal=sal*1.1 where empno=7934;
```

To execute this statement, the block of table data containing the row for employee number 7934 (and possibly several others rows, too, if the rows are smaller than the block) is copied into the database buffer cache, and a block of an undo segment is also copied into the cache. Then your server process writes to the log buffer the old version of the SAL column (which is the change to be applied to the block of undo) and the new version of the SAL column (which is the change to be applied to the block of table data). Lastly, the blocks themselves are updated in the database buffer cache. And remember that because SQL is a set-oriented language: if there are many rows in the EMP table with the same EMPNO, they would all be updated by the one statement. But because EMPNO will be a primary key, that won't happen.

Executing INSERT and DELETE Statements

Conceptually, INSERT and DELETE are managed in the same fashion as an UPDATE. The first step is to locate the relevant blocks in the database buffer cache, or to copy them into it if they are not there. Redo generation is exactly the same: all change vectors to be applied to data and undo blocks are first written out to the log buffer. For an INSERT, the change vector to be applied to the table block (and possibly index blocks) is the bytes that make up the new row (and possibly the new index keys). The vector to be applied to the undo block is the row ID of the new row. For a DELETE, the change vector to be written to the undo block is the entire row.

A crucial difference between INSERT and DELETE is in the amount of undo generated. When a row is inserted, the only undo generated is writing out the new row ID to the undo block. This is because to roll back an INSERT, the only information Oracle requires is the row ID. Therefore, the following statement can be constructed:

```
delete from table_name where rowid=rowid_of_the_new_row ;
```

Executing this statement will reverse the original change.

INSERT generates a minimal amount of undo data; DELETE generates much more.

For a DELETE, the whole row (which might be several kilobytes) must be written to the undo block, so that the deletion can be rolled back if need be by constructing a statement that will insert the complete row back into the table.

Transaction Control: COMMIT and ROLLBACK

Oracle's implementation of the relational database paradigm begins a transaction implicitly with the first DML statement. The transaction continues until a COMMIT or ROLLBACK statement. Note that this implementation is not the same as some competing products. Some software vendors think that a SELECT should begin a transaction, in order to ensure the repeatable reads; others require an explicit beginning of a transaction, or they will automatically commit each statement.

Executing a Rollback

Remember that if anything goes wrong, rollback of transactions in progress is completely automatic and is carried out by background processes. For example, if the session that initiated the transaction fails (perhaps a PC running a user process reboots, or the network link goes down), then PMON will detect that there is a problem with the session and roll back the transaction. If the server is rebooted while the database is in use, then on startup SMON will detect the problem and initiate a rollback of all active transactions.

A manual rollback requires the user to issue the **ROLLBACK** command. But, however the rollback is initiated, the mechanism is identical: in the case of an UPDATE, the pre-update versions of the columns, as stored in the block of undo segment, are used to construct another **UPDATE** command that will set the columns of the row in the table block back to their original values. To roll back an insert, Oracle retrieves the row ID of the inserted row from the undo block and uses it as the key for a DELETE statement on the table. To roll back a DELETE, Oracle constructs a complete INSERT statement from the data in the undo block. Thus, Oracle's implementation of the **ROLLBACK** command is to use undo data to construct and execute another statement that will reverse the effect of the first statement. Then Oracle will issue a COMMIT that will commit both the original change and the rollback change, as one transaction.

exam watch

A rollback will itself generate more redo as it executes, perhaps rather more than the original statement.

If you issue a **DML** command and omit a WHERE clause, like this,

```
delete from emp;
```

and thus delete all of the several million rows in the table when you meant to delete just one, you can roll back the changes. During the deletion, your server process will have copied the rows to an undo segment as it deleted them from the table: ROLLBACK will insert them back into the table, and no one will ever know you made the mistake. Unless, of course, you type COMMIT.

Executing a Commit

Commit processing is where many people (and even some experienced DBAs) show an incomplete (or indeed a completely inaccurate) understanding of the Oracle architecture. When you say COMMIT, all that happens physically is that LGWR flushes the log buffer to disk. DBWn does absolutely nothing. This is one of the most important performance features of the Oracle database.

To make a transaction durable, all that is necessary is that the changes that make up the transaction are on disk: there is no need whatsoever for the actual table data to be on disk, in the datafiles. If the changes are on disk, in the form of multiplexed redo log files, then in the event of damage to the database the transaction can be reinstantiated by restoring the datafiles from a backup taken before the damage occurred and applying the changes from the logs. Hang on to the fact that a COMMIT involves nothing more than flushing the log buffer to disk and flagging the transaction as complete. This is why a transaction involving millions of updates in thousands of files over many minutes or hours can be committed in a fraction of a second. Because LGWR writes in very nearly real time, virtually all the transaction's changes are on disk already, written as they were made. When you say COMMIT, LGWR actually does write in real time: your session will hang until the write is complete. This delay will be the length of time it takes to flush the last bit of redo from the log buffer to disk, which will take milliseconds. Your session is then free to continue, and from then on all other sessions will no longer be redirected to the undo blocks when they address the changed table, unless the principle of consistency requires it.

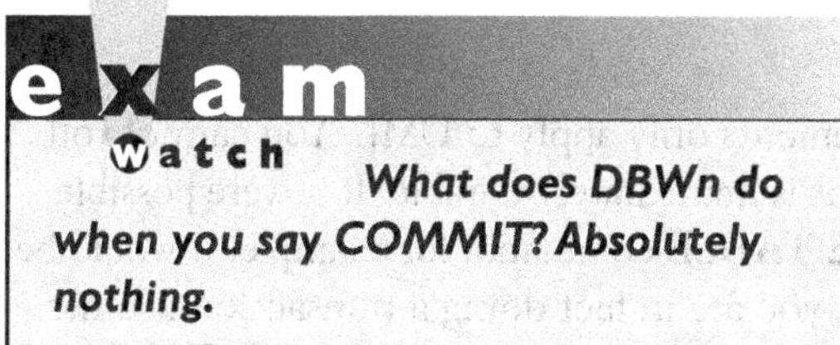

What does DBWn do when you say COMMIT? Absolutely nothing.

exam watch

The redo log stream includes all changes: those applied to data segments and to undo segments, for both committed and uncommitted transactions.

The change vectors written to the redo log are all the change vectors: those applied to data blocks (tables and indexes) and those applied to undo segments.

Having said that DBWn has nothing to do with commit processing, it does of course write changed (or "dirty") blocks to disk—eventually. The algorithm used is intended to ensure that while changed blocks do get to disk, they will not be written so quickly as to impact on normal working. If DBWn never wrote blocks to disk, there would be a huge amount of work for it do when a checkpoint is finally needed. The exception is when a checkpoint is issued; these are the rare occasions (typically only during an orderly shutdown of the database and instance) when CKPT instructs DBWn to write all dirty blocks to the datafiles.

Where there is often confusion is that the stream of redo written out to the log files by LGWR will contain changes for both committed and uncommitted transactions. Furthermore, at any given moment, DBWn may or may not have written out changed blocks of data segments or undo segments to the datafiles for both committed and uncommitted transactions. So in principle, your database on disk is corrupted: the datafiles may well be storing uncommitted work, and be missing committed changes. But in the event of a crash, the stream of redo on disk always has enough information to reinstantiate any committed transactions that are not in the datafiles (by use of the changes applied to data blocks) and to reinstantiate the undo segments (by use of the changes applied to undo blocks) needed to roll back any uncommitted transactions that are in the datafiles.

In normal running, DBWn writes only a few dirty buffers to disk; when a checkpoint is signaled, it writes all dirty buffers to disk.

DDL and Transaction Control

The COMMIT and ROLLBACK statements only apply to DML. You cannot roll back a DDL statement: once executed, it is immediately durable. If it were possible to see the source code for the **CREATE TABLE** command, for example, it would be obvious why. When you create a table, you are in fact doing a transaction against some data dictionary tables: at the very least, you are inserting a row into SYS.TAB$, which is a data dictionary table with one row to define every table in the database, and one or more rows into SYS.COL$, a data dictionary table with one row for the definition of every column of every table in the database. Then the command concludes with a COMMIT. This is to protect the data dictionary: if the COMMIT were not built into the **CREATE TABLE** command, the possibility of an incomplete transaction would arise, and an incomplete transaction in the data dictionary could have appalling side effects.

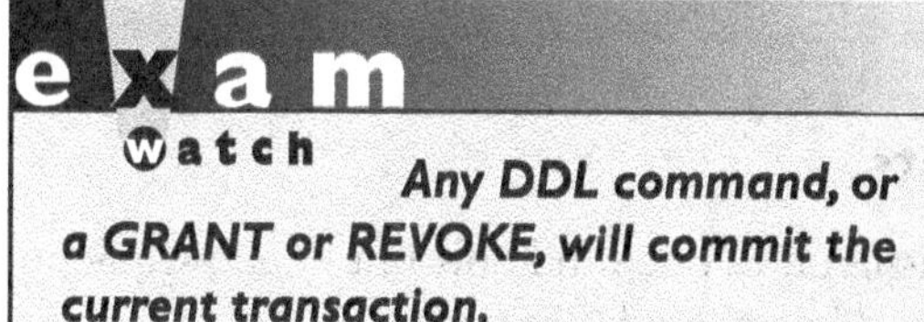

Any DDL command, or a GRANT or REVOKE, will commit the current transaction.

Because it is not possible to nest transactions (the SQL standard does not permit it), executing one or more **DML** commands followed by a **DDL** command will commit the whole lot: the DML statements as well as the DDL statement.

The So-Called "Autocommit"

To conclude this discussion of commit processing, it is necessary to remove any confusion about what is often called "autocommit," or sometimes "implicit commit." You will often hear it said that in some situations Oracle will autocommit. One of these situation is when doing DDL, which is described in the preceding section; another is when you exit from a user process such as SQL*Plus. Quite simply, there is no such thing as an automatic commit. When you execute a DDL statement, there is a perfectly normal COMMIT included in the source code that implements the **DDL** command. But what about when you exit from your user process? If you are using SQL*Plus on a Windows terminal (never mind what operating system the database server is running) and you issue a DML statement followed by an EXIT, your transaction will be committed. This is because built into the SQL*Plus **EXIT** command there is a COMMIT statement; if we could see the source code, it would be obvious. But what if you click in the top-right corner of the SQL*Plus window? The window will close, and if you log in again, you will see that the transaction has been rolled back. This is because the programmers who wrote SQL*Plus for Microsoft Windows included a ROLLBACK statement in the code that is executed when you close the window. The behavior of SQL*Plus on other platforms may well be different; the only way to be sure is to test it. So whether you get an "autocommit" when you exit from a program in various ways is entirely dependent on how your programmers wrote your user process. The Oracle server will simply do what it is told to do.

There is a SQL*Plus command **SET AUTOCOMMIT ON** that will cause SQL*Plus to modify its behavior: it will append a COMMIT to every DML statement issued. So all statements are committed immediately as soon as they are executed and cannot be rolled back. But this is happening purely on the user process side; there is still no autocommit in the database, and the changes made by a long-running statement will be isolated from other sessions until the statement completes. Of course, a disorderly exit from SQL*Plus in these circumstances, such as killing it with an operating system utility while the statement is running, will be detected by PMON and the active transaction will always be rolled back.

How Transactions Use Undo Segments

When a transaction starts, Oracle will assign it to one (and only one) undo segment. Any one transaction can only be protected by one undo segment—it is not possible for the undo data generated by one transaction to cut across multiple undo segments. This is not a problem, because undo segments are not of a fixed size. Therefore, if a transaction does manage to fill its undo segment, Oracle will automatically add another extent to the segment so that the transaction can continue. It is possible for multiple transactions to share one undo segment, but in normal running this should not occur. A tuning problem common with rollback segments was estimating how many rollback segments would be needed to avoid excessive interleaving of transactions within rollback segments without creating so many as to waste space. One feature of undo management is that Oracle will automatically spawn new undo segments on demand, in an attempt to ensure that it is never necessary for transactions to share undo segments. If Oracle has found it necessary to extend its undo segments or to generate additional segments, when the workload drops Oracle will shrink and drop the segments, again automatically.

As a transaction updates table or index data blocks, the information needed to roll back the changes is written out to blocks of the assigned undo segment. All this happens in the database buffer cache. Oracle guarantees absolutely the A, for atomicity, of the ACID test, meaning that all the undo data must be retained until a transaction commits. If necessary, the DBWn will write the changed blocks of undo data to the undo segment in the datafiles. By default, Oracle does not, however, guarantee the C, for consistency, of the ACID test. Oracle guarantees consistency to the extent that if a query succeeds, the results will be consistent with the state of the database at the time the query started—but it does not guarantee that the query will actually succeed. This means that undo data can be categorized as having different levels of necessity. *Active undo* is undo data that might be needed to roll back transactions in progress. This data can never be overwritten, until the transaction completes. At the other extreme, *expired undo* is undo data from committed transactions, which Oracle is no longer obliged to store. This data can

No transaction can ever span multiple undo segments, but one undo segment can support multiple transactions.

be overwritten if Oracle needs the space for another active transaction. *Unexpired undo* is an intermediate category; it is neither active nor expired. The transaction has committed, but the undo data might be needed for consistent reads, if there are any long-running queries in progress. Oracle will attempt not to overwrite unexpired undo.

The fact that undo information becomes inactive on commit means that the extents of undo segments can be used in a circular fashion. Eventually, the whole of the undo tablespace will be filled with undo data, so when a new transaction starts, or a running transaction generates some more undo, the undo segment will "wrap" around, and the oldest undo data within it will be overwritten—always assuming that this oldest data is not part of a long-running uncommitted transaction, in which case it would be necessary to extend the undo segment instead.

Active undo can never be overwritten; expired undo can be overwritten. Unexpired undo can be overwritten, but only if there is insufficient undo space for active transactions.

With the old manually managed rollback segments, a critical part of tuning was to control which transactions were protected by which rollback segments. A rollback segment might even be created and brought online specifically for one large transaction. Automatically managed undo segments make all of that unnecessary, because you as DBA have no control over which undo segment will protect any one transaction. Don't worry about this—Oracle does a better job that you ever could. But if you wish, you can still find out which segment has been assigned to each transaction by querying the view V$TRANSACTION, which has join columns to V$SESSION and DBA_ROLLBACK_SEGS, thus letting you build up a complete picture of transaction activity in your database: how many transactions there are currently running, who is running them, which undo segments are protecting those transactions, when the transactions started, and how many blocks of undo each transaction has generated. A related dynamic performance view is V$ROLLSTAT, which gives information on the size of the segments.

on the job

Undo segments are not the same as rollback segments, but the views DBA_ROLLBACK_SEGS and V$ROLLSTAT include rows for both without any flag to say which type of segment they are. The naming convention distinguishes them: undo segment names are automatically generated and prefixed with _SYSSMU.

EXERCISE 9-1

Use Undo Data

In this exercise, you will investigate the undo configuration and usage in your database. Use either SQL*Plus or SQL Developer. Here are the steps to follow:

1. Connect to the database as user SYSTEM.
2. Determine whether the database is using undo segments or rollback segments with this query:

   ```
   select value from v$parameter where name='undo_management';
   ```

   This should return the value AUTO. If it does not, issue the following command and then restart the instance:

   ```
   alter system set undo_management=auto scope=spfile;
   ```

3. Determine what undo tablespaces have been created, and which one is being used with these two queries:

   ```
   select tablespace_name from dba_tablespaces where contents='UNDO';
   select value from v$parameter where name='undo_tablespace';
   ```

4. Determine what undo segments are in use in the database, and how big they are:

   ```
   select tablespace_name,segment_name,segment_id,status
   from dba_rollback_segs;
   select usn,rssize from v$rollstat;
   ```

   Note that the identifying number for a segment has a different column name in the two views.

5. Find out how much undo data was being generated in your database in the recent past:

   ```
   alter session set nls_date_format='dd-mm-yy hh24:mi:ss';
   select begin_time, end_time,
   (undoblks * (select value from v$parameter where
   name='db_block_size'))
   undo_bytes from  v$undostat;
   ```

CERTIFICATION OBJECTIVE 9.02

Monitor and Administer Undo Data

A major feature of undo segments is that they are managed automatically, but you must set the limits within which Oracle will do its management. After considering the nature and volume of activity in your database, you set certain instance parameters and adjust the size of your undo tablespace in order to achieve your objectives.

Error Conditions Related to Undo

The principles are simple: First, there should always be sufficient undo space available to allow all transactions to continue. Second, there should always be sufficient undo data available for all queries to succeed. The first principle requires that your undo tablespace must be large enough to accommodate the worst case for undo demand. It should have enough space allocated for the peak usage of active undo data generated by your transaction workload. Note that this might not be during the highest number of concurrent transactions; it could be that during normal running you have many small transactions, but the total undo they generate might be less than that generated by a single end-of-month batch job. The second principle requires that there be additional space in the undo tablespace to store unexpired undo data that might be needed for read consistency.

If a transaction runs out of undo space, it will fail with the error "ORA-30036: unable to extend segment in undo tablespace." The statement that hit the problem is rolled back, but the rest of the transaction remains intact and uncommitted. The algorithm that assigns space within the undo tablespace to undo segments means that this error condition will only arise if the undo tablespace is absolutely full of active undo data.

If a DML statement runs out of undo space, the portion of it that had already succeeded will be rolled back. The rest of the transaction remains intact, and uncommitted.

If a query encounters a block that has been changed since the query started, it will go to the undo segment to find the pre-update version of the data. If, when it goes to the undo segment, that bit of undo data has been overwritten, the query will fail with the famous Oracle error "ORA-1555: snapshot too old."

If the undo tablespace is undersized for the transaction volume and the length of queries, Oracle has a choice: either let transactions succeed and risk queries failing with ORA-1555, or let queries succeed and risk transactions failing with ORA-30036. The default behavior is to let the transactions succeed, to allow them to overwrite unexpired undo.

Parameters for Undo Management

The following four parameters control undo:

- UNDO_MANAGEMENT
- UNDO_TABLESPACE
- UNDO_RETENTION (discussed in the section "Configure Undo Retention")
- TEMP_UNDO_ENABLED (discussed in the section "Temporary Undo")

UNDO_MANAGEMENT defaults to AUTO. It is possible to set this to MANUAL, meaning that Oracle will not use undo segments at all. This is for backward compatibility, and if you use this, you will have to do a vast amount of work creating and tuning rollback segments. Don't do it. Oracle Corporation strongly advises setting this parameter to AUTO, to enable use of undo segments. This parameter is static, meaning that if it is changed, the change will not come into effect until the instance is restarted. The other parameters are dynamic—they can be changed while the running instance is running.

If you are using UNDO_MANAGEMENT=AUTO (as you should), you must also specify UNDO_TABLESPACE. This parameter nominates a tablespace, which must have been created as an undo tablespace, as the active undo tablespace. All the undo segments within it will be brought online (that is, made available for use) automatically.

Sizing and Monitoring the Undo Tablespace

The undo tablespace should be large enough to store the worst case of all the undo generated by concurrent transactions, which will be active undo, plus enough unexpired undo to satisfy the longest running query. In an advanced environment, you may also have to add space to allow for flashback queries as well. The algorithm is simple: calculate the rate at which undo is being generated at your peak workload and multiply by the length of your longest query. There is a view, V$UNDOSTAT, that will tell you all you need to know.

Making your undo datafiles autoextensible will ensure that transactions will never run out of space, but Oracle will not extend them merely to meet the UNDO_RETENTION target; it is therefore still possible for a query to fail with "snapshot too old." However, you should not rely on the autoextend capability; your tablespace should be the correct size to begin with.

Figure 9-3 shows the undo configuration and usage, using SQL*Plus. The same information is available in graphical format in Database Express: on the database home page, take the Undo Management link on the Storage drop-down menu.

The first statement in the figure sets the session's date display format to show hours, minutes, and seconds. Then the SQL*Plus **SHOW** command shows the settings for the four instance parameters that include the string "undo" in their name. All four are set to their default: temporary undo is disabled, undo management is automatic (using undo segments, not antiquated rollback segments), the retention target is 900 seconds, and the undo tablespace is UNDOTBS1, which is the tablespace created when using DBCA to create a database. A query against V$UNDOSTAT shows undo activity,

FIGURE 9-3

Undo configuration and activity

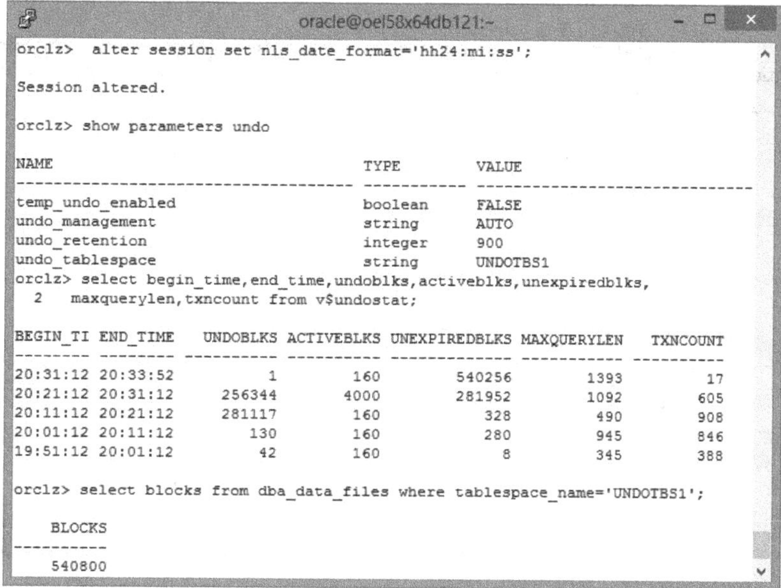

```
oracle@oel58x64db121:~
orclz>  alter session set nls_date_format='hh24:mi:ss';

Session altered.

orclz> show parameters undo

NAME                                 TYPE        VALUE
------------------------------------ ----------- ------------------------------
temp_undo_enabled                    boolean     FALSE
undo_management                      string      AUTO
undo_retention                       integer     900
undo_tablespace                      string      UNDOTBS1
orclz> select begin_time,end_time,undoblks,activeblks,unexpiredblks,
  2   maxquerylen,txncount from v$undostat;

BEGIN_TI END_TIME   UNDOBLKS ACTIVEBLKS UNEXPIREDBLKS MAXQUERYLEN   TXNCOUNT
-------- -------- ---------- ---------- ------------- ----------- ----------
20:31:12 20:33:52          1        160        540256        1393         17
20:21:12 20:31:12     256344       4000        281952        1092        605
20:11:12 20:21:12     281117        160           328         490        908
20:01:12 20:11:12        130        160           280         945        846
19:51:12 20:01:12         42        160             8         345        388

orclz> select blocks from dba_data_files where tablespace_name='UNDOTBS1';

    BLOCKS
----------
    540800
```

captured in 10 minute intervals. During the half hour shown, undo generation peaked at 281,117 blocks in one 10-minute interval and generated 908 transactions. The longest query was 1,393 seconds. Finally, querying DBA_DATA_FILES shows that the undo tablespace datafile is 540,800 blocks: about 4GB, assuming that the database was created using the default block size of 8KB.

Doing some simple arithmetic shows that the undo generation rate peaks at about 500 blocks a second, so if the longest query is about 1,000 seconds (which is pretty close to the undo_retention setting), one would need an undo tablespace of about half a million blocks to ensure that undo can always be kept for as long as the longest query. This database would appear to have undo configuration that is well matched to the workload.

The V$UNDOSTAT view is often referred to as the "undo advisor" because it lets you predict how long undo data can be kept for a given workload. Database Express represents this nicely, as shown in Figure 9-4.

The curve in the undo advisor window shows that if the undo tablespace were 5GB, it would be able to store undo data for between about 1,500 and 4,000 seconds (depending on activity). Larger or smaller sizes would increase or decrease the time for which undo would be kept.

FIGURE 9-4 Undo configuration in Database Express

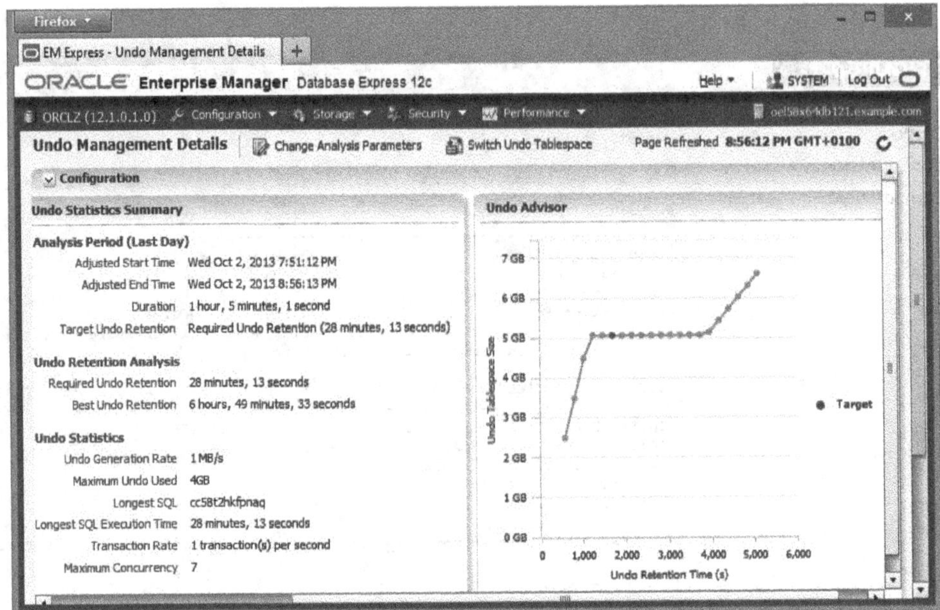

Temporary Undo

Temporary undo segments are used for storing undo generated by DML against global temporary tables. A global temporary table is a table whose definition may be visible to all sessions (hence "global") but whose rows are private to the session that inserted them. The duration of the rows is either until COMMIT or until the session terminates (hence "temporary").

Global temporary tables are often useful to developers. They offer a storage location for data that may be useful for interim result sets, without any need to worry about clearing the data when it is no longer needed or ensuring that sessions will not interfere with (or even see) data created by another session. From the DB's point of view, global temporary tables are very easy to manage. They exist as segments created (and dropped) automatically in a temporary tablespace.

Performance on temporary tables is usually superior to performance of permanent tables. This is for two reasons:

- The I/O is direct. The session reads and writes its temporary segment without going through the buffer cache, and without involving the database writer.
- No redo is generated on global temporary tables. There would be no reason: the purpose of redo is to make changes persistent, and global temporary tables do not store persistent data.

Undo data is generated by DML against temporary tables. This is necessary because the usual transactional rules apply. And it follows that redo is generated, because even though the table may be a temporary segment, the undo segment is not. In earlier releases this caused two problems:

- A performance hit, because of undo segment I/O going via the buffer cache and generating associated redo.
- The impossibility of transactions against temporary tables in a read-only database: the table might not exist in a read/write tablespace, but the undo segment does.

Release 12*c* has a facility that permits the creation of temporary undo segments in a temporary tablespace. This may significantly improve the performance of transactions against temporary tables without compromising the transactional integrity, and it also means that transactions can be run against read-only databases, such as a Data Guard physical standby database.

Creating and Managing Undo Tablespaces

So far as datafile management is concerned, an undo tablespace is the same as any other tablespace: files can be added, resized, taken online and offline, and moved or renamed. But it is not possible to specify any options regarding storage: you cannot specify automatic segment space management, and you cannot specify a uniform extent size. To create an undo tablespace, use the keyword UNDO:

```
CREATE UNDO TABLESPACE tablespace_name
DATAFILE datafile_name SIZE size [ M | G | T ]
 [ RETENTION NOGUARANTEE | GUARANTEE ] ;
```

By default, the tablespace will not guarantee undo retention. This characteristic can be specified at tablespace creation time or set later:

```
ALTER TABLESPACE tablespace_name
retention [ GUARANTEE | NOGUARANTEE ] ;
```

exam watch

Unless specified at creation time in the datafile clause, the datafile(s) of an undo tablespace will not be set to autoextend. But if your database is created with DBCA, it will enable automatic extension for the undo tablespace's datafile with maximum size unlimited. Automatic extension can be enabled or disabled at any time, as it can be for any datafile.

It is not possible to create segments in an undo tablespace, other than the undo segments that will be created automatically. Initially, there will be a pool of 10 undo segments created in an undo tablespace. More will be created if there are more than 10 concurrent transactions. Oracle will monitor the concurrent transaction rate and adjust the number of segments as necessary.

No matter how many undo tablespaces there may be in a database, generally speaking only one will be in use at a time. The undo segments in this tablespace will have a status of online (meaning that they are available for use); the segments in any other undo tablespaces will have a status of offline, meaning that they will not be used. If the undo tablespace is changed, all the undo segments in the old undo tablespace will be taken offline, and those in the new undo tablespace will be brought online. There are two exceptions to this:

- In a RAC database, every instance opening the database must have its own undo tablespace. This can be controlled by setting the UNDO_TABLESPACE parameter to a different value for each instance. Each instance will bring its own undo segments online.

- If the undo tablespace is changed by changing the undo_tablespace parameter, any segments in the previously nominated tablespace that were supporting a transaction at the time of the change will remain online until the transaction finishes.

EXERCISE 9-2

Work with Undo Tablespaces

In this exercise, you will create an undo tablespace and bring it into use. Here are the steps to follow:

1. Connect to your instance as user SYSTEM with SQL*Plus.
2. Create an undo tablespace:

   ```
   create undo tablespace undo2 datafile 'a_path_and_filename'
   size 100m;
   ```

   For the datafile's path and name, use anything suitable for your environment.
3. Run the following query, which will return one row for each tablespace in your database:

   ```
   select tablespace_name,contents,retention from dba_tablespaces;
   ```

   Note that your new tablespace has contents UNDO, meaning that it can only be used for undo segments and that retention is NOGUARANTEE.
4. Run the following query, which will return one row for each rollback or undo segment in your database:

   ```
   select tablespace_name, segment_name, status
   from dba_rollback_segs;
   ```

   Note that 10 undo segments have been created automatically in your new undo tablespace, but they are all offline.
5. Adjust your instance to use the new undo tablespace. Use a SCOPE clause to ensure that the change will not be permanent:

   ```
   alter system set undo_tablespace=undo2 scope=memory;
   ```

6. Rerun the query from step 4. You will see that the undo segments in the new tablespace have been brought online, and those in the previously active undo tablespace are offline.
7. Tidy up by setting the undo_tablespace parameter back to its original value and then dropping the new undo tablespace. Remember to use the INCLUDING CONTENTS AND DATAFILES clause.

CERTIFICATION OBJECTIVE 9.03

Describe the Difference Between Undo Data and Redo Data

This topic gets a special mention because many mistakes are made by many people when describing undo and redo. Here is a set of contrasts:

- Undo is transient, whereas redo is permanent. Undo data persists for at least the duration of the transaction that generates it, but possibly for no longer. Eventually, it will always be overwritten. Redo persists indefinitely, first in the online log files and then in the archive log files.
- Undo operates at the logical level, whereas redo operates at the physical level. Undo data is row oriented: changes are grouped according to the transaction that made them, and within an undo segment all the entries are related to rows of the same transaction. Redo is physically oriented: Change vectors are related to physical locations in blocks, by the row ID pointer. There is no relationship between consecutive change vectors in the log buffer or the log files.
- Undo can reverse changes, whereas redo can repeat changes. Undo data gives the ability to reverse committed transactions. Redo gives the ability to replay work that has been lost.
- Undo resides in tablespaces, whereas redo resides in files. Undo data is a segment structure, within the database. Redo is written out to operating system files.
- Undo and redo are not opposites. They have different functions: Undo is about transactional integrity, whereas redo is about preventing data loss.

CERTIFICATION OBJECTIVE 9.04

Configure Undo Retention

Automatic undo management will always keep undo data for as long as possible. This is usually all that is required. However, there are two cases where DBA action may be necessary: If it is necessary to ensure that queries will always succeed, even if this means that DML may fail, and if flashback queries are being used extensively.

Configuring Undo Retention to Support Long-Running Queries

UNDO_RETENTION, set in seconds, is usually optional. It specifies a target for keeping inactive undo data and determines when it becomes classified as expired rather than unexpired. If, for example, your longest running query is 30 minutes, you would set this parameter to 1800. Oracle will then attempt to keep all undo data for at least 1,800 seconds after COMMIT, and your query should therefore never fail with ORA-1555. If, however, you do not set this parameter, or set it to zero, Oracle will still keep data for as long as it can anyway. The algorithm controlling which expired undo data is overwritten first will always choose to overwrite the oldest bit of data; therefore, UNDO_RETENTION is always at the maximum allowed by the size of the tablespace.

on the job

Some queries can be very long running indeed. Queries lasting several days are not unheard of. You will need an undo tablespace the size of Jupiter if you are going to run such queries successfully during normal transaction processing. You may want to consider limiting the DML workload during long reporting runs, or tuning the SQL to reduce the time it needs.

Where the UNDO_RETENTION parameter is not optional is if you have configured guaranteed undo retention. The default mode of operation for undo is that Oracle will favor transactions over queries. If the sizing of the undo tablespace is such that a choice has to be made between the possibility of a query failing with ORA-1555 and the certainty of a transaction failing with ORA-30036, Oracle will choose to let the transaction continue by overwriting undo data that a query might need. In other words, the undo retention is only a target that Oracle will try to achieve. But there may be circumstances when successful queries are considered more important than successful transactions. An example might be the end-of-month billing run for a utilities company, when it might be acceptable to risk transactions being blocked for a short time while the reports are generating. Another case is if you are making use of flashback queries, which rely on undo data.

Guaranteed undo retention, meaning that undo data will never be overwritten until the time specified by the undo retention has passed, is enabled at the tablespace level. This attribute can be specified at tablespace creation time, or an undo tablespace can be altered later to enable it. Once you activate an undo tablespace for which retention guarantee has been specified, all queries will complete successfully, provided they finish within the undo retention time; you will never have "snapshot too old" errors again. The downside is that transactions may fail for lack of undo space.

If the UNDO_RETENTION tablespace parameter has been set, and the datafile (or datafiles) making up the undo tablespace is set to autoextend, then Oracle will increase the size of the datafile automatically if necessary to keep to the undo retention target. This combination of guaranteed undo retention and autoextending datafiles means that both queries and transactions will always succeed—assuming you have enough disk space. If you don't, the automatic extension will fail.

Flashback Query and Undo Retention

Flashback query can place additional demands on the undo system. Flashback query is a facility that allows users to see the database as it was at a time in the past. There are several methods of making flashback queries, but the simplest is a straightforward SELECT statement with an AS OF clause. Here is an example:

```
select * from scott.emp as of timestamp (systimestamp - 10/1440);
```

This statement will return all the rows in the SCOTT.EMP table that were there 10 minutes ago. Rows that have been deleted will be seen, rows that have been inserted will not be seen, and rows that have been updated will be seen with their old values. This is the case whether or not the DML statements have been committed. To execute a flashback query, undo data is used to roll back all the changes: the rows that have been deleted are extracted from the undo segments and inserted back into the result set; rows that have been inserted are deleted from the result set. A query, such as the preceding one, that attempts to go back 10 minutes will probably succeed. A query that tries to go back a week would almost certainly fail, because the undo data needed to reconstruct a version of the table as it was a week ago will have been overwritten.

Flashback query can be a very valuable tool. For example, if due to some mistake a deletion has occurred (and has been committed) at some time in the last hour, this command will reverse it by inserting all deleted rows back into the table:

```
insert into scott.emp
(select * from scott.emp as of timestamp (systimestamp - 1/24)
minus
select * from scott.emp);
```

If flashback query is likely to be used, then you must configure the undo system to handle it by setting the UNDO_RETENTION parameter to an appropriate value. If you want the ability to flash back a day, it must be set to 86,400 seconds. The undo tablespace must be appropriately sized. Then to be certain of success, either enable automatic extension for the undo tablespace's datafile(s) or enable the retention guarantee for the tablespace.

EXERCISE 9-3

Work with Transactions and Flashback Query

In this exercise, you'll demonstrate the manner in which undo data is used to provide transaction isolation and rollback as well as to implement flashback query. Use the REGIONS table in the HR demonstration schema. Here are the steps to follow:

1. Connect to the HR schema with two sessions, concurrently. These can be two SQL*Plus sessions, two SQL Developer sessions, or one of each. This table lists the steps to follow in each session:

Step	In Your First Session	In Your Second Session
1	`select * from regions;`	`select * from regions;`
Both sessions see the same data.		
2	`insert into regions values(100,'UK');`	`insert into regions values(101,'GB');`
3	`select * from regions;`	`select * from regions;`
Both sessions see different results: the original data plus their own changes.		
4	`commit;`	
5	`select * from regions;`	`select * from regions;`
One transaction has been published to the world, the other is still visible to only one session.		
6	`rollback;`	`rollback;`
7	`select * from regions;`	`select * from regions;`
The committed transaction was not reversed because it has already been committed, but the uncommitted one is now completely gone, having been terminated by the rolling back of the change. With all transactions terminated, both sessions see a consistent view of the table.		

2. Demonstrate the use of flashback query using one session connected as user HR:

   a. Adjust your time display format to include seconds:

```
alter session set nls_date_format='dd-mm-yy hh24:mi:ss';
```

b. Query and record the current time:

```
select sysdate from dual;
```

c. Delete the row inserted previously and then commit the deletion:

```
delete from regions where region_id=100;
commit;
```

d. Query the table as it was before the row was deleted:

```
select * from regions as of timestamp
to_timestamp('time_from_step_2','dd-mm-yy hh24:mi:ss');
```

The deleted row for region 100 will be listed, having been retrieved from an undo segment.

CERTIFICATION SUMMARY

Undo data is generated to enable atomic transactions, read consistency, and transaction isolation. The Oracle database guarantees transactional integrity absolutely, but not necessarily read consistency. If the undo system is not appropriately configured, queries may fail because of a lack of undo data—but if a query succeeds, it will be consistent. This behavior can be modified by enabling the RETENTION GUARANTEE, although this may mean that transactions fail.

Undo data is stored in an undo tablespace that can contain nothing other than automatically generated and managed undo segments. There may be more than one undo tablespace in a database, but only one will be in use at any given moment; this is controlled by the dynamic instance parameter UNDO_TABLESPACE.

TWO-MINUTE DRILL

Explain DML and Undo Data Generation

- ❑ All DML statements generate undo data.
- ❑ Undo data is used for transaction rollback and isolation, to provide read consistency, and for flashback queries.

Monitor and Administer Undo Data

- ❑ An instance will use undo segments in one nominated undo tablespace.
- ❑ More undo tablespaces may exist, but only one will be used at a time.
- ❑ The undo tablespace should be large enough to take account of the maximum rate of undo generation and the longest running query.
- ❑ Undo tablespace datafiles are datafiles like any others.

Describe the Difference Between Undo Data and Redo Data

- ❑ Undo protects transactions, whereas redo protects blocks changes. They are not opposites: they are complementary.

Configure Undo Retention

- ❑ Undo data will always be kept until the transaction that generated it completes with a COMMIT or a ROLLBACK. This is active undo.
- ❑ Undo data will be retained for a period after it become inactive to satisfy any read consistency requirements of long-running queries; this is unexpired undo.
- ❑ Expired undo is data no longer needed for read consistency and may be overwritten at any time as space in undo segments is reused.
- ❑ Configure undo retention by setting a target with the undo_retention parameter. This is only a target, and if the undo tablespace has insufficient space, it will not be attained—unless you set the tablespace to RETENTION GUARANTEE, which risks transactions failing for lack of undo space.

SELF TEST

Explain DML and Undo Data Generation

1. When a DML statement executes, what happens? (Choose the best answer.)
   A. Both the data and the undo blocks on disk are updated, and the changes are written out to the redo stream.
   B. The old version of the data is written to an undo segment, and the new version is written to the data segments and the redo log buffer.
   C. Both data and undo blocks are updated in the database buffer cache, and the updates also go to the log buffer.
   D. The redo log buffer is updated with information needed to redo the transaction, and the undo blocks are updated with information needed to reverse the transaction.
2. If you suspect that undo generation is a performance issue, what can you do to reduce the amount of undo data generated? (Choose the best answer.)
   A. Convert from use of rollback segments to automatic undo management.
   B. Set the UNDO_MANAGEMENT parameter to NONE.
   C. Reduce the size of the undo segments.
   D. There is nothing you can do because all DML statements must generate undo.
3. First, user JOHN initiates a query. Second, user ROOPESH updates a row that will be included in the query. Third, JOHN's query completes. Fourth, ROOPESH commits his change. Fifth, JOHN runs his query again. Which of the following statements are correct? (Choose all correct answers.)
   A. The principle of consistency means that both of JOHN's queries will return the same result set.
   B. When ROOPESH commits, the undo data is flushed to disk.
   C. When ROOPESH commits, the undo becomes inactive.
   D. JOHN's first query will use undo data.
   E. JOHN's second query will use undo data.
   F. The two queries will be inconsistent with each other.

Monitor and Administer Undo Data

4. If an undo segment fills up, what will happen? (Choose the best answer.)
   A. Another undo segment will be created automatically.
   B. The undo segment will increase in size.
   C. The undo tablespace will extend, if its datafiles are set to autoextend.
   D. Transactions will continue in a different undo segment.

5. Which of the following statements are correct about undo? (Choose all correct answers.)
   A. One undo segment can protect many transactions.
   B. One transaction can use many undo segments.
   C. One database can have many undo tablespaces.
   D. One instance can have many undo tablespaces.
   E. One undo segment can be cut across many datafiles.
   F. Undo segments and rollback segments cannot coexist.
6. Your undo tablespace has 10 undo segments, but during a sudden burst of activity you have 20 concurrent transactions. What will happen? (Choose the best answer.)
   A. Oracle will create another 10 undo segments.
   B. The transactions will be automatically balanced across the 10 undo segments.
   C. Ten transactions will be blocked until the first 10 commit.
   D. What happens will depend on your UNDO_RETENTION setting.
7. Your users are reporting "ORA-1555: Snapshot too old" errors. What might be the cause of this? (Choose the best answer.)
   A. You are not generating snapshots frequently enough.
   B. The undo data is too old.
   C. There is not enough undo data.
   D. Your undo tablespace is retaining data for too long.
8. Examine this query and result set:

```
SQL> select BEGIN_TIME,END_TIME,UNDOBLKS,MAXQUERYLEN
from V$UNDOSTAT;
BEGIN_TIME        END_TIME            UNDOBLKS MAXQUERYLEN
----------------- ----------------- ---------- -----------
02-01-08:11:35:55 02-01-08:11:41:33      14435          29
02-01-08:11:25:55 02-01-08:11:35:55     120248         296
02-01-08:11:15:55 02-01-08:11:25:55     137497          37
02-01-08:11:05:55 02-01-08:11:15:55     102760        1534
02-01-08:10:55:55 02-01-08:11:05:55     237014         540
02-01-08:10:45:55 02-01-08:10:55:55     156223        1740
02-01-08:10:35:55 02-01-08:10:45:55     145275         420
02-01-08:10:25:55 02-01-08:10:35:55      99074         120
```

   The block size of the undo tablespace is 4KB. Which of the following would be the optimal size for the undo tablespace? (Choose the best answer.)
   A. 1GB
   B. 2GB
   C. 3GB
   D. 4GB

Describe the Difference Between Undo Data and Redo Data

9. When do changes get written to the log buffer? (Choose all correct answers.)
   A. When a table block is updated
   B. When an index block is updated
   C. When an undo block is updated
   D. During rollback operations
   E. On COMMIT
   F. When queries are run that access blocks with uncommitted changes

Configure Undo Retention

10. Even though you are using automatic undo segments, users are still getting "snapshot too old" errors. What could you do? (Choose all correct answers.)
    A. Increase the UNDO_RETENTION parameter.
    B. Set the RETENTION_GUARANTEE parameter.
    C. Tune the queries to make them run faster.
    D. Increase the size of the undo tablespace.
    E. Enable RETENTION GUARANTEE.
    F. Increase the size of your undo segments.

LAB QUESTION

Simulate a problem with undo. You will need to be connected as user SYSTEM or some other user to whom you have granted the DBA role. The figures used on this exercise will be valid if the database block size is 8KB.

Create an undo tablespace with a single datafile of only 256KB. Do not set the file to autoextend. Set the database to use this small undo tablespace. Confirm that an undo segment has been created in this tablespace and that it is online by querying the views DBA_ROLLBACK_SEGS and V$ROLLSTAT. Why do you think that only one undo segment was created?

Create an empty table based on the ALL_OBJECTS view with this statement:

```
create table undotest as select * from all_objects where 1=2;
```

Populate this table with the contents of the ALL_OBJECTS view:

```
insert into undotest select * from all_objects;
```

The statement will fail with an error "ORA-30036: unable to extend segment by 8 in undo tablespace." Query the new table, and you will find that it is still empty. Why is this?

Adjust the undo tablespace's datafile to autoextend, and attempt to insert the contents of the ALL_OBJECTS view into the new table. This time, the insertion will succeed. Find out how many blocks of undo are needed to support the transaction so far by querying V$TRANSACTION as well as how big the new datafile is by querying V$DATAFILE.

Delete every row in the new table and then repeat the queries against V$TRANSACTION and V$DATAFILE. You will see that the deletion generated many more blocks of undo and required a much larger extension of the undo datafile than the insertion. Why is this?

Tidy up by switching back to the original undo tablespace and then dropping the test table and tablespace.

SELF TEST ANSWERS

Explain DML and Undo Data Generation

1. ☑ **C.** All DML occurs in the database buffer cache, and changes to both data blocks and undo blocks are protected by redo.
   ☒ **A, B,** and **D** are incorrect. **A** is incorrect because writing to disk is independent of executing the statement. **B** and **D** are incomplete: redo protects changes to both data blocks and undo blocks.

2. ☑ **D.** All DML generates undo, so the only way to reduce undo generation would be to redesign the application.
   ☒ **A, B,** and **C** are incorrect. **A** is incorrect because although automatic undo is more efficient, it cannot reduce undo. **B** is incorrect because there is no parameter setting that can switch off undo. **C** is incorrect because the size of the segments will only affect how quickly they are reused, not how much undo is generated.

3. ☑ **C, D, F.** Answer **C** is correct because undo becomes inactive on commit (although it does not necessarily expire). **D** is correct because the query will need undo data to construct a result consistent with the state of the data at the start of the query. **F** is correct because Oracle guarantees consistency within a query, not across queries.
   ☒ **A, B,** and **E** are incorrect. **A** is incorrect because Oracle guarantees consistency within a query, not across queries. **B** is incorrect because there is no correlation between a COMMIT and a write to the datafiles. **E** is incorrect because the second query is against a table that is not changed during the course of the query.

Monitor and Administer Undo Data

4. ☑ **B.** Undo segments extend as a transaction generates more undo data.
   ☒ **A, C,** and **D** are incorrect. **A** is incorrect because another undo segment will be created only if there are more concurrent transactions than segments. **C** confuses the effect of a segment filling up with that of the tablespace filling up. **D** is impossible because one transaction can only be protected by one undo segment.

5. ☑ **A, C, E.** Answer **A** is correct, although Oracle will try to avoid this. **C** is correct, although only one will be made active at any moment by the instance. **E** is correct because when it comes to storage, an undo segment is like any other segment: the tablespace abstracts the physical storage from the logical storage.
   ☒ **B, D,** and **F** are incorrect. **B** is incorrect because one transaction is protected by one undo segment. **D** is incorrect because one instance can only use one undo tablespace. **F** is incorrect because undo and rollback segments can coexist—but a database can use only one or the other.

6. ☑ **A.** Undo segments are spawned according to demand.
☒ **B, C,** and **D** are incorrect. **B** is incorrect because more segments will be created. **C** is incorrect because there is no limit imposed by the number of undo segments. **D** is incorrect because this parameter is not relevant to transactions, only to queries.

7. ☑ **C.** An "ORA-1555: snapshot too old" error is a clear indication that undo data is not being kept for long enough to satisfy the query workload: there is not enough undo data available.
☒ **A, B,** and **D** are incorrect. **A** is incorrect because it doesn't refer to undo at all—it refers to snapshots, which existed in earlier versions of the database but are now called materialized views. **B** and **D** are both incorrect because they describe the opposing situation: where undo data is being retained for longer than necessary. This is not a problem, but it may be a waste of space.

8. ☑ **C.** To calculate this, take the largest figure for UNDOBLKS, which is for a 10-minute period. Divide by 600 to get the rate of undo generation in blocks per second, and multiply by the block size to get the figure in bytes. Multiply by the largest figure for MAXQUERYLEN to find the space needed if the highest rate of undo generation coincided with the longest query, and then divide by a billion to get the answer in gigabytes:
237,014 / 600 * 4,096 * 1,740 = 2.6GB (approximately).
☒ **A, B,** and **D** are incorrect. These figures are derived from an incorrect understanding of the undo arithmetic (detailed for answer **C**).

Describe the Difference Between Undo Data and Redo Data

9. ☑ **A, B, C, D.** Changes to all data blocks are protected by redo. A rollback operation changes blocks and therefore also generates redo.
☒ **E** and **F** are incorrect. COMMIT does not write changes because they have already been written. Queries never read or write redo, although they may well read undo.

Configure Undo Retention

10. ☑ **C, D, E.** Answer **C** is correct because making the queries complete faster will reduce the likelihood of "snapshot too old." **D** is correct because it will allow more unexpired undo to be stored. **E** will solve the problem completely, although it may cause problems with transactions.
☒ **A, B,** and **F** are incorrect. **A** is incorrect because it won't help by itself—it is just a target, unless combined with **E. B** is incorrect because there is no such parameter (although it is a clause that can be applied to an undo tablespace). **F** is incorrect because this cannot be done manually—Oracle will already be doing its best automatically.

LAB ANSWER

Here is a possible solution:

```
create undo tablespace smallundo
datafile 'D:\ORADATA\SMALLUNDO.DBF' size 200k;
alter system set undo_tablespace=smallundo;
select segment_id, segment_name, tablespace_name,
status from dba_rollback_segs;
```

There is only one undo segment in the new tablespace, because the datafile is too small to store more than one.

```
create table undotest as select * from all_objects
where 1=2;
insert into undotest select * from all_objects;
select count(*) from undotest;
```

There are no rows in the table because the insertion was rolled back.

```
alter database datafile 'D:\ORADATA\SMALLUNDO.DBF' autoextend on;
insert into undotest select * from all_objects;
select xidusn,USED_UBLK from v$transaction;
select bytes from v$datafile
where name='D:\ORADATA\SMALLUNDO.DBF';
delete from undotest;
```

A deletion generates much more undo (in this example, perhaps 60 times as much) than an insertion—whereas an insertion only needs to write the new row ID to the undo segments, a deletion must write out the complete row.

Finally, tidy up:

```
alter system set undo_tablespace=undotbs1;
drop table undotest;
drop tablespace smallundo
including contents and datafiles;
```

10 Managing Data Concurrency

CERTIFICATION OBJECTIVES

10.01	Describe the Locking Mechanism and How Oracle Manages Data Concurrency	✓	Two-Minute Drill
10.02	Monitor and Resolve Locking Conflicts	Q&A	Self Test

Most database applications are multiuser. Perhaps they may have thousands of concurrent users. This means that there will be times when two or more sessions need to access the same data at the same time. The Oracle database has row- and table-locking mechanisms that will manage this, thus ensuring data integrity. The locking mechanisms can (and in most cases, should) be completely automatic. The database administrator must be aware of locking conflicts, and in some cases take action to solve locking problems.

CERTIFICATION OBJECTIVE 10.01

Describe the Locking Mechanism and How Oracle Manages Data Concurrency

There are many types of locks. Most are internal to the server: locks necessary for serializing execution of certain critical sections of code, or for protecting certain memory structures. The OCA exam does not cover these, although they are often very important for tuning. The topics covered are locks that are used at the application layer: locks taken and released as SQL statements execute. These locks are applied either to rows or to entire tables, automatically or manually (if developers really need to do this).

Serialization of concurrent access is accomplished by record- and table-locking mechanisms. Locking in an Oracle database is completely automatic. Generally speaking, problems only arise if software tries to interfere with the automatic locking mechanism with poorly written code, or if the business analysis is faulty and thus results in a business model where sessions will collide.

Shared and Exclusive Locks

The standard level of locking in an Oracle database guarantees the highest possible level of concurrency. This means that if a session is updating one row, the one row is locked and nothing else. Furthermore, the row is only locked to prevent other sessions from updating it—other sessions can read it at any time. The lock is held until the transaction completes, either with a COMMIT or a ROLLBACK. This is

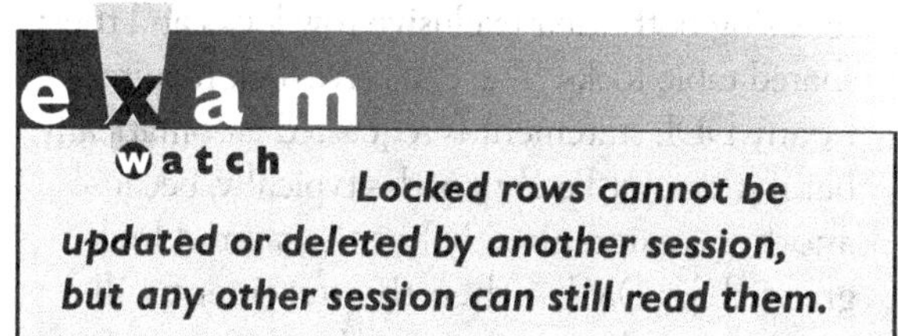

Locked rows cannot be updated or deleted by another session, but any other session can still read them.

an exclusive lock: the first session to request the lock on the row gets it, and any other sessions requesting write access must wait. Read access is permitted—although if the row has been updated by the locking session, as will usually be the case, then any reads will involve the use of undo data to make sure that reading sessions do not see any uncommitted changes.

Only one session can take an exclusive lock on a row, or a whole table, at a time—but *shared* locks can be taken on the same object by many sessions. It would not make any sense to take a shared lock on one row, because the only purpose of a row lock is to gain the exclusive access needed to modify the row. Shared locks are taken on whole tables, and many sessions can have a shared lock on the same table. The purpose of taking a shared lock on a table is to prevent another session acquiring an exclusive lock on the table: you cannot get an exclusive lock if anyone else already has a shared lock. Exclusive locks on tables are required to execute DDL statements. You cannot issue a statement that will modify an object (for instance, dropping a column of a table) if any other session already has a shared lock on the table.

To execute DML on rows, a session must acquire exclusive locks on the rows to be changed as well as shared locks on the tables containing the rows. If another session already has exclusive locks on the rows, the session will hang until the locks are released by a COMMIT or a ROLLBACK. If another session already has a shared lock on the table and exclusive locks on other rows, that is not a problem. An exclusive lock on the table could be a problem, but the default locking mechanism does not lock whole tables unless this is necessary for DDL statements.

on the job

It is possible to demand an exclusive lock on a whole table, but this has to be specifically requested, and programmers would need a good reason for doing it.

All DML statements require at least two locks: an exclusive lock on each row affected and a shared lock on the table containing the row. The exclusive lock prevents another session from interfering with the row, and the shared lock prevents another session from changing the table definition with a DDL statement. These locks are requested automatically. If a DML statement cannot acquire the exclusive row locks it needs, it will hang until it gets them.

To execute DDL commands requires an exclusive lock on the object concerned. This cannot be obtained until all DML transactions against the table have finished, thereby

Any uncommitted insert, update, or delete of a row will cause any attempted DDL on the table to fail immediately.

releasing both their exclusive row locks and their shared table locks. The exclusive lock required by any DDL statement is requested automatically, but if it cannot be obtained—typically, because another session already has the shared lock granted for DML—then the statement will terminate with an error immediately.

The Enqueue Mechanism

Requests for locks are queued. If a session requests a lock and cannot get it because another session already has the row or object locked, the session will wait. It may be that several sessions are waiting for access to the same row or object—in that case, Oracle will keep track of the order in which the sessions requested the lock. When the session with the lock releases it, the next session will be granted the lock, and so on. This is known as the *enqueue mechanism*.

If you do not want a session to queue up if it cannot get a lock, the only way to avoid this is to use the WAIT or NOWAIT clause of the **SELECT...FOR UPDATE** command. A normal SELECT will always succeed, because SELECT does not require any locks—but a DML statement will hang. The **SELECT...FOR UPDATE** command will select rows and lock them in exclusive mode. If any of the rows are locked already, the SELECT...FOR UPDATE statement will be queued and the session will hang until the locks are released, just as a DML statement would. To avoid sessions hanging, use either SELECT...FOR UPDATE NOWAIT or SELECT...FOR UPDATE WAIT <n>, where <n> is a number of seconds. Having obtained the locks with either of the SELECT...FOR UPDATE options, you can then issue the DML commands with no possibility of the session hanging.

on the job

It is possible to append the keywords SKIP LOCKED to a SELECT FOR UPDATE statement, which will return and lock only rows that are not already locked by another session.

Automatic and Manual Locking

Whenever any DML statement is executed, as part of the execution the session will automatically take a shared lock on the table and exclusive locks on the affected rows. This automatic locking is perfect for virtually all operations: it offers the highest possible level of concurrency (minimizing the possibilities for contention) and requires no programmer input whatsoever. These locks are released, also automatically, when the transaction is completed with either COMMIT or ROLLBACK.

Whenever any DDL statement is executed, the session will automatically take an exclusive lock on the entire object. This lock persists for the duration of the DDL statement and is released automatically when the statement completes. Internally, what is happening is that the DDL is in fact DML statements against rows in tables in the data dictionary. If one could see the source code of, for example, the **DROP TABLE** command, this would be clear: it will (among other things) be deleting a number of rows from the SYS.COL$ table, which has one row for every column in the database, and one row from the SYS.TAB$ table, which has one row for every table, followed by COMMIT. Most DDL statements are very quick to execute, so the table locks they require will usually not be noticed by users.

Manually locking objects can be done. The syntax is

```
lock table table_name in mode mode;
```

Five modes are possible, each of which may or may not be compatible with another lock request of a certain mode from another session:

- ROW SHARE
- ROW EXCLUSIVE
- SHARE
- SHARE ROW EXCLUSIVE
- EXCLUSIVE

The following table shows the lock compatibilities. If one session has taken the lock type listed across the top of the table, another session will (Y) or will not (N) be able to take the type of lock listed in the first column.

	Row Share	Row Exclusive	Share	Share Row Exclusive	Exclusive
Row Share	Y	Y	Y	Y	N
Row Exclusive	Y	Y	N	N	N
Share	Y	N	Y	N	N
Share Row Exclusive	Y	N	N	N	N
Exclusive	N	N	N	N	N

For example, if a session has taken a ROW SHARE lock on a table, other sessions can take any type of lock except EXCLUSIVE. On the other hand, if a session has an EXCLUSIVE lock on the object, no other session can take any lock at all. A ROW SHARE lock permits DML by other sessions, but will prevent any other session from taking an EXCLUSIVE lock on the table. An EXCLUSIVE lock is needed (and requested automatically) in order to drop the table. ROW SHARE will therefore ensure that the table is not dropped by another session. In practice, the only type of lock that is ever likely to be taken manually is the EXCLUSIVE lock. This will prevent any other sessions from performing any DML against the table.

Whenever a session does any DML against a table, it will (automatically) take a table lock in ROW EXCLUSIVE mode. Because this is not incompatible with other sessions taking a ROW EXCLUSIVE mode lock, many sessions can perform DML concurrently—as long as they do not attempt to update the same rows.

CERTIFICATION OBJECTIVE 10.02

Monitor and Resolve Locking Conflicts

When a session requests a lock on a row or object and cannot get it because another session has an exclusive lock on the row or object, it will hang. This is *lock contention*, and it can cause the database performance to deteriorate appallingly as all the sessions queue up waiting for locks. Some lock contention may be inevitable, as a result of normal activity: the nature of the application may be such that different users will require access to the same data. But in many cases, lock contention is caused by program and system design.

The Oracle database provides utilities for detecting lock contention, and it is also possible to solve the problem in an emergency. A special case of lock contention is the *deadlock*, which is always resolved automatically by the database itself.

on the job

Lock contention is a common reason for an application that performs well under test to grind to a halt when it goes production and the number of concurrent users increases. This is not the DBA's fault, but be prepared to detect such problems.

The Causes of Lock Contention

It may be that the nature of the business is such that users do require write access to the same rows at the same time. If this is a limiting factor in performance of the system, the only solution is business process reengineering, to develop a more efficient business model. However, although some locking is a necessary part of business data processing, some faults in application design can exacerbate the problem.

Long-running transactions will cause problems. An obvious case is where a user updates a row and then does not commit the change. Perhaps they even go off to lunch, leaving the transaction unfinished. You cannot stop this happening if users have access to the database with tools such as SQL*Plus, but it should never occur with well-written software. The application should take care that a lock is only imposed just before an update occurs and then released (with a COMMIT or ROLLBACK) immediately afterward.

Poorly written batch processes can also cause problems, if they are coded as long transactions. Consider the case of an accounting suite nominal ledger: it is a logical impossibility in accountancy terms for the ledger to be partly in one period and partly in another, so the end-of-month rollover to the next period is one business transaction. This transaction may involve updating millions of rows in thousands of tables, and take hours to complete. If the rollover routine is coded as one transaction with a COMMIT at the end, millions of rows will be locked for hours—but in accountancy terms, this is what should happen. Good program design would avoid the problem by updating the rows in groups, with regular commits—but the programmers will also have to take care of simulating read consistency across transactions and handle the situation where the process fails partway through. If it were one transaction, this wouldn't be a problem: the database would roll it back. If it involves many small transactions, they will have to manage a ledger that is half in one period and half in another. These considerations should not be a problem: your programmers should bear in mind the impact of long transactions on the usability of the system and design their systems accordingly.

Third-party user process products may impose excessively high locking levels. For example, some application development tools always do a SELECT...FOR UPDATE to avoid the necessity of requerying the data and checking for changes. Some other products cannot do row-level locking: if a user wants to update one row, the tool locks a group of rows—perhaps dozens or even hundreds. If your application software is written with tools such as these, the Oracle database will simply do what it is told to do: it will impose numerous locks that are unnecessary in business terms. If you suspect that the software is applying more locks than necessary, investigate whether it has configuration options to change this behavior.

Lastly, make sure your programmers are aware of the capabilities of the database. A common problem is repeatable reads. Consider this example:

```
SQL> select * from regions;
 REGION_ID REGION_NAME
---------- -------------------------
         1 Europe
         2 Americas
         3 Asia
         4 Middle East and Africa
SQL> select count(*) from regions;
  COUNT(*)
----------
         5
```

How can this be possible? The first query (the detail report) shows four rows, but then the second query (the summary report) shows five. The problem is that during the course of the first query, another session inserted and committed the fifth row. One way out of this would be to lock the table while running the reports, thus causing other sessions to hang. A more sophisticated way would be to use the SET TRANSACTION READ ONLY statement. This will guarantee (without imposing any locks) that the session does not see any DML on any tables, committed or not, until it terminates the read-only transaction with a COMMIT or ROLLBACK. The mechanism is based on the use of undo segments.

Detecting Lock Contention

Certain views will tell you what is going on with locking in the database, and Database Express offers a graphical interface for lock monitoring. Lock contention is a natural consequence of many users accessing the same data concurrently. The problem can be exacerbated by badly designed software, but in principle lock contention is part of normal database activity. It is therefore not possible for DBAs to resolve it completely—they can only identify that it is a problem, and suggest to system and application designers that they bear in mind the impact of lock contention when designing data structures and programs.

Lock contention can be seen in the V$SESSION view. This view has one row for each currently logged-on session. The unique identifier is the column SID (for Session IDentifier). If a session is blocked by another session, the SID of the blocking session is shown in the column BLOCKING_SESSION. Figure 10-1 shows a query that joins V$ESSION to itself, using the SID and BLOCKING_SESSION columns.

FIGURE 10-1

Finding and killing blocking sessions

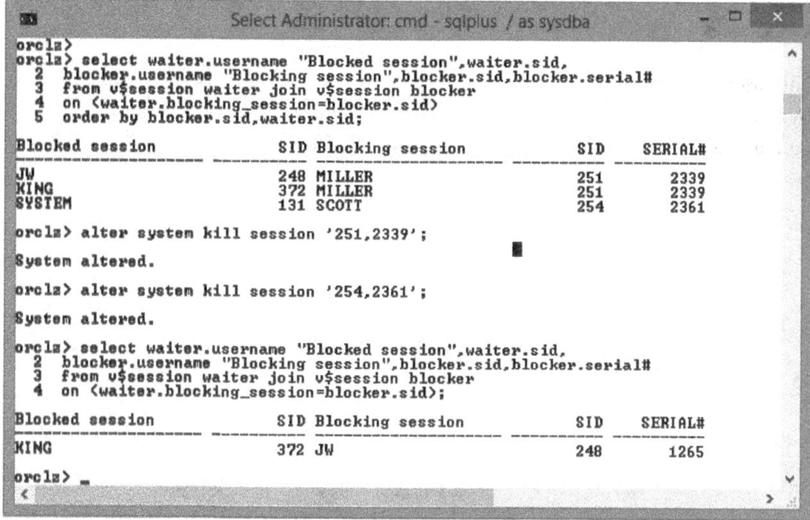

The only sessions listed are those that are blocked: all other sessions will have BLOCKING_SESSION=NULL, and will therefore not be included.

In the figure, user MILLER is blocking two other sessions: JW and KING. User SCOTT is blocking user SYSTEM. To identify lock contention in Database Express, click the Performance tab, click the link for Performance Hub, and then click the Current ADDM Findings tab. This will show current detected issues, with details visible if you click the Impact bar. Figure 10-2 shows a situation where one session, SID=256, is blocking two other sessions (SID=15 and SID=251) with row lock enqueues. It is also possible to understand the queue: Session SID=15 is blocked by both sessions 251 and 256, so killing 256 (which is suggested as Recommendation 1) will not be enough to free it. However, killing session 256 will free up session 251: this will allow 251 to complete its work, which may then free up session 15. All the sessions are identified by a three-faceted session ID, consisting of the instance number (which is always 1, because this is not a clustered database), the SID, and the SERIAL#.

Solving Lock Contention

In most circumstances, such blocks will be very short lived. The blocking sessions will commit their transactions, and the blocked sessions will then be able to work. In an emergency, however, it is possible for the DBA to solve the problem—by terminating the session (or sessions) holding too many locks for too long. When

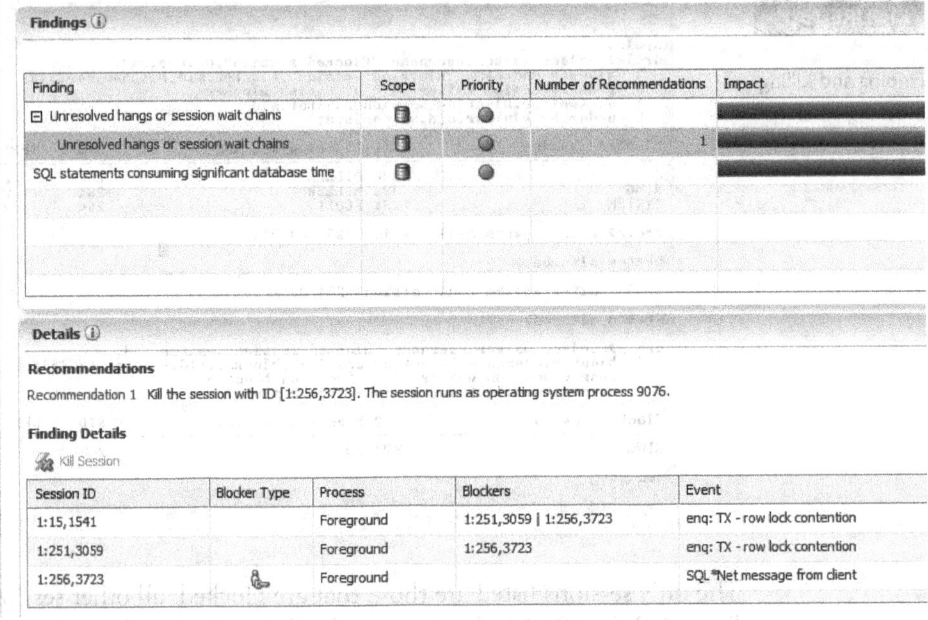

FIGURE 10-2 Lock contention as displayed in Database Express

a session is terminated forcibly, any locks it holds will be released as its active transaction is rolled back. The blocked sessions will then become free and can continue.

To terminate a session, use the **ALTER SYSTEM KILL SESSION** command. It takes the SID and SERIAL# of the session to identify which session to kill. SID is unique at any given moment, but as users log on and off, SIDs will be reused. SID plus SERIAL# is guaranteed to be unique for the lifetime of the instance, and both must be specified when a session is killed:

```
ALTER SYSTEM KILL SESSION ' sid , serial# ';
```

Deadlocks: A Special Case

It is possible to construct a position where two sessions block each other in such a fashion that both will hang, each waiting for the other to release its lock. This is a *deadlock*. Deadlocks are not the DBA's problem; they are caused by bad program design and resolved automatically by the database itself. Information regarding deadlocks is written out to the alert log, with full details in a trace file—part of your daily monitoring will pick up the occurrence of deadlocks and inform your developers that they are happening.

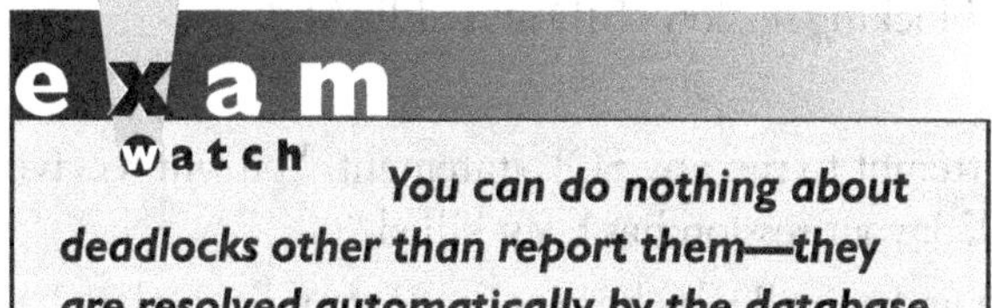

You can do nothing about deadlocks other than report them—they are resolved automatically by the database.

If a deadlock occurs, both sessions will hang, but only for a brief moment. One of the sessions will detect the deadlock within seconds, and it will roll back the statement that caused the problem. This will free up the other session, returning the message "ORA-00060 Deadlock detected." This message must be trapped by your programmers in their exceptions clauses, which should take appropriate action.

It must be emphasized that deadlocks are a program design fault. They occur because the code attempts to do something that is logically impossible. Well-written code will always request locks in a sequence that cannot cause deadlocks to occur, or will test whether incompatible locks already exist before requesting them.

EXERCISE 10-1

Monitor and Resolve Locking Conflicts

In the first part of this exercise, you will use SQL*Plus to cause a problem and then detect and resolve it. In the second part, you will learn how to handle deadlocks.

Here are the step to follow to demonstrate lock contention:

1. Using SQL*Plus, connect to your database with three sessions, as user SYSTEM.
2. In the first session, create a table:

   ```
   create table lockdemo as select * from all_users;
   ```

3. In the second session, update a row:

   ```
   update lockdemo set user_id=99 where username='SYS';
   ```

4. In the third session, issue the same statement as in step 2. The session will hang.
5. In the first session, run this query to identify which session is blocked:

   ```
   select username,sid,blocking_session from v$session
   where blocking_session is not null;
   ```

   And then run this query to retrieve the necessary details of the blocking session:

   ```
   select username,sid,serial# from v$session
   where sid=&blocking_session;
   ```

   When prompted, enter the blocking session's SID.

6. In the first session, kill the blocking session:

```
alter system kill session '&blocking_sid,&serial';
```

When prompted, enter the blocking session's SID and SERIAL#.

7. Tidy up.
   a. In the second session, attempt to run any SQL statement. You will receive the message "ORA-00028: your session has been killed."
   b. In the third session, the update will now have succeeded and completed. Terminate the transaction with COMMIT or ROLLBACK.

Here are the steps to follow to demonstrate deadlocks:

1. In your first session, update a row:

```
update lockdemo set user_id=99 where username='SYS';
```

2. In your third session, update a second row:

```
update lockdemo set user_id=99 where username='SYSTEM';
```

3. In your first session, attempt to update the second row:

```
update lockdemo set user_id=99 where username='SYSTEM';
```

This will hang, because the row is already locked.

4. Set up the deadlock by updating the first row in the third session:

```
update lockdemo set user_id=99 where username='SYS';
```

This will hang, but within three seconds the first session will become free with the message "ORA-00060: deadlock requested while waiting for resource."

5. Retrieve information about the deadlock from the alert log and trace files.
   a. From an operating system prompt, open the alert log in the database's trace directory. The location can be found with this query:

   ```
   select value from v$diag_info where name='Diag Trace';
   ```

   and the file will be called alert_*SID*.ora. The last entry in the file will be something like this (a Windows example):

   ```
   Tue Sep 24 10:54:41 2013
   ORA-00060: Deadlock detected. More info in file
   C:\APP\ORACLE\diag\rdbms\orclz\orclz\trace\orclz_ora_6000.trc.
   ```

b. Open the trace file with an editor. Toward the top of the file will be the critical message:

```
*** 2013-09-24 10:54:41.839

DEADLOCK DETECTED ( ORA-00060 )
[Transaction Deadlock]
The following deadlock is not an ORACLE error. It is a
deadlock due to user error in the design of an application
or from issuing incorrect ad-hoc SQL.
```

Note that this message places the responsibility firmly on the developers. Look lower down in the file, and you will find the SIDs of the sessions involved and the statements they executed that caused the deadlock.

6. Tidy up. In the first session, issue a ROLLBACK to roll back the update that did succeed. This will free up the third session, where you can now also issue a ROLLBACK. Drop the LOCKDEMO table.

CERTIFICATION SUMMARY

Record locking is completely automatic. The default mechanism ensures the highest possible level of concurrency: row-level locking whenever a DML statement is executed, and no locks for queries. Exclusive locks are taken on rows; shareable locks are taken on tables. Manual locking of entire tables is possible.

Excessive (that is, noticeable) lock contention may require DBA intervention by identifying the blocking session and then killing it. Deadlocks (which are programming logic errors) are resolved automatically.

TWO-MINUTE DRILL

Describe the Locking Mechanism and How Oracle Manages Data Concurrency

- The default level of locking is row level.
- Locks are required for all DML commands and are optional for SELECT.
- A DML statement requires shared locks on the objects involved and exclusive locks on the rows involved.
- A DDL lock requires an exclusive lock on the object it affects.

Monitor and Resolve Locking Conflicts

- Blocking caused by row locks can be identified by querying the V$SESSION view or through Database Express.
- Resolve lock contention either by terminating blocking transactions or by killing the blocking session.
- Deadlocks are resolved automatically.

SELF TEST

Describe the Locking Mechanism and How Oracle Manages Data Concurrency

1. Locks are needed to stop sessions working on the same data at the same time. If one user updates a row without specifying any locking, what will be the effect on other sessions?

A. Others will be able to read and write other rows, but not the affected rows.

B. Others will be able to read the affected rows, but not write to them.

C. Others will be able to read and write the affected rows, but a COMMIT will hang until the first session has committed or rolled back.

D. Others will not be able write any rows, because by default the first session will have taken a lock on the entire table.

2. Which of these commands will prevent other sessions from reading rows in the table?

A. LOCK TABLE SCOTT.EMP IN EXCLUSIVE MODE;

B. LOCK TABLE SCOTT.EMP IN ROW EXCLUSIVE MODE;

C. SELECT * FROM SCOTT.EMP FOR UPDATE;

D. DELETE FROM SCOTT.EMP;

E. Oracle does not provide a lock that will prevent others from reading a table.

Monitor and Resolve Locking Conflicts

3. If several sessions request an exclusive lock on the same row, what will happen? (Choose the best answer.)

A. The first session will get the lock; after it releases the lock there is a random selection of the next session to get the lock.

B. The first session will get an exclusive lock, and the other sessions will get shared locks.

C. The sessions will be given an exclusive lock in the sequence in which they requested it.

D. Oracle will detect the conflict and roll back the statements that would otherwise hang.

4. If a programmer does not request a type of lock when updating many rows in one table, what lock or locks will they be given? (Choose the best answer.)

A. No locks at all. The default level of locking is NONE, in order to maximize concurrency.

B. An exclusive lock on the table. This is the fastest method when many rows are being updated.

C. Shared locks on the table and on each row. This is the safest (although not the fastest) method.

D. An exclusive lock on each row and a shared lock on the table. This maximizes concurrency safely.

5. What happens if two sessions deadlock against each other? (Choose the best answer.)
   A. Oracle will roll back one session's statement.
   B. Oracle will roll back both sessions' statements.
   C. Both sessions will hang indefinitely.
   D. Oracle will terminate one session.
   E. Oracle will terminate both sessions.

LAB QUESTION

Create a table, and from several sessions, attempt some DML against it. Be sure to cause contention by attempting to hit the same rows. From another session, connected as SYSDBA, run the script utllockt.sql, which resides in the ORACLE_HOME/rdbms/admin directory. It will show the blocked and blocking sessions in a tree-like display. Open the script in an editor. It is well documented and instructive to study.

SELF TEST ANSWERS

Describe the Locking Mechanism and How Oracle Manages Data Concurrency

1. ☑ **B.** By default, a row exclusive lock will protect the row against write but not read.
☒ **A, C,** and **D** are incorrect. **A** is incorrect because reading the updated row (in its pre-update form) will always be possible. **C** is incorrect because it is DML that will be blocked, not COMMIT. **D** is incorrect because the default exclusive lock is on the affected row only.

2. ☑ **E.** Readers are never blocked.
☒ **A, B, C,** and **D** are incorrect. **A** will lock all rows against update, and **B** will lock any updated rows. Neither will block readers. **C** and **D** are incorrect because they will take shared locks on the table and exclusive locks on the rows: again, neither can prevent reads.

Monitor and Resolve Locking Conflicts

3. ☑ **C.** This correctly describes the operation of the enqueue mechanism.
☒ **A, B,** and **D** are incorrect. **A** is incorrect because locks are granted sequentially, not randomly. **B** is incorrect because the shared locks apply to the object; row locks must be exclusive. **D** is incorrect because this is more like a description of how deadlocks are managed.

4. ☑ **D.** This correctly describes the DML locking mechanism: a shared lock to protect the table definition, and exclusive locks to protect the rows.
☒ **A, B,** and **C** are incorrect. **A** is incorrect because locks are always imposed. **B** is incorrect because exclusive table locks are only applied if the programmer requests them. **C** is incorrect because exclusive locks must always be taken on rows.

5. ☑ **A.** One of the statements will be automatically rolled back, allowing the session to continue.
☒ **B, C, D,** and **E** are incorrect. **B** is incorrect because only one statement will be rolled back. The other will remain in effect, blocking its session. **C** is incorrect because this is exactly the effect that is avoided. **D** and **E** are incorrect because the deadlock-resolution mechanism does not terminate sessions, only statements.

LAB ANSWER

Here is an example of the utllockt.sql output:

```
orclz> @?\rdbms\admin\utllockt.sql

WAITING_SESSION   LOCK_TYPE        MODE_REQUESTED MODE_HELD
----------------- ---------------- -------------- ------------
251               None
9                 Transaction      Exclusive      Exclusive
372               None
131               Transaction      Exclusive      Exclusive
242               Transaction      Exclusive      Exclusive

orclz>
```

11 Implementing Oracle Database Auditing

CERTIFICATION OBJECTIVES

11.01	Explain DBA Responsibilities for Security and Auditing	✓	Two-Minute Drill
11.02	Enable Standard Database Auditing and Unified Auditing	Q&A	Self-Test

Database security has several aspects. Firstly, authentication: who can connect? How does one identify them? Secondly, authorization: what are users allowed to do? How does one restrict their actions? These aspects have been covered in Chapter 7. Now the third aspect: auditing. Given that users can connect and perform certain actions, how do you track what they are doing? In many environments, users will have permission to do certain things—but that doesn't mean that they should be able to do them without a record being kept. For example, a DBA will (usually) be able to read and write any row in any table in the database. This is part of their job. For example, if a business data corruption occurs (perhaps through user error, perhaps through application software issues), the DBA will need to use SQL*Plus or some other tool that can bypass all the application security and rules, and edit the data to fix it. But that does not mean he should be diving into tables of sensitive data without good reason. Actions such as this cannot be prevented—but they can, and must, be tracked. This is the purpose of auditing: to record actions that are permitted, but potentially harmful.

CERTIFICATION OBJECTIVE 11.01

Explain DBA Responsibilities for Security and Auditing

Audit is necessary to detect suspicious or even downright illegal activity. Audit is not an area where the DBA makes all the decisions: they do what they are told. If the business states that all access to certain tables must be tracked, the DBA must arrange this. In some jurisdictions, regulatory requirements make auditing certain actions mandatory. Apart from these business needs, two groups of users require special attention: developers and DBAs. Developers have great power within the database; DBAs have even more. Monitoring activity by these groups to ensure that they are not abusing their powers raises the issue of how to audit users who may be able to modify the audit trail (or "Quis custodiet ipsos custodes?" as Juvenal put it nearly 2,000 years ago).

Reasons for Audit

Why is audit considered necessary in virtually all databases? Typical reasons are:

- To enable accountability for actions. In order to hold users responsible for their actions, it is necessary to track what they have done.
- To deter users from inappropriate activity. Many users will have the ability to perform actions that are damaging or fraudulent. Knowing that they are monitored will dissuade them from doing this.
- To investigate suspicious activity. Security may be set up correctly, but it is still useful to know if people are trying to access data or run commands that are beyond their authorization.
- To notify an auditor of unauthorized activity. In some cases, users may have more capabilities than they need. Auditing can track the use of any privileges considered dangerous and access to sensitive data.
- Compliance issues. Many applications have quasi-legal requirements for audit. Typically, these are based around access to personal or financial information.

Auditing Techniques

Several auditing techniques are available in an Oracle environment. The most powerful is the Audit Vault. This is a separately installed and licensed product that is far beyond the scope of the OCP syllabus. Most environments will not need this: the internal techniques described in this section will be sufficient for the majority of business needs. Release 12*c* introduces a new auditing method: *unified auditing*. It is this technique that is tested.

Standard Database Auditing

Standard database auditing is enabled with one parameter: AUDIT_TRAIL. The default for this parameter is NULL, meaning that standard audit is disabled. However, if the database is created with DBCA, standard audit will have been enabled by setting this parameter to DB. If enabled in this way, a minimum set of information auditing use of privileges considered to be potentially dangerous is configured by default.

Standard auditing is configured with the **AUDIT** and **NOAUDIT** commands. It can track access to objects, use of privileges, and execution of certain statements.

Audit records can be gathered for all users or only some, once per session or once per action in the session, whenever the attempt was made, or filtered by successful or unsuccessful attempts. The audit records are either written to a database table (which is SYS.AUD$) and visible through a set of views or written to the operating system where they are stored as files external to the database.

This technique for auditing is fully supported, but in release 12.1, Oracle Corporation recommends that unified auditing should be used instead.

Fine Grained Auditing

Fine Grained Auditing (FGA) can be configured to focus on precise areas of concern. Rather than auditing access at the object level, FGA can track access to certain rows and columns. Without FGA, audit tends to produce a large number of "false positives": that is, audit records that report issues of no concern. Examples could be:

- Access to a table of employee data is fine in general, but if a SALARY column is accessed, that should be recorded.
- Perhaps a user has full rights to read a table when running an approved application. But if they query the table from SQL*Plus, that should be known.
- It may not be necessary to record access that occurs through normal means in the working day, but out-of-hours access from a device outside the corporate network should be tracked.

FGA will generate an audit record when certain conditions are met. The condition can be based on a predicate and also on a column list. As well as auditing the event, FGA can also execute a user-defined procedure. This is a very powerful facility: in effect, it is a trigger on SELECT. It is possible to define different audit policies for different statements. For example, one might want to record changes to data, but not reads.

The interface to FGA is a simple-to-use API—the DBMS_FGA package, with four procedures:

- **DBMS_FGA.ADD_POLICY** Create a policy for a table.
- **DBMS_FGA.DROP_POLICY** Drop a previously created policy.
- **DBMS_FGA.DISABLE_POLICY** Disable the policy. Policies are by default enabled.
- **DBMS_FGA.ENABLE_POLICY** Enable a policy that had been previously disabled.

The API is reasonably self-explanatory. Consider these examples:

```
execute dbms_fga.add_policy(-
      object_schema=>'scott',-
      object_name=>'emp',-
      policy_name=>'emp_d10_pol',-
      audit_condition=>'deptno=10',-
      statement_types=>'select,insert,update,delete');
execute dbms_fga.add_policy(-
      object_schema=>'scott',-
      object_name=>'emp',-
      policy_name=>'emp_sal_pol',-
      audit_column=>'sal');
execute dbms_fga.add_policy(-
      object_schema=>'scott',-
      object_name=>'emp',-
      policy_name=>'emp_del_pol',-
      handler_schema=>'sec',-
      handler_module=>'empdel',-
      statement_types=>'delete');
```

This example defines three policies on one table, SCOTT.EMP. The first policy, EMP_D10_POL, will generate an audit record whenever any statement is executed that accesses an employee in Department 10. Note that the policy does not include MERGE. A MERGE is captured according to the underlying DML statement that the MERGE implements. Using the default of NULL for AUDIT_COLUMNS means that there is no column restriction: no matter what columns are projected, the statement will be audited.

The second policy will capture all SELECT statements (SELECT is the default for the STATEMENT_TYPE argument) that read the SAL column. The default of NULL for AUDIT_CONDITION means that the audit will be made for any row.

The third policy will generate an audit record and will also run a procedure, SEC. EMPDEL, whenever a row is deleted. The procedure must conform to a defined interface: it must accept three VARCHAR2 arguments, which will be populated with the object schema (in this case, SCOTT), the object name (in this case, EMP), and the policy name (in this case, EMP_DEL_POL).

The audit records are visible in the data dictionary view DBA_FGA_AUDIT_TRAIL. This includes the actual SQL statement, along with details such as who executed it and when. The underlying storage for the view is the table SYS.FGA_LOG$, which by default resides in the SYSTEM tablespace.

Value-Based Auditing

The declarative techniques for audit (standard auditing, FGA, and unified auditing) do not capture the data themselves. They capture the action: who, what, when, and with which privilege. This means the statement executed, not the values that were actually seen or updated. If it is necessary to see the values, one must resort to value-base auditing, which is implemented with triggers.

A DML trigger designed to fire whenever any DML statement is executed can capture the row values and write them out to a user-defined audit table. Consider this example:

```
create or replace trigger emp_val_audit
after update or insert or delete on emp
for each row
begin
case
when updating then insert into sec.emp_aud
      values(user,sysdate,:new.empno,:old.sal,:new.sal);
when inserting then insert into sec.emp_aud
      values(user,sysdate,:new.empno,null,:new.sal);
when deleting then insert into sec.emp_aud
      values(user,sysdate,:new.empno,:old.sal,null);
end case;
end;
```

Depending on the nature of the DML, this trigger will capture appropriate values into a logging table. The trigger will fire as part of the DML, and the insert will be committed (or rolled back) with the calling transaction. It is therefore possible that performance may degrade. This should not be the case with standard or FGA auditing, where the capture is accomplished by routines that are internal to the instance, not by user-defined PL/SQL code.

Unified Auditing

Unified auditing is a new technique that replaces standard auditing, although the two can work concurrently. Unified auditing declares policies, which are then enabled for particular (or all) users. Five preconfigured policies are available to be implemented:

- ORA_SECURECONFIG declares similar audits to the default standard auditing.
- ORA_DATABASE_PARAMETER captures changes implemented with **ALTER DATABASE** and **ALTER SYSTEM** commands.

- ORA_ACCOUNT_MGMT captures changes made with ALTER, DROP, and CREATE roles and users, as well as GRANT and REVOKE.
- ORA_RAS_POLICY_MANAGEMENT, ORA_RAS_SESSION_MANAGEMENT. These are to do with Real Application Security, which is beyond the scope of the OCP examinations.

To confirm whether unified auditing is enabled, query the V$OPTION dynamic performance view. In this example, it is not enabled:

```
orclz>
orclz> select value from v$option where
  2  parameter ='Unified Auditing';

VALUE
----------------------------------------------------------------
FALSE

orclz>
```

The unified auditing mechanism is very efficient. By default, audit records are not written to the audit trail table (in the AUDSYS schema) in real time, but via a buffered queue. So sessions are writing only to a memory structure in the SGA. A background process, the GEN0 generic process, takes the strain of writing the records from the queue to the table asynchronously. This delayed write does raise the possibility of losing audit records in the event of an instance crash. Although enabled by default, this can be changed. To switch from delayed write mode to immediate write mode, use a procedure in the DBMS_AUDIT_MGMT package. This example enables immediate write and then switches back the default queued write:

```
orclz>
orclz> exec dbms_audit_mgmt.set_audit_trail_property(-
> dbms_audit_mgmt.audit_trail_unified,-
> dbms_audit_mgmt.audit_trail_write_mode,-
> dbms_audit_mgmt.audit_trail_immediate_write);

PL/SQL procedure successfully completed.

orclz>
orclz> exec dbms_audit_mgmt.set_audit_trail_property(-
> dbms_audit_mgmt.audit_trail_unified,-
> dbms_audit_mgmt.audit_trail_write_mode,-
> dbms_audit_mgmt.audit_trail_queued_write);
```

```
PL/SQL procedure successfully completed.

orclz>
```

Unified audit records are written to a table in the AUDSYS schema. The table has a system-generated name that may be different in every database and is read-only to any regular DDL or DML statements. It can be managed only through DBMS_AUDIT_MGMT.

Mandatory Auditing

A small number of operations are always audited, whether configured or not:

- Execution of the unified auditing commands **CREATE/ALTER/DROP AUDIT POLICY**
- Execution of the standard audit commands **AUDIT/NOAUDIT**
- Execution of the FGA package DBMS_FGA
- Execution of the management package DBMS_AUDIT_MGMT

Furthermore, all top-level statements executed by administrative users (sessions connected as SYSDBA, SYSOPER, SYSBACKUP, SYSDG, SYSKM, or SYSASM) while the database is in NOMOUNT or MOUNT mode are audited to the operating system audit trail. On Unix or Linux, the records are written to files in the directory specified by the AUDIT_FILE_DEST parameter; on Windows, they are written to the Windows application log. These statements include connect attempts, startup or shutdown, and any **ALTER SYSTEM** and **ALTER DATABASE** commands.

CERTIFICATION OBJECTIVE 11.02

Enable Standard Database Auditing and Unified Auditing

Standard auditing is enabled by default, although it may not have been configured. Unified auditing requires an appropriate dynamic library to be available, which is not the case following installation of the Oracle Home.

Enable Standard Auditing

Figure 11-1 shows a query that displays the current values of the standard auditing parameters as well as two commands to enable audit.

The parameters are:

audit_sys_operations	Records all SQL executed as an administrative user to the operating system audit trail. Default: false.
audit_file_dest	The location of audit records if auditing is to the operating system. Unix default: $ORACLE_BASE/admin/$ORACLE_SID/adump. Windows: always to the application log.
audit_syslog_level	Enables writing to the syslog daemon. Set according to your system administrator's instruction. Default: null (disabled).
audit_trail	Enables or disables standard audit to the operating system or the database, in various formats. Default: null (disabled).

The values in Figure 11-1 are typical of many installations. Once the parameters have been set (all of which are static), the **AUDIT** command enables audit of the execution of certain statements, the use of certain privileges, or the access to certain objects.

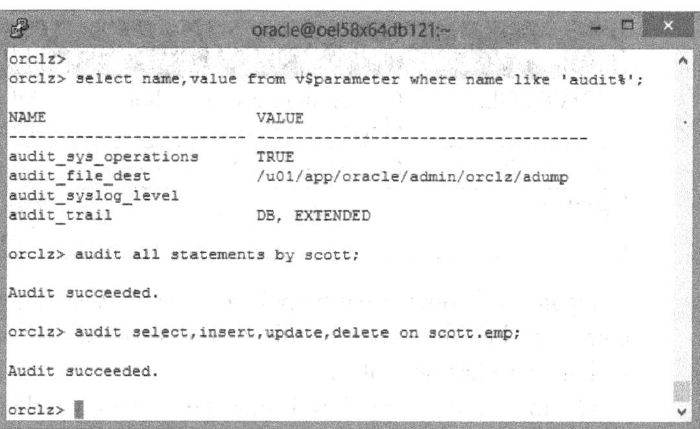
oracle@oel58x64db121:~
orclz>
orclz> select name,value from v$parameter where name like 'audit%';
NAME VALUE
audit_sys_operations TRUE
audit_file_dest /u01/app/oracle/admin/orclz/adump
audit_syslog_level
audit_trail DB, EXTENDED
orclz> audit all statements by scott;
Audit succeeded.
orclz> audit select,insert,update,delete on scott.emp;
Audit succeeded.
orclz>

FIGURE 11-1 Standard audit configuration

Enable Unified Auditing

If unified auditing is not enabled (which it is not, following a standard installation), it is necessary to enable it within the Oracle executable code: relink the Oracle executables for Linux or copy in a dynamic link library for Windows.

Here is how to relink the executables:

```
cd $ORACLE_HOME/rdbms/lib
make -f ins_rdbms.mk uniaud_on ioracle ORACLE_HOME=$ORACLE_HOME
```

On Windows, stop the Windows services for the database and the listener and then copy in the appropriate dynamic link library:

```
net stop oracleserviceORCL
net stop OracleOraDB12Home1TNSListener
cd %ORACLE_HOME%\bin
copy orauniaud12.dll.dbl orauniaud12.dll
net start oracleserviceORCL
net start OracleOraDB12Home1TNSListener
```

Restart the listener and database instance and then confirm in V$OPTION that unified auditing is now enabled.

To configure unified auditing, first grant the necessary roles to a user. These roles are AUDIT_ADMIN to administer unified auditing and AUDIT_VIEWER to view and analyze audit data. Then, as an AUDIT_ADMIN user, enable the supplied policies or create your own. A policy consists of specifying one (or more) of the three categories to audit:

Category	What to specify	What is audited
PRIVILEGES	One or more system and/or object privileges	All events that use any of the specified privileges
ACTIONS	One or more SQL commands	All invocations of the command
ROLES	One or more roles	Use of any privileges used through a direct grant to the role

Figure 11-2 shows creating policies of each type, followed by a mixed policy that combines the three types. Finally, it shows an example of an ACTION policy that will apply to just one table.

Having created the policy, it must be activated: either globally or for individual users. By default, an audit record is generated whenever the audit condition is met, whether the result was successful or not. Figure 11-3 shows activating policies in various ways.

FIGURE 11-2 Defining unified auditing policies

```
Administrator: cmd - sqlplus / as sysdba
orclz>
orclz> create audit policy privpol privileges select any table, create trigger;

Audit policy created.

orclz> create audit policy actpol actions drop table, alter trigger;

Audit policy created.

orclz> create audit policy rolepol roles dba;

Audit policy created.

orclz> create audit policy mixedpol
  2  privileges select any table, create trigger
  3  actions drop table, alter trigger
  4  roles dba;

Audit policy created.

orclz> create audit policy emppol actions insert,update,delete on scott.emp;

Audit policy created.

orclz> _
```

The first example in the figure enables the privpol policy for all users. Every attempt to use either of the privileges, whether successful or not, will be recorded. The next example enables the actpol policy, but will only record successful attempts to execute the statements. The third example will activate the rolepol policy for just two users, recording every time they use a privilege acquired through the nominated role. Then mixedpol is enabled for all users when attempts fail. The syntax to disable a policy is NOAUDIT POLICY <*policy name*>.

The last example in Figure 11-3 uses the DBMS_AUDIT_MGMT.FLUSH_UNIFIED_AUDIT_TRAIL procedure to flush all records currently buffered in the SGA to the audit trail within the database.

FIGURE 11-3 Enable and disable policies

```
Administrator: cmd - sqlplus scott/tiger
orclz>
orclz> audit policy privpol;

Audit succeeded.

orclz> audit policy actpol whenever successful;

Audit succeeded.

orclz> audit policy rolepol by scott,system;

Audit succeeded.

orclz> audit policy mixedpol whenever not successful;

Audit succeeded.

orclz>  noaudit policy actpol;

Noaudit succeeded.

orclz> exec dbms_audit_mgmt.flush_unified_audit_trail;

PL/SQL procedure successfully completed.

orclz>
```

EXERCISE 11-1

Use Unified Auditing

In this exercise, you will enable unified auditing. The method differs between Linux and Windows. Then you will create and configure audit policies as well as query the results. Connect as SYSDBA unless otherwise directed. Here are the steps to follow:

1. Determine whether unified auditing is enabled by running this query:

   ```
   select value from v$option where parameter='Unified Auditing';
   ```

   Following a standard install, this will return FALSE.

2. Shut down the Oracle services.
   Shut down all database instances and listeners. On Windows, also stop all Oracle-related Windows services.

3. Enable unified auditing.
   In Linux, relink the executables to include the unified auditing libraries:

   ```
   cd $ORACLE_HOME/rdbms/lib
   make -f ins_rdbms.mk uniaud_on ioracle ORACLE_HOME=$ORACLE_HOME
   ```

   In Windows, copy in the unified auditing dynamic link library:

   ```
   cd %ORACLE_HOME%\bin
   copy orauniaud12.dll.dbl orauniaud12.dll
   ```

4. Confirm that unified auditing is now enabled.
   Start the instance and listener (on Windows, start the relevant services) and rerun the query from step 1. This will return TRUE.

5. Enable a pre-supplied audit policy and then create and enable your own:

   ```
   audit policy ora_account_mgmt;
   create audit policy aud_dba_role roles dba;
   audit policy aud_dba_role by system;
   ```

   a. Confirm what has been configured:

   ```
   select policy_name, enabled_opt, user_name from
   audit_unified_enabled_policies;
   ```

   b. Note for whom the policies have been enabled. Are any policies enabled by default?

6. Confirm that unified auditing records are generated.

   a. Connect as user SYSTEM and perform a few actions. Here is an example:

   ```
   create user x identified by y;
   alter system set open_cursors=300 scope=memory;
   ```

b. Query the unified audit trail:

```
exec dbms_audit_mgmt.flush_unified_audit_trail
select dbusername,sql_text from unified_audit_trail;
```

7. Attempt to tamper with the audit trail.
Connected as SYSDBA, identify the name of the audit trail table and attempt to delete it:

```
select table_name from dba_tables where owner='AUDSYS';
delete from audsys."&audit_table_name";
truncate table audsys."&audit_table_name";
```

8. Clean the audit trail.
Execute a procedure to clear out the unified audit trail. This may throw an error message regarding initialization, but will function nonetheless:

```
select count(*) from unified_audit_trail;
execute dbms_audit_mgmt.clean_audit_trail(-
dbms_audit_mgmt.audit_trail_all,false)
select count(*) from unified_audit_trail;
```

CERTIFICATION SUMMARY

All databases perform certain mandatory audits: startup, shutdown, and connections with SYSDBA privileges. As configured following a default installation, standard auditing is enabled. This is configured with instance parameters and the **AUDIT** command. Audit records are written either to the SYS.AUD$ table or to operating system files.

Optional audits include auditing all SYSDBA actions (enabled with a parameter, written to the operating system audit trail) and Fine Grained Auditing (applied to selected SQL statements that conform to certain conditions). Value-based auditing can also be implemented, based on DML triggers.

Unified auditing combines all audit trails into one using a table in the AUDSYS schema that is protected from all DML and DDL, even when executed with SYSDBA privileges. Enabling unified auditing requires relinking the Oracle executables (Unix) or copying in the appropriate dynamic link library (Windows). Once unified auditing is enabled, standard auditing is disabled.

TWO-MINUTE DRILL

Explain DBA Responsibilities for Security and Auditing

- ❑ The DBA should configure auditing according to the organization's requirements.
- ❑ Unified auditing is the recommended approach.
- ❑ Value-based auditing can also be used, based on DML triggers.

Enable Standard Database Auditing and Unified Auditing

- ❑ Standard auditing is still supported and is enabled with instance parameters.
- ❑ Configure standard auditing with the **AUDIT** and **NOAUDIT** commands.
- ❑ Unified auditing requires linking appropriate modules into the Oracle executables.
- ❑ Unified auditing is configured by declaring audit policies.
- ❑ It is not possible to edit the unified audit trail with SQL commands.

SELF TEST

Explain DBA Responsibilities for Security and Auditing

1. You want to use unified auditing, and you run this query:

```
orclz> select value from v$option where parameter='Unified Auditing';
VALUE
----------------------------------------------------------------
TRUE
orclz>
```

What should you do to enable unified auditing? (Choose the best answer.)

A. Run ALTER SYSTEM SET AUDIT_TRAIL=DB,EXTENDED SCOPE=SPFILE; and then restart the database.

B. Relink the Oracle executables with the unified auditing libraries.

C. Create and enable one or more unified auditing policies.

D. Disable standard auditing.

2. It is necessary track all executions of SELECT by any users against a particular table. Which auditing tool will do this? (Choose the best answer.)

A. Standard auditing

B. Fine Grained Auditing

C. Unified auditing

D. All of the above

Enable Standard Database Auditing and Unified Auditing

3. What types of activity are mandatorily audited? (Choose three answers.)

A. Creating, altering, or dropping an audit policy

B. Creating, altering, or dropping a user

C. Execution of the **AUDIT** and **NOAUDIT** commands

D. All statements executed while connected AS SYSDBA

E. SYSDBA top-level statements in MOUNT or NOMOUNT

F. DDL against the data dictionary

4. Is it possible for the unified audit trail to lose audit records? (Choose the best answer.)

A. The unified audit trail is always protected in all circumstances.

B. Records cannot be lost, but they can be deleted or modified with **DML** commands.

C. The audit trail is protected against DML, but DDL (such as TRUNCATE) can lose records.

D. It is possible for records to be lost in the event of an instance failure.

SELF TEST ANSWERS

Explain DBA Responsibilities for Security and Auditing

1. ☑ **B.** It is necessary to link in the unified auditing libraries to the Oracle binaries.
☒ **A, C,** and **D** are incorrect. **A** is incorrect because the AUDIT_TRAIL parameter enables standard auditing, not unified auditing. **C** is necessary, but not sufficient. **D** is incorrect because standard and unified auditing can coexist.

2. ☑ **D.** Any of the auditing methods can do this.
☒ **A, B,** and **C** are incorrect. Each of these methods can track such access, although each has different means for configuration and different destinations for the audit records.

Enable Standard Database Auditing and Unified Auditing

3. ☑ **A, C, E.** Commands that configure audit are themselves audited as well as all top-level statements executed before the database is opened.
☒ **B, D,** and **F** are incorrect. These classes of commands are not mandatorily audited. Most DBAs will want to audit them, but this must be explicitly configured.

4. ☑ **D.** By default, records may be buffered in the SGA before being written to the audit trail. Therefore, an instance failure could lose records.
☒ **A, B,** and **C** are incorrect. **A** is incorrect because the audit trail can in fact lose records—if not configured to write them in real time. **B** and **C** are incorrect because the audit trail is protected against both DML and DDL.

12 Performing Database Maintenance

CERTIFICATION OBJECTIVES

12.01	Manage the Automatic Workload Repository (AWR)
12.02	Use the Automatic Database Diagnostic Monitor (ADDM)
12.03	Describe and Use the Advisory Framework
12.04	Set Alert Thresholds
12.05	Use Automated Tasks
✓	Two-Minute Drill
Q&A	Self Test

A 12c database is to a certain extent self-managing. Maintenance tasks run automatically (unless disabled) and diagnostic information is gathered at regular intervals. With earlier releases, monitoring the database in order to pick up developing problems before they become critical took much time. Identifying and diagnosing performance issues was not only time consuming but also required much skill. Use of the Alert system and the diagnostic advisors, installed as standard in every 12c database, frees the DBA from the necessity of devoting a large amount of effort to this work.

CERTIFICATION OBJECTIVE 12.01

Manage the Automatic Workload Repository (AWR)

Oracle collects a vast amount of statistical information regarding performance and activity. This information is accumulated in memory and periodically written to disk: to the tables that make up the AWR. The AWR exists as a set of tables and other objects in the SYSAUX tablespace. The AWR is related to the data dictionary, but unlike the data dictionary, the AWR is not essential for the database to function (although it may be necessary for it to function well). Data is written to the AWR, stored for a while, and eventually overwritten with more recent information.

Gathering AWR Statistics

The level of statistics gathered is controlled by the instance parameter STATISTICS_LEVEL. This can be set to BASIC, to TYPICAL (which is the default), or to ALL. The TYPICAL level will force the collection of all the statistics needed for normal tuning, without collecting any that would adversely impact performance. The BASIC level will disable virtually all statistics, all performance-tuning advisors, and the server-generated Alert system—with no appreciable run-time performance benefit. The ALL level will collect extremely detailed statistics on SQL statement execution; these may occasionally be necessary if you are doing

Setting STATISTICS_LEVEL=BASIC will disable all advisors and the server-generated Alert system.

advanced SQL statement tuning, but they may cause a slight performance drop while being collected.

Statistics are accumulated in memory, in data structures within the SGA. This causes no performance impact, because the statistics merely reflect what the instance is doing anyway. Periodically (by default, once an hour) they are flushed to disk, to the AWR. This is known as an AWR snapshot. The flushing to disk is done by a background process: the Manageability Monitor, or MMON. This use of a background process is the key to the efficiency of the statistics-collection process. In earlier releases of the database, accessing performance-tuning statistics was only possible by running queries against various views—the dynamic performance V$ views. Populating these views is an expensive process. The DBA must launch a session against the database and then issue a query. Executing this query forces Oracle to extract data from the SGA and present it to the session in a view. This approach is still possible—all the old views, and many more, are still available—but the AWR approach is far more efficient.

on the job

No third-party tool can ever have the direct memory access to the instance that MMON has. If your instance is highly stressed, you should think carefully before using any tuning products other than those provided by Oracle itself.

The MMON has direct access to the memory structures that make up the SGA, and therefore the statistics within them. It can extract data from the SGA without the need to go via a session, or to execute SQL. The only overhead involved is actually writing the snapshot of the data to the AWR. By default, this occurs only once an hour and therefore should not have a noticeable effect on run-time performance.

AWR statistics are saved as a snapshot to the AWR by the MMON process (by default, every 60 minutes). By default, the snapshots are stored for eight days before being overwritten.

The AWR is a set of tables located in the SYSAUX tablespace. These tables cannot be relocated; they exist in the SYSMAN schema. You can log on to the database with tools such as SQL*Plus as user SYSMAN, but this should never be necessary, and indeed Oracle Corporation does not support access to the AWR tables with SQL*Plus or with any tools other than the various APIs provided in the form of DBMS packages or through various views.

An AWR snapshot can be thought of as a copy of the contents of many V$ views at the time the snapshot was taken. However, never forget that the mechanism for copying the information is not to query the V$ views: the information is extracted directly from the data structures that make up the instance. The process that makes the copy is MMON. In addition to information from the dynamic performance (or V$) views, the AWR stores information otherwise visible in the DBA views, populated from the data dictionary. This category of information includes a history of object statistics. Without the AWR, the database would have no long-term record of how objects were changing. The statistics gathered with DBMS_STATS give current information, but it may also be necessary to have a historical picture of the state of the database objects. The AWR can provide this.

Managing the AWR

Snapshots of statistics data are kept in the AWR, by default, for eight days. This period is configurable, and it is also possible to mark a pair of snapshots as a baseline, to be kept indefinitely. Baseline snapshots are not automatically purged. As a rough guide for sizing, if the snapshot collection is left on every hour and the retention time is left on eight days, then the AWR may well require between 200MB and 300MB of space in the SYSAUX tablespace. But this figure is highly variable and will to a large extent depend on the number of sessions. Adjusting the AWR settings to save snapshots more frequently will make problem diagnosis more precise. If the snapshots are several hours apart, you may miss peaks of activity (and consequent dips in performance). But gathering snapshots too frequently will increase the size of the AWR and could possibly impact performance due to the increased workload of collecting and saving the information.

on the job

It is important to monitor the size and growth of the SYSAUX tablespace and the AWR within it. The Alert system will assist with the first task, and the view V$SYSAUX_OCCUPANTS should be used for the second.

Adjusting the AWR snapshot frequency and retention are done with the PL/SQL API, DBMS_WORKLOAD_REPOSITORY. Figure 12-1 shows examples of using this package. First, a query against the DBA_HIST_WR_CONTROL view shows the current values for snapshot retention and frequency. The values (which are of data type INTERVAL) are the default values. Then a call to

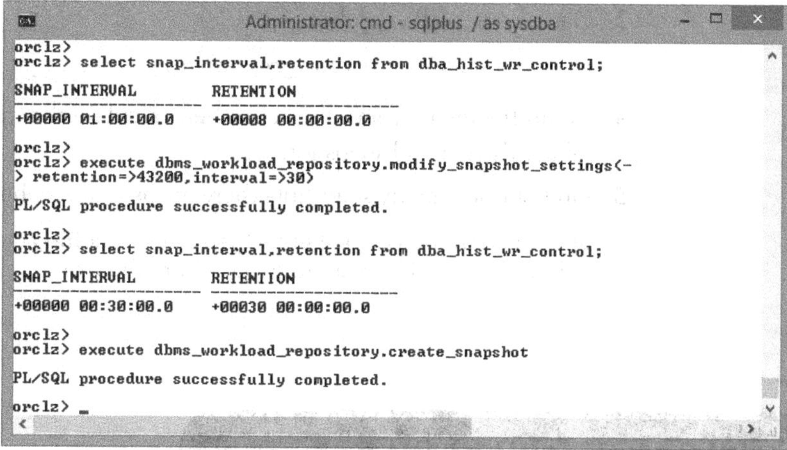

FIGURE 12-1 How to display and adjust the AWR snapshot settings

the MODIFY_SNAPSHOT_SETTINGS procedure changes them to 30 days and half an hour: the units are minutes. Finally, the CREATE_SNAPSHOT procedure forces gathering a snapshot, which will be made in addition to the regularly scheduled collections. Forcing collection of a snapshot would typically be done immediately before and after launching a job of some kind, so that reports can be generated focusing on a particular time frame.

exam watch

By default, AWR snapshots are taken every hour and saved for eight days. The AWR is located in the SYSAUX tablespace and cannot be relocated to anywhere else.

EXERCISE 12-1

Monitor the Automatic Workload Repository

In this exercise, you will determine the size of the AWR and monitor its growth as it stores more snapshots. Follow these steps:

1. Connect to your database with SQL*Plus as user SYSTEM.
2. The view V$SYSAUX_OCCUPANTS shows all the components installed into the SYSAUX tablespace. Find out how much space the AWR is taking up:

```
select occupant_desc,space_usage_kbytes from v$sysaux_occupants
where occupant_name='SM/AWR';
```

Note the size returned.

3. Gather an AWR snapshot:

```
execute dbms_workload_repository.create_snapshot
```

4. Rerun the query from step 2 and then calculate the increase in size caused by taking the manual snapshot.
5. Find out how many snapshots there are as well as what date range they cover:

```
select min(begin_interval_time), max(begin_interval_time),
count(snap_id) from dba_hist_snapshot;
```

CERTIFICATION OBJECTIVE 12.02

Use the Automatic Database Diagnostic Monitor (ADDM)

The database comes preconfigured with a set of advisors. First among these is the Automatic Database Diagnostic Monitor, or ADDM. Studying ADDM reports, which are generated automatically whenever an AWR snapshot is taken, will usually be a regular part of the DBA's routine. The ADDM reports are of great value in themselves and will highlight problems within the database and suggest solutions, but in many cases the recommendations will include suggesting that you run one or more other advisors. These advisors can give much more precise diagnostic information and advice than the ADDM.

The ADDM looks at data stored in two AWR snapshots: by comparing them, it can summarize the activity during the period between these snapshots and generate a report. The report attempts to detect any possible performance issues and make recommendations that will alleviate them. The issues that the ADDM can identify include the following:

- CPU bottlenecks
- Contention issues such as row locking
- Stress on the I/O system
- High-load SQL

ADDM reports are generated on demand as well as whenever a snapshot is gathered. A report requires two snapshots.

The ADDM runs automatically whenever an AWR snapshot is generated, and it will analyze activity between that snapshot and the preceding snapshot. Therefore, by default, reports are available per hour. It is also possible to generate a report on demand covering the time between any two snapshots. ADDM reports can be retrieved or generated either through Database Express (click the Performance Hub link on the Performance tab and then select the ADDM sub-tab) or by running the addmrpt.sql script. This script resides in the ORACLE_HOME/rdbms/admin directory. It presents all available snapshots, and prompts for the two over which the report should be generated.

ADDM reports will sometimes give precise advice (such as to change a parameter) but will more often identify particular statements and advise running another advisor against them. ADDM may also suggest restructuring objects, for example, perhaps to implement partitioning. It will always give reasons for its recommendations, which can be very instructive, even if you decide not to implement the advice.

on the job

ADDM will often recommend using facilities for which you may not be licensed, such as the SQL Tuning Advisor or Partitioning. This can be somewhat irritating.

EXERCISE 12-2

Generate an ADDM Report

In this exercise, you will generate an ADDM report. Follow these steps:

1. Connect to the database as user SYSTEM.
2. Generate the report by running this command from an SQL prompt:

   ```
   @?/rdbms/admin/addmrpt.sql
   ```

   When prompted, select any two snapshots.
3. Study the report. Note that it is possible that the time frame does not include enough activity to perform any meaningful analysis—if so, try again with a different period.

CERTIFICATION OBJECTIVE 12.03

Describe and Use the Advisory Framework

The advisors rely on activity statistics accumulated by the instance in memory and written to the AWR as snapshots. The ADDM and the SQL Tuning Advisor can be accessed through Database Express, on the Performance tab on the database home page. The other advisors have PL/SQL interfaces or are visible as data dictionary views. All the advisors are detailed in Chapters 13 and 14. For now, here is a summary description of each.

The Memory Advisors

The memory advisors predict the effect of varying the size of memory structures, reporting the estimates in terms of processing time saved (the Shared Pool, Java Pool, and Streams Pool advisors), disk activity reductions (the Database Buffer Cache advisor), or both (the PGA advisor). There is no advisor for the Large Pool. There is, however, an SGA advisor, which will report on the effect of varying the size of the entire SGA. If memory management has been automated via the parameter MEMORY_TARGET and all other memory parameters left on default, an overall memory advisor gives a single point from which to gauge whether allocating more memory to the instance would improve performance.

The memory advisors are exposed through these views:

- **V$DB_CACHE_ADVICE** The DB Cache advisor
- **V$JAVA_POOL_ADVICE** The Java Pool advisor
- **V$MEMORY_TARGET_ADVICE** The Automatic Memory Management advisor
- **V$PGA_TARGET_ADVICE** The PGA advisor
- **V$SGA_TARGET_ADVICE** The Shared Memory Management advisor
- **V$SHARED_POOL_ADVICE** The Shared Pool advisor
- **V$STREAMS_POOL_ADVICE** The Streams Pool advisor

The SQL Advisors

There are two SQL advisors: the SQL Access Advisor and the SQL Tuning Advisor. The SQL Access Advisor will observe a workload of SQL statements and make recommendations regarding segments so that the workload would run more quickly.

The workload can be a hypothetical workload, or it can be derived from the SQL actually executed during a certain time frame. The recommendations can be to create or drop indexes and materialized views, and to make use of segment partitioning. The SQL Tuning Advisor can analyze individual statements, as well as recommend schema changes (as the SQL Access Advisor does). It can recommend generating additional statistics on the statement's execution that will assist the optimizer in choosing the best execution plan, and rewriting the statement to eliminate some inefficiencies inherent in some SQL structures.

The SQL advisors are accessed through PL/SQL APIs: DBMS_ADVISOR and DBMS_SQLTUNE. The SQL Tuning Advisor is also accessible through Database Express.

The Automatic Undo Advisor

As discussed in Chapter 9, the Undo Advisor (exposed through the V$UNDOSTAT view) will observe the rate of undo data generation and the length of queries being run, and it will recommend a minimum size for the undo tablespace, which will ensure that queries do not fail with a "snapshot too old" error and that DML statements do not fail because of insufficient undo space.

The Mean Time to Recover (MTTR) Advisor

The mechanism for instance recovery after a failure is detailed in Chapter 18. In summary, if the instance terminates in a disorderly fashion (such as a power cut or server reboot while the database was open, or just a SHUTDOWN ABORT), then on the next startup it is necessary to reinstate all work in progress that had not been written to the datafiles at the time of the crash. This will happen automatically, but until it is done, users cannot log on. The MTTR Advisor (exposed in the V$INSTANCE_RECOVERY view) estimates how long this period of downtime for crash recovery will be, given the current workload.

The Data Recovery Advisor

If the database has been damaged in some way (such as files deleted or data blocks corrupted), it may take some time to identify the problem. Then there will often be several ways of recovering from the situation. For example, if a number of datafiles have been damaged by corruptions appearing on a disk, it will be necessary to find out which files as well as which blocks. Then a decision must be made as to whether to restore entire files or only the damaged blocks. If the database is protected by a physical standby, switching over to that would also be a possibility.

Following a failure, any DBA (no matter how experienced) will need time to determine the nature and extent of the problem, and then more time to decide upon the course of action that will repair the damage with the minimum disruption to work. The Data Recovery Advisor follows an expert system to advise the DBA on this. The expert system is essentially what the DBA would follow anyway, but the advisor can do it much faster. It is accessed with the DBMS_SQLDIAG package, invoked either through SQL*Plus or from the RMAN Recovery Manager tool.

The Segment Advisor

Segments grow automatically. As rows are inserted into table segments and index keys are inserted into index segments, the segments fill—and then Oracle will allocate more extents as necessary. But segments do not shrink automatically as data is removed or modified with DELETE and UPDATE commands; this only happens when the segment is deliberately reorganized. The Segment Advisor observes tables and indexes—both their current state and their historical patterns of use—and recommends appropriate reorganization when necessary. Invoke the Segment Advisor with the DBMS_ADVISOR package.

The SQL Repair Advisor

Occasionally, a SQL statement can fail because of an internal Oracle error. This will be reported with the ORA-600 error message. If the error condition (which is a polite name for a "bug") is only encountered for a particular execution plan, it follows that using a different execution plan could avoid the failure. The SQL Repair Advisor can investigate this and generate a patch to the statement that will force the optimizer to choose a safe plan, rather than a plan that hits the problem.

CERTIFICATION OBJECTIVE 12.04

Set Alert Thresholds

The Alert system is why the Oracle database can now be described as self-managing. In earlier releases, the DBA had to spend a great deal of effort on humdrum work that was essential but not always that interesting. They also had to devise methods of picking up exceptional conditions as they occurred. The Alert system can automate a large amount of work that previously fell into the DBA domain.

Alert Condition Monitoring and Notifications

A typical example of the humdrum work is space management, which, at its most basic, involves monitoring tablespaces to see when they are about to fill up. This could be done with scripts, such as this one:

```
SQL> select d.tablespace_name,sum(d.bytes) total,sum(f.bytes) free
  2  from dba_data_files d left outer join dba_free_space f
  3  on d.tablespace_name=f.tablespace_name
  4  group by d.tablespace_name;
TABLESPACE_NAME                      TOTAL       FREE
------------------------------ ---------- ----------
SYSAUX                          807337984   38928384
USERS                            24641536    1507328
SMALL                              401408
SYSTEM                         1509949440    4390912
EXAMPLE                         314572800   23396352
UNDO1                           209715200  208338944
```

But these scripts are prone to error—or at least, misinterpretation. For example, the view DBA_FREE_SPACE has one row for every bit of free space in every tablespace. But if a tablespace were full, there would be no rows at all; hence the need for the OUTER JOIN, without which the SMALL tablespace would not be listed, even though it is in a critical state. Then consider the effect of enabling AUTOEXTEND on the datafiles. Also, an UNDO tablespace will usually be 100-percent full, but this is not a problem, because a large part of the undo data will be inactive and can be overwritten. And what about temporary tablespaces? The query would have to be in a UNION with another query against DBA_TEMP_FILES. This second query would have to work out whether the space occupied by temporary segments is in use, or merely waiting to be used.

Many DBAs have written suites of SQL code to report on space usage and raise warnings before error conditions occur. This is fine, but the scripts have to be written, they have to be run regularly, and they have to be updated to take account of changes in technology. Many companies have written and marketed tools to do the same thing. The Alert system replaces a vast amount of this humdrum work. It will monitor many conditions that can cause problems, and will send notifications by a variety of methods. With regard to space management, it is by default configured to raise a warning alert when a tablespace reaches 85-percent full and a critical alert when a tablespace is 97-percent full, with account being taken of autoextension and the nature of the contents.

Alerts comes in two forms. *Stateful* alerts are based on conditions that persist and can be fixed. Tablespace space usage is an example, or the number of sessions hanging, or the average time it takes to complete an SQL statement execution. *Stateless* alerts are based on events; they happen and are gone. A query failing with "snapshot too old" and two transactions deadlocking are examples.

To configure the Alert system, you set thresholds. The thresholds are stored in the AWR. Then the MMON background process will monitor the database and the instance, in near real time, and compare the current state with the thresholds. If a threshold is crossed, it will raise the alert. The mechanism by which an alert is raised is simply to put an entry on the alert queue. A *queue* is a table of messages that other processes can read. What happens to the alert message next is a matter for further configuration. The default behavior is that Enterprise Manager Cloud Control will (if an agent has been installed) dequeue the message and display it on the database home page, but Enterprise Manager can be configured to send e-mails or SMS messages when it finds that an alert has been raised.

You can view the alerts by querying the view DBA_OUTSTANDING_ALERTS, and it is possible to write an alert handler in PL/SQL that will dequeue the messages and take any action desired.

Watch

Alerts are raised by the MMON process, not by Enterprise Manager. Enterprise Manager reads alerts, as can other event handlers written by you or by third parties.

Setting Thresholds

You can set over 200 metrics for thresholds. They are documented in the view V$METRICNAME, which gives the name of the metric, the units in which it is measured, and the ID number by which it is identified.

There is an API (the DBMS_SERVER_ALERT package) for setting thresholds. Here is an example:

```
execute dbms_server_alert.set_threshold(-
metrics_id=>dbms_server_alert.redo_generated_sec,-
warning_operator=>dbms_server_alert.operator_ge,-
warning_value=>'1000000',-
critical_operator=>dbms_server_alert.operator_ge,-
critical_value=>'2000000',-
```

```
7      observation_period=>1,-
8      consecutive_occurrences=>5,-
9      instance_name=>'ORCLZ',-
10      object_type=>dbms_server_alert.object_type_system,-
11      object_name=>null);
```

Taking this PL/SQL execution call line by line:

1. The procedure SET_THRESHOLD will create or update an alert threshold.
2. The metric being set is the rate of redo generation, measured in bytes per second.
3. The comparison operator for the warning level, which is "greater than or equal to."
4. The value for a warning alert, which is 1MB per second.
5. The comparison operator for the critical level, which is "greater than or equal to."
6. The value for a critical alert, which is 2MB per second.
7. The observation period, in minutes.
8. The number of consecutive occurrences before the alert is raised.
9. The instance for which the alert is being configured.
10. The type of object to which the alert refers.
11. The name of the object to which the alert refers.

Note that not all the arguments are relevant for all alerts.

The preceding example configures an alert for the rate of redo generation; a warning will be raised if this exceeds 1MB per second, and a critical warning if it goes over 2MB per second. The observation period is set to a minute and consecutive occurrences to five; this means that if the redo generation happens to hit a high level just a couple of times, it will not be reported—but if it stays at a high level consistently (for five consecutive minutes), it will be reported. Because this metric is one that could vary between instances in an RAC environment, the instance name must be specified, but the object name is not relevant. If the alert were for tablespace usage, the instance name would not be specified, the object type would be tablespace, and the object name would be set to the name of the tablespace.

When stateful alerts are raised, they are visible as rows in the DBA_OUTSTANDING_ALERTS view. They will remain visible until they are cleared.

They may be cleared because the DBA has fixed the problem, or in some cases the problem will go away in the natural course of events. For instance, a tablespace-usage alert would usually require DBA action (such as adding another datafile), whereas an activity-related alert such as the rate of redo generation might clear automatically when the activity reduces. When an alert is cleared, it is removed from the DBA_OUTSTANDING_ALERTS view and written to the DBA_ALERT_HISTORY view. Stateless alerts go straight to the history view.

Thresholds are configured by default for tablespace usage and blocking sessions. A space usage warning will be raised when a tablespace is 85-percent full and a critical warning when it is 97-percent full. The warning and critical values for blocked sessions are 2 and 4.

EXERCISE 12-3

Configure Alerts

In this exercise, you will enable an alert for the commit rate and demonstrate its use. Follow these steps:

1. Connect to your database with Database Control as user SYSTEM.
2. Create a rather small tablespace, as follows:

```
create tablespace small datafile 'small.dbf' size 1m
uniform size 128k;
```

   Given that the datafile will (by default) not autoextend and that each extent is a fixed size, it is impossible for this tablespace to contain more than eight extents.

3. Set a space usage alert that will raise a warning when the tablespace is half full and a critical warning when three quarters full. Confirm that the threshold has been set:

```
execute DBMS_SERVER_ALERT.SET_THRESHOLD(-
   metrics_id => DBMS_SERVER_ALERT.TABLESPACE_PCT_FULL,-
   warning_operator => DBMS_SERVER_ALERT.OPERATOR_GT,-
   warning_value => '50',-
   critical_operator => DBMS_SERVER_ALERT.OPERATOR_GT,-
   critical_value => '75',-
   observation_period => 1,-
   consecutive_occurrences => 1,-
   instance_name => NULL,-
   object_type => DBMS_SERVER_ALERT.OBJECT_TYPE_TABLESPACE,-
   object_name => 'SMALL')
select * from dba_thresholds where object_name='SMALL';
```

4. Create a table and fill the tablespace:

```
create table big (c1 date) tablespace small;
```

5. Fill the tablespace by allocating extents repeatedly until you receive the error "ORA-01653: unable to extend table SYSTEM.BIG by 16 in tablespace SMALL":

```
alter table big allocate extent;
```

6. Query the DBA_OUTSTANDING_ALERTS view. Note that it may take up to 10 minutes for the alert to be raised. This is because the timing of the space management alert is programmed internally and cannot be changed.

```
select * from dba_outstanding_alerts;
```

7. Resolve the problem by adding more space to the tablespace:

```
alter tablespace small add datafile 'small2.dbf' size 1m;
```

8. Confirm that the alert is cleared by querying the DBA_OUTSTANDING_ALERTS and DBA_ALERT_HISTORY views. Again, it may take up to 10 minutes for this to happen.

CERTIFICATION OBJECTIVE 12.05

Use Automated Tasks

The autotask system is a mechanism whereby certain maintenance jobs run automatically. These are jobs that Oracle recommends should be run regularly on all databases.

The Autotasks

There are three autotasks:

- Gathering optimizer statistics
- Running the SQL Tuning Advisor
- Running the Segment Advisor

Optimizer statistics are needed if the optimizer is to generate efficient plans for executing SQL statements. These statistics include information such as how big tables are, and the number of distinct values in columns. If these statistics are missing or inaccurate, code will certainly run but performance may degrade because the execution plans will not be appropriate to the state of the data. For example, using an index to retrieve rows rather than scanning an entire table may or may not be the best way to run a query, depending on the size of the table and the predicate: statistics will let the optimizer make the best decision. Statistics such as this are not static. As the application is used, they will become out of date and should be refreshed. The autotask that gathers statistics will do this. By default, any fresh statistics are made available for use immediately.

The SQL Tuning Advisor autotask identifies high-load SQLs that have been run, using information written to the AWR by snapshots, and attempts to tune them. The results of the tuning are stored in a *profile*, which is additional information on how best to run the statement that can be used by the optimizer the next time the statement is executed. By default, profiles are generated but are not actually brought into use. If this default is not changed, the DBA should check for any profiles that have been generated, and decide whether to implement them. To see the profiles, query the DBA_SQL_PROFILES view.

The Segment Advisor identifies table and index segments that contain a large amount of unused space, which could be released from the segment and returned to the tablespace by reorganizing the segment. Its recommendations cannot be implemented automatically.

Interpreting and implementing the result of the advisors is covered in later chapters on tuning the database and SQL.

Controlling the Autotasks

A prerequisite for running the autotasks is that the STATISTICS_LEVEL parameter should be set to either TYPICAL or ALL. The autotasks are launched by a background process: the ABP0 process. The tasks, if enabled, run within defined windows. The timing of the windows is to open at 22:00 on weekdays and remain open for four hours, and at 06:00 on weekend days and remain open for 20 hours. These windows are managed by the Scheduler, as described in Chapter 16. The intention is that the autotasks should run at times when the database is less likely to be in use by users. To limit further the impact on users, the resources used by the autotasks are restricted by the Resource Manager (detailed in Chapter 15) such that if the system is stressed, they will take up no more than 25 percent of CPU capacity.

on the job

The standard windows for the autotasks assume that your users are American, and may not be appropriate in a multinational environment. Just because it is night time in the database time zone does not mean that it is night time elsewhere. Furthermore, Saturday and Sunday are working days in some parts of the world.

The DBA_AUTOTASK_CLIENT view will show whether the tasks are enabled, and the DBMS_AUTO_TASK_ADMIN package has procedures to enable and disable them, as shown in Figure 12-2.

The first query in the figure shows that all three autotasks are enabled. Then the results of the last run of the SQL Tuning Advisor are shown. The advisor identified eight SQLs as being worthy of attention, but decided not to make any recommendations. Finally, the task is disabled.

on the job

Many databases are running the SQL Tuning autotask every night for no purpose, because no one ever looks at the results.

FIGURE 12-2

Controlling the autotasks

```
Select Administrator: cmd - sqlplus system/oracle
orclz> select client_name,status from dba_autotask_client;

CLIENT_NAME                                                STATUS
---------------------------------------------------------- --------
auto optimizer stats collection                            ENABLED
auto space advisor                                         ENABLED
sql tuning advisor                                         ENABLED

orclz> select dbms_auto_sqltune.report_auto_tuning_task from dual;

REPORT_AUTO_TUNING_TASK
--------------------------------------------------------------------------------
GENERAL INFORMATION SECTION
-------------------------------------------------------------------------------
Tuning Task Name                       : SYS_AUTO_SQL_TUNING_TASK
Tuning Task Owner                      : SYS
Workload Type                          : Automatic High-Load SQL Workload
Execution Count                        : 26
Current Execution                      : EXEC_1717
Execution Type                         : TUNE SQL
Scope                                  : COMPREHENSIVE
Global Time Limit(seconds)             : 3600
Per-SQL Time Limit(seconds)            : 1200
Completion Status                      : COMPLETED
Started at                             : 10/20/2013 06:00:03
Completed at                           : 10/20/2013 06:00:15
Number of Candidate SQLs               : 8
Cumulative Elapsed Time of SQL (s)     : 3

-------------------------------------------------------------------------------
There are no recommendations to improve the statements in the workload.

-------------------------------------------------------------------------------


orclz> execute dbms_auto_task_admin.disable('sql tuning advisor',null,null)

PL/SQL procedure successfully completed.
```

CERTIFICATION SUMMARY

Regular database maintenance tasks can be largely automated by enabling the autotasks. These provide the critical functions of gathering object statistics, identifying segments that need to be reorganized, and tuning high-load SQLs. The out-of-the-box configuration of a database created with the DBCA will also have automatic alerts for the most common problems: issues with space management and blocking sessions.

The enabling technology for the self-management capabilities is the AWR. This is created at database creation time as a set of tables in the SYSAUX tablespace. It is populated automatically and is self-managing—within limits set by the DBA.

The AWR and the facilities it supports are dependent on the STATISTICS_LEVEL instance parameter. Setting this to BASIC disables all facilities.

TWO-MINUTE DRILL

Manage the Automatic Workload Repository (AWR)

- By default, snapshots are taken every hour and stored for eight days.
- Additional snapshots can be taken on demand.
- MMON is responsible for creating snapshots and launching the ADDM.
- The AWR consists of tables (and related objects) in the SYSMAN schema, in the SYSAUX tablespace.
- The STATISTICS_LEVEL parameter must be set to TYPICAL or ALL; otherwise, the snapshots will not be made.

Use the Automatic Database Diagnostic Monitor (ADDM)

- The ADDM runs automatically whenever a snapshot is taken, and manually on demand.
- ADDM reports will give advice directly and may also recommend running other advisors.
- The ADDM requires two snapshots, generating reports on activity between them.

Describe and Use the Advisory Framework

- A set of advisors is provided for tuning purposes.
- The advisors depend on statistics stored as snapshots in the AWR.
- Access to some advisors is through Enterprise Manager, and all are accessible through views and PL/SQL APIs. By default, the SQL Tuning Advisor and the Segment Advisor will run automatically in the maintenance windows.

Set Alert Thresholds

- Stateful alerts must be configured with thresholds.
- If a stateful alert is raised, it will remain until the situation is cleared; stateless alerts are reported and do not need to be cleared.
- Thresholds are stored in the AWR.
- It is the MMON background process that raises an alert.
- Setting STATISTICS_LEVEL to BASIC will disable server alerts.

Use Automated Tasks

- ❑ The autotask framework automates execution of critical maintenance jobs.
- ❑ The three autotasks are gathering optimizer statistics, running the SQL Tuning Advisor, and running the Segment Advisor.
- ❑ By default, new statistics are published but the advisor tasks' recommendations are not implemented.
- ❑ The running of the autotasks is controlled by the Scheduler and the Resource Manager.

SELF TEST

Manage the Automatic Workload Repository (AWR)

1. The AWR is located in the SYSAUX tablespace. If you suspect that it is growing to such a size that it will fill the SYSAUX tablespace, what actions could you take to reduce the likelihood of this happening? (Choose all correct answers.)
   - A. Relocate the AWR to a tablespace created specifically for storing it.
   - B. Reduce the time between snapshots so that less data will generated by each one.
   - C. Increase the time between snapshots so that fewer snapshots will be generated.
   - D. Adjust the scheduling of the automatic maintenance tasks so that they will run less frequently.
2. By default, snapshots are removed from the AWR on a regular basis, making comparisons of activity over a long period of time (such as contrasting this year's year-end processing with last year's) impossible. What should you do to make this possible? (Choose the best answer.)
   - A. Save the year-end snapshots as a baseline.
   - B. Adjust the snapshot-retention period to the whole period: a little over a year.
   - C. Set the datafile(s) that make up the SYSAUX tablespace to AUTOEXTEND so that snapshots will not be purged.
   - D. Disable purging of snapshots by setting STATISTICS_LEVEL to ALL.

Use the Automatic Database Diagnostic Monitor (ADDM)

3. When will the ADDM run?
   - A. Whenever an alert is raised by the server Alert system
   - B. During the maintenance windows that run the autotasks
   - C. Following the gathering of an AWR snapshot
   - D. Only when explicitly requested
4. With regard to the collection of monitoring information, put these steps in the correct order:
   - A. Data accumulates in the SGA.
   - B. MMON generates an ADDM report.
   - C. MMON writes data to the AWR.
   - D. Reports are purged.
   - E. Snapshots are purged.

Describe and Use the Advisory Framework

5. Which advisors are run by the autotask system in the maintenance windows? (Choose all correct answers.)
   A. The ADDM
   B. The memory advisors
   C. The Segment Advisor
   D. The SQL Access Advisor
   E. The SQL Tuning Advisor
   F. The Undo Advisor
6. Under which circumstances would the advisors not be available? (Choose the best answer.)
   A. If the optimizer statistics-gathering autotask has been disabled.
   B. If the STATISTICS_LEVEL parameter is set to BASIC.
   C. If the AWR snapshots have been purged.
   D. If Enterprise Manager has not been configured.

Set Alert Thresholds

7. Which process raises alerts? (Choose the best answer.)
   A. MMON, the Manageability Monitor
   B. Enterprise Manager (Database Express or Cloud Control)
   C. The server process that detects the problem
   D. SMON, the System Monitor
8. End users are complaining that they receive "snapshot too old" error messages when running long queries. You look at the DBA_OUTSTANDING_ALERTS view and don't see any. Why might this be? (Choose the best answer.)
   A. The STATISTICS_LEVEL parameter is set to BASIC.
   B. The snapshots for the periods when the errors occurred have been purged.
   C. No alert has been configured for "snapshot too old."
   D. "Snapshot too old" is reported in DBA_ALERT_HISTORY.

Use Automated Tasks

9. How can you best automate the collection of optimizer statistics? (Choose the best answer.)
   A. The MMON process will collect them if STATISTICS_LEVEL is set to TYPICAL or to ALL.
   B. An automatic maintenance job will collect them if STATISTICS_LEVEL is set to TYPICAL or to ALL.
   C. Enterprise Manager Cloud Control will collect them if the agent is running.
   D. Schedule a job to execute the DBMS_STATS.GATHER_DATABASE_STATISTICS procedure.
10. Where are the object statistics used by the query optimizer stored? (Choose the best answer.)
   A. With the objects themselves.
   B. In the data dictionary.
   C. In the AWR.
   D. They are accumulated in the shared pool of the SGA.
11. You notice that the autotasks do not appear to be running. Why might this be? (Choose all correct answers.)
   A. The STATISTICS_LEVEL parameter is set to BASIC.
   B. The tasks have been explicitly disabled.
   C. The Enterprise Manager Agent is not running.
   D. The tasks have not been scheduled with the DBMS_SCHEDULER package.
   E. The tasks have not been scheduled with the DBMS_JOB package.

LAB QUESTION

Demonstrate that the Alert system is functioning by testing the alert for blocking sessions. Create a table, and from four separate sessions attempt to delete the same row. Three of the sessions will hang. In a fifth session, query the DBA_OUTSTANDING_ALERTS view. What is the alert raised? It is not raised immediately. Why not?

SELF TEST ANSWERS

Manage the Automatic Workload Repository (AWR)

1. ☑ **C.** Increasing the time between snapshots will reduce the number stored and therefore the space needed.
☒ **A, B,** and **D** are incorrect. **A** is incorrect because it is not possible to relocate the AWR. **B** is incorrect because the space needed to store a snapshot is not related to the snapshot frequency; this would actually have the opposite effect to that desired. **D** is incorrect because the automatic maintenance tasks do not control snapshots, and it is snapshots that take up the bulk of the space in the AWR.

2. ☑ **A.** This is exactly the type of situation for which baselines are intended.
☒ **B, C,** and **D** are incorrect. **B** would work, but you would need a SYSAUX tablespace the size of Jupiter; it is not a good solution. **C** is incorrect because the available space has no effect on the retention time. **D** is incorrect because STATISTICS_LEVEL controls how much information is gathered, not for how long it is kept.

Use the Automatic Database Diagnostic Monitor (ADDM)

3. ☑ **C.** The ADDM runs automatically whenever a snapshot is generated, contrasting that snapshot with the previous snapshot.
☒ **A, B,** and **D** are incorrect. **A** is incorrect because there is no integration between the Alert system and ADDM. **B** is incorrect because ADDM is not an autotask. **D** is incorrect because although you can request an ADDM report explicitly, they are also generated automatically.

4. ☑ **A, C, B, E, D** is the correct sequence.
☒ All other sequences are wrong.

Describe and Use the Advisory Framework

5. ☑ **C** and **E.** These run in every maintenance window, but implementing the recommendations is up to the DBA.
☒ **A, B, D,** and **F** are incorrect. **A** is incorrect because MMON invokes the ADDM. **B, D,** and **F** are incorrect because they are advisors that must be invoked manually.

6. ☑ **B.** The advisors are dependent on the STATISTICS_LEVEL.
☒ **A, C,** and **D** are incorrect. **A** is incorrect because optimizer statistics are not required by the advisors, although they may recommend collecting them. **C** is incorrect because the advisors can always be invoked using the information currently available in the instance. **D** is incorrect because although Enterprise Manager can invoke the advisors, there is no dependency between them.

Set Alert Thresholds

7. ☑ **A.** MMON raises alerts, by writing a message to the alert queue.
   ☒ **B, C,** and **D** are incorrect. **B** is incorrect because Enterprise Manager does not raise alerts; it reports them. **C** and **D** are incorrect because neither server sessions nor the SMON are part of the Alert system.

8. ☑ **D.** "Snapshot too old" is a stateless alert and therefore goes directly to the alert history.
   ☒ **A, B,** and **C** are incorrect. **A** is incorrect because the STATISTICS_LEVEL refers to statistics, not alerts. **B** is incorrect because outstanding alerts do not get purged on any schedule, only by being resolved. **C** is incorrect because "snapshot too old" is a stateless alert, and thresholds can only apply to stateful alerts.

Use Automated Tasks

9. ☑ **B.** A job will run in the maintenance windows unless STATISICS_LEVEL is set to BASIC.
   ☒ **A, C,** and **D** are incorrect. **A** and **C** are incorrect because they specify the wrong component to carry out the task. **D** is incorrect because although you could schedule a job yourself, letting the autotask facility do this is the best option.

10. ☑ **B.** The optimizer uses the latest published statistics, which are stored in the data dictionary.
    ☒ **A, C,** and **D** are incorrect. **A** is incorrect because the statistics are stored independently of the actual segments. **C** is incorrect because the AWR stores historical values, which are not used for real-time parsing. **D** is incorrect because the SGA stores the execution plan itself, not the information used to generate it.

11. ☑ **A** and **B.** Setting STATISTICS_LEVEL=BASIC will disable the autotasks (and a few other things). The tasks may also be disabled with the DBMS_AUTO_TASK_ADMIN.DISABLE procedure.
    ☒ **C, D,** and **E** are incorrect. **C** is incorrect because Enterprise Manager is not required to run autotasks. **D** and **E** are incorrect because although the Scheduler and the Resource Manager control when and how autotasks will run, they do not enable or disable them.

LAB ANSWER

These queries will show the alert raised and how it is configured:

```
select reason from dba_outstanding_alerts;
select metrics_name,
warning_operator,warning_value,
critical_operator,critical_value,
observation_period,consecutive_occurrences
from dba_thresholds;
```

13 Managing Performance

CERTIFICATION OBJECTIVES

13.01	Use Enterprise Manager to Monitor Performance	✓	Two-Minute Drill
13.02	Use Automatic Memory Management	Q&A	Self Test
13.03	Use the Memory Advisor to Size Memory Buffers		

Performance management is a huge subject. The treatment given in the core OCP syllabus is little more than an introduction. As an Oracle DBA, you will study performance monitoring and enhancement techniques throughout your whole career. Indeed, you may want "Don't worry, I'll find the problem soon" inscribed on your tombstone. The topics discussed here are the use of Enterprise Manager to monitor performance, followed by an in-depth discussion of memory management. Sorting out memory management will solve many performance issues, and it is a prerequisite step to tuning SQL statements. Tuning SQL is detailed in the next chapter.

CERTIFICATION OBJECTIVE 13.01

Use Enterprise Manager to Monitor Performance

Enterprise Manager has some nice facilities for displaying the results of monitoring queries, but before investigating these, it is necessary to appreciate what performance management is all about and how it should be approached.

A Performance Tuning Methodology

Tuning has one purpose only: to reduce response time for end users. Or to put it another way, all tuning should be oriented toward fixing a business problem. For example, no end user has ever telephoned the helpdesk to complain that "the shared pool is too small" or that "the indexing strategy is not correct." They telephone with complaints such as "the order entry screen does not refresh quickly enough" or "the overnight batch jobs didn't finish until lunchtime." It is very easy for a DBA to become sidetracked into tuning particular aspects of database operation, without considering whether they actually matter. It may well be that the memory structures or the indexes are not optimal for a given workload, but if end users are not facing any quantifiable problems related to this, there is no reason to expend effort on attempting to improve them.

Once one accepts that tuning should be focused on business needs, it becomes apparent that a top-down approach is required: start by analyzing, and if necessary re-engineering, the business processes. A performance tuning methodology should concentrate on business needs, and performance should be considered at all stages. Consider this as a possible application development life cycle:

- **Business analysis** Define the organization's business processes: what it needs to do.
- **Systems analysis** Model the business processes as an ideal system, using techniques such as entity-relationship modeling and data flow diagramming.
- **System design** Adapt the ideal system to reality. Consider the environment within which the application will run (including the fact that it is an Oracle database).
- **Application design** Write the SQL.
- **Implementation** Create the database and deploy the application.
- **Maintenance** Monitor and make adjustments during use.

A mistake made early on may be very hard to fix subsequently. For example, if the business analysis assumes that a customer name is unique and therefore at systems analysis time "customer name" is used as a primary key, it will be very difficult to adjust the application when at implementation time it turns out that several customers can have the same name. Similarly, performance should be considered right at the beginning. For example, systems analysts will model the data structures (typically) to third normal form. But although third normal form may be ideal theoretically, it is rarely optimal for performance. Selective denormalization should occur at the system design stage. If this is not done, the problems of managing over-normalized data will be hard to fix later on.

A tuning methodology should therefore have two major characteristics. First, it should be applied from the top down. Second, it should concentrate on business needs.

on the job

To say that tuning should be top down is all very well, but in many cases the DBA is presented with a finished product—and is forced to tune it from the bottom up, reacting to issues as they occur that perhaps were never properly considered earlier.

Performance Monitoring Data

Oracle collects a vast amount of information regarding activity and performance. This information is accumulated throughout the lifetime of the instance in a set of V$ views and periodically flushed to the AWR repository by the MMON background process (as described in Chapter 11). Two terms must be defined: *statistics* and *metrics*. In the Oracle world, a statistic is a figure that is meaningless by itself, whereas a metric is two or more statistics correlated together—and often correlated with time. For example, the number of disk reads is a statistic. Let us say this statistic is at 100,000,000. So what? That is useless. What one needs to know is disk reads per second, or disk reads per execution of a statement, or disk reads per transaction this week compared with disk reads per transaction last week. The conversion of statistics to metrics is to a large extent done by Oracle on the DBA's behalf, and the results are exposed through a set of views.

Execution of an SQL statement is rarely a continuous process. Usually, it is a set of stop-start events. For example, a statement such as SELECT COUNT(*) FROM EMP might require reading every block of the segment containing the EMP table. This could be many thousands of blocks. To accomplish this, the session's server process must ask the operating system to deliver a set of blocks—but not all of them in one go. The session will then hang while the operating system's I/O subsystem locates and delivers the blocks. Then the session can wake up, process the rows in the blocks, and issue another read request. It will hang until the next set of blocks is delivered. Many reasons are possible for a session to hang during execution of a statement. The reasons for hanging are known as *wait events*.

It is never possible to eliminate wait events completely (they are part of the normal SQL execution cycle), but if certain wait events are consuming an inordinate amount of time, the cause of the wait event should be investigated and if possible removed (or at least reduced). In the example of the query just given, the most significant wait event would probably be *db file scattered read*. This is the event that occurs during a full table scan, as groups of blocks are read for insertion into the buffer cache. Other wait events could also occur: *free buffer wait* as the server process searches for buffers in the cache into which to place the blocks, or *buffer busy wait*, which means that the block is already in the cache but temporarily inaccessible because another session is working on it.

Performance monitoring data is accumulated and metrics calculated on several dimensions. Here are some of the critical views:

- **V$STATNAME** A documentation view, listing every statistic gathered, grouping them into classes
- **V$SYSSTAT** The current value of each statistic for the entire instance, accumulated since the instance was started
- **V$SESSTAT** The current value of each statistic for each currently logged-on session, accumulated since the session started

- **V$MYSTAT** The statistics for your currently logged-on session
- **V$EVENT_NAME** A documentation view, listing every wait event, grouping them into classes
- **V$SYSTEM_EVENT** The number of times each wait event has occurred and the total time spent waiting on the event for the entire instance, accumulated since the instance was started
- **V$SESSION_EVENT** The number of times each wait event has occurred for each currently logged-on session and the total time spent by that session waiting on the event, accumulated since the session started

The Database Express Performance Pages

Enterprise Manager Database Express provides limited access to performance monitoring information. From the database home page, the Performance tab links to what is called the Performance Hub. When you are navigating around the Hub, the first step is to choose the time frame. By default this is real time, showing data for the last hour. The historical view lets you choose any time up to the limit of data within the AWR repository.

The following tabs on the Hub page give access to this information:

- **Summary** Shows an overall view of the performance activity of the system over the selected time period.
- **Activity** Currently active sessions, showing the SQL they are running and the wait events they are experiencing.
- **Workload** Charts showing the pattern of user calls, the logon rate, the redo generation, and the SQL being executed.
- **Monitored SQL** All statements that consume over five seconds of CPU or I/O time are monitored, with data regarding I/O, wait events, and the execution plan.
- **ADDM** Access to ADDM reports over whatever time period has been selected.

The other option on Database Express's Performance tab is to run the SQL Tuning Advisor, which is described in Chapter 14.

EXERCISE 13-1

Use Enterprise Manager to Monitor Activity

In this exercise, you generate a workload and inspect activity in Enterprise Manager. Follow these steps:

1. Connect to the database as user SYSTEM with SQL*Plus.
2. Determine the HTTP or HTTPS listening port, and set one if necessary. The following two function calls will list the port (returning zero if it has not been set). At least one, either HTTP or HTTPS, is needed. These two example procedure calls will create a listening end point and register it with the listener. Use either protocol, on any free port you wish. Confirm that the port is active by re-running the function calls and checking the status of the database listener—which will display the listening address and the protocol (either TCP or TCPS).

```
select dbms_xdb_config.gethttpport from dual;
select dbms_xdb_config.gethttpsport from dual;
exec dbms_xdb_config.sethttpport(5500)
exec dbms_xdb_config.sethttpsport(5501)
lsnrctl status
```

3. Connect to Database Express, logging on as user SYSTEM, with the appropriate URL. Here are two examples:

   http://127.0.0.1:5500/em
   https://127.0.0.0:5501/em

4. In the SQL*Plus session, launch a long-running query that should put some stress on the system:

```
select count(*) from
(select a.*,b.* from all_objects a,all_objects b);
```

5. In Database Express, observe the activity build up on the database home page. Then navigate to the Performance Hub, on the Performance tab, and investigate all the sub-tabs.

CERTIFICATION OBJECTIVE 13.02

Use Automatic Memory Management

Memory usage in the Oracle instance falls into two categories: Program Global Areas (the PGAs) that are private to each session, and the System Global Area (the SGA) that is shared by all the Oracle processes. From release 9*i* it has been possible to automate the management of the PGA. From release 10*g* it has been possible to automate the management of the SGA. Releases 11*g* and 12*c* can manage both the PGA and SGA together, fully automatically.

on the job

All Oracle memory usage is virtual memory. The Oracle processes have no way of knowing if the memory to which they are connecting is in RAM or has been swapped (or paged) to disk. However, swapping will cripple performance and should be avoided.

PGA Memory Management

A user session against an Oracle instance consists of a user process connected to a server process. The user process generates SQL statements and sends them to the server process for execution: this is the client-server split. Associated with the server process is a block of nonsharable memory: the PGA. When executing SQL, the server process makes use of the PGA to store session-specific data, including:

- Sorting rows
- Merging bitmaps
- Variables
- The call stack

For some data in the PGA, use of memory is nonnegotiable. For example, if the session needs memory for its call stack, that memory must be made available. For other structures (such as sort space), use of PGA is nice but not essential, because if necessary the data can be written out to a disk-based storage structure—although this will impact adversely on performance.

Every SQL statement uses memory in the SGA (specifically, the shared SQL area, in the shared pool) and also will require a minimum amount of PGA memory (sometimes referred to as the private SQL area), without which it cannot execute. Making more PGA memory available will often reduce execution time, but the reduction is not linear. Typically, there will be three stages of memory allocation: these are known as optimal, one-pass, and multipass. The optimal memory allocation will allow the statement to execute purely in memory, with no requirement to make use of temporary storage on disk. The optimal memory allocation is sufficient to accommodate all the input data and any auxiliary data structures that the statement must create. The one-pass memory allocation is insufficient for optimal execution and therefore forces an extra pass over the data. The multipass memory allocation is even smaller and means that several passes over the data will be needed.

As an example, consider a sort operation. The ideal situation is that all the rows to be sorted can be read into the PGA and sorted there. The memory required for this is the optimal memory allocation. If the optimal memory allocation is not available, then the rows must be separated into batches. Each batch will be read into memory, sorted, and written out to disk. This results in a set of sorted batches on disk, which must then be read back into memory and merged into a final sorted list of all the rows. The PGA memory needed for this is the one-pass allocation: the sort operation has had to become multiple sorts followed by a merge. If the one-pass memory allocation is not available, then the merge phase as well as the sort phase will require use of temporary disk storage. This is a multipass execution.

exam watch

A statement's shared SQL area is in the shared pool of the SGA; its private SQL area is in the session's PGA.

The ideal situation is that all SQL statements should execute optimally, but this goal may be impossible to reach. In data warehouse operations, the optimal memory allocation can be many gigabytes if the queries are addressing vast tables. In such environments, one-pass executions may be the best that can be achieved. Multipass executions should be avoided if at all possible. For example, to sort 10GB of data may require over 10GB of memory to run optimally, but only 40MB to run with one pass. Only if less than 40MB is available will the sort become multipass, and execution times will then increase substantially.

Managing PGA memory can be automatic, and Oracle Corporation strongly recommends that it should be. The older manual management techniques are supported only for backward compatibility and will not be discussed here. To implement automatic PGA memory management, you set a target for the total PGA memory allocation, summed up for all sessions. The Oracle instance will then pass out memory from this total to sessions on demand. When a session has finished executing its statement, the PGA it was using can be allocated to another session. This system relies on the fact that at any one moment only some of the connected sessions will need any negotiable PGA memory. They will all need a certain amount of PGA memory to retain the state of the session, even when the session is idle, but this will leave enough from the total so that those sessions actually running statements can have what they need. At least, that is what one hopes.

on the job

It is sometimes impossible to achieve optimal memory allocations, because the memory requirements can be huge. One-pass executions are bad but may be unavoidable. Multipass executions are disastrous, and if these are occurring, you should talk to the system administrators about available hardware and to the programmers about tuning their SQL.

Automatic PGA memory management is enabled with three instance parameters:

- WORKAREA_SIZE_POLICY
- PGA_AGGREGATE_TARGET
- PGA_AGGREGATE_LIMIT

The WORKAREA_SIZE_POLICY will default to AUTO, meaning that Oracle can assign PGA to sessions on demand, while attempting to keep the total allocated PGA within the PGA_AGGREGATE_TARGET. This parameter defaults to the greater of 10MB or 20 percent of the size of the SGA, and should be adjusted upward until a satisfactory proportion of statements are executing optimally, but not set so high that memory is over-allocated and the operating system has to page virtual memory to disk. Note that this is only a target—a soft limit. If set to a value that is too low for sessions to function (perhaps because the total of nonnegotiable memory requirements exceeds the target), the target will be broken and more memory will be allocated.

exam watch

What happens to sessions if the PGA_AGGREGATE_TARGET is exceeded? Nothing—that is, until the PGA_AGGREGATE_LIMIT is also exceeded, at which point statements will fail.

The PGA_AGGREGATE_LIMIT is a hard limit on the total PGA that can be used. The default is the greater of 2GB, or double the PGA_AGGREGATE_TARGET, or 3MB multiplied by the PROCESSES parameter. It cannot be set to less than 2GB. If this limit is exceeded, Oracle will terminate calls in progress in order to bring the PGA usage down below the limit.

on the job

If your PGA_AGGREGATE_TARGET is not sufficient for optimal and one-pass operations, your database will be performing badly. If the PGA_AGGREGATE_LIMIT is ever reached, the situation is disastrous. As a matter of urgency, tune the SQL to require less memory, and if possible add more memory to the system.

SGA Memory Management

The SGA contains several memory structures that can be sized independently:

- The shared pool
- The database buffer cache
- The large pool
- The Streams pool
- The Java pool
- The log buffer

As a general rule, the memory allocation to the large pool, the Java pool, and the Streams pool is not a matter for negotiation—either the memory is needed or it isn't. If these structures are undersized, there will be errors; if they are oversized, there will be no performance improvement. The memory allocation to the shared pool, the database buffer cache, and the log buffer is negotiable: if less than optimal, there will not be errors but performance will degrade. The exception is the shared pool: if this is chronically undersized, errors will occur.

on the job

Do not throw memory at Oracle unnecessarily. An oversized shared pool or log buffer can be bad for performance. An oversized buffer cache is less likely to be a problem, unless it is so oversized that the system is having to swap.

watch ***The log buffer is the only SGA structure that cannot be adjusted dynamically. It cannot therefore be automatically managed.***

SGA memory management can be automatic (and Oracle Corporation advises that it should be), with the exception of the log buffer. The DBA sets a total size for the SGA, and the instance will apportion this total to the various structures, thus ensuring that there are no errors from SGA components being undersized and that memory above this minimum is allocated where it will do the most good. The components will be resized on demand, so if a component needs more memory, it will be taken from a component that can spare it. The log buffer is the one SGA component whose size is fixed at instance startup and that cannot be automatically managed.

The parameters for manual management of the SGA are as follows:

- SHARED_POOL_SIZE
- DB_CACHE_SIZE
- LARGE_POOL_SIZE
- STREAMS_POOL_SIZE
- JAVA_POOL_SIZE

To enable automatic shared memory management (ASMM), leave all of these on default (or set to zero) and set one parameter instead: SGA_TARGET. Optionally, set SGA_MAX_SIZE as well.

When ASMM is used, the instance will monitor demand for memory in the various SGA components and pass out memory to the components as required, downsizing components if this is necessary to keep the total allocated memory within the target. Also included within the target is the log buffer. This is sized with the LOG_BUFFER parameter, which is static: the log buffer is created at instance startup and cannot be resized subsequently.

on the Job ***The default for LOG_BUFFER is probably correct. You can set the parameter to higher than the default, but this may well cause a degradation in performance. If you set it to less than the default, your setting will often be ignored.***

If you set any of the parameters that control the automatically managed SGA components, the value given will act as the minimum size below which ASMM will never reduce that component. Depending on activity, the size at any given moment may be above that requested by the parameter.

Watch ***The DBA can set minimum values for the automatically managed memory structures, but not maximum values.***

The SGA_TARGET parameter is dynamic: it can be adjusted to a lower value, and the instance will resize the variable components downward to meet the new target. It can also be raised—provided it is not raised above the value of the SGA_MAX_SIZE parameter. The SGA_MAX_SIZE defaults to the SGA_TARGET and is a static parameter. Therefore, by default, you can never make the total SGA larger than it was at instance startup time.

Automatic Memory Management

The Automatic Memory Management (AMM) mechanism lets the Oracle instance manage server memory usage as a whole via one parameter: MEMORY_TARGET. Optionally, you can set MEMORY_MAX_TARGET as well. This takes the automatic PGA management (enabled with PGA_AGGREGATE_TARGET) and the automatic shared memory management (enabled with SGA_TARGET) a step further, by letting Oracle transfer memory between PGAs and SGA on demand.

on the job

To make your life easy, set the parameter MEMORY_TARGET only and do not set any of the other parameters listed previously. Set MEMORY_MAX_TARGET to, perhaps, 20 percent higher—to give yourself some wiggle room if you need to tune later.

AMM is not just a tool to make database administration easy. It will often give big performance benefits as well. Many databases will experience different patterns of activity at different times, which could benefit from different memory configurations. For example, it is not uncommon for a database used for order processing to experience a very high transaction processing workload during most of the month, and then a heavy query processing workload during month-end reporting runs. Transaction processing will typically not be demanding on PGA memory but will require a large database buffer cache. Query processing will often require large PGA allocations, but not much buffer cache.

exam watch

The MEMORY_TARGET parameter is dynamic—it can be adjusted without shutting down the instance—but only within a limit set by another parameter: MEMORY_MAX_TARGET. This is static, so it can only be raised by adjusting with the SCOPE=SPFILE clause and restarting the instance.

Manually transferring memory between SGA and PGA in response to changing patterns of activity is not a practical option, and many systems will not be able to allocate enough memory to both concurrently to satisfy their peak demands. Automatic Memory Management is able to transfer memory between SGA and PGA as necessary to optimize performance within an overall memory constraint. This overall constraint must be determined by the DBA and the system administrator together. There is little point in the DBA setting an upper limit that is so large that the operating system has to page SGA and PGA to a swap device; the system administrator will be able to advise on a suitable maximum value.

exam watch

If you set the parameters PGA_AGGREGATE_TARGET and SGA_TARGET when AMM is enabled, the values you specify are a minimum size beneath which AMM will never reduce the PGA or SGA.

Generally speaking, memory allocations will stabilize within an instance after an application has been running for a while, until there is some dramatic change in the pattern of activity. Two views will be useful to monitor this:

- V$MEMORY_DYNAMIC_COMPONENTS shows the current sizes of the structures.
- V$MEMORY_RESIZE_OPS shows the history of the last 800 resizing operations.

AMM is implemented by the *memory broker*, which is made up of two background processes. The MMON Manageability Monitor process monitors activity and when advisable instructs the MMAN Memory Manager process to reassign memory between components. Memory transfers should occur at most only every few minutes for tuning purposes, and will usually occur much less frequently—perhaps never—once the system has stabilized. There will, however, be an immediate transfer in the event of an error condition being raised by a session: rather than the statement failing, the session will hang while memory is made available and will then resume.

on the job

AMM does have platform variations. For example, on Linux it is not possible to enable AMM if Huge Pages are in use. On Solaris, adequate Dynamic Intimate Shared Memory segments must be configured for the project under which the instance is running.

EXERCISE 13-2

Set the Memory Management Parameters

In this exercise, you will disable Automatic Memory Management (if it is enabled) and set the SGA and PGA targets independently. Make all the changes using syntax that will only affect the running instance: do not propagate the changes to the spfile, unless you are prepared to reverse them later. Here are the steps to follow:

1. Connect to your database with SQL*Plus as user SYSTEM.
2. Ensure that none of the parameters for managing the dynamic SGA memory structures manually are set:

```
alter system set db_cache_size=0 scope=memory;
alter system set shared_pool_size=0 scope=memory;
alter system set large_pool_size=0 scope=memory;
alter system set java_pool_size=0 scope=memory;
```

3. Disable Automatic Memory Management:

```
alter system set memory_target=0 scope=memory;
```

4. Set the parameters to size PGA and SGA independently, using very low values:

```
alter system set pga_aggregate_target=10m scope=memory;
alter system set sga_target=256m scope=memory;
```

   The second command may take a few minutes to complete, and it may fail if Oracle cannot reduce the SGA to the minimum. In this case, try a larger value.

5. Determine the actual size of the currently allocated PGAs by summing up the value for the statistic "session pga memory" across all sessions:

```
select sum(value) from v$sesstat natural join v$statname
where name='session pga memory';
```

   The figure will be significantly in excess of the 10MB requested in step 4. This is because 10MB is a value that is so low that Oracle cannot keep to it. The PGA target is only a target, not a hard limit.

6. Determine the actual size of the SGA:

```
select sum(bytes) from v$sgastat;
```

   This figure, too, may be greater than that requested in step 4.

CERTIFICATION OBJECTIVE 13.03

Use the Memory Advisor to Size Memory Buffers

The Oracle instance collects a vast amount of information regarding activity and performance. These statistics enable the memory advisors, which are tools that calculate the effect of varying the sizes of the SGA and PGA memory structures. The Automatic Memory Management facility uses the advisors to make decisions about memory allocation, and they are also visible to the DBA through various views and through Enterprise Manager. Figure 13-1 shows three queries that display memory advisor information.

The first query in Figure 13-1 shows the PGA advisor. The third selected column shows an estimate for the amount of disk I/O that would be needed if the PGA

FIGURE 13-1

Three memory advisors, queried with SQL*Plus

```
C:\WINDOWS\system32\cmd.exe - sqlplus / as sysdba
SQL> select pga_target_for_estimate,pga_target_factor,estd_extra_bytes_rw
  2  from v$pga_target_advice;

PGA_TARGET_FOR_ESTIMATE PGA_TARGET_FACTOR ESTD_EXTRA_BYTES_RW
----------------------- ----------------- -------------------
               13631488              .125           296644608
               27262976               .25           296644608
               54525952                .5           296644608
               81788928               .75           296644608
              109051904                 1            75833344
              130862080               1.2                   0
              152672256               1.4                   0
              174482432               1.6                   0
              196292608               1.8                   0
              218103808                 2                   0
              327155712                 3                   0
              436207616                 4                   0
              654311424                 6                   0
              872415232                 8                   0

14 rows selected.

SQL> select sga_size,sga_size_factor,estd_db_time from v$sga_target_advice;

  SGA_SIZE SGA_SIZE_FACTOR ESTD_DB_TIME
---------- --------------- ------------
       196               1         6053
       245            1.25         5661
       294             1.5         5647
       343            1.75         5647
       392               2         5647

SQL> select memory_size,memory_size_factor,estd_db_time
  2  from v$memory_target_advice;

MEMORY_SIZE MEMORY_SIZE_FACTOR ESTD_DB_TIME
----------- ------------------ ------------
        300                  1         6054
        375               1.25         4889
        450                1.5         4888
        525               1.75         4888
        600                  2         4888

SQL> _
```

target were set to the figure shown in the first column. The second column expresses this figure as a proportion of the actual setting. The fifth row of the output is the current setting: a PGA_TARGET_FACTOR of 1. It can be seen that if another 30MB of memory were added to the target, less I/O would be needed, but that adding more than this would give no further benefit.

The second query in Figure 13-1 shows the SGA advisor. This relates the size of the SGA to a projected value for DB_TIME, which is an overall figure for the amount of time taken by the database to execute SQL; minimizing DB_TIME is the overall objective of all tuning. It can be seen that if the SGA were raised from its current value of 196MB to 294MB, DB_TIME would reduce but that there would be no point in going further.

The third query is against the memory target advisor, which gives advice on the total (SGA plus PGA) memory allocation. This shows that the optimal value is 450MB, as opposed to the current value of 300MB. If Automatic Memory Management is in use (enabled with the MEMORY_TARGET parameter), then this last query is all that need be used. It can be seen that virtually all of the DB_TIME saving could be achieved by raising the target to 375MB, and if the system administrators say sufficient memory is not available to allocate the optimal amount, then this is what the DBA should ask for.

The advisors will not be enabled unless the STATISTICS_LEVEL parameter is set to TYPICAL or ALL.

In all, there are seven memory advisors. Each is exposed through a dynamic performance (or V$) view populated with current information in the SGA as well as a DBA view populated with historical data from tables in the AWR:

Advisor	V$ View	DBA View
PGA	V$PGA_TARGET_ADVICE	DBA_HIST_PGA_TARGET_ADVICE
SGA	V$SGA_TARGET_ADVICE	DBA_HIST_SGA_TARGET_ADVICE
Memory	V$MEMORY_TARGET_ADVICE	DBA_HIST_MEMORY_TARGET_ADVICE
DB cache	V$DB_CACHE_ADVICE	DBA_HIST_DB_CACHE_ADVICE
Java pool	V$JAVA_POOL_ADVICE	DBA_HIST_JAVA_POOL_ADVICE
Streams pool	V$STREAMS_POOL_ADVICE	DBA_HIST_STREAMS_POOL_ADVICE
Shared pool	V$SHARED_POOL_ADVICE	DBA_HIST_SHARED_POOL_ADVICE

EXERCISE 13-3

Use the Memory Advisors

In this exercise, you will gather advice about memory allocation by querying the relevant views. This exercise assumes that Exercise 13-2 has been completed. Here are the steps to follow:

1. Connect to your database as user SYSTEM with SQL*Plus.
2. Run this query to see the results of the SGA advisor:

```
select sga_size,sga_size_factor,estd_db_time,estd_physical_reads
from v$sga_target_advice;
```

   The value for SGA_SIZE_FACTOR=1 will be that specified in Exercise 13-2, step 6. Note the point at which there is no significant anticipated benefit to adding more memory.
3. Run this query to see the results of the PGA advisor:

```
select
pga_target_for_estimate,pga_target_factor,estd_extra_bytes_rw,
estd_pga_cache_hit_percentage,estd_overalloc_count
from v$pga_target_advice;
```

   This query will show the anticipated effect of various values for the PGA_AGGREGATE_TARGET. As the target increases, the ESTD_EXTRA_BYTES_RW will reduce. This is the amount of physical I/O necessary because SQL work areas do not need to be written out to temporary storage. The ESTD_PGA_CACHE_HIT_PERCENTAGE will tend toward 100 percent because queries can run optimally rather than one-pass or multipass. The ESTD_OVERALLOC_COUNT is the number of times Oracle would not be able to keep to the PGA target; this will tend toward zero if PGA is available.
4. Return your instance to the state it was in before Exercise 13-2 by restarting it.

CERTIFICATION SUMMARY

In a 12*c* database, memory management can be completely automatic. To enable this, set the appropriate instance initialization parameters. Automatic Memory Management (AMM) relies on statistics accumulated in the SGA and periodically flushed to disk as AWR snapshots. These statistics include a history of all activity in the database, and are the basis of the memory advisors. The advisors show the predicted effect of changing the sizes of the various SGA and PGA memory structures, and are used by the memory broker to resize the structures to achieve optimal performance.

TWO-MINUTE DRILL

Use Enterprise Manager to Monitor Performance

- ❑ Statistics are accumulated in memory, and metrics are calculated from these.
- ❑ Database Express exposes certain key statistics and metrics, represented graphically.

Use Automatic Memory Management

- ❑ All SGA structures except the log buffer can be dynamically resized.
- ❑ PGA is passed out, on demand, to sessions.
- ❑ AMM can transfer memory between SGA and PGA, within an overall target.
- ❑ Individual structures can be given minimum sizes with their own parameters.

Use the Memory Advisor to Size Memory Buffers

- ❑ There are seven memory advisors.
- ❑ The advisors are enabled if STATISTICS_LEVEL is set to TYPICAL or ALL.
- ❑ The memory broker uses the advisors to tune memory allocations.

SELF TEST

Use Enterprise Manager to Monitor Performance

1. Which advisors can be invoked through Database Express? (Choose two answers.)
   A. The SQL Access Advisor
   B. The SQL Tuning Advisor
   C. The Undo Advisor
   D. The memory advisors

Use Automatic Memory Management

2. Where are private SQL areas stored? (Choose the best answer.)
   A. In each session's PGA, always
   B. In each session's PGA, unless a PGA Aggregate Target has been set
   C. In the PGA, unless Automatic Memory Management has been enabled
   D. In the shared pool of the SGA, always
3. Which memory structure is fixed in size at instance startup? (Choose the best answer.)
   A. The shared pool.
   B. The large pool.
   C. The Java pool.
   D. The log buffer.
   E. None are fixed, if Automatic Memory Management has been enabled.
4. When Automatic Memory Management is enabled, what is not possible? (Choose the best answer.)
   A. Transfer of memory between sessions' PGAs.
   B. Transfer of memory between structures within the SGA.
   C. Transfer of memory from SGA to PGA, and vice versa.
   D. Increasing the total memory usage after instance startup.
   E. All of the above are possible.
5. Storage of what structures can exist in the PGA? (Choose all correct answers.)
   A. Shared SQL areas
   B. Private SQL areas
   C. Global temporary tables
   D. Sort areas
   E. Bitmap merge areas
   F. Cached object definitions

Use the Memory Advisor to Size Memory Buffers

6. Which instance parameter can disable the memory advisors? (Choose the best answer.)
   A. DB_CACHE_ADVICE
   B. MEMORY_TARGET
   C. STATISTICS_LEVEL
   D. TIMED_STATISTICS
7. Identify the true statement about Automatic Memory Management (AMM). (Choose the best answer.)
   A. MEMORY_TARGET and MEMORY_MAX_TARGET must both be set to enable AMM.
   B. MEMORY_TARGET enables AMM, and it is a static parameter.
   C. MEMORY_MAX_TARGET enables AMM, and it is a static parameter.
   D. MEMORY_TARGET enables AMM, and it is a dynamic parameter.

LAB QUESTION

Adjust your instance to disable AMM, and define an SGA of 350MB and PGA of 350MB. As user SYSTEM, create a couple large tables and attempt to join them, using a high degree of parallelism:

```
create table x as select * from all_objects;
create table y as select * from all_objects;
select /*+ parallel (64) */ count(*) from x natural join y;
```

The query will (probably) fail with an ORA-4031 error, stating that insufficient memory is available. Remove the fixed values for SGA and PGA and then enable AMM with a target of 700MB. Re-run the query and see that it succeeds (it should).

SELF TEST ANSWERS

Use Enterprise Manager to Monitor Performance

1. ☑ **B, C.** The Tuning Advisor is available on the Performance tab, the Undo Advisor on the Storage tab.
☒ **A** and **D** are incorrect. The Access Advisor and the various memory advisors can be reached through Cloud Control, but not through Database Express.

Use Automatic Memory Management

2. ☑ **A.** Private SQL areas are private to each session, in the session's PGA.
☒ **B, C,** and **D** are incorrect. **B** is incorrect because automatic PGA management is not relevant to where the private SQL area is stored, only to how it is managed. **C** and **D** are incorrect because private SQL areas are always in the PGA.

3. ☑ **D.** The log buffer cannot be changed after startup.
☒ **A, B, C,** and **E** are incorrect. **A, B,** and **C** are incorrect because all these structures can be resized. **E** is incorrect because not even Automatic Memory Management makes the log buffer resizable.

4. ☑ **E.** Memory can be transferred between all structures (except the log buffer), and the total can be increased.
☒ **A, B, C,** and **D** are incorrect. These are incorrect because all are possible—although **D** (the increase of total memory usage) is only possible up to the value specified by the MEMORY_MAX_TARGET parameter.

5. ☑ **B, C, D,** and **E.** These are all PGA memory structures, although they may spill to a temporary segment in the users' temporary tablespace.
☒ **A** and **F** are incorrect. These structures both exist in the shared pool of the SGA.

Use the Memory Advisor to Size Memory Buffers

6. ☑ **C.** STATISTICS_LEVEL must be on TYPICAL or FULL; otherwise, the advisors will not run.
☒ **A, B,** and **D** are incorrect. **A** and **D** are incorrect because these parameters (which still exist only for backward compatibility) are controlled by STATISTICS_LEVEL. **B** is incorrect because MEMORY_TARGET determines whether implementing the advice is automatic or manual.

7. ☑ **D.** MEMORY_TARGET enables AMM; it is a dynamic parameter and cannot be more than MEMORY_MAX_TARGET.
☒ **A, B,** and **C** are incorrect. **A** is incorrect because the MEMORY_MAX_TARGET can be left on default. **B** is incorrect because MEMORY_TARGET is dynamic. **C** is incorrect because although MEMORY_MAX_TARGET provides a limit for AMM, it does not enable it.

LAB ANSWER

Here is an example of how to configure the instance with inappropriate, fixed PGA and SGA:

```
alter system set memory_target=0 scope=spfile;
alter system set sga_target=350m scope=spfile;
alter system set pga_aggregate_target=350m scope=spfile;
startup force
```

And here is a typical error when an attempt is made to run the query:

```
orclz> select /*+ parallel (64) */ count(*) from x natural join y;
select /*+ parallel (64) */ count(*) from x natural join y
*
ERROR at line 1:
ORA-12801: error signaled in parallel query server P00T
ORA-12853: insufficient memory for PX buffers: current 48880K,
max needed 314880K
ORA-04031: unable to allocate 65560 bytes of shared memory
("large pool","unknown object","large pool","PX msg pool")
```

After you enable AMM, the query succeeds because memory can be transferred from PGA to the large pool.

CERTIFICATION OBJECTIVES

14.01	Manage Optimizer Statistics	✓	Two-Minute Drill
14.02	Use the SQL Tuning Advisor	Q&A	Self Test
14.03	Use the SQL Access Advisor to Tune Workload		

Chapter 13 introduced some aspects of instance tuning—principally, memory management. Although tuning the instance as a whole is important, it must be emphasized that all tuning should be oriented toward business problems. That means tuning SQL statements in order to meet business requirements for response time.

Generally speaking, the approach to take toward SQL tuning is to trust the optimizer. Oracle's Cost Based Optimizer (the CBO) may well be the most complex piece of software with which you will ever work. Many DBAs (including the author of this book) have spent years studying the operation of the CBO and will continue to study it throughout their working lives. Clearly, a comprehensive knowledge of the CBO is beyond the scope of the OCP (and the OCM) examination. But one aspect is discussed: the need to supply the CBO with the statistical information it needs to make decisions. These decisions are about how best to execute SQL statements, and if this information is missing or inaccurate, performance may degrade drastically. Developing execution plans based on statistics is known as *cost-based optimization*, and is one of the hottest topics in computer science.

Two advisors are relevant to SQL performance: the SQL Tuning Advisor, which looks at how a given statement runs, and the SQL Access Advisor, which looks at the segment structures against which the statement runs. Both these advisors are licensed as part of the Tuning Pack, available for Enterprise Edition installations.

CERTIFICATION OBJECTIVE 14.01

Manage Optimizer Statistics

Any one SQL statement may be executable in a number of different ways. For example, it may be possible to join tables in different orders; there may be a choice of whether to use indexes or table scans; or some execution methods may be more intensive in their use of disk I/O as against CPU resources. The method of executing a statement is known as the *execution plan*, and the choice of execution plan is critical for performance. In an Oracle database, execution plans are developed dynamically by the optimizer. The optimizer relies heavily on statistics to evaluate the effectiveness of many possible execution plans, and to choose which plan to use. For good performance, it is vital that these statistics are accurate. There are many types of statistics, but chief among these are the object statistics that give details of the tables that the SQL statements address.

on the job

Statistics are not relevant to PL/SQL, only to SQL—so gathering statistics will not improve PL/SQL performance. But most PL/SQL will include calls to SQL statements; statistics are as important for these statements as for any others.

Object Statistics

Analyzing a table gathers statistics on the table that will be of use to the optimizer. Some of the statistics are visible in the DBA_TABLES view; they include the following:

- The number of rows in the table
- The number of blocks (used and not yet used) allocated to the table
- The amount of free space in the blocks that are being used
- The average length of each row
- The number of "chained" rows—rows that cut across two or more blocks, either because they are very long or because of poor storage settings

Apart from statistics regarding the table as a whole, each column of the table is also analyzed. Column statistics are visible in the DBA_TAB_COLUMNS view; they include the following:

- The number of distinct values
- The highest and lowest values
- The number of nulls
- The average column length

When a table is analyzed, its indexes are analyzed implicitly. It is also possible to gather index statistics explicitly. The statistics on indexes are shown on the DBA_INDEXES view; they include the following:

- The depth of the index tree
- The number of distinct key values
- The clustering factor—how closely the natural order of the rows follows the order of the keys

These statistics, which are stored within the data dictionary, give the optimizer the information it needs to make vital decisions about how best to execute statements. If statistics are missing or incorrect, performance may degrade dramatically.

Object statistics are often imperfect, firstly, because they are static—until they are gathered again. This means that they become *stale*, or out of date, as a result of DML against the objects. Secondly, object statistics are often imperfect because as a general rule statistics are gathered through a sampling process. If an object is many gigabytes big, a complete analysis will take much time and resources and possibly have an impact on other work. Analyzing a sample of the object will usually give statistics that are representative of the whole at a much lower cost. In many cases, stale or sampled statistics are perfectly adequate. For example, if a table has a billion rows, one may be able to add millions more without disturbing the efficiency of execution plans, provided that the column values in the new rows fit within the frequency distributions already discovered. But in other cases, a relatively small amount of DML may have a significant effect.

Object statistics are static. They must be regenerated regularly to pick up changes in the state of the data.

How the Optimizer Uses Statistics

It is common for there to be several ways of running any given statement. Consider this trivial example: there is a table EMP with one row for each employee that includes a column for SAL with the employee's salary, and this column is indexed. A query retrieves the name of every employee whose salary is higher than a certain figure. To run this statement, Oracle could scan the entire table, checking each row against the criterion, or Oracle could search the index to identify those employees who meet the criterion and then use the index to retrieve exactly those employee rows. Consider these queries:

```
select ename from emp where sal > 1000000;
select ename from emp where sal > 0;
```

The first query will (almost certainly) be quicker if executed using the index method. Assuming that there are very few employees who meet the criterion, there is no point in reading the entire table to find them. Searching the index to find the relevant employees will be faster. The second query, however, is going to be faster (assuming everyone does have a positive salary) if one scans the table. All employees will be retrieved, so there is no point in using the index.

In making this choice of access method, one is using *object statistics*. Object statistics tell Oracle how many rows are in the table, how many blocks the table segment is occupying, the maximum and minimum values of the columns, the depth of the indexes, and much more. If the object statistics are missing or inaccurate, the optimizer will develop an inappropriate plan. To take this (somewhat contrived) example a step further, consider the situation where the object statistics say that the table is very small: that it contains only one row, and occupies only one block. In this case, there is no point in using the index: the entire table can be read by a single block read. Accessing the index would mean at least one read of the index, possibly followed by another read of the table: this could never be faster, so the optimizer would always choose to scan the table no matter what the criterion was. But if the statistics were in fact wrong, and the table consists of several million rows occupying many megabytes of space, this decision would be disastrous for some criteria. It becomes apparent that statistics should be both present and accurate if the optimizer is to develop efficient execution plans.

The optimizer bases its decisions on *cardinality estimates:* using the available statistics, it makes guesses about how many rows and blocks will be accessed by various execution methods. The accuracy of these guesses is critical for performance, and is generally dependent on the frequency of gathering statistics and the size of the sample. In some cases, these estimates will turn out to be wrong. Why? Typically because the statistics are either stale or based on an inadequate sample. Oracle has two facilities that allow it to correct this: SQL plan directives and adaptive execution plans.

During the execution of a statement, the CBO monitors how many rows are returned at each step and compares this figure for actual cardinality to the estimated cardinality used to derive the execution plan. If the figures deviate sufficiently, the CBO will generate a SQL plan directive for future use. A *directive* is an instruction to the optimizer to gather additional information regarding the objects through a mechanism known as *dynamic sampling*. A simple example would be that used previously: the statistics say that the EMP table has one row, but when querying it the optimizer finds that in fact it has millions of rows. In this case, Oracle will generate a directive that, in the future, will instruct the optimizer to check the size of the table when deciding upon an execution plan. A more complex example might be retrieving employees by city, state, and country. We know that Munich is the capital of Bavaria, and that Bavaria is in Germany. But Oracle does not. This will distort its assumptions about the number of rows returned if a predicate specifies values for all three columns. The directive would instruct the CBO to generate additional statistics regarding the correlation of values between columns. The directives are saved to the AWR in the SYSAUX tablespace and associated with the table to which they refer, and will thus be of benefit to any statements that hit the table from then on.

SQL plan directives are tied to tables, not to statements. They are persisted in the AWR.

The adaptive execution plan facility affects just one statement, at run time. If a choice has to be made between execution plans that would be more or less efficient depending on the number of rows retrieved, the CBO will determine a crossover point: if there are less than X rows, use plan A; if there are more than X rows, use plan B. Oracle will start to run the statement using the plan determined by the object statistics to be optimal, but if this turns out to be incorrect it will switch to the alternative plan during running. For example, if the crossover point were 100 rows and the cardinality estimate is 1,000, the statement would start with plan B and then switch to plan A if only 50 rows were returned by the first step of the plan. Adaptive execution is possible only if the plans have the same, or very similar, initial operations. Data is buffered until the crossover point is (or is not) reached, and then the final choice of plan is made.

on the job

The functionality of an adaptive execution plan is limited to switching between the join methods: either nested loop join or hash join. Both of these can start by scanning, and counting, rows from one table.

Gathering Statistics Manually

Object statistics are not real time; they are static, which means that they become out of date as DML operations are applied to the tables. It is therefore necessary to gather statistics regularly, to ensure that the optimizer always has access to statistics that reflect reasonably accurately the current state of the database. Statistics can be gathered manually by executing procedures in the DBMS_STATS package, as in Figure 14-1.

In Figure 14-1, first the table REGIONS is analyzed, using the DBMS_STATS package. Setting the argument ESTIMATE_PERCENT to 100 instructs Oracle to analyze the entire table, not just a sample of it. The following query shows that there are four rows in the table. Then a row is inserted, but the statistics haven't been updated: the number of rows is incorrect until the table is analyzed again—this time with the ESTIMATE_PERCENT set to enable sampling using Oracle's default sample size. Numerous arguments can be supplied to the GATHER_TABLE_STATS procedure to control what it does—this is the simplest form of its use.

on the job

The old ANALYZE TABLE command is still available. Do not use it! In some circumstances it may damage the much more sophisticated statistics that DBMS_STATS can gather.

FIGURE 14-1 Gathering statistics from the SQL*Plus prompt

```
Administrator: cmd - sqlplus scott/tiger
orclz> execute dbms_stats.gather_table_stats('HR','REGIONS',estimate_percent=>100)

PL/SQL procedure successfully completed.

orclz> select num_rows from dba_tables where owner='HR' and table_name='REGIONS';

  NUM_ROWS
----------
         4

orclz> insert into hr.regions values(99,'UK');

1 row created.

orclz> select num_rows from dba_tables where owner='HR' and table_name='REGIONS';

  NUM_ROWS
----------
         4

orclz> execute dbms_stats.gather_table_stats('HR','REGIONS',-
> estimate_percent=>dbms_stats.auto_sample_size)

PL/SQL procedure successfully completed.

orclz> select num_rows from dba_tables where owner='HR' and table_name='REGIONS';

  NUM_ROWS
----------
         5

orclz>
```

Gathering statistics will improve performance, but the actual gathering may impose a strain on the database that will have a noticeable effect on performance while the analysis is in progress. This paradoxical situation raises two questions. First, how frequently should statistics be gathered? The more frequently this is done, the better performance may be—but if it is done more frequently than necessary, performance will suffer needlessly. Second, what proportion of an object needs to be analyzed to gain an accurate picture of it? Analyzing a huge table will be a long and resource-intensive process—it may well be that analyzing a representative sample of the object would be enough for the optimizer and would not impose such a strain on the database.

exam watch

Object statistics are not real time; they are static until refreshed by a new analysis. If this is not done with sufficient frequency, they will be seriously out of date, and the optimizer may consequently develop inappropriate execution plans.

Object statistics can be gathered at various levels. These are the relevant procedures in the DBMS_STATS package:

- **gather_database_stats** Analyze the entire database
- **gather_schema_stats** Analyze all objects in one schema
- **gather_table_stats** Analyze one table
- **gather_index_stats** Analyze one index

When statistics are gathered at any level, a number of arguments can be passed. These can be specified in the procedure call, or set as saved preferences at each level. Consider this procedure call, which specifies the commonly used arguments giving the default value:

```
execute dbms_stats.gather_schema_stats(-
ownname=>'HR',-
cascade=>dbms_stats.auto_cascade,-
estimate_percent=>dbms_stats.auto_sample_size,-
degree=>dbms_stats.auto_degree,-
no_invalidate=>dbms_stats.auto_invalidate,-
granularity=>'auto',-
method_opt=>'for all columns size auto',-
options=>'gather')
```

Taking these arguments in turn:

- CASCADE will analyze indexes as well as tables. The setting given lets Oracle decide which indexes (if any) should be analyzed.
- ESTIMATE_PERCENT controls how much of each table to analyze. The setting given instructs Oracle to make an intelligent guess at the amount needed for a meaningful sample.
- DEGREE specifies whether to perform the analysis with parallel processing. The setting given lets Oracle decide the number of parallel processes according to the environment and the size of each table.
- NO_INVALIDATE controls whether or not to reparse any SQL with dependencies on the objects analyzed immediately. The setting given lets Oracle decide.
- GRANULARITY refers to how best to analyze objects consisting of a number of subobjects, such as a table that is divided into partitions. The setting given lets Oracle decide.

- METHOD_OPT controls for which columns to build up histograms, and how many buckets they should have. The setting given lets Oracle decide, according to the nature of the SQL being executed and the distribution of values in the data.
- OPTIONS determines which objects to analyze. The setting given instructs Oracle to analyze all objects.

The remaining point to consider is how frequently to run the command. An automatic statistics-gathering task will do this every day, during the maintenance window. The maintenance window runs for four hours every weekday night (starting at 2200) and for 20 hours on Saturday and Sunday (starting at 0600), though usually only a very small proportion of this time will be needed. Many databases will run well with statistics gathered by the automatic task, obviating any need to gather statistics manually.

EXERCISE 14-1

Gather Optimizer Statistics

In this exercise, you will use various techniques for gathering optimizer statistics.

1. Connect to your database as user SYSTEM with SQL*Plus.
2. Create a table and an index to be used for the exercise, and set your session's date format:

```
create table st as select * from all_users;
create index sti on st(username);
alter session set nls_date_format='dd-mm-yy hh24:mi:ss';
```

3. Investigate the statistics on the table and indexes:

```
select count(*) from st;
select num_rows,last_analyzed from user_tables where
table_name='ST';
select distinct_keys,last_analyzed from user_indexes where
index_name='STI';
```

Note that the statistics count of the rows in the table is missing because the table has never been analyzed. The number of distinct values recorded in the index is reported correctly (for now) because indexes are automatically analyzed on creation.

4. Analyze the table, using defaults for all optional arguments:

```
exec dbms_stats.gather_table_stats('SYSTEM','ST')
```

Rerun the queries from step 3. All the figures are now correct.

5. Insert some more rows into the table:

```
insert into system.st select * from all_users;
```

Rerun the queries from step 3. Note that the statistics are wrong.

6. Analyze the SYSTEM schema, relying on defaults:

```
exec dbms_stats.gather_schema_stats('SYSTEM')
```

Rerun the queries from step 3. The figures are now correct.

7. Tidy up as follows:

```
drop table st;
```

CERTIFICATION OBJECTIVE 14.02

Use the SQL Tuning Advisor

The SQL Tuning Advisor analyzes one or more SQL statements and potentially recommends gathering fresh object statistics, creating a SQL profile, creating additional indexes, or creating a revised SQL statement. You can run the SQL Tuning Advisor manually; however, it is run automatically during every maintenance window on the most resource-intensive SQL statements identified within the production workload. Optionally, you can specify that the analysis performed during the maintenance window automatically implements recommended SQL profiles.

The Capabilities of the SQL Tuning Advisor

Whether the SQL Tuning Advisor runs automatically or you run it on one or more SQL statements, it performs the same types of analyses:

- **Statistics Analysis** Check for stale or missing statistics, and recommend refreshing or creating them

- **SQL Profiling** Collect auxiliary statistics on a SQL statement along with partial execution statistics and store them in a SQL Profile
- **Access Paths** Analyze the impact of creating new indexes
- **Structure Analysis** Restructure the SQL statements to see if better execution plans are generated

When profiling a SQL statement, the optimizer partially runs the statement, experimenting with various execution plans. The execution statistics generated during this process update the profile. Information on how the statement actually ran can be used by the optimizer subsequently when the statement is encountered during normal database operation. Note that the SQL Tuning Advisor considers each SQL statement individually. If it recommends an index for a SELECT statement, it may help the performance of the query but may reduce the performance of DML activity against the table in a heavy OLTP environment. Thus, the SQL Access Advisor, discussed later in this chapter, may be a better tool to analyze all operations against one or more tables in a workload.

The SQL Tuning Advisor can use a number of sources for its analysis:

- The SQL statements currently cached in the library cache of the shared pool
- A precreated set of statements
- Statements retrieved from the AWR
- An individual ad hoc statement

The Tuning Advisor's segment advice is limited to index creation.

There is a graphical interface to the SQL Tuning Advisor, and also a set of PL/SQL APIs.

The SQL Tuning Advisor API: The DBMS_SQLTUNE Package

Database Express has an interface to the results of the SQL Tuning Advisor. Navigate to the SQL Tuning Advisor link on the Performance tab to reach this.

If you need to have more control over your tuning tasks or want to run a specific set of tuning tasks repeatedly, you can use the DBMS_SQLTUNE PL/SQL package to create, run, and monitor a SQL Tuning Advisor job.

For a basic analysis of a SQL statement, you will use the following procedures within DBMS_SQLTUNE:

- **CREATE_TUNING_TASK** Create a tuning task for a SQL statement or a SQL Tuning Set.

- **EXECUTE_TUNING_TASK** Execute a tuning task created with CREATE_TUNING_TASK.
- **REPORT_TUNING_TASK** Show the results and recommendations from the SQL Tuning Advisor.

In addition, you can use the following data dictionary views to query the name and status of tuning jobs:

- **DBA_ADVISOR_LOG** Task names, status, and execution statistics for all tasks
- **DBA_ADVISOR_TASKS** More detailed information about advisor tasks, such as advisor name, user-specified description, and execution type for the current user
- **V$ADVISOR_PROGRESS** More detailed information about the completion status and time remaining for an advisor task

EXERCISE 14-2

Run the SQL Tuning Advisor for a SQL Statement

In this exercise, you will use DBMS_SQLTUNE to generate recommendations for a SQL statement.

1. Connect to the database with SQL*Plus as user SYSTEM.
2. Create the schema and table to be used in this exercise:

```
create user user13 identified by user13;
grant dba to user13;
connect user13/user13
create table object_analysis as select * from all_objects;
```

3. These commands, executed at the SQL prompt, will create a variable to store the name of the task, create a task to tune one statement, and then run the task:

```
variable vtask varchar2(100);
execute :vtask := dbms_sqltune.create_tuning_task(-
sql_text=>'select max(object_id) from object_analysis')
execute dbms_sqltune.execute_tuning_task(:vtask)
```

The illustration shows steps 2 and 3.

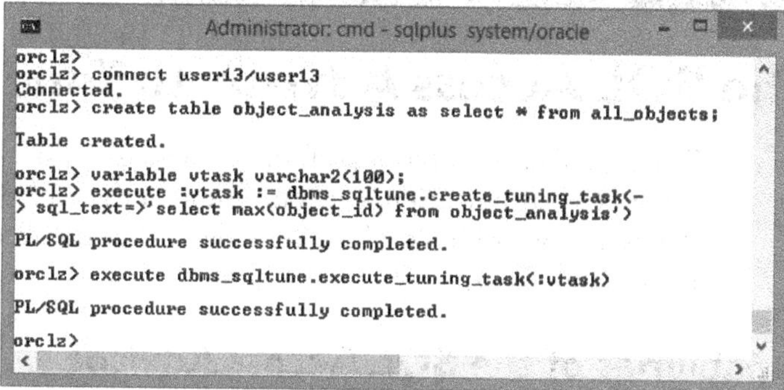

4. Retrieve the recommendations from the tuning task, first setting up SQL*Plus to display them:

```
set long 10000
set longchunksize 10000
select dbms_sqltune.report_tuning_task(:vtask) from dual;
```

5. Study the output of the tuning task, as retrieved in step 4. Following the detail of the task, there will be a recommendation to gather statistics on the table and an example of a procedure call to do this. Then there will be a recommendation to create an index, and an example of a suitable index-creation statement. Note that the rationale for the index creation will include this phrase (which, in the current release, includes a minor typing error):

```
Creating the recommended indices significantly improves
the execution plan of this statement. However, it might
be preferable to run "Access Advisor" using a representative
SQL workload as opposed to a single statement. This will
allow to get comprehensive index recommendations which takes
into account index maintenance overhead and additional space
consumption.
```

6. Tidy up as follows:

```
connect system/oracle

drop user user13 cascade;
```

CERTIFICATION OBJECTIVE 14.03

Use the SQL Access Advisor to Tune Workload

The SQL Access Advisor performs an analysis of overall SQL performance using a workload specification, concentrating on the segment structures. The Tuning Advisor may give basic advice on indexes, but the Access Advisor advice is much more comprehensive.

The Capabilities of the SQL Access Advisor

The workload specification can be one of the following:

- A single SQL statement
- A SQL statement tuning set
- Current SQL cache contents
- A hypothetical workload imputed from the DDL of a set of objects

A SQL statement tuning set is a stored set of statements. This set can be populated from a variety of sources, such as statements captured by an AWR snapshot or the recently executed code currently in the library cache of the shared pool. Statements are looked at individually, but reports will cover the entire set. Recommendations from the SQL Access Advisor include the following:

- Indexes (B-tree, bitmap, and function based)
- Materialized views and materialized view logs
- Partitioning strategies

It is always possible that recommendations that improve some aspect of the workload may have an adverse impact on another. This should be highlighted in the reports.

on the job

An advisor will never give advice that is definitively wrong, but often you can do better. Run the advisors, and when looking at the reports always consider whether the recommendations could be further improved.

The Tuning Advisor has its own API: DBMS_SQLTUNE. The Access Advisor does not. To invoke it, use either the Enterprise Manager interface or the DBMS_ADVISOR API. The DBMS_ADVISOR package is a generic API for running any of the advisors.

Using the SQL Access Advisor with DBMS_ADVISOR

Using the SQL Access Advisor via the DBMS_ADVISOR package can get quite complex. There is, however, one procedure designed to make the job easy.

DBMS_ADVISOR.QUICK_TUNE is straightforward and takes as input a single SQL statement to tune. As a result, it performs much like the SQL Tuning Advisor but can perform a much more in-depth analysis, producing more recommendations than the SQL Tuning Advisor, such as materialized view recommendations. The procedure requires (as a minimum) three arguments: the name of the advisor, the name of the task to be run, and the statement. Here's an example:

```
SQL> execute dbms_advisor.quick_tune(-
       dbms_advisor.sqlaccess_advisor,-
       'task1',-
       'select distinct object_id from object_analysis'-
       )
PL/SQL procedure successfully completed.

SQL>
```

The results of the tuning effort reside in the data dictionary view USER_ADVISOR_ACTIONS, but the output is not very readable. Therefore, you can use the procedure CREATE_FILE to create the script you use to implement the recommendations generated by the QUICK_TUNE procedure. First, create a directory object to point to a file system directory to hold the script:

```
SQL> create directory tune_scripts as '/u06/tune_scripts';

Directory created.

SQL>
```

Next, use CREATE_FILE to create the script containing the implementation recommendations:

```
SQL> begin
       dbms_advisor.create_file
          (dbms_advisor.get_task_script('task1'),
           'TUNE_SCRIPTS',
           'tune_fts.sql'
          );
     end;
     /
```

```
PL/SQL procedure successfully completed.

SQL>
```

In this example, the file tune_fts.sql looks like this:

```
Rem  SQL Access Advisor: Version 12.1.0.1.0 - Production
Rem
Rem  Username:          SCOTT
Rem  Task:              task4
Rem  Execution date:
Rem

CREATE MATERIALIZED VIEW LOG ON
    "SCOTT"."OBJECT_ANALYSIS"
    WITH ROWID, SEQUENCE("OBJECT_ID")
    INCLUDING NEW VALUES;

CREATE MATERIALIZED VIEW "SCOTT"."MV$$_03B80000"
    REFRESH FAST WITH ROWID
    ENABLE QUERY REWRITE
    AS SELECT MAX("SCOTT"."OBJECT_ANALYSIS"."OBJECT_ID") M1,
COUNT(*) M2 FROM SCOTT.OBJECT_ANALYSIS;

begin
  dbms_stats.gather_table_stats('"SCOTT"','"MV$$_03B80000"',
NULL,dbms_stats.auto_sample_size);
end;
/
```

The recommendations include creating a materialized view log, creating a materialized view that can be used for query rewrite, and collecting statistics on the materialized view. This advice is very different from that generated by the SQL Tuning Advisor for the same statement. Both advice sets would need to be tested to determine which is optimal.

You cannot run the Access Advisor against objects owned by internal users, such as SYSTEM. If you try to do this, you will receive the error "QSM-00794: the statement can not be stored due to a violation of the invalid table reference filter."

CERTIFICATION SUMMARY

Statistics are essential if the Cost Based Optimizer is to develop efficient execution plans. Any SQL statement may have many possible methods of execution. Object statistics are used by the CBO to determine the best method. Statistics are not updated in real time: they are gathered and remain static until they are gathered again. It is therefore necessary to analyze objects regularly. An autotask is configured by default that will gather statistics every night, using intelligent algorithms to determine which objects needs to be analyzed and in what way. It is also possible to gather statistics manually, as required.

The SQL Tuning Advisor and the SQL Access Advisor attempt to automate the tuning process. The Tuning Advisor can generate recommendations regarding the SQL statement and limited advice regarding segments: only b-tree index recommendations and detection of missing statistics. The Access Advisor takes segment recommendation much further, being capable of generating advice on all index types, materialized views, and partitioning strategies.

TWO-MINUTE DRILL

Manage Optimizer Statistics

- ❑ Object statistics are static until gathered again.
- ❑ An autotask gathers needed statistics every night.
- ❑ Statistics can be gathered manually for the database, a schema, a table, or an index.

Use the SQL Tuning Advisor

- ❑ The Tuning Advisor recommends the restructuring of SQL, gathering statistics, or b-tree index creation.
- ❑ The Tuning Advisor is run every night by an autotask against detected high-load SQL.
- ❑ Invoke the Tuning Advisor with Enterprise Manager or the DBMS_SQLTUNE package.
- ❑ The Tuning Advisor considers statements individually, not as a set.

Use the SQL Access Advisor to Tune Workload

- ❑ The Access Advisor can recommend all types of indexes, materialized views, and partitioning.
- ❑ Invoke the Access Advisor with Enterprise Manager or the DBMS_ADVISOR package.
- ❑ The Access Advisor can consider a set of SQL statements together.

SELF TEST

Manage Optimizer Statistics

1. How can you best automate the collection of optimizer statistics? (Choose the best answer.)
   A. The MMON process will collect them if STATISTICS_LEVEL is set to TYPICAL or ALL.
   B. An automatic maintenance job will collect them if STATISTICS_LEVEL is set to TYPICAL or ALL.
   C. Enterprise Manager (Database Express or Cloud Control) will collect them if STATISTICS_LEVEL is set to TYPICAL or ALL.
   D. Execute the DBMS_STATS.GATHER_DATABASE_STATISTICS procedure with OPTIONS=>'GATHER AUTO'.
2. You notice that the statistics on a table are not correct: the NUM_ROWS figure does not include any rows inserted in the day so far. Why might this be? (Choose the best answer.)
   A. The STATISTICS_LEVEL parameter is not set to TYPICAL or ALL.
   B. The statistics have been locked by the DBMS_STATS.LOCK_TABLE_STATS procedure.
   C. The statistics will not change until the table is next analyzed.
   D. The automatic maintenance tasks are not running.
3. Where are the object statistics used by the query optimizer stored? (Choose the best answer.)
   A. With the objects themselves.
   B. In the data dictionary.
   C. In the AWR.
   D. They are accumulated in the shared pool of the SGA.

Use the SQL Tuning Advisor

4. The SQL Tuning Advisor performs all but which of the following analyses? (Choose the best answer.)
   A. Structure analysis
   B. SQL Profile analysis
   C. Access paths
   D. Changes to materialized views
   E. Statistics analysis

5. Which of the following can you use as input for the SQL Tuning Advisor? (Choose all that apply.)
   A. A single SQL statement provided by a user
   B. An existing SQL Tuning Set (STS)
   C. A preprocessed Database Replay workload
   D. A schema name
   E. A SQL statement identified in EM as using excessive resources

Use the SQL Access Advisor to Tune Workload

6. Which of the following can you use as input for the SQL Access Advisor? (Choose all that apply.)
   A. A single SQL statement provided by a user
   B. An existing SQL Tuning Set (STS)
   C. A preprocessed Database Replay workload
   D. A schema name
   E. Current SQL cache contents
7. Which of the following changes can the SQL Access Advisor recommend? (Choose two answers.)
   A. Restructuring one or more SQL statements
   B. Gathering statistics for selected SQL statements
   C. Adding a materialized view log
   D. Enabling query rewrite

LAB QUESTION

Use the tables in the demonstration schema SCOTT to investigate the effect of missing statistics and use of the advisors. If SCOTT does not exist in your database, create the schema by running the script UTLSAMPL.SQL from the ORACLE_HOME/rdbms/admin directory. Note that the script will drop the SCOTT schema if it exists.

Delete any object statistics in the schema:

```
execute dbms_stats.delete_schema_stats('scott')
```

Here are some possible queries against which to run the advisors:

```
select ename from emp where deptno in
(select deptno from dept where dname='SALES');
select max(sal) from emp;
select sum(sal) from emp natural join dept where dname='SALES';
```

SELF TEST ANSWERS

Manage Optimizer Statistics

1. ☑ **B.** A job will run in the maintenance windows unless STATISICS_LEVEL is set to BASIC.
☒ **A, C,** and **D** are incorrect. **A** and **C** are incorrect because they specify the incorrect component to carry out the task. **D** is incorrect because the 'GATHER AUTO' option controls what objects to analyze, not whether to analyze at all.

2. ☑ **C.** Optimizer statistics are not maintained in real time, only refreshed when the object is analyzed.
☒ **A, B,** and **D** are incorrect. **A** and **D** are incorrect because they would affect the nightly refresh of the statistics, not a refresh during the day. **B** is incorrect because it would freeze the statistics permanently, not just for the day.

3. ☑ **B.** The optimizer uses the latest statistics, which are stored in the data dictionary.
☒ **A, C,** and **D** are incorrect. **A** is incorrect because the statistics are stored independently of the actual segments. **C** is incorrect because the AWR stores historical values, which are not used for real-time parsing. **D** is incorrect because the SGA stores the execution plan itself, not the information used to generate it.

Use the SQL Tuning Advisor

4. ☑ **D.** Only the SQL Access Advisor recommends changes to materialized views, including creating materialized view logs.
☒ **A, B, C,** and **E** are incorrect. The SQL Tuning Advisor performs statistics analysis, SQL Profiling, access paths, and structure analysis.

5. ☑ **A, B,** and **E.** The SQL Tuning Advisor can use currently running SQL statements, a single statement provided by any user, an existing SQL Tuning Set, or historical SQL statements from AWR snapshots.
☒ **C** and **D** are incorrect. **C** is incorrect because you cannot use Database Replay workloads to specify SQL for SQL Tuning Advisor. **D** is incorrect because you cannot specify a schema or table names; you can only specify SQL statements.

Use the SQL Access Advisor to Tune Workload

6. ☑ **A, B, D,** and **E.** In addition to a single SQL statement (using QUICK_TUNE), an existing STS, a schema name, and the current SQL cache contents, the SQL Access Advisor also uses statistics to analyze overall SQL performance.
☒ **C** is incorrect. You cannot use the captured Database Replay information as a source for the SQL Access Advisor.

7. ☑ C and D. The SQL Access Advisor recommends materialized views, materialized view logs, and enabling query rewrite. In addition, the SQL Access Advisor will also recommend new indexes or partitions.
☒ A and B are incorrect. The SQL Tuning Advisor recommends SQL statement restructuring and statistics gathering, not the SQL Access Advisor.

LAB ANSWER

A typical result from the Tuning Advisor for the statement

```
select ename from emp where deptno in
(select deptno from dept where dname='SALES');
```

is to recommend gathering statistics and also to create a SQL Profile:

```
3- SQL Profile Finding (see explain plans section below)
--------------------------------------------------------
A potentially better execution plan was found for this
statement.
Recommendation (estimated benefit: 35.71%)
------------------------------------------
- Consider accepting the recommended SQL profile.
execute dbms_sqltune.accept_sql_profile(task_name => 'TASK_967',
task_owner => 'SCOTT', replace => TRUE);
```

Other statements will result in recommendations for indexes and materialized views.

15

Managing Resources Using Database Resource Manager

CERTIFICATION OBJECTIVES

15.01	Configure the Database Resource Manager	✓	Two-Minute Drill
15.02	Access and Create Resource Plans	Q&A	Self Test
15.03	Monitor the Resource Manager		

Many computer systems will have several groups of users, each with different standards for the level of service it requires. If the system as a whole is highly stressed, it may be impossible to deliver the desired level of service to all groups. But if a priority structure can be negotiated, it should be possible to guarantee a certain level of service to certain groups—perhaps at the expense of other groups.

CERTIFICATION OBJECTIVE 15.01

Configure the Database Resource Manager

In a mainframe environment, the operating system itself handles allocating resources to tasks. But simpler operating systems such as Unix and Windows may not have proper resource scheduling capabilities. Oracle's Resource Manager brings mainframe-style resource management capabilities to all supported Oracle platforms, meaning that you as DBA can guarantee that certain groups of database users will always receive a certain level of service, no matter what the overall workload on the database may be. Configuring the Resource Manager is often easy, but testing its effect and monitoring what it is doing may be very difficult.

The Need for Resource Management

Operating systems such as Linux and Windows use a very simple algorithm to assign resources to different processes: round-robin time slicing. To the operating system, there is really no difference between any of the background processes that make up the Oracle instance and any of the many server processes that support user sessions: as far as the operating system is concerned, a process is a process; it will be brought onto CPU, given a few cycles of CPU time, and then switched off CPU so that the next process can be brought on. The operating system has no way of knowing that one server process is supporting a session doing completely trivial work while another server process is supporting a session doing work critical to the survival of the organization. The Resource Manager provides a mechanism whereby the operating system's time-slicing algorithm can be adjusted, to ensure that some users receive more processing capacity than others—and to ensure that any single query does not destroy performance for everyone else. The underlying mechanism is to place a cooperative multitasking layer controlled by Oracle on top of the operating system's preemptive multitasking system.

Throughout this chapter, the environment is assumed to be that of a telesales organization. There are several groups of users: of particular interest are the data entry clerks and the management accountants. There may be 200 data entry clerks in the call center, taking orders over the telephone. If their database sessions are running slowly, this is disastrous for the company. Customers will dial in only to be told, "You are number 964 in the queue. Your call is important to us. Please do not hang up." This is happening because the data entry clerks cannot process calls fast enough: they take an order, they click the Submit button, and then they wait… and wait… and wait… for the system to respond. This is costing money.

On the other hand, the management accountants' work is not so urgent. Perhaps an advertisement has been run on one local radio station, and the response in terms of sales inquiries needs to be evaluated before running the advertisement nationwide. This is important work, but it doesn't have to be real time. If the reports take ten minutes to run instead of five, does it really matter?

on the job

Do not adjust the priorities of Oracle processes by using the Unix* renice *command, or the Windows equivalent. Oracle assumes that the operating system is treating all processes equally, and if you interfere with this there may be unexpected (and disastrous) side effects.

What is needed is a technique for ensuring that if the database sessions supporting the data entry clerks need computing resources, they get them—no matter what. This could mean that at certain times of day when the call center is really busy, the clerks need 100 percent of computing resources. The Resource Manager can handle this, and during that time of peak usage the sessions supporting the management accountants may hang completely. But during other times of day, when the call center is not busy, plenty of resources will be available to be directed to the management accountants' work. At month end, another task will become top priority: the end-of-month billing runs, and the rollover of the ledgers into the next accounting period. The Resource Manager needs to be versatile enough to manage this too.

Clearly, the Resource Manager is only necessary in highly stressed systems, but when you need it, there is no alternative. In fact, you are using the Resource Manager whether you know it or not; it is configured by default in all databases to control the resources used by the Autotask system, but the default configuration has a minimal effect on normal work.

The Resource Manager Architecture

Users are placed in Resource Manager consumer groups, and Resource Manager plans, consisting of a set of directives, control the allocation of resources across the groups. Each session is assigned to a group, depending on attributes defined when the session was established and possibly modified subsequently. The underlying architecture places a cooperative multitasking layer on top of the preemptive multitasking provided by the operating system. The server process of a session in a low-priority group will, when brought onto CPU by a context switch, voluntarily relinquish the CPU earlier than it would have done if relying purely on the operating system's preemptive multitasking algorithm.

Consumer Groups

A Resource Manager consumer group is a set of users with similar resource requirements. One group may contain many users, and one user may be a member of many groups, but at any given moment, each session will have one group as its effective group. When a user first creates a session, his default consumer group membership will be active, but if he is a member of multiple groups, he can switch to another group, activating his membership of that group. The switch can be manual or automatic, depending on a number of factors.

In the telesales example, the 200 data entry clerks could be in a group called OLTP, and the half-dozen management accountants could be in a group called DSS. Some users could be in both groups; depending on what work they are doing, they will activate the appropriate group membership. Other groups might be BATCH, to be given top priority for month-end processing, and LOW, for people who happen to have accounts on the system but are of no great significance.

Eighteen groups are created by default when a database is created:

- **SYS_GROUP** This group is intended for the database administrators. By default, only the SYS and SYSTEM users are in this group.
- **DEFAULT_CONSUMER_GROUP** This group is for all users who have not been specifically assigned to any other group. By default, all sessions other than SYS and SYSTEM are in this group, and this membership is active when they first create a session.
- **OTHER_GROUPS** All users are members of this group. It is used as a catch-all for any sessions that are in groups not explicitly mentioned in the active Resource Manager plan.

- **Demonstration groups** The following groups are intended for separating different types of work: BATCH_GROUP, DSS_CRITICAL_GROUP, DSS_GROUP, ETL_GROUP, INTERACTIVE_GROUP, and LOW_GROUP.
- **ORA$AUTOTASK** The sessions running the autotasks will run under this group.
- **ORA$APPQOS_0 through ORA$APPQOS_7** These eight groups are used if Quality Of Service has been enabled; this is applicable only to clustered systems.

To view the groups in your database, query the views DBA_RSRC_CONSUMER_GROUPS and DBA_USERS. The latter shows the initial consumer group set for each session at connect time (see Figure 15-1).

Resource Manager Plans

A Resource Manager plan is of a certain type. The most basic (and most commonly used) type of plan is one that allocates CPU resources, but there are other resource allocation methods. Many plans can exist within the database, but only one plan is active at any one time. This plan applies to the whole instance: all sessions are controlled by it.

FIGURE 15-1

Resource Manager consumer groups

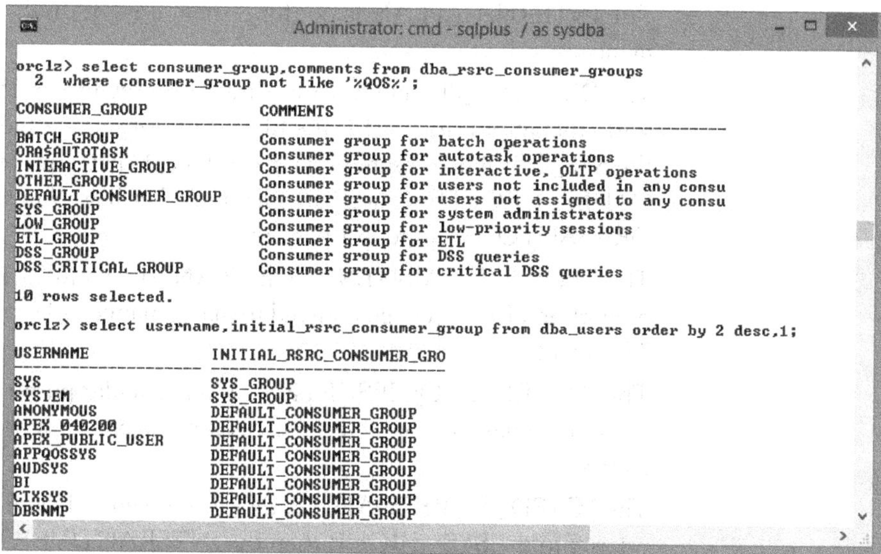

The resources that can be controlled by a plan are:

- Total CPU usage for all sessions in a group
- Degree of parallelism available to each session in a group
- Number of active sessions permitted per group
- Volume of undo space permitted per group
- Time before terminating idle sessions
- Maximum length of execution time for a call in a session, which can also trigger the switch of a session into another group

In the telesales example, there could be three plans based on CPU usage. A daytime plan would give top priority to the OLTP group. At times of peak activity, with the system working to full capacity, it is possible that the sessions of users in other groups would hang. At night, a different plan would be activated that guarantees the DSS jobs will run, though perhaps still not with the priority of the OLTP group. A month-end plan would give 100 percent of resources to the BATCH group, if it requires this.

A plan consists of a number of directives. Each directive assigns resources to a particular group at a particular priority level. Eleven plans are configured at database creation time:

- The INTERNAL_PLAN is not for normal use—it disables the resource manager.
- The DEFAULT_PLAN has three directives (see Figure 15-2). The first states that at priority level 1, the highest priority, any sessions connected to the SYS_GROUP consumer group can take 90 percent of CPU resources. OTHER_GROUPS sessions are guaranteed at least 9 percent, and the ORA$AUTOTASK group 1 percent.
- The DEFAULT_MAINTENANCE_PLAN (shown in Figure 15-2) raises the proportion of resources guaranteed to maintenance tasks and other users to 25 percent.
- The INTERNAL_QUIESCE plan has a particular purpose covered at the end of the chapter: it will freeze all sessions except those of the SYS_GROUP members.
- The MIXED_WORKLOAD_PLAN (also shown in Figure 15-2) gives top priority to the SYS_GROUP, then the INTERACTIVE_GROUP, and then the BATCH_GROUP. Other demonstration plans are DSS_PLAN and ETL_CRITICAL_PLAN.

FIGURE 15-2 The directives of the DEFAULT_PLAN, the DEFAULT_MAINTENANCE_PLAN, and the MIXED_WORKLOAD_PLAN

```
Administrator: cmd - sqlplus / as sysdba
orclz>
orclz> select group_or_subplan,cpu_p1,cpu_p2,cpu_p3 from dba_rsrc_plan_directives
  2  where plan='DEFAULT_PLAN';

GROUP_OR_SUBPLAN              CPU_P1     CPU_P2     CPU_P3
------------------------- ---------- ---------- ----------
SYS_GROUP                         90          0          0
OTHER_GROUPS                       9          0          0
ORA$AUTOTASK                       1          0          0

orclz> select group_or_subplan,cpu_p1,cpu_p2,cpu_p3 from dba_rsrc_plan_directives
  2  where plan='DEFAULT_MAINTENANCE_PLAN';

GROUP_OR_SUBPLAN              CPU_P1     CPU_P2     CPU_P3
------------------------- ---------- ---------- ----------
SYS_GROUP                         75          0          0
OTHER_GROUPS                      20          0          0
ORA$AUTOTASK                       5          0          0

orclz> select group_or_subplan,cpu_p1,cpu_p2,cpu_p3 from dba_rsrc_plan_directives
  2  where plan='MIXED_WORKLOAD_PLAN';

GROUP_OR_SUBPLAN              CPU_P1     CPU_P2     CPU_P3
------------------------- ---------- ---------- ----------
SYS_GROUP                         75          0          0
OTHER_GROUPS                       2          0          0
INTERACTIVE_GROUP                 20          0          0
BATCH_GROUP                        2          0          0
ORA$AUTOTASK                       1          0          0

orclz> _
```

- The ORA$AUTOTASK_PLAN is used by the Autotask system and cannot be adjusted.
- The ORA$ROOT_PLAN is relevant only to the multitenant container database.
- The ORA$QOS_PLAN is used by the Quality Of Service system.

To enable a plan, set the RESOURCE_MANAGER_PLAN instance parameter. This can be set automatically by the Scheduler (described in Chapter 16), manually with an ALTER SYSTEM command, or programmatically with the DBMS_RESOURCE_MANAGER.SWITCH_PLAN procedure. Following creation of a database with DBCA, the Scheduler will be configured to activate the DEFAULT_PLAN during normal working hours and the DEFAULT_MAINTENANCE_PLAN at night and weekends. It is assumed that these plans will be appropriate for most sites: they give the DBA staff top priority, followed by users, and restrict the resources that can be taken by maintenance jobs.

The instance parameter RESOURCE_LIMITS has nothing to do with the Resource Manager. It pertains to the older method of controlling resources through database profiles.

The Resource Manager works on a "trickle down" model. All resources not utilized at one priority level are available to the level lower down, and within a level any resources not needed by one group are available to the other groups. So, if the DEFAULT_PLAN is enabled, and no member of the SYS_GROUP are doing anything, the entire machine is available to the OTHER_GROUPS sessions, except for 1 percent, which may be used by the ORA$AUTOTASK group if it needs it.

Resource Manager Configuration

A PL/SQL API can be used to administer the Resource Manager. This API consists of two packages: DBMS_RESOURCE_MANAGER_PRIVS and DBMS_RESOURCE_MANAGER. DBMS_RESOURCE_MANAGER_PRIVS is used to put users into consumer groups and also to grant the system privilege necessary to administer the Resource Manager (see Figure 15-3).

FIGURE 15-3 The DBMS_RESOURCE_MANAGER_PRIVS package

```
oracle@vblin1:~
SQL> desc dbms_resource_manager_privs;
PROCEDURE GRANT_SWITCH_CONSUMER_GROUP
 Argument Name                  Type                    In/Out Default?
 ------------------------------ ----------------------- ------ --------
 GRANTEE_NAME                   VARCHAR2                IN
 CONSUMER_GROUP                 VARCHAR2                IN
 GRANT_OPTION                   BOOLEAN                 IN
PROCEDURE GRANT_SYSTEM_PRIVILEGE
 Argument Name                  Type                    In/Out Default?
 ------------------------------ ----------------------- ------ --------
 GRANTEE_NAME                   VARCHAR2                IN
 PRIVILEGE_NAME                 VARCHAR2                IN     DEFAULT
 ADMIN_OPTION                   BOOLEAN                 IN
PROCEDURE REVOKE_SWITCH_CONSUMER_GROUP
 Argument Name                  Type                    In/Out Default?
 ------------------------------ ----------------------- ------ --------
 REVOKEE_NAME                   VARCHAR2                IN
 CONSUMER_GROUP                 VARCHAR2                IN
PROCEDURE REVOKE_SYSTEM_PRIVILEGE
 Argument Name                  Type                    In/Out Default?
 ------------------------------ ----------------------- ------ --------
 REVOKEE_NAME                   VARCHAR2                IN
 PRIVILEGE_NAME                 VARCHAR2                IN     DEFAULT
```

Here is how to give user JOHN the capability of administering the Resource Manager, with the ability to pass on the privilege to other users:

```
SQL> execute dbms_resource_manager_privs.grant_system_privilege(-
grantee_name=>'JOHN',admin_option=>true);
```

This procedure call grants the system privilege ADMINISTER RESOURCE MANAGER. You can see this grant by querying the DBA_SYS_PRIVS view. To add a user to a group, use a call such as this:

```
SQL> exec dbms_resource_manager_privs.grant_switch_consumer_group(-
'ROOPESH','OLTP',false);
```

This call adds ROOPESH to the group OLTP, but without giving him the ability to add other users to the group. If ROOPESH is now a member of several groups, you should nominate one as his default group. This requires a procedure in a different package:

```
exec dbms_resource_manager.set_initial_consumer_group(-
user=>'ROOPESH',consumer_group=>'OLTP');
```

The DBMS_RESOURCE_MANAGER package is used to create consumer groups, plans, and directives. It is also used to create the "pending area." Before any work can be done with Resource Manager objects, you must create a pending area, which is an area of memory in the SGA used for storing the objects while they are being configured. A plan may consist of many directives, and each directive is created independently; it would therefore be possible to create a totally impossible plan: one that might, for example, allocate 500 percent of CPU. The pending area is provided to prevent this possibility: the plan is created in the pending area, and then when complete it is validated to check that it does make sense. Only then does the plan get saved to the data dictionary.

At connect time, a session will pick up the initial consumer group assigned to that user. If the user is a member of multiple consumer groups, the session can be switched to a different consumer group later on. This can be done either manually or by using more advanced techniques automatically, according to the work that the session is doing.

Any user can switch their active consumer group to any of the groups of which they are a member by using the SWITCH_CURRENT_CONSUMER_GROUP procedure in the DBMS_SESSION package. Alternatively, a user with the privilege to administer the Resource Manager can switch another session over by using one of two procedures in the DBMS_RESOURCE_MANAGER package. The SWITCH_CONSUMER_GROUP_FOR_USER procedure will switch all sessions logged on with a particular user name, or SWITCH_CONSUMER_GROUP_FOR_SESS will switch one particular session, identified by SID and SERIAL#:

```
SQL> exec dbms_resource_manager.switch_consumer_group_for_sess(-
session_id=>29,session_serial=>123,consumer_group=>'OLTP');
```

CERTIFICATION OBJECTIVE 15.02

Access and Create Resource Plans

A plan consists of a set of directives that divide resources between consumer groups. The following principles can be used to control this:

- CPU method
- Number of active sessions
- Degree of parallelism
- Operation execution time
- Idle time
- Volume of undo data

CPU Method

Continuing the telesales example, the daytime plan would give maximum resources to the OLTP group. All other sessions will hang if the OLTP users really do need the whole machine. The only exception is the SYS_GROUP. You should always give the SYS_GROUP priority over anything else: if you, the DBA, need to do something on the production system (such as rebuilding a broken index or doing a restore and recover), you should be able to do it as fast as possible. The plan could look like this:

Priority Level	Group	CPU %
1	SYS_GROUP	100
2	OLTP	100
3	DSS BATCH	50 50
4	OTHER_GROUPS	100

There are eight possible priority levels; this plan uses four of them. All CPU resources not used at one level trickle down to the next level. When this plan is active, the SYS_GROUP at level 1 can, if necessary, take over the whole machine; all other sessions will hang. But this shouldn't happen; in normal running, no CPU cycles will be taken by the SYS_GROUP, so the whole machine will be available at level 2, where the OLTP users can use it all. Any CPU resources they do not need drop down to level 3, where they are divided 50/50 between the DSS and the BATCH sessions. If, after the OLTP users have taken what they need, some capacity is still left, it will be available to members of other groups. It is possible, at times when the OLTP users are working nonstop and CPU usage has hit 100 percent, that the DSS and BATCH sessions will hang.

exam watch

The total CPU allocated at each level cannot exceed 100 percent. If it does, the pending area will fail to validate and the plan will not be saved to the data dictionary. It is possible to have a plan that allocates less than 100 percent at a level, but there is little purpose in doing this.

The nighttime plan will have different settings:

Priority Level	Group	CPU %
1	SYS_GROUP	100
2	OLTP DSS BATCH	50 25 25
3	OTHER_GROUPS	100

As with the daytime plan, if the SYS_GROUP needs to do something, it will get top priority. But at level 2, the DSS and BATCH users are guaranteed processing time. They still do not have as high a priority as the OLTP group, but their sessions will not hang. The month-end plan might change this further:

Priority Level	Group	CPU %
1	SYS_GROUP	100
2	BATCH	100
3	DSS OLTP	50 50
4	OTHER_GROUPS	100

When this plan is active, the BATCH jobs will take priority over everyone else, taking the whole machine if necessary. This would be advisable if the month-end processing actually means that the system is not usable, so it is vital to get it done as fast as possible.

on the job

If the CPU is not running at 100-percent usage, these plans will have no effect. They have an impact only if the CPU capacity cannot satisfy the demands on it.

A variation on the CPU method is that the "group" can itself be a plan. It is possible by this method to set up a hierarchy, where a top-level plan allocates resources between subplans. These subplans can then allocate resources between consumer groups. A case where this might be applicable would be an application service provider. Perhaps you have installed an application such as an accounting suite, and you lease time on it to several customers. Each customer will have their own groups of users. Your top-level plan will divide resources between subplans for each customer, perhaps according to the amount they are paying for access to the service. Then within that division, the customers can each allocate resources between their consumer groups.

exam watch

Every plan must include a directive for the group OTHER_GROUPS; otherwise, the validation will fail and you cannot save the plan from the pending area to the data dictionary.

To create a plan such as the daytime plan just described requires a series of procedure calls through the API. The first step is to create the pending area:

```
SQL> exec dbms_resource_manager.create_pending_area;
```

You then create the plan:

```
SQL> exec dbms_resource_manager.create_plan(-
plan=>'DAY',comment=>'plan for normal working hours');
```

Then you create the directives within it:

```
SQL> exec dbms_resource_manager.create_plan_directive(-
plan=>'DAY',group_or_subplan=>'SYS_GROUP',mgmt_p1=>100,-
comment=>'give sys_group users top priority');
SQL> exec dbms_resource_manager.create_plan_directive(-
plan=>'DAY',group_or_subplan=>'OLTP',mgmt_p2=>100,-
comment=>'give oltp users next priority');
SQL> exec dbms_resource_manager.create_plan_directive(-
plan=>'DAY',group_or_subplan=>'DSS',mgmt_p3=>50,-
comment=>'dss users have half at level 3');
SQL> exec dbms_resource_manager.create_plan_directive(-
plan=>'DAY',group_or_subplan=>'BATCH',mgmt_p3=>50,-
comment=>'batch users have half at level 3');
SQL> exec dbms_resource_manager.create_plan_directive(-
plan=>'DAY',group_or_subplan=>'OTHER_GROUPS',mgmt_p4=>100,-
comment=>'if there is anything left, others can have it');
```

Finally, validate the pending area and (if the validation returns successfully) save the plan to the data dictionary:

```
SQL> exec dbms_resource_manager.validate_pending_area;
SQL> exec dbms_resource_manager.submit_pending_area;
```

Here is how to activate the plan:

```
SQL> alter system set resource_manager_plan=day;
```

Use of the Ratio CPU Method

There is an alternative technique for allocating CPU resources. Rather than coding CPU usage as a percentage, you can specify ratios—and let Oracle work out the percentages. In the telesales example in the preceding section, the CPU resources at level 2 for the nighttime plan were as follows:

- OLTP 50%
- DSS 25%
- BATCH 25%

If you decide to add a fourth group (call it WEB) and want to make it equal in priority to OLTP, and to double DSS and BATCH, you will have to change all the directives to achieve this:

- OLTP 33%
- WEB 33%
- DSS 17%
- BATCH 17%

The ratio method lets you specify proportions. The absolute values have no significance. For example, the original ratios could have been

- OLTP 20
- DSS 10
- BATCH 10

Now, to add the WEB group with a priority equal to OLTP, you only have to add one new directive—WEB 20—and leave the others unchanged.

The Active Session Pool Method

It may be that investigation has shown that a certain number of jobs can be run concurrently by one group of users with no problems, but that if this number is exceeded, other groups will have difficulties. For example, it might be that the telesales company has six management accountants, logging on with Oracle usernames in the DSS group. If one, two, or even three of them generate reports at the same time, everything is fine, but if four or more attempt to run reports concurrently, the OLTP users begin to suffer.

The active session pool method of the Resource Manager lets the DBA limit the number of statements that will run concurrently for one group, without restricting the actual number of logins. To continue the example, all six accountants can be connected, and if three of them submit reports, they will all run, but if a fourth submits a job, it will be queued until one of the other three finishes. The nighttime plan would remove all restrictions of this nature.

An *active session* is defined as a session that is running a query or as a session that is in an uncommitted transaction. If parallel processing has been enabled, the individual parallel processors do not count against the session pool; rather, the entire parallel operation counts as one active session. By default, a session will be queued indefinitely, but if you wish, you can set a time limit. If a session from the pool does not become available within this limit, the statement is aborted and an error returned to the session that issued it. This call will adjust the DAY plan to limit the DSS group to three active sessions, queuing requests for one minute before returning an error:

```
execute dbms_resource_manager.update_plan_directive(-
plan=>'DAY',-
group_or_subplan=>'DSS',-
new_active_sess_pool_p1=>3,-
new_queueing_p1=>60)
```

A session that is not actually doing anything will still count against the active session pool for the group if it has made a change and not committed it.

To monitor the effect of the active session pool, the column CURRENT_QUEUE_DURATION in V$SESSION will show for every queued session the number of seconds it has been waiting. The view V$RSRC_CONSUMER_GROUP gives a global picture, showing how many sessions for each group are queued at any given moment.

What if the active session pool were set to zero for all groups? The result would be that all sessions would hang. This is in fact a very useful capability, and it is used by the command **ALTER SYSTEM QUIESCE RESTRICTED**. This command activates the Resource Manager plan INTERNAL_QUIESCE, which sets the active session pool for all groups other than the SYS_GROUP to zero. The effect is that statements in progress will continue until they finish, but that no one (other than members of the SYS_GROUP) can issue any more statements. If they do, the session will hang. In effect, the database is frozen for all but the administrators. This can be invaluable to get a stable system for a moment of maintenance work.

To cancel the quiesce, issue ALTER SYSTEM UNQUIESCE.

on the job

Quiesce is invaluable for DDL operations that require a very short exclusive object lock, such as an online index rebuild: quiesce the database, launch the operation, and then unquiesce. The rebuild operation will continue, and users may not have noticed that they were ever blocked.

Limiting the Degree of Parallelism

Parallel processing, both for SELECT statements and for DML, can greatly enhance the performance of individual statements, but the price you pay may be an impact on other users. It may be that your management accountants have discovered that if they run a query with the degree of parallelism set to 50 (and you cannot control this—it is done by hints in the code they write), the report generates faster. But do you really want one session to take 50 parallel execution servers from the pool? That may not leave enough for other work. Furthermore, the query may now run faster but cripple the performance of the rest of the database. The Resource Manager can control this, by setting a hard limit on the number of parallel processors that each session of any one group is allowed to use. In the daytime plan, for instance, you might limit the DSS and BATCH groups to no more than four per session, even if they ask for 50, and not permit OTHER_GROUPS sessions to use parallel processing at all. The nighttime plan could remove these restrictions. Here is an example:

```
execute dbms_resource_manager.update_plan_directive(-
plan=>'DAY',-
group_or_subplan=>'DSS',-
new_parallel_degree_limit_p1=>4,-
new_queueing_p1=>60)
```

Controlling Jobs by Execution Time

The problem of one large job killing performance for everyone else is well known in the database world. The Resource Manager solves this by providing a mechanism whereby large jobs can be completely eliminated from the system at certain times. Alternatively, a session can be allowed to launch the job, but if it exceeds (or is likely to exceed) a time threshold, the session can be switched to a lower priority group. This will allow the statement to run, but with reduced impact on other users. The relevant arguments to the DBMS_RESOURCE_MANAGER.CREATE_PLAN DIRECTIVE procedure are:

- SWITCH_GROUP
- SWITCH_TIME (measured as CPU time)
- SWITCH_ELAPSED_TIME (measured as wall-clock execution time)
- SWITCH_ESTIMATE
- MAX_EST_EXEC_TIME

The SWITCH_GROUP nominates a consumer group, probably one with lower priority in the plan, to which a session will be switched if a call takes longer than the number of seconds specified by SWITCH_TIME or SWITCH_ELAPSED_TIME to complete. If SWITCH_ESTIMATE is TRUE, the session will be switched before the statement starts running, if the optimizer thinks it might take more than that number of seconds. The MAX_EST_EXEC_TIME argument will block all statements that the optimizer believes would take longer than that number of seconds.

Terminating Sessions by Idle Time

Sessions that are not doing anything waste machine resources. Every session consists, on the server side, of a server process and a PGA. Even if the session is not executing a statement, the operating system must still bring it onto the CPU according to its round-robin time-slicing algorithm. This is known as a context switch. Every context switch forces the computer to do a lot of work as registers are loaded from main memory, the state of the session checked, and then the registers cleared again. If the PGA has been paged to disk, that too must be reloaded into main memory. The shared server mechanism, detailed in Chapter 5, will help to reduce idle processes, but it can't do anything about the number of sessions. The UGAs (in the SGA, remember) will still be taking up memory, and Oracle still has to check the state of the session on a regular basis.

The Resource Manager can disconnect sessions that are not working, according to two criteria. The first is simply based on idle time: how long is it since the session executed a statement? The second is more sophisticated: it not only checks how long since a session executed a statement, but also whether the session is holding any record or table locks that are blocking other sessions, which is much more serious problem. Remember from Chapter 10 that a record lock enqueue held by one session will cause another session that needs to lock the same row to hang indefinitely; this can cause the whole database to stop working if the problem escalates from session to session. It is possible for the DBA to detect this problem, identify the session that is holding the lock, and kill it—but this is a tricky procedure. By using the Resource Manager, you can configure automatic killing of any sessions that block other sessions for more than a certain length of time.

An important point is that "idle time" is time that the server process has been idle, not time that the user process has been idle. For example, your management accountant might be using a spreadsheet as his user process: he will have downloaded some information to it, to work on locally before saving it back to the database. While this is going on, the server process is indeed idle, but the user could be working flat out in the spreadsheet. He will not be pleased if, when he tries to pass the information back, he finds that you have disconnected him and perhaps lost all his work in progress.

The arguments to the DBMS_RESOURCE_MANAGER.CREATE_PLAN DIRECTIVE procedure that will enable idle session termination are:

- MAX_IDLE_TIME
- MAX_IDLE_BLOCKER_TIME

It is also possible to disconnect sessions by using profiles assigned to named users, which you must enable with the instance parameter RESOURCE_LIMITS. However, the Resource Manager is a better tool for this.

Restricting Generation of Undo Data

Management of undo data was covered in Chapter 9. All DML statements must generate undo data, and this data must be stored until the transaction has been committed or rolled back. Oracle has no choice about this; it is according to the rules of a relational database. If you have configured the UNDO_RETENTION instance parameter and set the RETENTION GUARANTEE attribute for your undo tablespace, the undo data may well be kept for some considerable time after the transaction has committed.

All your undo data will be written to a single undo tablespace, unless (against Oracle Corporation's advice) you are using the outdated rollback segment method of undo management. This means that transactions from all users are sharing a common storage area. A potential problem is that one badly designed transaction could fill this storage area, the undo tablespace. Programmers should not design large, long-running transactions. In business terms, though, huge transactions may be necessary to preserve the integrity of the system. For example, an accounting suite's nominal ledger cannot be partly in one accounting period and partly in the next: this is an impossibility in accountancy. So the rollover from one period to the next could mean updating millions of rows in thousands of tables over many hours, and then committing. This will require an undo tablespace the size of Jupiter and will also cause record-locking problems as the big transaction blocks other work. The answer is to break up the one business transaction into many small database transactions programmatically. If this is a problem, go back to the developers; there is nothing you as DBA can do to fix it.

As DBA, however, you can prevent large transactions by one group of users from filling up the undo tablespace. If your batch routines do not commit regularly, they will write a lot of undo data that cannot be overwritten. If too many of these batch jobs are run concurrently, the undo tablespace can fill up with active undo. This will cause all transactions to cease, and no more transactions can start until one of them commits. The Resource Manager provides a mechanism whereby the undo tablespace can in effect be partitioned into areas reserved for different consumer groups.

Your calculations on undo generated per second and your desired undo retention (as derived from the V$UNDOSTAT view, and your requirements for long-running queries and the flashback query capability) might show that the undo tablespace should be, for example, 8GB. To be safe, you size it at 12GB. But to ensure that the small OLTP transactions will always have room for their undo data, you can limit the space used by the BATCH group to, say, 6GB during normal working hours by assigning an undo pool in a Resource Manager plan. To calculate the undo space necessary for individual transactions, you can query the view V$TRANSACTION while the transaction is in progress. The column USED_UBLK shows how much undo is being used by each active transaction.

The undo pool per group has nothing to do with tablespace quotas, which are assigned per user. You cannot even grant quotas on undo tablespaces.

When the amount of active undo data generated by all sessions of a certain consumer group hits its pool limit, it will no longer be possible for members of that group to add more undo to current transactions or to start new transactions: they will hang until one transaction commits, thus freeing up space within the pool. Meanwhile, other groups can continue working in the remainder of the undo tablespace. This restricts the effect of generating too much undo to one group, rather than having it impact on all users. The argument to the DBMS_RESOURCE_MANAGER.CREATE_PLAN DIRECTIVE procedure that will define an undo pool is UNDO_POOL.

EXERCISE 15-1

Create and Implement a Resource Manager Plan

There is a shortcut to creating a Resource Manager plan: a single procedure call, CREATE_SIMPLE_PLAN. Use this to enable resource management in your database.

1. Connect to the database as user SYSTEM.
2. Create some users and grant them the CONNECT role:

```
grant connect to clerk identified by clerk;
grant connect to acct identified by acct;
grant connect to batch identified by batch;
grant connect to mgr identified by mgr;
```

3. Create two consumer groups. It is necessary to create a pending area first:

```
execute dbms_resource_manager.create_pending_area
execute dbms_resource_manager.create_consumer_group('OLTP')
execute dbms_resource_manager.create_consumer_group('DSS')
execute dbms_resource_manager.submit_pending_area
```

4. Assign the users to groups, and set their initial consumer group:

```
execute
dbms_resource_manager_privs.grant_switch_consumer_group-
('CLERK','OLTP',false)
execute
dbms_resource_manager_privs.grant_switch_consumer_group-
('MGR','OLTP',false)
execute
dbms_resource_manager_privs.grant_switch_consumer_group-
('ACCT','DSS',false)
execute
dbms_resource_manager_privs.grant_switch_consumer_group-
('BATCH','DSS',false)
execute dbms_resource_manager.set_initial_consumer_group-
('CLERK','OLTP')
execute dbms_resource_manager.set_initial_consumer_group-
('ACCT','DSS')
execute dbms_resource_manager.set_initial_consumer_group-
('BATCH','DSS')
execute dbms_resource_manager.set_initial_consumer_group-
('MGR','OLTP')
```

5. Create the plan:

```
execute dbms_resource_manager.create_simple_plan(-
simple_plan=>'my_plan',-
consumer_group1=>'OLTP',group1_percent=>80,-
consumer_group2=>'DSS',group2_percent=>20)
```

6. Activate the plan:

```
alter system set resource_manager_plan=my_plan
scope=memory;
```

CERTIFICATION OBJECTIVE 15.03

Monitor the Resource Manager

The Resource Manager configuration is documented in a set of DBA views, principally the following:

- DBA_RSRC_PLANS Plans and status
- DBA_RSRC_PLAN_DIRECTIVES Plan directives
- DBA_RSRC_CONSUMER_GROUPS Consumer groups

The current situation is documented in V$ views:

- V$SESSION The active consumer group of each session
- V$RSRC_PLAN The currently active plan
- V$RSRC_CONSUMER_GROUP Statistics for the groups

If a session has been impacted by the Resource Manager, this shows up as the wait event "resmgr:cpu quantum," which will be visible in the V$SESSION.EVENT column while the session is actually waiting as well as in the V$SESSION_EVENT view for the cumulative time waited since the session started.

on the job

It is difficult to test the effect of a Resource Manager configuration because until the system becomes stressed it will have no effect. This can mean that you see no occurrence of the "resmgr:cpu quantum" for months, and then one day everyone gets it.

EXERCISE 15-2

Test and Monitor a Resource Manager Plan

This exercise continues from Exercise 15-1, testing the effect of the plan.

1. Connect to the database as user SYSTEM.
2. Restrict the database instance to using only one CPU core, to ensure contention when multiple sessions work concurrently:

```
alter system set cpu_count=1 scope=memory;
```

3. In two more SQL*Plus sessions, log on as the ACCT and CLERK users:

```
sqlplus acct/acct
sqlplus clerk/clerk
```

4. In the SYSTEM session, run this query to confirm the group memberships of your sessions:

```
select username,resource_consumer_group from v$session
where username is not null;
```

5. In the SYSTEM session, run this query to show the CPU usage by each group so far:

```
select name, active_sessions, consumed_cpu_time
from v$rsrc_consumer_group;
```

   The figures for the DSS and OLTP groups will be low, and nearly identical.

6. In both the CLERK and ACCT sessions, run this query, concurrently, and let it run for a while:

```
select count(*) from all_objects,all_objects;
```

7. Repeat the query from step 5. Note that the OLTP group has used approximately four times as much CPU as the DSS group.
8. Run this query to see the wait time in sessions caused by the Resource Manager:

```
select s.username,e.event,e.time_waited from
v$session_event e join v$session s using (sid)
where e.event like 'resmgr:cpu%';
```

   Figure 15-4 shows typical results from steps 7 and 8: a much higher wait time for the ACCT user than the CLERK user.

9. Tidy up: drop the users and then return the database to its default Resource Manager and CPU configuration by restarting the instance.

FIGURE 15-4

Monitoring the effect of a Resource Manager plan

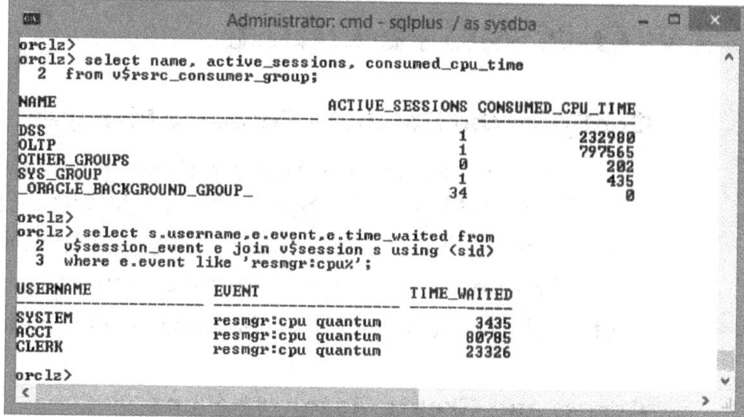

CERTIFICATION SUMMARY

The Resource Manager lets the DBA control the CPU (and other) resources available to sessions. Sessions are assigned to groups, and plan directives allocate resources to groups. Within a plan, all resources not used by one group at one level are available to other groups at the same level. All resources not used at any one level are available to groups at the next level down. Thus, if the system is not stressed, the Resource Manager will not in fact limit anything; it will come into action only when demand for resources has reached the maximum that the system can provide.

Only one plan can be active in the database at any given moment: the active plan can be assigned interactively by setting the RESOURCE_MANAGER_PLAN parameter or automatically by configuring the Scheduler. The default configuration of the Resource Manager gives top priority to the SYS_GROUP, whose membership is intended to be restricted to DBA staff. A low priority is given to the Autotask background jobs, with most of the capacity being available for regular users.

As well as limiting resources, the Resource Manager can also disconnect idle sessions.

TWO-MINUTE DRILL

Configure the Database Resource Manager

- Configure the Resource Manager with two APIs: DBMS_RESOURCE_MANAGER and DBMS_RESOURCE_MANAGER_PRIVS.
- Enable the Resource Manager by setting the RESOURCE_MANAGER_PLAN instance parameter, either interactively or through the Scheduler.
- A plan is a set of directives allocating resources to consumer groups.

Access and Create Resource Plans

- To configure the Resource Manager: first, create consumer groups; second, create a plan; third, create the plan directives that allocate resources to groups.
- A plan can limit several resources: CPU, active sessions, SQL statement execution time, use of parallel query, and undo space.
- The default plan (named DEFAULT_PLAN) gives top priority to the SYS_GROUP and lowest priority to the ORA$AUTOTASK group.

Monitor the Resource Manager

- The Resource Manager configuration is documented in a set of data dictionary views, DBA_RSRC_%.
- To monitor the Resource Manager, query the dynamic performance views.
- The Resource Manager will not appear to have any effect until the system comes under stress.

SELF TEST

Configure the Database Resource Manager

1. There are several steps involved in setting up the Resource Manager:
   - A. Assign users to consumer groups.
   - B. Create consumer groups.
   - C. Create directives.
   - D. Create the pending area.
   - E. Create the plan.
   - F. Submit the pending area.
   - G. Validate the pending area.

   What is the correct order for accomplishing these steps? (Choose the best answer.)
   - A. d-e-g-f-c-b-a
   - B. d-b-a-e-c-g-f
   - C. d-b-a-c-e-g-f
   - D. e-c-d-b-a-f-g.
   - E. b-a-d-e-c-f-g
2. Which of the following statements, if any, are correct about users and consumer groups? (Choose all correct answers.)
   - A. One user can only be a member of one consumer group.
   - B. One user can be a member of many consumer groups.
   - C. The SYS_GROUP is reserved for the user SYS.
   - D. By default, the initial group for all users is DEFAULT_CONSUMER_GROUP.
3. Some actions in the Resource Manager API are done with procedures in the package DBMS_RESOURCE_MANAGER_PRIVS, and others with procedures in the package DBMS_RESOURCE_MANAGER. Which package is needed for each of these actions?
   - A. Granting the privilege to administer the Resource Manager
   - B. Placing users in groups
   - C. Removing users from groups
   - D. Switching a session's effective group
   - E. Creating consumer groups
   - F. Configuring how to map sessions to groups

4. Resource Manager plans can use a number of methods to control resources. Which of the following are possible? (Choose three correct answers.)
   A. CPU usage
   B. Tablespace quota usage
   C. Number of active sessions
   D. Number of idle sessions
   E. Volume of redo data generated
   F. Volume of undo data generated
5. A CPU method plan allocates resources at two levels, as follows:
   Level 1: SYS_GROUP, 50% OLTP, 50%
   Level 2: DSS, 50% BATCH, 50%
   If the only users logged on are from the BATCH group, what percentage of CPU can they use? (Choose the best answer.)
   A. 12.5%.
   B. 25%.
   C. 50%.
   D. 100%.
   E. The plan will not validate because it attempts to allocate 200% of CPU resources.

Access and Create Resource Plans

6. You create a Resource Manager plan limiting the active session pool for the group DSS to 3. What will happen if three members of the group are logged on, and a fourth member attempts to connect? (Choose the best answer.)
   A. The new session will not be able to connect until an existing session disconnects.
   B. The new session will be able to connect but will hang immediately.
   C. The new session will be able to connect but will only be able to run queries, not DML statements.
   D. Any statements the new session issues may hang, depending on other activity.
7. If the active Resource Manager plan specifies that sessions belonging to a particular group may only have four parallel execution servers, what will happen if a session in that group issues a statement that requests six parallel execution servers? (Choose the best answer.)
   A. The statement will not run.
   B. The statement will run with four parallel servers.
   C. It will depend on the setting of the PARALLEL_MIN_PERCENT instance parameter.
   D. It will depend on the setting of the PARALLEL_AUTOMATIC_TUNING instance parameter.

8. When you use the Resource Manager to define an undo pool, what happens? (Choose the best answer.)

A. If a user exceeds their quota on the undo tablespace, their session will hang.

B. If a user exceeds their quota on the undo tablespace, the statement running will be rolled back but the rest of the statement will remain intact.

C. If a group fills its undo pool, all the group's transactions will hang until one session commits, rolls back, or is terminated.

D. The effect depends on whether RETENTION GUARANTEE is enabled for the undo tablespace.

Monitor the Resource Manager

9. How can you determine what is the active Resource Manager plan? (Choose two answers.)

A. SHOW PARAMETER RESOURCE_LIMIT

B. SHOW PARAMETER RESOURCE_MANAGER_PLAN

C. Query the DBA_RSRC_PLANS view

D. Query the V$RSRC_PLAN view

10. You notice that sessions have been waiting on the "resmgr:cpu quantum" wait event. What might this indicate? (Choose the best answer.)

A. That no Resource Manager plan been enabled

B. That the system has hit 100-percent CPU usage

C. That the number of sessions has reached the limit imposed by the SESSIONS parameter

D. That the CPU_COUNT has been exceeded

LAB QUESTION

Attempt to configure the Resource Manager in the manner described in the telesales example used in this chapter, which limits CPU, active sessions, and parallelism. The procedure calls have been provided. Create users and assign them to groups. Enable the plan and generate a workload in concurrent sessions attached to different groups. Monitor the effect.

SELF TEST ANSWERS

Configure the Database Resource Manager

1. ☑ **C.** This is the correct sequence, although d-b-e-c-g-f-a will also work.
   ☒ **A, B, D,** and **E** are incorrect. None of these sequences will work because the pending area must be active when working with groups and plans, and cannot be validated after it has been submitted.
2. ☑ **B.** One user can be a member of many groups, although only one membership is active at any time.
   ☒ **A, C,** and **D** are incorrect. **A** is incorrect because there can be a many-to-many relationship between users and groups. **C** is incorrect because it is possible to put other users in the SYS group. **D** is incorrect because SYS and SYSTEM are, by default, in the SYS_GROUP group.
3. ☑ DBMS_RESOURCE_MANAGER_PRIVS: **A, B, C**
   DBMS_RESOURCE_MANAGER: **D, E, F**
   The DBMS_RESOURCE_MANAGER_PRIVS package handles security, whereas the DBMS_RESOURCE_MANAGER package manages everything else.
   ☒ All other possibilities.
4. ☑ **A, C,** and **F.** The emphasis method controls CPU usage. Active sessions and volume of undo data are two of the absolute methods.
   ☒ **B, D,** and **E** are incorrect. Tablespace usage can be limited by quotas, not by the Resource Manager. Idle sessions can be timed out, but not limited in number. Redo volume is not a possible limit.
5. ☑ **D.** If no other sessions are connected, all CPU resources will be available to the connected sessions.
   ☒ **A, B, C,** and **E** are incorrect. **A, B,** and **C** misinterpret the "trickle down" nature of resource allocation. **E** fails to appreciate that CPU is allocated at each priority level, not across priority levels.

Access and Create Resource Plans

6. ☑ **D.** The session pool does not limit the number of sessions, only the number of active sessions.
   ☒ **A, B,** and **C** are incorrect. **A** is incorrect because it describes the effect of session limits in profiles, not the Resource Manager. **B** is incorrect because this result would only occur if the active session pool were full. **C** is incorrect because the Resource Manager makes no distinction between the types of SQL statements.

7. ☑ **B.** The limit will override the request.
   ☒ **A, C,** and **D** are incorrect. **A** is incorrect because the intent of the Resource Manager is not to block statements, but to control them. **C** and **D** refer to the instance parameters that drive the optimizer, not the Resource Manager.

8. ☑ **C.** Undo pools refer to whole groups, not to individual users or sessions. If a group fills its pool, all sessions that are part of the group will hang until one issues a COMMIT or a ROLLBACK.
   ☒ **A, B,** and **D** are incorrect. Tablespace quotas are relevant to neither undo in general nor the Resource Manager. RETENTION GUARANTEE does not apply either.

Monitor the Resource Manager

9. ☑ **B, C.** The active plan is set with the RESOURCE_MANAGER_PLAN parameter and displayed in the V$RSRC_PLAN dynamic performance view.
   ☒ **A** and **D** are incorrect. **A** is incorrect because the RESOURCE_LIMIT parameter is relevant to profiles, not to the Resource Manager. **D** is incorrect because the DBA_RSRC_PLANS data dictionary view shows the configuration of the Resource Manager, not its current state.

10. ☑ **B.** Once a system reaches 100-percent CPU usage, a CPU plan will come into effect and start limiting sessions' usage.
    ☒ **A, C,** and **D** are incorrect. **A** is incorrect because if no plan is enabled there can be no waits on this event. **C** and **D** are incorrect because although these parameters do control resource usage, they do not do this through the Resource Manager plan.

LAB ANSWER

It is sometimes difficult to simulate an environment where the system is under sufficient stress to force the Resource Manager to take action. However, the technique used in Exercise 15-2 should be sufficient to demonstrate its effect.

16

Automating Tasks by Using Oracle Scheduler

CERTIFICATION OBJECTIVES

16.01	Use Oracle Scheduler to Simplify Management Tasks
16.02	Use Job Chains to Perform a Series of Related Tasks
16.03	Use Scheduler Jobs on Remote Systems
16.04	Use Advanced Scheduler Features to Prioritize Jobs
✓	Two-Minute Drill
Q&A	Self Test

This chapter introduces the Scheduler: a facility to automate the running of jobs. These jobs may be procedures that execute within the database, or operating system commands and scripts. They can run locally or on remote machines and databases. They can run according to a schedule, according the results of a previous job, or in response to events. The Scheduler is integrated with the Resource Manager.

An alternative (and older) scheduling mechanism is DBMS_JOB. However, the Scheduler is far more capable (and complex) than this. A job-scheduling facility is also provided by Enterprise Manager, and of course your operating system will have a job scheduler. The Scheduler is probably more sophisticated than any alternative solution.

CERTIFICATION OBJECTIVE 16.01

Use Oracle Scheduler to Simplify Management Tasks

The Scheduler is configured by creating various objects. At a minimum, a job is all that is needed. But usually, more objects will be involved: at least programs and schedules. In many environments, job classes, windows, and chains are also useful. And at the instance level, the background processes control the environment and run the jobs.

The Scheduler Architecture

The data dictionary includes a table that is the storage point for all Scheduler jobs. You can query this table through the DBA_SCHEDULER_JOBS view. The job queue coordinator background process, the CJQ0 process, monitors this table and when necessary launches job queue processes, the J*nnn* processes, to run the jobs. The CJQ0 process is launched automatically if there are any defined and active Scheduler jobs. The J*nnn* processes are launched on demand, although the maximum number is limited by the JOB_QUEUE_PROCESSES instance parameter, which can have any value from 0 to 1000 (the default). If set to zero, the Scheduler will not function.

The job queue coordinator picks up jobs from the job queue table and passes them to job queue processes for execution. It also launches and terminates the job queue processes on demand. To see the processes currently running, query the V$PROCESS view:

```
SQL> select program from v$process
where program like '%J%';
PROGRAM
------------------------------------------------
oracle@vblin1.example.com (CJQ0)
oracle@vblin1.example.com (J000)
oracle@vblin1.example.com (J001)
```

This query shows that the job queue coordinator and two job queue processes are running. In a Unix instance, the processes will be separate operating system processes (as in this query); in a Windows instance, they execute as threads within the ORACLE.EXE process.

The JOB_QUEUE_ PROCESSES instance parameter must be greater than zero or the Scheduler cannot run. It is 1000 by default. The job queue coordinator will always be running if there are any defined and active jobs.

Jobs defined as procedures run within the database. Jobs can also be defined as operating system commands or shell scripts: these will run as external operating system tasks. The triggering factor for a job can be a time or an event. Time-based jobs may run once or repeatedly according to a schedule. Event-based jobs run when certain conditions arise. There are some preconfigured events, or you can use user-defined events. Jobs can be connected into a chain, using simple rules for branching depending on a job's success or failure.

An advanced feature of the Scheduler is to associate it with the Resource Manager. It may be that certain jobs should be run with certain priorities, and this can be achieved by linking a job to a Resource Manager consumer group, via a job class. It is also possible to use the Scheduler to activate a Resource Manager plan, rather than having to activate a plan manually by changing the RESOURCE_ MANAGER_PLAN instance parameter or using the DBMS_RESOURCE_ MANAGER.SWITCH_PLAN procedure call.

The API to administer the Scheduler is the DBMS_SCHEDULER package. Also, a graphical interface is provided by Enterprise Manager.

Scheduler Objects

The most basic object in the Scheduler environment is a job. A job can be completely self-contained: it can define the action to be taken and when to take it. In a more advanced configuration, the job is only a part of the structure consisting of a number of Scheduler objects of various types.

Jobs

A job specifies what to do and when to do it. The "what" can be an anonymous PL/SQL block (which could consist of just a single SQL statement), a PL/SQL stored procedure (which could invoke a Java stored procedure or an external procedure), or any executable file stored in the server's file system: either a binary executable or a shell script. A particularly powerful capability is the remote external job, which runs on a separate machine. The "when" specifies either the timestamp at which to launch the job and a repeat interval for future runs, or the triggering event.

You have several options when creating a job, as can be seen from looking at the DBMS_SCHEDULER.CREATE_JOB procedure. This procedure is overloaded; it has no less than six forms. Figure 16-1 shows part of the output

FIGURE 16-1

The specification of the CREATE_JOB procedure

```
oracle@oel58x64db121:~
PROCEDURE CREATE_JOB
 Argument Name                  Type                    In/Out Default?
 ------------------------------ ----------------------- ------ --------
 JOB_NAME                       VARCHAR2                IN
 JOB_TYPE                       VARCHAR2                IN
 JOB_ACTION                     VARCHAR2                IN
 NUMBER_OF_ARGUMENTS            BINARY_INTEGER          IN     DEFAULT
 START_DATE                     TIMESTAMP WITH TIME ZONE IN     DEFAULT
 REPEAT_INTERVAL                VARCHAR2                IN     DEFAULT
 END_DATE                       TIMESTAMP WITH TIME ZONE IN     DEFAULT
 JOB_CLASS                      VARCHAR2                IN     DEFAULT
 ENABLED                        BOOLEAN                 IN     DEFAULT
 AUTO_DROP                      BOOLEAN                 IN     DEFAULT
 COMMENTS                       VARCHAR2                IN     DEFAULT
 CREDENTIAL_NAME                VARCHAR2                IN     DEFAULT
 DESTINATION_NAME               VARCHAR2                IN     DEFAULT
PROCEDURE CREATE_JOB
 Argument Name                  Type                    In/Out Default?
 ------------------------------ ----------------------- ------ --------
 JOB_NAME                       VARCHAR2                IN
 JOB_TYPE                       VARCHAR2                IN
 JOB_ACTION                     VARCHAR2                IN
 NUMBER_OF_ARGUMENTS            BINARY_INTEGER          IN     DEFAULT
 START_DATE                     TIMESTAMP WITH TIME ZONE IN     DEFAULT
 EVENT_CONDITION                VARCHAR2                IN     DEFAULT
 QUEUE_SPEC                     VARCHAR2                IN
```

from a DESCRIBE of the DBMS_SCHEDULER package, showing the first two forms of CREATE_JOB.

All forms of the CREATE_JOB procedure must specify a JOB_NAME. This must be unique within the schema where the job is created. Note that jobs are schema objects. Then, taking the first form of the procedure, the JOB_TYPE must be one of the following:

- **PLSQL_BLOCK** An anonymous PL/SQL block
- **STORED_PROCEDURE** A named PL/SQL procedure
- **EXECUTABLE** Anything executable from an OS prompt
- **CHAIN** A named job chain object
- **EXTERNAL_SCRIPT** A script launched by the OS's command interpreter
- **SQL_SCRIPT** A SQL*Plus script
- **BACKUP_SCRIPT** An RMAN script

The JOB_ACTION is the command or script or chain to be run. The NUMBER_OF_ARGUMENTS parameter states how many arguments the JOB_ACTION should take.

The remaining arguments of the first form of the procedure shown in Figure 16-1 are details of when and how frequently to run the job. The first execution will be on the START_DATE; the REPEAT_INTERVAL defines a repeat frequency, such as daily, until END_DATE. JOB_CLASS has to do with priorities and integration of the Scheduler with the Resource Manager. The ENABLED argument determines whether the job can actually be run. Perhaps surprisingly, this defaults to FALSE. If a job is not created with this argument on TRUE, it cannot be run (either manually or through a schedule) without being enabled first. Finally, AUTO_DROP controls whether to drop the job definition after the END_TIME. This defaults to TRUE. If a job is created with no scheduling information, it will be run as soon as it is enabled, and then dropped immediately if AUTO_DROP is on TRUE, which is the default.

The second form of CREATE_JOB shown in Figure 16-1 creates an event-based job. The EVENT_CONDITION is an expression based on the definition of the messages enqueued to the queue table nominated by the QUEUE_SPEC argument. Between the start and end dates, Oracle will monitor the queue and launch the job whenever a message arrives that conforms to the condition.

Programs

Programs provide a layer of abstraction between the job and the action it will perform. They are created with the DBMS_SCHEDULER.CREATE_PROGRAM procedure:

```
PROCEDURE CREATE_PROGRAM
Argument Name           Type                    In/Out Default?
----------------------- ----------------------- ------ --------
PROGRAM_NAME            VARCHAR2                IN
PROGRAM_TYPE            VARCHAR2                IN
PROGRAM_ACTION          VARCHAR2                IN
NUMBER_OF_ARGUMENTS     BINARY_INTEGER          IN     DEFAULT
ENABLED                 BOOLEAN                 IN     DEFAULT
COMMENTS                VARCHAR2                IN     DEFAULT
```

By pulling the "what" of a job out of the job definition itself and defining it in a program, you can reference the same program in different jobs, and thus to associate it with different schedules and job classes, without having to define it many times. Note that (as for a job) a program must be ENABLED before it can be used; the default for this is FALSE.

Schedules

A schedule is a specification for when and how frequently a job should run. The basic principle of a schedule is to pull the "when" portion out of a job, thus associating it with different jobs. It is created with the DBMS_SCHEDULER.CREATE_SCHEDULE procedure:

```
PROCEDURE CREATE_SCHEDULE
Argument Name           Type                    In/Out Default?
------------------------------------------------------ --------
SCHEDULE_NAME       VARCHAR2                    IN
START_DATE          TIMESTAMP WITH TIME ZONE    IN     DEFAULT
REPEAT_INTERVAL     VARCHAR2                    IN
END_DATE            TIMESTAMP WITH TIME ZONE    IN     DEFAULT
COMMENTS            VARCHAR2                    IN     DEFAULT
```

The START_DATE defaults to the current date and time. This is the time that any jobs associated with this schedule will run. The REPEAT_INTERVAL specifies how frequently the job should run, until the END_DATE. Schedules without a specified END_DATE will run forever.

The REPEAT_INTERVAL argument can take a wide variety of calendaring expressions. These consist of up to three elements: a frequency, an interval (defaulting to 1), and possibly several specifiers. The frequency may be one of these values:

- YEARLY
- MONTHLY
- WEEKLY
- DAILY
- HOURLY
- MINUTELY
- SECONDLY

The specifiers can be one of these:

- BYMONTH
- BYWEEKNO
- BYYEARDAY
- BYMONTHDAY
- BYHOUR
- BYMINUTE
- BYSECOND

Using these elements of a REPEAT_INTERVAL makes it possible to set up schedules that should satisfy any requirement. For example,

```
repeat_interval=>'freq=hourly; interval=12'
```

will run the job every 12 hours, starting at the START_DATE. The next example,

```
repeat_interval=>'freq=yearly; bymonth=jan,mar,may;
bymonthday=2'
```

will run the job on the second day of each of the named four months, starting as early in the day as resources permit. A final example,

```
repeat_interval=>'freq=weekly; interval=2; byday=mon;
byhour=6; byminute=10'
```

will run the job at ten past six on alternate Mondays.

Using programs and schedules normalizes the job structure, allowing reuse of predefined programs and schedules for many jobs, as shown in Figure 16-2. Note that

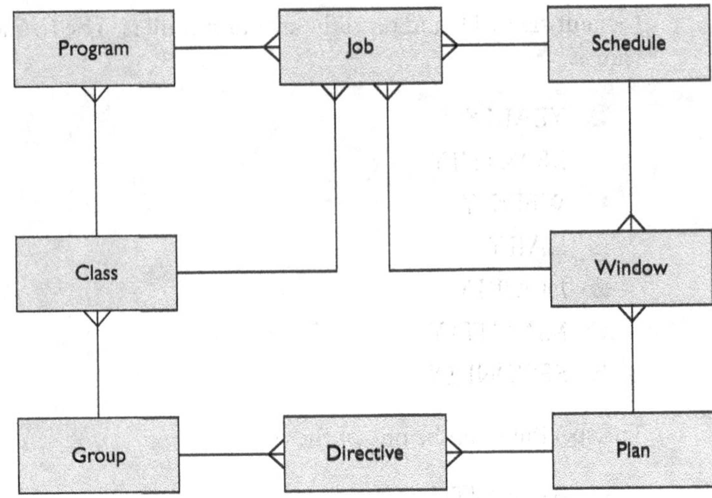

FIGURE 16-2 A normalized view of the Scheduler and Resource Manger objects

the figure includes other Scheduler objects and also refers to the Resource Manager objects Groups, Directives, and Plans.

A Self-Contained Job

To create and schedule a job with one procedure call, use the CREATE_JOB procedure. For example,

```
begin
dbms_scheduler.create_job(
job_name=>'hr.refresh_sums',
job_type=>'stored_procedure',
job_action=>'hr.refresh_summaries',
start_date=>trunc(sysdate)+23/24,
repeat_interval=>'freq=weekly;byday=mon,fri;byhour=23',
enabled=>true,
auto_drop=>false,
comments=>'update summary tables');
end;
```

will create an enabled job that calls the procedure HR.REFRESH_SUMMARIES at 11 o'clock on Mondays and Fridays, starting today. The job is created in the HR schema.

EXERCISE 16-1

Creating a Job with the Scheduler API

Use the DBMS_SCHEDULER package to create a job, and confirm that it is working.

1. Connect to your database as user SYSTEM using SQL*Plus.
2. Create a table to store times, and set your date format to show the date and time:

```
create table times (c1 date);
alter session set nls_date_format='dd-mm-yy hh24:mi:ss';
```

3. Create a job to insert the current time into the table every minute:

```
execute dbms_scheduler.create_job(-
job_name=>'savedate',-
job_type=>'plsql_block',-
job_action=>'insert into times values(sysdate);',-
start_date=>sysdate,-
repeat_interval=>'freq=minutely;interval=1',-
enabled=>true,-
auto_drop=>false)
```

4. Query the job table a few times to see that the job is scheduled and running:

```
select job_name,enabled,
to_char(next_run_date,'dd-mm-yy hh24:mi:ss'),run_count
from user_scheduler_jobs;
```

   Query the times table to demonstrate that the inserts are occurring:

```
select * from times;
```

5. Disable the job:

```
exec dbms_scheduler.disable('savedate')
```

6. Rerun the queries from step 4 to confirm that the job is disabled and that no more inserts are occurring.
7. Drop the job:

```
exec dbms_scheduler.drop_job('savedate')
```

CERTIFICATION OBJECTIVE 16.02

Use Job Chains to Perform a Series of Related Tasks

A chain represents a set of linked programs with execution dependencies. The logic connecting the steps in a chain is branching based on a success/failure test.

Here are the steps to follow to use job chains:

1. Create a chain object.
2. Define the steps (the individual programs) of the chain.
3. Define the rules connecting the steps.
4. Enable the chain.
5. Create a job to launch the chain.

This code fragment demonstrates the first four steps:

```
exec dbms_scheduler.create_chain(chain_name=>'mychain');
exec dbms_scheduler.define_chain_step(chain_name => 'mychain',-
step_name => 'step1',program_name => 'prg1');
exec dbms_scheduler.define_chain_step(chain_name => 'mychain',-
step_name => 'step2',program_name => 'prg2');
exec dbms_scheduler.define_chain_step(-
chain_name => 'mychain',-
step_name => 'step3',program_name => 'prg3');
exec dbms_scheduler.define_chain_rule(-
chain_name => 'mychain',-
rule_name => 'rule1',condition => 'step1 succeeded',-
action => 'start step2');
exec dbms_scheduler.define_chain_rule(-
chain_name => 'mychain',-
rule_name => 'rule2',condition => 'step1 failed',-
action => 'start step3');
exec dbms_scheduler.enable('mychain');
```

These commands create and enable a very simple chain of three steps. The execution of either the second or third step is dependent on the outcome of the first step. The syntax for creating rules permits the use of keywords such as SUCCEEDED and FAILED, which will test the outcome of another step. In this example it is assumed that the programs have already been created with CREATE_PROGRAM procedure calls.

To launch the chain, you must create a job. This could be based on a schedule or an event. This job will run the chain on the last Tuesday of alternate months:

```
exec dbms_scheduler.create_job(job_name=>'run_mychain',-
job_type=>'chain',-
job_action=>'mychain',-
start_date=>next_day(last_day(sysdate)-7,'tuesday'),-
repeat_interval=>'freq=monthly;interval=2',-
enabled=>true);
```

CERTIFICATION OBJECTIVE 16.03

Use Scheduler Jobs on Remote Systems

It is possible to schedule and run jobs on remote systems. These jobs can be database jobs (typically, calling a PL/SQL procedure) or external jobs (typically, shell scripts). The job definition exists in the calling database, but the procedure or shell script must reside at the remote site.

Every machine on which a remote job is to run requires a Scheduler Agent. Install this agent from the Oracle Client CD, selecting the Custom Install option. The agent process will, by default, listen on port 1500, although any port can be selected at install time. The protocol between agent and database is HTTP. The database and listener will already be configured to accept HTTP if Database Express has been configured. To confirm the listening port, and set it if it has not been configured, use procedures in the DBMS_XDB_CONFIG package:

```
orclz>
orclz> select dbms_xdb_config.gethttpport from dual;
GETHTTPPORT
-----------
          0
orclz> exec dbms_xdb_config.sethttpport(new_port=>5500)
PL/SQL procedure successfully completed.
orclz>
```

Once communications have been established between database and agent, create jobs that specify the DESTINATION_NAME argument of the CREATE_JOB procedure, giving the network name of the remote machine.

CERTIFICATION OBJECTIVE 16.04

Use Advanced Scheduler Features to Prioritize Jobs

The more advanced capabilities of the Scheduler enable you to integrate it with the Resource Manager, to control and prioritize jobs. These are the relevant components:

- **Job classes** Jobs can be assigned a class, and a class can be linked to a Resource Manager consumer group. Classes also control the logging level for their jobs.
- **Consumer groups** Resource Manager consumer groups are restricted in the resources they can use, being limited in, for instance, CPU usage or the number of active sessions.
- **Resource plans** A Resource Manager plan defines how to apportion resources to groups. Only one plan is active in the instance at any one time.
- **Windows** A window is a defined (probably recurring) period of time during which certain jobs will run and a certain plan will be active.
- **Window groups** It is possible to combine windows into window groups, for ease of administration.

Prioritizing jobs within a window is done at two levels. Within a class, jobs can be given different priorities by the Scheduler, but because all jobs in a class are in the same consumer group, the Resource Manager will not distinguish between them. But if jobs in different classes are scheduled within the same window, the Resource Manager will assign resources to each class according to the consumer groups for that class.

Using Job Classes

Create a class with the DBMS_SCHEDULER API. Here is an example:

```
SQL> exec dbms_scheduler.create_job_class(-
job_class_name=>'daily_reports',-
resource_consumer_group=>'dss',-
logging_level=>dbms_scheduler.logging_full);
```

Then assign the jobs to the class, either at job creation time by specifying the JOB_CLASS attribute or by modifying the job later. To assign a job to a class after creation, you must use the SET_ATTRIBUTE procedure. Here is how to create a job called REPORTS_JOB and place it in the class just created:

```
SQL> exec dbms_scheduler.create_job(job_name=>'reports_job',-
job_type=>'stored_procedure',-
job_action=>'run_reports')
SQL> exec dbms_scheduler.set_attribute(-
name=>'reports_job',-
attribute=>'job_class',-
value=>'daily_reports')
```

If there are several jobs in the one class, prioritize them with further SET_ATTRIBUTE calls:

```
SQL> exec dbms_scheduler.set_attribute(-
name=>'reports_job',-
attribute=>'job_priority',-
value=>2);
```

If several jobs in the same class are scheduled to be executed at the same time, the job priority determines the order in which jobs from that class are picked up for execution by the job coordinator process. It can be a value from 1 to 5, with 1 being the first to be picked up for job execution. The default for all jobs is 3. This could be critical if, for example, the class's consumer group has an active session pool that is smaller than the number of jobs: those jobs with the highest priority will run first, while the others are queued.

It is not possible to assign priorities when creating jobs with the CREATE_JOB procedures—you must use the SET_ATTRIBUTE procedure of the API subsequently.

Logging levels are also controlled by the job's class. There are three options:

- **DBMS_SCHEDULER.LOGGING_OFF** No logging is done for any jobs in this class.
- **DBMS_SCHEDULER.LOGGING_RUNS** Information is written to the job log regarding each run of each job in the class, including when the run was started and whether the job ran successfully.
- **DBMS_SCHEDULER.LOGGING_FULL** In addition to logging information about the job runs, the log will also record management operations on the class, such as creating new jobs.

To view logging information, query the DBA_SCHEDULER_JOB_LOG view:

```
SQL> select job_name,log_date,status from
dba_scheduler_job_log;
JOB_NAME     LOG_DATE                        STATUS
------------ ------------------------------- -----------
PURGE_LOG    16-OCT-13 13-00-03              SUCCEEDED
TEST_JOB     16-OCT-13 11-00-00              FAILED
NIGHT_INCR   16-OCT-13 01-00-13              SUCCEEDED
NIGHT_ARCH   16-OCT-13 01-00-00              SUCCEEDED
```

More detailed information is written to the DBA_SCHEDULER_JOB_RUN_DETAILS view, including the job's run duration and any error code it returned. Logging information is cleared by the automatically created PURGE_LOG job. By default, this runs daily according to the preconfigured schedule DAILY_PURGE_SCHEDULE and will remove all logging information more than 30 days old.

Using Windows

Create windows with the CREATE_WINDOW procedure. Here is an example:

```
SQL> exec dbms_scheduler.create_window(-
window_name=>'daily_reporting_window',-
resource_plan=>'night_plan',-
schedule_name=>'weekday_nights',-
duration=>'0 04:00:00',-
window_priority=>'low',-
comments=>'for running regular reports');
```

This window activates a Resource Manager plan called NIGHT_PLAN. This might be a plan that gives priority to the DSS consumer groups over the OLTP group. It opens according to the schedule WEEKDAY_NIGHTS, which might be Monday through Friday at 20:00. The window will remain open for four hours; the DURATION argument accepts an INTERVAL DAY TO SECOND value, as does the REPEAT_INTERVAL for a schedule. Setting the priority to LOW means that if this window overlaps with another window, the other window will be allowed to impose its Resource Manager plan. This would be the case if you created a different window for your end-of-month processing, and the end-of-month happened to be on a weekday. You could give the end-of-month window HIGH priority, to ensure that the end-of-month Resource Manager plan, which could give top priority to the BATCH group, does come into effect.

exam Watch

Even if a job has priority 1 within its class, it might still only run after a job with priority 5 in another class—if the second job's class is in a consumer group with a higher Resource Manager priority.

If two windows with equal priority overlap, the window with the longest duration will open (or remain open). If both windows have the same time to run, the window currently open will remain open.

on the Job

Oracle Corporation advises that you should avoid using overlapping windows.

EXERCISE 16-2

Use Scheduler Windows to Control the Resource Manager

In this exercise, you will use the Scheduler to automate the activation of the Resource Manager plan MY_PLAN created in Exercise 16-1.

1. Connect to your database as user SYSTEM with SQL*Plus.
2. Run this query to determine whether a window is currently open:

```
select WINDOW_NAME,ACTIVE from dba_scheduler_windows;
```

3. Run this query to determine which Resource Manager plan is currently active:

```
select * from v$rsrc_plan;
```

4. Temporarily clear whatever Resource Manager plan may be currently active:

```
alter system set resource_manager_plan='' scope=memory;
```

5. Confirm that there is no Resource Manager plan active.
   Re-run the query from step 3: this will show that the INTERNAL_PLAN is active, which is the plan used when no other has been set.
6. Execute this procedure call to create a window named MY_WINDOW that will activate the MY_PLAN plan:

```
execute dbms_scheduler.create_window(-
window_name=>'daytime',resource_plan=>'my_plan',-
start_date=>trunc(systimestamp) + 6/24,-
```

```
repeat_interval=>'freq=daily',-
duration=>'0 12:00:00',-
comments=>'daily at 6AM');
```

This will open the window from now onward, every morning at 6 o'clock, for 12 hours.

7. Force the database to open the new window immediately:

```
exec dbms_scheduler.open_window(-
window_name=>'daytime',duration=>'0 00:05:00',force=>true);
```

This procedure call will open the window immediately and activate its plan, but only for five minutes.

8. Rerun the queries from steps 2 and 3 to confirm that the DAYTIME window is open and the MY_PLAN plan is active.
9. After five minutes, repeat step 8. You will see that the window has closed and that no plan is active. This situation will persist until the next scheduled opening of a window.
10. Tidy up:

```
exec dbms_scheduler.drop_window('daytime')
```

CERTIFICATION SUMMARY

This chapter describes using the Scheduler to automate running jobs. Jobs can be PL/SQL running within the database, or operating system commands running on the host. By installing a Scheduler Agent on a remote machine, it is possible to run jobs on remote databases and hosts.

Basic configuration of the Scheduler is simple: one call to the CREATE_JOB procedure can define what to do, and when to do it. More complex configuration separates out the "what" and "when" into programs and schedules. A chain object lets one link a series of programs together, connected by branching based on whether a previous program succeeded or failed.

In an environment with many jobs configured, job priorities can be defined. This is done at two levels. Within the Scheduler environment, assign jobs to classes and give them priorities within the class. Alternatively, you can link the Scheduler to the Resource Manager by assigning the job classes to Resource Manager Consumer groups. The Resource Manager will then assign priorities based on the currently active Resource Manager plan. The use of Scheduler windows lets the Scheduler activate a particular plan, according to a schedule.

TWO-MINUTE DRILL

Use Oracle Scheduler to Simplify Management Tasks

- A job can specify what to do and when to do it, or it can point to a program and/or a schedule.
- A job (or its program) can be an anonymous PL/SQL block, a stored procedure, or an external operating system command or script.
- Jobs are launched by the CJQ0 background process and executed by J*nnn* processes.
- J*nnn* processes are launched on demand, up to the limit set by the JOB_QUEUE_PROCESSES parameter. Setting this to zero disables the job system.

Use Job Chains to Perform a Series of Related Tasks

- A chain object consists of a number of steps.
- Each step can launch a program.
- Simple logic (such as the success or failure of a previous step) can control the flow of execution through a job chain with branching steps.
- The chain itself is launched by a job, triggered by either an event or a schedule.

Use Scheduler Jobs on Remote Systems

- Remote jobs can run in remote databases or on remote hosts.
- Every system where a remote job may run must run a Scheduler Agent.
- Remote jobs are defined in the source database and sent to the remote agent with credentials.
- Create a remote job by specifying the DESTINATION argument of CREATE_JOB.

Use Advanced Scheduler Features to Prioritize Jobs

- Jobs can be prioritized at two levels: the Resource Manager will allocate resources via consumer groups to all the jobs in a class, and the class will prioritize the jobs within it according to the job priority set by the Scheduler.
- Scheduler priority varies between levels 1 to 5 (highest to lowest).

SELF TEST

Use Oracle Scheduler to Simplify Management Tasks

1. When a job is due to run, what process will run it? (Choose the best answer.)
   A. A CJQ*n* process
   B. A J*nnn* process
   C. A server process
   D. A background process
2. Which of the following is a requirement if the Scheduler is to work? (Choose the best answer.)
   A. The instance parameter JOB_QUEUE_PROCESSES must be set.
   B. A Resource Manager plan must be enabled.
   C. A schedule must have been created.
   D. All of the above.
   E. None of the above.
3. A Scheduler job can be of several types. Choose all that apply:
   A. An anonymous PL/SQL block
   B. An executable operating system file
   C. A PL/SQL stored procedure
   D. A Java stored procedure
   E. An operating system command
   F. An operating system shell script (Unix) or batch file (Windows)

Use Job Chains to Perform a Series of Related Tasks

4. How can jobs best be chained together?
   A. Put them in the same class, and use priorities to control the running order.
   B. Create them as programs, connected in a chain.
   C. Assign them to different schedules, timed to start consecutively.
   D. Run them within a window, giving them window priorities.

Use Scheduler Jobs on Remote Systems

5. Which process runs a remote database job?
   A. A job queue process on the originating machine
   B. A job queue process on the destination machine
   C. The Scheduler Agent on the destination machine
   D. The Enterprise Manager agent on the destination machine

Use Advanced Scheduler Features to Prioritize Jobs

6. You create a job with the syntax

```
exec dbms_scheduler.create_job(-
job_name=>'j1',-
program_name=>'p1',-
schedule_name=>'s1',-
job_class=>'c1');
```

   and find that it is not running when expected. What might be a reason for this? (Choose the best answer.)
   A. The schedule is associated with a window, which has not opened.
   B. The job has not been enabled.
   C. The class is part of a Resource Manager consumer group with low priority.
   D. The permissions on the job are not correct.
7. What are the possible priority levels of a job within a class? (Choose the best answer.)
   A. 1 to 5.
   B. 1 to 999.
   C. HIGH or LOW.
   D. It depends on the Resource Manager plan in effect.
8. You want a job to run every 30 minutes. Which of the following possibilities for the REPEAT_INTERVAL argument are correct syntactically and will achieve this result? (Choose three answers.)
   A. 'freq=minutely;interval=30'
   B. 'freq=hourly;interval=1/2'
   C. '0 00:30:00'
   D. 'freq=minutely;byminute=30'
   E. 'freq=byminute;interval=30'

9. You create a job class, and you set the LOGGING_LEVEL argument to LOGGING_RUNS. What will be the result? (Choose the best answer.)
   A. There will be a log entry for each run of each job in the class, but no information on whether the job was successful.
   B. There will be a log entry for each run of each job in the class, and information on whether the job was successful.
   C. There will be a single log entry for the class whenever it is run.
   D. You cannot set logging per class, only per job.

LAB QUESTION

Create a table with one column of data type timestamp and a procedure that will insert the current time into it:

```
create table times(runtime timestamp);
create or replace procedure gettime as begin
insert into times values (systimestamp);
end;

/
```

Create a program that will invoke the procedure, a schedule that will run every minute, and a job that will run the program according to the schedule. Confirm that the job runs.

SELF TEST ANSWERS

Use Oracle Scheduler to Simplify Management Tasks

1. ☑ **B.** Jobs are run by job queue processes.
☒ **A, C,** and **D** are incorrect. The job queue coordinator does not run jobs; it assigns them to job queue processes. These are ephemeral processes, not background processes that run continuously, and they are not server processes.

2. ☑ **E.** The Scheduler is available, by default, with no preconfiguration steps needed.
☒ **A, B, C,** and **D** are incorrect. **A** is incorrect because the JOB_QUEUE_PROCESSES instance parameter defaults to 1000; therefore, it does not need to be set. **B** and **C** are incorrect because the Resource Manager is not required, and neither are schedules.

3. ☑ **A, B, C, D, E,** and **F.** The JOB_TYPE can be PLSQL_BLOCK, or STORED_PROCEDURE (which can be PL/SQL or Java), or EXECUTABLE (which includes executable files and OS commands), or EXTERNAL_SCRIPT (either shell script or SQL*Plus script).
☒ All the answers are correct.

Use Job Chains to Perform a Series of Related Tasks

4. ☑ **B.** This is the best way, connecting them with branches based on success or failure.
☒ **A, C,** and **D** are incorrect. **A** and **C** are incorrect because although they might work, there is no guarantee of this. **D** is incorrect because window priorities control which window will open, not which job runs within a window.

Use Scheduler Jobs on Remote Systems

5. ☑ **B.** PL/SQL jobs are always run by job queue processes in the instance where the job runs.
☒ **A, C,** and **D** are incorrect. **A** is incorrect because a job queue process can run jobs only within its local instance. **C** is incorrect because although the agent launches the job, it does not actually run it. **D** is incorrect because the Enterprise Manager job system is not part of the Scheduler job system.

Use Advanced Scheduler Features to Prioritize Jobs

6. ☑ **B.** The job will, by default, not be enabled and therefore cannot run.
☒ **A, C,** and **D** are incorrect. **A** is incorrect because the job is not controlled by a window, but by a schedule. **C** is incorrect because although the Resource Manager can control job priority, it would not in most circumstances block a job completely. **D** is incorrect because although permissions might cause a job to fail, they would not stop it from running.

7. ☑ **A.** Job priorities are 1 to 5 (highest to lowest).
   ☒ **B, C,** and **D** are incorrect. **B** is incorrect because it is the wrong range. **C** is the choice for window priority, not job priority. **D** is incorrect because the Resource Manager controls priorities between classes, not within them.
8. ☑ **A, B,** and **D.** These will provide a half-hour repeat interval.
   ☒ **C** and **E** are incorrect. **C** is the syntax for a window's duration, not a repeat interval. **E** is syntactically incorrect.
9. ☑ **B.** With logging set to LOGGING_RUNS, you will get records of each run of each job, including the success or failure.
   ☒ **A, C,** and **D** are incorrect. **A** is incorrect because LOGGING_RUNS will include the success or failure. **C** and **D** are incorrect because even though logging is set at the class level, it is applied at the job level. Note that logging can also be set at the job level.

LAB ANSWER

Here is a possible solution, working in the SYSTEM schema:

```
exec dbms_scheduler.create_program(-
program_name=>'time_prog',-
program_type=>'plsql_block',-
program_action=>'gettime;',-
enabled=>true)
exec dbms_scheduler.create_schedule(-
schedule_name=>'one_minute',-
start_date=>systimestamp,-
repeat_interval=>'freq=minutely;interval=1')
exec dbms_scheduler.create_job(-
job_name=>'timing',-
program_name=>'time_prog',-
schedule_name=>'one_minute',-
enabled=>true,-
auto_drop=>false)
alter session set nls_date_format='dd-mm-yy hh24:mi:ss';

select * from times;
```

Do not forget to tidy up:

```
drop table times;
drop procedure gettime;
exec dbms_scheduler.drop_job('timing')
exec dbms_scheduler.drop_program('time_prog')
exec dbms_scheduler.drop_schedule('one_minute')
```

17 Moving Data

CERTIFICATION OBJECTIVES

17.01	Describe Ways to Move Data
17.02	Create and Use Directory Objects
17.03	Use SQL*Loader to Load Data from a Non-Oracle Database
17.04	Use External Tables to Move Data via Platform-Independent Files
17.05	Explain the General Architecture of Oracle Data Pump
17.06	Use Data Pump Export and Import to Move Data between Oracle Databases
✓	Two-Minute Drill
Q&A	Self Test

A common need in a database environment is to move data from one database to another. Oracle provides two facilities for this: Data Pump and SQL*Loader. Data Pump can transfer data between Oracle databases (across versions and platforms), whereas SQL*Loader can read data sets generated by non-Oracle systems.

CERTIFICATION OBJECTIVE 17.01

Describe Ways to Move Data

There are many situations where bulk transfers of data into a database or between databases are necessary. Common cases include populating a data warehouse with data extracted from transaction processing systems, and copying data from live systems to test or development environments. Because entering data with standard INSERT statements is not always the best way to do large-scale operations, the Oracle database comes with facilities designed for bulk operations. These are SQL*Loader and Data Pump. One also has the option of reading data without ever actually inserting it into the database; this is accomplished through the use of external tables.

If one wants to move data between databases using only SQL, this is also possible by using database links. For example, the commands

```
delete from emp@dev;
insert into emp@dev select * from emp;
commit;
```

will remove every row from the EMP table in the database to which the link DEV connects and then insert every row from the local database.

CERTIFICATION OBJECTIVE 17.02

Create and Use Directory Objects

Oracle directory objects allow sessions against the database to read and write operating system files. Some Oracle utilities (such as Data Pump) require directories.

Oracle directories provide a layer of abstraction between the user and the operating system: you as DBA create a directory object within the database, which points to a physical path on the file system. Permissions on these Oracle directories can then be granted to individual database users. At the operating system level, the Oracle user (the operating system account under which the Oracle instance is running) will need permissions against the operating system directories to which the Oracle directories refer.

exam watch ***Directories are always owned by user SYS, but any user to whom you have granted the CREATE ANY DIRECTORY privilege can create them.***

Directories can be created from a SQL*Plus prompt with the **CREATE DIRECTORY** command. To see information about directories, query the view DBA_DIRECTORIES. Each directory has a name, an owner, and the physical path to which it refers. Note that Oracle does not verify whether the path exists when you create the directory—if it does not exist, or if the operating system user who owns the Oracle software does not have permission to read and write to it, there will be an error only when an attempt is made to use the directory. Having created a directory, you must give the Oracle database user(s) who will be making use of the directory permission to read from and write to it, just as your system administrators must give the operating system users permission to read from and write to the physical path.

Figure 17-1 demonstrates how to create directories using SQL*Plus. In the figure, user SCOTT attempts to create a directory pointing to his operating system home directory on the database server machine. This fails because, by default, users do not have permission to do this. After being granted permission, he tries again. He then grants read permission on the directory (and therefore any files within it) to all users, and read and write permission to one user.

The query of ALL_DIRECTORIES in the figure shows that the directory (like all directories) is owned by SYS: directories are not schema objects. This is why SCOTT cannot drop the directory, even though he created it. To drop a directory requires another privilege: DROP ANY DIRECTORY.

on the job ***An Oracle directory always points to an operating system directory on the database server. There is no way to write to a directory on the client.***

FIGURE 17-1

Managing directories with SQL*Plus

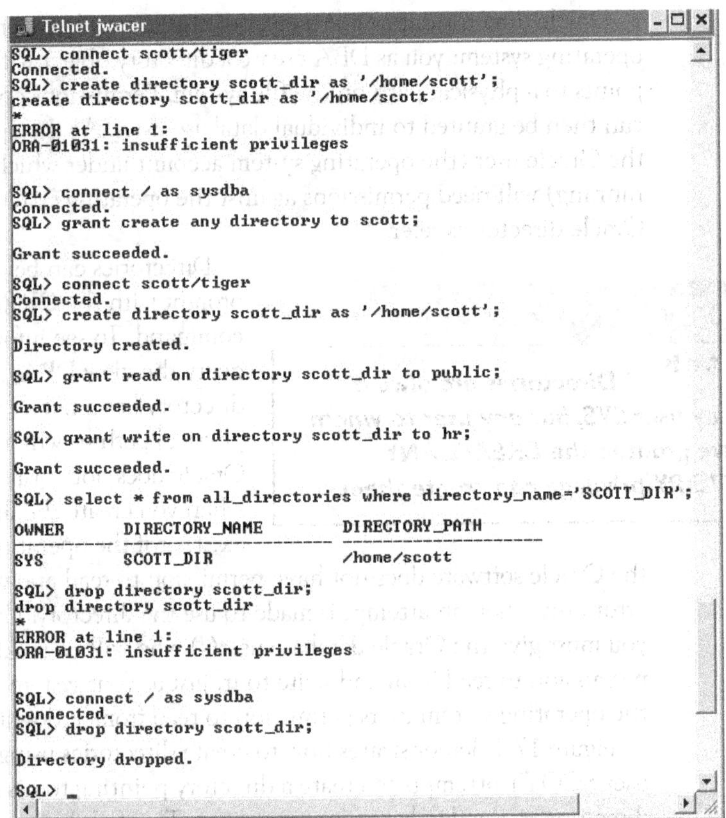

Telnet jwacer
SQL> connect scott/tiger
Connected.
SQL> create directory scott_dir as '/home/scott';
create directory scott_dir as '/home/scott'
*
ERROR at line 1:
ORA-01031: insufficient privileges
SQL> connect / as sysdba
Connected.
SQL> grant create any directory to scott;
Grant succeeded.
SQL> connect scott/tiger
Connected.
SQL> create directory scott_dir as '/home/scott';
Directory created.
SQL> grant read on directory scott_dir to public;
Grant succeeded.
SQL> grant write on directory scott_dir to hr;
Grant succeeded.
SQL> select * from all_directories where directory_name='SCOTT_DIR';
OWNER DIRECTORY_NAME DIRECTORY_PATH
SYS SCOTT_DIR /home/scott
SQL> drop directory scott_dir;
drop directory scott_dir
*
ERROR at line 1:
ORA-01031: insufficient privileges
SQL> connect / as sysdba
Connected.
SQL> drop directory scott_dir;
Directory dropped.
SQL> _

CERTIFICATION OBJECTIVE 17.03

Use SQL*Loader to Load Data from a Non-Oracle Database

In many cases you will be faced with a need to do a bulk upload of datasets generated from some third-party system. This is the purpose of SQL*Loader. The input files may be generated by anything, but as long as the layout conforms to something that SQL*Loader can understand, it will upload the data successfully. Your task as DBA is to configure a SQL*Loader controlfile that can interpret the contents of the input datafiles; SQL*Loader will then insert the data.

Using SQL*Loader

Architecturally, SQL*Loader is a user process like any other: it connects to the database via a server process, issuing a connect string that identifies a database listener, or (if SQL*Loader is running on the database server machine) it can connect using the ORACLE_SID environment variable. To insert rows, it can use one of two techniques: conventional or direct path. A conventional insert uses absolutely ordinary INSERT statements. The SQL*Loader user process constructs an INSERT statement with bind variables in the VALUES clause and then reads the source datafile to execute the INSERT once for each row to be inserted. This method uses the database buffer cache and generates undo and redo data: these are INSERT statements like any others, and normal commit processing makes them permanent.

The direct path load bypasses the database buffer cache. SQL*Loader reads the source datafile and sends its contents to the server process. The server process then assembles blocks of table data in its PGA and writes them directly to the datafiles. The write is above the high water mark of the table and is known as a *data save*. The high water mark is a marker in the table segment above which no data has ever been written: the space above the high water mark is space allocated to the table that has not yet been used. Once the load is complete, SQL*Loader shifts the high water mark up to include the newly written blocks, and the rows within them are then immediately visible to other users. This is the equivalent of a COMMIT. No undo is generated, and if you wish, you can switch off the generation of redo as well. For these reasons, direct path loading is extremely fast, and furthermore it should not impact on your end users because interaction with the SGA is kept to a minimum.

Direct path loads are very fast, but they do have drawbacks:

- Referential integrity constraints must be dropped or disabled for the duration of the operation.
- Insert triggers do not fire.
- The table will be locked against DML from other sessions.
- It is not possible to use direct path for clustered tables.

These limitations are a result of the lack of interaction with the SGA while the load is in progress.

exam watch

Only UNIQUE, PRIMARY KEY, and NOT NULL constraints are enforced during a direct path load. INSERT triggers do not fire, and the table is locked for DML.

SQL*Loader uses a number of files. The input datafiles are the source data that it will upload into the database. The controlfile is a text file with directives telling SQL*Loader how to interpret the contents of the input files, and what to do with the rows it extracts from them. Log files summarize the success (or otherwise) of the job, with detail of any errors. Rows extracted from the input files may be rejected by SQL*Loader (perhaps because they do not conform to the format expected by the controlfile) or by the database (for instance, insertion might violate an integrity constraint); in either case they are written out to a bad file. If rows are successfully extracted from the input but rejected because they did not match some record-selection criterion, they are written out to a reject file.

All files related to SQL*Loader are client-side files, not server-side files.

The controlfile is a text file instructing SQL*Loader on how to process the input datafiles. It is possible to include the actual data to be loaded on the controlfile, but you would not normally do this; usually, you will create one controlfile and reuse it, on a regular basis, with different input datafiles. The variety of input formats that SQL*Loader can understand is limited only by your ingenuity in constructing a controlfile.

Consider this table:

```
SQL> desc dept;
 Name                                      Null?    Type
 ----------------------------------------- -------- ---------------
 DEPTNO                                    NOT NULL NUMBER(2)
 DNAME                                              VARCHAR2(14)
 LOC                                                VARCHAR2(13)
```

And then consider this source datafile, named DEPT.DAT:

```
60,CONSULTING,TORONTO
70,HR,OXFORD
80,EDUCATION,
```

A SQL*Loader controlfile (with line numbers added) that could load this data is DEPTS.CTL:

```
load data
infile 'dept.dat'
badfile 'depts.bad'
discardfile 'depts.dsc'
append
```

```
6      into table dept
7      fields terminated by ','
8      trailing nullcols
9      (deptno integer external(2),
10      dname,
11      loc)
```

To perform the load, run this command from an operating system prompt:

```
sqlldr userid=scott/tiger@orcl control=depts.ctl
```

This command launches the SQL*Loader user process, connects to the local database as user SCOTT password TIGER, and then performs the actions specified in the controlfile DEPTS.CTL. Adding a DIRECT=TRUE argument would instruct SQL*Loader to use the direct path rather than a conventional insert (which is the default). The following explains the controlfile line by line:

Line	Purpose
1	Start a new load operation.
2	Nominate the source of the data.
3	Nominate the file to write out any badly formatted records.
4	Nominate the file to write out any unselected records.
5	Add rows to the table (rather than, for example, truncating it first).
6	The table into which to insert the rows.
7	Specify the field delimiter in the source file.
8	If there are missing fields, insert NULL values.
9, 10,11	The columns into which to insert the data.

This is a very simple example. The syntax of the controlfile can handle a wide range of formats with intelligent parsing to fix any deviations in format, such as length and data types. In general, you can assume that it is possible to construct a controlfile that will understand just about any input datafile. However, do not think that it is always easy.

on the Job

It may be very difficult to get a controlfile right, but once you have it, you can use it repeatedly, with different input datafiles for each run. It is then the responsibility of the feeder system to produce input datafiles that match your controlfile, rather than the other way around.

SQL*Loader Express Mode

There is a very simple way to use SQL*Loader that requires no controlfile. This is the express mode, demonstrated (on Windows) in Figure 17-2.

The directory listing in Figure 17-2 shows that there is one file present: dept.dat. This has been created according to the description given previously. Then the sqlldr.exe executable is launched, connecting as user SCOTT with the connect string orclz, and nominating the DEPT table and nothing else. The output shows that two rows were loaded, even though there are three in the datafile. The next directory listing shows that a file suffixed BAD has been generated that, when typed, contains one row from the input datafile. This is the third row, which was incomplete: no value for the LOC column of the table.

FIGURE 17-2 SQL*Loader running in express mode

```
cmd
$ dir
 Volume in drive C has no label.
 Volume Serial Number is 5A19-6F9C

 Directory of c:\Users\John\sqlldr

30/11/2013  16:01    <DIR>          .
30/11/2013  16:01    <DIR>          ..
30/11/2013  15:37                52 dept.dat
               1 File(s)             52 bytes
               2 Dir(s)  39,788,429,312 bytes free

$ sqlldr scott/tiger@orclz table=dept

SQL*Loader: Release 12.1.0.1.0 - Production on Sat Nov 30 16:01:55 2013

Copyright (c) 1982, 2013, Oracle and/or its affiliates.  All rights reserved.

Express Mode Load, Table: DEPT
Path used:      External Table, DEGREE_OF_PARALLELISM=AUTO

Table DEPT:
  2 Rows successfully loaded.

Check the log files:
  dept.log
  dept_%p.log_xt
for more information about the load.

$ dir *.bad
 Volume in drive C has no label.
 Volume Serial Number is 5A19-6F9C

 Directory of c:\Users\John\sqlldr

30/11/2013  16:01                15 dept_1832_9000.bad
               1 File(s)             15 bytes
               0 Dir(s)  39,788,421,120 bytes free

$ type dept_1832_9000.bad
80,EDUCATION,

$ _
```

Express mode is easy to use, but is demanding in its requirements:

- There must be a datafile with the same name as the table to be loaded, suffixed with .DAT.
- The columns must be a scalar data type: character, number, or date.
- The fields in the file must be comma delimited, and not enclosed in quotes.
- The input rows must have values for every column of the table.

The log files generated by express mode can be very instructive. Among other things, they include a SQL*Loader controlfile definition that could be used (or edited) for subsequent jobs.

CERTIFICATION OBJECTIVE 17.04

Use External Tables to Move Data via Platform-Independent Files

An external table is visible to SELECT statements as any other table, but you cannot perform DML against it. This is because it does not exist as a segment in the database: it exists only as a data dictionary construct, pointing toward one or more operating system files. The operating system files of external tables are located through Oracle directory objects.

A common use of external tables is to avoid needing to use SQL*Loader to read data into the database. This can give huge savings in the ETL (extract-transform-load) cycle typically used to update a DSS system with data from a feeder system. Consider the case where a feeder system regularly generates a dataset as a flat ASCII file, which should be merged into existing database tables. One approach would be to use SQL*Loader to load the data into a staging table, and then a separate routine to merge the rows from the staging table into the DSS tables. This second routine cannot start until the load is finished. Using external tables, the merge routine can read the source data from the operating system file(s) without having to wait for it to be loaded.

To create an external table, use the **CREATE TABLE** command with the keywords ORGANIZATION EXTERNAL. This tells Oracle that the table does not exist as a segment. Then specify the layout and location of the operating system file. Here is an example:

```
create table new_dept
  (deptno number(2),
  dname varchar2(14),
  loc varchar2(13))
organization external (
  type oracle_loader
  default directory ext_dir
  access parameters
    (records delimited by newline
    badfile 'depts.bad'
    discardfile 'depts.dsc'
    logfile 'depts.log'
    fields terminated by ','
    missing field values are null)
  location ('depts.dat'));
```

This command creates an external table that will be populated by the DEPTS.DAT file shown in the section "Using SQL*Loader," earlier in this chapter. The syntax for the ACCESS PARAMETERS is virtually identical to the SQL*Loader controlfile syntax and is used because the TYPE has been set to ORACLE_LOADER. The specification for the DEFAULT DIRECTORY gives the Oracle directory where Oracle will look for the source datafile, and where it will write the log and other files.

External tables can be queried in exactly the same way as internal tables. Any SQL involving a SELECT will function against an external table: external tables can be used in joins, views, and subqueries. They cannot have indexes, constraints, or triggers.

EXERCISE 17-1

Use Directories, SQL*Loader, and External Tables

In this exercise, you will install and use SQL*Loader to insert data into a table, and also to generate the CREATE TABLE script for an external table.

1. Connect to your database as user SYSTEM (in the examples, the SYSTEM password is oracle) with SQL*Plus.
2. Create a table to use for the exercise:

```
create table names(first varchar2(10),last varchar2(10));
```

3. Using any editor that will create plain text files, create a file called names.txt with these values (or similar):

```
John,Watson
Roopesh,Ramklass
Sam,Alapati
```

4. Using the editor, create a controlfile called names.ctl with these settings:

```
load data
infile 'names.txt'
badfile 'names.bad'
truncate
into table names
fields terminated by ','
trailing nullcols
(first,last)
```

   Note that this controlfile will truncate the target table before carrying out the insert.

5. From an operating system prompt, run SQL*Loader as follows:

```
sqlldr system/oracle control=names.ctl
```

6. Study the log file names.log that will have been generated.

7. With SQL*Plus, confirm that the rows have been inserted:

```
select * from names;
```

8. To generate a statement that will create an external table, you can use SQL*Loader and an existing controlfile:

```
sqlldr userid=system/oracle control=names.ctl
external_table=generate_only
```

9. This will have generated a CREATE TABLE statement in the log file names.log, which will look something like this:

```
CREATE TABLE "SYS_SQLLDR_X_EXT_NAMES"(
  "FIRST" VARCHAR2(10),
  "LAST" VARCHAR2(10))
ORGANIZATION external(
  TYPE oracle_loader
  DEFAULT DIRECTORY SYS_SQLLDR_XT_TMPDIR_00000
  ACCESS PARAMETERS(
    RECORDS DELIMITED BY NEWLINE CHARACTERSET WE8MSWIN1252
    BADFILE 'SYS_SQLLDR_XT_TMPDIR_00000':'names.bad'
```

```
LOGFILE 'names.log_xt'
READSIZE 1048576
FIELDS TERMINATED BY "," LDRTRIM
MISSING FIELD VALUES ARE NULL
REJECT ROWS WITH ALL NULL FIELDS(
  "FIRST" CHAR(255)
    TERMINATED BY ",",
  "LAST" CHAR(255)
    TERMINATED BY ","))
location(
  'names.txt'))
REJECT LIMIT UNLIMITED
```

10. From your SQL*Plus session, create an Oracle directory pointing to the operating system directory where your names.txt file is. Here is an example:

```
create directory system_dmp as '/home/oracle';
```

11. Make any edits you wish to the command shown in step 9. For example, you might want to change the name of the table being created ("SYS_SQLLDR_X_EXT_NAMES" isn't very useful) to something more meaningful. You will need to change both the DEFAULT DIRECTORY and BADFILE settings to point to the directory created in step 10.
12. Run the statement created in step 11 from your SQL*Plus session.
13. Query the table with a few SELECT and DML statements. You will find that a log file is generated for every SELECT, and that DML is not permitted.
14. Tidy up: delete the names.txt and names.ctl files; drop the tables; as SYS, drop the directory.

CERTIFICATION OBJECTIVE 17.05

Explain the General Architecture of Oracle Data Pump

Data Pump is a server-side utility. You initiate Data Pump jobs from a user process, but all the work is done by server processes. This improves performance dramatically over the old Export/Import utilities, because the Data Pump processes running on the server have direct access to the datafiles and the SGA; they do not have to go via a session. Also, it is possible to launch a Data Pump job and then detach from it, leaving it running in the background. You can reconnect to the job to monitor its progress at any time.

Involved in a Data Pump job are a number of processes, two queues, a number of files, and one table. The user processes are expdp and impdp (for Unix) or expdp.exe and impdp.exe (Windows). These are used to launch, control, and monitor Data Pump jobs. The expdp or impdp user process establishes a session against the database through a normal server process, either locally or via a listener. This session then issues commands to control and monitor Data Pump jobs. When a Data Pump job is launched, at least two processes are started: a Data Pump Master process (the DM*nn*) and one or more worker processes (named DW*nn*). If multiple Data Pump jobs are running concurrently, each will have its own DM*nn* process and its own set of DW*nn* processes. As the name implies, the master process controls the workers.

Two queues are created for each Data Pump job: a control queue and a status queue. The DM*nn* divides up the work to be done and places individual tasks that make up the job on the control queue. The worker processes pick up these tasks and execute them—perhaps making use of parallel execution servers. This queue operates on a deliver-exactly-once model: messages are enqueued by the DM*nn* and dequeued by the worker that picks them up. The status queue is for monitoring purposes: the DM*nn* places messages on it describing the state of the job. This queue operates on a publish-and-subscribe model: any session (with appropriate privileges) can query the queue to monitor the job's progress.

The files generated by Data Pump come in three forms: SQL files, dump files, and log files. SQL files are DDL statements describing the objects included in the job. You can choose to generate them (without any data) as an easy way of getting this information out of the database, perhaps for documentation purposes or as a set of scripts to re-create the database. Dump files contain the exported data. This is formatted in a fashion resembling XML tags. This means that there is considerable overhead in dump files for describing the data. A small table like the REGIONS table in the HR sample schema will generate a 94KB dump file, but although this overhead may seem disproportionately large for a tiny table like that, it becomes trivial for larger tables. The log files describe the history of the job run.

Data Pump can be invoked by a client, but it runs on the server. All the files are server-side files, with nothing on the client side.

Finally, there is the control table. This is created for you by the DM*nn* when you launch a job, and is used both to record the job's progress and to describe it. It is included in the dump file as the final item of the job.

Data Pump has two methods for loading and unloading data: the direct path and the external table path. The direct path bypasses the database buffer cache. For a direct path export, Data Pump reads the datafile blocks directly from disk, extracts and formats the content, and writes it out as a dump file. For a direct path import, Data Pump reads the dump file, uses its content to assemble blocks of table data, and writes them directly to the datafiles. The write is above the "high water mark" of the table, with the same benefits as those described earlier for a SQL*Loader direct load.

The external table path uses the database buffer cache. Even though Data Pump is manipulating files that are external to the database, it uses the database buffer cache as though it were reading and writing an internal table. For an export, Data Pump reads blocks from the datafiles into the cache through a normal SELECT process. From there, it formats the data for output to a dump file. During an import, Data Pump constructs standard insert statements from the content of the dump file and executes them by reading blocks from the datafiles into the cache, where the insert is carried out in the normal fashion. As far as the database is concerned, external table Data Pump jobs look like absolutely ordinary (though perhaps rather large) SELECT or INSERT operations. Both undo and redo are generated, as they would be for any normal DML statement. Your end users may well complain while these jobs are in progress. Commit processing is absolutely normal.

So what determines whether Data Pump uses the direct path or the external table path? You as DBA have no control; Data Pump itself makes the decision based on the complexity of the objects. Only simple structures, such as heap tables without active triggers, can be processed through the direct path; more complex objects such as clustered tables force Data Pump to use the external table path because it requires interaction with the SGA in order to resolve the complexities. In either case, the dump file generated is identical.

exam watch

The external table path insert uses a regular commit, like any other DML statement. A direct path insert does not use a commit; it simply shifts the high water mark of the table to include the newly written blocks. Data Pump files generated by either path are identical.

CERTIFICATION OBJECTIVE 17.06

Use Data Pump Export and Import to Move Data between Oracle Databases

Data Pump is commonly used for extracting large amounts of data from one database and inserting it into another, but it can also be used to extract other information such as PL/SQL code or various object definitions. There are several interfaces: command-line utilities, Enterprise Manager Cloud Control, and a PL/SQL API. Whatever purpose and technique are used, the files are always in the Data Pump proprietary format. It is not possible to read a Data Pump file with any tool other than Data Pump.

Capabilities

Whatever interface is used, Data Pump has these capabilities:

- Fine-grained object and data selection facilities mean that Data Pump can export either the complete database or any part of it. It is possible to export table definitions (with or without their rows), PL/SQL objects, views, sequences, or any other object type.
- If exporting a table, it is possible to apply a WHERE clause to restrict the rows exported (although this may make direct path impossible) or to instruct Data Pump to export a random sample of the table expressed as a percentage.
- Parallel processing can speed up Data Pump operations. Parallelism can come at two levels: the number of Data Pump worker processes, and the number of parallel execution servers each worker process uses.
- An estimate facility can calculate the space needed for a Data Pump export, without actually running the job.
- The Network Mode allows transfer of a Data Pump dataset from one database to another without ever staging it on disk. This is implemented by a Data Pump export job on the source database writing the data over a database link to the target database, where a Data Pump import job reads the data from the database link and inserts it.

- Remapping facilities mean that objects can be renamed or transferred from one schema to another and (in the case of data objects) moved from one tablespace to another as they are imported.
- When data is being exported, the output files can be compressed and encrypted.

Using Data Pump with the Command-Line Utilities

The executables expdb and impdp are installed into the ORACLE_HOME/bin directory. Following are several examples of using them. Note that in all cases the command must be a single one-line command; the line breaks are purely for readability.

Here is how to export the entire database:

```
expdp system/manager@orcl12g full=y
parallel=2
dumpfile=datadir1:full1_%U.dmp,datadir2:full2_%U.dmp
filesize=2g
compression=all
```

This command will connect to the database as user SYSTEM and launch a full Data Pump export, using two worker processes working in parallel. Each worker will generate its own set of dump files, uniquely named according to the %U template, which generates unique strings of eight characters. Each worker will break up its output into files of 2GB (perhaps because of underlying file system restrictions) of compressed data.

A corresponding import job (which assumes that the files generated by the export have all been placed in one directory) would be

```
impdb system/manager@dev12g full=y
directory=data_dir
parallel=2
dumpfile=full1_%U.dmp,full2_%U.dmp
```

This command makes a selective export of the PL/SQL objects belonging to two schemas:

```
expdp system/manager schemas=hr,oe
directory=code_archive
dumpfile=hr_oe_code.dmp
include=function,
include=package,
include=procedure,
include=type
```

This command will extract everything from a Data Pump export that was in the HR schema, and import it into the DEV schema:

```
impdp system/manager
directory=usr_data
dumpfile=usr_dat.dmp
schema=hr
remap_schema=hr:dev
```

Tablespace Export and Import

A variation on Data Pump export/import is the tablespace transport capability. This is a facility whereby entire tablespaces and their contents can be copied from one database to another. This is the routine:

1. Make the source tablespace(s) read-only.
2. Use Data Pump to export the metadata describing the tablespace(s) and the contents.
3. Copy the datafile(s) and Data Pump export file to the destination system.
4. Use Data Pump to import the metadata.
5. Make the tablespace(s) read-write on both the source and destination.

An additional step that may be required when transporting tablespaces from one platform to another is to convert the endian format of the data. A big-endian platform (such as Solaris on SPARC chips) stores a multibyte value such as a 16-bit integer with the most significant byte first. A little-endian platform (such as Windows on Intel chips) stores the least significant byte first. To transport tablespaces across platforms with a different endian format requires converting the datafiles: you do this with the RMAN command **CONVERT**.

To determine the platform on which a database is running, query the column PLATFORM_NAME in V$DATABASE. Then to see the list of currently supported platforms (which will vary depending on your exact release) and their endianness, query the view V$TRANSPORTABLE_PLATFORM:

```
orcl > select * from v$transportable_platform order by
platform_name;
PLATFORM_ID PLATFORM_NAME                        ENDIAN_FORMAT
----------- -------------------------------- --------------
          6 AIX-Based Systems (64-bit)          Big
```

```
        16 Apple Mac OS                          Big
        19 HP IA Open VMS                        Little
        15 HP Open VMS                           Little
         5 HP Tru64 UNIX                         Little
         3 HP-UX (64-bit)                        Big
         4 HP-UX IA (64-bit)                     Big
        18 IBM Power Based Linux                 Big
         9 IBM zSeries Based Linux               Big
        13 Linux 64-bit for AMD                  Little
        10 Linux IA (32-bit)                     Little
        11 Linux IA (64-bit)                     Little
        12 Microsoft Windows 64-bit for AMD Little
         7 Microsoft Windows IA (32-bit)     Little
         8 Microsoft Windows IA (64-bit)     Little
        20 Solaris Operating System (AMD64) Little
        17 Solaris Operating System (x86)    Little
         1 Solaris[tm] OE (32-bit)           Big
         2 Solaris[tm] OE (64-bit)           Big
19 rows selected.
```

When transporting tablespaces, there are certain restrictions:

- The tablespace(s) should be self-contained. This means that the objects within the tablespace(s) must be complete: not dependent on any other objects. For instance, if tables are in one tablespace and indexes on the tables in another, both tablespaces must be included in the set to be transported.
- The destination database must use the same (or a compatible) character set as the source database.
- The schemas that own the objects in the tablespace(s) must exist in the destination database, or the operation will fail.
- Any objects in the destination database with the same owner and object name as objects in the transportable tablespace set will not be lost: they will be ignored during the import.
- A tablespace of the same name must not already exist. Remember that it is possible to rename tablespaces.

Figure 17-3 shows the steps to generate a transport set. In the figure, the first command is the PL/SQL procedure call to confirm that a set of tablespaces (in the example, just one tablespace: TS1) is self-contained. Then the tablespace is made read-only. The Data Pump job, launched with the expdp command-line utility, connects as user SYSTEM and then specifies the tablespace to be transported.

FIGURE 17-3

Using command-line utilities to create a transportable tablespace set

```
SQL>
SQL> execute dbms_tts.transport_set_check('TS1')

PL/SQL procedure successfully completed.

SQL> alter tablespace ts1 read only;

Tablespace altered.

SQL> host
[oracle@oel58x64db121 ~]$ expdp system/oracle transport_tablespaces=ts1 \
> dumpfile=ts1.dmp directory=dp_out

Export: Release 12.1.0.1.0 - Production on Sun Dec 1 16:41:33 2013

Copyright (c) 1982, 2013, Oracle and/or its affiliates.  All rights reserve

Connected to: Oracle Database 12c Enterprise Edition Release 12.1.0.1.0 - 6
With the Partitioning, OLAP, Advanced Analytics and Real Application Testin
Starting "SYSTEM"."SYS_EXPORT_TRANSPORTABLE_01":  system/******** transport
out
Processing object type TRANSPORTABLE_EXPORT/PLUGTS_BLK
```

This will generate a dump file with metadata describing the contents of the TS1 tablespace in the Oracle directory DP_OUT. Then, while the tablespace is still read-only, copy its datafiles and the Data Pump dump file to a suitable location on the destination database server.

If the destination database is on a platform with a different endianness from the source, the files must be converted. To do this on the source, connect to the source database with RMAN and run a command such as this:

```
convert datafile '/u02/oradata/ts1.dbf' to platform
'Solaris[tm] OE (64-bit)' format '/to_solaris/ts1.dbf'
```

This command will write out a copy of the file, with the endianness changed. Alternatively, copy the unchanged file to the destination database, connect with RMAN, and run a command such as this:

```
convert datafile '/from_linux/ts1.dbf' from platform
'Linux IA (64-bit)' format '/u02/oradata/ts1.dbf';
```

This command will read the nominated datafile, and convert it from the named platform format to a new file in the format that is required for the destination database.

To import the tablespace(s) on the destination system, use a command such as that shown in Figure 17-4.

FIGURE 17-4 Using the impdp utility to import a transported tablespace

```
[oracle@oel58x64db121 ~]$
[oracle@oel58x64db121 ~]$ impdp system/oracle dumpfile=ts1.dmp \
> directory=dp_in transport_datafiles=/u02/oradata/ts1.dbf

Import: Release 12.1.0.1.0 - Production on Sun Dec 1 17:32:32 2013

Copyright (c) 1982, 2013, Oracle and/or its affiliates.  All rights reserved.

Connected to: Oracle Database 12c Enterprise Edition Release 12.1.0.1.0 - 64bi
With the Partitioning, OLAP, Advanced Analytics and Real Application Testing o
Master table "SYSTEM"."SYS_IMPORT_TRANSPORTABLE_01" successfully loaded/unload
Starting "SYSTEM"."SYS_IMPORT_TRANSPORTABLE_01":  system/******** dumpfile=ts1
Processing object type TRANSPORTABLE_EXPORT/PLUGTS_BLK
Processing object type TRANSPORTABLE_EXPORT/TABLE
Processing object type TRANSPORTABLE_EXPORT/TABLE_STATISTICS
Processing object type TRANSPORTABLE_EXPORT/STATISTICS/MARKER
Processing object type TRANSPORTABLE_EXPORT/POST_INSTANCE/PLUGTS_BLK
Job "SYSTEM"."SYS_IMPORT_TRANSPORTABLE_01" successfully completed at Sun Dec 1

[oracle@oel58x64db121 ~]$
```

The **impdp** command in Figure 17-4 reads a dump file to determine the name and contents of the tablespace consisting of the nominated datafile (previously converted, if necessary).

on the job

Do not forget the final step! Make the tablespace read/write, in both the source and the destination databases.

A generalization of the transportable tablespace feature makes it possible to transport an entire database from one machine to another.

EXERCISE 17-2

Use Data Pump Export/Import

In this exercise, use the Data Pump command-line utilities to copy a table from one schema to another.

1. Connect to the database as user SYSTEM.
2. Create two schemas to use for this exercise:

```
grant dba to artem identified by artem;
grant dba to ivana identified by ivana;
```

3. Create a table and index in one schema:

   ```
   create table artem.users as select * from all_users;
   create index artem.ui on artem.users(user_id);
   ```

4. There is a directory created by default for the use of Data Pump, named DATA_PUMP_DIR, which the Data Pump clients will use if no other directory is specified. Confirm its existence with this query, and create it (using any suitable operating system path) if it does not exist:

   ```
   select directory_path from dba_directories
   where directory_name='DATA_PUMP_DIR';
   ```

5. Export the ARTEM schema with this command:

   ```
   expdp system/<password> schemas=artem dumpfile=artem.dmp
   ```

6. Import the ARTEM schema into the IVANA schema:

   ```
   impdp system/<password> remap_schema=artem:ivana
   dumpfile=artem.dmp
   ```

7. Confirm that the objects have been imported:

   ```
   select object_name,object_type from dba_objects
   where owner='IVANA';
   ```

CERTIFICATION SUMMARY

To transfer data between Oracle databases, use Data Pump. A Data Pump export extracts data from a database in an Oracle proprietary format that can be read only by a Data Pump import. Data Pump jobs are controlled by a table that describes the job. This table is included within the export file. Architecturally, a Data Pump job consists of a master process and one or more worker processes. All the files used or created by Data Pump must reside in Oracle directories.

To read data generated by third-party systems into an Oracle database, use SQL*Loader. The format of the input file must be specified in a controlfile. SQL*Loader has an "express mode" that simplifies the syntax: if the input datafile is formatted as a comma-separated values file and is named with the name of the target table and suffixed with .DAT, then all that need be specified is the name of the table.

External tables are tables that exist as a data dictionary structure but have no segment within the database. The rows are read from an operating system file whose structure is defined using SQL*Loader syntax. Any SELECT command can be executed against an external table, but no DML commands.

TWO-MINUTE DRILL

Describe Ways to Move Data

- ❑ Data Pump can transfer data between Oracle databases.
- ❑ SQL*Loader can read files generated by third-party products.

Create and Use Directory Objects

- ❑ An Oracle directory maps a database object to an operating system path.
- ❑ The Oracle OS user must have permissions on the OS directory.
- ❑ Database users must be granted permissions on the Oracle directory.

Use SQL*Loader to Load Data from a Non-Oracle Database

- ❑ SQL*Loader reads operating system text files generated by any third-party system.
- ❑ Express mode simplifies usage hugely.

Use External Tables to Move Data via Platform-Independent Files

- ❑ External tables are operating system text files, defined with SQL*Loader syntax.
- ❑ No segment exists for an external table.
- ❑ External tables can be queried, but DML or indexes are not possible.

Explain the General Architecture of Oracle Data Pump

- ❑ Data Pump processes run on the instance, not the client.
- ❑ All files are accessed through Oracle directory objects.
- ❑ Direct path bypasses the buffer cache; external table path goes through the cache.

Use Data Pump Export and Import to Move Data between Oracle Databases

- ❑ Data Pump dump files are compatible across versions and platforms.
- ❑ Network mode avoids the need to stage data on disk.
- ❑ Tablespace transport mode permits copying of datafiles between databases.

SELF TEST

Describe Ways to Move Data

1. Which of these methods of moving data can transfer data from one platform to another? (Choose all correct answers.)
   A. Using CREATE TABLE AS with a SELECT statement that reads from a database link
   B. A Data Pump network mode export/import
   C. Data Pump tablespace transport
   D. Using the legacy exp and imp export/import utilities
   E. Using RMAN backup and restore with backup sets, not image copies

Create and Use Directory Objects

2. You create a directory with the statement

```
create directory dp_dir as 'c:\tmp';
```

   but when you try to use it with Data Pump, there is an error. Which of the following could be true? (Choose three answers.)
   A. The Oracle software owner has no permissions on c:\tmp.
   B. The Oracle database user has no permissions on dp_dir.
   C. The path c:\tmp does not exist.
   D. The path c:\tmp must exist or else the "create directory" statement would have failed.
   E. If you use Data Pump in network mode, there will be no need for a directory.
   F. Issuing the command **grant all** on 'c:\tmp' to public; may solve some permission problems.

3. What is a necessary condition to import a Data Pump file from a client? (Choose the best answer.)
   A. A directory object must be created pointing to the operating system directory where the file exists.
   B. A controlfile must exist that accurately describes the format of the file.
   C. The client and server operating systems must use the same endian format.
   D. It is not possible to import a file from a client.

Use SQL*Loader to Load Data from a Non-Oracle Database

4. Which of the following is not a SQL*Loader file? (Choose the best answer.)
   A. Bad file
   B. Controlfile
   C. Discard file
   D. Good file
   E. Log file

5. You run SQL*Loader on your PC to insert data into a remote database. Which of the following is true? (Choose the correct answer.)
   A. The input datafiles must be on your PC.
   B. The input datafiles must be on the server.
   C. Direct load is possible only if the input datafiles are on the server.
   D. Direct load is only possible if you run SQL*Loader on the server, not on the PC.
6. Study this SQL*Loader command:

```
sqlldr scott/tiger table=emp
```

   What will be the result? (Choose the best answer.)
   A. The load will fail unless there is a controlfile present named EMP.CTL.
   B. The load will succeed if there is a file present named EMP.DAT.
   C. The EMP table will be created if it does not exist, or appended to if it does.
   D. The user will be prompted for missing arguments, such as the datafile name.

Use External Tables to Move Data via Platform-Independent Files

7. Which of these SQL commands can reference an external table? (Choose two answers.)
   A. SELECT
   B. INSERT, UPDATE, DELETE
   C. CREATE VIEW
   D. CREATE INDEX

Explain the General Architecture of Oracle Data Pump

8. Which of the following is not a Data Pump file type? (Choose the best answer.)
   A. Dump file
   B. Log file
   C. Controlfile
   D. SQL file

Use Data Pump Export and Import to Move Data between Oracle Databases

9. You are using Data Pump to upload rows into a table, and you wish to use the direct path. Which of the following statements is correct? (Choose two answers.)
   A. You must include the DIRECT keyword in the Data Pump controlfile.
   B. This is not possible if the table is in a cluster.
   C. You have no control over this; Data Pump will use the direct path automatically if it can.
   D. Direct path is slower than the external table path because it doesn't cache data in memory.

10. You intend to transport a tablespace from database A on Windows to database B on AIX. These are the steps:
    A. Convert the files from little endian to big endian.
    B. Copy the files from A to B.
    C. Export the metadata describing the tablespace.
    D. Import the metadata describing the tablespace.
    E. Make the tablespace read-only in A.
    F. Make the tablespace read/write in B.

    In what order could the steps be carried out?
    A. c e b f a d
    B. e c b a d f
    C. e c d a b f
    D. c e b a d f

LAB QUESTION

In this exercise, create a copy of a demonstration schema (such as SCOTT or HR) in a new schema named DEV. Do the work as user SYSTEM.

The first step will be to perform a Data Pump export of the entire schema. You can use the default directory DATA_PUMP_DIR (query the data dictionary view DBA_DIRECTORIES to find to where this is mapped) or create your own. While the export is in progress, from a SQL*Plus session run this query:

```
select program from v$process order by program;
```

You will see two Data Pump processes listed, DM00 and DW00. These will persist for the duration of the Data Pump job. Once the job has completed, study the log file that will have been generated in the nominated directory.

To import the schema, use the REMAP_SCHEMA parameter to force the creation of the DEV schema into which the objects will be imported.

Confirm that the schema has been imported into a newly created schema by connecting to the new schema (in the example, called DEV). The password will be the same as that for HR (which is HR, by default). You will find that the HR tables exist.

SELF TEST ANSWERS

Describe Ways to Move Data

1. ☑ **A, B, C,** and **D.** All of these techniques have a cross-platform capability. **C** (tablespace transport) may require converting the files if the target platform is a different endian from the source.
   ☒ **E** is incorrect. This is incorrect because backup sets are not portable across platforms, although image copies may be.

Create and Use Directory Objects

2. ☑ **A, B,** and **C.** These conditions could all cause problems when using the directory, but not when creating it.
   ☒ **D, E,** and **F** are incorrect. **D** is incorrect because the existence of the directory is not checked at creation time. **E** is incorrect because although network mode does not need a directory for the dump file(s), it will need a directory for the log file(s). **F** is incorrect because it confuses the issue of Oracle permissions on directories with operating system permissions on physical paths.

3. ☑ **D.** It is not possible to import a file from the client: the dump must exist on the server.
   ☒ **A, B,** and **C** are incorrect. **A** is incorrect because a directory object can point only to a directory on the server. **B** is incorrect because a controlfile is used by SQL*Loader, not by Data Pump. **C** is incorrect because endianness is relevant to transportable tablespaces, not data import.

Use SQL*Loader to Load Data from a Non-Oracle Database

4. ☑ **D.** There is no "good" file—the acceptable rows are inserted into the table and are not logged by SQL*Loader.
   ☒ **A, B, C,** and **E** are incorrect. These are the file types that SQL*Loader can generate.

5. ☑ **A.** SQL*Loader is a client-server process: the input files must be local to the user process.
   ☒ **B, C,** and **D** are incorrect. **B** is incorrect because the input files must be on the PC, accessible to the client-side process. **C** and **D** are incorrect because direct load is not relevant to the location of the files.

6. ☑ **B.** Express mode relies on many defaults, one of which is that the datafile name must be the table name suffixed with .DAT.
   ☒ **A, C,** and **D** are incorrect. **A** is incorrect because express mode does not use a controlfile. **C** is incorrect because express mode cannot create a table: it can only append to an existing table. **D** is incorrect because express mode does not prompt.

Use External Tables to Move Data via Platform-Independent Files

7. ☑ **A** and **C.** Anything related to SELECT, including creating a view, can be executed against an external table.
   ☒ **B** and **D** are incorrect. DML is impossible against an external table, as is indexing.

Explain the General Architecture of Oracle Data Pump

8. ☑ **C.** SQL*Loader can use a controlfile; Data Pump does not.
   ☒ **A, B,** and **D** are incorrect. Data Pump export generates a dump file, an import can generate a SQL file, and both export and import generate log files.

Use Data Pump Export and Import to Move Data between Oracle Databases

9. ☑ **B** and **C.** Clusters are complex structures that cannot be directly loaded. Data Pump determines whether a direct load is possible automatically.
   ☒ **A** and **D** are incorrect. There is no DIRECT keyword because the choice is automatic. Direct is faster because it bypasses the SGA.
10. ☑ **B.** This is the correct sequence
   ☒ **A, C,** and **D** are incorrect. All these sequences are wrong. The only acceptable alternative would have been to convert the endianness on A before copying to B.

LAB ANSWER

Some sample commands, using the HR schema, are presented here:

```
expdp userid=system/<password> schemas=hr \
directory=data_pump_dir dumpfile=hr.dmp
impdp userid=system/<password> schemas=hr \
directory=data_pump_dir dumpfile=hr.dmp remap_schema=hr:dev
```

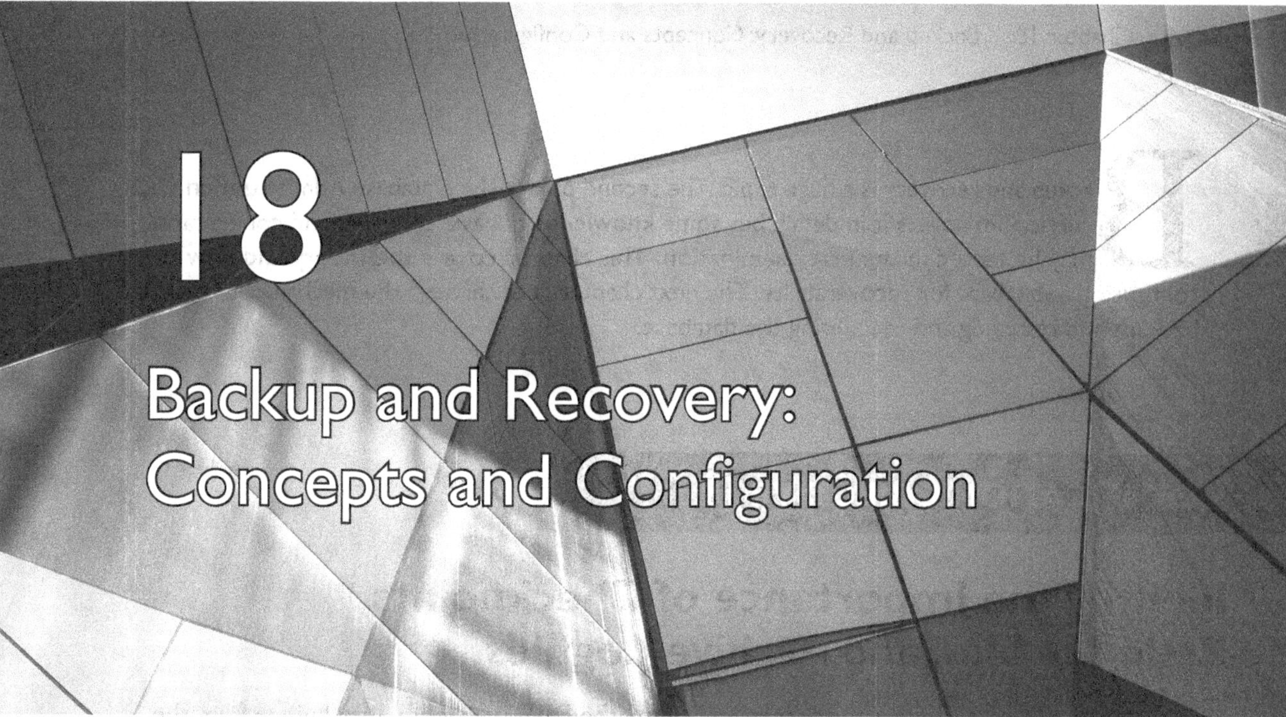

18

Backup and Recovery: Concepts and Configuration

CERTIFICATION OBJECTIVES

18.01	Identify the Importance of Checkpoints, Redo Logfiles, and Archive Logfiles	18.04	Configure ARCHIVELOG Mode
18.02	Backup and Recovery: Configuration	✓	Two-Minute Drill
18.03	Configure the Fast Recovery Area	Q&A	Self Test

Backup and recovery is a huge topic. The second part of the Database Administration OCP curriculum covers it in detail, but some knowledge of basic concepts and configuration may be tested in the first examination. This chapter covers the theory and how to configure the database for recoverability. The next chapter goes through the mechanics of making backups and restoring and recovering the database.

CERTIFICATION OBJECTIVE 18.01

Identify the Importance of Checkpoints, Redo Logfiles, and Archive Logfiles

Checkpointing is the process of forcing the DBWn to write dirty buffers from the database buffer cache to the datafiles. There are circumstances when this must be done to ensure that the instance and the database can be recovered. Also necessary for recovery are the online redo logs and the archive redo logs. Instance recovery is automatic and occurs after any instance failure. It requires online redo logs. Database recovery is a manually initiated process following damage to the disk-based structures that make up the database, and requires archive logfiles as well as online logfiles.

Instance Recovery

In principle, instance recovery is nothing more than using the contents of the online logfiles to rebuild the database buffer cache to the state it was in before the crash. This will replay all changes extracted from the online redo logfiles that refer to blocks that had not been written to disk at the time of the crash. Once this has been done, the database can be opened. This phase of recovery, known as the *roll forward*, reinstates all changes—changes to data blocks and changes to undo blocks—for both committed and uncommitted transactions. Each redo record has the bare minimum of information needed to reconstruct a change: the block address and the new values. During roll forward, each redo record is read, the appropriate block is loaded from the datafiles into the database buffer cache, and the change is applied. Then the block is written back to disk.

Once the roll forward is complete, it is as though the crash had never occurred. But at that point, there will be uncommitted transactions in the database—these must be rolled back, and Oracle will do that automatically in the rollback phase of instance recovery. However, that happens after the database has been opened for use. If a user connects and hits some data that needs to be rolled back and hasn't yet been, this is not a problem—the roll forward phase will have populated the undo segment that was protecting the uncommitted transaction, so the server can roll back the change in the normal manner for read consistency.

Instance recovery is automatic, and unavoidable—so how do you invoke it? By issuing a **STARTUP** command. When starting an instance, after mounting the controlfile and before opening the database SMON checks the file headers of all the datafiles and online redo logfiles. At this point, if there had been an instance failure, it is apparent because the file headers are all out of sync. So SMON goes into the instance recovery routine, and the database is opened only after the roll forward phase has completed.

on the job

You never have anything to lose by issuing a STARTUP command. After any sort of crash, try a STARTUP and see how far it gets. It might get all the way.

The Impossibility of Database Corruption

It should now be apparent that there is always enough information in the redo log stream to reconstruct all work done up to the point at which the crash occurred, and furthermore that this includes reconstructing the undo information needed to roll back transactions that were in progress at the time of the crash. But for the final proof, consider the following scenario.

User JOHN has started a transaction. He has updated one row of a table with some new values, and his server process has copied the old values to an undo segment. But before these updates were done, his server process wrote out the changes to the log buffer. User ROOPESH has also started a transaction. Neither has committed; nothing has been written to disk. If the instance crashed now, there would be no record whatsoever of either transaction, not even in the redo logs. So neither transaction would be recovered—but that is not a problem. Neither was committed, so they should not be recovered: uncommitted work must never be saved.

Then user JOHN commits his transaction. This triggers LGWR to flush the log buffer to the online redo logfiles, which means that the changes to both the table and the undo segments for both JOHN's transaction and ROOPESH's transaction are now in the redo logfiles, together with a commit record for JOHN's transaction. Only when the write has completed is the "commit complete" message returned to JOHN's user process. But there is still nothing in the datafiles. If the instance fails at this point, the roll forward phase will reconstruct both the transactions, but when all the redo has been processed, there will be no commit record for ROOPESH's update; that signals SMON to roll back ROOPESH's change but leave JOHN's in place.

But what if DBWR has written some blocks to disk before the crash? It might be that JOHN (or another user) was continually requerying his data, but that ROOPESH had made his uncommitted change and not looked at the data again. DBWn will therefore decide to write ROOPESH's changes to disk in preference to JOHN's; DBWn will always tend to write inactive blocks rather than active blocks. So now, the datafiles are storing ROOPESH's uncommitted transaction but missing JOHN's committed transaction. This is as bad a corruption as you can have. But think it through. If the instance crashes now—a power cut, perhaps, or a SHUTDOWN ABORT—the roll forward will still be able to sort out the mess. There will always be enough information in the redo stream to reconstruct committed changes; that is obvious, because a commit isn't completed until the write is done. But because LGWR flushes all changes to all blocks to the logfiles, there will also be enough information to reconstruct the undo segment needed to roll back ROOPESH's uncommitted transaction.

So to summarize, because LGWR always writes ahead of DBWn, and because it writes in real time on commit, there will always be enough information in the redo stream to reconstruct any committed changes that had not been written to the datafiles and to roll back any uncommitted changes that had been written to the datafiles. This instance recovery mechanism of redo and rollback makes it absolutely impossible to corrupt an Oracle database—so long as there has been no physical damage.

exam watch

Can a SHUTDOWN ABORT corrupt the database? Absolutely not! It is impossible to corrupt the database. The instance recovery mechanism will always repair any damage—so long as the online logfiles are available.

Checkpointing

The checkpoint position (the point in the redo stream from which instance recovery must start following a crash) is advanced automatically by the DBWn. This process is known as *incremental checkpointing*. In addition, there may be full checkpoints and partial checkpoints.

A *full checkpoint* occurs when all dirty buffers are written to disk. In normal running, there might be a hundred thousand dirty buffers in the cache, but the

DBWn would write just a few hundred of them for the incremental checkpoint. For a full checkpoint, it will write the lot. This entails a great deal of work: very high CPU and disk usage while the checkpoint is in progress, and reduced performance for user sessions. Full checkpoints are bad for business. Because of this, there will never be a full checkpoint except in two circumstances: an orderly shutdown and at the DBA's request.

on the job

Manually initiated checkpoints should never be necessary in normal running, although they can be useful when you want to test the effect of tuning. There is no full checkpoint following a log switch. This has been the case since release 8i, though to this day many DBAs do not realize this.

When the database is shut down with the NORMAL, IMMEDIATE, or TRANSACTIONAL option, there is a checkpoint: all dirty buffers are flushed to disk by the DBWn before the database is closed and dismounted. This means that when the database is opened again, no recovery will be needed. A clean shutdown is always desirable and is necessary before some operations (such as enabling archivelog mode). A full checkpoint can be signaled at any time with this command:

```
alter system checkpoint;
```

A *partial checkpoint* is necessary and occurs automatically as part of certain operations. Depending on the operation, the partial checkpoint will affect different buffers. These operations are detailed here:

Operation	What Buffers Will Be Flushed to Disk
Taking a tablespace offline	All blocks that are part of the tablespace
Taking a datafile offline	All blocks that are part of the datafile
Dropping a segment	All blocks that are part of the segment
Truncating a table	All blocks that are part of the table
Putting a tablespace into backup mode	All blocks that are part of the tablespace

Full checkpoints occur only with an orderly shutdown, or by request. Partial checkpoints occur automatically as needed.

Protecting the Online Redo Logfiles

Remember that an Oracle database requires at least two online logfile groups to function so that it can switch between them. You may need to add more groups for performance reasons, but two are required. Each group consists of one or more members, which are the physical files. Only one member per group is required for Oracle to function, but at least two members per group are required for safety.

on the job

Always have at least two members in each logfile group, for security. This is not just data security—it is job security, too.

The one thing that a DBA is not allowed to do is to lose all copies of the current online logfile group. If that happens, you will lose data. The only way to protect against data loss when you lose all members of the current group is to configure a Data Guard environment for zero data loss, which is not a trivial exercise. Why is it so critical that you do not lose all members of the current group? Think about instance recovery. After a crash, SMON will use the contents of the current online logfile group for roll forward recovery, to repair any corruptions in the database. If the current online logfile group is not available, perhaps because it was not multiplexed and media damage has destroyed the one member, then SMON cannot do this. And if SMON cannot correct corruptions with roll forward, you cannot open the database.

If a member of a redo logfile group is damaged or missing, the database will remain open if there is a surviving member. This contrasts with the controlfile, where damage to any copy will crash the database immediately. Similarly, groups can be added or removed and members of groups can be added or moved while the database is open, as long as there are always at least two groups, and each group has at least one valid member.

exam watch

The online redo log can be reconfigured while the database is open with no downtime, whereas operations on the controlfile can only be carried out when the database is in nomount mode or completely shut down.

If you create a database with DBCA, by default you will have three groups, but they will have only one member each. Two views will tell you the state of your redo logs: V$LOG will have one row per group, and V$LOGFILE will have one row per logfile member. Figure 18-1 shows an example of online redo logfile configuration.

FIGURE 18-1 Online redo logfile configuration

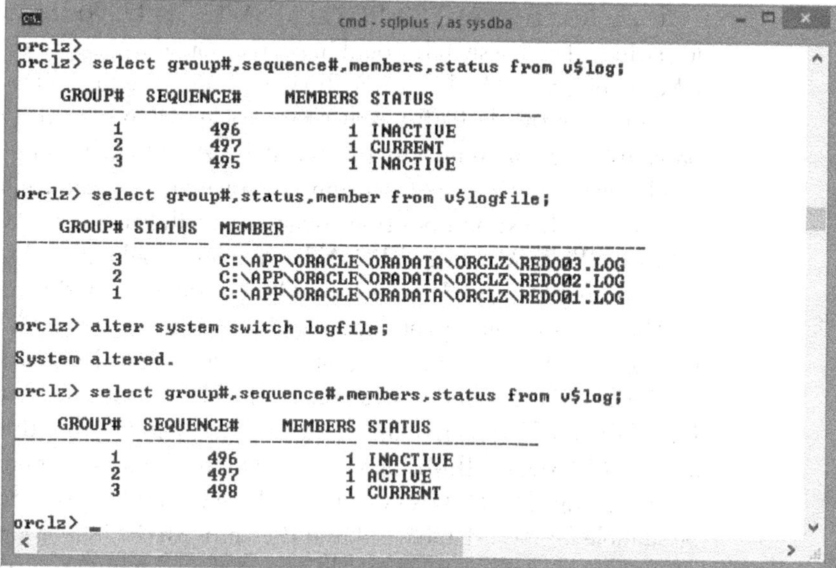

The first query shows that this database has three logfile groups. The current group—the one LGWR is writing to at the moment—is group 2; the other groups are inactive, meaning first that the LGWR is not writing to them, and second that in the event of an instance failure, SMON would not require them for instance recovery. In other words, the checkpoint position has advanced into group 2. The SEQUENCE# column tells us that there have been 497 log switches since the database was created. This number is incremented with each log switch. The MEMBERS column shows that each group consists of only one member—seriously bad news, which should be corrected as soon as possible.

The second query shows the individual online redo logfiles. Each file is part of one group (identified by GROUP#, which is the join column back to V$LOG) and has a unique name. The STATUS column should always be null, as shown. If the member has not yet been used, typically because the database has only just been opened and no log switches have occurred, the status will be INVALID; this will only be there until the first log switch. If the status is persistently INVALID, you have a problem.

on the Job

As with the controlfile and datafiles, Oracle does not enforce any naming convention for logfiles, but most organizations will have standards for this.

Then there is an **ALTER SYSTEM SWITCH LOGFILE** command to force a log switch. The log switch would happen automatically, eventually, if there were any DML in progress. The last query shows that after the log switch, group 3 is now the current group that LGWR is writing to, at log switch sequence number 498. The previously current group, group 2, has status ACTIVE. This means that it would still be needed by SMON for instance recovery if the instance failed now. In a short time, as the checkpoint position advances, it will become INACTIVE. Issuing an **ALTER SYSTEM CHECKPOINT** command would force the checkpoint position to come up to date, and group 2 would then become inactive immediately.

The number of groups and the members per group are restricted by settings in the controlfile, determined at database creation time. Turn back to the **CREATE DATABASE** command in Chapter 2 called by the CreateDB.sql script; the MAXLOGFILES directive limits the number of groups that this database can have, and the MAXLOGMEMBERS directive limits the maximum number of members of each group. The DBCA defaults for these (16 and 3, respectively) may well be suitable for most databases, but if they prove to be inappropriate, it is possible to re-create the controlfile with different values. However, as with all controlfile operations, this will require downtime.

To protect the database against loss of data in the event of damage to an online redo logfile group, multiplex it. Following the example in Figure 18-1, to add multiplexed copies to the online log, one would use a command such as this for each logfile group:

```
alter database add logfile member
'D:\APP\ORACLE\ORADATA\ORCLZ\REDO01A.log' to group 1;
```

Archivelog Mode and the Archiver Process(es)

Oracle guarantees that your database is never corrupted, through use of the online redo logfiles to repair any corruptions caused by an instance failure. This is automatic, and unavoidable. But to guarantee no loss of data following a media failure, it is necessary to have a record of all changes applied to the database since the last backup of the database; this is not enabled by default. The online redo logfiles are overwritten as log switches occur, so the history of change vectors is by default not kept—but the transition to archivelog mode ensures that no online redo logfile is overwritten unless it has been copied

An online redo logfile can be overwritten only if it is inactive, and (if the database is in archivelog mode) if it has been archived.

to an archive logfile first. So there will be a series of archive logfiles that represent a complete history of all changes ever applied to the database. If a datafile is damaged at any time, it will then be possible to restore a backup of the datafile and apply the changes from the archive log redo stream to bring it up to date.

By default, a database is created in *noarchivelog mode;* this means that online redo logfiles are overwritten by log switches with no copy being made first. It is still impossible to corrupt the database, but data would be lost if the datafiles were damaged by media failure. Once the database is transitioned to *archivelog mode*, it is impossible to lose data—provided that all the archive logfiles generated since the last backup are available.

Once a database is converted to archivelog mode, a new background process will start, automatically. This is the archiver process, ARCn. By default, Oracle will start four of these processes, but you can have up to 30. In earlier releases of the database it was necessary to start this process either with a SQL*Plus command or by setting the initialization parameter LOG_ARCHIVE_START, but from release 10g onward Oracle automatically starts the archiver processes if the database is in archivelog mode.

on the job ***In archivelog mode, recovery is possible with no loss of data up to and including the last commit. As a general rule, all databases where you cannot afford to lose data should run in archivelog mode. Don't exclude test and development systems from this rule; they are important too.***

The archiver processes will copy the online redo logfile to an archive logfile after each log switch, thus generating a continuous chain of logfiles that can be used for recovering a backup. The name and location of these archive logfiles is controlled by initialization parameters. For safety, the archive logfiles can be multiplexed, just as the online logfiles can be multiplexed—but eventually they should be migrated to offline storage, such as a tape library. The Oracle instance takes care of creating the archive logs with the ARCn process, but the migration to tape must be controlled by the DBA, either through operating system commands or by using the recovery manager utility RMAN.

exam watch ***Archiver processes launch automatically if the database is in archivelog mode.***

The transition to archivelog mode can be done only while the database is in mount mode after a clean shutdown, and it must therefore be done by a user with a SYSDBA connection. It is also necessary to set the initialization parameters that control the names and locations of the archive logs generated. Clearly, these names must be unique or archive logs could be overwritten by other archive logs. To ensure unique filenames, it is possible to embed variables such as the log switch sequence number in the archive logfile names. These variables may be used to embed unique values in archive logfile names:

Variable	Description
%d	A unique database identifier, necessary if multiple databases are being archived to the same directories.
%t	The thread number, visible as the THREAD# column in V$INSTANCE. This is not significant, except in a RAC database.
%r	The incarnation number. This is important if an incomplete recovery has been done, which will reset the log switch sequence number.
%s	The log switch sequence number. This will guarantee that the archives from any one database incarnation do not overwrite each other.

The minimum archiving necessary to ensure that recovery from a restored backup will be possible is to set one archive destination. But for safety, it will usually be a requirement to multiplex the archive logfiles by specifying two or more destinations, ideally on different disks served by different controllers. It is possible to specify up to 31 archive destinations, giving you that many copies of each filled online redo logfile. This is perhaps excessive for safety.

One archive destination? Good idea. Two destinations? Sure, why not. But 30?

The reason for so many possible destinations is distributed systems. For the purposes of this book and the OCP exam, an archive log destination will always be a directory on the machine hosting the database—and two destinations on local disks will usually be sufficient. But the destination can be an Oracle Net alias, specifying the address of a listener on a remote computer. This is the key to zero data loss: the redo stream can be shipped across the network to a remote database, where it can be applied to give a real-time backup. Remote destinations are also used for Streams, to propagate changes between independent databases.

CERTIFICATION OBJECTIVE 18.02

Backup and Recovery: Configuration

Configuring a database for recoverability means ensuring that certain critical files are multiplexed. These files are the online redo logfiles and the controlfile. Adjusting the online redo logfile configuration is an online operation, whereas adjusting the controlfile configuration requires a shutdown/startup.

A point of terminology: some DBAs say that a database should have multiple controlfiles, whereas others will say that it should have multiple copies of the controlfile. This book uses the latter terminology. The Oracle documentation is inconsistent.

To determine the names and locations of the controlfile copies, either query a view or a parameter:

```
orclz> select name from v$controlfile;
NAME
---------------------------------------------------
C:\APP\ORACLE\ORADATA\ORCLZ\CONTROL01.CTL
C:\APP\ORACLE\FAST_RECOVERY_AREA\ORCLZ\CONTROL02.CTL

orclz> select value from v$parameter2
where name='control_files';
VALUE
---------------------------------------------------
C:\APP\ORACLE\ORADATA\ORCLZ\CONTROL01.CTL
C:\APP\ORACLE\FAST_RECOVERY_AREA\ORCLZ\CONTROL02.CTL
orclz>
```

The preceding queries show that this database is running with two copies of the controlfile.

EXERCISE 18-1

Investigate and Adjust the Redo Log Configuration

In this exercise, you will investigate the configuration of the redo log.

1. Connect to your database as user SYSTEM using SQL*Plus.
2. Document the configuration of the redo log with this query:

   ```
   select * from v$log join v$logfile using (group#);
   ```

   This will show the logfile members, their status, their size, and the group to which they belong. If your database is the default database, it will have three groups each of one member, size 50MB.
3. Determine the archivelog mode of the database, and whether ARCn is running, with these commands:

   ```
   select log_mode from v$database;
   select archiver from v$instance;
   ```

Note that the mode is an attribute of the database, but archiving is an attribute of the instance.

4. Add another member to each of the online logfile groups. Choose any directory and filename suitable for your operating system. For example, following the situation described in Figure 18-1, the commands could be as follows:

```
alter database add logfile member
'c:\app\oracle\oradata\orclz\redo01a.log' to group 1;
alter database add logfile member
'c:\app\oracle\oradata\orclz\redo02a.log' to group 2;
alter database add logfile member
'c:\app\oracle\oradata\orclz\redo03a.log' to group 3;
```

5. Run this query to check the status of your logfile members:

```
select * from v$logfile;
```

Note that the new members will be INVALID.

6. Cycle through the logfile groups by executing this command a few times:

```
alter system switch logfile;
```

7. Rerun the query from step 5. The status of each member should now have cleared. If it still invalid, something is wrong: look at the database instance alert log to diagnose what the problem might be.

CERTIFICATION OBJECTIVE 18.03

Configure the Fast Recovery Area

The fast recovery area is a disk destination used as the default location for recovery-related files. It is controlled with two instance parameters:

- db_recovery_file_dest
- db_recovery_file_dest_size

The first of these parameters nominates the location. This can be a file system directory or an ASM disk group. It is possible for several databases to share a common destination; each database will have its own directory structure (created automatically) in the destination. The second parameter limits the amount of space in the destination that the database will occupy; it says nothing about how much space is actually available in the destination. The configuration and usage of the fast recovery area is shown in two views:

- v$recovery_file_dest
- v$recovery_area_usage

on the Job

Release 10.x introduced the* flash *recovery area. In release 11.2.x it was renamed to the* fast *recovery area (a major upgrade). Some old views (and some old DBAs) still use the original name.

The files that will be written to the fast recovery area (unless specified otherwise) include

- Recovery Manager backups
- Archive redo logfiles
- Database flashback logs

RMAN, the Recovery Manager, can manage space within the fast recovery area: it can delete files that are no longer needed according to its configured policies for retaining copies and backup of files. In an ideal situation, the fast recovery area will be large enough to store a complete copy of the database, plus any archive logs and incremental backups that would be necessary to recover the copy if necessary.

The database backup routines should also include backing up the fast recovery area to tape, thus implementing a strategy of primary, secondary, and tertiary storage:

- Primary storage is the live database, on disk.
- Secondary storage is a copy of the database plus files needed for fast recovery.
- Tertiary storage is long-term backups, usually in a tape library.

RMAN can manage the whole cycle: backup of the database from primary to secondary, and migration of backups from secondary to tertiary storage. Such a system can be implemented in a fashion that will allow near-instant recovery following a failure, combined with the ability to take the database back in time if this is ever necessary.

FIGURE 18-2

Determining the fast recovery area configuration

```
orclz> select name,value from v$parameter where name like 'db_recovery%';

NAME                                 VALUE
------------------------------------ ------------------------------------
db_recovery_file_dest                /u01/app/oracle/fast_recovery_area
db_recovery_file_dest_size           5033164800

orclz> select name,space_limit,space_used from v$recovery_file_dest;

NAME                                 SPACE_LIMIT SPACE_USED
------------------------------------ ----------- ----------
/u01/app/oracle/fast_recovery_area    5033164800          0

orclz> alter system set db_recovery_file_dest_size=10g;

System altered.

orclz> alter system set db_recovery_file_dest='/u02/fra';

System altered.

orclz>
```

The fast recovery area can be reconfigured at any time, without affecting any files within it: changes will apply only to files created subsequently. Figure 18-2 shows how to determine the fast recovery area configuration, followed by statements to adjust both its location and its size.

CERTIFICATION OBJECTIVE 18.04

Configure Archivelog Mode

A database is by default created in noarchivelog mode. The transition to archivelog mode is straightforward, but it does require downtime. The process is as follows:

- Shut down the database, cleanly.
- Start up in mount mode.
- Issue the command ALTER DATABASE ARCHIVELOG;.

- Open the database.
- Perform a full backup.

Following a default installation; the archive logs will be written to only one destination, which will be the fast recovery area. This is specified by an implicit setting for LOG_ARCHIVE_DEST_1 parameter, visible in the V$ARCHIVE_DEST view. If the parameters that enable the fast recovery area have not been set, they will go to a platform-specific destination (the $ORACLE_HOME/dbs directory for Unix systems).The final command in Figure 18-3, ARCHIVE LOG LIST, shows summary information about the archiving configuration: that the database is running in archivelog mode, that the ARCn process is running, and that the archive logfiles are being written to the fast recovery area.

exam watch ***The change to archivelog mode can only be done in mount mode, after a clean shutdown.***

A full backup is an essential step for the transition to archivelog mode. Following the transition, all backups made earlier are useless. The backup can be made while the database is open or closed, but until it is made, the database is not protected at all.

on the job ***If the shutdown is not clean (for instance, SHUTDOWN ABORT), the transition will fail. Not a problem—open the database and shut it down again: this time, cleanly.***

FIGURE 18-3 Enabling and verifying archivelog mode with SQL*Plus

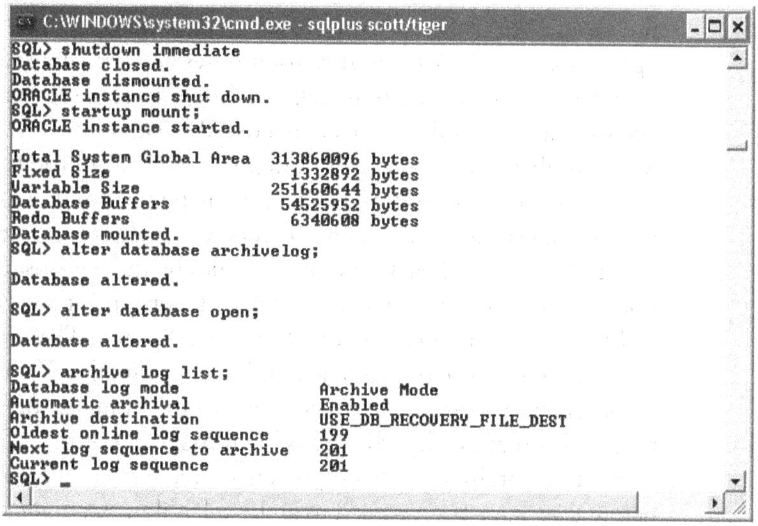

```
C:\WINDOWS\system32\cmd.exe - sqlplus scott/tiger
SQL> shutdown immediate
Database closed.
Database dismounted.
ORACLE instance shut down.
SQL> startup mount;
ORACLE instance started.

Total System Global Area  313860096 bytes
Fixed Size                  1332892 bytes
Variable Size             251660644 bytes
Database Buffers           54525952 bytes
Redo Buffers                6340608 bytes
Database mounted.
SQL> alter database archivelog;

Database altered.

SQL> alter database open;

Database altered.

SQL> archive log list;
Database log mode              Archive Mode
Automatic archival             Enabled
Archive destination            USE_DB_RECOVERY_FILE_DEST
Oldest online log sequence     199
Next log sequence to archive   201
Current log sequence           201
SQL> _
```

EXERCISE 18-2

Enable Archivelog Mode

In this exercise, you will transition your database into archivelog mode. This is an essential procedure for completing the next chapter on backup and recovery.

1. Connect to your database with Database Control as user SYS. (Why SYS? Because you will have to stop and start the instance.)
2. Follow the steps shown in Figure 18-3 to enable archivelog mode.
3. Confirm that archiving is working by forcing a log switch and an archive:

```
alter system archive log current;
```

4. Confirm that the archive log file has been generated, in the fast recovery area:

```
select name,is_recovery_dest_file from v$archived_log;
```

CERTIFICATION SUMMARY

This chapter is an introduction to material studied in greater detail later in the OCP curriculum.

It is vital to understand the mechanism of instance recovery following an instance failure: the use of change vectors read from the online redo log to rebuild the instance to the state it was in before the crash. This process of forward recovery operates at the block level. It reinstantiates all work, committed or not, including changes to undo segments as well as changes to data segments. Instance recovery occurs in mount mode. Once completed, the database opens and recovery completes with a rollback of transactions in flight at the time of the failure.

The checkpoint position represents the point in the redo stream from which recovery must start. All change vectors earlier than this refer to blocks that have already been copied back into the datafiles by the database writer: these blocks do not need to be recovered, because the disk version is the latest version.

Many sites will make use of a fast recovery area. This can simplify database administration by acting as a default location for all recovery-related files. Space management within the fast recovery area is automatic: files are created and then removed automatically when possible if the area is full.

Enabling archivelog mode prevents Oracle from overwriting online logfiles before they have been copied to archive logfiles. Archiver processes are launched automatically to do this.

TWO-MINUTE DRILL

Identify the Importance of Checkpoints, Redo Logfiles, and Archive Logfiles

- ❑ Full checkpoints occur only on orderly shutdown or on demand.
- ❑ Partial checkpoints occur automatically when necessary.
- ❑ Incremental checkpoints advance the point in the redo stream from which recovery must begin after an instance failure.
- ❑ The redo log consists of the disk structures for storing change vectors. The online log is essential for instance recovery.
- ❑ The archive log consists of copies of online logfile members, created as they are filled. These are essential for datafile recovery after media failure.

Backup and Recovery: Configuration

- ❑ Online logfiles and archive logfiles and the controlfile should all be multiplexed.
- ❑ Operating in archivelog mode is essential for recoverability.
- ❑ The redo log can be reconfigured with zero downtime, whereas changing the controlfile configuration cannot be done online.

Configure the Fast Recovery Area

- ❑ The fast recovery area is an optional default location for recovery-related files.
- ❑ Configure the FRA with instance parameters, which are dynamic.

Configure ARCHIVELOG Mode

- ❑ The change to archivelog mode can be accomplished only in mount mode.
- ❑ In archivelog mode, archiver processes are launched automatically.
- ❑ Oracle will never overwrite an unarchived logfile group when the database is in archivelog mode.

SELF TEST

Identify the Importance of Checkpoints, Redo Logfiles, and Archive Logfiles

1. When will a full checkpoint occur? (Choose all correct answers.)
   A. As part of a NORMAL shutdown
   B. As part of an IMMEDIATE shutdown
   C. When a tablespace is taken offline
   D. When a log switch occurs
2. Which of these operations cannot be accomplished while the database is open? (Choose all correct answers.)
   A. Adding a controlfile copy
   B. Adding an online logfile member
   C. Changing the location of the fast recovery area
   D. Changing the archivelog mode of the database
3. Which of these files is *not* required for instance recovery? (Choose the best answer.)
   A. Archive logfiles
   B. Controlfile
   C. Datafiles
   D. Online logfiles

Backup and Recovery: Configuration

4. If the database is in archivelog mode, what will happen if the archiving fails for any reason? (Choose the best answer.)
   A. The instance will abort.
   B. All non-SYSDBA sessions will hang.
   C. DML operations will hang.
   D. The database will revert to noarchivelog mode.
5. To configure the database for recoverability, which files types can (and should) be multiplexed? (Choose three answers.)
   A. Archive redo logfile
   B. Controlfile
   C. Online redo logfile

D. Server parameter file
E. System tablespace datafile
F. Undo tablespace datafile

Configure the Fast Recovery Area

6. What file types will, by default, be stored in the fast recovery area if it has been defined? (Choose all correct answers.)

A. Archive redo log files
B. Background process trace files
C. RMAN backup sets
D. RMAN image copies
E. Undo data

Configure Archivelog Mode

7. Several steps are involved in transitioning to archivelog mode. Put these in the correct order:

1 alter database archivelog
2 alter database open
3 alter system archive log start
4 full backup
5 shutdown immediate
6 startup mount

A. 5, 6, 1, 2, 4; 3 not necessary
B. 5, 4, 6, 1, 2, 3
C. 6, 1, 3, 5, 4, 2
D. 1, 5, 4, 6, 2; 3 not necessary
E. 5, 6, 1, 2, 3; 4 not necessary

8. What conditions must hold before an online logfile member can be reused if the database is operating in archivelog mode? (Choose all correct answers.)

A. It must be inactive.
B. It must be multiplexed.
C. It must be archived.
D. The archive must be multiplexed.

LAB QUESTION

Check whether your database is configured for recoverability. These are some points to look at:

- Online redo log files should be multiplexed.
- The controlfile should be multiplexed.
- The database should be in archivelog mode.
- Archiver processes should be running.
- Archive logs should be multiplexed.
- The fast recovery area should be enabled.

SELF TEST ANSWERS

Identify the Importance of Checkpoints, Redo Logfiles, and Archive Logfiles

1. ☑ **A** and **B**. Any orderly shutdown will trigger a full checkpoint.
   ☒ **C** and **D** are incorrect. **C** is incorrect because this would trigger only a partial checkpoint. **D** is incorrect because log switches do not trigger checkpoints.

2. ☑ **A** and **D**. Anything to do with the controlfile can only be done in nomount or shutdown mode. Changing the archivelog mode can only be done in mount mode.
   ☒ **B** and **C** are incorrect. **B** is incorrect because the online redo log can be configured while the database is open. **C** is incorrect because DB_RECOVERY_FILE_DEST is a dynamic parameter.

3. ☑ **A**. Archive logfiles are used for media recovery, not instance recovery.
   ☒ **B**, **C**, and **D** are incorrect. **B** is incorrect because the controlfile stores the critical values needed to determine the checkpoint position and control the recovery. **C** and **D** are incorrect because during instance recovery, change vectors from the online logfiles are used to update blocks read from the datafiles.

Backup and Recovery: Configuration

4. ☑ **C**. Once all the online logfiles need archiving, DML commands will be blocked.
   ☒ **A**, **B**, and **D** are incorrect. **A** is incorrect because the instance will remain open. **B** is incorrect because only sessions that attempt DML will hang; those running SELECTs can continue. **D** is incorrect because this cannot happen automatically.

5. ☑ **A**, **B**, and **C**. These file types can all be multiplexed, with Oracle ensuring that copies are identical.
   ☒ **D**, **E**, and **F** are incorrect. These files cannot be multiplexed by Oracle (although you can of course mirror them with operating system facilities, or with ASM).

Configure the Fast Recovery Area

6. ☑ **A**, **C**, and **D**. These will go to the fast recovery area, unless directed elsewhere.
   ☒ **B** and **E** are incorrect. **B** is incorrect because background trace files will go to a directory in the DIAGNOSTIC_DEST directory. **E** is incorrect because undo data is stored in the undo tablespace.

Configure Archivelog Mode

7. ☑ **A.** This is the correct sequence
   ☒ **B, C, D,** and **E** are incorrect. **B, C,** and **D** are incorrect because enabling archiving is not necessary (it will occur automatically). **E** is incorrect because a backup is a necessary part of the procedure.
8. ☑ **A** and **C.** These are the two conditions.
   ☒ **B** and **D** are incorrect. Although these are certainly good practices, they are not requirements.

LAB ANSWER

The information can be obtained using these queries:

```
select group#,members from v$log;
select count(*) from v$controlfile;
select log_mode from v$database;
select archiver from v$instance;
select dest_name,destination from v$archive_dest;
select name,value from v$parameter
where name like 'log_archive_dest%';
select value from v$parameter
where name='db_recovery_file_dest';
```

If the database is the default database created by DBCA and the exercises have been completed as written, the results of these queries will show that there is one potential problem: the archive redo logfiles are going to only one destination, which is the fast recovery area.

19

Backup and Recovery Operations

CERTIFICATION OBJECTIVES

19.01	Create Consistent Database Backups
19.02	Back Up Your Database Without Shutting It Down
19.03	Create Incremental Backups
19.04	Automate Database Backups
19.05	Manage Backups
19.06	Determine the Need for Performing Recovery
19.07	Use Recovery Manager (RMAN) and the Data Recovery Advisor to Perform Recovery of the Controlfile, Redo Logfile, and Datafile
✓	Two-Minute Drill
Q&A	Self Test

This chapter introduces backup and recovery. These are vital topics of which every DBA must have complete mastery, and they cannot be covered in one chapter. The final OCP exam has many objectives on these topics, and tests them comprehensively. It is possible that general knowledge of techniques could be tested in the first exam, and even if it is not, this subject matter is useful preparation for the second exam. Certainly even the most junior DBAs should be familiar with backup and recovery, if only so that they can protect the databases they use for their own experimentation and development.

Oracle Corporation's recommended tool for backup and recovery is the Recovery Manager (RMAN), which is invoked from an executable program that acts as a client to the database: it logs on and establishes sessions as does any other user process. RMAN backups are often referred to as *server-managed* backups, because the work is done by server processes. It is possible to perform backup and recovery operations without using RMAN: these are usually referred to as *user-managed* backups.

CERTIFICATION OBJECTIVE 19.01

Create Consistent Database Backups

A *consistent backup* is a backup taken while the database is closed. You may hear offline backups referred to as closed or cold backups. The term "closed" is self-explanatory and "cold" is just slang, but "consistent" requires an understanding of the Oracle architecture. For a datafile to be consistent, every block in the datafile must have been checkpointed and the file closed by the operating system. In normal running, the datafiles are inconsistent: there will be a number of blocks that have been copied into the database buffer cache, updated, and not yet written back to disk. The datafile itself, on disk, is therefore not consistent with the real-time state of the database; some parts of it will be out of date. To make a datafile consistent, all changed blocks must be flushed to disk and the datafile closed. As a general rule, this only happens when the database is shut down cleanly—with the IMMEDIATE, TRANSACTIONAL, or NORMAL shutdown option. An *inconsistent backup* is a backup taken while the database is in use. Other terms for online backups are "open" and "hot" backups. A datafile that is backed up online will not be synchronized with any particular SCN, nor is it synchronized with the other datafiles or the controlfile. It is backed up while it is in use—being read from by server processes and written to by DBWn.

A server-managed consistent backup can be accomplished only when the database is in mount mode. This is because the datafiles must be closed, or they would not be consistent. RMAN needs to read the controlfile in order to find the datafiles, and will also write to the controlfile details of the backup operation. To back up the mounted controlfile, RMAN avoids the problem of inconsistency by taking a read-consistent snapshot of the controlfile and backing that up.

An RMAN backup is launched from the RMAN executable. The RMAN executable is a tool supplied by Oracle and installed into the Oracle Home. RMAN logs on to the database (like any other user process) and then launches additional server processes to copy files. In general, there are three techniques for using RMAN: an interactive interface, for performing ad hoc tasks; a script interface, for running jobs through the operating system's scheduler; and an Enterprise Manager interface, for generating scripts and defining jobs to be scheduled by Enterprise Manager.

This is an RMAN script for performing an offline full backup:

```
run {
shutdown immediate;
startup mount;
allocate channel d1 type disk;
backup as backupset database
format '/u02/backup/orcl12c/offline_full_whole.bset';
alter database open;
}
```

The first two commands within the run{} block perform a clean shutdown and then bring the database back up in mount mode. Then the script launches a server process to perform the backup. This is known as a *channel*. In this case, the channel is a disk channel because the backup is being directed to disk; the alternative channel type is SBT_TAPE, which is used for backups directed to a tape device. The next command launches a backup operation. This will be of type BACKUPSET. Backup sets are an RMAN-proprietary structure that can combine many input files into one output file. Backup sets have other advantages, such as compression (not enabled in this example) and the ability to reduce the size of the backup by ignoring blocks in the input datafiles that have never been used. The keyword DATABASE instructs RMAN to back up the entire set of datafiles and the controlfile. RMAN will never back up online redo logfile members or tempfiles. The FORMAT keyword names the file that will contain the backup set. Finally, the script opens the database.

RMAN will never back up the online redo logfiles, or the tempfiles. It will back up datafiles, archivelog files, the controlfile, and the spfile.

An operating system command that could be scheduled to run this script is

```
rman target sys/oracle@orcl12c @offline_full_whole.rman
```

This command launches the RMAN executable, with the SYS login (necessary because of the **SHUTDOWN** and **STARTUP** commands) and then the name of the script, which must be preceded by an "@" symbol. Note that the connect string uses a net alias, so the connection will be made via a database listener.

RMAN can generate three types of backup:

- A backup set is a proprietary format that can contain several files and will not include never-used blocks.
- A compressed backup set has the same content as a backup set, but RMAN will apply a compression algorithm as it writes out the backup set.
- An image copy is a backup file that is identical to the input file. An image copy is immediately interchangeable with its source, whereas to extract a file from a backup set requires an RMAN restore operation.

EXERCISE 19-1

Consistent Server-Managed Backup

In this exercise, you will perform a full offline backup using RMAN.

1. Set the environment variables ORACLE_SID, ORACLE_HOME, and PATH to allow connection to your local database, in the same manner that you would before launching SQL*Plus.
2. Launch the RMAN executable (it is called rman on Unix and Linux, rman.exe on Windows) and connect using operating system authentication. The command is

   ```
   rman target /
   ```

3. Shut down the database and mount it. This can be done from SQL*Plus or from within RMAN:

   ```
   shutdown immediate;
   startup mount;
   ```

The illustration shows steps 2 and 3, executed with RMAN.

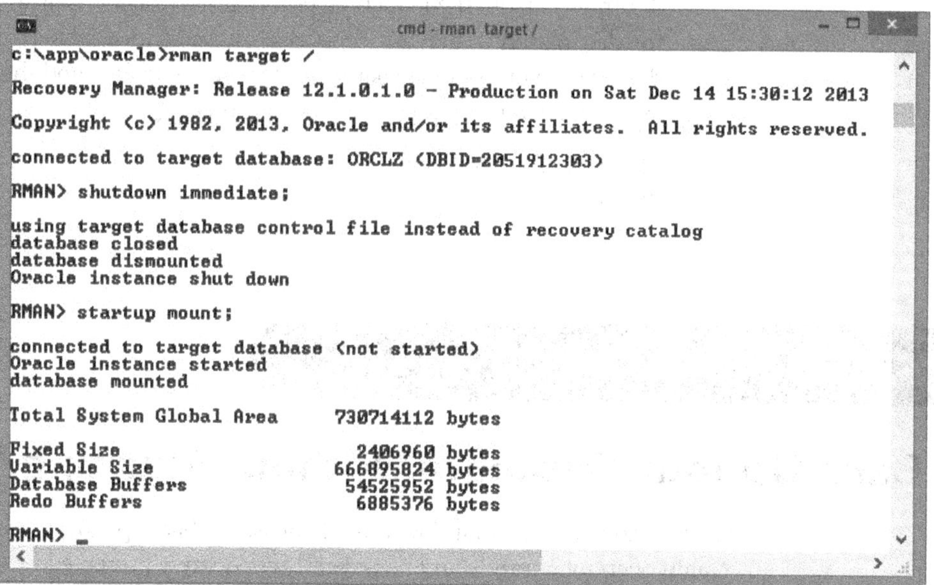

```
c:\app\oracle>rman target /

Recovery Manager: Release 12.1.0.1.0 - Production on Sat Dec 14 15:30:12 2013

Copyright (c) 1982, 2013, Oracle and/or its affiliates.  All rights reserved.

connected to target database: ORCLZ (DBID=2051912303)

RMAN> shutdown immediate;

using target database control file instead of recovery catalog
database closed
database dismounted
Oracle instance shut down

RMAN> startup mount;

connected to target database (not started)
Oracle instance started
database mounted

Total System Global Area     730714112 bytes

Fixed Size                     2406960 bytes
Variable Size                666895824 bytes
Database Buffers              54525952 bytes
Redo Buffers                   6885376 bytes

RMAN> _
```

4. Perform a full backup. The command from the RMAN prompt is

   ```
   backup database;
   ```

   This will, by default, back up the entire database to the fast recovery area. The next illustration shows the command on a Windows system.

```
RMAN> backup database;

Starting backup at 2013-12-14 15:34:43
allocated channel: ORA_DISK_1
channel ORA_DISK_1: SID=124 device type=DISK
channel ORA_DISK_1: starting full datafile backup set
channel ORA_DISK_1: specifying datafile(s) in backup set
input datafile file number=00003 name=C:\APP\ORACLE\ORADATA\ORCLZ\SYSAUX01.DBF
input datafile file number=00006 name=C:\APP\ORACLE\ORADATA\ORCLZ\USERS01.DBF
input datafile file number=00005 name=C:\APP\ORACLE\ORADATA\ORCLZ\UNDOTBS01.DBF
input datafile file number=00001 name=C:\APP\ORACLE\ORADATA\ORCLZ\SYSTEM01.DBF
input datafile file number=00002 name=C:\APP\ORACLE\ORADATA\ORCLZ\EXAMPLE01.DBF
channel ORA_DISK_1: starting piece 1 at 2013-12-14 15:34:44
channel ORA_DISK_1: finished piece 1 at 2013-12-14 15:35:09
piece handle=C:\APP\ORACLE\FAST_RECOVERY_AREA\ORCLZ\BACKUPSET\2013_12_14\O1_MF_
214T153443 comment=NONE
channel ORA_DISK_1: backup set complete, elapsed time: 00:00:25
channel ORA_DISK_1: starting full datafile backup set
channel ORA_DISK_1: specifying datafile(s) in backup set
including current control file in backup set
including current SPFILE in backup set
channel ORA_DISK_1: starting piece 1 at 2013-12-14 15:35:12
channel ORA_DISK_1: finished piece 1 at 2013-12-14 15:35:13
piece handle=C:\APP\ORACLE\FAST_RECOVERY_AREA\ORCLZ\BACKUPSET\2013_12_14\O1_MF_
214T153443 comment=NONE
channel ORA_DISK_1: backup set complete, elapsed time: 00:00:01
Finished backup at 2013-12-14 15:35:13

RMAN> _
```

5. Study the feedback in the RMAN session, some of which is shown in the illustration. Note the launching of a channel, the identification of the datafiles, the destination in the fast recovery area, and (not visible in the illustration) the creation of a second backup set for the controlfile and the spfile.
6. Open the database and then exit from RMAN:

```
alter database open;
exit;
```

CERTIFICATION OBJECTIVE 19.02

Back Up Your Database Without Shutting It Down

There is no reason to shut down the database for backups. An Oracle database can remain open indefinitely and be perfectly adequately protected by open backups—provided that it is running in archivelog mode. It is not possible to take an open backup in noarchivelog mode, because the change vectors stored in the archive logfile generated while the inconsistent backup was being made are required to make the datafiles consistent when they are restored.

Hot backup is impossible in noarchivelog mode. RMAN will not permit it.

An absolutely reliable open backup can be made with RMAN with a four-word command: **BACKUP DATABASE PLUS ARCHIVELOG.** This command relies on configured defaults for the destination of the backup (disk or tape library), the names of the backup files generated, the number of server channels to launch to carry out the backup, and the type of backup (image copies of the files, backup sets, or compressed backup sets).

This RMAN script performs a full whole online backup of the database and the archive logfiles:

```
run {
allocate channel t1 type sbt_tape;
allocate channel t2 type sbt_tape;
```

```
backup as compressed backupset filesperset 4 database;
backup as compressed backupset archivelog all delete all input;
}
```

The script launches two channels that will write to the tape library. The device driver for the tape library (supplied by the hardware vendor) must have been installed. The use of multiple channels (possible related to the number of tape drives in the library) will parallelize the backup operation, which should make it run faster. The first backup command backs up the complete database, but rather than putting every file into one huge (even though compressed) backup set, it instructs RMAN to divide the database into multiple backup sets of four files each; this can make restore operations faster than if all the files are interleaved in one backup set. The second backup command will back up all the archive logfiles, removing them from disk as it does so.

watch ***When creating backup sets, or compressed backup sets, RMAN will never back up blocks that have never been used. This results in considerable space savings.***

EXERCISE 19-2

Perform Server-Managed Open Backups

In this exercise, you will perform a hot backup of a datafile with RMAN.

1. Connect to the database using RMAN, as in Exercise 19-1.

```
rman target /
```

2. Back up a tablespace using defaults:

```
backup tablespace sysaux;
```

3. Back up your archive logfiles, again using defaults:

```
backup archivelog all;
```

4. Study the output of steps 3 and 4. An example is shown in the next illustration.

```
cmd - rman target /
RMAN> backup tablespace sysaux;

Starting backup at 2013-12-14 15:58:13
using channel ORA_DISK_1
channel ORA_DISK_1: starting full datafile backup set
channel ORA_DISK_1: specifying datafile(s) in backup set
input datafile file number=00003 name=C:\APP\ORACLE\ORADATA\ORCLZ\SYSAUX01.DBF
channel ORA_DISK_1: starting piece 1 at 2013-12-14 15:58:13
channel ORA_DISK_1: finished piece 1 at 2013-12-14 15:58:38
piece handle=C:\APP\ORACLE\FAST_RECOVERY_AREA\ORCLZ\BACKUPSET\2013_12_14\O1_MF_
214T155813 comment=NONE
channel ORA_DISK_1: backup set complete, elapsed time: 00:00:25
Finished backup at 2013-12-14 15:58:38

RMAN> backup archivelog all;

Starting backup at 2013-12-14 15:58:48
current log archived
using channel ORA_DISK_1
channel ORA_DISK_1: starting archived log backup set
channel ORA_DISK_1: specifying archived log(s) in backup set
input archived log thread=1 sequence=588 RECID=553 STAMP=834163129
channel ORA_DISK_1: starting piece 1 at 2013-12-14 15:58:49
channel ORA_DISK_1: finished piece 1 at 2013-12-14 15:58:50
piece handle=C:\APP\ORACLE\FAST_RECOVERY_AREA\ORCLZ\BACKUPSET\2013_12_14\O1_MF_
214T155849 comment=NONE
channel ORA_DISK_1: backup set complete, elapsed time: 00:00:01
Finished backup at 2013-12-14 15:58:50
```

5. Exit from the RMAN utility.

CERTIFICATION OBJECTIVE 19.03

Create Incremental Backups

Incremental backups can be made with server-managed backups, but not with user-managed backups. As far as an operating system utility is concerned, the granularity of the backup is the datafile: an operating system utility cannot look inside the datafile to extract changed blocks incrementally. Incremental backups must always be as backup sets or compressed backup sets. It is logically impossible to make an image copy incremental backup, because an incremental backup can never be identical to the source file. If it were, it wouldn't be incremental.

An incremental backup relies on a starting point that contains all blocks: this is known as the incremental level 0 backup. Then an incremental level 1 backup will extract all blocks that have changed since the last level 1 backup, or the last level 0 backup if there have been no intervening level 1 backups. A cumulative backup will extract all blocks that have changed since the last level 0 backup, irrespective of whether there have been any level 1 backups in the meantime.

An RMAN command to make a level 0 backup is

```
backup as backupset incremental level 0 database;
```

This command relies on configured defaults for launching channels, for the number of files to place in each backup set, and to where the backup set will be written. The backup set will contain all blocks that have ever been used. Many sites will make an incremental level 0 backup every weekend. Then a level 1 backup can be made with this command:

```
backup as backupset incremental level 1 database;
```

If there is no level 0 backup when you attempt a level 1 backup, RMAN will realize this and rather than returning an error will in fact perform a level 0 backup.

CERTIFICATION OBJECTIVE 19.04

Automate Database Backups

Enterprise Manager can schedule backups. The mechanism is not related to the operating system's job scheduler, nor to the job scheduling system within the database. It is purely an Enterprise Manager facility and is available only if Cloud Control has been deployed. You cannot automate backups with Database Express.

In a Cloud Control–managed environment, every machine runs an Enterprise Manager agent. Cloud Control launches jobs according to a specified schedule by contacting the agent and passing it appropriate instructions: what to do, how to do it, and the database and operating system credentials to use. The agent then runs the job. Backup jobs are in fact RMAN scripts. The backups can be of any type but will always be server managed: using RMAN.

Enterprise Manager offers a one-click implementation of the "Oracle Suggested Backup." This consists of making a once-only complete copy (an image copy of all files, rather than a backup set) of the database, followed by daily incremental backups. The incremental backups are applied to the copy a day after their creation, thus rolling it forward such that the copy is always between 24 and 48 hours behind the live database. This allows for very fast recovery in the event of a problem: a damaged datafile can be restored from the copy and brought up to date by applying any necessary archive logfiles. Alternatively, in the event of some terrible user error (such as dropping a schema), the database can be taken back in time at least 24 hours and rolled forward to the instant before the error occurred. Enterprise Manager will create a job that automates this backup strategy.

CERTIFICATION OBJECTIVE 19.05

Manage Backups

RMAN uses a repository to store details of all the backup operations it has carried out. This repository is the key to automated restore and recovery, and the source of reports on backups. By default, server-managed backups will go to the fast recovery area. RMAN will attempt to manage space in the fast recovery area, but the DBA must monitor it as well.

The RMAN Repository

During a backup operation, RMAN will write to its repository all detail of the backup: what was backed up, where the backup files are, the time and system change number of certain events, and so on.

For a datafile restore operation, RMAN must determine the most recent backup (either full or level 0) from which the file should be extracted. Then to recover it, RMAN must determine which incremental backups (if any) are available and then extract and apply them. Then it must determine what archive logfiles are needed and (if they are no longer available on disk) restore them too from backups, and apply them. Finally, it will apply change vectors from the online logfiles to bring the restored file right up to date.

The RMAN repository is always stored in the target database's controlfile—though it is possible to have a copy of it in a separate database, known as the Recovery Manager Catalog.

The repository is the source of the information RMAN needs. Whenever it does anything, it will consult the repository. The repository is stored in the database's controlfile. This does raise the question of what to do if the controlfile itself needs to be restored. There are techniques to cover this situation (dealt with in the second OCP examination) by creating a separate database known as the Recovery Manager Catalog, and by creating automatic backups of the controlfile to a well-known location. At this stage, the assumption is that the controlfile is protected by multiplexing, so there will always be at least one copy of it available.

Reports on Backups

RMAN has two commands that will tell you the state of your backups: LIST will tell you what backups there are; REPORT will tell you what backups are needed. Examples from the RMAN command line are

```
list backup of database;
list backup of archivelog all;
report need backup;
report obsolete;
```

The first of these commands will list all the backups that have been made and are still recorded in the repository. The second command lists all backups of archived redo logfiles. The third command lists everything that needs to be backed up according to the Recovery Manager's configured retention policy (such as three backups of every file). The final command lists all backups that are no longer needed according to the Recovery Manager's configured retention policy.

Figure 19-1 shows two RMAN commands that interrogate the repository.

The **LIST** command shows a backup of the SYSTEM tablespace. There is one only, which is a FULL backup, not any sort of incremental. The **REPORT** command shows (by default) all files where RMAN does not have one backup: this is the REDUNDANCY LEVEL. The two files listed should be backed up without delay.

Administering Backups

Using server-managed backups, management should be largely automatic. That is the whole idea. But there are circumstances where intervention will be necessary—typically, when something has been done that RMAN doesn't know

FIGURE 19-1 LIST and REPORT commands

```
RMAN> list backup of tablespace system;


List of Backup Sets
===================


BS Key  Type LV Size       Device Type Elapsed Time Completion Time
------- ---- -- ---------- ----------- ------------ ---------------
6       Full    680.30M    DISK        00:00:39     14-DEC-13
        BP Key: 6   Status: AVAILABLE  Compressed: NO  Tag: TAG20131214T180755
        Piece Name: /u02/fra/ORCLZ/backupset/2013_12_14/o1_mf_nnndf_TAG20131214T
180755_9bs7mvqg_.bkp
  List of Datafiles in backup set 6
  File LV Type Ckp SCN    Ckp Time  Name
  ---- -- ---- ---------- --------- ----
  1       Full 3184261    14-DEC-13 /u01/app/oracle/oradata/orclz/system01.dbf

RMAN> report need backup;

RMAN retention policy will be applied to the command
RMAN retention policy is set to redundancy 1
Report of files with less than 1 redundant backups
File #bkps Name
---- ----- -----------------------------------------------------
8    0     /u01/oradata/ORCLZ/datafile/o1_mf_omfts_92s6g205_.dbf
11   0     /u02/oradata/ts1.dbf

RMAN>
```

about. If backup files are removed or damaged or relocated, then RMAN must be informed of what has happened. For example, backups may reside on tape, in an automated tape library. The tape library will often have a retention policy: it will automatically delete all files over a certain age. The RMAN repository will not know that this has happened. Alternatively, if the tape library is not deleting old files, then RMAN must do it. From the RMAN command line, there are four critical commands:

- **CROSSCHECK** A crosscheck forces RMAN to compare its repository with the real world. It will check that all the backups it has made do still exist, on disk or tape. Any that it finds to be missing are flagged as EXPIRED.
- **DELETE EXPIRED** This will remove all references from the repository to expired backups. If the backups have merely been moved (offsite, perhaps), an alternative is to mark them as UNAVAILABLE.

- **DELETE OBSOLETE** This will force RMAN to apply its retention policy. It will delete all backups that it considers to be no longer necessary from disk or tape, and remove the references to them from its repository.
- **CATALOG** This command lets you inform RMAN about relocated backups, so that RMAN can include them in its repository in their current location.

CERTIFICATION OBJECTIVE 19.06

Determine the Need for Performing Recovery

The terms *restore* and *recover* have precise meanings in the Oracle environment. To restore a file is to extract it from a backup and return it to the place from which it came. If a datafile is damaged or missing, a restore operation will replace it with a copy extracted from a backup. So far so good, but the restored file will be out of date compared to the rest of the database. To recover the file, extract the relevant change vectors from the redo log stream and apply them to bring the file forward in time until it is synchronized with the rest of the database.

To open a database, the following conditions must be met:

- All copies of the controlfile must be available.
- Each online logfile group must have at least one available member.
- All online datafiles must be present.

The controlfile and the online logfile members will usually be protected by multiplexing. So if a controlfile copy is missing or damaged, it can be replaced with a copy of a surviving controlfile. This must be done while the database instance is shut down, or possibly started in nomount mode. Loss off a multiplexed logfile member is not critical, but it should be replaced without unnecessary delay in order to reestablish the desired level of safety. Never forget that losing *all* members of a logfile group may result in loss of data. A database can be opened with a missing datafile—if the file is taken offline. This can be done while the database is in mount mode, and then the file can be restored and recovered while the database is open.

The technique for determining the need for restore and recovery will depend on the nature of the problem:

- A damaged controlfile means that the instance gets stuck in nomount mode. Inspect the alert log to determine which copy of the controlfile is damaged.
- A damaged datafile will mean that the database mounts, but cannot open. Query the V$DATAFILE view to determine which file or files are in trouble.
- A damaged online redo logfile member will allow the database to open (assuming the file is multiplexed) and the problem will be reported in the V$LOGFILE view.

CERTIFICATION OBJECTIVE 19.07

Use Recovery Manager (RMAN) and the Data Recovery Advisor to Perform Recovery of the Controlfile, Redo Logfile, and Datafile

The Data Recovery Advisor (DRA) is a facility for diagnosing and repairing problems with a database. There are two interfaces: the RMAN executable and Enterprise Manager. The DRA is capable of generating scripts to repair damage to datafiles and (in some circumstances) the controlfile: it does not advise on problems with the spfile or with the online redo logfiles. It is dependent on the Automatic Diagnostic Repository (ADR) and the Health Monitor. The information the Health Monitor gathers and the advice the DRA gives follow the same diagnosis and repair methods that the DBA would follow without them—but they make the process quicker and less prone to error.

The Health Monitor and the ADR

The Health Monitor is a set of checks that run automatically when certain error conditions arise, or manually in response to the DBA's instructions. The results of the checks are not stored in the database, but in the file system. This is because the nature of some errors is such that the database is not available: it is therefore essential to have an external repository for the Health Monitor results. This repository is the ADR, which is located in the directory specified by the DIAGNOSTIC_DEST instance parameter.

Different Health Monitor checks can run only at various stages:

- In nomount mode, only the "DB Structure Integrity" check can run, and it can only check the integrity of the controlfile.
- In mount mode, the "DB Structure Integrity" check will check the integrity of the controlfile, and of the online redo logfile and the datafile headers. The "Redo Integrity Check" can also run, which will check the online and archive logfiles for accessibility and corruption.
- In open mode, it is possible to run checks that will scan every data block for corruption, and check the integrity of the data dictionary and the undo segments.

The DRA can do nothing unless the instance is in nomount mode, or higher. It follows that it cannot assist if there is a problem with the initialization file. In nomount mode, it can diagnose problems with the controlfile and generate scripts to restore it, either by using an existing valid copy or (if none is available) by extracting a copy from a backup set—provided it can find one. Once the database can reach mount mode, the DRA can diagnose problems with missing or damaged datafiles and missing online logfile groups, and generate repair scripts.

Using the DRA

The Data Recovery Advisor makes use of information gathered by the Health Monitor to find problems, and then it constructs RMAN scripts to repair them. As with any RMAN-based utility, the instance must be started. To start an instance in nomount mode, all that is required is a parameter file. RMAN is in fact capable of starting an instance without a parameter file, using the ORACLE_SID environment variable as a default for the one parameter for which there is no default value: the DB_NAME parameter. This ability may mean that is possible to bootstrap a restore and recovery operation from nothing.

The flow for using the DRA is as follows:

- **Assess data failures** The Health Monitor, running reactively or on demand, will write error details to the ADR.
- **List failures** The DRA will list all failures, classified according to severity.
- **Advise on repair** The DRA will generate RMAN scripts to repair the damage.
- **Execute repair** Run the scripts.

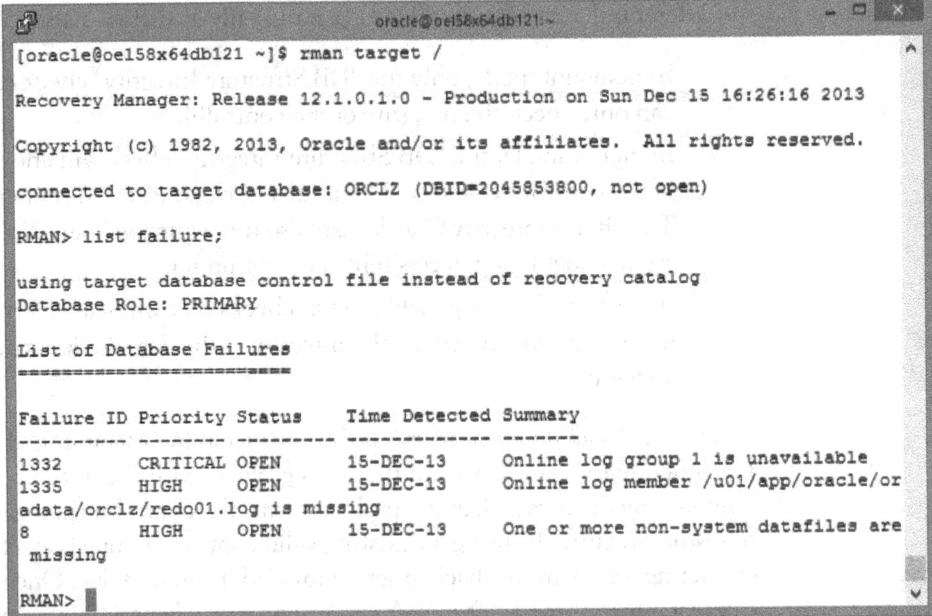

oracle@oel58x64db121:~
[oracle@oel58x64db121 ~]$ rman target /
Recovery Manager: Release 12.1.0.1.0 - Production on Sun Dec 15 16:26:16 2013
Copyright (c) 1982, 2013, Oracle and/or its affiliates. All rights reserved.
connected to target database: ORCLZ (DBID=2045853800, not open)
RMAN> list failure;
using target database control file instead of recovery catalog
Database Role: PRIMARY
List of Database Failures
=========================
Failure ID Priority Status Time Detected Summary
---------- -------- --------- ------------- -------
1332 CRITICAL OPEN 15-DEC-13 Online log group 1 is unavailable
1335 HIGH OPEN 15-DEC-13 Online log member /u01/app/oracle/or
adata/orclz/redo01.log is missing
8 HIGH OPEN 15-DEC-13 One or more non-system datafiles are
missing
RMAN>

FIGURE 19-2 Diagnosing a problem with the RDA

Run the commands from the RMAN executable. The advice will be generated only for errors previously listed and still open. No advice will be generated for additional errors that have occurred since the listing, or for errors fixed since the listing. Figure 19-2 shows a DRA session, launched from the RMAN executable. The situation is that the instance started and mounted the controlfile, but failed to open the database.

The **LIST FAILURE** command in Figure 19-2 identifies three problems. A critical problem is that one online logfile group is unavailable. This is considered "critical" because it will prevent the database from functioning. The second problem is that an online logfile member is missing. This is considered to be "high" priority, because the loss of one member may mean that the database can continue to function, although not in this case, because the member is not multiplexed. A second "high" priority problem is a missing datafile: this is not critical because it is a non-system datafile, and therefore can be taken offline before opening the database.

Figure 19-3 shows the next command in the DRA usage cycle: ADVISE FAILURE.

FIGURE 19-3 The DRA's recommendations

```
oracle@oel58x64db121:~
RMAN> advise failure;

Database Role: PRIMARY

List of Database Failures
=========================

Failure ID Priority Status    Time Detected Summary
---------- -------- --------- ------------- -------
1332       CRITICAL OPEN      15-DEC-13     Online log group 1 is unavailable
1335       HIGH     OPEN      15-DEC-13     Online log member /u01/app/oracle/or
adata/orclz/redo01.log is missing
8          HIGH     OPEN      15-DEC-13     One or more non-system datafiles are
 missing

analyzing automatic repair options; this may take some time
using channel ORA_DISK_1
analyzing automatic repair options complete

Mandatory Manual Actions
========================
no manual actions available

Optional Manual Actions
=======================
1. If file /u01/app/oracle/oradata/orclz/users01.dbf was unintentionally renamed
 or moved, restore it
2. If file /u01/app/oracle/oradata/orclz/redo01.log was unintentionally renamed
or moved, restore it

Automated Repair Options
========================
Option Repair Description
------ ------------------
1      Clear redo log group 1; Restore and recover datafile 6
  Strategy: The repair includes complete media recovery with no data loss
  Repair script: /u01/app/oracle/diag/rdbms/orclz/orclz/hm/reco_2681575513.hm

RMAN>
```

The first suggestion is that some error by the system administrators could be responsible for the problems and could be fixed manually. Then there is an automatic repair: clear the logfile group, and restore and recover the damaged file. This is in the form of an RMAN script. The contents of the script (not shown in the figure) are:

```
# clear redo log group
sql "begin
sys.dbms_ir.execsqlscript(filename =>
''/u01/app/oracle/diag/rdbms/orclz/orclz/hm/reco_2270m'' );
end;";
```

```
# restore and recover datafile
restore ( datafile 6 );
recover datafile 6;
sql 'alter database datafile 6 online';
```

Executing the **REPAIR FAILURE** command will cause RMAN to run the script, which will fix the problems. Note that the DRA does not generate the **CLEAR LOGFILE** command that one would use within SQL*Plus, but rather uses a PL/SQL procedure that has the same effect.

If the damage is to a controlfile copy, the instance will stop in nomount mode. Figure 19-4 shows the output of ADVISE FAILURE in this circumstance.

The script will replace the missing file by making use of the multiplexed copy.

FIGURE 19-4 Diagnosing a problem with the RDA

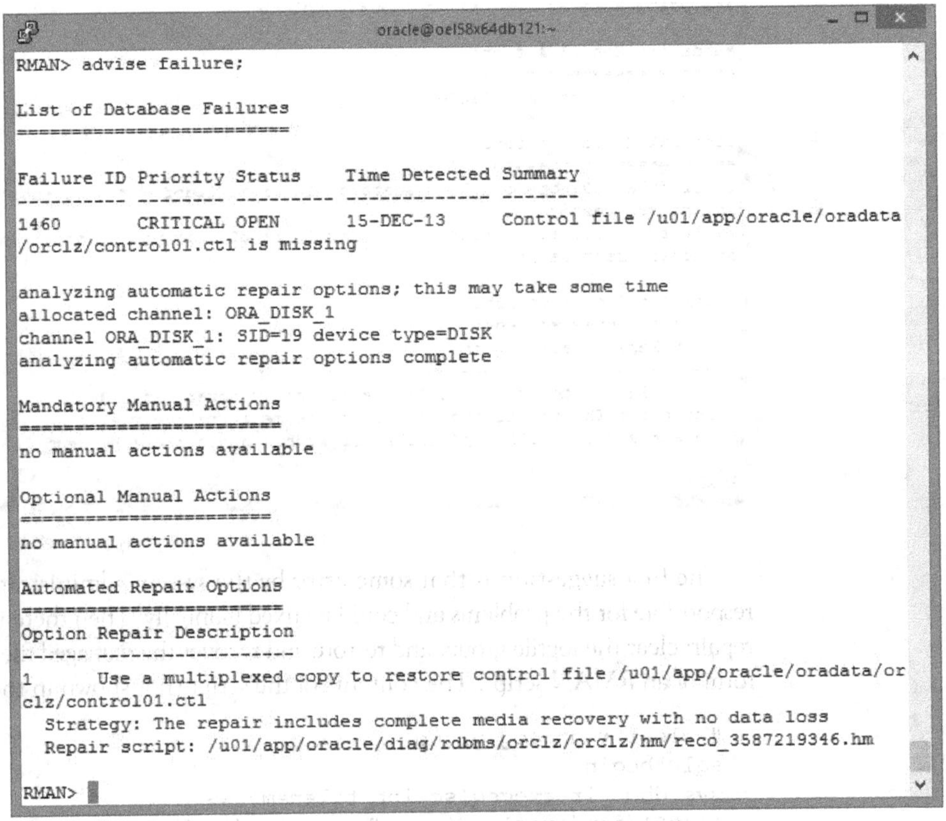

```
oracle@oel58x64db121:~
RMAN> advise failure;

List of Database Failures
=========================

Failure ID Priority Status    Time Detected Summary
---------- -------- --------- ------------- -------
1460       CRITICAL OPEN      15-DEC-13     Control file /u01/app/oracle/oradata
/orclz/control01.ctl is missing

analyzing automatic repair options; this may take some time
allocated channel: ORA_DISK_1
channel ORA_DISK_1: SID=19 device type=DISK
analyzing automatic repair options complete

Mandatory Manual Actions
========================
no manual actions available

Optional Manual Actions
=======================
no manual actions available

Automated Repair Options
========================
Option Repair Description
------ ------------------
1      Use a multiplexed copy to restore control file /u01/app/oracle/oradata/or
clz/control01.ctl
  Strategy: The repair includes complete media recovery with no data loss
  Repair script: /u01/app/oracle/diag/rdbms/orclz/orclz/hm/reco_3587219346.hm

RMAN>
```

EXERCISE 19-3

Use the DRA to Diagnose and Repair a Problem

In this exercise, you will cause a problem with the database and then use the DRA to fix it.

1. From an operating system prompt, connect to your database with RMAN.
2. Confirm that there is a backup of the SYSAUX tablespace:

   ```
   list backup of tablespace sysaux;
   ```

   If this does not return at least one backup set of type FULL, repeat Exercise 19-2.
3. Shut down the instance and exit from RMAN:

   ```
   shutdown immediate;
   exit;
   ```

4. Using an operating system utility, delete the datafile(s) for the SYSAUX tablespace that were listed in step 2. If using Windows, you may have to stop the Windows service under which the instance is running to release the Windows file lock before the deletion is possible.
5. Connect to the database with SQL*Plus and attempt a startup. This will stop in mount mode, with an error regarding the missing file. If you are using Windows, make sure the service has been started.
6. Launch the RMAN executable and connect, as in step 1.
7. Diagnose the problem:

   ```
   list failure;
   ```

   This will return a message to the effect that one or more non-system datafiles are missing.
8. Generate advice on the failure:

   ```
   advise failure;
   ```

   This will suggest that you should restore and recover the datafile, and generate a repair script. Open the script with any operating system editor and study its contents.
9. Repair the failure:

   ```
   repair failure;
   ```

   This will run the script, which will restore and recover the missing datafile(s). At the conclusion, there will be a prompt to open the database.

CERTIFICATION SUMMARY

This chapter introduces material vital for any DBA of any level to understand, but is unlikely to be tested in the OCA examinations. It is tested exhaustively in the second OCP examination.

The RMAN tool can back up datafiles and the controlfile while the database is mounted or (if the database is in archivelog mode) open. The spfile is included with controlfile backups. RMAN can also back up archive logfiles. The default destination for backups is the fast recovery area.

Restore and recovery with RMAN can be completely automatic. The Data Recovery Advisor will identify problems and run scripts that will fix them.

TWO-MINUTE DRILL

Create Consistent Database Backups

- Consistent (aka "closed" or "cold") backups are taken by RMAN when in mount mode.
- A full closed backup is the complete set of datafiles plus the controlfile.

Back Up Your Database Without Shutting It Down

- Open (aka "hot") backups are taken by RMAN while the database is in use.
- Open backups are possible only if the database is running in archivelog mode.
- Archive logfiles must also be backed up, or an open backup of the database will be useless.

Create Incremental Backups

- A level 0 incremental backup is the whole datafile, and can be used as the base for subsequent level 1 backups.
- A level 1 incremental backup is all blocks changed since the last level 1 backup, or the level 0 backup if no level 1 has yet been taken.
- A level 1 cumulative backup is all blocks changed since the last level 0 backup.

Automate Database Backups

- Enterprise Manager can schedule automatic backups.
- Scheduled backups use RMAN, invoked by the Enterprise Manager agent.

Manage Backups

- RMAN uses a repository. This is stored in the target database controlfile and (optionally) in a Recovery Catalog database.
- The repository stores information regarding all backups that have been made, and is vital for automating restore and recovery operations.

Determine the Need for Performing Recovery

- Information regarding problems is visible in the database alert log and various dynamic performance views.
- The database cannot mount if the controlfile is damaged.
- The database cannot open if datafiles are damaged—unless they are taken offline.
- Damage to a multiplexed redo logfile member is not critical.

Use Recovery Manager (RMAN) and the Data Recovery Advisor to Perform Recovery of the Controlfile, Redo Logfile, and Datafile

- The DRA automates the process of diagnosis and repair.
- The DRA process is:

```
LIST FAILURE;

ADVISE FAILURE;

REPAIR FAILURE;
```

SELF TEST

Create Consistent Database Backups

1. What file types can be backed up by RMAN? (Choose all correct answers.)

A. Archive logfiles
B. Controlfile
C. Online logfiles
D. Password file
E. Permanent tablespace datafiles
F. Server parameter file
G. Static parameter file
H. Temporary tablespace tempfiles

2. RMAN backup sets are smaller than RMAN image copies because…. (Choose the best answer.)

A. They always use compression.
B. They always skip unused blocks.
C. They never include tempfiles.
D. They can be written directly to tape.

Back Up Your Database Without Shutting It Down

3. Which of the following statements are correct about RMAN offline backup? (Choose all correct answers.)

A. The database must be in NOMOUNT mode.
B. The database must be in MOUNT mode.
C. The backup will fail if the shutdown mode was SHUTDOWN IMMEDIATE.
D. Noarchivelog databases can only be backed up offline.
E. Archivelog databases cannot be backed up offline.
F. Offline backups can be incremental.

4. You need to back up the controlfile while the database is open. What will work? (Choose the best answer.)

A. The controlfile can be included in an RMAN backup set, but not backed up as an image copy.
B. The **ALTER DATABASE BACKUP CONTROLFILE TO TRACE** command will make an image copy of the controlfile.
C. You cannot back up the controlfile while it is in use—it is protected by multiplexing.
D. None of the above.

Create Incremental Backups

5. You are setting up an incremental backup strategy. Which of these statements is correct?

   A. Before running an INCREMENTAL LEVEL 1 backup, you must run an INCREMENTAL LEVEL 0 backup.

   B. Either a FULL backup or an INCREMENTAL LEVEL 0 backup can be the basis for an INCREMENTAL LEVEL 1 backup.

   C. When restoring and recovering with incremental backups, archive logfiles are not needed.

   D. You cannot make an incremental backup of a database in NOARCHIVELOG mode.

   E. Running an INCREMENTAL LEVEL 1 backup will automatically perform an INCREMENTAL LEVEL 0 if none exits.

Automate Database Backups

6. What processes must be running if an RMAN backup scheduled within the Oracle environment is to run? (Choose all correct answers.)

   A. The database instance must be started.

   B. The Cloud Control management server must be running.

   C. The Enterprise Manager agent must be running.

   D. The operating system scheduler must be running.

Manage Backups

7. What is true about the **CROSSCHECK** command? (Choose the best answer.)

   A. Crosscheck will check the validity of the backup pieces.

   B. Crosscheck will delete references to files that no longer exist.

   C. Crosscheck will verify the existence of backup set pieces.

   D. Crosscheck only works with backup sets, not image copies.

8. If the volume of data in the fast recovery area has reached the limit defined by DB_RECOVERY_FILE_DEST_SIZE, what will happen when RMAN attempts to write more data to it? (Choose the best answer.)

   A. If AUTOEXTEND has been enabled and the MAXSIZE has not been reached, the fast recovery area will extend as necessary.

   B. The operation will fail.

   C. This will depend on whether warning and critical alerts have been enabled for the fast recovery area.

   D. RMAN will automatically delete OBSOLETE backups.

   E. RMAN will automatically delete EXPIRED backups.

Determine the Need for Performing Recovery

9. Loss of which of these files will cause an open database to crash? (Choose all correct answers.)

A. A multiplexed controlfile
B. A multiplexed online logfile
C. A multiplexed archive logfile
D. An active undo tablespace datafile
E. An active temporary tablespace tempfile
F. A datafile from the SYSAUX tablespace
G. A datafile from the SYSTEM tablespace
H. A datafile containing critical user data

10. Which of the following conditions will prevent a database from opening? (Choose three answers.)

A. Loss of a multiplexed controlfile
B. Loss of a multiplexed online logfile member
C. Loss of an offline datafile that is part of the SYSTEM tablespace
D. Loss of the tempfiles that make up the default temporary tablespace
E. Loss of all members of an inactive online logfile group

Use Recovery Manager (RMAN) and the Data Recovery Advisor to Perform Recovery of the Controlfile, Redo Logfile, and Datafile

11. These are three DRA commands:

```
ADVISE FAILURE;

LIST FAILURE;

REPAIR FAILURE;
```

In what order must they be run to fix a problem? (Choose the best answer.)

A. ADVISE, LIST, REPAIR
B. LIST, ADVISE, REPAIR
C. LIST, REPAIR (ADVISE is not necessary)
D. ADVISE, REPAIR (LIST is not necessary)

12. Where is the Automatic Diagnostic Repository stored? (Choose the best answer.)

A. In the Automatic Workload Repository
B. In the SYSAUX tablespace
C. In the data dictionary
D. In operating system files
E. In the Enterprise Manager repository

LAB QUESTION

Prepare for this extended exercise by taking a full backup of the database with RMAN. Be absolutely certain you do have a backup. Also confirm that you have at least two copies of the controlfile, and that your online redo logfiles are multiplexed.

Abort the database instance and then simulate a major failure by deleting a datafile, a controlfile copy, and a redo logfile member.

Attempt to start the database. To begin with, the instance will not be able to mount the database. In nomount mode, the DRA will be able to generate a script to copy a surviving controlfile to the missing location. The database can then be mounted but will not open until the missing datafile has been restored and recovered. The missing online redo logfile member can be replaced by clearing the logfile group after the database has been opened.

SELF TEST ANSWERS

Create Consistent Database Backups

1. ☑ **A, B, E,** and **F.** These are the database file types that the Recovery Manager can back up and restore.
   ☒ **C, D, G,** and **H** are incorrect. RMAN will never back up online redo logs or tempfiles because it is not necessary to back them up, and it cannot back up a static parameter file or the external password file.

2. ☑ **B.** A backup set will never include blocks that have never been used.
   ☒ **A, C,** and **D** are incorrect. **A** is incorrect because compression is an option, not enabled by default. **C** is incorrect because it applies to image copies as well as backup sets. **D** is incorrect because it is not relevant: an image copy can't go to tape, because if it did, it wouldn't be an image.

Back Up Your Database Without Shutting It Down

3. ☑ **B, D,** and **F.** Offline backups must be done in mount mode. This is the only backup type for a noarchivelog mode database, but it can be incremental.
   ☒ **A, C,** and **E** are incorrect. **A** is incorrect because the database must be mounted, or RMAN won't be able to connect to its repository or find the location of the datafiles. **C** is incorrect because an IMMEDIATE shutdown is clean—it is only an ABORT that would cause problems. **E** is incorrect because an archivelog mode database can certainly be backed up offline—it just isn't necessary.

4. ☑ **D.** In this case, **A, B,** and **C** are all incorrect.
   ☒ **A, B,** and **C** are incorrect. **A** is incorrect because a copy of the controlfile can be created while the database is open, via a read-consistent snapshot. **B** is incorrect because this command will generate a CREATE CONTROLFILE script, not a file copy. **C** is incorrect because the file multiplexing is an additional precaution, not the only one.

Create Incremental Backups

5. ☑ **E.** RMAN will detect the absence of a suitable backup on which to base the incremental, and will therefore make a level 0 backup.
   ☒ **A, B, C,** and **D** are incorrect. **A** is incorrect because this will occur automatically. **B** is incorrect because FULL cannot be used as the base for any INCREMENTAL. **C** is incorrect because redo is required to fill the gap between the last incremental backup and the current time. **D** is incorrect because an incremental strategy can be used with NOARCHIVELOG mode, so long as the backup is made while the database is closed.

Automate Database Backups

6. ☑ **A, B,** and **C.** The Enterprise Manager will instruct the agent to run the backup. The database instance must be running, or the agent will not be able to contact it and start RMAN.
   ☒ **D** is incorrect. Oracle-scheduled backups do not use the operating system scheduler.

Manage Backups

7. ☑ **C.** The **CROSSCHECK** command verifies that the repository does accurately reflect reality.
   ☒ **A, B,** and **D** are incorrect. **A** is incorrect because crosscheck does not validate whether the backups are good—only whether they exist. **B** is incorrect because crosscheck doesn't delete references to missing backups; it only flags them as expired. **D** is incorrect because crosscheck confirms the existence of both backup sets and image copies.
8. ☑ **D.** Backups that are OBSOLETE according to RMAN's retention policy will be removed.
   ☒ **A, B, C,** and **E** are incorrect. **A** is incorrect because this describes datafiles, not the fast recovery area. **B** is incorrect because the operation will not necessarily fail—it may be possible to free up space automatically. **C** is incorrect because the alert system will only report the problem; it won't fix it. **E** is incorrect because EXPIRED refers to the status of the backup record in the repository, not the backup itself.

Determine the Need for Performing Recovery

9. ☑ **A, D,** and **G.** If any files of these types are lost, the instance will abort immediately.
   ☒ **B, C, E, F,** and **H** are incorrect. **B** is incorrect because the whole purpose of multiplexing the redo log is to survive a failure. **C** is incorrect because nothing that happens to an archived logfile can affect the instance. **E, F,** and **H** are incorrect because the instance can take these file types offline automatically and so remain open.
10. ☑ **A, C,** and **E.** It is not possible to open a database if any copy of the controlfile is damaged, or if all members of any logfile group are missing. Datafiles that are part of the SYSTEM tablespace cannot be taken offline.
   ☒ **B** and **D** are incorrect. **B** is incorrect because online logfile member is not a critical file—if it is multiplexed. **D** is incorrect because tempfiles are never considered critical. They will be re-created automatically if they are missing.

Use Recovery Manager (RMAN) and the Data Recovery Advisor to Perform Recovery of the Controlfile, Redo Logfile, and Datafile

11. ☑ **B.** This is the only sequence that will work.
   ☒ **A, C,** and **D** are incorrect. **A** is incorrect because the sequence is incorrect. **C** is incorrect because ADVISE is necessary to generate the repair script. **D** is incorrect because LIST is necessary to identify the problem.

12. ☑ **D.** The ADR resides in files in the DIAGNOSTIC_DEST directory.
☒ **A, B, C,** and **E** are incorrect. **A, B,** and **C** are incorrect because they all imply storage within the database, which is not correct. **E** is incorrect because although Enterprise Manager can read the ADR, it does not manage it.

LAB ANSWER

Once you are in nomount mode, connect with RMAN. Use LIST FAILURE, ADVISE FAILURE, and REPAIR FAILURE. At this stage, this will only detect and repair the controlfile problem, but you can now mount the database. Repeat the LIST-ADVISE-REPAIR cycle to repair the datafile damage and the missing online logfile member, and open the database.

20

Installing Oracle Grid Infrastructure for a Standalone Server

CERTIFICATION OBJECTIVES

20.01	Configure Storage for Oracle Automatic Storage Management (ASM)	✓	Two-Minute Drill
20.02	Install Oracle Grid Infrastructure for a Standalone Server	Q&A	Self Test

This chapter describes the installation of Grid Infrastructure (GI). GI is a separately installed product that provides clustering, networking, storage, and high availability services for Oracle databases. It is required for Real Application Clusters (RAC) databases, and can also be used with single-instance databases. In a single-instance environment, GI is usually used to provide Automatic Storage Management (ASM) devices for storing database files (as described in this chapter) and to provide an automatic restart capability in the event of failures (as described in Chapter 21). The treatment of GI in the OCA syllabus is limited to using the restart capability in the single-instance environment, although concepts of ASM may also be examined.

CERTIFICATION OBJECTIVE 20.01

Configure Storage for Oracle Automatic Storage Management (ASM)

Grid Infrastructure includes the capability to manage storage to be used for Oracle database files: ASM. In earlier releases (up to release 11.1.x) ASM was shipped as part of the database software, but from 11.2.x onward it is part of GI. GI is a set of processes that run as part of the operating system: on Windows, services that run with Administrator privileges; on Linux, daemons that run with root privileges. The GI processes start an ASM instance. In some ways, an ASM instance resembles the RDBMS instance with which all DBAs are familiar, but its purpose is very different: it manages devices that are made available to RDBMS instances for file storage. These devices must be configured by the system administrator before installing GI.

GI Architecture

GI consists of a set of processes, all of which are protected against failure. The core process is the High Availability Services daemon, the OHASD. This is protected by the operating system. If it fails, the OS will restart it. The OHASD then starts and monitors a set of other processes, which in turn will start and monitor resources used by database instances. These resources are ASM and database listeners.

on the job

You can run database listeners from a database home or from a GI home. It is considered to be best practice to run them from the GI home if GI has been installed.

GI maintains a registry of resources that run under its control. These resources may include any or all of the following:

- Database listeners
- Virtual IP addresses
- An ASM instance (one only)
- ASM disk groups
- Database instances
- Third-party products

The registry exists in a file: the Oracle Local Registry, or OLR. The location of the OLR is specified by a platform-specific pointer. On Linux, the pointer is the file /etc/oracle/olr.loc. On Windows, it is the registry key HKEY_LOCAL_MACHINE/SOFTWARE/Oracle/olr/olrconfig_loc.

Resources are registered in the OLR using the crsctl utility. These registrations include details of how to start and stop the resources, the operating accounts under which they should run, and what to do if they fail. The GI daemons make use of this information to manage the resources.

watch

GI processes and any resources can be administered with the crsctl utility. The srvctl utility can manage only Oracle resources: it cannot manage GI or third-party resources.

The crsctl utility is also used to stop and start the GI processes themselves, including the OHASD, and to administer registered resources. An alternative administration tool is the srvctl utility. srvctl can manage Oracle resources, but not any third-party products that may have been registered and placed under GI control. It is generally much easier to use syntactically (and is less prone to error) than the crsctl utility.

ASM Architecture

ASM is a logical volume manager (LVM) that can be used to configure striped and mirrored volumes for storing Oracle database files. These volumes are known as disk groups. Disk groups are not formatted with a file system that is visible to the operating system: they can be used only for Oracle database files, and these files can be managed only with Oracle products and utilities.

To understand the relationship between an ASM file and an Oracle database file, study the entity-relationship diagram presented in Figure 20-1.

In the leftmost column of Figure 20-1 is the logical storage structure with which all DBAs must be familiar. The next column over shows the usual physical structures: datafiles formatted into operating system blocks. The ASM structures are shown in the two right-hand columns. In an ASM environment, the datafile becomes an ASM file. ASM files reside on a disk group, consisting of one or more ASM disks. The ASM disks are formatted into allocation units (or AUs). AUs are grouped into file extents, and a file consists of one or more file extents. There is, in effect, a many-to-one relationship between ASM files and ASM disks: one file can be spread across many disks, and one disk can hold parts of many files. This many-to-one relationship is resolved in two ways: by the disk group entity, and by the file extent and AU route. Any one file extent consists of consecutive AUs on one physical disk. An ASM file is defined by its *extent map*—that is, the list of pointers to the physical locations of its file extents.

FIGURE 20-1 The ASM storage model

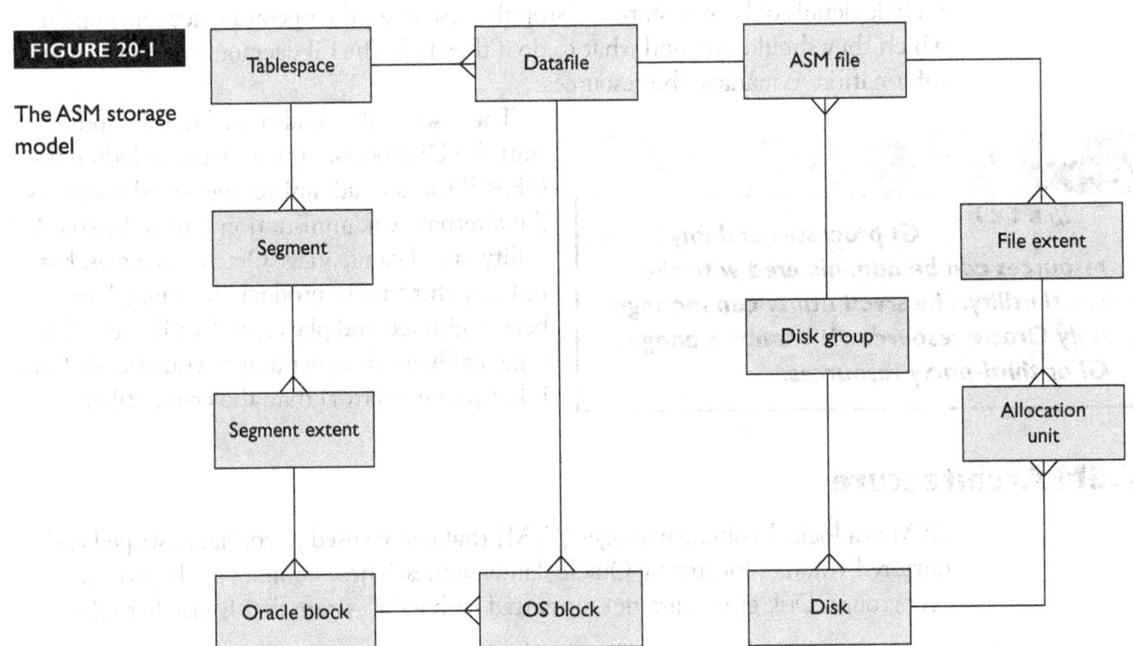

ASM is managed by the ASM instance. The ASM instance is memory components and background processes: a lightweight structure that manages the ASM environment. It tracks the extent maps that define file locations, adding or removing file extents to or from files according to demands from the RDBMS instance using the file.

The ASM instance has an SGA, and it accepts sessions in the same way that an RDBMS instance does, but it is never in any mode other than NOMOUNT. An ASM instance never mounts a controlfile; it has no data dictionary. Therefore, the only way to log on is by using operating system authentication or password file authentication.

The ASM bootstrap:

1. The operating system starts the GI processes.
2. GI starts the ASM instance.
3. The ASM instance locates the ASM disk devices.
4. The ASM instance mounts the disk groups and registers them with GI.
5. The RDBMS instance identifies that a file is on an ASM disk group.
6. The RDBMS requests the ASM instance address from GI.
7. The RDBMS instance logs on to the ASM instance and requests access to the ASM file.
8. The ASM instance returns the file's extent map.
9. The RDBMS instance opens the file.

In summary, when opening an ASM file, GI facilitates the connection between the RDBMS and ASM instances, then the ASM instance facilitates the connection between the RDBMS instance and the file.

No data ever passes through an ASM instance. All I/O is between the RDBMS instance and the file. The ASM instance is only a control structure.

An ASM disk group can store only database files, but it is a broad definition of database files and incudes these files types:

- Controlfiles
- Datafiles

- Tempfiles
- Online logfiles
- Archive logfiles
- Server parameter file, the spfile
- Password file
- RMAN backups
- Data Pump dump files

These file types cannot be stored on an ASM disk group:

- The Oracle Home
- Trace files or the alert log
- A pfile initialization file
- User-managed backups

ASM Disks

The term "ASM disk" is a little misleading, because the devices are not actually disks. The possibilities are:

- Partitions of directly attached storage (DAS) devices
- Storage area network (SAN) devices
- Network-attached storage (NAS) devices

DAS devices are disks physically attached to the server. Typically, this means SCSI disks or some variation thereof. In earlier releases, it was possible to give the entire, raw disk to ASM to use as an ASM disk. This was rarely advisable, and is no longer possible. It is now required that the disks have a partition table, even if this defines only one partition covering the entire disk. The partition is then presented to ASM.

SAN devices will usually be striped (and possibly mirrored) volumes managed by a storage array and attached to the server over a fiber optic channel. They will be presented to ASM as LUNs. There is no practical limit to the size that these volumes may be. Striping the volumes with whatever RAID algorithm is considered appropriate will improve performance. Mirroring can be enabled at the SAN level or managed by ASM.

NAS devices will typically be iSCSI volumes or NFS files. An iSCSI device is exported to the network by an iSCSI target machine, and mounted on the database server by an iSCSI initiator. NFS files will exist as large zero-filled files on an NFS volume exported from an NFS server and mounted by the database server. The underlying storage for NAS devices may of course be a RAID device: the NAS layer will conceal this from ASM. The local area network connection between database server and storage server should be high speed and dedicated to this function. Multipathing is advisable to add bandwidth and resilience against network failures.

DAS, SAN, or iSCSI devices (which should not be formatted with any file system) are identified by their device drivers. NFS files are identified by their fully qualified filename. Either way, the ASM instance needs to determine what devices it should use. An ASM instance is controlled by a parameter file, in the same way as an RDBMS instance. One critical parameter is ASM_DISKSTRING. This is a comma-separated list of values (which may include wildcard characters) that identify the ASM disks. The manner of naming the devices, and therefore the values to include in the ASM_DISKSTRING, is platform specific. These are the default values for some popular operating systems:

AIX	/dev/rhdisk*
HP-UX	/dev/rdisk/*
Solaris	/dev/rdsk/*
Windows	\\.\ORCLDISK*
Linux	/dev/raw/*
On Linux if using ASMLib Kernel Driver	ORCL:*

It is important to note that the default value may find disks that are not intended for ASM's use. If this is the case, it is imperative to set the parameter such that it will find only appropriate devices.

Creating ASM Disks

Disk creation will be done by your system administrator. Subsequently, each disk device will be accessed through a device driver. Device drivers are created by the operating system as it boots. During boot-up, the operating system scans the various I/O buses and creates a device driver for each device it finds. Because this is a dynamic process, it is possible that any one device may be assigned to a different device driver on each boot. Furthermore, following creation the device drivers will be root owned.

To make devices usable by ASM, it is necessary that the names should be persistent across system restarts and that the drivers should be readable and writeable by the Oracle processes. On Linux, there are two techniques for this:

- **The ASMLib kernel library** This library is available for some Linux distributions, depending on your Linux license.
- **The udev facility** This facility runs scripts written by your system administrator that identify devices and set appropriate ownership and permissions.

To configure devices on Windows, Oracle supplies the asmtool.exe utility. Other operating systems will have their own platform-specific techniques for managing device ownership and name persistence.

If you are using NFS files as ASM disks, create them with commands such as these, which create a 1TB file, and give access to the Oracle owner:

```
dd if=/dev/zero of=/asm/disk1 bs=1048576 count=1048576
chown oracle:dba /asm/disk1
chmod 660 /asm/disk1
```

The details of creating ASM disks are beyond the scope of the OCA examination, and there are many platform variations.

CERTIFICATION OBJECTIVE 20.02

Install Oracle Grid Infrastructure for a Standalone Server

GI is installed into a dedicated Oracle Home. The release of GI must be greater than or equal to the release of any database that intends to use the GI services. It is, for example, possible for a 12.1.x GI installation to service an 11.2.x database—but not the other way around. GI must always be running on the same nodes as the database instances. It is, however, possible in a clustered environment to configure Flex ASM, where only a small number of nodes (by default, three) run ASM instances.

The GI installation media include a copy of the Oracle Universal Installer (OUI). Run this (the executable is the runInstaller.sh shell script on Unix, the setup.exe file on Windows) and follow the prompts. These are the major choices:

- **Download Software Updates** Choose whether to register the installation with My Oracle Support, to facilitate downloading patches and updates.
- **Select Installation Option** What type of dialog box should the OUI present? The options are:
  - Install and Configure Oracle Grid Infrastructure for a Cluster
  - Install and Configure Oracle Grid Infrastructure for a Standalone Server
  - Upgrade Oracle Grid Infrastructure or Oracle Automatic Storage Management
  - Install Oracle Grid Infrastructure Software Only
- **Create ASM Disk Group** Set the ASM_DISKSTRING discovery path and choose disks to be used for a disk group.

Figure 20-2 shows the window that prompts for creating a disk group. This window is part of the dialog box presented by the Install and Configure installation options.

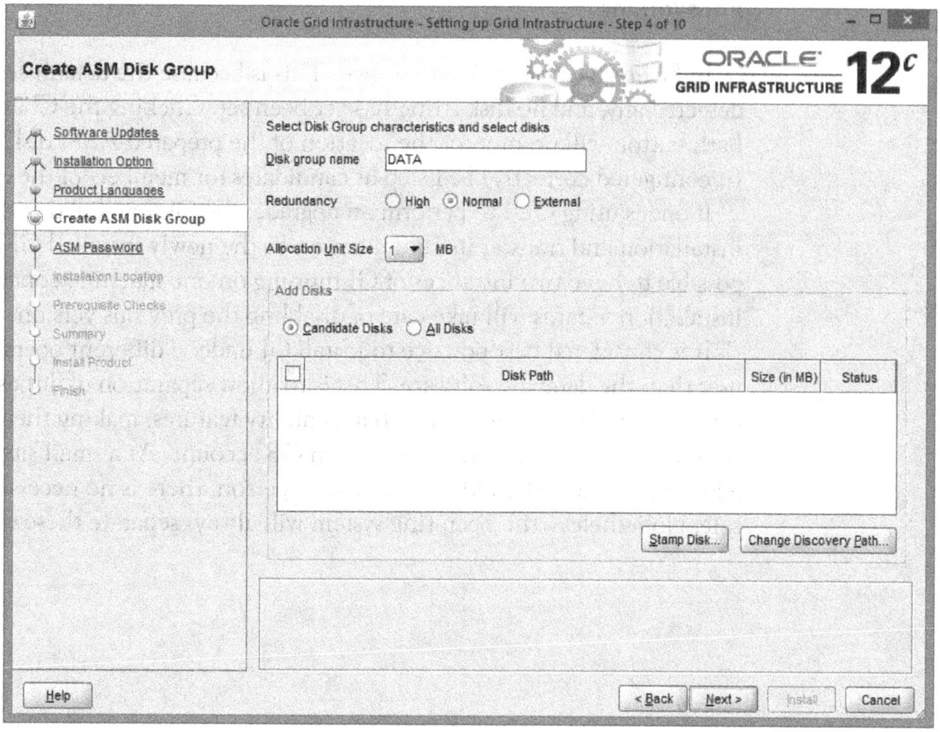

FIGURE 20-2

Creating an ASM disk group during GI install

In the figure, note that by default, Redundancy is set to Normal, meaning that unless specified otherwise every extent of every file created on this disk group will be mirrored. This means that the group must consist of at least two disks, because there would be little point in creating a mirror copy on the same device as the primary copy, and ASM will not permit this. The other radio buttons are High, meaning that three copies will be made of each extent (and at least three disks required), and External, meaning that ASM will not mirror at all but rather rely on fault tolerance provided by the storage medium.

The allocation unit (AU) size defaults to 1MB. This has a knock-on effect on the file extent size. The first 20,000 extents of any file are one AU, the next 20,000 extents are four AUs, and beyond that they are 16 AUs. AU size can be set to 1, 2, 4, 8, 16, 32, or 64MB. It applies to all files on the disk group, and can never be changed after disk group creation.

on the job

Opinion is tending toward 4MB being the optimal AU size for large systems, and is recommended by Oracle for Exadata installations. But in the context of ASM, "large" does mean "very large indeed." In fact, 1MB will be fine for most installations.

In Figure 20-2, no disks are shown. This is because the default search path has not detected any, and no disk string has yet been set. Clicking the Change Discovery Path button will prompt for the location of the prepared ASM disks, which will then (if configured correctly) be listed as candidates for members of the disk group.

If one is using OUI to perform an upgrade, the OUI will detect the existing installation and transfer its configuration to the newly installed GI home. It is not possible to have two instances of GI running on one machine concurrently, and the installation wizards will take care of disabling the previous version.

It is considered best practice to install GI under a different operating system user than the database software. This is to allow separation of duties: one OS user can manage GI's storage and high availability features, making them available to several DBAs who each have their own OS account. At a small site, where the GI administrator and the DBA are the same person, there is no necessity to follow this rule. Nonetheless, the operating system will always separate these roles through the use of operating system groups. The GI administrator must be a member of the OSASM group. The name of this group is hardcoded on Windows as ORA_ASMDBA, and the group is created implicitly. On Unix, the group can be named anything and must be created before running OUI.

EXERCISE 20-1

Install Grid Infrastructure

In this exercise, you will install the GI software and configure it for use. It is assumed that the software has been downloaded and unzipped. The routine is slightly different on Windows and Linux.

1. Follow these steps on Windows:
   a. Launch the OUI dialog box by running the setup.exe file. You will need to do this from a command prompt started with the Run As Administrator privilege.
   b. In the Download Software Updates window, select the Skip Software Updates radio button. Click Next.
   c. In the Select Installation Option window, select the Install Grid Infrastructure Software Only radio button. Click Next.
   d. In the Select Install Type window, select the Install Oracle Grid Infrastructure for a Standalone Server radio button. Click Next.
   e. In the Select Product Languages window, choose any languages you want. Click Next.
   f. In the Specify Installation Location, adjust the directory if you wish (the default is usually fine). Click Next.
   g. In the Perform Prerequisite Checks window, any "failed" checks should be addressed and a decision made about whether they are likely to matter in your case. Warnings (for example, regarding Windows security issues) can usually be ignored. Check the Ignore All box, and click Next.
   h. In the Summary window, click Install.

i. After the install completes, the Finish window, shown next, will prompt you to run the operating system command necessary to configure GI for a standalone server.

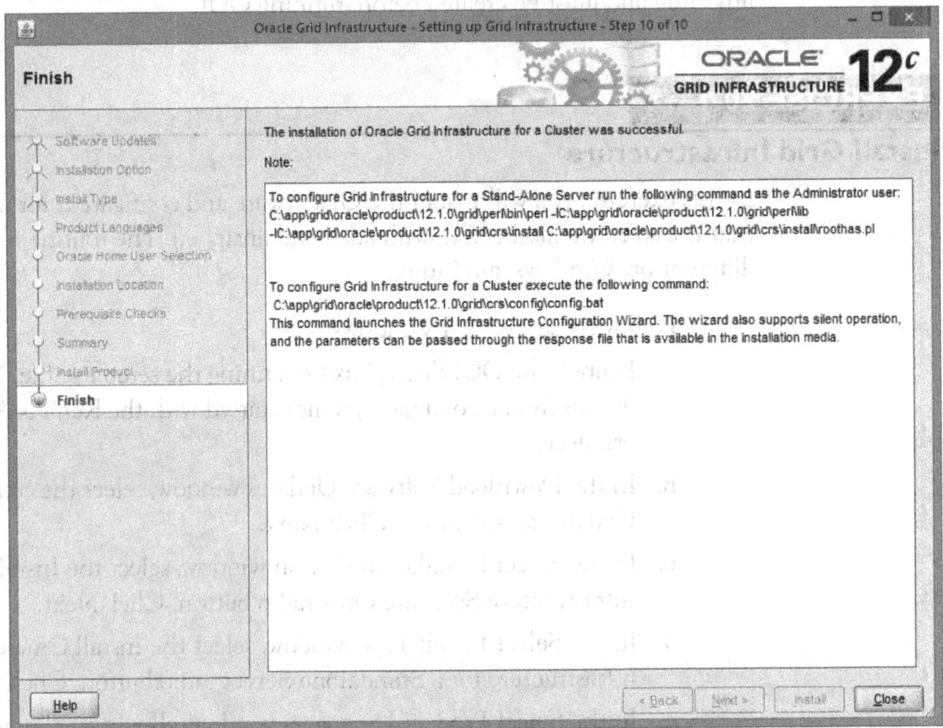

In the illustration, the command, which must be run as Administrator, and is one long command with no line breaks (copy/paste will be useful), is:

```
C:\app\grid\oracle\product\12.1.0\grid\perl\bin\perl
-IC:\app\grid\oracle\product\12.1.0\grid\perl\lib
-IC:\app\grid\oracle\product\12.1.0\grid\crs\install
C:\app\grid\oracle\product\12.1.0\grid\crs\install\roothas.pl
```

After running the command, click Close to exit from the installer.

2. Follow these steps on Linux:
   a. Launch the OUI dialog box in a graphical session by running the runInstaller shell script. This cannot be done as the root user. Using the same account that was used for the Oracle software install will be fine (although for a production site, one would usually create a separate OS user to install GI).
   b. In the Download Software Updates window, select the Skip Software Updates radio button. Click Next.
   c. In the Select Installation Option window, select the Install Grid Infrastructure Software Only radio button. Click Next.
   d. In the Select Product Languages window, choose any languages you want. Click Next.
   e. In the Privileged Operating System Groups window, if you are running the installer as the same user who installed the Oracle software, select the group dba for all three groups (OSASM, OSDBA for ASM, and OSOPER for ASM).
   f. In the Specify Installation Location window, adjust the directory if you wish (the default is usually fine). Click Next.
   g. In the Perform Prerequisite Checks window, you can usually ignore Warnings. Any "failed" checks should be addressed. For instance, a failure of the test for an NTP daemon will not matter; a failure on file permissions would. Check the Ignore All box, and click Next.
   h. In the Summary window, click Install.
   i. Execute Configuration Scripts is a popup window that will prompt you to run a script named something like /u01/app/12.1.0.grid/root.sh as root.

Execute this script from a root session, accepting the defaults for any prompts. The following illustration shows the result of a typical run.

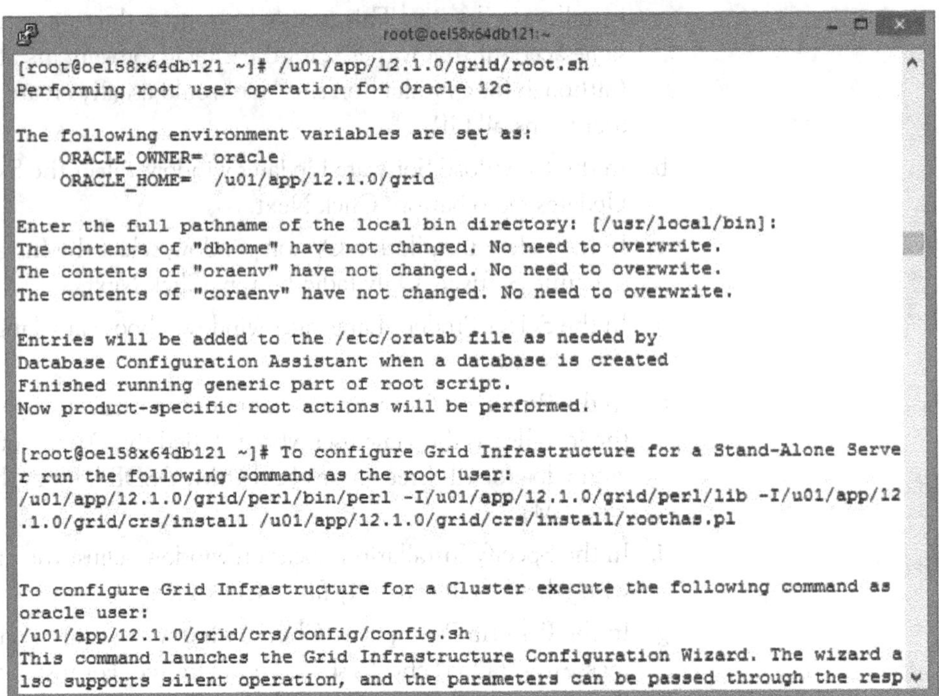

j. Still in your root session, run the command generated by the root.sh script that will complete the configuration for a standalone server. This is one long command, with no line breaks. In the preceding illustration, the command is:

```
/u01/app/12.1.0/grid/perl/bin/perl
-I/u01/app/12.1.0/grid/perl/lib
-I/u01/app/12.1.0/grid/crs/install
/u01/app/12.1.0/grid/crs/install/roothas.pl
```

Following completion, return to the OUI window and click OK and Close.

3. To confirm the successful installation, use the crsctl utility. This will be in the bin directory beneath the directory chosen for the installation. Here is an example on Windows:

```
cd \app\grid\oracle\product\12.1.0\grid\bin
crsctl config has
crsctl status resource
```

And on Linux:

```
cd /u01/app/12.1.0/grid/bin
./crsctl config has
./crsctl status resource
```

These commands will show that the High Availability Service (HAS) is enabled and that the Event Management Daemon is running, as shown in the following illustration:

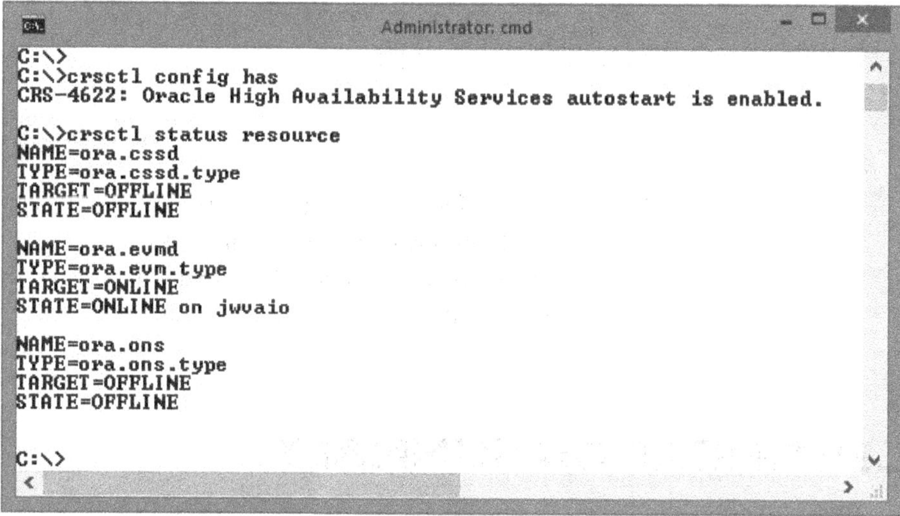

4. Investigate the automatic startup of the GI processes.

   a. On Windows, GI is launched by a Windows service. Check its configuration and status with the sc utility, as shown in this illustration:

```
c:\>sc qc OracleOHService
[SC] QueryServiceConfig SUCCESS

SERVICE_NAME: OracleOHService
        TYPE               : 10  WIN32_OWN_PROCESS
        START_TYPE         : 2   AUTO_START
        ERROR_CONTROL      : 1   NORMAL
        BINARY_PATH_NAME   : C:\app\grid\oracle\product\12.1.0\grid\bin\ohasd.exe
        LOAD_ORDER_GROUP   :
        TAG                : 0
        DISPLAY_NAME       : OracleOHService
        DEPENDENCIES       :
        SERVICE_START_NAME : LocalSystem

c:\>sc query OracleOHService

SERVICE_NAME: OracleOHService
        TYPE               : 10  WIN32_OWN_PROCESS
        STATE              : 4  RUNNING
                                (STOPPABLE, PAUSABLE, ACCEPTS_SHUTDOWN)
        WIN32_EXIT_CODE    : 0  (0x0)
        SERVICE_EXIT_CODE  : 0  (0x0)
        CHECKPOINT         : 0x0
        WAIT_HINT          : 0x0

c:\>
```

   b. On Linux, GI is launched through the rc system. Look for the file /etc/rc.d/init.d/init.ohasd and links to it in the various rc directories. There will also be an entry in /etc/inittab that will respawn the init.ohasd process if it fails.

CERTIFICATION SUMMARY

Grid Infrastructure provides support services for Oracle databases and other products. These services may include:

- Virtual IP addresses
- Storage
- Monitoring and restart in the event of failure

The processes that make up GI are launched, and protected, automatically by whatever mechanism is provided by the operating system for running background services. The GI configuration is stored in the Oracle Local Registry (OLR). The OLR is a file created at install time and located via a platform-specific mechanism.

A major function of GI is to run an ASM instance that will manage storage for Oracle databases. Storage is made available in the form of ASM disk groups. A disk group is a logical volume striped across one or more physical volumes. The physical volumes are known as ASM disks, although in practice they are probably not disks: they are more likely to be SAN or NAS devices. Whatever they are, they are presented as raw devices, not formatted with any file system. Files are stored in disk groups as a set of file extents composed of one or more allocation units. The ASM instance serves out the extent maps that act as locators for the files to RDBMS instances as necessary. The RDBMS instances are then responsible for all I/O on the files.

TWO-MINUTE DRILL

Configure Storage for Oracle Automatic Storage Management (ASM)

- ❑ An ASM disk group stores only database files; it has no normal file system.
- ❑ ASM disks are unformatted DAS, SAN, or NAS devices.
- ❑ The ASM instance is a control structure only: no data passes through it.

Install Oracle Grid Infrastructure for a Standalone Server

- ❑ GI must be installed into its own Oracle home.
- ❑ To configure GI requires root (Linux) or Administrator (Windows) privileges.
- ❑ The ASM disk search string can be set at install time, or changed later.
- ❑ The GI daemons are launched by the operating system on boot-up.

SELF TEST

Configure Storage for Oracle Automatic Storage Management (ASM)

1. What file types and directories can be stored with ASM? (Choose all that apply.)
   - A. Alert log
   - B. Controlfiles
   - C. Datafiles
   - D. Online redo logfiles
   - E. Oracle Home directory
   - F. Tempfiles

2. Which of the following recovery files can be stored with ASM? (Choose all that apply.)
   - A. Archive redo logfiles
   - B. RMAN backup sets
   - C. RMAN image copies
   - D. User-managed backups
   - E. The flash recovery area

3. What are the default characteristics of ASM files? (Choose the best answer.)
   - A. The files will be striped for performance but not mirrored for safety.
   - B. The files will be mirrored for safety but not striped for performance.
   - C. The files will be both striped and mirrored.
   - D. The files will be neither striped nor mirrored.

4. What statement is correct about ASM and logical volume managers (LVMs)? (Choose the best answer.)
   - A. ASM is itself an LVM and cannot work with a third-party LVM.
   - B. ASM can use LVM volumes, if they are formatted with a file system.
   - C. You can use ASM for striping and the LVM for mirroring.
   - D. You can use ASM for mirroring and the LVM for striping.

5. How can you connect to an ASM instance? (Choose the best answer.)
   - A. By using operating system authentication only
   - B. By using password file authentication only
   - C. By using data dictionary authentication only
   - D. By using either operating system or password file authentication

6. What does ASM stripe? (Choose the best answer.)
   A. Files across all disk groups
   B. Disks across all disk groups
   C. Disk groups across all disks
   D. Files across all disks in a group

Install Oracle Grid Infrastructure for a Standalone Server

7. You want to make Grid Infrastructure services available to your database. Where can the software be installed? (Choose the best answer.)
   A. Into the database Oracle Home, if it is the same release
   B. Into an Oracle Home on a machine accessible to all databases over a network
   C. Into a dedicated Oracle Home on each machine running a database
   D. All of the above
8. What utilities can you use to start and stop the GI High Availability Services? (Choose two correct answers.)
   A. crsctl
   B. SQL*Plus
   C. srvctl
   D. Windows net start utility

LAB EXERCISE

In this extended exercise, you will attempt to set up ASM. Following completion of Exercise 20-1, you will have the HAS (the GI High Availability Services) running, but you will not have an ASM instance. If you have an environment where you can create raw devices, do this and proceed straight to step 2.

Step 1: Create simulated raw devices.
On Linux, use the **dd** command to create a set of files for use as ASM devices, filled with NULLs. For example, this command will create a 2GB file and clear all access restrictions:

```
mkdir /u01/asm
dd if=/dev/zero of=/u01/asm/d1 bs=1024 count=2147483648
chmod 777 /u01/asm
chmod 666 /u01/asm/d1
```

Windows does not ship with an equivalent of the dd utility. Therefore, on Windows, use any third-party tool you wish to create the files. Note that the size must be a multiple of 1KB.

Step 2: Create an ASM parameter file.
The file should be named init+ASM.ora and placed in the dbs directory beneath the GI home on Linux or in the database directory beneath the GI home on Windows. Only one parameter is needed: the parameter that sets the disk string to the location of the disks. If you are using simulated devices, also include an undocumented parameter that permits the use of files rather than disks. This technique is certainly not supported by Oracle Corporation, but is useful for research and development. This is an example of what the file should contain:

```
_asm_allow_only_raw_disks=false
asm_diskstring='/u01/asm/d*'
```

Step 3: Start the CSSD daemon.
The CSSD resource must be running. This is the process with which ASM instances register. Set your search path and Oracle Home, and then start the CSSD.

Here is an example on Linux:

```
export ORACLE_HOME=/u01/app/12.1.0/grid
export Path=$ORACLE_HOME/bin:$PATH
export ORACLE_SID=+ASM
crsctl start resource ora.cssd
```

Here is an example on Windows:

```
set ORACLE_HOME=C:\app\grid\oracle\product\12.1.0\grid
set PATH=%ORACLE_HOME%\bin;%PATH%
set ORACLE_SID=+ASM
crsctl start resource ora.cssd
```

Step 4: Start the ASM instance.
With the environment set as for step 3, launch SQL*Plus, connect AS SYSASM, and start the ASM instance. On Windows, the service must be created first. The following illustration shows this:

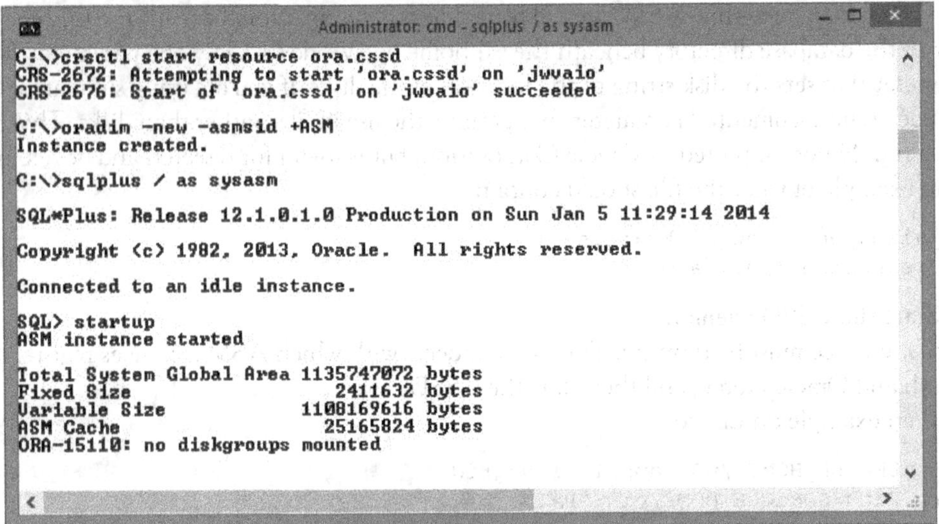

```
C:\>crsctl start resource ora.cssd
CRS-2672: Attempting to start 'ora.cssd' on 'jwvaio'
CRS-2676: Start of 'ora.cssd' on 'jwvaio' succeeded

C:\>oradim -new -asmsid +ASM
Instance created.

C:\>sqlplus / as sysasm

SQL*Plus: Release 12.1.0.1.0 Production on Sun Jan 5 11:29:14 2014

Copyright (c) 1982, 2013, Oracle.  All rights reserved.

Connected to an idle instance.

SQL> startup
ASM instance started

Total System Global Area 1135747072 bytes
Fixed Size                  2411632 bytes
Variable Size            1108169616 bytes
ASM Cache                  25165824 bytes
ORA-15110: no diskgroups mounted
```

Step 5: Investigate the disks available and create a disk group. Here is an example:

```
select path, header_status, os_mb from v$asm_disk;
create diskgroup dg1 external redundancy
disk 'c:\tmp\asm\d1','c:\tmp\asm\d2';
select name,state,total_mb from v$asm_diskgroup;
```

Step 6: Tidy up.
In SQL*Plus, connect AS SYSASM and abort the ASM instance. Stop the CSSD resource with the crsctl utility. On Windows, use the oradim utility to delete the Windows ASM service.

SELF TEST ANSWERS

Configure Storage for Oracle Automatic Storage Management (ASM)

1. ☑ **B, C, D,** and **F.** You can use ASM for database files, such as the controlfile, the datafiles, the tempfiles, and the online logfiles.
   ☒ **A** and **E** are incorrect. Your Oracle Home and the alert and trace files must be on conventional storage.
2. ☑ **A, B, C,** and **E.** Archive logs, RMAN backups and image copies, and indeed the whole flash recovery area can be on ASM.
   ☒ **D** is incorrect. You cannot direct user-managed backups to ASM, because operating system utilities cannot write to ASM devices.
3. ☑ **C.** By default, files are both striped and mirrored, because this is the default when creating a disk group and will be applied to all files unless specified otherwise.
   ☒ **A, B,** and **D** are incorrect. You can disable the mirroring by using the EXTERNAL REDUNDANCY option when you create the disk group, or by specifying this for any particular file. You cannot disable the striping (and you would not want to).
4. ☑ **C.** This is probably the best way to use ASM: to rely on an LVM to provide fault tolerance, and ASM to provide Oracle-aware striping.
   ☒ **A, B,** and **D** are incorrect. ASM can use any devices presented by the operating system, even LVM devices, but they should not be formatted by a file system. You can use an LVM to mirror volumes, and then ASM will stripe files on top of this.
5. ☑ **D.** Both password file and operating system authentication will work.
   ☒ **A, B,** and **C** are incorrect. ASM instances do not open a database, so you cannot use data dictionary authentication, but both of the other methods are available.
6. ☑ **D.** ASM stripes files across all disks in the group.
   ☒ **A, B,** and **C** are incorrect. ASM striping is managed per file, not per disk or disk group.

Install Oracle Grid Infrastructure for a Standalone Server

7. ☑ **C.** GI must be installed into its own home directory.
   ☒ **A, B,** and **D** are incorrect. It is not possible for the GI and database binaries to coexist in one Oracle home. Neither is it possible for a database to contact GI over a network connection.
8. ☑ **A** and **D.** crsctl is the Oracle-provided tool that can manage the GI processes, and on Windows the service manager can also be used.
   ☒ **B** and **C** are incorrect. SQL*Plus can manage an ASM instance, but not GI. srvctl can manage GI registered resources, but not GI itself.

LAB ANSWER

The following illustrations show some queries and commands that can be used in steps 5 and 6, first on Windows and then Linux.

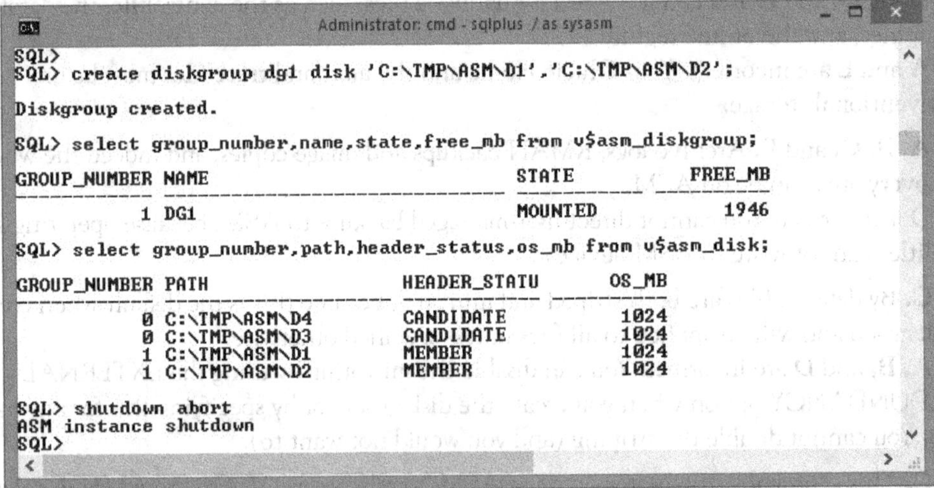

```
Administrator: cmd - sqlplus / as sysasm
SQL>
SQL> create diskgroup dg1 disk 'C:\TMP\ASM\D1','C:\TMP\ASM\D2';

Diskgroup created.

SQL> select group_number,name,state,free_mb from v$asm_diskgroup;

GROUP_NUMBER NAME                           STATE       FREE_MB
------------ ------------------------------ ----------- ----------
           1 DG1                            MOUNTED     1946

SQL> select group_number,path,header_status,os_mb from v$asm_disk;

GROUP_NUMBER PATH                 HEADER_STATU      OS_MB
------------ -------------------- ------------ ----------
           0 C:\TMP\ASM\D4        CANDIDATE          1024
           0 C:\TMP\ASM\D3        CANDIDATE          1024
           1 C:\TMP\ASM\D1        MEMBER             1024
           1 C:\TMP\ASM\D2        MEMBER             1024

SQL> shutdown abort
ASM instance shutdown
SQL>
```

```
oracle@oel58x64db121:/u01/asm

SQL> select group_number,name,state,type,total_mb from v$asm_diskgroup;

GROUP_NUMBER NAME                           STATE       TYPE     TOTAL_MB
------------ ------------------------------ ----------- ------ ----------
           1 DG1                            MOUNTED     NORMAL       2048

SQL> select path,name,state,group_number from v$asm_disk;

PATH                           NAME                           STATE    GROUP_NUMBER
------------------------------ ------------------------------ -------- ------------
/u01/asm/d4                                                   NORMAL              0
/u01/asm/d3                                                   NORMAL              0
/u01/asm/d1                    DG1_0000                       NORMAL              1
/u01/asm/d2                    DG1_0001                       NORMAL              1

SQL>
```

21 Using Oracle Restart

CERTIFICATION OBJECTIVES

21.01	Use Oracle Restart to Manage Components	✓	Two-Minute Drill
		Q&A	Self Test

This chapter details the use of Oracle Restart, which is the non-clustered version of Grid Infrastructure. It provides the ability to manage a range of Oracle resources: once placed under GI control, they can be started and stopped with the GI utilities, and restarted automatically in the event of failure.

CERTIFICATION OBJECTIVE 21.01

Use Oracle Restart to Manage Components

Oracle Restart is a service provided by GI. It consists of a set of processes started and monitored by the operating system. Some of these processes run with root (or Administrator) privileges, and others as the user under which GI was installed. Oracle Restart may be configured to start automatically or manually.

A *resource* is, in this context, something that can be managed by GI. All resources are registered in the Oracle Local Registry (OLR). Once registered, they are under the control of Oracle Restart. Some configuration tools will implicitly register resources if they detect the presence of an Oracle Restart configuration; others will not. In the latter case, the resource must be explicitly registered. Once registered, a resource can be started or stopped either with GI utilities (which also will take care of stopping or starting any dependent resources) or with the utilities native to the resource.

Of great importance is the high availability capability. GI includes an event-monitoring mechanism that will detect any state change for a registered resource, propagate messages regarding state changes, and if necessary attempt an automatic restart of failed resources.

Administering the Oracle Restart Processes

Following installation of GI, the Oracle Restart processes will be started automatically on booting the server. On Linux, the core process is the init.ohasd daemon. This is launched through an rc script, with monitoring and respawn enabled by an entry in the /etc/inittab file. Should the daemon die (or be killed), init will restart it. On Windows, the same function is provided by the OracleOHService Windows service, which launches, monitors, and restarts the ohasd.exe process.

To control Oracle Restart manually, use the crsctl utility. Figure 21-1 shows the use of the most frequently used crsctl commands for administering Oracle Restart, on a Windows system. The commands are syntactically identical on Linux. Note that most of these commands can be executed only by a user with Administrator (Windows) or root (Linux) privileges.

These are the commands used in Figure 21-1:

Command	Description
crsctl config has	Oracle Restart is configured to start on boot-up.
crsctl check has	Oracle Restart is currently running.
crsctl stop has	Stop the Oracle Restart process.
crsctl start has	Start the Oracle Restart process.

Figure 21-2 shows some more crsctl commands, this time on a Linux system. These are the commands used in Figure 21-2:

Command	Description
crsctl query softwareversion	The software that is installed.
crsctl config has	Oracle Restart is not configured to start on boot-up.
crsctl enable crs	From now on, Oracle Restart will start on boot-up.
crsctl disable crs	Except that it is now disabled again.

FIGURE 21-1 Using the crsctl utility to manage Oracle Restart (Windows)

```
Administrator: cmd
C:\WINDOWS\system32>
C:\WINDOWS\system32>crsctl config has
CRS-4622: Oracle High Availability Services autostart is enabled.

C:\WINDOWS\system32>crsctl check has
CRS-4638: Oracle High Availability Services is online

C:\WINDOWS\system32>crsctl stop has
CRS-2791: Starting shutdown of Oracle High Availability Services-managed resourc
es on 'jwvaio'
CRS-2673: Attempting to stop 'ora.evmd' on 'jwvaio'
CRS-2677: Stop of 'ora.evmd' on 'jwvaio' succeeded
CRS-2793: Shutdown of Oracle High Availability Services-managed resources on 'jw
vaio' has completed
CRS-4133: Oracle High Availability Services has been stopped.

C:\WINDOWS\system32>crsctl check has
CRS-4639: Could not contact Oracle High Availability Services

C:\WINDOWS\system32>crsctl start has
CRS-4123: Oracle High Availability Services has been started.

C:\WINDOWS\system32>crsctl check has
CRS-4638: Oracle High Availability Services is online

C:\WINDOWS\system32>
```

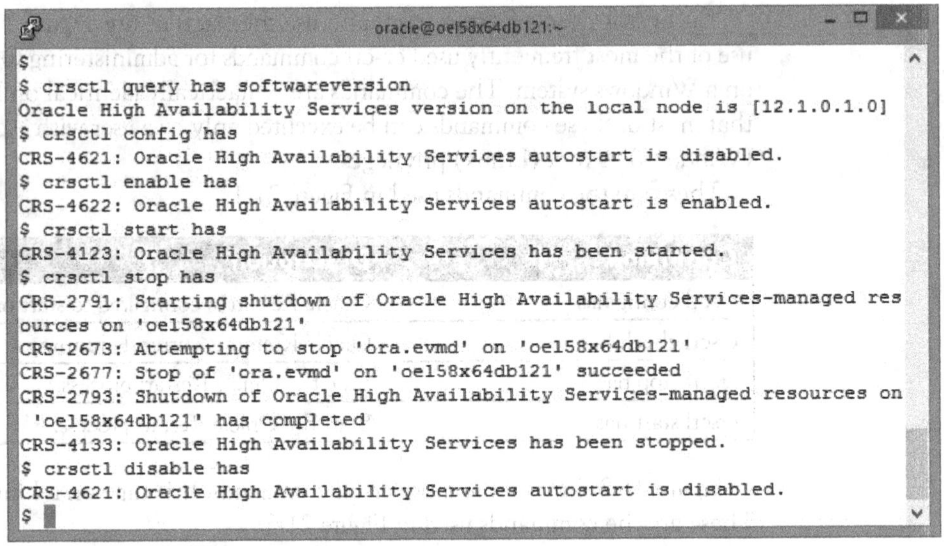

FIGURE 21-2 Using the crsctl utility to manage Oracle Restart (Linux)

```
$
$ crsctl query has softwareversion
Oracle High Availability Services version on the local node is [12.1.0.1.0]
$ crsctl config has
CRS-4621: Oracle High Availability Services autostart is disabled.
$ crsctl enable has
CRS-4622: Oracle High Availability Services autostart is enabled.
$ crsctl start has
CRS-4123: Oracle High Availability Services has been started.
$ crsctl stop has
CRS-2791: Starting shutdown of Oracle High Availability Services-managed res
ources on 'oel58x64db121'
CRS-2673: Attempting to stop 'ora.evmd' on 'oel58x64db121'
CRS-2677: Stop of 'ora.evmd' on 'oel58x64db121' succeeded
CRS-2793: Shutdown of Oracle High Availability Services-managed resources on
 'oel58x64db121' has completed
CRS-4133: Oracle High Availability Services has been stopped.
$ crsctl disable has
CRS-4621: Oracle High Availability Services autostart is disabled.
$
```

Administering Registered Resources

Resources must be registered with Oracle Restart if it is to provide a high availability service for them. Some tools will register resources as they are created; others will not. For example, if you create a database with the DBCA utility, it will detect the presence of Oracle Restart and run commands to register the database. You can see these commands in the scripts that DBCA generates. If you create the database with SQL*Plus, you must register it yourself. If you create a listener with Net Configuration Assistant, it will be registered; if you create one with the Net Manager, it will not be registered. If GI has been installed after other products have already been installed, all previously created resources must be explicitly registered.

It is possible to register resources with the crsctl utility, but this is a very general-purpose tool and the syntax for adding a resource is, to put it mildly, awkward. When registering a resource, you need to give Oracle Restart, at a minimum, this information:

- Exactly how to start, stop, and monitor the resource
- What to do if the resource fails
- On what other resources it may depend

Furthermore, the nature of the information needed will be different for different types of resources. A much better alternative when working with Oracle resources is to use the srvctl utility. This is preconfigured with commands for working with all the resources that a DBA is likely to need. It is, however, limited to Oracle resources: you cannot use it to (for example) register an Apache web listener as a managed resource.

The general syntax of the srvctl utility is:

```
srvctl <command> <object> <options>
```

The commonly used <commands> are:

Command	Description
add | remove	Register or deregister a resource
enable | disable	Allow or disallow Oracle Restart to manage the resource
start | stop	Start or stop a registered (and enabled) resource
config	Show the configuration of the resource
modify	Adjust the configuration of the resource
status	Show whether the resource is started or stopped

The commonly used <objects> are:

Object	Description
database	A database, including the instance that opens it
service	A database service
listener	A database listener
asm	The node's ASM instance
diskgroup	An ASM disk group

The <options> used in an srvctl command depend on the <command> and the nature of the <object>.

on the job

The srvctl utility has a superb help facility. Run `srvctl -help` and you will see the full syntax of every command for every resource type. Unfortunately, you can't do this in the exam.

To register a database, use a command such as this:

```
srvctl add database -db orclz -oraclehome /u01/db_home1
```

The first option is the DB_UNIQUE_NAME of the database, which will (usually) be the DB_NAME. The second option is the Oracle Home off which the instance that opens the database will run. Other not infrequently used options let one specify required disk groups, nominate the spfile and the password file, and control the automatic start. By default, the database will be configured such that Oracle Restart will start it in OPEN mode automatically. To show the configuration of the database orclz, use this command:

```
srvctl config database -db orclz -all
```

Here is how to start, stop, and check the status of a database:

```
srvctl start database -db orclz -startoption open
srvctl stop database -db orclz -stopoption immediate
srvctl status database -db orclz
```

The arguments STARTOPTION and STOPOPTION default to OPEN and IMMEDIATE (as shown). Other possible STARTOPTION values are NOMOUNT, MOUNT, and READONLY. Other STOPOPTION values are NORMAL, TRANSACTIONAL, and ABORT.

exam watch

The srvctl utility is installed in both a database Oracle Home and the GI Oracle Home, and can be run from either. The crsctl utility is available only in the GI Oracle Home.

The Restart Capability

When a resource is placed under the control of Oracle Restart, it will be monitored by GI and restarted in the event of failure. A controlled shutdown of the resource (whether with the srvctl utility or with a tool native to the resource) will not trigger a restart.

There is no "reality check" when using SRVCTL ADD. The fact that a database is successfully registered in the OLR does not mean that it actually exists.

Restart behavior is determined by the POLICY argument passed to the **SRVCTL ADD** command, or to the **SRVCTL MODIFY** command subsequently. The default value is to enable automatic restart:

```
-POLICY AUTOMATIC | MANUAL | NORESTART
```

EXERCISE 21-1

Configure a Database for Oracle Restart

In this exercise, you register your database with Oracle Restart. It is assumed that Exercise 20-1 has been completed.

1. From an operating system prompt, confirm that the HAS is configured and running. Note that you will need Administrator or root privileges, and ensure that your search path includes the bin directory in the GI home. Then use the crsctl utility as follows:

   ```
   crsctl config has
   crsctl check has
   ```

2. Demonstrate that the GI process that implements Oracle Restart is itself protected against failure by the operating system. On Linux, as the root user, identify the process number of the daemon and then kill it. Use these commands, substituting whatever the process number of your init.ohasd process is for 12345:

   ```
   ps -ef | grep init.ohasd
   kill -9 12345
   ps -ef | grep init.ohasd
   ```

   On Windows, use the Task Manager to locate the ohasd.exe process and then click the End Task button to kill it. Observe that the process is restarted, with a different process ID, within seconds.

3. Use the srvctl utility to register your database with Oracle Restart. You can rely on defaults for all arguments except the database unique name and the Oracle Home. If you have the ORACLE_HOME environment variable set to the database home, you can use it. Here is an example on Linux with a database named orclz:

   ```
   srvctl add database -d orclz -oraclehome $ORACLE_HOME
   ```

4. Confirm that the database has been successfully registered and then check its status:

```
srvctl config database -d orclz
srvctl status database -d orclz
```

The database will be reported as "not running," whether it is or not. This is because it has not been started since it was registered.

5. Force GI to perform a reality check by issuing a start command, and then check the status again:

```
srvctl start database -db orclz
srvctl status database -db orclz
```

The following illustration shows steps 2 through 4 on a Windows system.

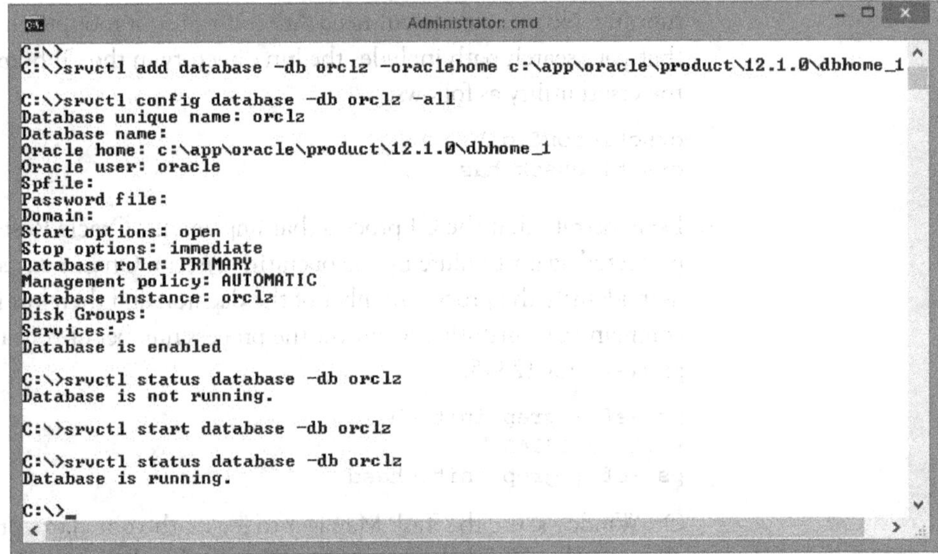

6. Experiment with startup and shutdown commands, both with srvctl and with SQL*Plus. Check the status each time.

7. While the database is running, demonstrate the restart capability. On Linux, use the **ps** command to identify the smon background process and then kill it. This will terminate the instance immediately. On Windows, use the Task Manager "End task" button to kill the oracle.exe process. Observe that the instance will restart within seconds.

The following illustration shows the instance restart test on Linux.

```
oracle@oel58x64db121:~
$
$ srvctl status database -db orclz
Database is running.
$
$ ps -ef | grep smon
oracle    9454     1  0 22:14 ?        00:00:00 ora_smon_orclz
oracle    9599  2958  0 22:14 pts/1    00:00:00 grep smon
$
$ kill -9 9454
$
$ srvctl status database -db orclz
Database is not running.
$
$ srvctl status database -db orclz
Database is running.
$
$ ps -ef | grep smon
oracle    9812     1  0 22:16 ?        00:00:00 ora_smon_orclz
oracle    9945  2958  0 22:17 pts/1    00:00:00 grep smon
$
```

CERTIFICATION SUMMARY

This chapter describes the Oracle Restart functionality, which is a part of Grid Infrastructure. Restart provides high availability capability to databases and related services. It monitors registered resources, restarting them in the event of failure. The restart daemon itself is protected by the operating system.

Oracle Restart is managed with the crsctl utility. Much of its functionality requires root or Administrator privileges. The utility for managing Oracle resources is srvctl, which is available from both database and GI Oracle Homes.

Key to the Oracle Restart capability is the Oracle Local Registry, the OLR. Use srvctl to register resources in the OLR and to manage them subsequently. Native management tools can still be used.

TWO-MINUTE DRILL

Use Oracle Restart to Manage Components

- ❑ Control Oracle Restart with the crsctl utility.
- ❑ Administer Oracle Restart–managed resources with the srvctl utility.
- ❑ The HAS daemon is protected by the operating system.
- ❑ Protected components may be databases, database listeners, the ASM instance, and ASM disk groups.
- ❑ If dependencies have been configured (such as between a database and a disk group), Oracle Restart will stop and start them in an appropriate sequence.

SELF TEST

Use Oracle Restart to Manage Components

1. Under what circumstances will Oracle Restart restart a database? (Choose two answers.)
   A. If it is stopped with SQL*Plus
   B. If it fails after being started with SQL*Plus
   C. If it fails after being started with the srvctl utility
   D. If it is stopped with the crsctl utility
2. There are several techniques for registering a database with Oracle Restart. Which of these techniques will not result in a successful registration?
   A. Use the SRVCTL ADD DATABASE command from the database home to add the database to the OLR, then create the database with SQL*Plus.
   B. Create the database with the DBCA.
   C. Create a database and leave it running, then install GI and run the GI configuration scripts.
   D. Create the database with SQL*Plus, then use the SRVCTL ADD DATABASE command from the Grid Infrastructure home to add the database to the OLR.
3. Following a standard installation, the GI processes will start automatically when a machine is booted. How can you change this behavior, such that they must be started manually? (Choose the best answer.)
   A. Use the srvctl utility:

   ```
   srvctl config has -startoption manual
   ```

   B. Use the crsctl utility:

   ```
   crsctl disable has
   ```

   C. Edit the /etc/inittab file to remove the entry that launches the HAS daemon.
   D. Use the DBCA graphical utility to adjust the start mode.
4. Your database uses the ASM disk groups DATA and FRA for its storage. You register the database with this command:

   ```
   srvctl add database -db orcl -diskgroup DATA,FRA \
   -oraclehome $ORACLE_HOME
   ```

   Which of the following statements is correct? (Choose the best answer.)
   A. If you attempt to use srvctl to start the database before the ASM instance has mounted the disk groups, the database will not start.

B. If you attempt to use srvctl to start the database before the ASM instance has started, the ASM instance will start automatically.

C. The $ORACLE_HOME variable must be set to the ASM home so that the database instance can find the ASM instance.

D. The registration command will fail if the database does not exist.

LAB EXERCISE

Place your database listener under Oracle Restart control and demonstrate its effectiveness. The command you will need (no line breaks) is:

```
srvctl add listener
[ -listener <lsnr_name> ]
[ -oraclehome <path> ]
[ -endpoints "<port>" ]
```

The default values for the arguments assume that the listener is named LISTENER, that the listening endpoint is 1521, and that the Oracle Home is the GI home (which will not be correct if you have followed the exercises so far). Then check its configuration and status, stop and start the listener, and observe the effect of killing the listener process with an operating system utility.

SELF TEST ANSWERS

Use Oracle Restart to Manage Components

1. ☑ **B** and **C.** Oracle Restart will restart automatically after any failure, no matter how the database was started.
   ☒ **A** and **D** are incorrect. These are incorrect because Oracle Restart will not restart a database that is stopped in an orderly fashion, no matter what utility is used for this.
2. ☑ **C.** The GI installation and configuration does not include any facility for detecting and registering databases, whether or not they are running at the time.
   ☒ **A, B,** and **D** are incorrect. **B** is incorrect because if DBCA detects the presence of GI, it will generate and run appropriate commands. **A** and **D** are incorrect because registration in the OLR can be done before or after database creation, running the utility from either home.
3. ☑ **B.** The crsctl utility is the supported technique for disabling the autostart of the GI processes.
   ☒ **A, C,** and **D** are incorrect. **A** is incorrect because the srvctl utility can manage an Oracle Restart registered resource, not Oracle Restart itself. **C** is incorrect because although you could hack at the operating system inittab and rc files, it is not a supported technique. **D** is incorrect because the DBCA cannot manage any GI components, only databases.
4. ☑ **B.** Oracle Restart is aware of dependencies, and it will start ASM and mount any required disk groups.
   ☒ **A, C,** and **D** are incorrect. **A** is incorrect because registered dependencies will take care of this. **C** is incorrect because when you are registering a database, the ORACLE_HOME argument must point to the home off which the RDBMS instance will run. **D** is incorrect because there is no "reality" check when adding entries to the OLR: the errors will come later.

LAB ANSWER

Possible commands are:

```
srvctl add listener -listener listener -oraclehome c:\app\oracle\product
\12.1.0\dbhome_1
srvctl config listener -listener listener
srvctl stop listener -listener listener
srvctl start listener -listener listener
```

This is one way to simulate a failure on Windows:

```
net stop OracleOraDB12Home1TNSListener
```

On Linux, find the process ID of the tnslsnr process and kill it.
Note that the listener will restart in a few seconds.

22

Upgrading Oracle Database Software and Migrating Data

CERTIFICATION OBJECTIVES

22.01	Describe Upgrade Methods
22.02	Describe Data Migration Methods
22.03	Describe the Upgrade Process
22.04	Migrating Data by Using Oracle Data Pump
✓	Two-Minute Drill
Q&A	Self Test

This chapter covers the technique for upgrading the database software and migrating data from a database of one release to a database of another.

From release 11.2.x, the routine for upgrade is the same whether one is applying a patchset (to move from, for example, release 12.1.0.1 to release 12.1.0.2) or performing a major release upgrade (from, for example, 11.2.0.3 to 12.1.0.1). In either case, it is necessary to install a new Oracle Home. Before release 11.2.x, a major release required a new Oracle Home, but a patchset was applied to the existing Oracle Home. Now, only individual patches or patchset updates are applied, in place, to an existing home.

Having upgraded the database software, you must either upgrade the database itself or create a new database with the new software and move the data into it. Database upgrade is described in the following chapter. Data migration to a new database using the Data Pump utility is described in this chapter.

CERTIFICATION OBJECTIVE 22.01

Describe Upgrade Methods

Moving from one release of the database to another involves two distinct processes: upgrading the database software and upgrading the database. The software and the database must always be at the same release level, except for the short period while the database is being upgraded. The software upgrade is accomplished with the Oracle Universal Installer (OUI). Then there are two options for the database upgrade: using the Database Upgrade Assistant (DBUA), which automates most of the steps, and performing all the steps manually.

Software Upgrade

Oracle products have a multifaceted release number, with five elements:

- Major release number
- Database maintenance release number
- Application server release number (always zero for a database)

- Component-specific release number
- Platform-specific release number

To determine the release of your database, query the V$VERSION view. Within the database, it is possible for some installed components to be at different releases. To determine what is installed at what release, query the DBA_REGISTRY view. Figure 22-1 shows these queries on a database running on 64-bit Windows.

In the figure, the database release is 12.1.0.1.0, which was the first 12*c* production version: release 12, the first maintenance release. The fourth digit indicates the patchset. Patchset 1 is included in the first production release (the final beta release, used for developing much of this book, was 12.1.0.0.0). The second query in the figure shows that all the components installed in the database are also at release 12.1.0.1.0, with the exception of Application Express (APEX). APEX has its own upgrade routine, and the release of APEX is largely independent of the release of the database.

on the Job

Terms such as 12c and 11g are pretty meaningless in a technical context: they are little more than marketing labels. You will find that professional DBAs always identify their version with the release number, to four decimals.

FIGURE 22-1 Determining the release of the database

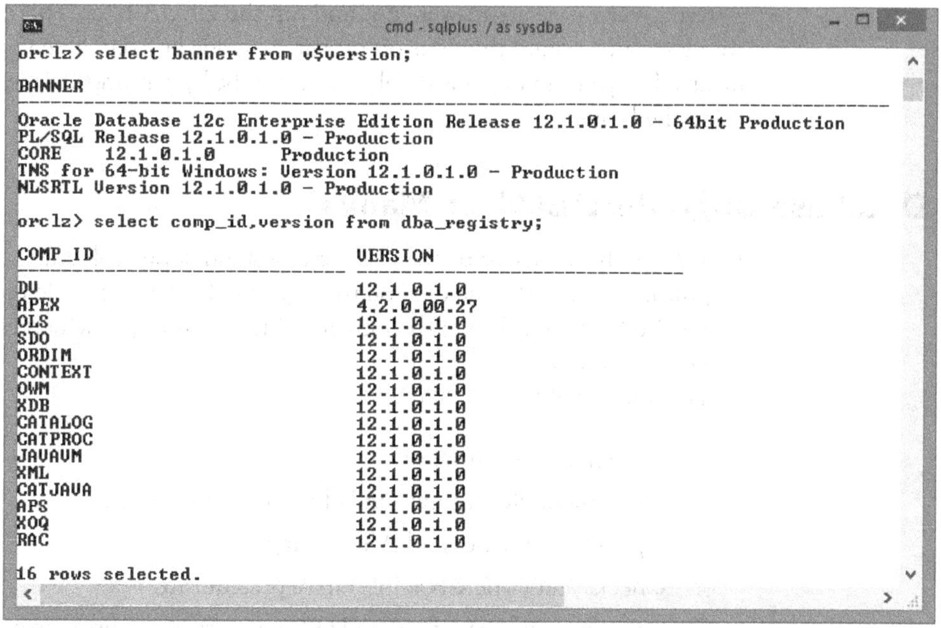

```
cmd - sqlplus / as sysdba
orclz> select banner from v$version;

BANNER
--------------------------------------------------------------------------------
Oracle Database 12c Enterprise Edition Release 12.1.0.1.0 - 64bit Production
PL/SQL Release 12.1.0.1.0 - Production
CORE    12.1.0.1.0      Production
TNS for 64-bit Windows: Version 12.1.0.1.0 - Production
NLSRTL Version 12.1.0.1.0 - Production

orclz> select comp_id,version from dba_registry;

COMP_ID                        VERSION
------------------------------ ------------------------------
DV                             12.1.0.1.0
APEX                           4.2.0.00.27
OLS                            12.1.0.1.0
SDO                            12.1.0.1.0
ORDIM                          12.1.0.1.0
CONTEXT                        12.1.0.1.0
OWM                            12.1.0.1.0
XDB                            12.1.0.1.0
CATALOG                        12.1.0.1.0
CATPROC                        12.1.0.1.0
JAVAVM                         12.1.0.1.0
XML                            12.1.0.1.0
CATJAVA                        12.1.0.1.0
APS                            12.1.0.1.0
XOQ                            12.1.0.1.0
RAC                            12.1.0.1.0

16 rows selected.
```

It is not necessary to install a base release of the product before installing a patchset. Patchsets are complete installable software images.

The method for software upgrade is to use the OUI. A patchset (identified by the fourth element of the release number) of the database is delivered as a self-contained installable image that includes a copy of OUI that is appropriate for the patchset. Launch OUI by running the runInstaller.sh script (Linux) or the setup.exe file (Windows) that is included with the patchset, and follow exactly the installation routine detailed in Chapter 1. The software must be installed into a newly created Oracle Home. OUI will prompt for the location. Best practice is to create the new home beneath the Oracle Base directory, next to the existing Oracle Home. To start using the newly installed version of the software, adjust your ORACLE_HOME and PATH environment variables to point to the new home. Then create (or upgrade) a database.

When using OUI to install an Oracle database home (whether a base release or a patchset), the OUI will detect all previous installations. It can do this by reading the content of the OUI Inventory, which will have been created during the first installation. If OUI detects a previous installation, it will prompt for whether any existing databases should be upgraded. Should you answer "yes," following the installation OUI will launch the DBUA to perform these database upgrades. Alternatively, you can answer "no" and run the DBUA later. This approach means that you can separate the tasks of software upgrade and database upgrade. It also means that you can upgrade databases manually, by running scripts, rather than using the DBUA.

Database Upgrade: DBUA or Manual

DBUA can be launched by the OUI or as a standalone tool at any time. It is a graphical interface that guides you through the database upgrade process, although it can also be driven through a command-line interface, in which case no prompts need be answered.

The functionality is as follows:

- Automates the entire process
- Supports single-instance and clustered environments
- Upgrades databases and ASM storage
- Checks and (where possible) fixes prerequisites
- Logs errors and generates an HTML report of the upgrade process

Using the DBUA is undoubtedly the easiest way to upgrade, and is less prone to error than a manual technique. But it is not always appropriate. For example, if downtime is critical, it may be faster to upgrade manually. DBUA generally does all steps sequentially, many of them while the database is not available for use: a manual upgrade may be able to perform some steps in parallel, and others either before or after the essential downtime period.

A manual upgrade will typically involve these tasks:

- Space check of the SYSTEM and SYSAUX tablespaces
- Adjust newly obsoleted or deprecated parameters
- Run scripts to upgrade the data dictionary and installed components
- Recompile all stored code

Whether you are using DBUA or a manual method, direct upgrade to 12.1 is possible from these releases:

- 10.2.0.5 (the terminal release of 10g)
- 11.1.0.7 (the terminal release of 11g R1)
- 11.2.0.2 or later

All other releases must be upgraded to one of those listed before you upgrade to 12.1.

CERTIFICATION OBJECTIVE 22.02

Describe Data Migration Methods

A database upgrade has two major restrictions. First, it must be performed on the same platform. You cannot move from, for example, Windows to AIX during an upgrade. Second, you cannot carry out any form of reorganization or implementation of new features during the upgrade: after it has completed, nothing has really changed. Data migration gets around both these limitations.

A migration is the process of transferring data from one database into another. In the context of upgrade, this means creating a new database of the new release and copying the entire user dataset from the old database into the new. The new database can be configured, in advance, with all the new features enabled that one wishes to use. Then as the data is inserted, it will take on the characteristics of the new release. Furthermore, the new database can be on a different platform. The downside of data migration as an upgrade technique is the necessary downtime. An upgrade of a database with DBUA might involve downtime of less than an hour; a migration could take days, depending on the volume of data to be moved.

on the job

Many DBAs prefer migration to upgrade because it results in a new, "clean" data dictionary: no rubbish left behind by years of (ab)use.

Data migration is usually accomplished with the Data Pump export/import utility. Particular advantages are:

- Data Pump can work across platforms.
- Source and destination character sets need not be the same.
- The source can be any release from 10.0 upward.
- It is not necessary to transfer the entire database if only a subset is actually needed.
- Data segments will be reorganized as part of the process.

If the migration is from a pre-10g database, it can still be accomplished by using the legacy exp/imp utilities.

CERTIFICATION OBJECTIVE 22.03

Describe the Upgrade Process

Database upgrade is an operation that is fraught with peril. Theoretically, an upgrade can do nothing but good, but there is always the possibility that the behavior of the applications using the database will change. For that reason, testing is vital. There are typically six steps to an upgrade:

1. *Prepare to upgrade*. Choose an upgrade method, install the new Oracle Home, develop a test plan, and determine what new features to implement.
2. *Upgrade a test database*. Test the upgrade process on a non-production clone of the database. In particular, note the necessary downtime.
3. *Test the upgraded database*. Complete the planned tests. In particular, ensure that performance has not regressed. Iterate steps 2 and 3 as necessary until all issues are resolved.

4. *Prepare the production database*. Stop all user activity according to an agreed schedule for downtime and then take a full backup.
5. *Upgrade the production database*. Follow the tried and tested upgrade procedure. Take a full backup after completion. The downtime will now be over.
6. *Tune the upgraded database*. As the system comes back into use, monitor performance and carry out normal proactive and reactive tuning work.

CERTIFICATION OBJECTIVE 22.04

Migrating Data by Using Oracle Data Pump

The use of Data Pump for transferring individual tables, schemas, and various object types between databases was discussed in Chapter 17. Data Pump can also be used to copy an entire database: all user objects can be read from one database and created in another. Because the objects are represented in a Data Pump dump file logically rather than physically, there is no reason why they cannot be read from a database of one release on one platform and written into a database of another release, possibly on another platform. Thus, the database can (in effect) be upgraded by the export/import process. It is possible to downgrade through the same technique, but only if the objects in the source database do not require any features that are not available in the destination.

If the new database is configured with various features enabled, the data will take on these features during the import. If run completely on defaults, a full import will create tablespaces, schemas, and objects as they were in the source before inserting data—but they can be pre-created. For example, the tablespaces in the source database might be using the old storage mechanisms of dictionary-managed extents and freelist-managed segments; the destination tablespaces would be created, in advance, with the current defaults of local extent management and automatic segment space management.

One issue with using Data Pump for upgrade is the space requirement. A large database will require a great deal of space for the dump file(s) generated by the export. Furthermore, if the upgrade is to a destination database on a different machine, the dump will have to be copied over to the remote machine—where the same amount of space will be required again. There is also a time penalty: the export must complete before the copy can begin, and the copy must complete before the import can begin. A *network mode* import avoids both the space and the time issues.

To use the network mode of Data Pump, a database link must exist from the destination database to the source database. This link must connect to a user with the DATAPUMP_EXP_FULL_DATABASE role. Then, running the import on the destination database (as a user with the DATAPUMP_IMP_FULL_DATABASE role) will launch worker processes on the source database that read the data and write it through the database link to the destination database, where more worker processes write the data to the database. This mechanism avoids the need to stage the data on disk as a dump file, and also means that the export, the copy, and the import all run concurrently. Figure 22-2 shows the initiation of this operation.

In Figure 22-2, the user is connected to a database named orclb. This is a release 12.1.0.1 database. The database link orcla connects to an 11.2.0.3 database. Then the **impdp** command starts a job that will perform a complete migration of all user data from orcla into orclb, through the database link. Schemas and tablespaces will be created as they were in the source database, although they can be pre-created with appropriate characteristics if desired. During the import there will be many messages of the form "ORA-31684: Object ... already exists" as the import encounters objects that are part of Oracle's seeded schemas: these can safely be ignored. The end result will be a complete migration of all user data.

FIGURE 22-2 Launching a full import in network mode

```
Select Administrator: cmd - impdp system/oracle network_link=orcla full=y
orclb> select banner from v$version where rownum=1;

BANNER
--------------------------------------------------------------------------------
Oracle Database 12c Enterprise Edition Release 12.1.0.1.0 - 64bit Production

orclb> create database link orcla connect to system identified by oracle
  2 using 'orcla';

Database link created.

orclb> select banner from v$version@orcla where rownum=1;

BANNER
--------------------------------------------------------------------------------
Oracle Database 11g Enterprise Edition Release 11.2.0.3.0 - 64bit Production

orclb> exit
Disconnected from Oracle Database 12c Enterprise Edition Release 12.1.0.1.0
With the Partitioning, OLAP, Advanced Analytics, Real Application Testing
and Unified Auditing options

C:\>impdp system/oracle network_link=orcla full=y

Import: Release 12.1.0.1.0 - Production on Sun Jan 19 13:39:55 2014

Copyright (c) 1982, 2013, Oracle and/or its affiliates.  All rights reserved

Connected to: Oracle Database 12c Enterprise Edition Release 12.1.0.1.0 - 64
With the Partitioning, OLAP, Advanced Analytics, Real Application Testing
and Unified Auditing options
Starting "SYSTEM"."SYS_IMPORT_FULL_02":  system/******** network_link=orcla
Estimate in progress using BLOCKS method...
```

EXERCISE 22-1

Perform a Data Pump Full Database Migration

In this exercise, you simulate a data migration from one database to another. It is assumed that the source database is a database created from the General Purpose template, with the sample schemas installed.

1. Create a full export of the database, using the default DATA_PUMP_DIR directory:

   ```
   expdp system/oracle full=y dumpfile=full_exp.dmp
   ```

2. Drop any tablespaces and schemas that hold user data. These commands will be needed:

   ```
   drop tablespace users including contents and datafiles;
   drop tablespace example including contents and datafiles;
   drop user scott cascade;
   drop user hr cascade;
   drop user sh cascade;
   drop user oe cascade;
   drop user pm cascade;
   drop user ix cascade;
   ```

   At this point, you have a database that is devoid of user data.

3. Import the user data into the database:

   ```
   impdp system/oracle full=y dumpfile=full_exp.dmp
   ```

4. Confirm that the tablespaces and users dropped in step 2 have been created, and that the schemas are populated with tables and other objects.

CERTIFICATION SUMMARY

This chapter describes the two-stage upgrade process: first, upgrade the software; second, upgrade the database. Software upgrades are accomplished by installing a new Oracle Home, of whatever release is desired, with the OUI. The databases can be upgraded to the new release either by using the DBUA or by running commands and scripts manually. The OUI will detect existing installations and databases, and prompt for whether to run the DBUA following the installation. The DBUA automates the database upgrade process. It is an in-place mechanism: existing structures are modified as necessary, rather than being re-created.

An alternative to upgrading a database is to create a new database and transfer the user data from the existing database into the new database. As the objects are created and rows inserted, they will take on the characteristics of the new release. Generally speaking, a data migration will be significantly slower than an upgrade, but it does have the advantage that new features can be implemented and data reorganized as part of the process.

A data migration is accomplished with the Data Pump utility. Because Data Pump can work across releases and platforms, it is more versatile than the DBUA. It is not an in-place operation, and at the end there are two databases, but the requirement for interim storage can be reduced by using a network mode import that avoids the need to stage a dump file on disk.

TWO-MINUTE DRILL

Describe Upgrade Methods

- The Database Upgrade Assistant automates the upgrade, and also all before and after checks.
- A manual upgrade gives the DBA full control of all steps: a more complex process, but possibly faster.
- An upgrade is an in-place operation: it is not possible to change platform, physical location, character set, or indeed anything except the release.
- Upgrade is possible only from a defined list of previous releases.

Describe Data Migration Methods

- A Data Pump migration exports from one database and imports into another.
- A migration can go across platforms as well as releases.
- The source database can be any release from 10.0 onward.
- A network mode import obviates the need to stage a dump file on disk.

Describe the Upgrade Process

- A new Oracle Home, of the new release, must be installed with the OUI.
- Determine whether to use DBUA or a manual upgrade.
- Design and implement a test plan.
- Perform the production upgrade.
- Verify the success of the operation.

Migrating Data by Using Oracle Data Pump

- A new Oracle Home, of the new release, must be installed with the OUI.
- Create a new database.
- Create any objects that you want to configure (such as tablespaces).
- Perform a full export of the source database.
- Transfer the dump file to the destination database.
- Import the dump file.
- Redirect users to the new database.

SELF TEST

Describe Upgrade Methods

1. What can be accomplished during an upgrade when using the Database Upgrade Assistant? (Choose two answers.)
   A. Conversion from a legacy character set to Unicode
   B. Direct upgrade from any release of 11g to 12c
   C. Direct upgrade from the terminal release of 10g to 12c
   D. Verification of prerequisite conditions
2. What considerations are needed for space usage during an upgrade? (Choose the best answer.)
   A. None: an upgrade is an in-place operation, and requires no significant additional storage.
   B. It is possible that the SYSTEM and SYSAUX tablespaces will expand during an upgrade.
   C. Up to double the space needed for data will be needed during the upgrade.
   D. No archivelogs will be generated, because an upgrade is not recoverable and no redo is generated.

Describe Data Migration Methods

3. Which of the following can be accomplished with a Data Pump migration? (Choose all correct answers.)
   A. Upgrade from any release of 10g or 11g
   B. Character set conversion
   C. A move from a 32-bit to a 64-bit platform
   D. Direct upgrade from the terminal release of 9*i*
4. Which of these correctly describes a network mode Data Pump operation? (Choose the best answer.)
   A. Create database links in both the source and destination databases, and run expdp on the source and impdp on the destination.
   B. Create a database link in the source pointing to the destination, and run expdp on the source.
   C. Create a database link in the destination pointing to the source, and run impdp on the destination.
   D. Run expdp in the source, writing a dump file to a pipe, and run impdp on the destination, reading the dump file from the pipe.

Describe the Upgrade Process

5. What does the Database Upgrade Assistant upgrade? (Choose the best answer.)
   A. Oracle database software and databases
   B. Oracle database software
   C. Oracle databases
   D. User data storage structures and user data logical attributes

Migrating Data by Using Oracle Data Pump

6. Under which circumstance must a Data Pump export be performed when carrying out a database migration? (Choose the best answer.)
   A. The database must be open read-only.
   B. The database must be in mount mode.
   C. The database must have restricted session enabled.
   D. The database must be open.
7. If a full database import operation attempts to import objects into a tablespace that does not exist, what will happen? (Choose the best answer.)
   A. The tablespace must be pre-created, or the operation will fail.
   B. The tablespace will be created if Oracle Managed Files has been enabled in the destination database.
   C. The import will succeed if the tablespace is specified with the TABLESPACES parameter.
   D. The objects will be imported into the database's default permanent tablespace.

SELF TEST ANSWERS

Describe Upgrade Methods

1. ☑ **C** and **D.** Direct upgrade is possible from the terminal release of 10*g*, but not from earlier releases. The DBUA runs verification scripts before and after the upgrade.
   ☒ **A** and **B** are incorrect. **A** is incorrect because character set conversion is not part of DBUA's functionality: you must use other utilities for this. **B** is incorrect because direct upgrade from 11*g* is possible only for the terminal release of 11.1 or any release from 11.2.0.2.

2. ☑ **B.** It is usual for data dictionary objects to increase in size as a result of an upgrade (Oracle keeps getting bigger...).
   ☒ **A, C,** and **D** are incorrect. **A** is incorrect because space will often be required for data dictionary objects. **C** is incorrect because user data is not affected by an upgrade: the changes are usually limited to metadata. **D** is incorrect because an upgrade involves executing a large amount of DML and DDL against the data dictionary, which does generate redo.

Describe Data Migration Methods

3. ☑ **A, B,** and **C.** Data Pump is compatible across all versions that support it, from 10.0 onward. It can move data across any supported platforms, performing character set conversion as it does so.
   ☒ **D** is incorrect. This is incorrect because Data Pump was introduced with release 10*g*. To migrate from 9*i*, one must use the legacy exp/imp utilities.

4. ☑ **C.** A network mode import is initiated by impdp, although worker processes will run at both the source and the destination.
   ☒ **A, B,** and **D** are incorrect. **A** and **B** are incorrect because a network mode operation is managed from the destination only. **D** is incorrect because it is not possible to import a dump file until it has been completed. The technique described does, however, function with the legacy imp/exp utilities.

Describe the Upgrade Process

5. ☑ **C.** The DBUA upgrades databases—and nothing else.
   ☒ **A, B,** and **D** are incorrect. **A** and **B** are incorrect because the software must be upgraded with the OUI, not the DBUA. **D** is incorrect because restructuring storage and objects is a task that must be done after the upgrade, not during the upgrade.

Migrating Data by Using Oracle Data Pump

6. ☑ **D.** The export is a perfectly normal export operation with no special requirements.
   ☒ **A, B,** and **C** are incorrect. **A** and **B** are incorrect because the database must be open read/write; otherwise it is not possible for Data Pump to create its master table. **C** is incorrect because although restricted mode might be a good idea, it is not a requirement.

7. ☑ **B.** If OMF has been enabled, tablespaces will be created accordingly.
   ☒ **A, C,** and **D** are incorrect. **A** is incorrect because the import will attempt to create the tablespace, using either OMF or the datafile definition from the source database. **C** is incorrect because the TABLESPACES parameter identifies a list of tablespaces to import: it is not relevant for a full import. **D** is incorrect because if a suitable tablespace neither exists nor can be created, there will be an error.

23

Database Upgrade: Preparation, Upgrading, and Post-Upgrade Tasks

CERTIFICATION OBJECTIVES

23.01 Describe Upgrade Requirements when Certain Features or Options Are Used in Oracle Database

23.02 Use the Pre-Upgrade Information Tool Before Performing an Upgrade

23.03 Prepare the New Oracle Home Prior to Performing an Upgrade

23.04 Upgrade the Database to Oracle Database 12*c* by Using the Database Upgrade Assistant (DBUA)

23.05 Perform a Manual Upgrade to Oracle Database 12*c* by Using Scripts and Tools

23.06 Migrate to Unified Auditing

23.07 Perform Post-Upgrade Tasks

✓ Two-Minute Drill

Q&A Self Test

This chapter describes the process of upgrading an Oracle database. This could be an upgrade to a new major release (such as from 11.2.0.4 to 12.1.0.1) or applying a patchset within a major release (such as from 12.1.0.1 to 12.1.0.2). Either way, the principle is the same. Assuming that the software has already been upgraded (by using the OUI to create a new Oracle Home), certain steps must be followed before, during, and after the upgrade process.

CERTIFICATION OBJECTIVE 23.01

Describe Upgrade Requirements when Certain Features or Options Are Used in Oracle Database

An upgrade involves running scripts against the data dictionary that will upgrade various database features and options. Depending on what options have been installed and configured, some preparatory work may be needed.

Oracle Label Security and Oracle Data Vault

These options are beyond the scope of the OCP curriculum, but their impact on upgrade may be tested. In summary, Oracle Label Security (OLS) is a technique for filtering access by users to rows. This is in addition to the usual mechanism of privileges. Two users may have the same SELECT or DML privileges on a table, but even though they run identical SQL statements, they will see a different subset of the table. The filtering is based on session attributes over which the users have no control, and they will not be aware that the filtering has occurred.

Oracle Data Vault adds an additional layer to Oracle's privilege and role model. Users can be placed in groups, and policies can be designed that control groups' access to user objects even though they may have the requisite privilege. These policies apply to all users, including those with the SYSDBA privilege. This is the only way to limit access to data by the otherwise all-powerful database administrators.

To determine if either OLS or Data Vault has been installed in the database, run this query:

```
select * from v$option where parameter in
('Oracle Database Vault','Oracle Label Security');
```

If either option is installed, then it is possible that the SYS.AUD$ table will need to be relocated. A script is provided in the new 12.x Oracle Home to accomplish this:

ORACLE_HOME/rdbms/admin/olspreupgrade.sql

The script is very well documented, and includes precise instructions on what to do if either OLS or Data Vault or both are installed, with variations depending on the exact release of the database to be upgraded. Copy the script from the newly installed 12.x Oracle Home to the Oracle Home currently in use, study the instructions in the script, and then run it while connected AS SYSDBA.

Oracle Warehouse Builder

Oracle Warehouse Builder (OWB) is a graphical tool for designing, building, managing, and maintaining data integration processes in business intelligence systems. It is beyond the scope of the OCP curriculum. OWB is not shipped with the 12*c* database; therefore, if it is installed in the database to be upgraded, the upgrade routine will not upgrade it and it will no longer be usable. It is, however, possible for a 12*c* database to interoperate with a separate release 11.2.0.3 (nothing earlier) OWB installation. There are three techniques for this:

- Give the upgraded 12*c* database access to an existing standalone (that is, not installed as part of an 11*g* database) OWB installation.
- Retain an already configured OWB installation in an 11*g* database running of the 11*g* home, and continue to use this.
- Configure a new standalone OWB installation.

All these methods come down to the same thing: you can no longer use OWB in the database after upgrade, and must therefore provide an OWB installation external to the upgraded database.

To determine whether OWB is installed in the database, run this query:

```
select comp_name,version,status from dba_registry
where comp_id='OWB';
```

CERTIFICATION OBJECTIVE 23.02

Use the Pre-Upgrade Information Tool Before Performing an Upgrade

Following the installation of the new 12*c* database home, you will have access to the Pre-Upgrade Information Tool. This is a script, preupgrd.sql, installed into the ORACLE_HOME/rdbms/admin directory. Run this script against the database to be upgraded. It will generate a report detailing any issues as well as a "fix-up" script that will fix some issues; other issues will have to be addressed manually.

Figure 23-1 shows an example of running this script on a Windows database. In the figure, the database is currently at release 11.2.0.3. The script is run from the newly installed (but not yet used) 12*c* Oracle Home. It produces three files, generated in a directory (cfgtoollogs\<db_name>\preupgrade) below the Oracle Base directory:

- preupgrade.log details all the checks that were run with advice on items that should be addressed.

FIGURE 23-1

Running the Pre-Upgrade Information Tool

Select cmd - sqlplus / as sysdba

```
orcla>
orcla> select banner from v$version where rownum=1;
Oracle Database 11g Enterprise Edition Release 11.2.0.3.0 - 64bit Production
orcla>
orcla> @c:\app\oracle\product\12.1.0\dbhome_1\rdbms\admin\preupgrd.sql
Loading Pre-Upgrade Package...
Executing Pre-Upgrade Checks...
Pre-Upgrade Checks Complete.
      ************************************************************

Results of the checks are located at:
 C:\app\oracle\cfgtoollogs\orcla\preupgrade\preupgrade.log

Pre-Upgrade Fixup Script (run in source database environment):
 C:\app\oracle\cfgtoollogs\orcla\preupgrade\preupgrade_fixups.sql

Post-Upgrade Fixup Script (run shortly after upgrade):
 C:\app\oracle\cfgtoollogs\orcla\preupgrade\postupgrade_fixups.sql

      ************************************************************

         Fixup scripts must be reviewed prior to being executed.

      ************************************************************

      ************************************************************
                  ====>> USER ACTION REQUIRED  <<====
      ************************************************************
```

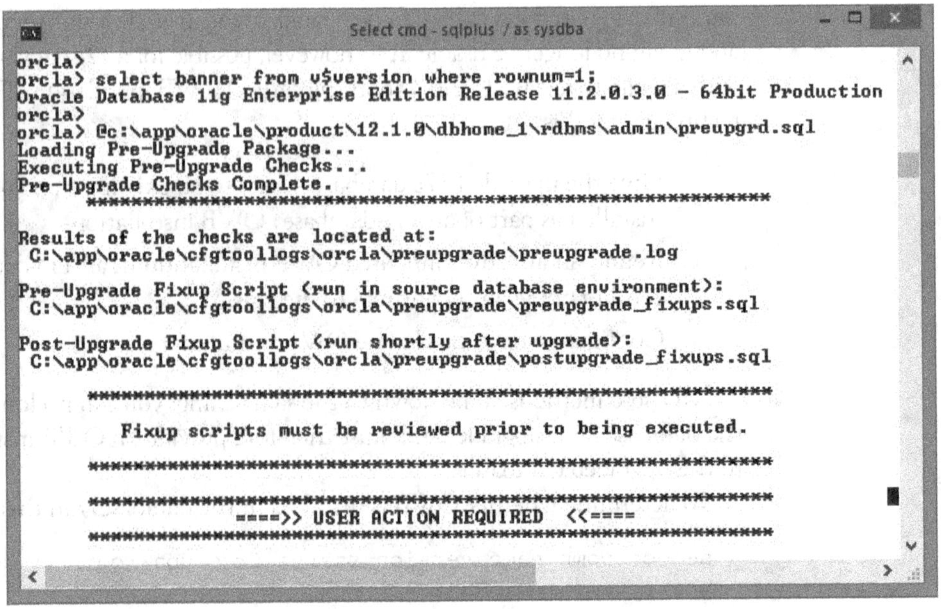

- preupgrade_fixups.sql contains commands that should be run in the database before commencing the upgrade to fix any problems.
- postupgrade_fixups.sql contains commands that should be run in the database after the upgrade has completed.

The logfile and the scripts should be studied with care: they give information and instructions that may make the upgrade run more smoothly.

CERTIFICATION OBJECTIVE 23.03

Prepare the New Oracle Home Prior to Performing an Upgrade

The new Oracle Home must be installed, using the OUI. This installation (either interactive, or a silent install driven by a response file) should be a software-only install, as shown in Figure 23-2.

FIGURE 23-2 Installing an Oracle Home preparatory to upgrading a database

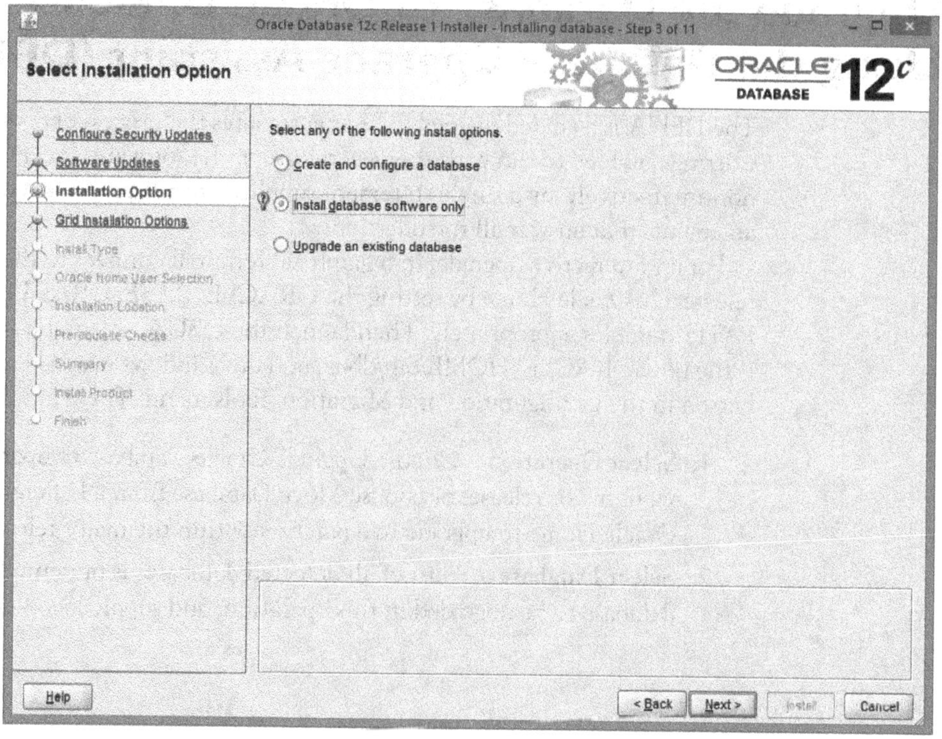

Do not take the option to create a database. It is possible to select the option to upgrade an existing database. This will chain the software install to a run of the DBUA. There is nothing wrong with this in theory, but most DBAs will want to separate these two processes in order to take the time to run the Pre-Upgrade Information Tool manually and consider thoroughly its advice.

At this point, consider the database listener. If you are using a database listener running from a Grid Infrastructure home, no further action is needed. A GI listener can support connections to any release of the database. But if your database listener is running off the database home, you will want to shut down the listener running off the old Oracle Home and replace it with a listener from the new Oracle Home. This listener upgrade need not be related to the database upgrade, and can be carried out before or after. The process is to copy the Oracle Net configuration files from the old home to the new, and make any edits that may be necessary to entries that include directory paths.

CERTIFICATION OBJECTIVE 23.04

Upgrade the Database to Oracle Database 12c by Using the Database Upgrade Assistant (DBUA)

The DBUA is a guided dialog box that automates the process of configuring an existing database to run with the new release of the software. It can also be run non-interactively, by a single statement supplied with appropriate command-line arguments that answer all the questions.

For an interactive upgrade, in a graphical terminal connect to the newly installed release 12*c* Oracle Home by setting the ORACLE_BASE, ORACLE_HOME, and PATH variables appropriately. Then launch the DBUA executable. On Linux, this is the file $ORACLE_HOME/bin/dbua, and on Windows it will be on your Start button in the Configuration and Migration Tools menu. These are the major steps:

1. **Select Operation** Choose Upgrade Oracle Database to upgrade from a previous major release, or choose Move Database from a Different Release 12.1 Oracle Home to upgrade to a patchset within the major release.
2. **Select Database** A list of all detected databases is presented. Choose the database to be upgraded in this operation, and supply logon details for a

database user with SYSDBA privileges. On Windows, you must supply the Windows password for the operating system account under which the 12c Oracle Home is installed.

3. **Prerequisite Checks** DBUA runs some checks (similar to the Pre-Upgrade Information Tool checks) against the database. In Figure 23-3, two issues have been identified. The first issue shown in Figure 23-3 is informative. DBUA has detected that Enterprise Manager Database Control (the management facility shipped with release 10g and 11g databases) is installed. This will be removed during the upgrade. The second issue is that the database has been configured to work with an LDAP directory, and some adjustments to this will be needed. DBUA can do this during the upgrade, or it can be ignored for now and dealt with later.

FIGURE 23-3 The third step of the DBUA dialog box

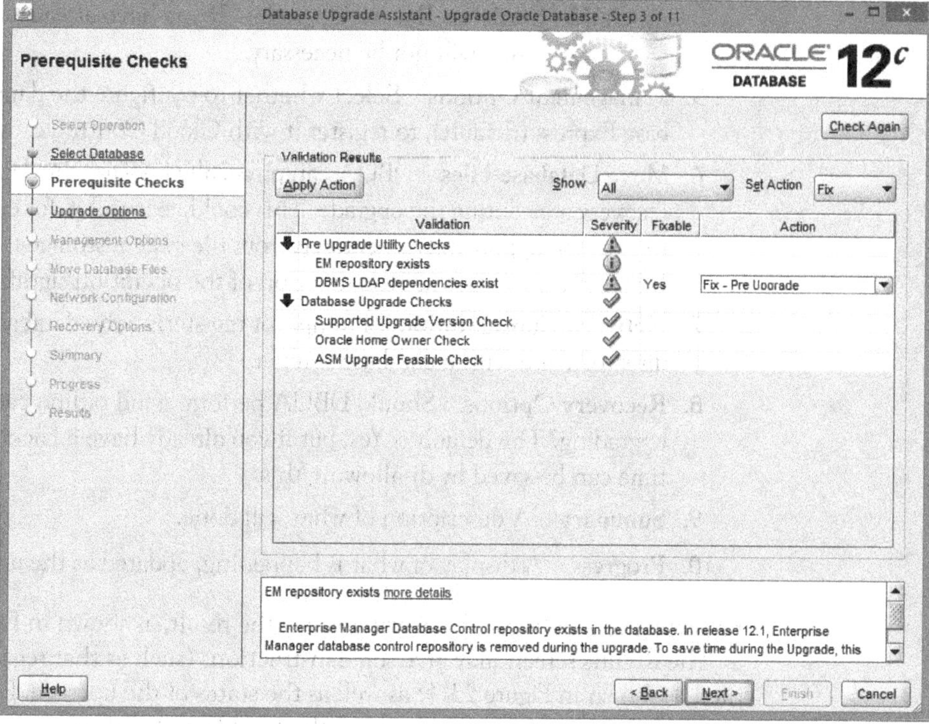

4. **Upgrade Options** There are some choices that give a limited amount of control over the upgrade process and how long it will take. The defaults are usually correct. Choices to consider are:
   - **Select Upgrade Parallelism** The default is based on the number of CPUs detected. You might think it is too high and would flood the machine with work, or too low and that a higher value would push the upgrade through faster.
   - **Recompile Invalid Objects During Post Upgrade, Recompilation Parallelism** Allowing DBUA to recompile during the upgrade will make the operation comprehensive, but will also delay the post-upgrade restart. You may want to recompile manually afterward instead.
   - **Upgrade Timezone Data** Depending on what is already installed, you may need to update the database's time zone files, either as part of the upgrade or later.
   - **Gather Statistics Before Upgrade** If you have already analyzed the database, this will not be necessary.
5. **Management Options** Select whether to configure the database with Database Express (default), to register it with Cloud Control, or neither.
6. **Move Database Files** DBUA can physically relocate the database and the fast recovery area during the upgrade. This could be useful if, for example, you want to take the opportunity to convert from file system storage to ASM storage. It will of course increase the duration of the operation significantly.
7. **Network Configuration** Prompt for registering the database with an LDAP directory, and with a database listener.
8. **Recovery Options** Should DBUA perform a full offline backup before upgrading? The default is Yes, but if you already have a backup, considerable time can be saved by disallowing this.
9. **Summary** A description of what will done.
10. **Progress** A display of what is happening, updated as the upgrade proceeds.

Following completion, DBUA will display the result, as shown in Figure 23-4.

The Results screen may give some instructions (such as that regarding time zone files, as shown in Figure 23-4) as well as the status of the upgrade. Follow them, as well as following any steps advised by the Pre-Upgrade Information Tool.

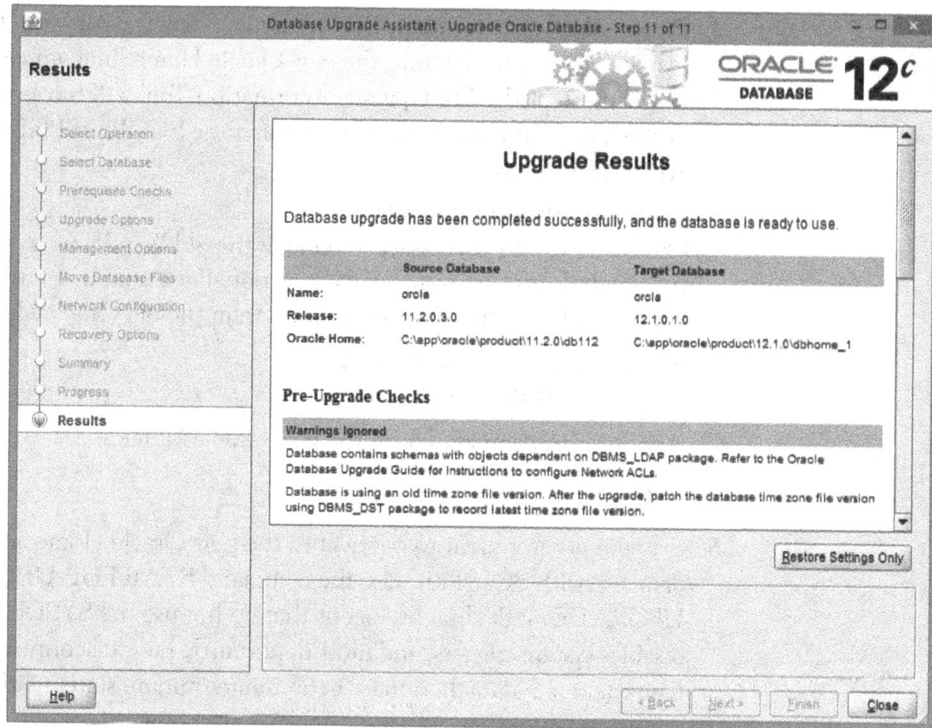

FIGURE 23-4 The completion of a DBUA upgrade exercise

CERTIFICATION OBJECTIVE 23.05

Perform a Manual Upgrade to Oracle Database 12c by Using Scripts and Tools

A manual upgrade is perhaps a little more work than using DBUA, but it does give more control. These are the steps to follow:

1. While connected to the old Oracle Home and with the database open, log on to the database and run the Pre-Upgrade Information Tool provided with the new software. Study the logfile and scripts it generates, and take any appropriate action.
2. Back up the source database.

3. Prepare the newly installed Oracle Home. Copy the password file and the instance parameter file into the new Oracle Home. If any parameters need to be adjusted (the Pre-Upgrade Information Tool will have informed you of this), make the adjustments first, using the SCOPE=SPFILE clause of ALTER SYSTEM.
4. Shut down the source database.
   On Windows, it is necessary to remove the old Windows service under which the database runs and to create a new one. For example, for the database named ORCLA, run these commands from the old Oracle Home:

   ```
   net stop OracleServiceORCLA
   oradim -delete -sid ORCLA
   ```

   And run this command from the new Oracle Home:

   ```
   oradim -new -sid ORCLA
   ```

5. Set your environment to connect to the new Oracle Home, and open the database with SQL*Plus. Use the command **STARTUP UPGRADE**. The UPGRADE mode disables logons that do not use the SYSDBA privilege, disables system triggers, and most importantly permits connections to a database that has a data dictionary in an indeterminate state: neither one release nor another.
6. Execute the parallel upgrade script, which is provided in the ORACLE_HOME/rdbms/admin directory. This is a Perl script that invokes parallelism to reduce the necessary downtime. A suitable Perl interpreter is provided in the Oracle Home. On Windows:

   ```
   cd %ORACLE_HOME%\rdbms\admin
   %ORACLE_HOME%\perl\bin\perl catctl.pl catupgrd.sql
   ```

   Or on Linux:

   ```
   cd $ORACLE_HOME/rdbms/admin
   $ORACLE_HOME/perl/bin/perl catctl.pl catupgrd.sql
   ```

7. The parallel upgrade script finishes by shutting down the database. Open it as normal.
8. Run the Post-Upgrade Status Tool to generate a summary of the result of the upgrade exercise. If it shows any errors or any components as not VALID, take appropriate action. To run the tool, execute the script utlu121s.sql:

   ```
   SQL> @?/rdbms/admin/utlu121s.sql
   ```

9. Run scripts to complete the post-upgrade operations. The catuppst.sql script attempts to fix any problems encountered by the upgrade, and the ultrp.sql script recompiles all invalid PL/SQL. Here is a Linux example:

```
SQL> @?/rdbms/admin/ctuppst.sql
SQL> @?/rdbms/admin/utlrp.sql
```

Rerun the Post-Upgrade Status tool to ensure that there are no remaining issues.

CERTIFICATION OBJECTIVE 23.06

Migrate to Unified Auditing

Detail of how to configure and enable unified audit has been given in Chapter 11. Here is a summary:

- By default, the 12*c* unified audit facility is not enabled.
- All previous auditing (standard audit, fine-grained audit, component-specific audit) will continue to function unchanged in the upgraded database.
- Grant the AUDIT_ADMIN and AUDIT_VIEWER roles as necessary.
- Configure unified audit policies that match the existing audit regime.
- During a period of downtime, enable unified audit: on Linux, relink the executables; on Windows, copy in the appropriate dynamic link library.

CERTIFICATION OBJECTIVE 23.07

Perform Post-Upgrade Tasks

In addition to the steps identified by the Pre-Upgrade Information Tool and documented in the postupgrade_fixups.sql script, various actions may or may not be necessary depending on the environment and whether the upgrade was manual or done with DBUA. All these items should, however, be considered:

- Update environment variables in all relevant scripts. Critical variables are ORACLE_HOME, PATH, and ORACLE_SID.

- On Linux, update the /etc/oratab file.
- On Windows, check all registry settings for the database.
- If an RMAN catalog database is in use, connect with the RMAN executable and upgrade the catalog (it is not necessary to upgrade the catalog database itself).
- If Database Express has been installed as part of the upgrade, confirm and (if necessary) configure its listening ports(s). The routine for this is:

```
select dbms_xdb_config.gethttpport from dual;
select dbms_xdb_config.gethttpsport from dual;
execute dbms_xdb_config.sethttpport(<your desired port>)
execute dbms_xdb_config.sethttpsport(<your desired port>)
```

- Enable the Database Vault (if installed):

```
execute dvsys.dbms_macadm.enable_dv
```

- Reset all passwords. If the upgrade is from release 10.x, all passwords should be changed to take on the password attributes of the current release.
- Set thresholds for tablespace usage alerts. Tablespace alerts are disabled by the upgrade and will need to be reestablished.
- Implement new features as appropriate.

EXERCISE 23-1

Simulate Some Upgrade Tasks

For this exercise, it is assumed that there is not in fact a database that needs to be upgraded. It is, however, possible to run some of the tasks that would be required.

1. Determine what components are installed in the database:

   ```
   select comp_name,version,status from dba_registry;
   ```

2. Run the Pre-Upgrade Information Tool:

   ```
   SQL> @?/rdbms/admin/preupgrd.sql
   ```

   Study the output and also the files generated. These are the logfile preupgrade.log, and the fix-up scripts preupgrade_fixups.sql and postupgrade_fixups.sql.

3. Open the database in UPGRADE mode, confirm this, and attempt to connect as a non-SYSDBA user. Restart the database. Use commands such as these:

```
connect / as sysdba
shutdown immediate
startup upgrade
select status from v$instance;
connect scott/tiger
connect / as sysdba
startup force
```

4. From a command prompt, display all the options for running DBUA:

```
dbua -help
```

Observe the wide range of options that can be applied when running DBUA—many more than are prompted for when running it interactively.

5. Run the script to identify and recompile all invalid objects:

```
@?/rdbms/admin/utlrp.sql
```

Study the output of the script.

CERTIFICATION SUMMARY

This chapter describes the database upgrade process: the preparatory steps, the upgrade itself, and some post-upgrade tasks. The Database Upgrade Assistant (the DBUA) automates the whole process, or it can be carried out manually. Both ways follow the same routine.

First, the Pre-Upgrade Information Tool generates a report on what needs to be done before and after the upgrade. The tool is a SQL script shipped with the new version of the Oracle software, and run against the source database while it is opened with the old version of the Oracle software.

During the upgrade itself, the database is opened from the new Oracle Home with the UPGRADE clause. This is necessary because during the course of the upgrade, the data dictionary and other components will be in an inconsistent state, which would otherwise prevent the database from opening. The upgrade involves running SQL scripts to upgrade the database and installed components. These scripts are launched by a Perl script and (where possible) parallelism is used in order to carry out the process as fast as possible.

After the upgrade, the database is shut down and then reopened in the normal open mode. There will usually be some necessary post-upgrade actions, depending on what components have been installed, and also it will usually be advisable to enable some new features, such as unified auditing.

TWO-MINUTE DRILL

Describe Upgrade Requirements when Certain Features or Options Are Used in Oracle Database

- ❑ Installed components, their version, and status are listed in the DBA_REGISTRY view.
- ❑ Some components (such as APEX) have their own upgrade mechanisms; others (such as Oracle Warehouse Builder, Label Security, and Data Vault) have particular requirements.

Use the Pre-Upgrade Information Tool Before Performing an Upgrade

- ❑ The Pre-Upgrade Information Tool is a SQL script provided with the new software that is run while still using the previous release.
- ❑ The tool inspects the database and generates a report that describes the necessary actions and provides fix-up scripts with commands to be run before and after the upgrade.

Prepare the New Oracle Home Prior to Performing an Upgrade

- ❑ The new Oracle Home must be instantiated before you upgrade the database.
- ❑ If performing a manual upgrade, you must copy certain configuration files (such as the instance parameter file and the password file) to the new home.

Upgrade the Database to Oracle Database 12c by Using the Database Upgrade Assistant (DBUA)

- ❑ The DBUA is run from the new Oracle home, and automates the entire upgrade process.
- ❑ DBUA can be run interactively or for silent upgrade can be executed from the command line with arguments that replace the dialog box.

Perform a Manual Upgrade to Oracle Database 12c by Using Scripts and Tools

- A manual upgrade follows the same steps as the DBUA, but they are invoked individually from the command line.

Migrate to Unified Auditing

- Following upgrade to 12c, unified auditing is not enabled.
- To enable unified auditing, configure appropriate audit policies and then relink the Oracle executable.

Perform Post-Upgrade Tasks

- The Pre-Upgrade Information Tool (run either manually or by DBUA) will have generated instructions on necessary post-upgrade tasks.
- Optional (but advisable) post-upgrade tasks include analyzing the database and recompiling all invalid objects.
- Bringing new features into use is a step that can be done at any time after the upgrade.

SELF TEST

Describe Upgrade Requirements when Certain Features or Options Are Used in Oracle Database

1. Which of these components is no longer available in the database following an upgrade to 12*c*? (Choose the best answer.)
   - A. Data Vault
   - B. Oracle Label Security
   - C. Oracle Warehouse Builder
   - D. Standard database auditing

Use the Pre-Upgrade Information Tool Before Performing an Upgrade

2. Before running the Pre-Upgrade Information Tool, preupgrd.sql, how should you start the database? (Choose the best answer.)
   - A. Start the database with STARTUP UPGRADE from the old Oracle Home.
   - B. Start the database with STARTUP OPEN from the old Oracle Home.
   - C. Start the database with STARTUP UPGRADE from the new Oracle Home.
   - D. Start the database with STARTUP OPEN from the old Oracle Home.
3. What is the output of the Pre-Upgrade Information Tool, preupgrd.sql? (Choose the best answer.)
   - A. Fix-up scripts with commands to be run before and after upgrade
   - B. Scripts to run during the upgrade
   - C. Instructions for how to run the upgrade
   - D. The script prompts for what reports and scripts should be generated

Prepare the New Oracle Home Prior to Performing an Upgrade

4. When you are upgrading a database manually, what files would usually be copied from the old Oracle Home to the new? (Choose all correct answers.)
   - A. Database controlfile
   - B. Instance parameter file
   - C. Password file
   - D. Time zone files
   - E. The AUDIT_FILE_DEST directory

Upgrade the Database to Oracle Database 12c by Using the Database Upgrade Assistant (DBUA)

5. What is the correct method for using the DBUA? (Choose the best answer.)

A. Start the database in UPGRADE mode from the new Oracle Home, and then run DBUA from the new Oracle Home.

B. Start the database in UPGRADE mode from the old Oracle Home, and then run DBUA from the new Oracle Home.

C. Start the database in OPEN mode from the old Oracle Home, and then run DBUA from the new Oracle Home.

D. Shut down the database, and then run DBUA from the new Oracle Home.

Perform a Manual Upgrade to Oracle Database 12c by Using Scripts and Tools

6. In order to minimize downtime for your users, which of these operations can be carried out while the database is open for use? (Choose all correct answers.)

A. The backup before starting the upgrade

B. Running the Pre-Upgrade Information Tool, the script preupgrd.sql

C. Running the catctl.pl Perl script that parallelizes the upgrade process

D. Recompiling all invalid PL/SQL after upgrade

E. Gathering statistics on the data dictionary after upgrade

F. Running the Post-Upgrade Status Tool, the utlu121s.sql script

7. You are performing a manual upgrade of a database and have opened the database in UPGRADE mode. If a user attempts to connect to the database at this time, what will be the result? (Choose the best answer.)

A. The connection will succeed, but may compromise the success of the upgrade.

B. The connection will succeed, but all DML and DDL will be blocked.

C. The connection will fail, because the database listener will not spawn sessions against a database in UPGRADE mode.

D. The connection will fail, unless the user has the SYSDBA privilege.

Migrate to Unified Auditing

8. What options do you have following the 12*c* upgrade, if you have configured both standard audit and fine-grained audit in the source 11*g* database? (Choose the best answer.)

A. You must disable both standard and fine-grained audit before the upgrade, and configure unified audit after the upgrade.

B. After upgrade, you can enable unified audit and leave the standard and fine-grained audit running in parallel for a while to ensure that the results are the same.

C. After upgrade, the standard audit and fine-grained audit will continue to run until you enable unified audit, at which time they will cease to function.

D. After upgrade, you can migrate first the standard audit to unified auditing and then the fine-grained audit to unified auditing.

Perform Post-Upgrade Tasks

9. Some of the post-upgrade tasks are time consuming, and you may wish to perform them after opening the database for use. If you choose to open the database for use before recompiling invalid PL/SQL with the utlrp.sql script, what may result? (Choose the best answer.)

A. The database will not open if any of the SYS-owned supplied PL/SQL packages are invalid.

B. The database will open, but if any users attempt to use invalid PL/SQL that has not yet been recompiled, they will receive errors.

C. The database will open, but if any users attempt to use invalid PL/SQL that has not yet been recompiled, it will be compiled automatically.

D. The database will open, but if any users attempt to use invalid PL/SQL that has not yet been recompiled, it will run in interpreted mode rather than native mode.

10. Following a successful upgrade with the DBUA, you find that remote users can no longer connect to the database. What might be the problem? (Choose two correct answers.)

A. You are running your database listener off the Grid Infrastructure home, and it must be reconfigured to point to the new release of the database.

B. You have shut down the database listener running off the old home and have not started a listener from the new home.

C. You have omitted copying the tnsnames.ora file from the old home to the new home.

D. You have omitted copying the password file from the old home to the new home.

E. You did not restart the database after the upgrade.

LAB QUESTION

If you have an 11*g* environment, upgrade it. Ideally, create two databases and upgrade one with the DBUA and the other using a manual upgrade.

If you do not have an 11*g* environment and wish to work through the upgrade process, you will need to download the software. As of the time of writing, release 11.2.0.1 is available for download through the edelivery.oracle.com website, but earlier releases are no longer available. The routine for installing 11*g* and creating a database is broadly similar to the 12*c* routine.

SELF TEST ANSWERS

Describe Upgrade Requirements when Certain Features or Options Are Used in Oracle Database

1. ☑ **C.** Following an upgrade, Oracle Warehouse Builder can still be used, but it must be installed externally.
   ☒ **A, B,** and **D** are incorrect. **A** and **B** are incorrect, because although the Data Vault and OLS have special requirements for upgrade, they are still available. **D** is incorrect because standard auditing is enabled after upgrade, although you may wish to convert to unified auditing instead.

Use the Pre-Upgrade Information Tool Before Performing an Upgrade

2. ☑ **B.** The tool is supplied with the new Oracle Home, but run against a database opened from the old Oracle Home.
   ☒ **A, C,** and **D** are incorrect. **A** and **C** are incorrect because STARTUP UPGRADE (from the new Oracle Home) is used for the upgrade itself, not the preparatory steps. **D** is incorrect because the database cannot be opened from the new home at this point.
3. ☑ **A.** The scripts are preupgrade_fixups.sql and postupgrade_fixups.sql.
   ☒ **B, C,** and **D** are incorrect. **B** and **C** are incorrect because the tool is concerned with steps before and after upgrade, not during. **D** is incorrect because the tool is not interactive: there are no prompts.

Prepare the New Oracle Home Prior to Performing an Upgrade

4. ☑ **B** and **C.** The parameter file and password file must be copied, as their default location is derived from the Oracle Home.
   ☒ **A, D,** and **E** are incorrect. **A** is incorrect because no datafiles should be moved: an upgrade is an in-place operation. **D** is incorrect because the new Oracle Home will have new time zone files. **E** is incorrect because the AUDIT_FILE_DEST remains unchanged following upgrade.

Upgrade the Database to Oracle Database 12c by Using the Database Upgrade Assistant (DBUA)

5. ☑ **C.** The DBUA must be run from the new home, and will take care of all the necessary startups and shutdowns.
   ☒ **A, B,** and **D** are incorrect. **A** and **B** are incorrect because the DBUA will manage the start in UPGRADE mode. **D** is incorrect because the DBUA automates the whole process, including the shutdown before upgrade.

Perform a Manual Upgrade to Oracle Database 12c by Using Scripts and Tools

6. ☑ **A, B, D, E,** and **F.** All of these steps can be performed against an open database.
☒ **C** is incorrect. The catctl.pl script can be run only when the database is in UPGRADE mode, during which time no regular users can connect.

7. ☑ **D.** A database instance started in UPGRADE mode will not accept any logons other than those with the SYSDBA privilege.
☒ **A, B,** and **C** are incorrect. These are incorrect because a database in UPGRADE mode is protected against all non-SYSDBA connections.

Migrate to Unified Auditing

8. ☑ **C.** There is no necessity to enable unified auditing, but when you do other audits will stop.
☒ **A, B,** and **D** are incorrect. **A** is incorrect because you can continue to use older methods of audit after upgrade. **B** and **D** are incorrect because it is not possible to run the older methods in conjunction with the new.

Perform Post-Upgrade Tasks

9. ☑ **C.** Invalid packages are recompiled when necessary, but they will be a performance hit on the session that does this.
☒ **A, B,** and **D** are incorrect. **A** and **B** are incorrect because recompilation is automatic when needed. **D** is incorrect because whether the PL/SQL is set for native compilation or interpretation, it will still be recompiled on demand.

10. ☑ **B** and **E. B** is correct because if you stop the old listener, you must configure and start a replacement. **E** is correct because following upgrade, DBUA leaves the database shutdown.
☒ **A, C,** and **D** are incorrect. **A** is incorrect because the new release of the database will register with the GI listener, as it did before the upgrade. **C** and **D** are incorrect because although failing to copy these files may cause problems for the DBA, it should not be relevant to users.

LAB ANSWER

Having assembled the necessary items, you are ready to proceed with your studies. Enjoy.

A

About the CD-ROM

The CD-ROM included with this book comes with Total Tester practice exam software, two complete practice exams, and a PDF copy of the book. The software can be installed on any Windows XP/Vista/7/8 computer and must be installed to access the Total Tester practice exams.

System Requirements

The software requires Windows XP or higher; a current or prior major release of Chrome, Firefox, Internet Explorer, or Safari; and 30MB of hard disk space for full installation.

Installing and Running Total Tester

From the main screen you may install the Total Tester by clicking the Software Installers button, then selecting the Total Tester OCA Oracle Database 12*c*: Installation and Administration Exam Guide (Exam 1Z0-062) Practice Exams button. This will begin the installation process and place an icon on your desktop and in your Start menu. To run Total Tester, navigate to Start | (All) Programs | Total Seminars or double-click the icon on your desktop.

To uninstall the Total Tester software, go to Start | Settings | Control Panel | Add/Remove Programs (XP) or Programs and Features (Vista /7/8) and then select the OCA Oracle Database 12*c*: Installation and Administration Exam Guide (Exam 1Z0-062) Total Tester program. Select Remove, and Windows will completely uninstall the software.

Total Tester

Total Tester provides you with a simulation of the OCA Oracle Database 12*c*: Installation and Administration Exam Guide (Exam 1Z0-062) exam. Exams can be taken in either Practice or Final mode. Practice mode provides an assistance window with hints, references to the book, an explanation of the answer, and the option to check your answer as you take the test. Both Practice and Final modes provide an overall grade and a grade broken down by certification objective. To take a test, launch the program and select OCA Oracle Database 12*c*: Installation and Administration Exam Guide (Exam 1Z0-062) from the Installed Question Packs list on the left. Select Practice Exam or Exam Simulation, or create a custom exam.

Free PDF Copy of the Book

The contents of this book are provided in PDF format on the CD. This file is viewable on your computer and many portable devices.

To view the file on your computer, Adobe's Acrobat Reader is required and has been included on the CD.

Note: For more information on Adobe Reader and to check for the most recent version of the software, visit Adobe's website at www.adobe.com and search for the free Adobe Reader or look for Adobe Reader on the product page.

To view the electronic book on a portable device, copy the PDF file to your computer from the CD, and then copy the file to your portable device using a USB or other connection. Adobe offers a mobile version of Adobe Reader, the Adobe Reader mobile app, which currently supports iOS and Android. The Adobe website also has a list of recommended applications.

Technical Support

For questions regarding the Total Tester software or operation of the CD-ROM, visit www.totalsem.com or e-mail support@totalsem.com.

For questions regarding the PDF copy of the book, e-mail techsolutions@mhedu.com or visit http://mhp.softwareassist.com.

For questions regarding book content, please e-mail customer.service@mheducation.com. For customers outside the United States, e-mail international.cs@mheducation.com.

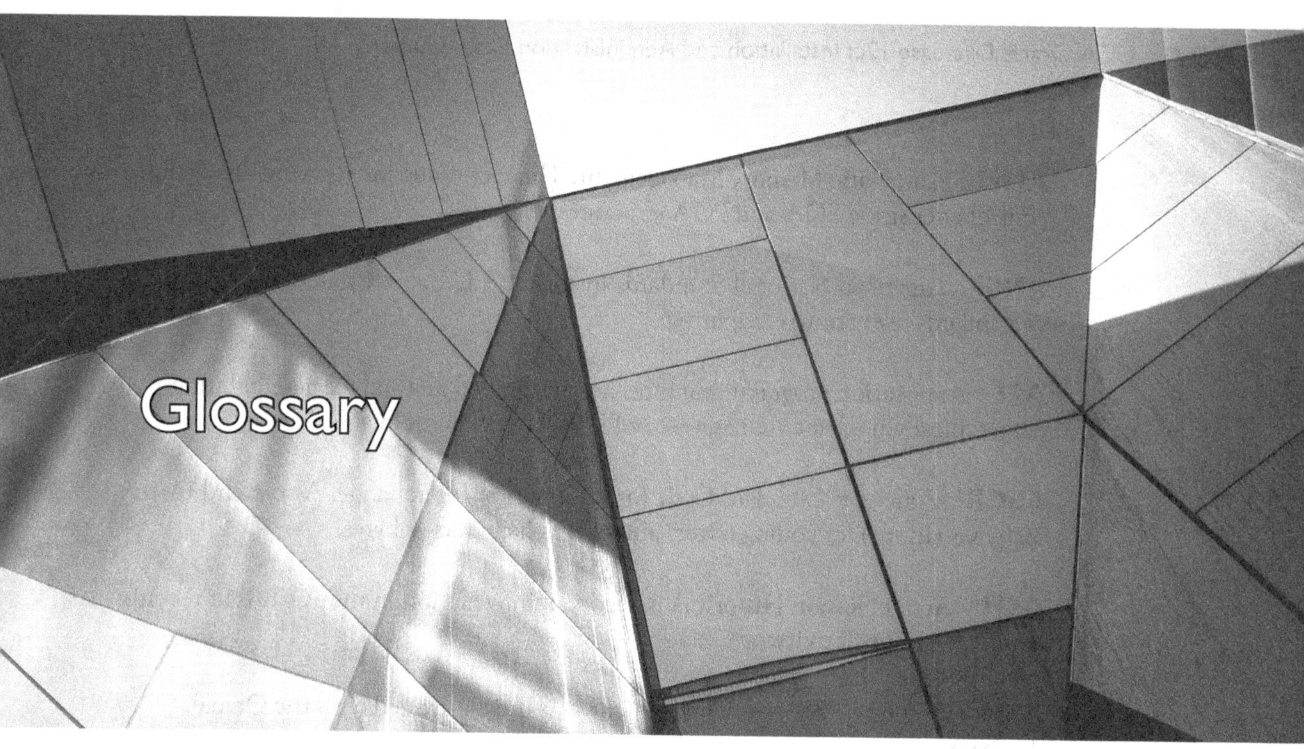

Glossary

ACID Atomicity, Consistency, Isolation, and Durability. Four characteristics that a relational database must be able to maintain for transactions.

ADDM Automatic Database Diagnostic Monitor. A tool that generates performance-tuning reports based on snapshots in the AWR.

ADR Automatic Diagnostic Repository. Default location for the alert log, trace files, and other information useful for fault finding.

ADRCI The ADR command-line interface.

AES Advanced Encryption Standard. A widely used data encryption method.

AL16UTF16 A Unicode fixed-width two-byte character set, commonly specified for the NLS character set used for NVARCHAR2, NCHAR, and NCLOB data types.

AMM Automatic Memory Management. The technique for allowing Oracle full control over sizing SGA and PGA structures.

ANSI American National Standards Institute. A U.S. body that defines a number of standards relevant to computing.

API Application programming interface. A defined method for manipulating data, typically implemented as a set of PL/SQL procedures in a package.

ASCII American Standard Code for Information Interchange. A standard (with many variations) for coding letters and other characters as bytes.

ASH Active Session History. A category of information in the AWR that records details of session activity.

ASM Automatic Storage Management. An LVM provided with the Oracle database.

ASMM Automatic Shared Memory Management. The technique for allowing Oracle full control over sizing SGA structures.

ASSM Automatic Segment Space Management. The method of managing space within segments by use of bitmaps.

AWR Automatic Workload Repository. A set of tables in the SYSAUX tablespace, populated with tuning data gathered by the MMON process.

Background process A process that is part of the instance: launched at startup.

BFILE A large object data type that is stored as an operating system file. The value in the table column is a pointer to the file.

Bind variable A value passed from a user process to a SQL statement at statement execution time.

BLOB Binary large object. A LOB data type for binary data, such as photographs and video clips.

Block The units of storage into which datafiles are formatted. The size can be 2KB, 4KB, 8KB, 16KB, 32KB, or 64KB.

BMR Block Media Recovery. An RMAN technique for the restore and recovery of individual data blocks, rather than complete datafiles.

Character set The encoding system for representing data within bytes. Different character sets can store different characters, and may not be suitable for all languages. Unicode character sets can store any character.

Check constraint A simple rule enforced by the database that restricts the values that can be entered into a column.

Checkpoint An event that forces the DBWn to write dirty buffers from the database buffer cache to the datafiles.

CKPT The Checkpoint process. The background process responsible for recording the current redo byte address—the point in time up to which the DBWn has written changed data blocks to disk—and for signaling checkpoints, which forces DBWn to write changed blocks to disk immediately.

Client-server architecture A processing paradigm where the application is divided into client software that interacts with the user and server software that interacts with the data.

CLOB Character large object. A LOB data type for character data, such as text documents, stored in the database character set.

Cluster A hardware environment where more than one computer shares access to storage.

Cluster segment A segment that can contain one or more tables, denormalized into a single structure.

Column An element of a row: tables are two-dimensional structures, divided horizontally into rows and vertically into columns.

Commit To make a change to data permanent.

Complete recovery Following a restore of damaged database files, a complete recovery applies all redo to bring the database up to date with no loss of data.

Connect identifier An Oracle Net service name.

Connect role A pre-seeded role retained only for backward compatibility.

Connect string The database connection details needed to establish a session: the address of the listener and the service or instance name.

Consistent backup A backup made while the database is closed.

Constraint A mechanism for enforcing rules on data: that a column value must be unique, or may only contain certain values. A primary key constraint specifies that the column must be both unique and not null.

Controlfile The file containing pointers to the rest of the database, critical sequence information, and the RMAN repository.

CPU Central processing unit. The chip that provides the processing capability of a computer, such as an Intel i7 or a Sun SPARC.

CTWR Change Tracking Writer. The optional background process that records the addresses of changed blocks, to enable fast incremental backups.

Data blocks The units into which datafiles are formatted.

Data dictionary The tables owned by SYS in the SYSTEM tablespace that define the database and the objects within it.

Data dictionary views Views on the data dictionary tables that let the DBA investigate the state of the database.

Data Guard A facility whereby a copy of the production database is created and updated (possibly in real time) with all changes applied to the production database.

Data Pump A facility for transferring large amounts of data at high speed into, out of, or between databases.

Database buffer cache An area of memory in the SGA used for working on blocks copied from datafiles.

Database link A connection from one database to another, based on a username and password and a connect string.

Datafile The disk-based structure for storing data.

DBA Database administrator. The person responsible for creating and managing Oracle databases—this could be you.

DBA role A pre-seeded role provided for backward compatibility that includes all the privileges needed to manage a database, except those needed to start up and shut down.

DBCA The Database Configuration Assistant. A GUI tool for creating, modifying, and dropping instances and databases.

DBID Database identifier. A unique number for every database, visible in the DBID column of the V$DATABASE dynamic performance view.

DBMS Database management system. Often used interchangeably with RDBMS.

DBWn or DBWR The Database Writer. The background process responsible for writing changed blocks from the database buffer cache to the datafiles. An instance may have up to 100 Database Writer processes: DBW0–DBW9, DBWa–DBWz, and BW36–BW99.

DDL Data Definition Language. The subset of SQL commands that change object definitions within the data dictionary: CREATE, ALTER, DROP, and TRUNCATE.

Deadlock A situation where two sessions block each other, such that neither can do anything. Deadlocks are detected and resolved automatically.

DHCP Dynamic Host Configuration Protocol. The standard for configuring the network characteristics of a computer, such as its IP address, in a changing environment where computers may be moved from one location to another.

DIAG The diagnosability process that generates diagnostic dumps.

Direct path A method of I/O on datafiles that bypasses the database buffer cache.

Directory object An Oracle directory: an object within the database that points to an operating system directory.

Dirty buffer A buffer in the database buffer cache that contains a copy of a data block that has been updated and not yet written back to the datafile.

DML Data Manipulation Language. The subset of SQL commands that change data within the database: INSERT, UPDATE, DELETE, and MERGE.

DMnn The Data Pump Master process. The process that controls a Data Pump job—there will be one launched for each job that is running.

DNS Domain Name Service. The TCP mechanism for resolving network names into IP addresses.

Domain The set of values an attribute is allowed to take. Terminology: tables have rows, and rows have columns with values. Alternatively, relations have tuples, and tuples have attributes with values taken from their domain.

DSS Decision Support System. A database, such as a data warehouse, optimized for running queries as against OLTP work.

DWnn The Data Pump Worker process. There will be one or more of these launched for each Data Pump job that is running.

Easy connect A method of establishing a session against a database by specifying the address on the listener and the service name, without using an Oracle Net alias.

EBCDIC Extended Binary Coded Decimal Interchange Code. A standard developed by IBM for coding letters and other characters in bytes.

Environment variable A variable set in the operating system shell that can be used by application software and by shell scripts.

Equijoin A join condition using an equality operator.

Fact table The central table in a star schema, with columns for values relevant to the row and columns used as foreign keys to the dimension tables.

Fast recovery area (previously known as the flash recovery area) A default location for all recovery-related files.

FGA Fine Grained Auditing. A facility for tracking user access to data, based on the rows that are seen or manipulated.

Full backup A backup containing all blocks of the files backed up, not only those blocks changed since the last backup.

GMT Greenwich Mean Time. Now referred to as UTC, this is the time zone of the meridian through Greenwich Observatory in London.

Grid computing An architecture where the delivery of a service to end users is not tied to certain server resources but can be provided from anywhere in a pool of resources.

GUI Graphical user interface. A layer of an application that lets users work with the application through a graphical terminal, such as a PC with a mouse.

HTTP Hypertext Transfer Protocol. The protocol that enables the World Wide Web (both invented at the European Organization for Nuclear Research in 1989), this is a layered protocol that runs over TCP/IP.

HWM High water mark. This is the last block of a segment that has ever been used—blocks above this are part of the segment, but are not yet formatted for use.

I/O Input/output. The activity of reading from or writing to disks—often the slowest point of a data processing operation.

IBM International Business Machines. A well-known computer hardware, software, and services company.

Image copy An RMAN copy of a file.

Inconsistent backup A backup made while the database was open.

Incremental backup A backup containing only blocks that have been changed since the last backup was made.

Instance recovery The automatic repair of damage caused by a disorderly shutdown of the database.

IOT Index Organized Table. A table type where the rows are stored in the leaf blocks of an index segment.

IP Internet Protocol. Together with the Transmission Control Protocol, IP makes up the de facto standard communication protocol (TCP/IP) used for client-server communication over a network.

IPC Inter-Process Communications protocol. The platform-specific protocol, provided by your OS vendor, used for processes running on the same machine to communicate with each other.

ISO International Standards Organization. A group that defines many standards, including SQL.

J2EE Java 2 Enterprise Edition. The standard for developing Java applications.

Join The process of connecting rows in different tables, based on common column values.

JVM Java Virtual Machine. The run-time environment needed for running code written in Java. Oracle provides a JVM within the database, and there will be one provided by your operating system.

Large pool A memory structure within the SGA used by certain processes: principally shared server processes and parallel execution servers.

LDAP Lightweight Directory Access Protocol. The TCP implementation of the X25 directory standard, used by the Oracle Internet Directory for name resolution, security, and authentication. LDAP is also used by other software vendors, including Microsoft and IBM.

LGWR The Log Writer. The background process responsible for flushing change vectors from the log buffer in memory to the online redo log files on disk.

Library cache A memory structure within the shared pool, used for caching SQL statements parsed into their executable form.

Listener The server-side process that listens for database connection requests from user processes, and launches server processes to establish sessions.

LOB Large object. A data structure that is too large to store within a table. LOBs (Oracle supports several types) are defined as columns of a table, but physically are stored in a separate segment.

Log switch The action of closing one online logfile group and opening another: triggered by the LGWR process filling the first group.

LREG The background process responsible for registering database services with the listener.

LRU Least Recently Used. LRU lists are used to manage access to data structures, using algorithms that ensure the data that has not been accessed for the longest time is the data that will be overwritten.

LVM Logical Volume Manager. A layer of software that abstracts the physical storage within your computer from the logical storage visible to an application.

MMAN The Memory Manager background process, which monitors and reassigns memory allocations in the SGA for automatically tunable SGA components.

MML Media Management Layer. Software that lets RMAN make use of automated tape libraries and other SBT devices.

MMNL Manageability Monitor Light. The background process responsible for flushing ASH data to the AWR, if MMON is not doing this with the necessary frequency.

MMON The Manageability Monitor background process, responsible for gathering performance-monitoring information and raising alerts.

Mounted database A situation where the instance has opened the database controlfile, but not the online redo logfiles or the datafiles.

MTBF Mean Time Between Failure. A measure of the average length of running time for a database between unplanned shutdowns.

MTS Multi-Threaded Server. Since release 9*i*, renamed to Shared Server. This is the technique whereby a large number of sessions can share a small pool of server processes, rather than requiring one server each.

MTTR Mean Time To Recover. The average time it takes to make the database available for normal use after a failure.

Multiplexing To maintain multiple copies of files.

Namespace A logical grouping of objects within which no two objects may have the same name.

NCLOB National character large object. A LOB data type for character data, such as text documents, stored in the alternative national database character set.

NLS National Language Support. The capability of the Oracle database to support many linguistic, geographical, and cultural environments—now usually referred to as Globalization.

Node A computer attached to a network.

Null The absence of a value, indicating that the value is not known, missing, or inapplicable.

OC4J Oracle Containers for J2EE. The control structure provided by the Oracle Application Server for running Java programs.

OCA Oracle Certified Associate.

OCI Oracle Call Interface. An API, published as a set of C libraries, that programmers can use to write user processes that will use an Oracle database.

OCP Oracle Certified Professional. The qualification you are working toward.

ODBC Open Database Connectivity. A standard developed by Microsoft for communicating with relational databases. Oracle provides an ODBC driver that will allow clients running Microsoft products to connect to an Oracle database.

Offline backup A backup made while the database is closed.

OLAP Online Analytical Processing. Select, intensive work involving running queries against a (usually) large database. Oracle provides OLAP capabilities as an option, in addition to the standard query facilities.

OLTP Online Transaction Processing. A pattern of activity within a database typified by a large number of small, short transactions.

Online backup A backup made while the database is open.

Online redo log The files to which change vectors are streamed by the LGWR.

Oracle Net Oracle's proprietary communications protocol, layered on top of an industry-standard protocol.

ORACLE_BASE The root directory into which Oracle products are installed.

ORACLE_HOME The root directory of any one Oracle product.

OS Operating system. Typically, in the Oracle environment this will be a version of Unix (perhaps Linux) or Microsoft Windows.

Parse To convert SQL statements into a form suitable for execution.

PGA Program Global Area. The variable-sized block of memory used to maintain the state of a database session. PGAs are private to the session and controlled by the session's server process.

PL/SQL Procedural Language / Structured Query Language. Oracle's proprietary programming language, which combines procedural constructs, such as flow control, and user interface capabilities with SQL.

PMON The Process Monitor. The background process responsible for monitoring the state of users' sessions against an instance.

Primary key The column (or combination of columns) whose value(s) can be used to identify each row in a table.

RAC Real Application Clusters. Oracle's clustering technology, which allows several instances in different machines to open the same database for scalability, performance, and fault tolerance.

RAID Redundant Array of Inexpensive Disks. Techniques for enhancing performance and/or fault tolerance by using a volume manager to present a number of physical disks to the operating system as a single logical disk.

RAM Random access memory. The chips that make up the real memory in your computer hardware, as opposed to the virtual memory presented to software by the operating system.

Raw device An unformatted disk or disk partition.

RDBMS Relational database management system. Often used interchangeably with DBMS.

Referential integrity A rule defined on a table specifying that the values in a column (or columns) must map onto those of a row in another table.

Relation A two-dimensional structure consisting of tuples with attributes (aka a table).

RMAN Recovery Manager. Oracle's backup and recovery tool.

Rowid The unique identifier of every row in the database, used as a pointer to the physical location of the row.

RVWR The Recovery Writer background process. An optional process responsible for flushing the flashback buffer to the flashback logs.

SBT System Backup to Tape. An RMAN term for a tape device.

Schema The objects owned by a database user.

SCN System Change Number. The continually incrementing number used to track the sequence and exact time of all events within a database.

Segment A database object, within a schema, that contains a data object (such as a table or index).

Sequence A database object, within a schema, that generates unique numbers.

Service name A logical name registered by an instance with a listener, which can be specified by a user process when it issues a connect request.

Session A user process and a server process, connected to the instance.

SGA System Global Area. The block of shared memory that contains the memory structures that make up an Oracle instance.

SID System identifier. The name of an instance, which must be unique on the computer the instance is running on.

Alternatively, session identifier. The number used to identify uniquely a session logged on to an Oracle instance.

SMON The System Monitor. The background process responsible for opening a database and monitoring the instance.

Spfile The server parameter file: the file containing the parameters used to build an instance in memory.

SQL Structured Query Language. An international standard language for extracting data from and manipulating data in relational databases.

SSL Secure Sockets Layer. A standard for securing data transmission using encryption, checksumming, and digital certificates.

Synonym An alternative name for a database object.

Sysdba The privilege that lets a user connect with operating system or password file authentication, and create or start up and shut down a database.

Sysoper The privilege that lets a user connect with operating system or password file authentication, and start up and shut down (but not create) a database.

System A pre-seeded schema used for database administration purposes.

Table A logical two-dimensional data storage structure, consisting of rows and columns.

Tablespace The logical structure that abstracts logical data storage in tables from physical data storage in datafiles.

TCP Transmission Control Protocol. Together with the Internet Protocol, TCP makes up the de facto standard communication protocol (TCP/IP) used for client-server communication over a network.

TCPS TCP with SSL. The secure sockets version of TCP.

Tempfile The physical storage that makes up a temporary tablespace, used for storing temporary segments.

TNS Transparent Network Substrate. The heart of Oracle Net, TNS is a proprietary layered protocol running on top of whatever underlying network transport protocol you choose to use—probably TCP/IP.

Transaction A logical unit of work, which will complete in total or not at all.

Tuple A one-dimensional structure consisting of attributes (aka a row).

UGA User Global Area. That part of the PGA stored in the SGA for sessions running through shared servers.

UI User interface. The layer of an application that communicates with end users—nowadays, frequently graphical: a GUI.

URL Uniform Resource Locator. A standard for specifying the location of an object on the Internet, consisting of a protocol, a hostname and domain, an IP port number, a path and file name, and a series of parameters.

UTC Coordinated Universal Time, previously known as Greenwich Mean Time (GMT). UTC is the global standard time zone; all others relate to it as offsets, ahead or behind.

X As in X-Windows, the standard GUI environment used on most computers—except those that run Microsoft Windows instead.

XML Extensible Markup Language. A standard for data interchange using documents, where the format of the data is defined by tags within the document.

INDEX

SYMBOLS

A

B

D

E

F

J

K

L

N

Q

R

S

T

U

V

W

X

LICENSE AGREEMENT

THIS PRODUCT (THE "PRODUCT") CONTAINS PROPRIETARY SOFTWARE, DATA AND INFORMATION (INCLUDING DOCUMENTATION) OWNED BY McGRAW-HILL EDUCATION AND ITS LICENSORS. YOUR RIGHT TO USE THE PRODUCT IS GOVERNED BY THE TERMS AND CONDITIONS OF THIS AGREEMENT.

LICENSE: Throughout this License Agreement, "you" shall mean either the individual or the entity whose agent opens this package. You are granted a non-exclusive and non-transferable license to use the Product subject to the following terms:
(i) If you have licensed a single user version of the Product, the Product may only be used on a single computer (i.e., a single CPU). If you licensed and paid the fee applicable to a local area network or wide area network version of the Product, you are subject to the terms of the following subparagraph (ii).
(ii) If you have licensed a local area network version, you may use the Product on unlimited workstations located in one single building selected by you that is served by such local area network. If you have licensed a wide area network version, you may use the Product on unlimited workstations located in multiple buildings on the same site selected by you that is served by such wide area network; provided, however, that any building will not be considered located in the same site if it is more than five (5) miles away from any building included in such site. In addition, you may only use a local area or wide area network version of the Product on one single server. If you wish to use the Product on more than one server, you must obtain written authorization from McGraw-Hill Education and pay additional fees.
(iii) You may make one copy of the Product for back-up purposes only and you must maintain an accurate record as to the location of the back-up at all times.

COPYRIGHT; RESTRICTIONS ON USE AND TRANSFER: All rights (including copyright) in and to the Product are owned by McGraw-Hill Education and its licensors. You are the owner of the enclosed disc on which the Product is recorded. You may not use, copy, decompile, disassemble, reverse engineer, modify, reproduce, create derivative works, transmit, distribute, sublicense, store in a database or retrieval system of any kind, rent or transfer the Product, or any portion thereof, in any form or by any means (including electronically or otherwise) except as expressly provided for in this License Agreement. You must reproduce the copyright notices, trademark notices, legends and logos of McGraw-Hill Education and its licensors that appear on the Product on the back-up copy of the Product which you are permitted to make hereunder. All rights in the Product not expressly granted herein are reserved by McGraw-Hill Education and its licensors.

TERM: This License Agreement is effective until terminated. It will terminate if you fail to comply with any term or condition of this License Agreement. Upon termination, you are obligated to return to McGraw-Hill Education the Product together with all copies thereof and to purge all copies of the Product included in any and all servers and computer facilities.

DISCLAIMER OF WARRANTY: THE PRODUCT AND THE BACK-UP COPY ARE LICENSED "AS IS." McGRAW-HILL EDUCATION, ITS LICENSORS AND THE AUTHORS MAKE NO WARRANTIES, EXPRESS OR IMPLIED, AS TO THE RESULTS TO BE OBTAINED BY ANY PERSON OR ENTITY FROM USE OF THE PRODUCT, ANY INFORMATION OR DATA INCLUDED THEREIN AND/OR ANY TECHNICAL SUPPORT SERVICES PROVIDED HEREUNDER, IF ANY ("TECHNICAL SUPPORT SERVICES"). McGRAW-HILL EDUCATION, ITS LICENSORS AND THE AUTHORS MAKE NO EXPRESS OR IMPLIED WARRANTIES OF MERCHANTABILITY OR FITNESS FOR A PARTICULAR PURPOSE OR USE WITH RESPECT TO THE PRODUCT. McGRAW-HILL EDUCATION, ITS LICENSORS, AND THE AUTHORS MAKE NO GUARANTEE THAT YOU WILL PASS ANY CERTIFICATION EXAM WHATSOEVER BY USING THIS PRODUCT. NEITHER McGRAW-HILL EDUCATION, ANY OF ITS LICENSORS NOR THE AUTHORS WARRANT THAT THE FUNCTIONS CONTAINED IN THE PRODUCT WILL MEET YOUR REQUIREMENTS OR THAT THE OPERATION OF THE PRODUCT WILL BE UNINTERRUPTED OR ERROR FREE. YOU ASSUME THE ENTIRE RISK WITH RESPECT TO THE QUALITY AND PERFORMANCE OF THE PRODUCT.

LIMITED WARRANTY FOR DISC: To the original licensee only, McGraw-Hill Education warrants that the enclosed disc on which the Product is recorded is free from defects in materials and workmanship under normal use and service for a period of ninety (90) days from the date of purchase. In the event of a defect in the disc covered by the foregoing warranty, McGraw-Hill Education will replace the disc.

LIMITATION OF LIABILITY: NEITHER McGRAW-HILL EDUCATION, ITS LICENSORS NOR THE AUTHORS SHALL BE LIABLE FOR ANY INDIRECT, SPECIAL OR CONSEQUENTIAL DAMAGES, SUCH AS BUT NOT LIMITED TO, LOSS OF ANTICIPATED PROFITS OR BENEFITS, RESULTING FROM THE USE OR INABILITY TO USE THE PRODUCT EVEN IF ANY OF THEM HAS BEEN ADVISED OF THE POSSIBILITY OF SUCH DAMAGES. THIS LIMITATION OF LIABILITY SHALL APPLY TO ANY CLAIM OR CAUSE WHATSOEVER WHETHER SUCH CLAIM OR CAUSE ARISES IN CONTRACT, TORT, OR OTHERWISE. Some states do not allow the exclusion or limitation of indirect, special or consequential damages, so the above limitation may not apply to you.

U.S. GOVERNMENT RESTRICTED RIGHTS: Any software included in the Product is provided with restricted rights subject to subparagraphs (c), (1) and (2) of the Commercial Computer Software-Restricted Rights clause at 48 C.F.R. 52.227-19. The terms of this Agreement applicable to the use of the data in the Product are those under which the data are generally made available to the general public by McGraw-Hill Education. Except as provided herein, no reproduction, use, or disclosure rights are granted with respect to the data included in the Product and no right to modify or create derivative works from any such data is hereby granted.

GENERAL: This License Agreement constitutes the entire agreement between the parties relating to the Product. The terms of any Purchase Order shall have no effect on the terms of this License Agreement. Failure of McGraw-Hill Education to insist at any time on strict compliance with this License Agreement shall not constitute a waiver of any rights under this License Agreement. This License Agreement shall be construed and governed in accordance with the laws of the State of New York. If any provision of this License Agreement is held to be contrary to law, that provision will be enforced to the maximum extent permissible and the remaining provisions will remain in full force and effect.